International Investment Law and General International Law

FRANKFURT INVESTMENT AND ECONOMIC LAW SERIES

Series Editors: Rainer Hofmann, *University of Frankfurt, Germany,* Stephan W. Schill, *University of Amsterdam, the Netherlands* and Christian J. Tams, *University of Glasgow, UK*

The Frankfurt Investment and Economic Law Series addresses a core field of international law whose importance is likely to increase further as globalization progresses: international economic law. Serving as a forum for dialogue and cutting-edge debate, its scope takes in the legal regime governing international economic relations at large with a particular focus on international investment law.

Seeking to look beyond practical concerns raised in this field, the series addresses conceptual and foundational issues relating to the theory of international investment law – including questions of legitimacy and policy, the interaction with other fields of international and domestic law (both public and private), and interdisciplinary approaches to investment law and policy. Its intellectual foundations link to the workshops held in Frankfurt in connection with the annual Frankfurt Investment Arbitration Moot Court.

Titles in the series include:

International Investment Law and Development
Bridging the Gap
Edited by Stephan W. Schill, Christian J. Tams and Rainer Hofmann

International Investment Law and the Global Financial Architecture
Edited by Christian J. Tams, Stephan W. Schill and Rainer Hofmann

International Investment Law and History
Edited by Stephan W. Schill, Christian J. Tams and Rainer Hofmann

International Investment Protection and Constitutional Law
Edited by Stephan W. Schill and Christian J. Tams

International Investment Law and General International Law
Radiating Effects?
Edited by Christian J. Tams, Stephan W. Schill and Rainer Hofmann

International Investment Law and General International Law

Radiating Effects?

Edited by

Christian J. Tams

Professor of International Law, University of Glasgow, UK

Stephan W. Schill

Professor of International and Economic Law and Governance, University of Amsterdam, the Netherlands

Rainer Hofmann

Professor of Public Law, International Law and European Law, University of Frankfurt, Germany

with

Jeanne Gillet

Assistant Editor

FRANKFURT INVESTMENT AND ECONOMIC LAW SERIES

Edward Elgar PUBLISHING

Cheltenham, UK • Northampton, MA, USA

Published by
Edward Elgar Publishing Limited
The Lypiatts
15 Lansdown Road
Cheltenham
Glos GL50 2JA
UK

Edward Elgar Publishing, Inc.
William Pratt House
9 Dewey Court
Northampton
Massachusetts 01060
USA

A catalogue record for this book
is available from the British Library

Library of Congress Control Number: 2022946680

This book is available electronically in the **Elgar**online
Law subject collection
http://dx.doi.org/10.4337/9781800884069

Printed on elemental chlorine free (ECF)
recycled paper containing 30% Post-Consumer Waste

ISBN 978 1 80088 405 2 (cased)
ISBN 978 1 80088 406 9 (eBook)

Printed and bound in the USA

Contents

Contributors

Christina Binder E.MA, holds the Chair for International Law and International Human Rights Law at the University of the Bundeswehr Munich since April 2017. Before, she was University Professor of International Law at the Department of European, International and Comparative Law at the University of Vienna. Christina is member of the ILA Committee on Human Rights in Times of Emergency. She is member of the Executive Board and former Vice-President of the European Society of International Law (ESIL). Her research focuses on a number of public international law issues, including human rights, the law of treaties, international investment law as well as international environmental law. She is co-editor of the European Yearbook of International Economic Law, the Hungarian Yearbook of International and European Law and the Zeitschrift für Menschenrechte.

Berta Boknik is an Associate at Cleary Gottlieb Steen & Hamilton LLP in Cologne. She has previously worked at the International Investment Law Centre Cologne. She studied law at the Universities of Cologne and Paris I and wrote her doctoral thesis on the relationship between the CJEU and arbitral tribunals based on intra-EU BITs.

James G. Devaney is a Senior Lecturer at the University of Glasgow. His research interests include international courts and tribunals, state succession, and legal theory and reasoning. He is also a Member of the Bar of the State of New York.

Tarcisio Gazzini is a Professor of International Law at the University of Padua. He has previously taught at the Universities Glasgow, VU Amsterdam and East Anglia. He is a founding member of the editorial board of International Investment Law Series (Brill).

Jeanne Gillet holds a Bachelor and a Master in Law from Belgium. She continued her studies at the University of Glasgow, where she obtained an LLM and a PhD in International Law, looking at online surveillance and privacy issues in international law. During her time in Glasgow, she was a Research Assistant, LLM Dissertation Supervisor, and Graduate Teaching Assistant. She is mainly interested in International Public Law, International Human Rights Law, and International Humanitarian Law. She is currently working as

Policy Assistant at the European Commission, focusing on the disinformation phenomenon.

Jane A. Hofbauer LLM, is postdoctoral Researcher and Lecturer at the Bundeswehr University Munich. Previously she worked at the University of Vienna, where she obtained her doctorate in international law, and the Ludwig Boltzmann Institute of Human Rights. Her research particularly focuses on the field of international dispute settlement, the interaction between different regimes, and international environmental law. She is co-editor of the Austrian Review of International and European Law (ARIEL) and of the Zeitschrift für das Recht der nachhaltigen Entwicklung (NR).

Rainer Hofmann is Professor of Public Law, International Law and European law at Frankfurt University and Co-Director of its Wilhelm Merton Centre for European Integration and International Economic Order. His research focuses on general international law and human rights law, with a special interest in migration law and the law of national minorities, and investment law.

Federica I. Paddeu is Derek Bowett Fellow in Law at Queens' College, Cambridge, and a Fellow of the Lauterpacht Centre for International Law. Her research focuses on State responsibility (in particular defences and exceptions), the law on the use of force, international investment law, and recognition of Governments.

Dirk Pulkowski is a Senior Legal Counsel at the Permanent Court of Arbitration. He has broad experience as registrar in arbitrations between States under public international law and as institutional secretary in investor-State arbitrations and contract-based arbitrations administered by the PCA. He has represented the PCA at various intergovernmental fora, including the Sixth Committee of the United Nations General Assembly, UNCITRAL and the OECD. He teaches international investment law at Université libre de Bruxelles (ULB).

Michail Risvas is a Lecturer in Southampton Law School and specialises in public international law, WTO law, and international arbitration. Dr Risvas's experience includes acting as counsel in investment and commercial arbitration cases under the ICSID, UNCITRAL, LCIA, and ICC rules in the different sectors.

Stephan W. Schill is Professor of International and Economic Law and Governance at the University of Amsterdam. He is admitted to the Bar in Germany and New York, is a Member of the Panel of Arbitrators of the International Centre for Settlement of Investment Disputes (ICSID), and regularly acts as arbitrator in international investment arbitrations. He is also General Editor of the Publications of the International Council for Commercial Arbitration (ICCA) and Co-Editor-in-Chief of The Journal of World Investment & Trade.

Christoph Schreuer is a former professor of international law at the University of Vienna, Johns Hopkins University and Salzburg University. He is currently of counsel at Zeiler Floyd Zadkovich in Vienna.

Frédéric Gilles Sourgens is the Senator Robert J. Dole Distinguished Professor of Law at Washburn University School of Law in Topeka, Kansas. Freddy is the co-author with Kabir Duggal and Ian Laird of 'Evidence in International Investment Arbitration' (Oxford University Press: 2018). He serves as Editor in Chief of InvestmentClaims.com and currently is a member of the Executive Council of the American Society of International Law. He holds a candidatus magisterii in Philosophy and Latin from the University of Oslo, a Master of Arts in Political Philosophy (The Idea of Toleration) from the University of York (UK), a Juris Doctor from Tulane University School of Law, and a PhD in Law from the Johann Wolfgang Goethe Universität Frankfurt am Main.

Christian J. Tams is Professor of International Law at the University of Glasgow where he directs the Glasgow Centre of International Law and Security (GCILS). His research centres on dispute resolution, the law of treaties and State responsibility, with a particular focus on international investment law and arbitration. Christian is an academic member of Matrix Chambers, London.

Stephan Wittich is Professor of Public International Law at the University of Vienna and Adjunct Professor at the Vienna School of International Studies. He is interested in questions of general international law with research focuses on sources, international responsibility, jurisdiction and immunities, international procedural law, and international law in Austrian courts.

Preface and acknowledgments

International investment law is a special regime, but it remains embedded in the framework of general (public) international law. The interactions between the special regime and the general framework are manifold. They have been studied before, at times in detail, but typically from a particular angle: the bulk of the existing scholarship assesses how the general framework influences the special regime, and often inquires how international investment could be better integrated into general international law. The contributions to the present volume reverse the perspective. They ask whether investment law influences general international law, and more specifically: whether approaches adopted by investment lawyers (including those sitting on investment tribunals) have radiated, or should radiate, into other fields of international law. This question is addressed with a focus on three broad areas in which investment law approaches has potential to leave a mark, viz. the general law of treaties, the law of State responsibility, and general principles governing the process of resolving international disputes. Perhaps predictably, the question eschews a straightforward answer. Much depends on the context, on the persuasiveness of the approach adopted by investment lawyers, and on the willingness of international lawyers elsewhere to be open to persuasion. Reflecting the need for nuance, this book does not attempt to prove, or argue for, 'radiation'; the question mark at the end of its title is there for a reason. But read together, the book's 12 chapters are a plea for a fuller engagement directed not least at general international lawyers who will benefit from paying close attention to how investment lawyers have applied, interpreted, and at times moulded, rules of general international law.

* * *

To say that this book has not been rushed to press may be an understatement. Whether investment law might have radiating effects is a question that has puzzled us for a long time. In the process of moving from our initial curiosity to the eventual manuscript, we have incurred many debts. The team of the Wilhelm Merton Centre, led by then Dr. (and now Professor) Philipp B. Donath, provided vital assistance in organising a meeting of authors in Frankfurt, where early ideas for many of the book‘s chapters were tested. At Glasgow, our assistant editor, Dr. Jeanne Gillet, provided valuable editorial and research assistance, while Ms. Aleksandra Sobieraj shepherded the book through the later stages of the production process.

Throughout, we have benefited from the generous support by our host institutions, which we gratefully acknowledge. Stephan W. Schill would particularly like to acknowledge support in the preparation of this book and the research leading up to it by a European Research Council Starting Grant on 'Transnational Private-Public Arbitration as Global Regulatory Governance: Charting and Codifying the Lex Mercatoria Publica' (LexMercPub, Grant agreement no: 313355).

Finally, our thanks are due to Edward Elgar Publishing, especially to Ben Booth, Jane Bayliss, and Amber Watts for their continued support for this series and to Emily Wright, Holly Doogood, and Sally Philip for their careful work on the manuscript. To all of them, we are grateful.

Christian J. Tams, Stephan W. Schill and Rainer Hofmann
Glasgow, Amsterdam and Frankfurt, April 2022

PART I

Overarching perspectives

1. Radiating effects: The gentle impact of international investment law on general international law

Christian J. Tams, Stephan W. Schill and Rainer Hofmann

I. INTRODUCTION

Consider three problems that have arisen, in one way or another, in recent investment disputes:[1] (i) An investor complains of measures taken by a State enterprise exercising elements of governmental authority. Could such conduct amount to a breach of an international investment agreement (IIA) entered into by the host State of the investment? (ii) A tribunal is presented with documents that have been obtained unlawfully. Could it take account of this evidence? (iii) A new State proclaims its independence after seceding from an existing State. Does the new State have to observe commitments made in bilateral investment treaties (BITs) entered into by its predecessor?

The express rules of international investment law — notably those found in IIAs[2] and in the constituent documents governing the arbitral process — are mostly silent on these questions; to the extent that they address the issues at all, they seldom provide conclusive answers. Investment lawyers seeking responses to such questions have looked around and sought guidance from elsewhere. In the three instances mentioned above, such guidance might, for example, come from (i) the regime of State responsibility, notably the

[1] For considerations of similar issues, see, e.g., *Bosh International, Inc v Ukraine*, ICSID Case No ARB/08/11, Award (25 October 2012) para 183; *Methanex Corporation v United States of America,* UNCITRAL/NAFTA, Final Award of the Tribunal on Jurisdiction and Merits (3 August 2005) paras 55–56; *Gold Pool Limited Partnership v Republic of Kazakhstan*, PCA Case No 2016-23, Award (30 July 2020) (unpublished, summarised in the set-aside judgment of the High Court of Justice [2021] EWHC 3422 (Comm)).

[2] This term encompasses rules on investment protection in bilateral, regional, or sectoral investment treaties, as well as investment chapters in free trade agreements.

rules governing the attribution of conduct to a State; (ii) general principles of international dispute resolution governing the admissibility of evidence; and (iii) the rules regulating the succession of States to treaties. Put differently, guidance comes from regimes and rules that are not particular to international investment law, but general in character, because they in principle purport to apply to all fields of international law (State succession, State responsibility) or to different forms of international dispute resolution. For reasons of convenience, we refer to these in the following, as 'general international law', or as 'general frameworks', reflecting their 'systemic importance to international law'.[3]

A quick glance at international investment law textbooks or investment awards is sufficient to appreciate that investment lawyers, especially those with a background in public international law and international dispute settlement, regularly seek guidance from the general international law rules 'surrounding' the regime of international investment law, and regularly interpret and apply them in the particular context of investor-State relations. They mostly do so competently (although there certainly are exceptions), and typically in a routine manner, almost intuitively.[4]

So far, the resulting engagement of investment tribunals with general international law has been analysed mostly in terms of how the tribunals apply general international law, whether they apply it 'correctly', or whether regime-specific adaptations occur that fuel the much-lamented fragmentation of international law.[5] The starting premise of the contributions in the present volume is different. They do not simply consider investment tribunals as

---

[3] See Christoph Schreuer, 'The Development of International Law by ICSID Tribunals' (in this volume) 31, 36. Along similar lines, Damian Charlotin describes these 'general frameworks' as belonging to a 'shared corpus of international law' that is 'predicated upon … universality' and to a body of rules reflecting 'a common international judicial function': see Damian Charlotin, 'The Place of Investment Awards and WTO Decisions in International Law: A Citation Analysis' (2017) 20(2) *JIEL* 279, 284–85.

[4] As discussed below in Sections II.B, and III, investment tribunals adjudicating treaty claims have adopted this 'intuitive approach' from early on; it is, e.g., reflected in the approach of the *AAPL* tribunal, which described the applicable bilateral investment treaty as 'not a self-contained closed legal system' but considered that it had to be 'envisaged within a wider juridical context in which rules from other sources are integrated through implied incorporation methods, or by direct reference to certain supplementary rules': see *Asian Agricultural Products Ltd v Democratic Socialist Republic of Sri Lanka*, ICSID Case No ARB/87/3, Award (27 June 1990) para 21.

[5] See, e.g., Freya Baetens (ed), *Investment Law within International Law: Integrationist Perspectives* (CUP 2012), as well as Rainer Hofmann and Christian J. Tams (eds), *International Investment Law and General International Law: From Clinical Isolation to Systemic Integration?* (Nomos 2011); see also below Section III.

rule-takers that consume general international law, and may use its tools and rules correctly or incorrectly, or adapt them to a regime-specific understanding. They instead explore to which extent investment tribunals are actors in their own right that do not simply receive general international law (or, at a maximum, project a certain sense of authority on the meaning of general international law within the regime of international investment law), but ask whether their interpretation and application of rules of general international law has repercussions on international law as a whole, that is, beyond the borders of the investment treaty regime. Proceeding from this vantage point, contributors ask questions such as the following: Are the rules of general international law affected by their encounter with investment law? Do investment lawyers, through their engagement, influence, perhaps even shape, general international law? Can investment law be a motor for the development of general international law more generally? This book is, in other words, an attempt to assess whether investment law, through its engagement with rules outside of its own, narrow field, has an impact on general international law.

Drawing on earlier studies interrogating the interaction between different fields of law, we refer to this impact as a 'radiating effect', namely 'the centrifugal flow of influence outward from [international investment law]' and 'into the wider world [of general international law]'.[6] We distinguish such 'outward flowing' radiating effects from influences flowing in the opposite direction, namely 'inward', that is, from general international law into the special regime of international investment law. We do not assume that investment law radiates outwards, but want to assess whether it does, or whether there is at least potential for investment law to radiate and impact general international law.

With that perspective in mind, Section II of this introduction lays the basics in describing international investment law as a special regime of international

---

[6] Our adaptation in the text draws on Marc Galanter's prominent description of the 'radiating effects of courts', which 'produce not only decisions, but messages': see Marc Galanter, 'The Radiating Effects of Courts' in Keith O. Boyum and Lynn Mather (eds), *Empirical Theories about Courts* (Longman 1983) 117–19 and 126. While Galanter used 'radiating effects' to describe a wide range of indirect effects of court decisions outside the courtroom, our focus in the following is on a particular form of outward-flowing influence, namely an impact on the understanding of the rules of general international law. For earlier uses of the term 'radiating effect' in this context, see, e.g., Theodor Meron, *The Humanization of International Law* (Brill 2006) xv, studying 'the radiation, or the reforming effect, that human rights and humanitarian law has had, and is having, on other fields of public international law'; and the voluminous literature inspired by German debates about the radiating effects (*Ausstrahlungswirkung*) of constitutional law on private law: see, e.g., Robert Alexy, 'Constitutional Rights, Balancing and Rationality' (2003) 16(2) *Ratio Juris* 131, 133, 'a "radiating effect" of constitutional rights over the entire legal system'.

law that is nevertheless embedded in general international law. This explains why rules of general international law impact international investment law and the activity of investment tribunals. Sections III and IV then look at the interactions between the special regime and the general international law framework from two different perspectives: Section III briefly summarises the hitherto dominant perspective and outlines the mechanisms that ensure a measure of inward-flowing influence from general international law into the special regime of international investment law. Section IV shifts perspective and looks in more depth at the research question that underlies the contributions to the present volume, that is whether and how investment law itself could radiate outwards, 'into the wider world [of general international law]'.[7] Section V distills the main takeaways of the contributions to the present book. Section VI concludes with an outlook and a plea for a fuller engagement, encouraging international lawyers to tap into the rich potential of investment law practice on general international law.

II. SPECIAL AND EMBEDDED: INTERNATIONAL INVESTMENT LAW AND GENERAL INTERNATIONAL LAW

In broaching investment law's radiating effects on general international law, the contributions to the present volume proceed from two assumptions about the relationship between international investment law and international law: First, that international investment law is a special regime of international law and in many ways is purposefully different from general international law; and, second, that notwithstanding its specialty, international investment law remains embedded in the general framework of international law and is in many ways shaped by it. The first assumption has never been in doubt; the second no longer seriously is (and should never have been). Taken together, the two assumptions define the parameters for interactions between general international law and international investment law. They are the basis not only of asking how investment tribunals apply general international law, but also whether their interpretation and application of it have radiating effects in general international law. We set out both assumptions briefly in turn.[8]

---

[7] See Galanter (n 6).

[8] The discussion in the remainder of this second section draws on Christian J. Tams, 'International Investment Law and General International Law: Comments on a Special Relationship' in Stephan Hobe and Julian Scheu (eds), *Evolution, Evaluation and Future Developments in International Investment Law: Proceedings of the 10 Year Anniversary Conference of the International Investment Law Centre in Cologne* (Nomos/Hart 2021) 61–70.

A. A Special Regime

International investment law is, of course, a special regime of international law, and there is nothing problematic about it. Like other special fields of international law (such as international refugee law or international environmental law), international investment law protects particular interests, addresses particular audiences, and emphasises particular modalities for resolving disputes. In fact, at first sight, one might be forgiven for feeling that it has 'specialty' written all over it: in important respects, it is based on special rules that have been agreed with the express or implied aim of opting out of the general regime of international law. Three examples illustrate the point.

(i) In IIAs, international investment law enshrines a set of special rights benefiting foreign investors that purposefully exceed those granted under general international law. To be sure, the various treaty standards are not sealed off from general international law: some treaties explicitly tie treaty rights to a general international law standard (as is, famously, the case for Articles 5 and 6 of the 2012 United States Model Bilateral Investment Treaty[9]). However, in the absence of such *renvoi*, and unless IIAs merely codify general international law, it is clear that investment treaty standards exist (to borrow a phrase coined in human rights litigation) 'over and above'[10] standards granted under general international law. International investment law purposefully confers on foreign investors a special level of protection. The right to national treatment is a clear example of such a treaty standard going beyond general international law.[11]

(ii) By offering foreign investors the opportunity to bring arbitral proceedings against host States, investment law offers a special mechanism for resolving investment-related disputes. This is doubly special in fact: first, because it relies on a binding method for settling disputes, which, notwithstanding the rise of international adjudication and arbitration

---

[9] According to Art 5, two treaty standards (fair and equitable treatment and full protection and security) are to be granted 'in accordance with customary international law', while States' obligations under Art 6 on expropriation and compensation 'intended to reflect customary international law concerning the obligation of States with respect to expropriation': see 2012 US Model BIT, https://ustr.gov/sites/default/files/BIT%20text%20for%20ACIEP%20Meeting.pdf accessed 14 August 2022.

[10] See *Ireland v UK* (1978) Series A No 25 para 239 (ECtHR).

[11] See, e.g., August Reinisch and Christoph Schreuer, *International Protection of Investments: The Substantive Standards* (CUP 2020) 605: 'Although national treatment provisions are routinely included in both trade and investment treaties, there is consensus that this has not led to an obligation under customary international law.'

over the past few decades, remains exceptional in public international law; and, second, because it grants the right to initiate binding dispute settlement to a privileged set of non-State actors (that are not otherwise so empowered under general international law or other regimes of international law, with the exception of human rights law). Looked at from the perspective of general international law, and the general regime for the peaceful settlement of disputes, which is dominated by diplomatic forms of dispute resolution and premised on the principle of free choice of means,[12] the emergence of the system of investment treaty arbitration marks indeed 'a highly exceptional development in the context of international law,'[13] and certainly makes it special.

(iii) The specialty of investment law can also be felt at the more granular level. To illustrate, broadly worded definitional clauses in IIAs are construed to permit independent claims of shareholders for violations of company rights, in a conscious departure from the general position shaped by the International Court of Justice (ICJ) in its judgments in the *Barcelona Traction* and *Diallo* cases.[14] A range of quite diverse provisions define who qualifies as a 'foreign investor' for the purposes of investment protection, among them provisions in EU member States BITs that extend protection to other EU nationals, which disapply the general rules on nationality.[15] Sunset clauses that extend the protection of an IIA beyond the date of the treaty's termination deviate from the general law of treaties, pursuant to which, as a default, termination

---

[12] In the *Fisheries Jurisdiction* case, the International Court of Justice (ICJ) restated the general position in the following terms: '[D]isputes are required to be resolved by peaceful means, the choice of which, pursuant to Article 33 of the Charter [listing negotiation, mediation and other non-binding means alongside arbitration and adjudication], is left to the parties' (*Fisheries Jurisdiction (Spain v Canada)* [1998] *ICJ Reports* 432, 456, para 56).

[13] Gus Van Harten, *Investment Treaty Arbitration and Public Law* (OUP 2007) 8.

[14] *Pars pro toto*, see *Camuzzi International SA v Argentina,* ICSID Case No ARB/03/2, Decision on Jurisdiction (11 May 2005) paras 141–42, noting that 'whatever may have been the merits of *Barcelona Traction*, that case was concerned solely with the diplomatic protection of nationals by their State, while the case here disputed concerns the contemporary concept of direct access for investors to dispute resolution by means of arbitration between investors and the State'; as well as the tribunal's discussion in *CMS v Argentina*, ICSID Case No ARB/01/8, Decision on Objections to Jurisdiction (17 July 2003) paras 43–48.

[15] See, e.g., Art 2 of the 2021 Italy Model BIT, https://investmentpolicy.unctad.org/international-investment-agreements/treaty-files/6390/download accessed 14 August 2022.

immediately 'releases the parties from any obligation further to perform the treaty.'[16] And so on and so forth.

None of this, to reiterate, is a problem. The framework of general international law is no straightjacket: unless core principles of peremptory law are concerned (which exclude or discourage deviation),[17] it regularly permits States to opt out.[18] International law as a loosely integrated system combining general frameworks and special regimes needs to strike a balance that ensures a degree of unity (avoiding complete fragmentation), while benefiting from the diversity of the special regimes that do opt out.[19] What is more, opting out is common. As noted above, investment law is by no means the only special regime of international law. In fact, points similar to the ones made above could be made to characterise two other prominent special regimes, viz. international human rights law and world trade law, which also rely on treaties supplementing and going beyond general international law standards, and on special procedures for the settlement of disputes. By doing just that for the special field of investment protection, international investment law contributes to international law's diversity.

B. An Embedded Regime

'Opting out' captures only one aspect of the relationship between international investment law and general international law. While special in many important ways, investment law remains embedded in the framework of general international law. Again, this is neither problematic nor unusual: as an embedded sub-system of international law, international investment law shares

---

16 Contrast Art 70 of the Vienna Convention on the Law of Treaties (adopted 23 May 1969, entered into force 27 January 1980) 1155 UNTS 331 (VCLT), providing for parties, upon termination, to be immediately released from their obligations, to, e.g., Art 38(3) of the 2015 India Model BIT, providing for treaty provisions to remain in force for five years post termination (https://investmentpolicy.unctad.org/international-investment-agreements/treaty-files/3560/download accessed 14 August 2022).

17 See, most prominently, Arts 53 and 64 VCLT (n 16), declaring treaties conflicting with peremptory rules to be invalid.

18 See ILC, 'Fragmentation of International Law: Difficulties Arising from the Diversification and Expansion of International Law, Report of the Study Group, finalised by Martti Koskenniemi' (13 April 2006) UN Doc A/CN.4/L.682, para 108 (ILC Fragmentation Report): 'Most of general international law may be derogated from by *lex specialis*.

19 Similarly, though using slightly different terms, Anne Peters refers to '[f]ragmentation … as an opportunity': see Anne Peters, 'The Refinement of International Law: From Fragmentation to Regime Interaction and Politicization' (2017) 15(3) *ICON* 671, 680.

the fate of many other special regimes of international law. None of them can operate fully outside the general framework. 'No regime', in the words of the International Law Commission (ILC), 'is self-contained',[20] at least not in the ambitious sense of the term that dominates the general international law discourse, which would require a special regime to 'prescribe and control all reactions to breaches of their norms'[21] and to 'totally exclude the application of the general legal consequences of wrongful acts'.[22]

This is not as such remarkable — in fact, general international lawyers used to decades of debates about the 'myth' of self-contained regimes[23] may find it trite, having accepted that 'general international law provides a systemic fabric from which no special legal regime is completely decoupled',[24] and even considering the notion of self-contained regime to be 'obsolete'.[25] But it deserves to be mentioned, as investment law's rise to prominence has been accompanied by prominent claims of exceptionalism and autonomy, especially coming from arbitrators and commentators approaching the field from a commercial arbitration background. Jan Paulsson's much-cited comment illustrates this perspective: in 'Arbitration without Privity', one of the seminal accounts in the early literature, investment arbitration was described as 'not a sub-genre of an existing discipline', but 'dramatically different from anything previously known in the international sphere'.[26] This could be read to suggest that it operated on a new level, and outside any general framework. Frequent assertions of the allegedly 'self-contained' nature of the investment arbitration system[27] add

---

20 ILC Fragmentation Report (n 18) para 192.

21 Peters (n 19) 675.

22 Bruno Simma and Dirk Pulkowski, 'Of Planets and the Universe: Self-Contained Regimes in International Law' (2006) 17(3) *EJIL* 483, 493. See also the literal meaning ascribed by the Cambridge Dictionary: to 'ha[ve] everything necessary to be independent or to work independently'; see https://dictionary.cambridge.org/dictionary/english/self-contained accessed 14 August 2022.

23 See, e.g., Bruno Simma, 'Self-Contained Regimes' (1985) 16 *NYIL* 111; Alexander Marschik, *Subsysteme im Völkerrecht* (Duncker & Humblot 1997). Peters (n 19) 675, considers the term to be 'obsolete'.

24 Simma and Pulkowski (n 22) 529.

25 Peters (n 19) 675.

26 Jan Paulsson, 'Arbitration Without Privity' (1995) 10 *ICSID Review* 232, 256.

27 Abby Cohen Smutney, 'Procedural Review' (2005) 2 *TDM* 35; OECD Secretariat, 'Improving the System of Investor-State Dispute Settlement' (OECD, 12 December 2005) paras 9, 19, 22, www.oecd.org/industry/inv/internationalinvestmenta greements/35808448.pdf accessed 14 August 2022; Georges R. Delaume, 'ICSID Arbitration in Practice' (1983) 2 *Int'l Tax & Bus L* 58, 67; see also *Itisaluna v Iraq*, ICSID Case No ARB/17/10, Award (3 April 2020) para 41: 'the ICSID Convention and ICSID Arbitration Rules establish a self-contained and sui generis arbitration regime for the arbitration of investment disputes between Contracting States and the nation-

to this: among investment lawyers, the notion of 'self-contained regimes' (now widely derided in the wider debate among international lawyers), is anything but 'obsolete'.[28] What is more, certain statements by general international lawyers equally seemed to suggest that the special regime of investment law did not really fit within general international law. To illustrate, in its Report on 'Fragmentation of International Law' issued on 2006 (Fragmentation Report) — finalised 40 years after the adoption of the ICSID Convention, and nearly two decades after the first-ever IIA-based request for arbitration in *AAPL v Sri Lanka* — the ILC described investment law as 'exotic',[29] betraying a surprising degree of hesitation, reservation, and perhaps even ignorance.

It only requires a slightly closer look to dispel these myths of 'exoticism' and 'radical difference', and to identify the source of confusion about the allegedly 'self-contained' nature of investment arbitration. To begin with this latter aspect, in the investment context, the term 'self-contained' is typically taken to describe the absence of any 'external control', by domestic courts, of ICSID awards or their enforcement.[30] This may be a plausible use of the term, but it is clearly different from the more 'ambitious' understanding of the term favoured by the ILC and in general international law scholarship.[31] While the fact that investment lawyers often fail to acknowledge their particular use of the term invites misunderstandings,[32] the fact that ICSID arbitration is not subject to any 'external control' from domestic courts does not stop it from remaining embedded in the framework of general international law.

And in fact, as general international lawyers and investment lawyers have looked a little more closely, they have found that investment law does not look that 'radically different' or 'exotic'[33] at all.[34] It is a special system based on

---

als of other Contracting States'. See also the reflections in Ole-Kristian Fauchald, 'The Legal Reasoning of ICSID Tribunals – An Empirical Analysis' (2008) 19(2) *EJIL* 301, 313–14.

28 Cf. Peters (n 19) 675.

29 ILC Fragmentation Report (n 18) para 8.

30 See, e.g., OECD (n 27) para 9.

31 See above nn 20–22, for examples.

32 This is especially because, as noted in Section I, the Tribunal in one of the discipline's classic cases clearly disavowed the 'self-contained regime' terminology: see *AAPL* (n 4), noting that a BIT was:

> not a self-contained closed legal system limited to provide for substantive material rules of direct applicability, but it has to be envisaged within a wider juridical context in which rules from other sources are integrated through implied incorporation methods, or by direct reference to certain supplementary rules.

33 See Paulsson (n 26); and the ILC Fragmentation Report (n 18) para 8.

34 For detailed engagements with the question, see notably Eric De Brabandere, *Investment Treaty Arbitration as Public International Law* (CUP 2014).

a standard source of public international law,[35] namely treaties, which dominate international law in its age of 'treatification' in a wide range of areas.[36] The breach of such treaties results in general international law's 'normal' consequence of unlawful conduct, viz. State responsibility, requiring investment lawyers to work closely with one of general international law's 'few basic tools and techniques'.[37] Whether a treaty has been breached and whether responsibility has been incurred, in turn, depends on a relatively limited set of principles governing, respectively, the application and interpretation of treaties, and 'the general conditions under international law for the State to be considered responsible for wrongful actions or omissions'.[38] Put differently, investment law in its 'BIT generation'[39] remains unusual in certain ways (among them its reliance on bilateral treaties, and on compulsory arbitration as the central agency of rule-clarification and development — two features that set it apart from many other sectoral regimes that are based on multilateral treaties and/or create permanent institutions tasked with overseeing the evolution of its rules). But when applied and interpreted, investment law has a fairly standard 'public international law feel' to it.

To illustrate, investment lawyers do what most international lawyers do: they try to identify the proper meaning of treaty provisions, guided by the protocols of Articles 31–33 of the Vienna Convention on the Law of Treaties (VCLT), which mandate a serious interrogation of the treaty's text, context and telos, but suggest that the treaty ought not 'to be regarded as inhabiting its own watertight compartment'.[40] Just as lawyers active in many other fields of international law, investment lawyers inquire whether a particular actor qualifies for protection under the standards set out in a treaty. In international investment law the issue is whether that actor qualifies as a foreign investor, in other fields the test may be whether an individual qualifies as a 'refugee' (under the 1951 Refugee Convention), or as a 'child' (for the purposes of the

---

35 See, e.g., Campbell McLachlan, 'Investment Treaties and General International Law' (2008) 57(2) *ICLQ* 361, 369 ('International law is a legal system, and investment treaties are creatures of it and governed by it.'); and James Crawford, 'Keynote Address: International Protection of Foreign Direct Investment: Between Clinical Isolation and Systemic Integration' in Hofmann and Tams (n 5) 22, noting that 'all international investment law derives from the law of treaties'.

36 See Jeswald W. Salacuse, 'The Treatification of International Investment Law' (2007) 13(1) *Law and Business Review of the Americas* 155.

37 James Crawford, *State Responsibility: The General Part* (CUP 2013) 52

38 ILC, Draft Articles on Responsibility of States for Internationally Wrongful Acts, with commentaries (2001) II(2) *ILC Yearbook* 31, General Commentary, para 1.

39 Cf. the subtitle of Santiago Montt, *State Liability in Investment Treaty Arbitration. Global Constitutional and Administrative Law in the BIT Generation* (Hart 2009).

40 McLachlan (n 35) 364.

Convention on the Rights of the Child).[41] In ascertaining whether host State conduct breaches a treaty, and in identifying consequences flowing from such a wrongful act, investment lawyers — like international lawyers of many other specialisations — work with the rules of State responsibility: in fact they refer to them enthusiastically, though perhaps (as the late James Crawford once noted drily) often 'by way of signposting rather than actually integrating the substance of the [ILC] Articles into the decision'.[42]

Fundamentally, investment lawyers — like international criminal lawyers, international human rights lawyers, or WTO lawyers, to name but a few — participate in one of the central projects of international law: that of assessing how States can be held to account under rules agreed at the international level.[43] In that sense, international investment law in its 'treatified' incarnation certainly 'cannot' (as the *Phoenix* tribunal rightly noted), 'be read and interpreted in isolation from public international law and its general principles'.[44] And as this is so, claims investment law's exceptionalism should be viewed with caution. Just as Mr Jourdain, Molière's *bourgeois gentilhomme*, belatedly realised that he had been speaking prose for over 40 years,[45] so investment lawyers seem to have come to realise that they have been 'doing' international law all along: working with a special regime that remains firmly embedded in international law's general framework.

---

[41] See Art 1 of the Convention relating to the Status of Refugees (adopted 28 July 1951, entered into force 22 April 1954) 189 UNTS 137, and Art 1 of the Convention on the Rights of the Child (adopted 20 November 1989, entered into force 2 September 1990) 1577 UNTS 3.

[42] James Crawford, 'Investment Arbitration and the ILC Articles on State Responsibility' (2010) 25(1) *ICSID Review* 127, 132. That, too, is no exception, nor is the fact that 'the universe of [investment] cases is, on the whole, of variable quality' (ibid.): like human rights lawyers, or international criminal lawyers, investment lawyers occasionally struggle with the ILC's work on State responsibility.

[43] See, e.g., Crawford (n 35) 22: '[Investment law] is about the way in which we bring the state under some measure of control, which is the main aspiration of general international law.'

[44] *Phoenix Action Ltd v Czech Republic*, ICSID Case No ARB/06/5, Award (15 April 2009) para 78. citing the WTO's Appellate Body Report in *United States–Standards for Reformulated and Conventional Gasoline*, WT/DS2/AB/R, 29 April 1996, 18.

[45] *Par ma foi! Il y a plus de quarante ans que je dis de la prose sans que j'en susse rien, et je vous suis le plus obligé du monde de m'avoir appris cela.*

III. THE INWARD-FLOWING INFLUENCE OF GENERAL INTERNATIONAL LAW ON INTERNATIONAL INVESTMENT LAW: INTEGRATIONIST PERSPECTIVES

The special regime of international investment law and the general framework in which it is embedded clearly do not exist in isolation from each other; they interact. Schematically such interactions can take two forms — which are not mutually exclusive, but reflect different directions of influence: First, the general framework can shape the special regime, which — while remaining special — is moulded by the general framework. Second, it is possible for the special regime to influence the general framework, which would draw on special approaches and perhaps over time 'generalize' them. These interactions can be usefully described by adapting (and adopting) the terminology of "radiating effects" mentioned at the start of this chapter: influence can flow 'inwards' (from the general regime to the special regime), or 'outwards' (from the special regime to the general framework).[46]

Perhaps curiously, commentators addressing the relationship between the special regime of international investment law and the framework of general international law have almost exclusively focused on 'inward flows' of influence: they have set out to 'critically examine and appraise the role of general public international law within investment arbitration.'[47] Very often, in fact, such inquiries have adopted (as the subtitle of a prominent book-length treatment put it) an express or implied 'integrationist perspective', reflecting on how international investment law might be subtly moulded by generalist international law.[48]

The two main modes of such 'inward influence' are not peculiar to international investment law; they reflect insights on how general international law influences any of its special regimes. In the words of the ILC's Fragmentation Report, '[g]eneral international law … fulfils [sic] gaps in the special regime

---

[46] See Galanter (n 6).

[47] See Laurence Boisson de Chazournes and Campbell McLachlan, 'Preface: The Intersection of Investment Arbitration and Public International Law' (2016) 31(2) *ICSID Review* 255, describing the interest of the journal's Special Focus Issue on the topic, comprising 11 perspectives on 'the influence to be accorded to doctrines of general international law in investment disputes' (ibid.)).

[48] See, e.g., the contributions to the symposium convened by Boisson de Chazournes and MacLachlan (n 47), and to the volumes edited by Baetens (n 5) and Hofmann and Tams (n 5). See further the account of De Brabandere (n 34) 203, which the author summarises as an effort to highlight 'the various procedural ways in which the public international law character is revealed in or has influenced the arbitral proceedings'.

and provides interpretative direction for its operation'.[49] Both forms of inward influence — 'gap-filling' and 'interpretative direction' — clearly affect the special regime of international investment law.

Gap-filling is the obvious impact: to the extent that international investment law does not lay down special rules, general international law applies by default. This is particularly important because international investment law leaves many gaps to be filled. Some of these have been referred to already, e.g., in the examples mentioned in the introductory section. As hinted at there, the general rules governing attribution of conduct are regularly relied on to determine whether a contested measure is attributable to the host State — e.g., where it has been taken by a bankruptcy judge or a State-owned entity competent to exercise certain regulatory powers.[50] Unless investment treaties formulate their own primary rules of attribution (which they rarely do),[51] the special regime of international investment law leaves a gap, which the general standards of attribution set out in the ILC Articles on State Responsibility fill. As a result, as noted by James Crawford, '[q]uestions surrounding attribution are the primary subject area in which arbitral tribunals have referred to the ILC Articles'.[52] Similar considerations apply to other gaps in the investment law regime that require being filled — among them questions as to the scope of reparation for unlawful conduct, and (in more unusual cases) the principles governing succession to treaties. In these instances, and many more, general international law (often as construed by the ICJ whose jurisprudence is regularly cited and treated, in the words of Alain Pellet, with 'particular deference')[53] indeed 'fulfils [sic] gaps in the special regime'[54] of investment law, and thereby ensures that influence flows 'inwards', from the general to the special regime.

There is more to integrationist approaches than gap-filling, though. Much effort has gone into establishing that, even where international investment law does address matters expressly (i.e., when it does not leave a gap), it does not fully escape the influence of general international law. General international law provides, in the words of the ILC, 'interpretative direction for [the] operation'[55]

---

[49] ILC Fragmentation Report (n 18) para 194(2)(a).

[50] See, e.g., *Gavrilovic v Croatia*, ICSID Case No ARB/12/39, Award (26 July 2018) paras 760 ff; and *United Parcel Service of America Inc v Canada*, UNCITRAL/NAFTA, Award on the Merits (11 June 2007) paras 45ff.

[51] But see the Award in *UPS v Canada*, ibid., paras 59–62.

[52] Crawford (n 42) 132.

[53] Alain Pellet, 'The Case Law of the ICJ in Investment Arbitration' (2013) 28(2) *ICSID Review* 223, 230.

[54] ILC Fragmentation Report (n 18) para 194(2)(a).

[55] Ibid.

of special regimes, such as international investment law. It does so notably by encouraging investment treaty rules to be construed in light of the 'the general international law principle[s]' surrounding it.[56] 'Systemic integration' is the leitmotif of this particular line of reasoning: drawing on Article 31(3)(c) VCLT, scholars have emphasised that 'other rules of international law applicable in the relation between the parties' could very well guide the interpretation of investment treaty standards[57] — and that an interpretation so guided would better embed investment law in its wider normative context.[58] This in turn is said to reflect a broader principle of interpretation that has been referred to as the 'presumption against normative conflict',[59] or in Jennings' and Watts' slightly fuller description: a 'presumption that the parties [to a treaty] intend something not inconsistent with generally recognized principles of international law'.[60]

This second form of inward-flowing influence seems to clash with the idea that international investment law is special and that it opts out of the general international law framework. Seeking to avoid this tension, commentators have emphasised that systemic integration could not resolve 'true conflicts of norms in international law', but could usefully operate 'before an irreconcilable conflict of norms has arisen'.[61] 'Interpretative direction' is therefore just that: one element in the interpreta-

---

[56] See, e.g., CJEU, Case C-386/08 *Brita* [2010] ECR I-1289, paras 43–44; *Al-Adsani v United Kingdom*, App No 35763/97, 21 November 2001, paras 55–56 (ECtHR); *Oil Platforms (Iran v USA)* (Merits) [2003] *ICJ Reports* 161, 181–82, paras 40–41.

[57] See McLachlan (n 35); and further Duncan French, 'Treaty Interpretation and the Incorporation of Extraneous Legal Rules' (2006) 55(2) *ICLQ* 281; Rumiana Yotova, 'Systematic Integration: An Instrument for Reasserting the States' Control in Investment Arbitration?' in Andreas Kulick (ed), *Reassertion of Control over the Investment Treaty Regime* (CUP 2016) 182.

[58] Systemic integration has been described as 'one of the most elegant attempts to locate specific treaty-based regimes within the context of broader principles' (Kalderimis) and 'a darling of recent international legal literature' (Simma): see Daniel Kalderimis, 'Systemic Integration and International Investment Law – Some Practical Reflections' (2012) *SIEL Working Paper* 2012/46 http://arbitrationlaw.com/files/free_pdfs/2012_-_d_kalderimis_-_systemic_integration_and_iil_-_some_practical_reflections.pdf accessed 14 August 2022; and Bruno Simma, 'Foreign Investment Arbitration: A Place For Human Rights?' (2011) 60(3) *ICLQ* 573, 584.

[59] ILC Fragmentation Report (n 18) para 37; see already *Georges Pinson (France v Mexico)* (1928) 5 RIAA 327, para 50 subpara 4: '*Toute convention internationale doit être réputée s'en référer tacitement au droit international commun, pour toutes les questions qu'elle ne résout pas elle-même en termes exprèset d'une façon différente.*'

[60] Robert Jennings and Arthur Watts (eds), *Oppenheim's International Law* (9th edn, OUP 1992) 1275.

[61] Campbell McLachlan, 'The Principle of Systemic Integration and Article 31(3)(c) of the Vienna Convention on the Law of Treaties' (2005) 54(2) *ICLQ* 279, 318; and further Christopher J. Borgen, 'Resolving Treaty Conflicts' (2005) 37(3)

tive process among others, such as respect for the text, context, and purpose of a treaty provision. As one element of interpretation, it is not designed to fully streamline international investment law into the general international law framework. But systemic integration can help broaden the view: it can encourage treaty interpreters to draw on themes and concepts that international investment law does not expressly take up. What is more, it can reflect the 'willingness [of investment lawyers, and investment tribunals in particular] to integrate themselves in a common international adjudicative practice'.[62] In that sense, it can indeed inform (and has informed) the interpretation of investment treaty standards, e.g., by unlocking arguments derived from proportionality discourse, from debates in other fields of international law, notably international human rights, or from the jurisprudence of other international courts and tribunals on general issues of dispute resolution.[63]

IV. REVERSING THE PERSPECTIVE: INVESTMENT LAW'S RADIATING EFFECTS

The contributions to the present volume need to be seen against the backdrop of the debate about the place of international investment law within the framework of general international law. They are part of this debate, but they approach it from a different angle. Rather than inquiring whether (or how) influence flows inward, from general international law to international investment law, they reverse the perspective and ask whether (and how) international investment law, as applied in arbitral practice, radiates outward and influences general international law. At some level, this might be said to

---

George Washington ILR 573, 640 (stating that systemic integration 'cannot resolve genuine conflicts').

62 See Charlotin (n 3) 289. On the basis of a computerised analysis comparing citations by different international courts and tribunals, Charlotin notes 'the sheer magnitude of external citations [to other international courts and tribunals] in the investment jurisprudence' (ibid., 288).

63 *Pars pro toto,* see, e.g., *Técnicas Medioambientales Tecmed, SA v The United Mexican States,* ICSID Case No ARB (AF)/00/2, Award (29 May 2003) para 122 (drawing on the jurisprudence of the European Court of Human Rights in assessing whether an impugned state measure was proportionate). See further *PL Holdings Sàrl v Republic of Poland*, SCC Case No V2014/163, Partial Award (28 June 2017) para 355 (noting that 'the [proportionality] principle is understood in largely similar terms across jurisdictions'); *Salini Costruttori SpA and Italstrade SpA v Hashemite Kingdom of Jordan,* ICSID Case No ARB/02/13, Award (31 January 2006) paras 72 and 74 (drawing on other courts' approaches to burden of proof); *Chevron Corporation and Texaco Petroleum Corporation v The Republic of Ecuador,* UNCITRAL, PCA Case No 2009-23, Third Decision on Jurisdiction (27 February 2012) paras 4.60–4.71 (regarding the absence of indispensable third parties).

be a fairly obvious question. The relationship between special regimes and general framework should not be a one-way street after all; international law as a system (however loosely integrated) depends on impulses from its various sub-systems, which (as Judge Greenwood has noted) do not 'functio[n] in isolation from [each other]'.[64] And, in the abstract, the possibility that investment law should radiate into general international law, is readily admitted, as reflected, for example, in Bruno Simma's and Dirk Pulkowski's succinct claim that 'general international law does not remain unaffected by the encounter with the modern investment system'.[65]

Quite how, concretely, general international law should be affected by this encounter is by no means clear, though. Assertions that international investment law should shape general international law have been received very cautiously, at least by general international lawyers and the ICJ. The debate about the relationship between BITs and customary international law is illustrative. Stephen Schwebel's view that 'customary international law governing the treatment of foreign investments has been reshaped to embody the principles of law found in two thousand concordant bilateral investment treaties'[66] is much cited, but outside the field of investment law, as a general proposition, meets with a significant measure of caution.[67] Emblematically, in

---

[64] *Ahmadou Sadio Diallo (Guinea v DRC)* (Compensation) [2012] *ICJ Reports* 324, Declaration Greenwood, 394, para 8.

[65] Bruno Simma and Dirk Pulkowski, 'Two Worlds, But Not Apart: International Investment Law and General International Law' in Marc Bungenberg et al (eds), *International Investment Law: A Handbook* (Nomos 2015) 362.

[66] Stephen M. Schwebel, 'Investor-State Disputes and the Development of International Law: The Influence of Bilateral Investment Treaties on Customary International Law' (2004) 98 *ASIL Proceedings* 27; and further Ian A Laird, 'A Community of Destiny: The *Barcelona Traction Case* and the Development of Shareholder Rights to Bring Investment Claims' in Todd Weiler (ed), *International Investment Law and Arbitration: Leading Cases from the ICSID, NAFTA, Bilateral Treaties and Customary International Law* (Cameron May 2005) 77, 95–96.

[67] To illustrate, Patrick Dumberry emphasises differences between treaties and argues that 'they are not entered into by States based on any perceived legal obligation'; while Jean d'Aspremont warns of the 'perils' of 'conflating practice and *opinio juris*': see Patrick Dumberry, 'Are BITs Representing the "New" Customary International Law in International Investment Law?' (2010) 28(4) *Penn State ILR* 675, 692; Jean d'Aspremont, 'International Customary Investment Law: Story of a Paradox' in Tarcisio Gazzini and Eric De Brabandere (eds), *International Investment Law: The Sources of Rights and Obligations* (Brill 2012) 34; see further Abdullah Al Faruque, 'Creating Customary International Law Through Bilateral Investment Treaties. A Critical Appraisal' (2004) 44(2) *Indian JIL* 292. But note that it is a separate question whether particular standards of treatment recognised in IIAs have come to reflect customary international law. This issue has been much discussed, notably by reference to the FET standard and the international minimum standard, on the customary

the *Diallo* case, when discussing one particular 'principle of law found in … concordant' provisions of IIAs, the ICJ was clear that the routine acceptance of independent shareholder claims in investment treaties and contracts left the general regime of diplomatic protection unaffected. In the words of the Court, 'the fact that various international agreements … have established special legal regimes governing investment protection … is not sufficient to show that there has been a change in the customary rules of diplomatic protection; it could equally show the contrary'.[68]

At least in ICJ proceedings, other attempts to rely on investment arbitration case law have not fared much better. In *Obligation to Negotiate Access to the Pacific Ocean*, the ICJ held that, while 'references to legitimate expectations may be found in arbitral awards' applying the fair and equitable treatment (FET) standard, 'it does not follow from such references that there exists in general international law a principle that would give rise to an obligation on the basis of what could be considered a legitimate expectation'.[69] In other proceedings, the ICJ has simply not responded to parties' reliance on investment treaty cases, which had been advanced to support points of general international law, but drew on its own precedent and other authorities.[70]

The ICJ's approach is not necessarily representative of other international tribunals, which have at times been less cautious.[71] For example, the arbi-

---

basis of which tribunals are divided: contrast e.g. *Mondev International Ltd v United States of America*, ICSID Case No ARB(AF)/99/2, Award (11 October 2002) para 125, and *United Parcel Service of America Inc v Government of Canada*, ICSID Case No UNCT/02/1, Award on Jurisdiction (22 November 2002) paras 84–97.

68 *Ahmadou Sadio Diallo (Guinea v DRC)* (Preliminary Objections) [2007] *ICJ Reports* 582, 615, para 90 — a passage that, in the view of one commentator, 'seems to have paralysed' the possible 'development of a customary international law of investment protection', see Campbell McLachlan, 'Is There an Evolving Customary International Law on Investment?' (2016) 31(2) *ICSID Review* 257, 258.

69 *Obligation to Negotiate Access to the Pacific Ocean (Bolivia v Chile)* [2018] *ICJ Reports* 507, 559, para 162.

70 See Stephan W. Schill and Katrine Tvede, 'Mainstreaming Investment Treaty Jurisprudence: The Contribution of Investment Treaty Tribunals to the Consolidation and Development of General International Law' (2015) 14(1) *LPICT* 94, 114–18. In contrast, investment arbitral awards have at times been considered in the judges' individual opinions: see, e.g., *Questions Relating to the Seizure and Detention of Certain Documents and Data (Timor-Leste v Australia)* (Provisional Measures), Order of (3 March 2014) [2014] *ICJ Reports* 147, Separate Opinion Cançado Trindade, 179–80, para 34, referring to *Libananco Holdings Co Ltd v Turkey*, ICSID Case No ARB/06/8, Decision on Preliminary Issues (23 June 2008) 42 para 2.

71 Nor is the ICJ's approach above criticism: Alain Pellet in fact found the treatment of investment law decisions in *Diallo* (n 64) to be 'quite cavalier': see Pellet (n 53) 226.

tral tribunal in the *Abyei Arbitration*,[72] the WTO Appellate Body,[73] and the Iran-United States Claims Tribunal[74] have relied on investment arbitration rules and case law as expressions of general principles or rules of international dispute settlement procedure.[75] But these references remain selective, as remains the academic discussions assessing whether investment law has 'radiated', or has even become a motor for the development of general international law in the way outlined in the opening section of this chapter.[76]

The eleven chapters that follow do engage more fully and across a variety of issues with this question. They offer a nuanced picture of how approaches pursued within 'the modern investment system' (adapting Simma's and

---

[72] *Government of Sudan v The Sudan People's Liberation Movement/Army (Abyei Arbitration)*, PCA Case No 2008-07, Final Award (22 July 2009) paras 412–24, 512, 526, 528–31, considering investment law decisions in relation to the possible partial annulment of arbitral awards and the standard of review in annulment, as well as the duty to give reasons.

[73] See, e.g., *United States–Final Antidumping Measures on Stainless Steel from Mexico*, WT/DS344/AB/R, 30 April 2008, para 160, relying on *Saipem SpA v The People's Republic of Bangladesh*, ICSID Case No ARB/05/07, Decision on Jurisdiction and Recommendation on Provisional Measures (21 March 2007) para 67, concerning the duty to follow, in principle, earlier case law; see further *United States–Anti Dumping Act of 1916*, WT/DS136/AB/R, 28 August 2000, para 54, referring to Art 41(2) of the ICSID Arbitration Rules to support the position that some jurisdictional objections are of such a serious nature that they have to be addressed by the panel regardless of the timing of the objections.

[74] *Iran v USA*, Partial Award (No 601-A3/A8/A9/A14/B61) (17 July 2009) 38 Iran-USCTR para 119, relying on *Waste Management, Inc v Mexico*, ICSID Case No ARB(AF)/00/3, Decision on Mexico's Preliminary Objections concerning the Previous Proceedings (26 June 2002) when considering *res judicata* effects.

[75] National courts have also gradually begun to engage with investment practice; e.g., in its decision on sovereign bonds, the German Constitutional Court considered investment treaty case law (amongst other decisions by international courts and tribunals) to have clarified and concretised the scope of the general defence of necessity under international law: see Bundesverfassungsgericht (BVerfG), Case No 2 BvM 1/03-5/03, 1/06, 1 2/06, Order (8 May 2007) www.bundesverfassungsgericht.de accessed 14 August 2022, discussing *CMS v Argentina* and *LG&E v Argentina*; and further Stephan W Schill and Yun-I Kim, 'Sovereign Bonds in Economic Crisis: Is the Necessity Defense under International Law Applicable to Investor-State Relations?' (2012) 3 *Yearbook Int'l Inv L & Pol'y 2010–2011* 489.

[76] For earlier treatments, see, e.g., Charlotin (n 3), who aptly notes that 'the "dialogue" between international economic fora and other international courts and tribunals (to the extent it exists), appears to take place mostly on a one-way basis' (ibid., 294); for comments by present authors, see Schill and Tvede (n 70); and Christian J. Tams and Rainer Hofmann, 'International Investment Law: Situating an Exotic Special Regime Within the Framework of General International Law' in Hofmann and Tams (n 35) 9, 15.

Pulkowski's words)[77] have 'affected general international law', or how they could or should affect it. Certainly, this is not a comprehensive account of the interactions between international investment law and general international law, which are too many to be covered in one volume. But it is by no means a narrow or selective inquiry either. Rather, following this introductory chapter, the volume offers two overarching inquiries, by Christoph Schreuer and Stephan Schill, and nine more focused studies of concrete 'interfaces' between the special regime of international investment law and different aspects of the general international legal framework.

The overarching inquiries, together with this chapter, lay the groundwork: Christoph Schreuer's general account of 'The Development of International Law by ICSID Tribunals' underlines that, in terms of their jurisdiction and applicable law clauses, ICSID tribunals are not 'restricted to their separate field … [but] apply international law in general'.[78] Their 'rich practice', Schreuer stresses, while not a 'source of law' within the meaning of Article 38(1)(d) of the ICJ Statute, is more than the mere application of international law, but can have an 'indirect and subtle' impact outside their own field.[79] Stephan Schill's chapter focuses on this 'indirect and subtle' impact: it notably emphasises the role of arbitral (*de facto*) precedent as a 'lodestar' for the development of the law, which has not only clarified the meaning of investment treaty standards, but transformed 'the use and conceptualisation of sources of international investment law'.[80] 'Norm production' in investment law, in an era of 'compulsory dispute settlement', Schill argues, is no longer 'an exclusively State-driven enterprise, as was traditionally the case in international law, but shared with international adjudicators'.[81]

The subsequent nine chapters assess to what extent investment law's adjudicators and other decision-makers partake in the process of 'norm production' outside the investment treaty regime. Their focus is partly on actual, partly on potential radiating effects of investment law on 'core areas' of international law that (as Christoph Schreuer notes) 'are of systemic importance to international law'.[82] We have grouped them into three broad fields:

1. The (general) law of treaties writ large — of obvious relevance to investment law in its present, treatified era — is the first of these. Three

[77] Simma and Pulkowski (n 65).
[78] Schreuer (n 3) 34.
[79] Ibid., 41, 44, 46, respectively.
[80] Stephan W. Schill, 'Sources of International Investment Law: Sonderweg or Lodestar in International Dispute Settlement?' (in this volume) 47, 76.
[81] Ibid., 77.
[82] Schreuer (n 3) 36.

inquiries assess whether the engagement, by investment lawyers, with the general international legal regime has radiated: Berta Boknik and Tarcisio Gazzini focus on the principles of treaty interpretation, Christina Binder and Jane Hofbauer on the scope of application of treaties, and Christian J. Tams, moving beyond the core issues covered in the VCLT, on the regime of State succession to treaties.

2. The (general) regime of State responsibility is the second interface addressed. As with the (general) law of treaties, it is of great significance for investment lawyers, which have for long drawn on the ILC Articles on State Responsibility. Three dedicated inquiries assess whether this investment law practice has radiated: Stephan Wittich covers the rules governing attribution of conduct, Federica Paddeu the circumstances precluding wrongfulness, and Dirk Pulkowski the regime of remedies.
3. The final three inquiries address general principles of dispute resolution applicable in proceedings before international courts and tribunals. While not (unlike the general law of treaties or State responsibility) codified in one canonical text, these have long been the subject of discussion, with commentators distilling aspects of a 'common law of international adjudication'.[83] Three chapters of the volume assess whether investment law contributes to such a 'common law:' Frédéric Sourgens and James Devaney, in two chapters, focus on the collection and assessment of evidence and Michail Risvas addresses the review and enforcement of awards.

The chapters studying those interfaces are not reports, in which contributors respond, point-by-point, to a centrally produced questionnaire, recording radiating effects (or noting their absence). But they do engage with two overarching sets of questions: (i) How have investment lawyers approached the particular 'interface' in question (sources, succession, remedies, etc.)? Has a specific investment law approach emerged, and if so, how does it relate to the general framework? (ii) Has the specific investment law approach influenced the general international law framework? More specifically, has it been noted and adopted by actors outside international investment law, and would such adoption be desirable? The combination of overarching and more focused inquiries, we submit, offers a fuller understanding of the real and potential radiating effects of international investment law on the wider world of general international law.

---

[83] As put in the title of Brown's influential study; see Chester Brown, *A Common Law of International Adjudication* (OUP 2007).

V. RADIATING EFFECTS: A ROADMAP AND FIVE STARTING POINTS

Contributors' assessments of investment law's radiating effects indicate a broad range of positions and views, partly reflecting the particular features of the respective interfaces, partly diverse normative starting points. To illustrate, while James Devaney's chapter firmly encourages international courts and tribunals to draw on the 'rich investment arbitral practice' and explore the 'untapped potential of investment arbitration',[84] Berta Boknik and Tarcisio Gazzini point to weaknesses in investment tribunals' approaches to treaty interpretation: to them, the particular investment law approach to treaty interpretation is an 'unconvincing departur[e] from the rules contained in the VCLT'; radiation should be contained, not encouraged.[85] But notwithstanding these differences, the contributions to the present volume do yield general lessons. Five of these are summarised in the following, in fairly condensed and simplified form, not to paper over the nuances brought out by the subsequent chapters, but as a roadmap to them.

Regular and systematic engagement: First, the modern international investment system regularly and systematically engages with the general international legal framework. This is true across the various forms of investment law activity, from treaty-making to law enforcement. However, investment arbitration is the key site of engagement: in dozens, indeed hundreds, of awards, investment tribunals apply and mould the general law of treaties, as well as general principles of dispute resolution. To say that there is now a 'critical mass' of engagement would be an understatement. Indeed, if numbers are any guide, investment arbitrations have long become (as has been noted) 'a prominent forum — perhaps the most frequent — for ever more nuanced interpretations of … general public international law rules:'[86] a laboratory for applying, and 'testing', general international law concepts. Contributors partly state this expressly (e.g., noting that international investment law had prompted the 'by far the largest number of decisions',[87] or referring to

[84] See James G. Devaney, 'On the Contribution of Investment Arbitration to Issues of Evidence and Procedure Before other International Courts and Tribunals' (in this volume) 343, 361 and 364, respectively.

[85] See Berta Boknik and Tarcisio Gazzini, 'Questions of Treaty Interpretation' (in this volume) 80, 105.

[86] José E. Alvarez, 'A BIT on Custom' (2009) 42 *NYU JILP* 17, 67.

[87] See Federica I. Paddeu, 'The Impact of Investment Arbitration on the Development of State Responsibility Defences' (in this volume) 209, 242.

the 'sheer number of cases' decided by tribunals,[88] and the 'consistent and steady flow of precedent'),[89] and partly assume as much. In the laboratory of investment arbitration, 'investment tribunals … apply all or major parts of international law and not just a specialized segment',[90] and in the process these parts are interpreted and occasionally stretched, in what Dirk Pulkowski refers to as a 'collective learning experience'.[91] The fact that it is such a regular and systematic experience would seem to suggest that there is a lot of potential for international investment law to have radiating effects, at least where it is indeed 'consistent and steady'.[92]

Engagement 'from within': Second, in engaging with general international law, international investment law typically works 'from within' the general legal framework. Stephan Wittich concludes his discussion of attribution standards by pointing to the 'remarkable "embeddedness" of investment law in general international law' and notes that 'tribunals overwhelmingly have discarded [the] option' of asserting that international investment law would be governed by special rules.[93] There are, no doubt, concerns about investment tribunals working from within this framework, as reflected in the statement by Boknik and Gazzini, quoted above, that tribunals depart from the rules in the VCLT.[94] However, such concerns stop short of suggesting that investment tribunals had moved out of the general framework for treaty interpretation; it rather reflects Boknik's and Gazzini's view that the tribunals had misconstrued certain of the VCLT's rules.

The fact that international investment law works 'from within' has two important implications. First, the subsequent contributions reflect the relevance of the major texts of general international law for international investment law, among them the VCLT, the ILC Articles on State Responsibility, and the amorphous body of general principles of international dispute settlement. Second, as it engages 'from within' the general frameworks, international investment law certainly has the potential of radiating and impacting general international

---

[88] See Christina Binder and Jane A. Hofbauer, 'The Temporal Scope of Application of Investment Treaties and the Effects on General International Law' (in this volume) 107, 145.

[89] See Frédéric Gilles Sourgens, 'Investment Arbitration as Incubator of Evidentiary Principles in International and Transnational Law' (in this volume) 280, 320.

[90] See Schreuer (n 3) 41.

[91] Dirk Pulkowski, 'Remedies for Wrongful Conduct: Lessons from Investment Arbitration' (in this volume) 246, 278.

[92] Sourgens (n 89) 320.

[93] Stephan Wittich, 'Investment Arbitration as an Engine of Development of the Rules of Attribution – With Particular Focus on *lex specialis* and *de facto* State Organs' (in this volume) 181, 206.

[94] See Boknik and Gazzini (n 85) 105.

law: investment tribunals after all interpret and apply concepts, notions, and doctrines that are not particular to international investment law, but form part and parcel of general international law. Frédéric Sourgens' statement that the investment law approach is not 'alien to a public international law way of thinking about evidence'[95] captures this second aspect, and it reflects a view shared by many contributors: extending Sourgens' point, one could summarise the subsequent chapters by noting that international investment law and jurisprudence approach questions of attribution, succession, and remedies in ways that are anything but 'alien' to general international law. The fact that general international law typically is just a framework leaving room for adaptation and adjusting (or that it, in fact, merely provides the 'bare bones' or is even 'skeletal'),[96] of course helps: it means that mostly it is not necessary to move out of the framework, as so much can be done 'from within'.

Concretising the general framework: Third, the subsequent chapters bring out clearly how much is being done 'from within'. In many of the areas under review, international investment law and investment arbitration are building on the general framework to offer greater specificity. In Federica Paddeu's 'bare bones' metaphor, which is also used by Stephan Wittich, the rich body of investment arbitration in particular has 'the important role of fleshing out [the] skeletal rules'.[97] The fleshing out primarily takes place (in Dirk Pulkowski rival imagery) in the 'laboratory'[98] of investment arbitration, in which the general rules are applied, tested, and above all concretised and specified. The outcomes of such a move towards concreteness and specificity can be seen in many areas, as brief snippets from the subsequent chapters illustrate. The investment law laboratory, amongst other things, is said to offer 'a more rigorous use of formal valuation methods and modelling in assessing … compensation',[99] and a 'rich jurisprudence' detailing grounds for the 'review of arbitral awards'.[100] It provides 'extensive consideration' of the 'admissibility of illegally-obtained evidence'[101] and also a 'detailed examination of … burdens and standards of proof' that could 'greatly assist in the development of more precise general international law rules'.[102] Some awards are credited with having added weighty arguments suggesting that 'provisionally applied

95 Sourgens (n 89) 282.

96 Paddeu (n 87) 242 and 245, respectively.

97 Ibid., 245. See also Wittich (n 93) 207.

98 Pulkowski (n 92) 276.

99 Ibid., 277.

100 Michael Risvas, 'Review and Enforcement of Arbitral Awards in International Investment Law and General Public International Law' (in this volume) 368, 390.

101 Devaney (n 84) 343.

102 Sourgens (n 89) 303.

treaties have legal effect' (a hitherto controversial question),[103] and with having offered 'extremely useful' guidance on 'the requirements for [States to succeed to treaties] based on conduct and tacit agreement'.[104] Finally, in the field of responsibility, investment law decisions have 'add[ed] flesh to the bone' of the concept of *de facto* organs,[105] and provided observers with 'a better sense of what interests of the State are "essential",' and thus capable of being relied on for purposes of the defence of necessity.[106]

Notwithstanding their differences in focus, and the commentators' diverse normative starting points, these snippets illustrate the central promise of the special regime of international investment law and arbitration: its '[fairly] consistent and steady flow'[107] of decisions is an ongoing exercise in applying concepts, notions, and doctrines recognized in the general international law of treaties, in the field of State responsibility, and in the practice of international dispute settlement; in clarifying these concepts in the face of real disputes; and in moulding them to fit 'circumstances which the most imaginative writers [as well as the codifiers of the general frameworks] never thought of'.[108] Across the board, this exercise results in a body of arbitral pronouncements enunciating rules that are more specific, more tangible, and often more 'grounded' than those comprising the general framework.[109] Developed against the background of the general framework and using its concepts, this body of concretised and specified rules is certainly capable of radiating outwards into the wider field of general public international law.

Engagement through persuasion: Fourth, while the subsequent contributions note the added value (or more rarely, the dangers) of having the more specific investment law guidance radiate into the wider field of general international law, they are clear that such 'radiating effects' are a matter of predilection. The point may be trite, but given the fetishisation of arbitral precedent in the investment law debates (and investment law practice), it is worth stating explicitly: while investment tribunals may have quite a lot to offer to public international lawyers, it is clear that when looking at the effects of their decisions outside international investment law, their pronouncements have persuasive force

---

103 Binder and Hofbauer (n 88) 136.

104 Christian J. Tams, 'Ways out of the Marshland: International Investment Law and the Law of State Succession' (in this volume) 150, 168.

105 Wittich (n 93) 207.

106 Paddeu (n 87) 243.

107 Sourgens (n 89) 320.

108 See Robert Y. Jennings, 'What Is International Law and How Do We Tell It When We See It?' in *Collected Writings of Sir Robert Jennings,* vol 2 (Brill 1998) 744.

109 For the clearest example, see the text of 'Evidentiary Principles in Investor-State Arbitration' appended to Sourgens' chapter: see Sourgens (n 89) 321ff.

only. In fact, if there is a notable absence in the subsequent discussion, it is the idea of binding (*de iure*) precedent. Investment tribunals do not determine, and have no binding authority on, how the general rules are to be read. Binding precedent (at least precedent across regimes)[110] is absent from the discussion in the subsequent contributions, which centre around the power of persuasion, the strength of convincing construction, and the common-sense argument that there is virtue in looking (from a general international law perspective) at how others (here investment tribunals) have dealt with similar questions before. The language used by contributors makes this plain: According to Christoph Schreuer, 'it is not any legislative power but their intellectual persuasiveness that will determine the influence of investment tribunals on the development of international law'.[111] Others agree, describing investment law guidance as 'illuminating',[112] rather than binding; it is widely noted that 'other courts and tribunals would have to embrace' or 'adopt' investment law approaches;[113] and even where international investment law approaches are described as an 'incubator',[114] a 'lodestar',[115] or a 'role model',[116] it is clear that they need to be seen as such by others and cannot decree that role themselves.

Whether international investment law's guidance is taken up needs to be assessed on a case-by-case basis, but is likely to depend on a range of fairly straightforward factors. As a threshold issue, guidance is more likely to radiate if it addresses cross-cutting issues that arise, in the same way, in other regimes, and if it is based on reasoning that is not tied to the particularities of international investment law, but capable of generalisation.[117] What is more,

---

[110] Whether arbitral decisions have greater authority within 'their' regime is a separate question. As is well-known, the Tribunal in *Saipem* seemed to endorse some form of soft precedential power, but even this (the high-water mark of a precedential approach) was subject to 'compelling contrary grounds': see *Saipem* (n 73), where the Tribunal put on record its:

> belie[f] that, subject to compelling contrary grounds, it has a duty to adopt solutions established in a series of consistent cases. It also believes that, subject to the specifics of a given treaty and of the circumstances of the actual case, it has a duty to seek to contribute to the harmonious development of investment law and thereby to meet the legitimate expectations of the community of States and investors towards certainty of the rule of law.

[111] Schreuer (n 3) 45.

[112] Risvas (n 100) 362.

[113] Devaney (n 84) 364; Paddeu (n 87) 244.

[114] Sourgens (n 89) 280.

[115] Schill (n 80) 77.

[116] Boknik and Gazzini (n 85) 106.

[117] For the most part, contributors assume that approaches by investment tribunals are in principle generalisable — and sometimes, they note so explicitly, e.g., by describing the issues as 'cross-cutting', 'identical', etc. But see Binder and Hofbauer (n

guidance is more likely to persuade if it is consistent — whereas a cacophony of inconsistent decisions is less likely to persuade others. All of this is not only straightforward, but also fully in line with the proper understanding of the effects of judicial and arbitral decisions in international law more generally.[118] International courts and tribunals do not make law by *fiat*, and they certainly do not do so across regimes. They settle disputes, and in so doing, may advance normative propositions about the proper interpretation of a treaty, about the state of customary international law, or about the existence of a general principle of law. Their propositions need to be accepted to have any force beyond the immediate dispute before them, which will likely depend on the scope and consistency of the reasoning of tribunals. None of this excludes judicial contributions to the law-making process, which especially within special regimes (such as investment law, human rights law, WTO law) are common; but it means that the 'fate' of a dictum needs to be studied carefully. Whether international investment law radiates depends on whether its normative propositions and its reasoning persuade, and on how they are received by decision-makers outside the special regime of international investment law.

Relatively limited uptake to date: Fifth, when looking at the reception by decision-makers outside the special regime of international investment law, the subsequent chapters suggest that the promise of relying on international investment law for guidance is by no means fully realised. Conversely, for those who view international investment law approaches critically, the dangers so far have not materialised. In fact, many contributors point to a marked gap between potential and actual radiating effects.[119] Partly, this may be due to the straightforward factors mentioned in the preceding paragraph, such as investment tribunals arguing narrowly, and emphasising the specific features

88) 148, wondering whether investment tribunals 'afford special attention to the specific features of investment law', which are simply not shared by other fields, and thus not capable of being generalised.

[118] For much more on this, see Christian J. Tams, 'The World Court's Role in the International Law-Making Process' in Jost Delbrück et al (eds), *Aus Kiel in die Welt: Kiel's Contribution to International Law – Essays in Honour of the 100th Anniversary of the Walther Schücking Institute for International Law* (Duncker & Humblot 2014) 139.

[119] To add this, at least in some fields, investment law itself does not seem keen on radiation: As regards succession to treaties, important investment awards have not been published. So it is difficult for them to shape international law more generally. In other fields, investment tribunals seem keen to argue narrowly, emphasising the specific features of 'their' area of law — which is not wrong, but makes it less likely for them to be considered persuasive. For illustrations, see, e.g., Binder and Hofbauer (n 88) 114–7, (discussing the temporal application of investment treaties) and Tams (n 104) 168–72, (discussing non-published awards on questions of succession).

of 'their' area of law, which makes it less likely for their approach to be generalised and taken up elsewhere. Similarly, as highlighted by reference to investment law decisions on necessity, where the reasoning of a tribunal 'has not worn well' in subsequent investment jurisprudence, it is unlikely to radiate into other fields.[120] For the most part, however, the subsequent contributions suggest that the gap between potential and actual radiating effects is due to a relative failure to listen: decision-makers outside international investment law seem to have been selective in engaging with the 'rich practice'[121] of investment tribunals, at least if formally acknowledged references in the form of citations are any guide. To illustrate, in relation to the review of awards, Michael Risvas 'to date' sees 'limited influence of international investment law … on the practice of other international courts and tribunals';[122] Dirk Pulkowski considers 'the effect of investor-State case law regarding remedies on courts and tribunals under general international law [to have] been rather limited'.[123] Similarly, Christina Binder and Jane Hofbauer note that standard VCLT commentaries contain 'scarce[ly] [any] reference … to existing investment case law';[124] and James Devaney is critical of the *Chagos* tribunal's decision to seek guidance, on the question of arbitrator challenges, only from 'the law and practice of courts and tribunals concerned … with inter-State cases'.[125]

The picture is by no means uniform, though, and it may be changing. As James Devaney also notes, the *Chagos* tribunal's approach stands in contrast to that of the *Abyei* and *Kishenganga* tribunals, which seemed more open to consider investment arbitration practice.[126] In the field of State responsibility, international organisations and scholars have done a lot to document (and occasionally critique) investment tribunals' 'almost ubiquitous reliance … on the ILC Articles';[127] this is particularly true for the investment jurisprudence on necessity (discussed by Federica Paddeu)[128] and for the rules of attribution (which, as Stephan Wittich notes, 'has attracted a considerable body of literature [addressing] these questions already in great detail').[129] What is more,

---

[120] Paddeu (n 87) 241 (discussing the fate of the *CMS v Argentina,* ICSID Case No ARB/01/8, Decision on Annulment (25 September 2007)).

[121] Schreuer (n 3) 46.

[122] Risvas (n 100) 389.

[123] Pulkowski (n 91) 275.

[124] Binder and Hofbauer (n 88) 148.

[125] Devaney (n 84) 351 (citing the *Chagos Marine Protected Area Arbitration (Mauritius v UK)*, PCA Case No 2011-03, Award (18 March 2015) para 165).

[126] Devaney (n 84) 353–5.

[127] Esmé Shirlow and Kabir Duggal, 'The ILC Articles on State Responsibility in Investment Treaty Arbitration' (2022) 37 *ICSID Review* 378, 390.

[128] Paddeu (n 87) 238–41.

[129] Wittich (n 93) 184.

during its work on State responsibility, the ILC took note of investment awards and earlier forms of decisions bearing on rights of aliens, which 'the ILC's Commentary … frequently refers to';[130] investment arbitration decisions rendered before the completion of the Commission's work in 2001 clearly influenced the 'collective learning experience'[131] of drafting the general regime of State responsibility. For another topic currently under consideration in the ILC, namely 'evidence before international courts and tribunals', Frédéric Sourgens hopes for, and expects, a similar uptake: 'Given the ILC's current composition, it certainly is familiar with investor-state arbitration;' its work may thus mark a more 'open engagement by general international legal bodies with the jurisprudence of investor-State tribunals'.[132] These considerations suggest that, while investment law's radiating effects continue to be resisted or ignored, general international lawyers seem to open up.

VI. A PLEA FOR FULLER ENGAGEMENT

The present volume takes stock of interactions between international investment law and the wider field of general international law, as they present themselves at the time of writing. It illustrates how deeply, and how systematically, the special regime and the general framework surrounding it are intertwined. And yet, reading the contributions, one is bound to observe that, to date, influence between the two has mainly flown 'inward', namely from the general framework towards the special regime. By contrast, outward flows — or radiating effects — are not (yet) as clearly established: while international investment law does occasionally radiate, 'general international law' often seems to 'remain unaffected by the encounter with the modern investment system'.[133]

The subsequent chapters suggest that this is a missed opportunity — and that it may be about to change. It is a missed opportunity because investment lawyers have for decades engaged with the general framework: their engagement is too rich and too pervasive to be ignored in general international law. General international lawyers ignoring it (or selectively engaging with it) do so at their peril. They deprive international law of a wealth of experience generated, above all, in the laboratory of investment arbitration. The subsequent chapters illustrate how much international lawyers could benefit from letting international investment law radiate: by considering investment law's 'more

---

[130] Paddeu (n 87) 219, referring also to earlier decisions, by mixed claims commissions, concerning the protection of alien property.

[131] Pulkowski (n 91) 278.

[132] Sourgens (n 89) 283.

[133] Cf. Simma and Pulkowski (n 65) 362.

granular understanding'[134] of inferences and presumptions, by taking guidance from how investment tribunals have construed the ILC's rules on counter-measures, necessity and reparation; or by working with the significant number of awards on State succession, to name but a few examples.

And so, in concluding this introductory chapter, we end with a plea for fuller engagement, directed at decision-makers and scholars working primarily outside international investment law: a plea to move from a 'one-way street' engagement, i.e., the reception of general international law in the investment treaty regime, to a true dialogue, and to tap into the rich body of investment practice whose potential often remains 'untapped'.[135] The goal of such engagement is not to adopt international investment law's treatment of general international law (in the words used by Judge McNair to describe the impact of private law institutions on international law) 'lock, stock and barrel', but to weigh that practice, and to scrutinise whether it could offer 'an indication of policy and principles'.[136] The goal is rather to assess whether international investment law yields findings, ideas or approaches that can be generalised, or that could flow outwards and inform the application and interpretation of international law elsewhere. Precisely because it is neither 'radically different' nor 'exotic',[137] the rich practice of international investment law to us seems capable of radiating a lot more widely than it presently does. The contributions to the present volume suggest that, while this has not happened sufficiently to date, things are about to change, albeit slowly and gradually. Perhaps indeed, as noted by Alain Pellet, it is only a matter of time until even those in generalist bodies that so far have remained cautious, 'it will have to [admit] that the critical mass' of investment law practice can no longer be ignored.[138]

---

134 Sourgens (n 89) 316.

135 Devaney (n 84) 361.

136 *International Status of South West Africa* (Advisory Opinion) [1950] *ICJ Reports* 128, Separate Opinion McNair, 148.

137 Paulsson (n 26); ILC Fragmentation Report (n 18) para 8.

138 Pellet (n 53) 226, discussing the relationship between claims under investment treaties and those brought by way of diplomatic protection.

2. The development of international law by ICSID tribunals

Christoph Schreuer[1]

I. ARBITRATION AND INTERNATIONAL LAW

In 1899 Russia initiated the First Hague Peace Conference with a bold proposal. Its suggestion was to introduce compulsory arbitration to replace war. The motive behind this revolutionary idea was less humanitarian than economic. The impossibility of financing a new artillery prompted Russia towards this unusual proposal.

With hindsight at the events of the 20th century, the idea of replacing war by arbitration seems unrealistic and naïve. But at the time, arbitration instead of war was seen as a real hope or a real threat depending on from which side you looked at it. The German representatives at the Peace Conference were instructed in no uncertain terms to reject the arbitration proposals and we all know the outcome: the PCA was established but the idea of compulsory arbitration was dropped.[2]

Today, over 100 years later, we have become far more modest. Nobody suggests that arbitration can revolutionise international law in one bold stroke. In fact, investment arbitration finds itself on the defensive. Public opinion (or a vociferous segment of it), far from seeing it as the saviour of peace, regards it as a problem that needs to be tackled through radical reform or even outright abolition.

But we should not be too modest nor too defensive. Investment arbitration is not just an arcane specialisation in international economic relations. It does have a role in depoliticising international disputes and defusing potentially disruptive or even dangerous conflicts between States.

The theme of this chapter is even more modest than that. To what extent has ICSID arbitration contributed to the development of international law?

---

[1] This chapter appeared as an article in (2016) 31 *ICSID Review* 728–739.

[2] Norman Rich, *Friedrich von Holstein. Politics and Diplomacy in the Era of Bismarck and Wilhelm II*, vol 2 (CUP 1965) 603ff.

A preliminary question is whether ICSID tribunals apply international law. The answer may seem obvious. Of course, they do. However, a look into the drafting history of the ICSID Convention shows that the application of international law was not a foregone conclusion. During the drafting of what ultimately became Article 42 of the Convention, there was some debate as to whether international law should be included at all. Some representatives insisted on the application of domestic law, in particular the host State's law.[3] Eventually a compromise was achieved that included international law as well as host State law.[4] Mr Broches argued tirelessly in favour of the application of international law both during the drafting of the Convention and thereafter.[5]

Over time, there has been a marked shift towards the application of international law. Early doctrine and practice still subscribed to the theory of a mere supplemental and corrective role for international law. According to this theory, the law of the host State would be applied in the first instance. The result would then be tested against international law. This would lead to not applying domestic law where it conflicted with international law.[6]

This approach was criticised by the second tribunal in *Amco v Indonesia* under the presidency of Judge Rosalyn Higgins. The Tribunal said that the classification of international law as only supplemental and corrective seemed a distinction without a difference.[7]

Gaillard and Banifatemi, in an article published in 2003, have pointed out that under Article 42 international law and host State law are equivalent and should be applied without any hierarchy or sequence.[8] Tribunals have since generally accepted this view.

The rise of treaty arbitration has accelerated the shift towards international law. Nowadays, the majority of investment cases are based on offers of consent to arbitration in treaties, mostly BITs. Therefore, we tend to perceive investment arbitration primarily as an exercise in the interpretation of the relevant treaties.

---

3 ICSID, History of the Convention, vol II, 267, 501, 513/4, 571, 801ff, 804, 984.

4 Ibid., 419, 421, 800–804.

5 See Aron Broches, 'The Convention on the Settlement of Investment Disputes between States and Nationals of Other States: Applicable Law and Default Procedure' in Pieter Sanders (ed), *International Arbitration Liber Amicorum for Martin Domke* (Nijhoff 1967) 12.

6 Aron Broches, 'The Convention on the Settlement of Investment Disputes between States and Nationals of Other States' (1972-II) 136 *Recueil des Cours* 331, 392.

7 *Amco v Indonesia*, ICSID Case No ARB/81/1, Award (5 June 1990) para 40.

8 Emmanuel Gaillard and Yas Banifatemi, 'The Meaning of "and" in Article 42(1), Second Sentence, of the Washington Convention: The Role of International Law in the ICSID Choice of Law Process' (2003) 18(2) *ICSID Review* 375.

The recent revised CETA text for a treaty between the European Union and Canada, confirms the trend towards international law at the cost of domestic law. It states that the Tribunal is to apply the Agreement and other rules and principles of international law applicable between the parties. The host State's domestic law is to be considered only as a fact.[9]

II. FRAGMENTATION OR INTEGRATION

It is beyond doubt that nowadays international law is very much at the centre of the activity of ICSID tribunals. That recognition is neither remarkable nor surprising. More interesting is the question to what extent investment tribunals apply international law. Put differently, is investment law, as applied by tribunals, a specialisation on the fringes of international law or is it part of the mainstream of international law? Or even more drastically, is investment law a self-contained regime that merely shares certain structural elements with general international law?

The fragmentation of international law has attracted much attention, including a detailed report of the ILC.[10] In the context of international investment law, the phenomenon of fragmentation is reflected in the attitude of some tribunals towards human rights law.[11] A procedural order in *Pezold v Zimbabwe*,[12] offers a good illustration of such an isolationist attitude. In response to an *amicus curiae* petition that sought to rely on human rights arguments, the Tribunal found that the BIT's reference to international law did not incorporate all of international law and that there was no basis to the assertion that international investment law and international human rights law are interdependent. Consideration of human rights was not part of the Tribunal's mandate.[13]

There is a widespread perception that investment arbitration is essentially a means to monitor compliance with the treaties that contain offers of arbitration. But is it really true that because a tribunal derives its jurisdiction from

---

9 Comprehensive Economic and Trade Agreement (29 February 2016) Art 8.31 (CETA).

10 ILC, Report of a Study Group on Fragmentation of International Law: Difficulties Arising from the Diversification and Expansion of International Law (13 April 2006) UN Doc A/CN.4/L.682, paras 410–480.

11 *Biloune and Marine Drive Complex Ltd v Ghana Investments Centre and the Government of Ghana*, Award on Jurisdiction and Liability (27 October 1989) 95 *ILR* 184, 203; *Spyridon Roussalis v Romania*, ICSID Case No ARB/06/1, Award (7 December 2011) para 312; *The Rompetrol Group NV v Romania*, ICSID Case No ARB/06/3, Award (6 May 2013) paras 170, 172.

12 *Bernhard von Pezold and Others v Republic of Zimbabwe*, ICSID Case No ARB/10/15, Procedural Order No 2 (26 June 2012).

13 Ibid., paras 57–60.

a particular treaty, the legal basis for its decision on the merits is necessarily confined to that treaty's substantive standards of protection? Are ICSID Tribunals restricted to their separate field or do they apply international law in general?

International investment law is part of general international law and it is the task of investment tribunals to apply all of international law. Three main factors afford the theoretical underpinnings for this proposition. They are the scope of a tribunal's *jurisdiction*, the *applicable law*[14] and the methodology of *treaty interpretation*.

A. Jurisdiction

The scope of the jurisdiction of tribunals, as determined by treaty clauses providing for consent to arbitration, is by no means uniform. Under many treaties jurisdiction goes beyond the treaties' substantive standards. These BITs in their consent clauses contain phrases such as 'disputes concerning investments' or 'any legal dispute concerning an investment'.[15] A tribunal operating under such a wide jurisdictional clause, that refers to investment disputes in general, is not restricted to applying the substantive protections of the respective treaty.

Other jurisdictional clauses are narrower. Under some treaties jurisdiction for investor-State disputes is indeed limited to disputes arising out of the interpretation and application of the treaty's substantive standards. This is the case under some BITs.[16] Under NAFTA, Article 1116, the scope of the consent to arbitration is limited to claims arising from alleged breaches of the NAFTA itself. Also under Article 26(1) of the Energy Charter Treaty (ECT) the scope of the consent is limited to disputes concerning an alleged violation of the ECT.

Under wide jurisdictional treaty clauses that refer to all disputes concerning investments a claimant is not restricted to rights arising from the treaty's substantive standards. Apart from contract claims, the claimant may pursue claims based on sources of international law beyond the treaty that provides for jurisdiction. These may be other treaties, bilateral as well as multilateral and

---

[14] On the relationship between jurisdiction and applicable law see Christoph Schreuer, 'Jurisdiction and Applicable Law in Investment Treaty Arbitration' (2014) 1(1) *McGill J Disp Res* 1.

[15] For comparative analysis, see Chester Brown, *Commentaries on Selected Model Investment Treaties* (OUP 2013).

[16] Some treaties, especially those of former communist countries, do not even allow claimants to rely on all of the BIT's substantive standards. Rather, they restrict consent to arbitration to claims arising from expropriation.

customary international law. Examples for pertinent treaties would be double taxation agreements or human rights treaties. Of course, the requirement remains that the dispute arises directly from an investment.

Practice confirms that under a wide jurisdictional clause tribunals are not restricted to applying the substantive protections of the treaty that offers consent to arbitration.[17] The *ad hoc* Committee in *Vivendi,* in its Decision on Annulment, described the scope of a wide jurisdictional clause in the following terms:

> ... Article 8 deals generally with disputes 'relating to investments made under this Agreement between one Contracting Party and an investor of the other Contracting Party'. ... Article 8 does not use a narrower formulation, requiring that the investor's claim allege a breach of the BIT itself. Read literally, the requirements for arbitral jurisdiction in Article 8 do not necessitate that the Claimant allege a breach of the BIT itself: it is sufficient that the dispute relate to an investment made under the BIT.[18]

B. Applicable Law

The second factor that determines what parts of international law will be applied by ICSID tribunals is the applicable law. Under Article 42(1) of the ICSID Convention, the applicable law is determined either by agreement of the disputing parties or by a combination of host State law and international law.[19] Some BITs contain their own provisions on applicable law, typically combin-

---

[17] *SGS v Philippines*, ICSID Case No ARB/02/6, Decision on Jurisdiction (29 January 2004) paras 131–135; *Tokios Tokelės v Ukraine,* ICSID Case No ARB/02/18, Decision on Jurisdiction (29 April 2004) para 52, fn 42; *Siemens v Argentina*, ICSID Case No ARB/02/8, Award (6 February 2007) para 205; *Salini v Jordan*, ICSID Case No ARB02/13, Decision on Jurisdiction (29 November 2004) paras 97–101; *Impregilo v Pakistan*, ICSID Case No ARB/03/3, Decision on Jurisdiction (22 April 2005) paras 57, 82, 102, 188; *Parkerings v Lithuania*, ICSID Case No ARB/05/8, Award (11 September 2007) paras 261–266; *MCI Power Group LC and New Turbine, Inc v Republic of Ecuador*, ICSID Case No ARB/03/6, Decision on Annulment (19 October 2009) paras 71–72; *Alpha Projektholding GmbH v Ukraine*, ICSID Case No ARB/07/16, Award (8 November 2010) para 243; *SGS Société Générale de Surveillance SA v The Republic of Paraguay*, ICSID Case No ARB/07/29, Decision on Jurisdiction (12 February 2010) paras 129, 183; *Metal-Tech Ltd v Republic of Uzbekistan*, ICSID Case No ARB/10/3, Award (4 October 2013) para 378. For a contrary view see *SGS v Pakistan*, ICSID Case No ARB/01/13, Decision on Jurisdiction (6 August 2003) para 161.

[18] *Compañía de Aguas del Aconquija, SA & Compagnie Générale des Eaux v Argentine Republic*, ICSID Case No ARB/07/3, Decision on Annulment (3 July 2002) para 55.

[19] ICSID Convention, Art 42(1).

ing host State law and international law.[20] By accepting an offer of arbitration under the BIT, an investor accepts its clause on applicable law. In this way, the BIT's provision on applicable law becomes part of the agreement between the parties to the dispute. Practically all these provisions on applicable law include general references to rules or principles of international law.

Where jurisdiction is based on a BIT that does not contain a provision on governing law, some tribunals have found a choice of law in the parties' pleadings. Invocation of the BIT is seen as a choice of law. In the first BIT arbitration, *AAPL v Sri Lanka*, the Tribunal found that the BIT was not a self-contained closed legal system but had to be seen in a wider legal context, which integrated other sources of international law.[21] Other ICSID Tribunals have also reached the conclusion that the choice of a BIT as the applicable law implied a choice of international law in general.[22]

Therefore, the acceptance of the theory that by pleading on the basis of the BIT the parties have made an implicit choice of law in favour of the BIT, leads to the conclusion that all relevant parts of international law are applicable.

This leads to the question: what are the relevant parts of international law? The relevant parts of international law clearly include certain core areas of international law. These core areas consist of rules that are of systemic importance to international law. They are the law of treaties (especially the rules on treaty interpretation), the law of State responsibility and the international law of dispute settlement.

But do the relevant rules of international law also include substantive rules beyond the narrow confines of the treaty that is primarily applicable?

---

[20] See, e.g., Art 10(7) of the Argentina-Netherlands BIT of 1992:

> The arbitration tribunal addressed in accordance with paragraph (5) of this Article shall decide on the basis of the law of the Contracting Party which is a party to the dispute (including its rules on the conflict of law), the provisions of the present Agreement, special Agreements concluded in relation to the investment concerned as well as such rules of international law as may be applicable.

[21] *AAPL v Sri Lanka,* ICSID Case No ARB/87/3, Award (27 June 1990) paras 20, 21.

[22] *Wena Hotels v Egypt*, ICSID Case No ARB/98/4, Award (8 December 2000) paras 78, 79; *MTD v Chile*, ICSID Case No ARB/01/7, Award (25 May 2004) para 87, Decision on Annulment (21 March 2007) paras 61–62; *ADC v Hungary*, ICSID Case No ARB/03/16, Award (2 October 2006) paras 288–291; *Saipem v Bangladesh*, ICSID Case No ARB/05/07, Award (30 June 2009) para 99; *Bayindir v Pakistan*, ICSID Case No ARB/03/29, Award (27 August 2009) paras 109–110; *Ulysseas v Ecuador*, Final Award (12 June 2012) para 111; *Emmis International Holding, BV, Emmis Radio Operating, BV, MEM Magyar Electronic Media Kereskedelmi és Szolgáltató Kft v The Republic of Hungary*, ICSID Case No ARB/12/2, Decision on Respondent's Objection Under ICSID Arbitration Rule 41(5) (11 March 2013) para 78.

The need to apply standards beyond the treaty that establishes jurisdiction is particularly evident in cases involving intertemporal questions. A treaty may provide for jurisdiction over disputes arising from events that took place before its entry into force. In such a situation, in accordance with Article 13 of the ILC's Articles on State Responsibility,[23] the law in force at the time of the relevant events and not the treaty that establishes jurisdiction must be applied to the merits of the case. The tribunal may have to apply the substantive provisions of an earlier treaty that has since been replaced or rules of customary international law.[24]

The importation of extraneous international standards of protection also takes place through so-called 'preservation of rights' clauses in treaties. Under these clauses, any better treatment granted by other treaties shall be preserved.

What about multilateral treaties of general application? Investment tribunals apply some of these as a matter of course without any debate. This would be the case for the ICSID Convention and for the Vienna Convention on the Law of Treaties (VCLT). Another treaty frequently applied by tribunals is the New York Convention.[25] The relevance of these treaties is beyond doubt either because they belong to the core areas of international law mentioned earlier or because they are specific to investment law.

But investment tribunals have also relied on a number of other multilateral treaties of general application and on decisions of bodies created by these treaties.[26]

---

[23] See ILC, Draft Articles on Responsibility of States for Internationally Wrongful Acts, with commentaries (2001) II(2) *ILC Yearbook*.

[24] *Island of Palmas*, Reports of International Arbitral Awards, vol II, 829, 845 (1949); *Tradex Hellas SA (Greece) v Republic of Albania*, ICSID Case No ARB/94/2, Decision on Jurisdiction (24 December 1996) 14 *ICSID Review* 161, 191 (1999); *SGS v Philippines*, ICSID Case No ARB/02/6, Decision on Jurisdiction (29 January 2004) para 166; *Impregilo v Pakistan*, ICSID Case No ARB/03/3, Decision on Jurisdiction (22 April 2005) paras 309, 311; *Salini v Jordan*, ICSID Case No ARB/02/13, Decision on Jurisdiction (29 November 2004) paras 176, 177; *Ioan Micula, Viorel Micula, SC European Food SA, SC Starmill SRL and SC Multipack SRL v Romania*, ICSID Case No ARB 05/20, Decision on Jurisdiction and Admissibility (24 September 2008) para 157; *Jan de Nul NV and Dredging International NV v Arab Republic of Egypt*, ICSID Case No ARB/04/13, Award (6 November 2008) paras 132–134.

[25] Convention on the Recognition and Enforcement of Foreign Arbitral Awards (New York, 10 June 1958) (New York Convention) 330 UNTS 38. See, e.g., *World Duty Free v Kenya*, ICSID Case No ARB/00/7, Award (4 October 2006) para 138; *Saipem v Bangladesh*, ICSID Case No ARB/05/07, Decision on Jurisdiction (21 March 2007) paras 141–142.

[26] See Moshe Hirsch, 'Interactions between Investment and Non-Investment Obligations' in Peter Muchlinski, Federico Ortino and Christoph Schreuer (eds), *The Oxford Handbook of International Investment Law* (OUP 2008) 154–81.

In a considerable number of cases, investment tribunals apply GATT/WTO law.[27] Numerous tribunals have relied on the respective treaties and on WTO decisions including those of the Appellate Body.[28]

In a number of cases, investment tribunals have treated European Community (Union) Law and decisions of the Court of Justice of the European Community (Union) as part of the applicable law.[29]

Tribunals have also relied on multilateral treaties for the protection of human rights. The relevant treaties include the International Covenant on Civil and Political Rights (ICCPR)[30] and the European Convention on Human Rights (ECHR), including the case law of the European Court of Human Rights.[31]

Other multilateral treaties of general application relied upon by investment tribunals deal with protected cultural heritage,[32] with the control of hazardous waste,[33] and with corruption.[34]

---

27 See generally Friedl Weiss, 'Trade and Investment' in Muchlinski, Ortino and Schreuer, ibid., 182.

28 *SD Myers v Canada*, First Partial Award (13 November 2000) paras 244–6, 291–3, 298; *Occidental v Ecuador*, LCIA Case No UN3467, Award (1 July 2004) paras 93, 153, 174–6; *Intl Thunderbird v Mexico*, Award (26 January 2006), Sep Op Wälde, paras 29, 37; *Canfor v United States*, Decision on Preliminary Questions (6 June 2006) paras 183, 187, 327, 333; *United Parcel Service v Canada*, Award (24 May 2007) paras 61; *Corn Products v Mexico*, ICSID Case No ARB(AF)/04/1, Decision on Responsibility (15 January 2008) paras 110–11, 121–3, 156–7, 160; *Continental Casualty v Argentina*, ICSID Case No ARB/03/9, Award (5 September 2008) paras 192–5; *Phoenix v Czech Republic*, ICSID Case No ARB/06/5, Award (15 April 2009) para 77; *Cargill v Mexico*, ICSID Case No ARB(AF)05/2, Award (18 September 2009) para 194; *Paushok v Mongolia*, Award (28 April 2011) para 315.

29 *Maffezini v Spain*, ICSID Case No ARB 97/7, Award (13 November 2000) paras 67–71. For a more reserved approach, see *AES v Hungary*, ICSID Case No ARB/07/22, Award (23 September 2010) paras 7.6.3–7.6.12.

30 *Toto v Lebanon*, ICSID Case No ARB/07/12, Decision on Jurisdiction (11 September 2009) paras 157–160. See also the non-ICSID case *Hesham Talaat M Al-Warraq v Indonesia*, Final Award (15 December 2014) paras 556–621.

31 *ADC v Hungary*, ICSID Case No ARB/03/16, Award (2 October 2006) para 497; *Rompetrol v Romania*, ICSID Case No ARB/06/3, Decision on the Participation of a Counsel (14 January 2010) para 20; *Tulip v Turkey*, ICSID Case No ARB/11/28, Decision on Annulment (30 December 2015) paras 146, 152.

32 The 1972 UNESCO World Heritage Convention was applied in *SPP v Egypt*, ICSID Case No ARB/84/3, Award (20 May 1992) paras 75–78 and *Parkerings v Lithuania*, ICSID Case No ARB/05/8, Award (11 September 2007) paras 382–383, 385, 389, 392, 394.

33 The 1989 Basel Convention was addressed in *SD Myers v Canada*, First Partial Award (13 November 2000) paras 105–107, 210–215.

34 The 2003 UN Convention against Corruption was applied in *World Duty Free v Kenya*, ICSID Case No ARB/00/7, Award (4 October 2006) para 145.

These examples illustrate that the inclusion of international law in the governing law, whether through a party agreement or by virtue of the default rule of Article 42(1) of the ICSID Convention, may lead to the applicability of the entire universe of international law. There is no convincing reason why the applicable rules of international law should be restricted to a particular treaty or even to rules dealing with the subject matter of international investment law.

A word of caution may be appropriate at this point. Not every invocation of a rule of law amounts to its application. In some cases tribunals' reliance on these 'extraneous rules' is not for the purpose of their application in the strict sense but as inspiration or authority for the interpretation of provisions in investment related treaties, such as the ICSID Convention or a BIT. A good example is the reliance by some ICSID tribunals on the case law of the European Court of Human Rights in cases against States that are not Parties to the European Convention on Human Rights.[35]

C. Treaty Interpretation

Article 31(3)(c) of the VCLT directs that, in the interpretation of a treaty, together with the context, 'any relevant rules of international law applicable in the relations between the parties' are to be taken into account.[36]

The International Law Commission in its Fragmentation Report[37] has discussed Article 31(3)(c) of the VCLT extensively. It has described the function

---

[35] *Mondev v United States*, ICSID Case No ARB(AF)/99/2, Award (11 October 2002) para 143; *TECMED v Mexico*, ICSID Case No ARB(AF)/00/2, Award (29 May 2003) para 122; *Saipem v Bangladesh*, ICSID Case No ARB/05/07, Decision on Jurisdiction (21 March 2007) paras 130, 132; *Azurix v Argentina*, ICSID Case No ARB/01/12, Award (14 July 2006) para 311; *Intl Thunderbird v Mexico*, Award (26 January 2006) Sep. Op. Wälde, para 27; *Société Générale v Dominican Republic*, LCIA Case No UN7927, Award on Jurisdiction (19 September 2008) para 93; *Perenco v Ecuador*, ICSID Case No ARB/08/6, Decision on Provisional Measures (8 May 2009) para 70; *Total v Argentina*, ICSID Case No ARB/04/01, Decision on Liability (27 December 2010) para 129; *El Paso v Argentina*, ICSID Case No ARB/03/15, Award (31 October 2011) para 598. In *Fireman's Fund v Mexico*, ICSID Case No ARB(AF)/02/1, Award (17 July 2006) the Tribunal questioned whether the case law under the ECHR is a viable source to interpreting Art 1110 of the NAFTA. See also reference to case law of the Court of Justice of the European Union in cases involving non-Member States: *Intl Thunderbird v Mexico*, Award (26 January 2006) Sep. Op. Wälde, para 27; *Total v Argentina*, ICSID Case No ARB/04/01, Decision on Liability (27 December 2010) para 130.

[36] For detailed treatment see Campbell McLachlan, 'The Principle of Systemic Integration and art 31(3)(c) of the Vienna Convention' (2005) 54 *ICLQ* 279; Richard Gardiner, *Treaty Interpretation* (OUP 2008) 250–91.

[37] ILC Fragmentation Report (n 10) paras 410–480.

of that provision as follows: '… if it is indeed the point of international law to coordinate the relations between States, then it follows that specific norms must be read against other norms bearing upon those same facts as the treaty under interpretation'.[38]

The ILC's study group has rejected any suggestion that tribunals should restrict themselves to the treaty upon which their jurisdiction is based. In the words of the ILC:

> … although a tribunal may only have jurisdiction in regard to a particular instrument, it must always *interpret* and *apply* that instrument in its relationship to its normative environment – that is to say 'other' international law. This is the principle of systemic integration to which article 31(3)(c) VCLT gives expression.[39]

Bruno Simma and Theodore Kill have explained how investment tribunals may make use of the rules on the protection of human rights through an interpretation in accordance with Article 31(3)(c) of the VCLT.[40] Their methodology is valid also for other parts of international law.

Article 31(3)(c) of the VCLT contains three conditions for its application:

- the extraneous material must amount to '*rules* of international law';
- the rules in question must be '*relevant*';
- the relevant rules must be '*applicable* in the relations between the parties'.

Clearly, the reference in Article 31(3)(c) of the VCLT to 'relevant rules of international law' includes customary international law as well as other treaties.[41] International courts and tribunals, when interpreting the provisions of a particular treaty, have relied on the terms of other treaties that contained relevant rules applicable in the relations between the parties.[42]

---

38 Ibid., para 416.

39 Ibid., para 423 (footnotes omitted, italics in the original).

40 Bruno Simma and Theodore Kill, 'Harmonizing Investment Protection and International Human Rights: First Steps Towards a Methodology' in Christina Binder et al (eds), *International Investment Law for the 21st Century* (OUP 2009) 678.

41 See also McLachlan (n 36) 290; Simma and Kill (n 40) 695; Gardiner (n 36) 260–63 with references to the VCLT's preparatory work as well as to subsequent practice.

42 *Oil Platforms (Iran v United States of America)* (Merits), Judgment (6 November 2003) *ICJ Reports* 2003, 161, paras 41, 42; *Certain Questions of Mutual Assistance in Criminal Matters* (*Djibouti v France*), Judgment (4 June 2008) *ICJ Reports* 2008, 177, para 112; *Southern Bluefin Tuna* (*Australia & New Zealand v Japan*) 39 *ILM* 1359 (2000) para 52. For additional pertinent practice of the PCIJ and the ICJ, see Simma and Kill (n 40) 682–91. See also Zachary Douglas, *The International law of Investment Claims* (2009) 86.

The requirement that the rules must be 'relevant' means that they must be related to the dispute as well as to the subject matter of the treaty provision that is to be interpreted. How close this relationship must be is subject to some discussion.

The relevant rules must be 'applicable in the relations between the parties'. This means that the rules must be in force at the time of the interpretation between the parties of the treaty to be interpreted. This may create difficulties if the treaty to be interpreted is multilateral, unless all its parties are also parties to the treaty that is to serve as background for the interpretation. If the treaty to be interpreted is bilateral, this is less likely to create a problem.

A complication arises from the fact that in investment arbitration one of the parties to the dispute is a private investor who cannot be a party to either of the treaties. The most sensible solution to this problem is to look at the States parties to the treaty in question and not at the parties to the dispute. In other words, if both States parties to a BIT are also parties to the treaty that is to serve as interpretive authority, Article 31(3)(c) applies.[43]

The Decision on Annulment in *Tulip v Turkey* offers an example for the systemic integration of international law through the application of Article 31(3)(c). The *ad hoc* Committee interpreted the concept of a fundamental rule of procedure in Article 52(1)(d) of the ICSID Convention in light of provisions in human rights instruments dealing with the right to a fair trial as well as judicial practice thereto.[44]

III. DEVELOPMENT OF INTERNATIONAL LAW

It follows from the above that investment tribunals should and actually do apply all or major parts of international law and not just a specialised segment. However, do these tribunals, in addition to applying it, also develop international law?

Article 38(1)(d) of the Statute of the ICJ refers to judicial decisions not as sources of international law but only as subsidiary means for the determination of rules of law. In the words of Judge Gilbert Guillaume '[a] judicial decision, even issued by the International Court of Justice, is not, as such, a source of international law'.[45]

---

43 Simma and Kill (n 40) 698–700.

44 *Tulip Real Estate v Turkey*, ICSID Case No ARB/11/28, Decision on Annulment (30 December 2015) paras 86–92, 146, 152.

45 Gilbert Guillaume, 'Can Arbitral Awards Constitute a Source of International law under Article 38 of the Statute of the International Court of Justice?' in Emmanuel Gaillard and Yas Banifatemi (eds), *Precedent in International Arbitration* (Juris 2008) 105.

An easy way out would be to downplay the difference between the sources and evidences of international law, reflected in Article 38(1) of the ICJ Statute, and to argue that every application of the law necessarily leads to its development.

Sir Hersch Lauterpacht was not overly impressed by the distinction between application and development of the law. In his famous book *The Development of International Law by the International Court*, he wrote:

> The distinction between the evidence and the source of many a rule of law is more speculative and less rigid than is commonly supposed. … the legal profession is not unduly troubled by the phenomenon of the mysterious birth of an authoritative source [of] law out of what is supposed to be no more than evidence of the existing law.[46]
>
> Judicial legislation, so long as it does not assume the form of deliberate disregard of the existing law, is a phenomenon both healthy and unavoidable.[47]

This might lead to the somewhat fatalistic conclusion that, in the face of judicial practice, development of the law is inevitable. However, it is possible to take the discussion further and to add a few theoretical and empirical observations on the development of international law through the activities of investment tribunals.

One theoretical approach would regard the practice of tribunals as delegated State practice. Under this theory, by endowing tribunals with the authority to decide on the application of the respective treaties, States have delegated to them the power to develop relevant practice.[48]

Anthea Roberts has described this approach in the following terms:

> In theory, states and states alone make international law while decisions of international courts and tribunals are merely subsidiary means of determining international law rather than sources of international law *per se*. In practice, when states delegate power to international courts and tribunals to resolve disputes under treaties and/or to interpret and apply those treaties, they impliedly delegate some law-making functions to those judicial bodies. Those judicial decisions are then routinely cited as evidence of what the law is, even when these decisions clearly develop rather than merely apply the law.[49]

---

[46] Sir Hersch Lauterpacht, *The Development of International Law by the International Court* (reprint, CUP 1982) 21.

[47] Ibid., 156.

[48] State practice has a dual function in the development of international law. First, as one of the essential elements in the creation of customary international law. Second, as an element in the interpretation of treaties under Art 31(3)(b) of the VCLT.

[49] Anthea Roberts, 'Subsequent Agreements and Practice: The Battle over Interpretive Power' in Georg Nolte (ed), *Treaties and Subsequent Practice* (OUP 2013) 95.

A more traditional approach would view the pleadings of States before investment tribunals as part of State practice or as expression of *opinio juris*. The problem with such a theory is that these pleadings are made in adversarial situations as part of a litigation strategy. Therefore, they do not necessarily reflect the considered position of the State concerned. Moreover, where a law firm hired to fend off a claim represents the State, it is even less obvious that a particular argument corresponds to the State's genuine position. Investment tribunals have taken conflicting positions on the legal value of arguments made by States and their representatives in the course of previous proceedings.[50]

In fact, the practice of investment tribunals affects the evolution of international law in a number of ways. Here, it may be more appropriate to speak of the influence of tribunal practice on international law rather than of its development by tribunals.

One area is the drafting of treaties. The more recent treaties in the field of investment protection display a number of features that clearly are in reaction to tribunal practice.

This influence of judicial practice on the development of treaty law is actually quite complex. On some points, the treaty drafters take guidance from tribunal practice. On other points, they try to settle questions left open by conflicting decisions. In yet other contexts, they attempt to counteract tendencies in judicial practice that seem undesirable.

The Consolidated CETA text for an agreement between the EU and Canada[51] contains a number of provisions that are obviously in response to the practice of investment tribunals. These provisions offer examples for all three of the categories just mentioned.

The definition of fair and equitable treatment in the CETA draft mostly reproduces practice by summarising concepts developed by tribunals.[52] On the other hand, the provision on most-favoured nation treatment seeks to settle a contentious question. It gives an unmistakably negative answer to the question whether MFN clauses apply to dispute settlement.[53] Similarly, the CETA text takes a clear position in the debate on the meaning of full protection and security: it only relates to physical and not to legal security.[54] An attempt to 'correct' tribunal practice addresses the ostensible incursions by investment

---

[50] *Canadian Cattlemen for Fair Trade v United States*, Award on Jurisdiction (28 January 2008) paras 171–189; *Urbaser v Argentina*, ICSID Case No ARB/07/26, Decision on Jurisdiction (19 December 2012) para 51.

[51] See CETA (n 9).

[52] Ibid., Art 8.10, para 2.

[53] Ibid., Art 8.7, para 4.

[54] Ibid., Art 8.10, para 5.

tribunals into the host States' regulatory space: a separate provision reaffirms the host State's right to regulate to achieve legitimate policy objectives.[55]

The practice of investment tribunals can also influence the development of customary international law. The discussion about the relationship of the fair and equitable treatment standard to the international minimum standard is a good example. Tribunals have suggested that the much-debated difference between fair and equitable treatment and the customary law minimum standard is more apparent than real.[56] This has led some tribunals and academic observers[57] to the conclusion that nowadays the driving force in the development of the customary international law minimum standard is the practice of tribunals on fair and equitable treatment.[58]

The impact of the activities of investment tribunals on legal developments can also be more indirect and subtle. Stephan Schill and Katrine Tvede have described how the case law of investment tribunals is beginning to influence the practice of other international courts and tribunals.[59] Similarly, the ILC has relied on and cited decisions of investment tribunals in its work on State Responsibility[60] as well as on Most-Favoured-Nation clauses.[61]

---

55 Ibid., Art 8.9, para 1.

56 *Saluka v Czech Republic*, Partial Award (17 March 2006) para 291. See also *Azurix v Argentina*, ICSID Case No ARB/01/12, Award (14 July 2006) para 361, 364; *Occidental Exploration and Production Co v Ecuador*, LCIA Case No UN3467, Award (1 July 2004) para 190; *CMS Gas Transmission Company v Argentina*, ICSID Case No ARB/01/8, Award (12 May 2005) 44 *ILM* 1205 (2005) paras 282–284; *Biwater Gauff v Tanzania*, ICSID Case No ARB/05/22, Award (24 July 2008) para 592; *Rumeli v Kazakhstan*, ICSID Case No ARB/05/16, Award (29 July 2008) para 611; *Duke Energy v Ecuador*, ICSID Case No ARB/04/19, Award (18 August 2008) paras 332–337; *Impregilo v Argentina*, ICSID Case No ARB/07/17, Award (21 June 2011) paras 287–289; *El Paso v Argentina*, ICSID Case No ARB/03/15, Award (31 October 2011) para 335.

57 Rudolf Dolzer and André von Walter, 'Fair and Equitable Treatment and Customary Law – Lines of Jurisprudence' in Federico Ortino et al (eds), *Investment Treaty Law: Current Issues II* (BIICL 2007) 99; Ioana Tudor, *The Fair and Equitable Treatment Standard in International Law of Foreign Investment* (OUP 2008) 83–85.

58 *Intl Thunderbird v Mexico*, Award (26 January 2006) para 194; *Azurix v Argentina*, ICSID Case No ARB/01/12, Award (14 July 2006) paras 365–372; *Compañiá de Aguas del Aconquija SA and Vivendi Universal v Argentina*, ICSID Case No ARB/97/3, Award (20 August 2007) fn 325; *Chemtura v Canada*, Award (2 August 2010) paras 121, 236.

59 Stephan W. Schill and Katrine R. Tvede, 'Mainstreaming Investment Treaty Jurisprudence' (2015) 14 *LPICT* 94, 106.

60 ILC Articles on State Responsibility (n 23), Commentary to Article 36.

61 ILC, Final Report, Study Group on the Most-Favoured-Nation Clause (29 May 2015) A/CN.4/L.852 http://legal.un.org/docs/?symbol=A/CN.4/L.852 accessed 4 April 2016.

It is not entirely clear to what extent ICSID tribunals perceive themselves as agents of the development of international law. A number of tribunals have called for consistency of practice in the interest of developing international investment law. The Tribunal in *Saipem v Bangladesh* has coined a formula that other tribunals have since repeated:[62]

> [The Tribunal] believes that, subject to compelling contrary grounds, it has a duty to adopt solutions established in a series of consistent cases. It also believes that, subject to the specifics of a given treaty and of the circumstances of the actual case, it has a duty to seek to contribute to the harmonious development of investment law and thereby to meet the legitimate expectations of the community of States and investors towards certainty of the rule of law.[63]

Academic analysis may support this process of harmonious development. Systematic description and appraisal of tribunal practice may lead to generalised conclusions, which in turn, affect the subsequent activity of tribunals.

Ultimately, it is not any legislative power but their intellectual persuasiveness that will determine the influence of investment tribunals on the development of international law. To quote once more Sir Hersch Lauterpacht: 'It is in their intrinsic power, and not in the fourth subparagraph of Article 38(1) of the Statute … that lies the source of the authority of the Court's pronouncements and the explanation of their actual influence.'[64]

The authority or intrinsic power of an investment tribunal and its influence on the development of international law depends on a number of factors:

- the persuasiveness and cogency of a decision's reasoning. Variations in quality are the consequence not only of the composition of tribunals but

---

[62] *Noble Energy v Ecuador*, ICSID Case No ARB/05/12, Decision on Jurisdiction (5 March 2008) para 50; *Duke Energy v Ecuador*, ICSID Case No ARB/04/19, Award (18 August 2008) para 117; *Bayindir v Pakistan*, ICSID Case No ARB/03/29, Award (27 August 2009) para 145; *Austrian Airlines v Slovakia*, Final Award (9 October 2009) para 84; *Oostergetel v Slovakia*, Decision on Jurisdiction (30 April 2010) para 62; *Fakes v Turkey*, ICSID Case No ARB/07/20, Award (14 July 2010) para 96; *Chemtura v Canada*, Award (2 August 2010) para 109; *Bosh v Ukraine*, ICSID Case No ARB/08/11, Award (25 October 2012) para 211; *Burlington v Ecuador*, ICSID Case No ARB/08/5, Decision on Liability (14 December 2012) para 187; *Metal-Tech v Uzbekistan*, ICSID Case No ARB/10/3, Award (4 October 2013) para 116; *KT Asia v Kazakhstan*, ICSID Case No ARB/09/8, Award (17 October 2013) para 83; *Renée Rose Levy and Gremcitel SA v Republic of Peru*, ICSID Case No ARB/11/17, Award (9 January 2015) para 76.

[63] *Saipem v Bangladesh*, ICSID Case No ARB/05/7, Decision on Jurisdiction (21 March 2007) para 67, footnotes omitted.

[64] Lauterpacht (n 46) 22.

also of the parties' pleadings and the need to find a compromise within a tribunal;

- it will add to a tribunal's authority if all its members are perceived as being genuinely impartial;
- unanimity within a tribunal is not necessarily a decisive factor. A powerful majority decision or even a convincing dissenting opinion may leave an important mark;
- over time, a consistent line of decisions by different tribunals may build up compelling authority on a point of international law.

IV. CONCLUSION

The domain of ICSID tribunals is not just an exotic sub-discipline of international law. Their activity lies in the mainstream of international law and touches upon many of its central questions. Through their rich practice, investment tribunals have made an important impact on the development of international law.

3. Sources of international investment law: Sonderweg or lodestar in international dispute settlement?

Stephan W. Schill[1]

I. INTRODUCTION

Since the 1990s, the production of primary norms of international investment law in the form of international investment agreements (IIAs) and their interpretation and application in investor-State dispute settlement have proliferated. As a result, international investment law today is equivalent to the law of investment treaties as interpreted and applied by investor-State arbitration tribunals.[2] In addition, the frequent recourse of foreign investors to treaty-based arbitration has generated its own epistemic community of international investment lawyers and a new sub-field of international legal study.[3] This field has also started attracting attention from the mainstream of international law, not least because investment treaty arbitrations raise manifold issues of general

[1] The present text in parts draws on, updates, and further develops the analysis presented in Stephan W. Schill, 'Sources of International Investment Law: Multilateralization, Arbitral Precedent, Comparativism, Soft Law' in Jean d'Aspremont and Samantha Besson (eds), *The Oxford Handbook on the Sources of International Law* (OUP 2017) 1095.

[2] By contrast, the application of investment treaties and the resolution of investor-State disputes in other institutional courts and tribunals, such as the International Court of Justice (ICJ), is a rather peripheral phenomenon. For examples of investment disputes before the ICJ, see *Elettronica Sicula SpA (ELSI) (United States v Italy)* (Judgment) [1989] *ICJ Reports* 15; *Ahmadou Sadio Diallo (Republic of Guinea v Democratic Republic of the Congo)* (Merits) [2010] *ICJ Reports* 639. For examples of inter-State arbitrations dealing with investment disputes, see Anthea Roberts, 'State-to-State Investment Treaty Arbitration: A Hybrid Theory of Interdependent Rights and Shared Interpretive Authority' (2014) 55 *Harvard ILJ* 1.

[3] On the mainstreaming of investment law, see Stephan W. Schill, 'W(h)ither Fragmentation? On the Literature and Sociology of International Investment Law' (2011) 22 *EJIL* 875.

international law and international dispute settlement, whether in respect of the law of treaties, State responsibility, State succession, immunities, arbitral jurisdiction, or dispute settlement procedure. In all of these areas, questions can be raised to which extent international investment law merely adapts to preconceived structures and concepts of public international law or also actively shapes and contributes to the further development of international law writ large.[4]

To which extent 'radiating effects' of international investment law also exist in respect of the sources of international law is the topic of the present chapter.[5] It shows that international investment law, while principally involving the interpretation and application of IIAs, also has recourse to all other sources of international law laid down in Article 38 of the Statute of the International

---

[4] For writings considering the interactions between general international law and international investment law, see, e.g., Rainer Hofmann and Christian J. Tams (ed), *International Investment Law and General International Law – From Clinical Isolation to Systemic Integration?* (Nomos 2011); Eric De Brabandere, *Investment Treaty Arbitration as Public International Law – Procedural Aspects and Implications* (CUP 2014); Bruno Simma and Dirk Pulkowski, 'Two Worlds, But Not Apart: International Investment Law and General International Law' in Marc Bungenberg and others (eds), *International Investment Law: A Handbook* (CH Beck 2015) 368; Stephan W. Schill and Katrine R. Tvede, 'Mainstreaming Investment Treaty Jurisprudence: The Contribution of Investment Treaty Tribunals to the Consolidation and Development of General International Law' (2015) 14 *LPICT* 94; Christoph Schreuer, 'The Development of International Law by ICSID Tribunals' (2016) 31 *ICSID Review* 728. See also the contributions in Laurence Boisson de Chazournes and Campbell McLachlan (eds), 'Special Focus Issue: The Intersection Between Investment Arbitration and Public International Law' (2016) 31 *ICSID Review* 255–503.

[5] This chapter concentrates on the different legal forms in which rights and obligations are cast, but does not address or assess their material content, i.e., the substantive rights and obligations that arise under different sources in international investment law. For a general overview over substantive investment law and its implementation, see, e.g., Rudolf Dolzer, Ursula Kriebaum and Christoph Schreuer, *Principles of International Investment Law* (3rd edn, OUP 2022); Campbell McLachlan, Laurence Shore, and Matthew Weiniger, *International Investment Arbitration—Substantive Principles* (2nd edn, OUP 2017); Andrew Newcombe and Lluís Paradell, *Law and Practice of Investment Treaties: Standards of Treatment* (Kluwer Law International 2009). In focusing on the impact of international investment law on the sources of international law, the chapter does also not address the role domestic law plays in the resolution of foreign investment disputes by investment tribunals and its interaction with international law. On these issues, see Monique Sasson, *Substantive Law in Investment Treaty Arbitration: The Unsettled Relationship between International Law and Municipal Law* (Kluwer Law International 2010); Hege Elisabeth Kjos, *Applicable Law in Investor-State Arbitration: The Interplay Between National and International Law* (OUP 2013); Jarrod Hepburn, *Domestic Law in International Investment Arbitration* (OUP 2017).

Court of Justice (ICJ Statute),[6] that is, custom, and general principles of law, and makes use of judicial decisions and writings of publicists as well.[7] The purpose of recourse to these sources is usually to concretise and clarify the meaning of the often vague standards of treatment in investment treaties, such as the prohibition of indirect expropriation without compensation or the requirement to treat investors fairly and equitably. Still, international investment law displays certain notable specificities. To which extent these specificities are a Sonderweg of international investment law that has little relevance outside the field, or whether investment law can serve as a lodestar for how the use and relative importance of sources of international law more generally may change also elsewhere in international law is the focus of the present chapter.

This chapter's principal argument is that the specificities one can observe in the use of sources in international investment law are principally due to the existence of compulsory dispute settlement mechanisms in the form of investment arbitration and the frequent recourse investors have to this mechanism. Because of the burgeoning tribunal practice, it is ultimately investment arbitrators that determine what counts as a source in international investment law, how that source and its content are identified, and what the relative weight of a source of investment law is.[8] In performing this task, investment arbitrators

---

6 Statute of the International Court of Justice (San Francisco, 26 June 1945) (ICJ Statute) 33 UNTS 993.

7 Ole K. Fauchald, 'The Legal Reasoning of ICSID Tribunals' (2008) 19 *EJIL* 301, 303. For analyses on the sources of international law, see Patrick Juillard, 'L'évolution des sources du droit des investissements' (1994) 250 *Recueil des cours* 9; Tarcisio Gazzini and Eric De Brabandere (eds), *International Investment Law: The Sources of Rights and Obligations* (Martinus Nijhoff 2012); Moshe Hirsch, 'Sources of International Investment Law' in Andrea K Bjorklund and August Reinisch (eds), *International Investment Law and Soft Law* (Edward Elgar 2012) 9; Florian Grisel, 'The Sources of Foreign Investment Law' in Zachary Douglas, Joost Pauwelyn and Jorge E Viñuales (eds), *The Foundations of International Investment Law: Bringing Theory into Practice* (OUP 2014) 213.

8 The reason for this is that the substantive control over the decision-making of investment treaty tribunals is very limited. In respect of investment arbitrations under the Convention on the Settlement of Investment Disputes Between States and Nationals of Other States (adopted 18 March 1965; entered into force 14 October 1966) (ICSID Convention) 575 UNTS 159 control is limited to the grounds for annulment listed in Art 52 of the Convention. In respect of non-ICSID arbitrations, domestic courts at the seat of arbitration may exercise supervisory jurisdiction over the outcome of tribunal decisions, but their control is equally limited and usually concerns questions of procedure, but not the substantive outcome. See, e.g., the provisions on the review powers of domestic courts contained in the United Nations Commission on International Trade Law (UNCITRAL) Model Law on International Commercial Arbitration (1985, amended 2006) art 34 https://uncitral.un.org/sites/uncitral.un.org/files/media-documents/uncitral/en/19-09955_e_ebook.pdf accessed 14 September 2022.

generally stay well within the traditional canon of the law of sources in the sense of Article 38 of the ICJ Statute, and do not create idiosyncracies that would be contrary to that traditional canon. But still, the approach of arbitral tribunals to the field's sources diverges from the approach taken by other international courts, such as the ICJ, in important respects. The peculiarities the sources of international investment law display, this chapter argues, are a lodestar also for other areas of international law, as well as general international and dispute settlement, as international investment law is indicative for how the views on and use of sources may change whenever compulsory dispute settlement mechanisms are established under any system of international law.

In addressing the transformation that the sources of international law may undergo due to the existence of a frequently-used compulsory dispute settlement mechanism, this chapter does not go through the sources laid down in Article 38 of the ICJ Statute step by step.[9] Instead, it will look at a selected number of issues that appear most promising in showing the radiating effects international investment law has in respect of the sources of international law. First, the chapter discusses how the network of (principally bilateral) IIAs can lead to the emergence of a genuinely multilateral regime that behaves almost as if it was based on a multilateral source of international law, whether customary international or a widely adopted multilateral convention (Section II). Second, the chapter addresses the preeminent importance played by arbitral

[9] Some sources of international law that are applied by investment tribunals to settle disputes are rather unremarkable from a general international law perspective. The way, e.g., the tribunal looks at the formation and identification of customary international law is very much in line with how these issues are addressed elsewhere in international law. At the most, international investment law displays some peculiarities in respect of what documents and statements count as evidence of State practice and *opinio juris*. Thus, the weight given to pleadings of States in investment disputes is less than that of State pleadings in other international courts; the role of model treaties is rather unique, and so are statements by treaty organs set up for issuing joint interpretations and non-disputing party interventions that several IIAs explicitly permit and encourage. For details, see the study by Patrick Dumberry, *The Formation and Identification of Customary International Law in International Investment Law* (CUP 2016). Similarly, the recourse to scholarly writings is not further addressed in the present chapter. As compared to dispute settlement in other areas of international law, notably before the ICJ, references to scholarship in investment arbitration are more frequent, including to authors that are still alive, an aspect that in the ICJ so far generally only occurs in individual opinions. Recourse to scholarship could indicate a greater impact of scholars on the construction of international investment law, and the rights and obligations it contains. For discussion, see Tony Cole, 'Non-Binding Documents and Literature' in Gazzini and De Brabandere (n 7) 289; Niccolò Ridi and Thomas Schultz, 'Empirically Mapping Invetsmnet Arbitration Scholarship: Networks, Authorities, and the Research Front' in Katia Fach Gomez (ed), *Private Actors in International Investment Law* (Springer 2020) 209, 227–256.

decisions as a source of international investment law, a fact that is not appropriately captured by the idea that such decisions are only 'subsidiary means for the determination of rules of law' (Section III).[10] Third, the chapter analyses the increasing influence of comparative law in international investment law and the renaissance of general principles of law connected to it (Section IV). Finally, the chapter will turn to how soft law instruments increasingly harden as a result of compulsory dispute settlement, although such instruments are not formally binding law (Section V). In respect of all of these issues, international investment law can serve as a lodestar for international law more generally on how the sources of international law may change under the impact of compulsory dispute settlement. This lays open not only the transformative potential core features of international investment law have, but also some of the problems this entails for the legitimacy of the use and transformation of the sources of international law (Section VI).

II. MULTILATERALISATION THROUGH BILATERAL TREATIES

The sources of a specific field of international law are not only relevant for ascertaining and determining the content of the rights and obligations of the actors involved. Sources also mirror a field's underlying ordering paradigm, that is, whether it reflects multilateralism in enshrining broadly shared rules that balance the interests of all participating actors (whether under custom or multilateral conventions) or is fragmented into bilateral *quid pro quo* bargains that not only differ greatly from treaty to treaty, but usually also give preferential treatment to the interests of hegemonic States who have superior bargaining power in bilateral as compared to multilateral settings.[11] International investment law is a field that is clearly dominated by bilateral treaties, with custom and general principles (both of them multilateral in nature, in that they apply to a plurality of States) being limited to concretise and serve as interpretative background for investment treaty norms.[12] Investment law could

---

[10] See ICJ Statute (n 6) Art 38(1)(d).

[11] For a general discussion of the difference between bilateralism and multilateralism, see John G. Ruggie, 'Multilateralism: The Anatomy of an Institution' in John G. Ruggie (ed), *Multilateralism Matters: The Theory and Praxis of an Institutional Form* (Columbia UP 1993) 3. See also Bruno Simma, 'From Bilateralism to Community Interest in International Law' (1994) 250 *Recueil des cours* 217, 233: 'The antithesis of the bilateralism thus described consists of the assertion of community interest in the development of international law …'.

[12] For a comprehensive assessment of the role of custom in international investment law, see Dumberry (n 9).

therefore be seen as a typical example of a fragmented patchwork of bilateral bargains, and hence the anti-thesis to a multilateral regime.[13] This would seem all the more true considering that attempts to create multilateral conventions that address the substantive rights and obligations have been unsuccessful at various points in time since the end of World War II.[14]

Curiously however, international investment law can be understood as a case in which multilateral structures have developed on the basis of bilateral treaties despite the margenalisation of custom and the failure of several multilateral treaty projects.[15] Notably, the large number of bilateral IIAs that has been negotiated in reaction to the failures of establishing a multilateral treaty addressing substantive rights and obligations in international investment relations has not resulted, as should be expected in bilateral settings, in a large amount of variation across treaties. On the contrary, IIAs (even the more recent ones that have engaged in a recalibration of rights and obligations in reaction to the extensive criticism of the field),[16] are generally cast in a remarkably similar fashion in respect of their core clauses, including the definitions of 'investment' and 'investor,' the different substantive standards of protection, and access to investment dispute settlement.

---

[13] In this sense, Eyal Benvenisti and George W Downs, 'The Empire's New Clothes: Political Economy and the Fragmentation of International Law' (2007) 60 *Stanford LR* 595, 597–98, 609ff.

[14] On the various failed attempts to establish multilateral treaties governing international investment relations in substance, whether as part of the International Trade Organization (ITO) in 1948, the Organization for Economic Co-operation and Development (OECD) in 1967 and 1998, or the World Trade Organization (WTO) during the Uruguay and Doha Rounds, see Stephan W. Schill, *The Multilateralization of International Investment Law* (CUP 2009) 23–64.

[15] For an in-depth analysis of how bilateral investment treaties make up a multilateral regime, see Schill (n 14). For a similar argument that the function of custom in international investment law is filled by the network of bilateral treaties and the interpretation by arbitral tribunals, see Jean d'Aspremont, 'International Customary Investment Law: Story of a Paradox' in Gazzini and De Brabandere (n 7) 5.

[16] While States are actively involved in recalibrating investment treaties to provide a better balance between the protection of foreign investors and States' right to regulate, these modifications do not challenge the basic underlying principles and characteristics of IIAs, but rather adjust the system from within. The changes increase the complexity of the system, but leave the foundational multilateral features of international investment untouched. In fact, recent attempts at reforming investment dispute settlement under the auspices of UNCITRAL are likely to lead to even more convergence, rather than fragmentation, with the introduction of more centralised features, including potentially a multilateral investment court. For further information, see the website of UNCITRAL Working Group III addressing 'Investor-State Dispute Settlement Reform' https://uncitral.un.org/en/working_groups/3/investor-state accessed 14 September 2022.

Moreover, the similarity of IIAs is not a result of chance, but the product of deliberate planning capital-exporting countries undertook in order to promote and protect foreign investments and reduce political risk in countries with weak domestic institutions at a time when customary rules on the protection of aliens were challenged by the calls of many capital-importing countries for a New International Economic Order in the 1970s.[17] To this end, IIAs are based on model treaties that were first developed by a handful of capital-exporting countries (particularly Germany, The Netherlands, the United Kingdom, and the United States) who coordinated their investment policies and IIA programs within the Organization for Economic Co-operation and Development (OECD) and later promoted as instruments for development by international organisations, such as the United Nations Conference for Trade and Development (UNCTAD).[18] Meanwhile, IIAs are losing their North-South pedigree as investment flows not only from developed to developing countries, but also in the reverse directions, as well as among developed and developing countries; this suggests that acceptable levels of investment protection under international law are in the shared interest of all States.

In addition, the treaties provide for a number of mechanisms that reduce divergence amongst them and increase harmonisation in the field. First, MFN clauses regularly included in IIAs contribute to the multilateralisation of international investment law.[19] Within their scope of application, which usually encompasses substantive standards of treatment, but may also apply to questions of dispute settlement,[20] such clauses ensure that a host State must extend any more favourable treatment it may offer to third States and their investors also to the State benefiting from MFN treatment and its investors. This prevents that different investment standards apply depending on the investor's nationality, leading to a harmonisation and hence multilateralisation of international investment law.

---

[17] For in-depth treatment of these challenges to customary international law, with a specific focus on the international law of expropriation, see Rudolf Dolzer, *Eigentum, Enteignung und Entschädigung im geltenden Völkerrecht* (Springer 1985).

[18] See Zachary Elkins, Andrew T. Guzman and Beth A. Simmons, 'Competing for Capital: The Diffusion of Bilateral Investment Treaties, 1960–2000' (2006) 60 *Int'l Org* 811, 818–19.

[19] For a typical MFN clause, see Agreement between the Government of Australia and the Government of the People's Republic of China on the Reciprocal Encouragement and Protection of Investments (signed and entered into force 11 July 1988) Art 3(c), which requires a State to 'treat investments and activities associated with investments in its own territory … on a basis no less favourable than that accorded to investments and activities associated with investments of nationals of any third country'.

[20] On the debate about the scope of application, see Schill (n 14) 121–96.

Second, nationality planning through corporate structuring, a practice that has been validated widely by arbitral tribunals, allows investors to opt into their preferred IIA rather independently of their own nationality.[21] To do so, foreign investors can use corporate vehicles established in another jurisdiction in order to channel their investment into the host State and see it protected under the IIA between the host State and the jurisdiction in question. This is possible because IIAs often determine corporate nationality based on incorporation and independently of the nationality of controlling shareholders. Nationality planning undermines strict connections between investment protection and nationality and suggests that international investment is better understood as a multilateral regime that does not effectively impose different levels of investment protection depending on the source of the investment and the nationality of an investor.

Finally, the dispute settlement mechanisms under IIAs make a key contribution to the multilateralisation of international investment law. Disputes under the treaties are resolved by arbitrators chosen from a relatively small pool of specialists who are appointed in a considerable number of cases.[22] While arbitrators do not share identical views on all aspects of international investment law, they do have a broadly consistent understanding of the main structural features and substantive principles of investment law. Also, investment tribunals do not interpret IIAs in a compartmentalised, IIA-by-IIA fashion, but generally embed their interpretations within a treaty-overarching framework that is comprised of the entire universe of IIAs. As addressed in more depth in the next section, tribunals regularly cite and refer to decisions of other tribunals that have previously dealt with similar issues as persuasive precedent, independently of whether the piece of precedent dealt with the same or another IIA. Such cross-treaty citation suggests a multilateral conceptualisation of bilateral IIAs by investment tribunals.

The multilateralisation of international investment law, however, should not be understood as leading to absolute uniformity; rather, the point is that the investment treaty system should be understood and examined as a system that functions, despite the bilateral form of its predominant source, on the basis of multilateral rather than bilateral rationales. Notably, this is so independently

---

[21] For comprehensive analysis of this phenomenon, see Jorun Baumgartner, *Treaty Shopping in International Investment Law* (OUP 2016); Björn Ebert, *Forum Shopping in International Investment Law – Forum Planning, Forum Enhancement, and Facilitation of Procedure* (Mohr Siebeck 2017); Anil Yilmaz, *The Nationality of Corporate Investors under International Investment Law* (Hart 2020).

[22] See Sergio Puig, 'Social Capital in the Arbitration Market' (2014) 25 *EJIL* 387; Joost Pauwelyn, 'The Rule of Law Without the Rule of Lawyers? Why Investment Arbitrators Are from Mars, Trade Adjudicators from Venus' (2015) 109 *AJIL* 761.

of the much discussed question of whether the large number of IIAs contribute themselves to the formation of customary law – a question that itself is of little relevance for investment treaty arbitrations, given that these proceedings generally presuppose the existence of an investment treaty as a basis for the disputing parties' consent.[23] Instead, multilateralisation relies mainly on how investment tribunals, as the principal dispute settlement mechanism established under investment treaties, interpret and apply the treaties, namely as part of a broader multilateralised regime created by the network of IIAs rather than as isolated *quid pro quo* bargains. Functionally, IIAs are therefore largely equivalent to a single multilateral convention, or to the role traditionally performed by customary international law, in laying down the basic norms that govern international investment relationship in the global economy as a whole.

The phenomenon of multilateralisation of bilateral treaties is a specificity of how treaties as a source of international investment law are interpreted and applied by investment tribunals. Yet, it is a phenomenon that does not need to be limited to the field of foreign investment, but can have radiating effects in other fields of international law, as well as in general international law and dispute settlement. It could play out whenever networks of bilateral treaties are applied in international dispute settlement mechanisms, particularly when recourse to such mechanisms is compulsory and does not only occur in an interstitial manner. Examples from other fields of international law where formally bilateral treaties dominate are the fields of consular relations, cultural cooperation, extradition and judicial assistance, double taxation, or preferential trade agreements (PTAs).

In all of these fields, the treaties in question are usually looked at and analysed only in respect of the impact they have on the bilateral relationship of the contracting parties, but not as bringing about overarching governance structures for the broader field in which they operate. This view may still be defensible when the implementation of these treaties relies on domestic courts, inter-State diplomacy, or occasional inter-State dispute settlement before the ICJ or some other international body, whether permanent or one-off, as in such cases no judicial centre or integrated network of judicial bodies exists for the application and interpretation of the bilateral treaties in question. But it becomes difficult to maintain if such treaties become applied in compulsory dispute settlement mechanisms, a scenario that is not unlikely in particular

---

[23] On the classical question to which extent IIAs contribute to the formation of custom, see, e.g., Steffen Hindelang, 'Bilateral Investment Treaties, Custom and a Healthy Investment Climate – The Question of Whether BITs Influence Customary International Law Revisited' (2004) 5 *JWIT* 789; José E. Alvarez, 'A BIT on Custom' (2009) 42 *NYU JILP* 17; Dumberry (n 9) 188–205, 334–350.

in the field of PTAs,[24] but also in double-taxation where compulsory dispute settlement mechanisms are becoming more prevalent. In all of these cases, international investment law can stand as a lodestar and have radiating effects for how a compulsory dispute settlement mechanism can bring about the paradoxical transformation of bilateral treaties into a source of multilateralism and create a regime that is functionally equivalent to a multilateral convention or customary international law, without however having to result itself in the formation of customary law. But even without an adjudicatory centre that can develop a network of bilateral treaties into a quasi-multilateral regime, the similarity of underlying bilateral treaty relationship, coupled with an interest of States to create uniform rules, could give rise to a presumption that formally separate, but substantively similar and connected rules in bilateral treaties should receive coherent and consistent interpretations.

III. THE ROLE OF ARBITRAL PRECEDENT

The introduction of, and frequent recourse to, compulsory dispute settlement mechanisms not only have an impact on the understanding and nature of the sources of international law, as discussed in relation to treaties above. It also has an impact on how decisions produced by the dispute settlement mechanism itself fare as a source for the ascertainment and content determination of international investment law. Decisions by investment treaty tribunals themselves are assuming an importance that is increasingly difficult to square with the inferior position attributed to 'judicial decisions' in Article 38(1)(d) of the ICJ Statute as 'subsidiary means for the determination of rules of law'.

Instead, arbitral tribunals, and their pronouncements on the rights and obligations in international investment law, have become the principal reference point for determining what the rights and obligations are of foreign investors and host States and what the powers are of arbitral tribunals in resolving investor-State disputes. In other words, when asking what rights and duties, or powers, the different actors involved in foreign investment relations or investor-State disputes have, it is not so much the often vague rules and principles in IIAs, or the procedural rules applicable in arbitration proceedings, that are outcome determinative. Rather, what is the focus both of arguments of the disputing parties, and much of the reasoning of arbitral tribunals, is

---

[24] See in this context Adrian M. Johnston and Michael J. Trebilcock, 'Fragmentation in International Trade Law: Insights from the Global Investment Regime' (2013) 12 *World Trade Rev* 621, arguing that if international investment law is used as a model, the fear that PTAs will fragment international trade law is not well-founded given that the same features that are responsible for the multilateralisation of international investment law are also present in the world of PTAs.

the way in which these rules and principles have been applied, shaped, and further developed by investment tribunals in past cases. Arbitral precedent, in other words, becomes the principal reference point to determine the content of international investment law and interpret and apply the law to resolve investor-State disputes.[25]

Already from a purely quantitative perspective, the legal authority investment treaty tribunals most often make reference to in their decisions are pronouncements of other investment treaty tribunals. In 2007, Jeffrey Commission summarised the findings of a quantitative citation analyses as follows: 'citations to supposedly subsidiary sources, such as judicial decisions, including arbitral awards, predominate'.[26] Today, decisions and awards without reference to arbitral precedent are rather exceptional.[27] Unlike in commercial arbitrations that are held behind closed doors, this development is possible because the decisions and awards of investment tribunals regularly become public (often almost instanteously online) and are intensively discussed not only by parties to other investment treaty cases, but also analysed in the growing legal literature on international investment law. The ways precedent is used by arbitral tribunals, of course, differs and ranges from its cautious use as a 'source of inspiration' in treaty interpretation or as an indication of the ordinary meaning of a treaty provision, to cases where precedent further develops international investment law or even becomes an instrument of system-wide lawmaking.[28]

Even though arbitral tribunals do not become tired of emphasising that arbitral precedent is not binding, they attach importance to it up to a point where a *jurisprudence constante* becomes more authoritative as an argument than reference to a formal source of international law. The statement of the Tribunal in *Saipem v Bangladesh*, which was made in 2007, and since has been reproduced in a large number of arbitral awards,[29] is representative of a position that is widely, even though not unanimously, shared among investment arbitrators:

---

[25] On this and the following, see in more detail, including references to arbitral case law, Stephan W. Schill, 'System-Building in Investment Treaty Arbitration and Lawmaking' (2011) 12 *German LJ* 1083. See also Schill (n 14) 321–61.

[26] Jeffery P. Commission, 'Precedent in Investment Treaty Arbitration: A Citation Analysis of a Developing Jurisprudence' (2007) 24 *J Int'l Arb* 129, 148. See also Fauchald (n 7) 333–43.

[27] For a rare example, see *Hochtief AG v Argentine Republic*, ICSID Case No ARB/07/31, Decision on Jurisdiction (24 October 2011).

[28] On the different uses of precedent in international law, see Marc Jacob, 'Precedents: Lawmaking Through International Adjudication' (2011) 12 *German LJ* 1005.

[29] For a recent example, see *Muszynianka Spółka v Slovak Republic*, UNCITRAL, PCA Case No 2017-08, Award (7 October 2020) para 166.

> The Tribunal considers that it is not bound by previous decisions. At the same time, it is of the opinion that it must pay due consideration to earlier decisions of international tribunals. It believes that, subject to compelling contrary grounds, it has a duty to adopt solutions established in a series of consistent cases. It also believes that, subject to the specifics of a given treaty and of the circumstances of the actual case, it has a duty to seek to contribute to the harmonious development of investment law and thereby to meet the legitimate expectations of the community of States and investors towards certainty of the rule of law.[30]

While precedent, in this view, does not bind later tribunals, it shifts the burden of argumentation by demanding a reasoned justification for departing from established precedent, not least because, as stated by another tribunal, 'it is a fundamental principle of the rule of law that "like cases should be decided alike," unless a strong reason exists to distinguish the current case from previous ones'.[31] The more established a precedent becomes, and the more investment treaty tribunals align themselves with a certain line of jurisprudence, the more difficult it becomes for parties and tribunals to meet that burden and to deviate from prior practice.[32]

Consequently, through the process of referencing arbitral precedent, the true meaning of the rights and obligations under IIAs is not so much enshrined anymore in what passes as a formal source, but rather in the decisions of investment treaty tribunals. For this reason, almost all textbooks on international investment law concentrate on describing and analysing the juris-

---

[30] *Saipem SpA v People's Republic of Bangladesh*, ICSID Case No ARB/05/07, Decision on Jurisdiction and Provisional Measures (21 March 2007) para 67. For criticism of the focus on precedent by arbitrators themselves, see, e.g., the orthodox position in *Muszynianka Spółka* (n 29), Partial Dissenting Opinion of Robert G Volterra (7 October 2020) paras 4–13, who explains that arbitral decisions do not constitute a source of international law in the sense of Art 38 of the ICJ Statute, that no doctrine of precedent exists in public international law, that it does not matter to what extent investment treaty tribunals have previously reached the same conclusion, that there is no system of investment treaty arbitration enacted by States and hence no basis on which coherence to such a system could be given. For earlier criticism that does not take issue with the idea to treat like cases alike, but that criticised the lawmaking activity of arbitral tribunals, see *Suez, Sociedad General de Aguas de Barcelona, SA and Vivendi Universal, SA v Argentina*, ICSID Case No ARB/03/19 and *AWG Group v Argentina* (joint cases), Separate Opinion of Arbitrator Pedro Nikken (30 July 2010) paras 2427.

[31] *Daimler Financial Services AG v Argentine Republic*, ICSID Case No ARB/05/1, Award (22 August 2012) para 52 (internal footnotes omitted).

[32] *International Thunderbird Gaming Corp v United Mexican States*, UNCITRAL (NAFTA), Arbitral Award (26 January 2006), Separate Opinion of Thomas Wälde, para 16, '[a] deviation from well and firmly established jurisprudence requires an extensively reasoned justification'.

prudence of arbitral tribunals to illustrate the content of rights and duties of investors and States, as well as the powers of investment treaty tribunals. Similarly, arbitration proceedings at times resemble argumentative battles about the better precedent[33] and demands are increasingly raised that a tribunal should not even diverge from precedent.[34] All of this shows that understanding international investment law, as well as applying it in practice, is equivalent to needing to know, and be able to play on the keyboard of, the jurisprudence of investment tribunals.

Most importantly, arbitral precedent does not only inform the interpretation of IIAs, but has an impact in creating rights and obligations that govern investor-State relations and in shaping the powers of arbitral tribunals more generally. Investment treaty tribunals, in other words, do not only apply existing sources, but actively make investment law themselves. Tribunals have, for example, declared provisional measures in ICSID arbitrations to be binding, even though Article 47 of the ICSID Convention envisaged them as mere recommendations.[35] Similarly, tribunals have developed the rule to award compound instead of simple interest.[36]

But above all, the role of investment tribunals as lawmakers becomes clear when considering how they transform the vague and open-ended principles of international investment law, such as fair and equitable treatment (FET), full protection and security, indirect expropriation, or national treatment, into concrete rules that limit how the executive, legislator, and judiciary in host States ought to conduct themselves in relation to foreign investors. Most notably,

---

[33] A particularly prominent example about which line of precedent should be applied are the controversies about whether MFN clauses apply to questions of dispute settlement procedures and arbitral jurisdiction and whether to follow the line of cases associated with *Maffezini v Spain* or *Plama v Bulgaria*. For discussion in arbitral proceedings, see, e.g., *Christian Doutremepuich and Antoine Doutremepuich v Mauritius*, UNCITRAL, PCA Case No 2018-37, Award on Jurisdiction (23 August 2019) paras 156–236.

[34] See, e.g., *The PV Investors v Spain*, UNCITRAL, PCA Case No 2012-14, Final Award (28 February 2020), Concurring and Dissenting Opinion of Charles N Brower, para 16, who concludes after reviewing precedent on the interpretation and application of the same treaty, the Energy Charter Treaty, to the same host State measures involving the reregulation of feed-in tariffs for renewable energies, that there is 'no reason to depart from such sound reasoning, repeatedly applied without exception by eleven predecessor tribunals confronting the same problem'.

[35] See Chester Brown, 'Article 47' in Stephan W. Schill and others (eds), *Schreuer's Commentary on the ICSID Convention* (3rd edn, CUP 2022) Art 47 paras 19–33.

[36] See Grisel (n 7) 225–33; Mark Beeley, 'Approaches to the Award of Interest' in Christina L. Beharry, *Contemporary and Emerging Issues on the Law of Damages and Valuation in International Investment Arbitration* (Brill Nijhoff 2018) 371, 387–392.

tribunals develop the content of investment treaty standards not primarily through the application of methods of treaty interpretation, as enshrined in the Vienna Convention on the Law of Treaties (VCLT),[37] or through recourse to customary international law, but by turning to and relying on arbitral precedent as the main source of law ascertainment and content determination.

The NAFTA award in *Waste Management v Mexico*, an Award from the earlier years of investment arbitration (2004), is representative of arbitral practice in this respect; but virtually any other case could be referred to. In that case, the Tribunal extensively described prior investment awards applying FET in order to clarify the standard's normative content. After discussing arbitral precedent at length, the Tribunal concluded:

> Taken together, the *S.D. Myers*, *Mondev*, *ADF* and *Loewen* cases suggest that the minimum standard of treatment of fair and equitable treatment is infringed by conduct attributable to the State and harmful to the claimant if the conduct is arbitrary, grossly unfair, unjust, or idiosyncratic, is discriminatory and exposes the claimant to sectional or racial prejudice, or involves a lack of due process leading to an outcome which offends judicial propriety—as might be the case with a manifest failure of natural justice in judicial proceedings or a complete lack of transparency and candour in an administrative process.[38]

As can be glanced from this quote, the Tribunal's understanding of FET was not derived from an independent application of methods of treaty interpretation but from how the standard has been developed and applied in arbitral jurisprudence. Similar forms of argumentation are not specific to NAFTA, nor is reference to arbitral jurisprudence limited to awards that interpreted the same governing IIA; instead, reference to arbitral precedent is a phenomenon that can be found in virtually any arbitral award, and with respect to virtually any question of international investment law and arbitration. What is more, the power of precedent even plays out in cases of conflicting and inconsistent arbitral decisions.[39] In such cases, tribunals, often at length, engage in distinguishing precedent based on the facts of the case, the procedural posture, or based on the applicable treaty, seek to reconcile irreconcilable results through meta-rules, such as redefining an earlier holding on a point of law from a precise rule to a broader principle that allows for exceptions, or by considering an earlier holding itself as an exception to yet another principle, or suggest

[37] Vienna Convention on the Law of Treaties (VCLT) (Vienna, 23 May 1969, 1155 UNTS 331).

[38] *Waste Management, Inc v United Mexican States*, ICSID Case No ARB(AF)/00/3 (NAFTA), Award (30 April 2004) para 98.

[39] For the following, including references to arbitral jurisprudence, see Schill (n 14) 339–55.

that a prior case should be overruled as a matter of principle and with effect for the entire investment treaty regime.

Overall, reliance on precedent illustrates how investment treaty tribunals move from institutions that settle individual investment disputes to lawmakers for the entire investment treaty regime. Even beyond that regime, decisions by investment tribunals may contribute to the further development of general international law, as discussed in some of the other contributions to the present volume. Tribunal decisions, while *de iure* non-binding beyond the individual case, *de facto* determine how investment treaties are interpreted and investment disputes decided in the future and in entirely unrelated cases. Their practical impact in governing international investment relations and influencing the future behaviour of investors and States goes much beyond the limited status accorded to them in Article 38(1)(d) of the ICJ Statute as 'subsidiary means for the determination of rules of law', even though from a formal perspective, tribunal decisions do no more than determining and concretising the content of treaty rules within the investment treaty regime.

This peculiarity of international investment law is one that will likely be shared by any other field of international law that has already introduced a compulsory dispute settlement mechanisms or will do so in the future. Certainly, in the context of world trade law, pronouncements of the Appellate Body of the World Trade Organization (WTO), are among the principal reference points for the interpretation and application of the WTO's covered agreements and will likely remain so despite the current dysfunctionality of the WTO's appellate tier; judgments of the European Court of Human Rights determine the content and application of the European Convention of Human Rights; and judgments of the Inter-American Court of Human Rights are the most important drivers of the understanding of rights and obligations under the Inter-American Convention on Human Rights. But even in institutionally less centralised dispute settlement systems, such as the those provided for under Part XV of the United Nations Convention on the Law of the Seas (UNCLOS), the different dispute settlement bodies (the ICJ, the International Tribunal for the Law of Seas, and arbitration tribunals established under UNCLOS Annex VII and VIII)[40] make reference to each other's jurisprudence and therefore have been appropriately described as being part of a 'collective interpretative

[40] See United Nations Convention on the Law of the Sea (adopted 10 December 1982, entered into force 16 November 1994) 1833 UNTS 397 (UNCLOS), Art 287. For an instructive overview over the design features of dispute settlement under UNCLOS, see Alan E. Boyle, 'Dispute Settlement and the Law of the Sea Convention: Problems of Fragmentation and Jurisdiction' (1997) 46 *ICLQ* 37.

endeavor'.[41] The example of investor-State arbitration certainly shows that the further development of international law is not limited to permanent international courts, but that arbitral tribunals are equally capable of contributing to it.

Similar to other international courts and tribunals, the importance investment treaty tribunals give to their own pronouncements on and understanding of the law will serve as a lodestar and thus have radiating effects beyond the field of foreign investment for any situation in which the creation of compulsory dispute settlement mechanisms under international law is envisaged or where the question arises as to whether the jurisdiction of existing international courts or tribunals should be extended. As the example of international investment law shows, such steps will not only lead to more effective compliance mechanisms for the international legal obligations in question, and to peaceful means to settle international legal disputes, it will also have an impact on increasing the relative importance of judicial and arbitral decisions as *de facto* sources of international law. International investment law therefore provides a reference area for considering how the legitimacy and continuous State control of such international dispute settlement bodies can be ensured. Although it might go too far to claim that the canon of sources in Article 38(1)(d) of the ICJ Statute should be rewritten and decisions by international courts and tribunal put at par with the principal sources of international law, in particular treaties and custom, the impact international courts and tribunals can have as *de facto* lawmakers should be accompanied by more probing inquiries into the conditions under which their contribution to international law is legitimate. The dismantling of the Tribunal of the Southern African Development Community (SADC) or the dysfunctionality of the WTO Appellate Body are forceful reminders of the limits international courts and tribunals face in pushing the boundaries of international law and further developing its content.

IV. THE USE OF COMPARATIVE LAW AND THE RENAISSANCE OF GENERAL PRINCIPLES OF LAW

The inclusion of compulsory dispute settlement mechanisms in international investment law does not only enhance the importance of arbitral precedent, it

---

41 *Dispute Concerning Delimitation of the Maritime Boundary Between Bangladesh and Myanmar in the Bay of Bengal (Bangladesh/Myanmar)*, ITLOS Case No 16, Judgment (14 March 2012), Declaration of Judge Tullio Treves, ITLOS Reports 2012, 141. Judge Rüdiger Wolfrum went a step further, arguing that UNCLOS 'requires [courts and tribunals applying it] to harmonize their jurisprudence with the view to avoiding any fragmentation' (ibid., Declaration of Judge Wolfrum, ITLOS Reports 2012, 136, 137).

also has an effect on bringing instruments into the process of resolving investment disputes and interpreting IIAs that do not form part of the conventional canon of sources or that have played a relatively minor role in international law so far. One notable development, in this context, is the influence of comparative law in the interpretation and application of IIAs, notably comparative public law and the importance this gives to general principles of public law.[42] In fact, comparative references to both domestic legal systems and other international legal regimes (other than the applicable law) are frequently found in investment tribunal decisions. While comparative analysis does not make the *droit comparé* into an independent source of international investment law, it still gives the 'foreign' law a degree of authority for the determination of the content of treaty norms or rules of arbitral procedure. The use of comparative law comes in different degrees of methodological sophistication, from simple and loose comparative reference to the more sophisticated development of general principles of law.

At one end of the spectrum, one can observe a simple and methodically loose use of comparative law as mere inspiration for the interpretation of international investment law. At the other end, we see a more sophisticated, even if not irreproachable, recourse to comparative law in order to distill general principles of law. An example of a loose use of comparative law is the decision in *Lemire v Ukraine*, which considered, in a rather selective and unsystematic fashion, when determining whether the requirement to radio-broadcast a certain percentage of Ukrainian music was contrary to FET, the use of similar requirements in a variety of domestic legal systems of third countries.[43]

Often, however, tribunals will attempt to use comparative law in a more methodical fashion. The Tribunal in *Saar Papier v Poland*, for example, made use of the domestic law on expropriation of the two contracting parties to circumscribe the concept of indirect expropriation under the Germany-Poland bilateral investment treaty (BIT).[44] Arbitral tribunals also regularly refer to comparable norms in other international legal regimes to concretise IIA treaty standards. The Tribunal in *Tecmed v Mexico*, for example, drew on the case law of the European Court of Human Rights and of the Inter-American Court

---

[42] For detailed discussion, see further Valentina Vadi, *Analogies in International Investment Law and Arbitration* (CUP 2016); Daniel Peat, *Comparative Reasoning in International Courts and Tribunals* (CUP 2019).

[43] *Joseph Charles Lemire v Ukraine*, ICSID Case No ARB/06/18, Decision on Jurisdiction and Liability (14 January 2010) para 506. Similarly, *Noble Ventures, Inc v Romania*, ICSID Case No ARB/01/11, Award (12 October 2005) para 178; *Plama Consortium Ltd v Republic of Bulgaria*, ICSID Case No ARB/03/02, Award (27 August 2008) para 269.

[44] *Saar Papier v Poland*, UNCITRAL, Final Award (16 October 1995) paras 78ff.

of Human Rights to determine what constitutes an indirect expropriation in IIAs.[45] Numerous tribunals have also drawn on WTO law and jurisprudence to concretise the ambit of national treatment,[46] or the meaning of necessity clauses and non-precluded-measures clauses in IIAs.[47]

There are, however, also cases where investment treaty tribunals develop more sophisticated and ambitious ways to use comparative law in order to develop general principles.[48] The tribunals in *Total v Argentina* and *Gold Reserve v Venezuela*, for example, drew heavily on domestic legal orders of various common and civil law jurisdictions, in Europe and overseas, in addition to general international law, human rights law, and EU law, to normatively ground and give concrete meaning to the concept of legitimate expectations as a restriction of a State's regulatory powers.[49] The Tribunal in *Cairn Energy v India*, in turn, when asked to assess the compliance of retroactive tax legislation with the FET obligations, reasoned that FET had to be interpreted in light of the concept of the rule of law, which constituted a general principle of law recognised as such in numerous domestic legal systems, and which provided for a number of more specific sub-elements, including legal certainly, stability, and predictability; the type of retroactive tax legislation Respondent had enacted violated such an understanding of FET.[50]

---

[45] See *Tecnicas Medioambientales Tecmed SA v United Mexican States*, ICSID Case No ARB (AF)/00/2, Award (29 May 2003) paras 113–122. Similarly, *Mondev Int'l Ltd v United States of America*, ICSID Case No ARB (AF)/99/2, Award (11 October 2002) paras 138, 141–144, concerning immunities of public authorities.

[46] For further discussion, including reference to case law, see Jürgen Kurtz, *The WTO and International Investment Law: Converging Systems* (CUP 2016) 79–135; Nicholas A. DiMascio and Joost Pauwelyn, 'Non-Discrimination in Trade and Investment Treaties: Worlds Apart or Two Sides of the Same Coin?' (2008) 102 *AJIL* 48.

[47] *Continental Casualty Company v Argentine Republic*, ICSID Case No ARB/03/9, Award (5 September 2008) paras 192–195.

[48] More generally on the role of general principles in international investment law, see Tarcisio Gazzini, 'General Principles of Law in the Field of Foreign Investment' (2009) 10 *JWIT* 103; Ursula Kriebaum, 'Article 42' in Schill and others (n 35) paras 245–249; Stephan W. Schill, 'General Principles of Law in International Investment Law' in Gazzini and De Brabandere (n 7) 133, 142–143, 154–157; Andrea Gattini, Attila Tanzi and Filippo Fontanelli (eds), *General Principles of Law and International Investment Arbitration* (Brill Nijhoff 2018); Patrick Dumberry, *A Guide to General Principles of Law in International Investment Arbitration* (OUP 2020);

[49] See *Total SA v Argentine Republic*, ICSID Case No ARB/04/1, Decision on Liability (27 December 2010) para 111; *Gold Reserve Inc v Bolivarian Republic of Venezuela*, ICSID Case No ARB(AF)/09/1, Award (22 September 2014) para 576.

[50] *Cairn Energy PLC and Cairn UK Holdings Limited v Republic of India*, UNCITRAL, PCA Case No 2016-7, Award (21 December 2020) paras 1715–1817.

Other tribunals focus predominantly on other international legal regimes in order to ground certain general principles of law. The Tribunal in *Mobil Corporation et al v Venezuela*, for example, engaged in a detailed analysis of the jurisprudence of various international courts and tribunals, including the ICJ, the Permanent Court of International Justice, the WTO Appellate Body, the Administrative Tribunal of the International Labour Organization, and the Court of Justice of the European Union to ground the concept of misuse of law/abuse of rights.[51]

The difference in how tribunals use comparative law reflects different functions comparative analysis can have. These range from serving as mere instruments of inspiration for the interpretation of vague treaty standards, via the determination of the ordinary meaning States attribute to certain concepts of international investment law, to developing general principles of law in the sense of Article 38(1)(c) of the ICJ Statute, a source of international law that must be taken into account as 'relevant rules of international law applicable in the relations between the parties' in the interpretation of IIAs pursuant to Article 31(3)(c) of the VCLT. These different functions notwithstanding, the extent to which comparative law can impact international investment law, depends on the interpretative leeway the applicable treaty norms leave. Comparative legal analysis does not control the interpretation and application of IIAs as an independent source, or overwrite clear treaty rules, but serves primarily as an instrument to determine the content of vague treaty standards.

What is notable, in this context, is the increasing recourse in comparative analysis to systems of public rather than private law, including in the growing development of general principles of public law by investment treaty tribunals. The Tribunal in *Cairn Energy v India* justified this by stating that general principles of law 'have emerged mostly in the context of municipal laws and contains various principles of individual-to-State relations that are usually at stake in the context of investment protection', whereas '[o]ther sources of international law, such as treaties and customary international law, traditionally regulate State-to-State affairs and offer limited guidance as to the particularities of the relationship between an individual and the State'.[52]

---

[51] *Mobil Corporation, Venezuela Holdings, BV and others v Bolivarian Republic of Venezuela*, ICSID Case No ARB/07/27, Decision on Jurisdiction (10 June 2010) paras 169–185. See also *Orascom TMT Investments Sàrl v People's Democratic Republic of Algeria*, ICSID Case No ARB/12/35, Award (31 May 2017) para 541, denoting abuse of rights as a 'general principle applicable in international law as well as in municipal law' – quoting Robert Kolb, General Principles of Procedural Law' in Andreas Zimmermann and others (eds), *The Statute of the International Court of Justice: A Commentary* (2nd edn, OUP 2012) 904.

[52] *Cairn Energy* (n 50) para 1715.

Consequently, general principles of public law, as well as comparative public law reasoning have gained increasing importance in investment arbitration.

One such general principle of public law is the principle of proportionality, which is used by a large number of domestic courts, as well as other international courts and tribunals, to balance and reconcile competing interests, such as investment protection and environmental protection, labour standards, or human rights.[53] As recently stated by the Tribunal in *Muszynianka Spółka v Slovak Republic* in a case involving the assessment under a BIT of a constitutional amendment that prohibited the export of underground water in order to preserve natural resources, the environment, and health of the host State's population, under the principle of proportionality a State measure must

> be suitable to achieve a legitimate public purpose (a); necessary to achieve the objective pursued in that no less burdensome or intrusive, yet feasible and equally effective measures exist (b); and not excessive in consideration of the relative weigh of the interests at issue (i.e., proportionality strictu sensu) (c).[54]

Another genuinely public law approach that is increasingly used in investment arbitration, but also in other international courts and tribunals, is recourse to public law doctrines of deference, such as the margin of appreciation doctrine used by the European Court of Human Rights, when asking whether the host State's agency has violated existing investment treaty obligations.[55] In the words of the *Muszynianka Spółka* tribunal

---

[53] For the use of proportionality analysis in domestic legal systems, see in particular Alec Stone Sweet and Jud Mathews, 'Proportionality Balancing and Global Constitutionalism' (2008) 47 *Columbia JTL* 73; Aharon Barak, *Proportionality: Constitutional Rights and Their Limitations* (CUP 2012) 175–210; Alec Stone Sweet and Jud Matthews, *Proportionality Balancing and Constitutional Governance: A Comparative and Global Approach* (OUP 2019). For the use in international legal regimes, including international investment law, see Alec Stone Sweet and Giacinto della Cananea, 'Proportionality, General Principles of Law, and Investor-State Arbitration: A Response to José Alvarez' (2014) 46 *NYU JILP* 911; Gebhard Bücheler, *Proportionality in Investor-State Arbitration* (OUP 2015); Benedict Kingsbury and Stephan W. Schill, 'Public Law Concepts to Balance Investors' Rights with State Regulatory Actions in the Public Interest: The Principle of Proportionality' in Stephan W. Schill (ed), *International Investment Law and Comparative Public Law* (OUP 2010) 75–106; Caroline Henckels, *Proportionality and Deference in Investor-State Arbitration* (CUP 2015); Thomas Cottier and others, 'The Principle of Proportionality in International Law: Foundations and Variations' (2017) 18 *JWIT* 628; Valentina Vadi, *Proportionality, Reasonableness and Standards of Review in International Investment Law and Arbitration* (Edward Elgar 2018) 54-128.

[54] *Muszynianka Spółka*, Award (n 29) para 566.

[55] Henckels (n 53) 69ff. Vadi (n 53) 186–240. For criticism of the use of doctrines, such as the margin of appreciation doctrine, in investment arbitration, see *Philip Morris*

> arbitral tribunals must pay deference to the choices States make when deciding how to implement policy objectives. Such deference or margin of appreciation makes sense because arbitral tribunals are not embedded within the host State and State authorities are better placed to assess national the [sic] conditions, needs, sensitivities, priorities, technical specificities and interests of the stakeholders.[56]

Overall, recourse to comparative public law, whether in the looser form of comparative public law reasoning or the more demanding development of general principles of public law, reflects the understanding that international investment law constitutes a public law system that is no longer restricted to governing inter-State relations, but directly addresses the relations between public and private actors and limits, similar to domestic administrative or constitutional law, how governments exercise authority vis-à-vis private economic actors.[57]

The use of comparative law is not without problems though, as it may distort the content of rights and obligations enshrined in IIAs. Similarly, if comparative analysis aims at the distillation of general principles, there is the danger that the legal orders drawn on are not well understood in their social, legal, and institutional context and are not sufficiently representative, perhaps even Eurocentric, so as to reflect a globally acceptable solution.[58] It is because of these methodological challenges that the use of comparative law has raised the criticism of being 'manipulable according to subjective preferences'.[59] To avoid such manipulation, and to pre-empt charges of selectiveness and bias,

---

Brands Sàrl, Philip Morris Products SA and Abal Hermanos SA v Oriental Republic of Uruguay, ICSID Case No ARB/10/7, Award (8 July 2016), Concurring and Dissenting Opinion by Mr Gary Born, Arbitrator (28 June 2016) paras 85, 87, 138, 181–191. Critical also Julian Arato, 'The Margin of Appreciation in International Investment Law' (2014) 54 *Va JIL* 545. For the use of deference by other international courts and tribunals, see the contributions in Lukas Gruszczynski and Wouter Werner (eds), *Deference in International Courts and Tribunals* (OUP 2014).

[56] *Muszynianka Spółka*, Award (n 29) para 558.

[57] See Stephan W. Schill, 'International Investment Law and Comparative Public Law—An Introduction' in Schill (n 53) 3, 17. See also Gus Van Harten, *Investment Treaty Arbitration and Public Law* (OUP 2008) 5; Santiago Montt, *State Liability in Investment Treaty Arbitration: Global Constitutional and Administrative Law in the BIT Generation* (Hart 2009) 21–2. For the first elaboration of this analogy, see the Separate Opinion of Thomas Wälde in *International Thunderbird Gaming Corp v United Mexican States*, UNCITRAL (NAFTA), Arbitral Award (26 January 2006) paras 12ff.

[58] See José E. Alvarez, '"Beware: Boundary Crossings"—A Critical Appraisal of Public Law Approaches to International Investment Law' (2016) 17 *JWIT* 171; Jaye Ellis, 'General Principles and Comparative Law' (2011) 22 *EJIL* 949, 955–8, 968.

[59] M. Sornarajah, *The International Law on Foreign Investment* (3rd edn, CUP 2010) 418.

a methodologically rigorous, sophisticated, and critical use of comparative law is necessary. These challenges notwithstanding, the use of comparative (domestic and international) law is likely to remain a persisting feature in the application of international investment law by investment treaty tribunals.

The reference to comparative law by investment treaty tribunal as well as recourse to general principles of public law are not features that are likely going to remain limited to international investment law. In fact, comparative reasoning is a feature that is present, to different degrees, in many international courts and tribunals, whether the ICJ, the WTO Appellate Body, the European Court of Human Rights, or international criminal tribunals.[60] Similarly, general principles of law are used frequently by many international courts and tribunals.[61] This notwithstanding, the practice in international investment law may well have radiating effects outside its narrow context – for three interrelated reasons.

First, investment treaty tribunals may contribute to the concretisation and further development of specific general principles that are also used, but not yet well-developed in other international dispute settlement fora. The doctrine of abuse of rights/abuse of process or the principle of good faith may be just two examples where the practice of investment tribunals is growing and meets a dearth of settled practice elsewhere in international dispute settlement.[62] But the same could hold true for any of the other general principle used and further

---

[60] For discussion of the use of comparative law in these dispute settlement systems, see Peat (n 42). See also An Hertogen, 'The Persuasiveness of Domestic Law Analogies in International Law' (2018) 29 *EJIL* 1127.

[61] See, e.g., Bin Cheng, *General Principles of Law as Applied by International Courts and Tribunals* (Stevens & Sons 1953); Fabián O. Raimondo, *General Principles of Law in the Decisions of International Criminal Courts and Tribunals* (Martinus Nijhoff 2008); Charles T. Kotuby and Luke A. Sobota, *General Principles of Law and International Due Process – Principles and Norms Applicable in Transnational Disputes* (OUP 2017); Marija Đorđeska, *General Principles of Law Recognized by Civilized Nations (1922–2018)* (Brill Nijhoff 2020); Imogen Saunders, *General Principles as a Source of International Law: Art 38(1)(c) of the Statute of the International Court of Justice* (Hart 2021).

[62] On the use of these principles in investment arbitration and in other international courts and tribunals, see, e.g., Eric De Brabandere, '"Good Faith", "Abuse of Process" and the Initiation of Investment Treaty Claims' (2012) 3 *JIDS* 609; Yuka Fukunaga, 'Abuse of Process under International Law and Investment Arbitration' (2018) 33 *ICSID Rev* 181; Luke Tattersall and Azfer A. Khan, 'Taking Stock: Abuse of Process within the International Court of Justice' (2020) 10 *LPICT* 229; Robert Kolb, *Good Faith in International Law* (Hart 2017); Andrew D. Mitchell, M. Sornarajah and Tania Voon (eds), *Good Faith and International Economic Law* (OUP 2015); Jan Paulsson, *The Unruly Notion of Abuse of Rights* (CUP 2020); Emily Sipiorski, *Good Faith in International Investment Arbitration* (OUP 2019); Ahmed El Far, *Abuse of Rights in International Arbitration* (OUP 2020).

developed by investment tribunals.[63] It may thus only be a matter of time until these other dispute settlement mechanisms will draw on how investment tribunals have concretised and further developed the general principles in question. Simply put: the growing number of precedent of arbitral tribunals on questions of relevance for general international law and international dispute settlement will simply be difficult to ignore outside international investment law proper. In fact, we already see counsel in other international dispute settlement systems, and at times another international court or tribunal itself, draw on precedent generated by investment tribunals as supporting and at times even principal authority for points of international law.[64]

Second, international investment dispute settlement could have a particularly strong impact on the development of principles of public law and comparative public law reasoning as it is a field of international law that directly deals with the relationship between States and private economic actors and is not limited to inter-State relations. With the increasing penetration of international law into private-public relations also in fields other than investment law, for example in energy, financial markets, data protection, or cyber-activities, taxation, public heath, or environmental protection, public law analysis is set to gain broader traction. With the existing and growing practice of public law analogies, or even the development of general principles of public law, international investment law may serve as an engine in helping public law thinking to penetrate international law more generally.

Finally, the way investment tribunals make use of general principles can also make a contribution to the theory of general principles of international law, for example, by clarifying the methodology to develop general principles, including the identification of principles that are common to domestic legal orders, distilling the essence of the general principle, and modifying the principle to suit the particularities of international law.[65] The practice of investment tribunals could help, for instance, in the debates about which legal orders to draw on, how to ensure the representativeness of these legal orders, and how to avoid pitfalls in developing general principles of law.

---

[63] For a detailed overview over the different principles applied in investment arbitration, see Dumberry (n 48) ch 4.

[64] For examples, see Stephan W. Schill and Katrine R. Tvede, 'Mainstreaming Investment Treaty Jurisprudence: The Contribution of Investment Treaty Tribunals to the Consolidation and Development of General International Law' (2015) 14 *LPICT* 94, 106-119. For more on this point, see, e.g., Dirk Pulkowski, 'Remedies for Wrongful Conduct: Lessons from Investment Arbitration' (in this volume) 246; James G. Devaney, 'On the Contribution of Investment Arbitration to Issues of Evidence and Procedure before Other International Courts and Tribunals' (in this volume) 343.

[65] For a summary of the methodology of developing a general principle of law, see Ellis (n 58) 954.

All in all, investment tribunal practice therefore has the potential of having radiating effects in promoting the use of comparative law analysis in particular in fields of international law that concern private-public relations and contribute to a renaissance of general principles of law, in particular general principles of public law. The precedents developed by investment tribunals will be, without doubt, the main driver and source of that development.

V. HARDENING OF SOFT LAW

The final area for discussion where international investment law could have radiating effects in its use of sources for other areas of international law and dispute settlement concerns its engagement with soft law. International investment law is no exception when it comes to the widely noted rise in soft law in international law and global governance.[66] Indeed, non-binding soft law instruments, which are created by a variety of different actors, including inter-governmental and international organisations, but also by private, non-governmental bodies, have an impact on international investment law.[67] Soft law instruments play a particularly important role in the management of arbitration procedures, but also influence how different substantive economic and non-economic interests are balanced. What is most remarkable in international investment law is how arbitral tribunals contributes to hardening soft law and to developing normative expectations outside the traditional processes of international lawmaking.

A first strand of soft law that finds application in investment arbitration consists of instruments relating to arbitral procedure. Often they are instruments that find their origin in professional communities dealing with international commercial arbitration, rather than dispute settlement under public international law. Prominent examples of such instruments are the rules and guidelines adopted by the International Bar Association (IBA), an organisation of the legal profession with national bar associations as members, such as the IBA

---

[66] On the growth of soft law, see, e.g., Timothy L. Meyer, 'Soft Law as Delegation' (2009) 32 *Fordham ILJ* 888; Andrew T. Guzman and Timothy L. Meyer, 'International Soft Law' (2010) 2 *J Legal Analysis* 171; Gregory C. Shaffer and Mark A. Pollack, 'Hard vs. Soft Law: Alternatives, Complements, and Antagonists in International Governance' (2010) 94 *Minn LR* 706; Armin von Bogdandy and others (eds), *The Exercise of Public Authority by International Institutions* (Springer 2009); Matthias Goldmann, *Internationale öffentliche Gewalt: Handlungsformen internationaler Institutionen im Zeitalter der Globalisierung* (Springer 2015).

[67] See in depth Marc Jacob and Stephan W. Schill, 'Going Soft: Towards a New Age of Soft Law in International Investment Law?' (2014) 8 *WAMR* 1. See also the contributions in Bjorklund and Reinisch (n 7).

Rules on the Taking of Evidence in International Commercial Arbitration,[68] the IBA Guidelines on Conflicts of Interests in International Arbitration,[69] and the IBA Rules on Party Representation in International Arbitration.[70] These instruments are important in concretising what are at times unclear and vague rules relating to arbitral procedure, such as the rules on the taking of evidence or the rules on conflicts of interests of arbitrators and counsel.

Soft law instruments that address questions of investment arbitration procedure exercise normative guidance independently of the disputing parties' consent and express standards of behaviour or default procedures that those involved as lawyers (counsel or arbitrator) in the settlement of investment disputes follow as a matter of professional best practices. As pointed out by Gabrielle Kaufmann-Kohler:

> Even though the law may be soft, even though it need not be incorporated into the parties' contract, soft law exercises a significant influence over the way arbitration proceedings are conducted. The IBA Rules of Evidence, for instance, have become standard practice, whether they are referred to expressly or not. Similarly, in all likelihood no arbitrator would make a decision on a delicate disclosure issue without consulting the IBA Guidelines on Conflicts of Interest.[71]

A second strand of soft law instruments relating to international investment relations aims at rebalancing investment protection and competing rights in response to the criticism that investment law one-sidedly favours the protection of foreign investment at the expense of competing public interests. A particularly important area of soft law that has developed in this context in recent years concerns what is often referred to as corporate social responsibility (CSR), responsible business conduct (RBC), or business and human rights (BHR).[72] In this field, several soft law instruments have been developed by

---

[68] IBA Rules on the Taking of Evidence in International Arbitration (adopted 17 December 2020) www.ibanet.org/resources accessed 14 September 2022.

[69] IBA Guidelines on Conflicts of Interest in International Arbitration (adopted 23 October 2014) www.ibanet.org/resources accessed 14 September 2022.

[70] IBA Guidelines on Party Representation in International Arbitration (adopted 25 May 2013) www.ibanet.org/resources accessed 14 September 2022.

[71] Gabrielle Kaufmann-Kohler, 'Soft Law in International Arbitration: Codification and Normativity' (2010) 1 *JIDS* 283–99.

[72] For an overview over instruments on business and human rights, see Barnali Choudhury, 'Balancing Soft and Hard Law for Business and Human Rights' (2018) 67 *ICLQ* 961. See also Surya Deva, *Regulating Corporate Human Rights Violations – Humanizing Business* (Routledge 2012); John Ruggie, *Just Business – Multinational Corporations and Human Rights* (Norton 2013); Robert C. Bird, Daniel R. Cahoy and Jamie Darin Prenkert (eds), *Law, Business and Human Rights – Bridging the Gap* (Edward Elgar 2014); Jena Martin and Karen E. Bravo (eds), *The Business and Human*

international organisations, including the UN Global Compact, the UN Norms on the Responsibilities of Transnational Corporations and Other Business Enterprises with Regard to Human Rights, the UN Guiding Principles on Business and Human Rights, or the OECD Guidelines for Multinational Enterprises. These instruments aim at counterbalancing investor rights through the codification of obligations investors are expected to comply with independently of their rights under IIAs.

References to CSR/RBC/BHR instruments are not only included more and more in IIAs themselves,[73] they are also referred to with increasing frequency by parties to investment arbitrations, by *amici curiae*, and by investment treaty tribunals in order to concretise the otherwise vague standards of treatment in IIAs[74] and to impose obligations on foreign investors.[75] Investment tribunals integrate CSR/RBC/BHR obligations through a number of different gateways, some of which go to arbitral jurisdiction or the admissibility of claims, others concern the assessment of liability and remedies.[76]

Rights Landscape – Moving Forward, Looking Back (CUP 2015); Nadia Bernaz, *Business and Human Rights: History, Law and Policy – Bridging the Accountability Gap* (Routledge 2016); Dorothée Baumann-Pauly and Justine Nolan (eds), *Business and Human Rights: From Principles to Practice* (Routledge 2016); Surya Deva and David Bilchitz (eds), *Building a Treaty on Business and Human Rights: Context and Contours* (CUP 2017); Dalia Palombo, *Business and Human Rights: The Obligations of the European Home States* (Hart 2020).

[73] See Kathryn Gordon and others, 'Investment Treaty Law, Sustainable Development and Responsible Business Conduct: A Fact Finding Survey' *OECD Working Papers on International Investment 2014/01* (2014).

[74] For an example of a Tribunal making reference to a soft law instrument to concretise the duties of the host State under the standards of treatment in IIAs, see *Hesham Talaat M Al-Warraq v Republic of Indonesia*, UNCITRAL, Final Award (15 December 2014) para 577.

[75] For examples of parties and *amici* making reference to soft law instruments to suggest the existence of duties of foreign investors under international law, see *Bear Creek Mining Corporation v Republic of Peru*, ICSID Case No ARB/14/21, Award (30 November 2017) paras 218, 227, 256–260 and ibid., Partial Dissenting Opinion Professor Philippe Sands QC (12 September 2017) paras 7–14; *South American Silver Ltd v Plurinational State of Bolivia*, PCA Case No 2013-15, Award (22 November 2018) paras 186–205.

[76] For an overview of the different ways investment treaty tribunals use to integrate CSR/RBC/BHR obligations in their decisions-making, see Jorge E. Viñuales, 'Investor Diligence in Investment Arbitration: Sources and Arguments' (2017) 32 *ICSID Review* 346; Johannes H. Fahner, 'Assessing Investor Misconduct in Mining Disputes – Legality Requirements, Clean Hands, and Contributory Fault' in Cory H. Kent and others (eds), *Social License and Dispute Resolution in the Extractive Industries* (Brill Nijhoff 2021) 50. See also Martin Jarrett, *Contributory Fault and Investor Misconduct in Investment Arbitration* (CUP 2019).

One of the most daring uses of soft law instruments can be found in the way the Tribunal in *Urbaser v Argentina*, in a case that involved a dispute concerning a water and sewage concession in Buenos Aires, dealt with the Respondent's counterclaim.[77] It involved a request by the host State for damages of some USD 400 million because the investor had failed to make investments into the water and sewage concession. It was presented, however, not as a claim for breach of the concession, but as a breach of the investor's duties under the international human right to water.[78] Although the Tribunal ultimately rejected the counterclaim as the right to water did not, in its reading, require the investor to make capital injections independently of the concession,[79] it found that international law could, in principle, impose direct obligations on a private investor. Developments in respect of CSR/RBC/BHR and references to soft law instruments played a key role for the Tribunal's finding. It stated:

> [I]nternational law accepts corporate social responsibility as a standard of crucial importance for companies operating in the field of international commerce. This standard includes commitments to comply with human rights in the framework of those entities' operations conducted in countries other than the country of their seat or incorporation. In light of this more recent development, it can no longer be admitted that companies operating internationally are immune from becoming subjects of international law. On the other hand, even though several initiatives undertaken at the international scene are seriously targeting corporations [sic] human rights conduct, they are not, on their own, sufficient to oblige corporations to put their policies in line with human rights law. The focus must be, therefore, on contextualizing a corporation's specific activities as they relate to the human right at issue in order to determine whether any international law obligations attach to the non-State individual.[80]

In this context, the Tribunal relied on a number of binding instruments, such as the International Covenant on Economic, Social and Cultural Rights, the principle of systemic integration laid down in Article 31(3)(c) of the Vienna Convention on the Law of Treaties, the notion of *ius cogens*, and the law applicable under the BIT and the ICSID Convention, but also on various non-binding soft law instruments, such as the Universal Declaration of Human Rights, the General Comment and the UN General Assembly Resolution on the 'Right to Water', the International Labour Organization (ILO) Tripartite

---

[77] *Urbaser SA and Consorcio de Aguas Bilbao Bizkaia, Bilbao Biskaia Ur Partzuergoa v Argentina*, ICSID Case No ARB/07/26, Award (8 December 2016).

[78] Ibid., paras 1110–1220.

[79] Ibid., paras 1206–1220.

[80] Ibid., para 1195 (referencing John G. Ruggie, 'Guiding Principles on Business and Human Rights: Implementing the United Nations "Protect, Respect and Remedy" Framework' UN Doc No A/HRC/17/31 (Final Report) (21 March 2011)).

Declaration of Principles Concerning Multilateral Enterprises and Social Policy, and concluded that the position that foreign investors could not be addressees of obligations under international law was no longer tenable.[81] Although the *Urbaser* tribunal ultimately rejected the finding of a violation of the right to water by the investor because this right could not be translated into a duty to perform specific acts,[82] the Award illustrates the potential of investment arbitration mechanisms to enforce not only obligations investors have undertaken under domestic law or in investor-State contracts,[83] but also duties directly under international law whose content is concretised in non-binding instruments.

Similar developments could also take place in respect of other soft law instruments, such as the Principles on Promoting Responsible Sovereign Lending and Borrowing,[84] which aim at laying down rights and obligations for lenders and borrowers in sovereign debt transactions and restructurings,[85] of the Principles for Responsible Agricultural Investment, which *inter alia* deal with the issue of land-grabbing,[86] or the so-called Santiago Principles, which lay down general principles and practices relating to sovereign wealth funds.[87] All of these soft law instruments help to fill blind spots left by the vague treaty

---

[81] *Urbaser v Argentina* (n 77) paras 1196–1203.

[82] Ibid., paras 1205–1210.

[83] For examples, see *Perenco Ecuador v Ecuador*, ICSID Case No ARB/08/6, Interim Decision on the Environmental Counterclaim (11 August 2015) and *Burlington Resources v Ecuador*, ICSID Case No ARB/08/5, Decision on Counterclaims (7 February 2017).

[84] UNCTAD, 'Principles on Promoting Responsible Sovereign Lending and Borrowing (amended and restated as of 10 January 2012) https://unctad.org/topic/debt-and-finance/Sovereign-Lending-and-Borrowing accessed 14 September 2022; see also UNGA Res 68/304 (9 September 2014) UN Doc A/RES/68/304.

[85] For a reference to these Principles in investment arbitration, see *Ambiente Ufficio SpA and others v Argentine Republic*, ICSID Case No ARB/09/9, Decision on Jurisdiction and Admissibility (8 February 2013) Dissenting Opinion of Santiago Torres Bernárdez, para 330.

[86] See Inter-Agency Working Group on the Food Security Pillar of the G20 Multi-Year Action Plan on Development, 'Options for Promoting Responsible Investment in Agriculture, Report to the High-Level Development Working Group' (3 June 2011) Annex 1 https://unctad.org/system/files/information-document/diae_dir_2011-06_G20_en_0.pdf accessed 14 September 2022. See also Lorenzo Cotula, *The Great African Land Grab? Agricultural Investments and the Global Food System* (Zed 2013); Lorenzo Cotula et al., 'Land Grab or Development Opportunity? Agricultural Investment and International Land Deals in Africa' (FAO, IIED and IFAD 2009) www.ifad.org/documents/10180/a2ea06a0-d0b2-4e99-a9b4-1f23e0491afb accessed 14 September 2022.

[87] International Working Group of Sovereign Wealth Funds (IWG), 'Sovereign Wealth Funds: Generally Accepted Principles and Practices' (October 2008) www

standards contained in IIA and could be hardened in the process of settling investor-State disputes before investment tribunals.

The use of soft law, however, comes with its own problems and challenges, not least since reliance on it can bypass, or undermine, traditional modes of international lawmaking.[88] Legitimacy concerns are particularly astute when soft law instruments are developed by technocratic expert groups that may share a common professional bias; but also the elaboration of soft law by international organisations can raise questions about representativeness and procedural propriety. Similarly, reference to and application of soft law instruments by investment tribunals, while contributing to hardening the underlying obligations, may also lead to changes in the instruments' application to individual cases and the further development of their content. After all, it should be borne in mind that investment arbitrators are an epistemic community with a certain outlook and approach to interpretation that may well differ from those who traditionally engage with CSR/RBC/BHR instruments. Investment arbitrators, for once, are typically not human rights or labour rights lawyers, but live and work in a world influenced by the considerations relevant for international commerce and dispute settlement. This does not mean that arbitrators would not be capable of properly interpreting and applying CSR/RBC/BHR instruments, but the hermeneutic context in which they will make their determinations may well shape the application given to the instruments in question.

These concerns notwithstanding, soft law is part of the instruments used to resolve investor-State disputes, to concretise the meaning of IIA standards, and to integrate international investment law with other areas of international law and dispute settlement. Although its use is not as prevalent as that of comparative law in present-day investment arbitration, the growing amount of soft law instruments that bear on investor-State relations is likely going to be reflected in increasing references to these instruments in future disputes, thus ensuring soft law an important place among the instruments taken into account in determining the content of rights and obligations of foreign investors and host States.

Reference to and use of soft law instruments is also an issue where international investment law can have radiating effects for other fields of international law and dispute settlement. Above all, investment arbitration can be looked at not only for the fact that the establishment of compulsory dispute settlement mechanisms contributes to hardening soft law, but also for how it hardens it. Questions that are highly relevant for the hardening of soft law that can

---

.ifswf.org/sites/default/files/santiagoprinciples_0_0.pdf accessed 14 September 2022 (Santiago Principles).

[88] On this concern, see, e.g., Goldmann (n 66) 394–8.

be studied in relation to international investment law with a view to learning lessons for other dispute settlement contexts include for example the question which impact party-appointed arbitrators have on hardening the soft law in question, as compared to the application of soft law by permanent courts. This issue is relevant, for example, when considering the idea to settle business and human rights disputes through especially adapted arbitration procedures, as proposed under The Hague Rules on Business and Human Rights Arbitration.[89] Does the appointment process for arbitrators, as well as their sociological and professional background impact the way they harden soft law relating to CSR/RBC/BHR? These and other questions that are relevant for the hardening of soft law in any context, could be assessed in respect of how investment treaty tribunals engage with soft law instruments. In that sense, international investment law can have radiating effects for other areas of international law and dispute settlement and serve as a lodestar for developments in these fields. All of this will depend, of course, on whether other courts and tribunals are willing to draw inspiration from international investment law, but the sheer number of precedent generated by investment tribunals will be increasingly difficult to ignore.

VI. CONCLUSION

As the previous discussions has shown, international investment law displays a number of specificities in its use of sources. The main reason for these specificities is the existence of a compulsory dispute settlement mechanism in the form of investment arbitration. The existence of this mechanism has not only been a force for transforming international investment law from an inter-State system of diplomatic protection into a judicialised regime in which affected investors have direct access to pursue claims under international law. Investor-State arbitration has also had significant impact on the use and conceptualisation of sources of international investment law. Unlike in an inter-State system, it is no longer solely, or even principally, the view of States on, and argumentative practices relating to, sources that are key for ascertaining the existence of a specific rule or for determining its content. Instead, in investment arbitration, it is arbitral tribunals that determine what counts as a source and how it is given content.[90] Norm production in international law is,

---

89 The Hague Rules on Business and Human Rights Arbitration (December 2019) www.cilc.nl/cms/wp-content/uploads/2019/12/The-Hague-Rules-on-Business-and-Human-Rights-Arbitration_CILC-digital-version.pdf accessed 14 September 2022.

90 Arbitral tribunals are therefore at the core of determining what is law and what is not, what is lawful and what is not. For the underlying theory, see Niklas Luhmann, *Law as a Social System* (OUP 2004) 297–337.

as a consequence, not anymore an exclusively State-driven enterprise, as was traditionally the case in international law,[91] but shared with international adjudicators. While State consent is still a necessary condition for the participation of international courts and tribunals in the further development of the law, and although these courts and tribunals base the resolution of disputes (also) on the recognised sources of law, the relative weight given to these sources, and the content given to the rights and obligations contained therein, depends to a large extent on the views of investment tribunals, rather than the views of States.

For this reason, the choice of decision-makers, their acculturation and interpretative mindset become important criteria for the legal culture and doctrinal reconstruction of a field, including but not limited to its use of sources. In light of the composition of the investment arbitration community, which goes much beyond classical public international lawyers, it is hardly surprising that investment tribunals draw on a variety of non-conventional sources, in particular references to arbitral precedent, comparative law, or soft law instruments, to determine the content of the often vague treaty standards in IIAs and motivate their decisions. International investment law is therefore a good example to illustrate how the understanding of sources in a specific sub-field of international law depends to a large degree on the practice of the dispute settlement mechanism and its sociological and epistemic embeddedness.[92]

The existence of compulsory dispute settlement mechanisms and their frequent use by foreign investors also indicates which radiating effects international investment law can have on other areas of international law and dispute settlement. It is a field that produces a steady flow of decisions that become public and thereby shape and concretise the content of the disputing parties' rights and obligations, but also the very understanding of the use of sources itself. In this respect, international investment law and arbitration are unlikely to have embarked on a Sonderweg that has no impact on other areas of international law. Instead, it is highly likely that international investment law will constitute a lodestar for how other areas of international law may develop if a frequently used, compulsory dispute settlement mechanisms is installed. As illustrated above, the multilateralisation of bilateral treaties, the importance of precedent for the interpretation and application of international law, the recourse to comparative reasoning and the renaissance of general principles

---

[91] On this view, see Martti Koskenniemi, *From Apology to Utopia* (2nd edn, CUP 2006).

[92] On the uncertain disciplinary identity of international investment law, which sits at the confluence of public international law, international commercial arbitration, and (internationalized) public law, see Anthea Roberts, 'Clash of Paradigms: Actors and Analogies Shaping the Investment Treaty System' (2013) 107 *AJIL* 45; Schill (n 3) 878–83.

of law, as well as the increasing reference to and hardening of soft law instruments are some of the elements in which international investment law may play a guiding role for other areas of international law.

Its radiating effects should not be understood, however, as implying that any other field would necessarily take the same developments as international investment law once compulsory dispute settlement mechanisms are introduced. On the contrary, the developments in international investment law can also serve as an example for what developments may not be desirable for, and intended by, States and should be better avoided by appropriately reacting in dispute settlement design. Among the important lessons to be learnt from international investment law is certainly that the significant lawmaking activities by investment tribunals need to be legitimate and find acceptance by States and other stakeholders.

While the search for legitimacy may explain some the recourse we see by investment tribunals to soft law instruments or comparative reasoning, the significant interpretative authority exercised by investment tribunals and their command over the impact of the sources of law on the outcome of disputes, also fuels calls for establishing better control mechanisms that would allow States to correct jurisprudential developments they disagree with. The creation of treaty organs for the issuance of interpretative statements may be one example of such control mechanisms; another example are projects for the creation of a permanent investment court with a legislative counterweight. All of this shows that, while the sources of law are the foundations of the law that is applied to settle international legal disputes, their creation by States is not sufficient to shape the future of a field of international law. What is also necessary is continuous and ideally institutional mechanisms to enable the checks and balances between legislative and adjudicatory functions at the international level that are tested and accepted as legitimate in any system that embodies the rule of law.

PART II

Investment law and the general law of treaties

4. Questions of treaty interpretation

Berta Boknik and Tarcisio Gazzini

I. INTRODUCTION

Investment treaties are quite peculiar. They formally pursue several objectives, most prominently the creation of a stable and predictable legal environment for foreign investments, the promotion of the economic development of the host State and the enhancement of the economic co-operation between the States parties. Yet, they have traditionally been, and largely remain, manifestly unbalanced, as they normally impose substantive obligations exclusively upon States and grant rights solely to foreign investors.[1]

As a rule, investment treaties not only provide a mechanism for the settlement of disputes between the parties, but also grant qualified investors access to international arbitration. Indeed, the latter form of dispute settlement is by far the most commonly used (so-called investor-State arbitration). The idea behind investor-State arbitration is to avoid the real or perceived hazards of delays and political pressures of adjudication in national courts.[2] Due to the absence in these treaties of obligations incumbent upon foreign investors or, at least, their exclusion from the scope of the relevant arbitral clauses, the claimant in investor-State arbitration is virtually always the foreign investor.[3]

---

[1] In *Spyridon Roussalis v Romania*, ICSID Case No ARB/06/1, Award (7 December 2011) para 871, the Tribunal conceded that the BIT between Greece and Romania 'imposes no obligation on investors, only on contracting States'.

[2] See, for instance, *Gas Natural SDG v Argentine Republic*, ICSID Case No ARB/03/10, Jurisdiction (17 June 2005) paras 29ff.

[3] See Mehmet Toral and Thomas Schultz, 'The State, a Perpetual Respondent in Investment Arbitration? Some Unorthodox Considerations' in Michael Waibel et al (eds), *The Backlash against Investment Arbitration: Perceptions and Reality* (Kluwer 2010) 577. For counterclaims, see, for instance, *Perenco Ecuador Limited v Republic of Ecuador*, ICSID Case No ARB/08/6, Decision on Perenco's Application for Dismissal of Ecuador's Counterclaims (18 August 2017); *Burlington Resources Inc v Ecuador*, ICSID Case No ARB/08/5, Decision on Ecuador's Counterclaims (7 February 2017); *Spyridon Roussalis v Romania*, ICSID Case No ARB/06/1, Decision Concerning the Respondent's Counter-Claim (31 March 2009) (not public); *Saluka Investments*

Opposing a private subject, normally a multinational company, to a sovereign State, investor-State arbitration can be seen as a hybrid form of arbitration,[4] in which the parties to the dispute and the parties to the treaty do not coincide. Investment tribunals are thus called to exercise a 'particular duty of caution' when interpreting these treaties,[5] which requires the most scrupulous application of the Vienna Convention on the Law of Treaties (VCLT).[6] The argument that the hybrid nature of investment arbitration demands a departure from or an adjustment of the rules on interpretation codified in the VCLT can safely be dismissed by pointing out that a treaty bears the same meaning regardless whether it is applied for the purpose of settling a dispute between States or between an investor and a State.

Investment tribunals have delivered an impressive body of decisions in almost 1,000 known cases.[7] It is therefore stimulating to examine whether arbitral tribunals dealing with the interpretation of these treaties have developed new canons, principles or techniques which already have or could generate radiating effects across international law and whose application has or could be extended to treaty interpretation outside the specific realm of international investment law.

This chapter briefly recalls the rules on interpretation (Section II) and then discusses their application by investment tribunals with regard to treaty provisions which were problematic due to their vague or imprecise content or the use of generic terms (Section III). It also examines a few instances in which investment tribunals have applied these rules in a rather peculiar fashion with a view to detecting departures from these rules and discern them from the development of new canons, principles or techniques (Section IV). Finally, it considers how States may ensure that investment treaties are given the meaning they intended to record in their texts (Sections V and VI). In line with the thrust of this volume, the chapter seeks to identify whether approaches adopted by investment tribunals have radiated, or could radiate into other fields of international law.

BV v Czech Republic, UNCITRAL, Decision on Jurisdiction over Czech Republic's Counterclaim (7 May 2004).

4 See Zachary Douglas, 'The Hybrid Foundations of Investment Treaty Arbitrations' (2003) *74 BYIL* 151.

5 *Empresas Lucchetti, SA and Lucchetti Peru, SA v Republic of Peru*, ICSID Case No ARB/03/4, Annulment (5 September 2007) Franklin Berman, Dissenting Opinion, para 9.

6 Vienna Convention on the Law of Treaties (adopted 23 May 1969, entered into force 27 January 1980) 1155 UNTS 331 (116 parties).

7 At the end of March 2020, UNCTAD website has recorded 983 cases, see UNCTAD, Investment Policy Hub, 'Case name and number' (*UNCTAD*) https://investmentpolicyhub.unctad.org/ISDS accessed 10 January 2021.

II. RULES APPLICABLE TO THE INTERPRETATION OF INVESTMENT TREATIES

Investment agreements are written agreements concluded between two or more sovereign States and governed by international law. They fall squarely within the definition of a treaty given by the VCLT and must therefore be interpreted in accordance with the rules on interpretation contained in Articles 31–33 VCLT.[8] Since these articles reflect customary international law,[9] they apply irrespective of whether States have ratified the VCLT. It is worth noting, nonetheless, that several investment treaties expressly indicate that their provisions are to be interpreted in accordance with the VCLT.[10]

Not surprisingly, investment tribunals have aligned themselves to all other international tribunals – with the possible exception of the Court of Justice of the European Union – and systematically proclaimed that investment treaties must be interpreted in accordance with Articles 31–33 VCLT,[11] to the point that a reference to these articles has become a *clause de style*.[12] Yet, these rules on interpretation 'are often briefly referred to or solemnly reproduced verbatim, and then largely ignored. A failure to apply the rules of interpretation perforce distorts the resulting interpretation of the parties' agreement'.[13]

---

[8] In the literature, see Ian Sinclair, *The Vienna Convention on the Law of Treaties* (2nd edn, Manchester University Press 1984); Robert Kolb, *Interprétation et création du droit international. Esquisse d'une herméneutique juridique moderne pour le droit international public* (Bruylant 2006); Ulf Linderfalk, *On the Interpretation of Treaties. The Modern International Law as Expressed in the 1969 Vienna Convention on the Law of Treaties* (Springer 2007); Malgosia Fitzmaurice et al (eds), *The Issue of Treaty Interpretation and the Vienna Convention on the Law of Treaties: 30 Years On* (Kluwer 2010); Ingo Venzke, *How Interpretation Makes International Law. On Semantic Change and Normative Twists* (OUP 2012); Richard Gardiner, *Treaty Interpretation* (2nd edn, OUP 2017); Andrea Bianchi et al (eds), *Interpretation in International Law* (OUP 2015).

[9] See *Question of the Delimitation of the Continental Shelf between Nicaragua and Colombia beyond 200 nautical miles from the Nicaraguan Coast (Nicaragua v Colombia)* [2016] *ICJ Reports* 100, para 35, as well as the decisions referred to.

[10] See, for instance, Comprehensive Economic and Trade Agreement between Canada, of the one part, and the European Union and its Member States, of the other part (CETA) [2017] OJ L11/23, art 8.31 – Applicable law and interpretation.

[11] On the interpretation of investment treaties, see in particular J. Romesh Weeramantry, *Treaty Interpretation in Investment Arbitration* (OUP 2012); Trinh Hai Yen, *The Interpretation of Investment Treaties* (Brill 2014); Tarcisio Gazzini, *Interpretation of International Investment Treaties* (Hart 2016).

[12] *Pac Rim Cayman LLC v Republic of El Salvador*, ICSID Case No ARB/09/12, Opinion of Michael Reisman on the International Legal Interpretation of the Waiver Provision in CAFTA Chapter 10 (22 March 2010) para 19.

[13] Ibid.

The interpretative process defined in the VCLT can be considered a 'well-formulated compromise',[14] combining the elements that characterised the main schools of interpretation that were in competition before the Vienna Conference, namely the 'textual', the 'founding father', and the 'teleological' schools.[15] As metaphorically pointed out by the UN International Law Commission, '[a]ll the various elements … would be thrown into the crucible, and their interaction would give the legally relevant interpretation'.[16]

Article 31, in particular, attaches paramount importance to the text of the treaty, including subsequent agreements, but also requires the interpreter to put terms, expressions and provisions into context and to take into account the purpose(s) and object(s) of the treaty. It also directs the interpreter to consider how the parties have applied the treaty as well as other rules of international law applicable between them.

Yet, the VCLT takes a rather minimalist approach to treaty interpretation and in good substance offers a broad framework whose degree of guidance still leaves the interpreter room for manoeuvre. From an internal perspective, the only hierarchical feature of the VCLT rules of interpretation relates to the supplementary nature of the preparatory work of the treaty and the circumstances of its conclusion under Article 32 VCLT. As several tribunals have correctly pointed out, recourse to Article 32 VCLT is required 'only in case of insufficient elements of interpretation in connection with the rule laid down in Article 31'.[17] In *El Paso v Argentina*, on the contrary, the Tribunal seems to have misunderstood the role of supplementary means and blurred the distinction between Articles 31 and 32 VCLT when it held that they can be used 'to establish a special meaning; to confirm or invalidate interpretations obtained by applying the elements listed in Article 31; to correct results so obtained if they are ambiguous, obscure, manifestly absurd or unreasonable'.[18] The crux of the matter is that the interpreter has to resort to Article 32 VCLT when the application of Article 31 VCLT leaves the meaning of the treaty ambiguous or obscure, or leads to a manifestly absurd or unreasonable result. The interpreter may also resort to Article 32 VCLT with a view to confirming the interpreta-

---

[14] Thomas W. Wälde, 'Interpreting Investment Treaties: Experiences and Examples' in Christina Binder et al (eds), *International Investment Law for the 21st Century. Essays in Honour of Christoph Schreuer* (OUP 2009) 724, 746.

[15] See Gerald Fitzmaurice, 'The Law and Procedure of the International Court of Justice: Treaty Interpretation and Certain Other Treaty Points' (1951) 28 *BYIL* 1.

[16] ILC, 'Report of the International Law Commission on the work of its eighteeth session' (1966) 18 (II) *ILC Yearbook* 219–20.

[17] *Enron Corporation and Ponderosa Assets, LP v Argentine Republic*, ICSID Case No ARB/01/3, Decision on Jurisdiction (Ancillary Claim) (2 August 2004) para 32.

[18] *El Paso Energy International Company v Argentine Republic*, ICSID Case No ARB/03/15, Award (31 October 2011) para 606.

tion reached under Article 31 VCLT, but this exercise would put the interpreter in an uncomfortable position if the supplementary means contradict, instead of confirming, such an interpretation.[19]

From an external perspective, the VCLT is framed in open terms in the sense that it allows the interpreter to resort to canons, principles and techniques that are not expressly provided for in the convention. As long as they are consistent with the rules of interpretation under Articles 31 to 33, the interpreter may resort to any aids that might shed some light on the meaning the contracting parties intended to attach to and record in the treaty.

Most investment tribunals have indeed emphasised that the text of the treaty is 'the authentic expression of the intentions of the parties and its elucidation, rather than wide-ranging searches for the supposed intentions of the parties, is the proper object of interpretation',[20] even when it may lead to a 'surprising and unsatisfactory result'.[21] Yet, the text of the treaty is the obvious point of departure of the process of interpretation, which has been effectively described, with regards to Article 31 VCLT, in the following terms:

> [i]nterpretation … is a process of progressive encirclement where the interpreter starts under the general rule with (1) the ordinary meaning of the terms of the treaty, (2) in their context and (3) in light of the treaty's object and purpose, and by cycling through this three step inquiry iteratively closes in upon the proper interpretation.[22]

Several tribunals have carefully and meticulously considered all relevant elements of the interpretative process in a holistic manner,[23] as required under

---

[19] In this regard, Justice Blackmun, Dissenting Opinion in *Sale v Haitian Centers Council, Inc*, 509 US 155, 194 (1993), warns that, '[r]eliance on a treaty's negotiating history (*travaux préparatoires*) is a disfavored alternative of last resort, appropriate only where the terms of the document are obscure or lead to "manifestly absurd or unreasonable" results'.

[20] *Methanex Corp v United States of America*, UNCITRAL (NAFTA), Final Award (3 August 2005) Part II, Chapter B, para 22. For another example, see *Wintershall Aktiengesellschaft v Argentine Republic*, ICSID Case No ARB/04/14, Award (8 December 2008) para 78.

[21] *Planet Mining Pty Ltd v Indonesia*, ICSID Case No ARB/12/14 and 12/40, Decision on Jurisdiction (24 February 2014) para 169. The decision echoed the ICJ decision in *Aegean Sea Continental Shelf Case (Greece v Turkey)* [1978] *ICJ Reports* 3, 22.

[22] *Aguas del Tunari v Republic of Bolivia*, ICSID Case No ARB/02/3, Decision on Respondent's Objections to Jurisdiction (21 October 2005) paras 91–93. This position is reminiscent of the *encirclement progressif* described by Max Huber, 'Commentaire de l'interpretation des traités' (1952) 44 *Annuaire IDI* 198, 200.

[23] In WTO, *EC – Customs Classification of Frozen Boneless Chicken Cuts – Report of the Appellate Body* (12 September 2005) WT/DS269/AB/R, para 176, the World

the VCLT.[24] Others have applied the relevant rules in a rather fragmented and partial way.[25]

Importantly, investment treaties – as any other treaties – must be interpreted in a balanced and unbiased manner in order to establish the intention of both or all parties as recorded in the text of the treaty. As unambiguously held by a tribunal, 'there is no principle either of extensive or restrictive interpretation of jurisdictional provisions in treaties. In the end the question is what the relevant provisions mean, interpreted in accordance with the applicable rules of interpretation of treaties'.[26] Regrettably, an inaccurate or incomplete understanding of the objects and purposes of investment treaties has induced a few investment tribunals to solve uncertainties either in favour of the host State or, more frequently, of the investor.[27]

III. INTERPRETATION OF PROBLEMATIC TREATY PROVISIONS

Interpretation, being 'the process of determining the meaning of a text',[28] becomes arduous when the text is poorly drafted. It must be recognised that this does not occur too infrequently in the case of investment treaties. The English authentic text of Article VII.2 of the BIT between Turkey and

---

Trade Organisation Appellate Body, stressed that interpretation is a 'holistic exercise that should not be mechanically subdivided into rigid components'.

[24] See, for instance, *Philip Morris Brands Sàrl, Philip Morris Products SA and Abal Hermanos SA v Oriental Republic of Uruguay*, ICSID Case No ARB/10/7, Award (8 July 2016) paras 106–113; *Continental Casualty Company v Argentine Republic*, ICSID Case No ARB/03/9, Decision on the Claimant's Preliminary Objection to Argentina's Application for Annulment (23 October 2009) paras 23ff.

[25] See, for instance, *Malaysian Historical Salvors SDN BHD* v *Malaysia*, ICSID Case No ARB/05/10, Award on Jurisdiction (17 May 2007) section IV, part E. For a matrix offering an overview of the application by investment tribunals of arts 31 and 32, see Hai Yen (n 11) Appendix A.

[26] *Mondev International Ltd v United States*, ICSID Case No ARB(AF)/99/2 (NAFTA), Award (11 October 2002) para 43 (footnote omitted). Amongst many other examples, see also *ICS Inspection and Control Services Ltd* v *Argentina*, UNCITRAL, PCA No 2010-9, Award on Jurisdiction (10 February 2012) para 282; *Grand River Enterprises Six Nations Ltd et al v United States of America*, UNCITRAL, Award (12 January 2011) para 69.

[27] For a recent example of the criticised approach, see *Mera Investment Fund Limited v Serbia*, ICSID Case No ARB/17/2, Decision on Jurisdiction (30 November 2018) para 123. The Tribunal relied on *SGS Société Générale de Surveillance SA v Philippines*, ICSID Case No ARB/02/6, Decision on Objections to Jurisdiction (29 January 2004) para 116.

[28] Harvard Law School, 'Draft Convention on the Law of Treaty' (1935) 29 *AJIL Supp* 657, 938, Comment to Article 19.

Turkmenistan, for instance, has been described by a tribunal and a dissenting arbitrator, respectively, as 'grammatically incorrect',[29] and 'undisputedly defective'.[30] Another tribunal found the use of the term 'entitled' in Article 25 of the Organisation of Islamic Cooperation Agreement 'clumsy and ambiguous' and the opening phrase of Article 17 of the same agreement 'ambiguously drafted'.[31] Since shortcomings in treaty drafting are not restricted to the area of investment law, the approach international investment tribunals adopt when dealing with poorly formulated IIAs can serve as a role model for international tribunals in other areas of law.

When treaty provisions present syntax and grammatical problems it can hardly be expected that the application of the VCLT rules always leads to a convincing interpretation. The problem concerns the drafting of the treaty rather than the rules on treaty interpretation or the skills of the interpreter. Sometimes even the assistance of linguistic experts may be of limited value.

Likewise, interpretation is likely to be particularly problematic when the treaty contains imprecise or vague provisions, as well as generic terms. The following three examples, related, respectively, to most-favoured-nation (MFN) clauses, fair-and-equitable-treatment (FET) clauses and the generic term 'investment', are illustrative.

A. MFN Clauses

MFN clauses included in several investment treaties are imprecise or susceptible to different plausible interpretations. They often do not expressly indicate whether their scope of application does or does not include procedural matters. According to some tribunals, limitations to the scope of the clause must be specifically agreed upon by the parties, since the clause is meant 'to eliminate the effect of specially negotiated provisions unless they have been excepted'.[32]

---

[29] *Kılıç İnşaat İthalat İhracat Sanayi ve Ticaret Anonim Şirketi v Turkmenistan,* ICSID Case No ARB/10/01, Decision on Article VII.2 of the Turkey-Turkmenistan Bilateral Investment Treaty (7 May 2012) para 9.14. See also *Muhammet Çap & Sehil Inşaat Endustrive Ticaret Ltd Sti v Turkmenistan,* ICSID Case No ARB/12/6, Jurisdiction under Article VII (2) of the Turkey-Turkmenistan Bilateral Investment Treaty (13 February 2015) paras 207 and 212.

[30] *Kılıç İnşaat İthalat İhracat Sanayi ve Ticaret Anonim Şirketi v Turkmenistan,* ICSID Case No ARB/10/01, Separate Opinion of Professor William W Park (20 May 2013) para 8.

[31] *Hesham Talaat M Al-Warraq v Republic of Indonesia,* UNCITRAL, Award on Respondent's Preliminary Objections to Jurisdiction and Admissibility of the Claims (21 June 2012) paras 72.5 and 75.

[32] See, for instance, *Siemens v Argentine Republic,* ICSID Case No ARB/02/8, Decision on Jurisdiction (3 August 2004) para 106; *Gas Natural v Argentina* (n 2) para

Conversely, other tribunals have held that the inclusion of procedural rights within the scope of application of the MFN clause requires a sufficiently clear language or context in this sense.[33] This question has provoked a significant number of diverging decisions on jurisdiction and can hardly be solved by arbitral tribunals as both interpretations are compatible with the open texture of the clause.

It is, therefore, rather for the States to clarify the meaning of the clause. This can be simply and efficiently done at the time of the conclusion of the treaty by clarifying the scope of the MFN clause in the clause itself,[34] in a footnote to the clause, or an annex.[35] An example of a well-drafted provision in this regard is the MFN clause included in the Comprehensive Economic and Trade Agreement (CETA), which provides that no dispute settlement provision is to be imported through the MFN clause. Article 8.7(4) CETA reads:

> For greater certainty, the 'treatment' referred to in paragraphs 1 and 2 does not include procedures for the resolution of investment disputes between investors and states provided for in other international investment treaties and other trade agreements. Substantive obligations in other international investment treaties and other trade agreements do not in themselves constitute 'treatment', and thus cannot give rise to a breach of this Article, absent measures adopted or maintained by a Party pursuant to those obligations.

After the conclusion of the treaty itself, States can still have recourse to other means permitted under the law of the treaties in order to dissipate any doubts on the scope of the MFN provision. Thus, they can, for instance, exchange letters, which amount to a subsequent agreement between the parties for the purpose of Article 31(3)(a) VCLT. Surprisingly, States have been rather reluctant to seek and reach such an agreement.[36] Given the lack of an original

---

49.

[33] See, for instance, *Telenor Mobile Communications AS v Hungary*, ICSID Case No ARB/04/15, Award, (13 September 2006) para 92; *Plama Consortium Ltd v Bulgaria*, ICSID Case No ARB/03/24, Decision on Jurisdiction (8 February 2005) para 223.

[34] See, for instance, BIT (United Kingdom-Nicaragua) (adopted 4 December 1996, entered into force 21 December 2001) art 3(3) and United Kingdom Model BIT (2008) art 3(3).

[35] See, for instance, Free Trade Agreement (Chile-Colombia) (adopted 27 November 2006, entered into force 8 May 2009) Annex 9.3 and Free Trade Agreement (Canada-Peru) (adopted 29 May 2008, entered into force 1 August 2009) Annex 804.1.

[36] See, for instance, the diplomatic notes exchanged between Argentina and Panama to the effect that the MFN clause contained in the BIT they concluded in 1996 does not extend to dispute resolution clauses. See also the Joint Interpretative Notes of India and Bangladesh, in which they clarify that the MFN clause in the BIT concluded between them 'does not apply to the mechanism for settlement of investment disputes

interpretative approach of investment arbitral tribunals in this problematic area, the only thing that can be transferred from it to the sphere outside investment law is that the authors of a treaty should take care to ensure its clear and unambiguous wording.

B. FET Clauses

Investments tribunals have also struggled to interpret vague provisions, like FET clauses, which, today, probably constitute the most important and most litigated provisions in investment treaties. Traditionally, FET provisions are limited to proclaim in just three words ('fair and equitable') the main standard of treatment of foreign investors, without providing any indication on its content. Yet, investment tribunals were called upon to put some flesh on its bones in order to settle dozens of disputes in which the claimant complained about alleged breaches of the standard. Given the general nature of the standard and its applicability to investments of any kind and in any sector, tribunals have refrained from attempting to establish *in abstracto* its content. Apart from some rather sterile efforts to define the standard through synonyms, tribunals have adopted a case-by-case approach and have broken down the standard into a series of concrete principles, mostly borrowed from the experience of domestic courts. This led to a progressive elaboration of an operative standard based on substantially similar combinations of procedural and substantive principles, without any ambition to provide a comprehensive list. In other words, tribunals 'have endeavoured to pinpoint some typical obligations that may be included in the standard, as well as types of conduct that would breach the standard, in order to be guided in their analysis of the issue before them'.[37] This can be considered a new interpretative method developed under the auspices of the VCLT and, potentially, transferable to other fields of international law. So far, however, it does not appear that the approach has been followed or even noticed in other areas of international law.

---

contained in the Agreement or to other procedural and jurisdiction issues under any circumstance', 'Joint Interpretative Notes on the Agreement between the Government of the Republic of India and the Government of the People's Republic of Bangladesh for the Promotion and Protection of Investments' (4 October 2017) 5 https://dea.gov.in/sites/default/files/Signed%20Copy%20of%20JIN.pdf accessed 10 January 2021. In addition to deleting the MFN provision from its new Model BIT (2015), India has also sent draft join interpretative statements to 25 BIT partners, proposing to explicitly delimit the scope of the MFN clause in the respective treaty accordingly. See also Section V below.

[37] *Total SA v Argentine Republic*, ICSID Case No ARB/04/01, Decision on Liability (27 December 2010) para 109.

A good example of this interpretative technique is offered in *Rumeli v Kazakhstan*. According to the Tribunal, the standard:

> encompasses *inter alia* the following concrete principles: the State must act in a transparent manner; the State is obliged to act in good faith; the State's conduct cannot be arbitrary, grossly unfair, unjust, idiosyncratic, discriminatory, or lacking in due process; the State must respect procedural propriety and due process. The case law also confirms that to comply with the standard, the State must respect the investor's reasonable and legitimate expectations.[38]

An interesting process can be detected here with regard to the evolution of FET clauses. First, States have concluded rather vague treaty provisions. Next, arbitral tribunals progressively have shaped the meaning of the standard via the application of concrete principles well-established in domestic law. Inspired by the practice of arbitral tribunals, finally, States have started drafting increasingly sophisticated treaty provisions that borrow some of the concrete principles indicated by arbitral tribunals.

Over time, thus, a flow of consistent arbitral decisions has triggered the refinement of FET clauses and contributed to enhancing legal accuracy and predictability. Concrete principles have eventually found their way into investment treaties. Currently, treaty practice offers clear examples in which States have explicitly defined the scope of the included FET standard by naming concrete principles previously developed in investment arbitration. An example for this treaty practice is Article 8.10 CETA,[39] which reads in part:

> A Party breaches the obligation of fair and equitable treatment referenced in paragraph 1 if a measure or series of measures constitutes:
> (a) denial of justice in criminal, civil or administrative proceedings;
> (b) fundamental breach of due process, including a fundamental breach of transparency, in judicial and administrative proceedings;
> (c) manifest arbitrariness;
> (d) targeted discrimination on manifestly wrongful grounds, such as gender, race or religious belief;
> (e) abusive treatment of investors, such as coercion, duress and harassment; or
> (f) a breach of any further elements of the fair and equitable treatment obligation adopted by the Parties in accordance with paragraph 3 of this Article … .

---

[38] *Rumeli Telekom AS and Telsim Mobil Telekomikasyon Hizmetleri AS v Kazakhstan*, ICSID Case No ARB/05/16, Award (29 July 2008) para 609.

[39] For a comparable clause, see also European Union Commission, 'Proposal on Transatlantic Trade and Investment Partnership' (16 September 2015) Chapter II, Section 2, art 3(2).

In the new Indian model BIT, which was approved by the Indian government in December 2015, Article 3(1) does not even mention the term FET anymore, but merely enumerates some specific principles normally associated with it. It reads:

> No Party shall subject investments made by investors of the other Party to measures which constitute a violation of customary international law through:
> (i) denial of justice in any judicial or administrative proceedings; or
> (ii) fundamental breach of due process; or
> (iii) targeted discrimination on manifestly unjustified grounds, such as gender, race or religious belief; or
> (iv) manifestly abusive treatment, such as coercion, duress and harassment.

C. Notion of 'Investment'

Lastly, investment tribunals have experienced problems in interpreting generic terms, like 'investment'. Arbitral tribunals have disagreed on the criteria suggested in *Salini v Morocco* to define an investment for the purpose of Article 25 ICSID Convention.[40] Some of them have preferred to search for a combination of characteristics that define an economic operation as an investment but do not need to be satisfied cumulatively. Other tribunals opted for the identification of a certain number of constitutive elements that need to be satisfied cumulatively for an operation to qualify as an investment.[41] Occasionally, arbitral tribunals have preferred a completely deferential or subjective approach and refrained from reading Article 25 ICSID Convention as constraining the definition of investment freely and deliberately agreed upon by the contracting parties in the relevant investment treaty.[42] The qualification of governmental bonds as investments, furthermore, has provoked a sharp division within arbitral tribunals, has triggered harsh dissenting opinions and has attracted a good deal of criticism.[43]

---

[40] *Salini Costruttori SpA and Italstrade SpA v Morocco*, ICSID Case No ARB/00/4, Decision on Jurisdiction (31 January 2001) para 56.

[41] The two approaches have been described in *Saba Fakes v Republic of Turkey*, ICSID Case No ARB/07/20, Award (14 July 2010) paras 99–102. In the literature, see, in particular, Emmanuel Gaillard, 'Identify or Define? Reflections on the Evolution of the Concept of Investment in ICSID Practice' in Binder et al (n 14) 403.

[42] *Malaysian Historical Salvors v Malaysia* (n 25), Decision on Annulment (16 April 2009), para 62.

[43] See, in particular, *Abaclat and Others v Argentine Republic*, ICSID Case No ARB/07/5, Decision on Jurisdiction and Admissibility (4 August 2011) with Dissenting Opinion of Georges Abi-Saab (28 October 2011); and *Ambiente Ufficio SpA and others v Argentine Republic*, ICSID Case No ARB/08/9, Decision on Jurisdiction and Admissibility (8 Feburary 2013) with Dissenting Opinion of Santiago Torres Bernárdez

In *Romak v Uzbekistan*, the tribunal developed an interesting argument based on the text and the structure of Article 1(2) of the BIT between Switzerland and Uzbekistan. The chapeau of Article 1(2) indicates that the term 'investments' refers to every kind of assets and particularly those indicated in the non-exhaustive list that follows. The tribunal held that the non-inclusion of any given type of investment enumerated in the non-comprehensive list does not prevent its qualification as investment for the purpose of Article 1(2). More importantly, it also found that such an inclusion does not automatically bring an investment within the scope of application of Article 1(2). In both cases, the interpreter must search the ordinary – or inherent – meaning of the term 'investment'.[44] Such an approach is fully consistent with the VCLT rules on interpretation and, indeed, the tribunal did consider carefully all elements of Article 31 VCLT, including the context of Article 1(2) and the object and purpose of the treaty.[45]

Aware of the difficulties concerning the definition of investment, States are much more attentive and have included in investment treaties increasingly elaborated definitions. A good example is the definition in the BIT between Nigeria and Morocco, which combines a chapeau largely reminiscent of the criteria identified in the *Salini* decision, with a comprensive list of categories of investments.[46] The definition also expressly excludes from the scope of the agreement governmental loans, debt securities and portfolio investments. Again, this kind of definitions are clearly designed with the relevant arbitral decisions in mind.

IV. PROBLEMATIC INTERPRETATION OF TREATY PROVISIONS

Although investment tribunals have systematically proclaimed their loyalty to the VCLT rules on interpretation, in a significant number of instances they have applied these rules in a rather peculiar manner. This begs the question whether these instances are to be considered as departures – whether intentional or not – from the generally accepted rules, or as evidence of the emergence of new approaches to treaty interpretation, possibly justified by the

(2 May 2013). For M. Sornarajah, *The International Law on Foreign Investments* (4th edn, CUP 2017) 233, the two decisions indicate 'the unfortunate trend to expand jurisdiction of investment arbitration'.

44 *Romak SA v Uzbekistan*, PCA No AA280 (UNCITRAL), Award (26 November 2009) paras 176–190.

45 The reference to art 32(b) in para 184 of the award, however, seems inaccurate.

46 BIT between Nigeria and Morocco (3 December 2016, not entered into force yet).

peculiar nature of investment treaties. In the latter case, it is worth examining whether these approaches have contaminated or may contaminate other areas of international law. The following examples are particularly significant.

A. Relevance of Preambular Language

The first case concerns the significance of preambles for the purpose of interpretation. According to Article 31(1) and (2) VCLT, a treaty shall be interpreted in good faith in accordance with the ordinary meaning to be given to its terms in their context and in the light of the treaty's object(s) and purpose(s). As a result, the preamble of a treaty plays an important double role. On the one hand, it forms part of the context of the treaty, which has to be considered in the interpretative process in accordance with the principle of integration, that treaties are to be interpreted as a whole. On the other hand, it can shed light on and is usually the primary source for defining the treaty's object(s) and purpose(s).[47]

An investment tribunal has observed that:

> [t]he Preamble sets out the general purposes and objectives of the Treaty but … cannot add substantive requirements to the provisions of the Treaty. The Treaty articles and its Preamble have different roles that should not be confused. Their confluence in the context of treaty interpretation relates to a situation in which the ordinary meaning of the text cannot be clearly established by the pertinent provisions themselves … .[48]

However, the value of preambles in the interpretative process should not be overestimated.[49] Investment treaties normally do not have a 'single, undiluted object and purpose but a variety of differing and possibly conflicting objects and purposes'.[50]

---

[47] *Adel A Hamadi Al Tamimi v Sultanate of Oman*, ICSID Case No ARB/11/33, Award (3 November 2015) fn 777; *Total v Argentina* (n 37) para 116.

[48] *Société Générale In Respect of DR Energy Holdings Ltd and Empresa Distribuidora de Electricidad del Este, SA v Dominican Republic*, LCIA No UN 7927, Award on Preliminary Objections to Jurisdiction (19 September 2008) para 32.

[49] *HICEE BV v Slovak Republic*, UNCITRAL, PCA No 2009-11, Partial Award (23 May 2011) para 116.

[50] Cf. WTO, *United States – Import Prohibition of Certain Shrimp and Shrimp Products – Report of the Appellate Body* (12 October 1998) WT/DS58/AB/R, para 17. The CETA (n 10) preamble, e.g., refers to 12 objects. Wälde (n 14) 724, 759, identifies 23 objects in Energy Charter Treaty's preamble. Giorgio Gaja, 'The Perspective of International Law' in Guglielmo Maisto (ed), *Multilingual Texts and Interpretation of Tax Treaties and EC Tax Law* (IBFD 2005) 91, 94, notes that 'treaties … may have a plurality of objects and purposes, without establishing any clear hierarchy'.

In such a situation, the search for 'the' object and purpose of the treaty can be frustrating.[51]

From this angle, it may be argued, that in *Bayindir Insaat Turizm Ticaret Ve Sanayi AŞ v Pakistan*[52] the tribunal misconstrued the preamble and eventually wrongly interpreted the BIT between Turkey and Pakistan. In the case, the relevant treaty did not contain any substantive provision on the FET standard, but in its preamble the parties had explicitly agreed that the inclusion of FET standard was 'desirable' in order to maintain a stable framework for investment. The tribunal found that:

> [i]t is true that the reference to FET in the preamble together with the absence of a FET clause in the Treaty might suggest that Turkey and Pakistan intended not to include an FET obligation in the Treaty. The Tribunal is, however, not persuaded that this suggestion rules out the possibility of importing an FET obligation through the MFN clause expressly included in the Treaty. The fact that the States parties to the Treaty clearly contemplated the importance of the FET rather suggests the contrary. Indeed, even though it does not establish an operative obligation, the preamble is relevant for the interpretation of the MFN clause in its context and in the light of the Treaty' s object and purpose pursuant to Article 31 (1) VCLT. ... The ordinary meaning of the words used in Article II(2) [MFN clause] together with the limitations provided in Article II(4) show that the parties to the Treaty did not intend to exclude the importation of a more favourable substantive standard of treatment accorded to investors of third countries. This reading is supported by the preamble's insistence on FET.[53]

The decision is not convincing. The reference to FET in the preamble of the treaty is hortatory, as clearly demonstrates the use of the adjective 'desirable' and cannot be (mis)used to introduce into the treaty substantive obligations that might subsequently trigger the invocation of a MFN treatment. According to the tribunal itself 'it is doubtful that, in the absence of a specific provision in the BIT itself, the sole text of the preamble constitutes a sufficient basis for a self-standing fair and equitable treatment obligation under the BIT'.[54] It even admitted that the preamble 'does not establish any operative obligation', where the adjective 'operative' presumably means 'substantive'.[55]

---

[51] See Jan Klabbers, 'Some Problems Regarding the Object and Purpose of Treaties' (1997) 8 *Finn YIL* 138; Malgosia Fitzmaurice, 'The Practical Working of the Law of Treaties' in Malcolm Evans (ed), *International Law* (5th edn, OUP 2018) 138.

[52] *Bayindir Insaat Turizm Ticaret Ve Sanayi AŞ v Pakistan*, ICSID Case No ARB/03/29, Award (27 August 2009).

[53] Ibid., paras 155–157.

[54] *Bayindir Insaat Turizm Ticaret Ve Sanayi AŞ v Pakistan,* ICSID Case No ARB/03/29, Decision on Jurisdiction (14 November 2005) para 230.

[55] *Bayindir v Pakistan*, Award (n 52) para 155.

Nonetheless, the tribunal described the text as 'of little assistance' and downgraded the interpretation of the preamble (not imposing upon the parties any substantive obligations) to a 'suggestion'.[56] It then postulated that such a suggestion was not necessarily an obstacle to the importation of the FET standard into the treaty via the MFN clause. Quite the contrary, for the tribunal, the importance attached to FET treatment by the parties in the preamble militates in favour of the functioning of the MFN clause with regard to FET obligations.

In a rather unpredictable twist, the tribunal moved to the interpretation of the MFN clause and found the preamble to be relevant as context and as expression of the object and purpose of the treaty. It established that the MFN clause functioned with regards to all substantive standards accorded to investors of third countries – apart from those expressly excluded in the MFN clause, which did not include FET. The tribunal thus deduced that the FET clause fell within the scope of the MFN provision.

In doing so, the tribunal turned the clear meaning of the preamble upside down. Its interpretation eventually imposed upon the parties a substantive obligation they had not even contemplated to include in the treaty, although agreeing on its importance and desirability. Thus, the tribunal showed a complete disrespect of the intention of the parties as clearly recorded in the text of the treaty, as well as for the *ejusdem generis* rule. Its approach departs from the interpretative rules laid down by the VCLT and cannot be viewed as the emergence of a new way of interpreting treaties worth of imitation outside the realm of international investment law. Fortunately, this seems to have remained an outlier without radiating effects.

B. Role of Subsequent Practice

The second case to be mentioned here is related to the relevance of subsequent practice of the parties to a treaty for the purpose of interpretation under Article 31(3)(b) VCLT. As is well known, the investment treaty regime is particularly fragmented. In the absence of multilateral treaties comparable to global trade agreements, investment treaty law is based on a dense web of BITs (of which, according to UNCTAD, 2,342 were in force at the end of March 2020) as well as free trade agreements dealing also with the protection of foreign investment (according to UNCTAD at the end of March 2020 they are 319 such agreements in force).[57] These treaties often present the same structure and similar, if

---

[56] Ibid.

[57] See UNCTAD, Investment Policy Hub, 'Most Recent IIAs' (*UNCTAD*) https://investmentpolicyhub.unctad.org/IIA accessed 10 January 2020. On their contribu-

not substantially identical provisions. This is especially true for BITs, although their provisions have become increasingly sophisticated over the years in order to strike a better balance between the private and public interests of the various stakeholders.

States normally pursue a coherent policy when concluding BITs and bring their experience from earlier treaty conclusions to the negotiating table when entering new negotiations. Even if the new treaties might eventually differ as a result of the negotiations, they inevitably share common features with their predecessors. This is hardly surprising, since:

> [e]ach state brings to the negotiating table a lexicon which is derived from prior treaties (bilateral or multilateral) into which it has entered with other states. The resulting text in each case may be different. It is, after all, the product of a specific negotiation. But it will inevitably share common elements with what has gone before.[58]

In order to interpret the text before them, several investment tribunals have looked at other treaties concluded by the parties under the guise of subsequent practice. In *National Grid v Argentina*, for instance, the tribunal considered, for the purpose of interpreting the BIT between the United Kingdom and Argentina, the practice of each State in relation to their respective BIT with third States. It concluded that while such practice of the UK demonstrates that the MFN clause has been understood as applying to treaty provisions on dispute resolution, no definite conclusion could be reached regarding Argentina's position.[59] The tribunal was therefore unable to detect a 'concordant, consistent and common practice' within the meaning of Article 31(3)(b) VCLT.[60]

The tribunal was undoubtedly correct in stating that subsequent practice must be concordant, consistent and common to both parties in order to fall under Article 31(3)(b) VCLT. However, it distorted the perspective. In accordance with Article 31(3)(b) VCLT, the subsequent practice the interpreter

---

tion to the formation and evolution of customary rules, see Patrick Dumberry, *The Formation and Identification of Rules of Customary International Law in International Investment Law* (CUP 2016).

[58] Campbell McLachlan, 'The Principle of Systemic Integration and Article 31(3)(c) of the Vienna Convention' (2005) 54 *ICLQ* 279, 283–4.

[59] *National Grid PLC v Argentina*, UNCITRAL, Decision on Jurisdiction (20 June 2006) para 85.

[60] In *Emilio Agustín Maffezini v Spain*, ICSID Case No ARB/97/7, Decision on Objections to Jurisdiction (25 January 2000) paras 58ff, the Tribunal in order to interpret the BIT Argentina-Spain unconvincingly 'examined in detail the practice followed by Spain in respect of bilateral investment treaties with other countries'.

must take into account is the subsequent practice of 'the parties to the treaty'. The purpose of the exercise is to ascertain how the parties to a treaty have interpreted it in practice in search of a 'concordant, common and consistent practice'.[61] As observed by a NAFTA tribunal, Article 31(3)(b) VCLT requires 'evidence of a sequence of facts and acts that amounts to a practice that is concordant, common and consistent'.[62] In the case referred to above, therefore, the tribunal's duty was to examine how Argentina and the UK have interpreted their BIT, and not the treaties each of them has negotiated and concluded with third States. Only this approach is in line with the principle *res inter alios acta*, which is enshrined in Article 34 VCLT.

The arbitral tribunal in *RosInvest v Russian Federation* therefore rightly stated, that the subsection (b) of Article 31(3) VCLT requires some relation or connection to the treaty to be interpreted, which is not fulfilled by the separate practice of either party.[63] In this sense, the arbitral tribunal in *Wintershall Aktiengesellschaft v Argentina* accurately rejected the idea that a conclusion concerning the content of the BIT between Argentina and Germany could be drawn from an overall assessment of the BITs concluded by Argentina. It stressed, that the content of the other BITs entered into by Argentina was not relevant for its analysis as its task in the case was limited to interpreting the particular treaty in question.[64] The misguided practice of some investment arbitral tribunals consisting in referring to the treaty practice of a State with third countries within the framework of Article 31(3)(b) VCLT is a misapplication of the VCLT and cannot, as such, serve as a role model. Unsurprisingly, it has not been consciously imitated by other international courts.

C. Drawing on Non-Investment Jurisprudence

The third case concerns the relevance for the purpose of interpretation of decisions of other tribunals, including investment tribunals. In a string of decisions on the nature of preliminary measures, in particular, investment tribunals have systematically held that these measures are mandatory. Under Article 47 ICSID Convention, a tribunal may 'recommend' any provisional measures,

---

[61] See WTO, *Japan – Measures Alcoholic Beverages – Report of the Appellate Body* (4 October 1996) WT/DS8/AB/R, WT/DS10/AB/R, WT/DS11/AB/R, para 106. The expression 'concordant, common and consistent practice' was borrowed from Sinclair (n 8) 137.

[62] *Canadian Cattleman for Fair Trade v United States*, UNCITRAL, Award on Jurisdiction (28 January 2008) para 189.

[63] *RosInvest v Russian Federation*, SCC Case No V079/2005, Award on Jurisdiction (1 October 2007) para 119.

[64] *Wintershall v Argentina* (n 20) para 128.

which should be taken to preserve the respective interests of either party. Under Arbitration Rule 39, a party may request that provisional measures for the preservation of its rights be 'recommended' by the tribunal, although the Spanish version of the Arbitration Rule uses the term 'dictación'.

Starting with the decision in *Maffezini v Spain*,[65] investment tribunals have heavily relied on ICJ jurisprudence and more specifically the decision in the *LaGrand* case, where the Court held that it had the power to adopt binding provisional measures. Article 41 of the ICJ Statute provides that the Court has the power to 'indicate',[66] if it considers that circumstances so require, any provisional measures which ought to be taken to preserve the rights of either party.

Subsequent investment tribunals have laconically relied on 'a well-established principle laid down by the jurisprudence of the ICSID tribunals'.[67] In *PNG v Papua New Guinea*, the tribunal merely reiterated the power of ICSID tribunals to order provisional measures[68] and, without elaborating any legal arguments, relied upon one single decision, namely *Occidental v Ecuador*, which in turn made a reference to 'numerous international tribunals', but expressly indicated only the one rendered in *Tokios Tokeles v Ukraine*.[69]

The weakness of the legal argument upholding the mandatory nature of provisional measures in ICSID arbitration was summarised in *Quiborax v Bolivia* as follows:

> It is true that the ordinary meaning of this provision, especially the terms 'recommend' and 'should be taken' do not convey the notion of a binding order. The same can be said for the context; other provisions of the ICSID Convention use different language when referring to binding obligations. Similarly, the *travaux préparatoires* of the ICSID Convention, to the extent relevant as supplementary

---

65 *Emilio Agustín Maffezini v Spain*, ICSID Case No ARB/97/7, Procedural Order No. 2 (28 October 1999) para 9.

66 *LaGrand Case (Germany v United States of America)* [2001] *ICJ Reports* 466, para 102. In the literature, see in particular, Robert Y. Jennings, 'The *LaGrand* Case' (2002) 1 *LPICT* 50; Christian Tams and Martin Mennecke, 'The *LaGrand* Case' (2002) 51 *ICLQ* 449; Robert Kolb, 'Note on the New International Case-Law Concerning the Binding Character of Provisional Measures' (2005) 74 *Nordic JIL* 117.

67 *Tokios Tokelés v Ukraine*, ICSID Case No ARB/02/18, Procedural Order No. 1 (1 July 2003) para 4.

68 *PNG Sustainable Development Program Ltd v Papua New Guinea*, ICSID Case No ARB/13/33, Decision on Provisional Measures (21 January 2015) para 102.

69 *Occidental Petroleum Corporation and Occidental Exploration and Production Company v Ecuador*, ICSID Case No ARB/06/11, Decision on Provisional Measures (17 August 2007) para 58.

> means of interpretation, show that an earlier draft using the word 'prescribe' was then changed to 'recommend'.[70]
>
> Despite this, the Tribunal recognized that several ICSID tribunals had made binding orders for provisional measures and further explained that the mandatory force of those orders derives from the function of provisional remedies, which is to secure the applicant's rights while the proceedings are pending as emphasised by the ICJ decision in *LaGrand*. While conceding that Article 41 of the ICJ Statute and Article 47 of the ICSID Convention are not identical, the Tribunal found it decisive that the function of the measures in the two legal instruments is the same

It is argued that this interpretation is hardly convincing. ICSID tribunals are certainly allowed to look at the ICJ jurisprudence as a source of inspiration to interpret investment treaties.[71] What is inappropriate, under the Vienna Convention regime, is to mechanically transpose the interpretation of Article 41 of the ICJ Statute to the relevant ICSID provisions in spite of the evident textual differences. Furthermore, it is important that investment tribunals carefully consider previous arbitral decisions, although there is no strict doctrine of *stare decisis* in international investment law, in order to contribute to 'the harmonious development of investment law and thereby to meet the legitimate expectations of the community of States and investors towards certainty of the rule of law'.[72] Again, this should not be a mechanical exercise and even less a substitute for the interpretative process as designed in Articles 31 to 33 VCLT. In general, the reference to the decisions of other international courts cannot be understood as a method of interpretation specific to investment arbitration courts, so that a discussion of its radiating effects is not expedient.

Finally, and quite obviously, ICSID tribunals must consider the object(s) and purpose(s) of the relevant treaties or provisions, without departing from the clear textual meaning of the provision being interpreted, when there are no cogent reasons to do so. Conversely, investment tribunals have refrained from performing a thorough analysis under the lense of the VCLT, going through all different elements of the interpretative process as required. Instead, they have often limited themselves to the development of rudimentary teleological arguments and vague references to the *LaGrand* case and previous arbitral decisions.

Although acquiescence by the generality of States that have ratified the ICSID Convention can be considered as concordant, consistent and common

---

[70] *Quiborax SA and Non Metallic Minerals SA v Bolivia*, ICSID Case No ARB/06/2, Award (16 September 2015) paras 578–579.

[71] Alain Pellet, 'The Case Law of the ICJ in Investment Arbitration' (2013) 28 *ICSID Review* 223.

[72] See *Saipem SpA v Bangladesh*, ICSID Case No ARB/05/07, Award (30 June 2009) para 90 (footnote omitted).

subsequent practice leading to the informal modification of the treaty, the interpretation of Article 47 ICSID Convention and Arbitration Rule 39 by those tribunals remains rather questionable.[73]

All the decisions discussed above seem to be instances of misapplication of the VCLT rules on interpretation, rather than the elaboration of new techniques or canons of interpretation compatible with those rules. It would therefore be hardly worth examining whether these approaches have influenced – in fact, 'contaminated' – other areas of international law, or might do so in the future. When dealing with vague or imprecise treaty provisions as well as with generic terms, investment tribunals – as any interpreter – must scrupulously follow the VCLT rules on interpretation and carefully consider each relevant element.

V. AUTHORITATIVE INTERPRETATION OF TREATIES

Keeping in mind the hybrid nature of investment arbitration as well as the sovereign character of investment tribunals,[74] States have a significant role to play in ensuring that the meaning attached to an investment treaty is indeed the one they intended to record in its text. The importance of drafting the treaty as precisely and meticulously as possible does not need much elaboration. A clear text, which takes into account previously rendered decisions and difficulties faced by investment tribunals, is the best guarantee for the correct interpretation of a treaty.

However, not all uncertainties can be eliminated by clear treaty drafting. States, which undoubtedly remain the masters of the treaty, have different tools to ensure that the meaning attached by tribunals to a given treaty correlates with the meaning they agreed upon. These tools include authoritative interpretations (discussed in this section) and non-disputing party submissions (discussed in the next section).

Through authoritative interpretations, the parties to a treaty formally indicate the meaning they intended to record in the treaty. Such interpretations are legally binding for domestic and arbitral tribunals as well as, more generally, anybody interpreting and applying the treaty. The parties to the authoritative

---

[73] For a more detailed discussion, see Tarcisio Gazzini and Robert Kolb, 'Provisional Measures in ICSID Arbitration. From "Wonderland's Jurisprudence" to Informal Modification of Treaties' (2017) 16 *LPICT* 159.

[74] In *AES Corp v Argentine Republic*, ICSID Case No ARB/02/17, Decision on Jurisdiction (26 April 2005) para 30, for example, the Tribunal held that '[e]ach tribunal remains sovereign and may retain, as it is confirmed by ICSID practice, a different solution for resolving the same problem'.

interpretation must coincide with the parties to the treaty being interpreted.[75] Moreover, authoritative interpretations cannot be transferred to other treaties, even if those treaties provide for the exact same provision in wording.[76]

Conversely, a declaration containing the interpretation of the treaty unilaterally issued by a party is not legally binding. Yet, it might serve as a starting point and lead to the conclusion of an authoritative interpretation if the other party or parties either consent to it or adopt the identical interpretation in the same or an equivalent document.

Depending on whether the authoritative interpretation is made concordantly or subsequently to the conclusion of the respective treaty, its legally binding nature derives from Article 31(2) VCLT or Article 31(3)(a) VCLT.

A recent example of the first category is the joint interpretative instrument agreed by Canada and the European Union and its Member States upon the conclusion of CETA. The instrument also played an important role at the political level for in the specific case the conclusion of the agreement would not have taken place without an interpretation agreement addressing several concerns of CETA opponents, *inter alia* concerning the Investment Court System (point 6(i)).[77]

Additionally, parties to a treaty continuously monitor the interpretation of their treaty and can address interpretative issues throughout the life of the treaty. For instance, India and Bangladesh considered it necessary, eight years after the conclusion of the BIT itself, to clarify the meaning they intended to give certain of its provisions through a Joint Interpretative Note.[78]

The conclusion of a subsequent authoritative interpretation may or may not already be foreseen in the text of the treaty. Either way, it is important that a convergence of wills concerning the interpretation at a later moment in time is discernable between the parties. Some treaties even establish entities (so-called joint committees, commissions or conferences) entitled *inter alia* to

[75] It is therefore not convincing when *Caratube International Oil Company LLP v Kazakhstan*, ICSID Case No ARB/08/12, Award (5 June 2012) para 333 qualifies a BIT as a subsequent agreement regarding the interpretation of the ICSID Convention.

[76] Not really convincing therefore *Daimler Financial Services AG v Argentine Republic*, ICSID Case No ARB/05/1, Award (22 August 2012) para 272, assigning an indicative value for the interpretation of the BIT between Chile and Argentina to the interpretative declaration by Argentina and Panama concerning the BIT between Argentina and Panama.

[77] Joint Interpretative Instrument on the Comprehensive Economic and Trade Agreement (CETA) between Canada and the European Union and its Member States [2017] OJ L 11/3.

[78] Joint Interpretative Notes on the Agreement between India and Bangladesh (n 36).

adopt authoritative interpretations. Under Article 8.31(3) CETA, for instance,[79] a Joint Committee may adopt interpretations where 'serious concerns arise as regards matters of interpretation that may affect investment' and such interpretations shall be binding on investment tribunals.[80] Importantly, authoritative interpretations are intended 'to avoid and correct any misinterpretation of CETA by Tribunals'.[81] From this perspective, the parties maintain an effective control on the interpretation of the treaty and may intervene when they believe that the interpretation given by a tribunal does not reflect their intentions as recorded in the treaty. This obviously presupposes an agreement on this point amongst all parties.

Authoritative interpretations by the parties are meant to protect the parties against distorted interpretations and clarify the meaning of the treaty in order to ensure legal certainty and coherence. However, there remains a potential of abuse deriving from the dual role of the host State as party to the treaty and potential respondent in a dispute. This dual nature has attracted some scepticism regarding the State's proposed interpretative approaches and solutions.[82] States might be tempted to take advantage of the institutional mechanisms provided for by BITs and issue authoritative interpretations in order to influence the outcome of judicial and arbitral procedures in which they act as defendant.[83]

However, the potential for abuse is severely limited by the fact that an authoritative interpretation always requires the consent of the other contracting party or parties. Furthermore, temporal limitations can be inserted in authoritative interpretations in order to ensure that pending disputes are not unduly

---

[79] Other examples include the North American Free Trade Agreement (United States-Canada-Mexico) (adopted 17 December 1992, entered into force 1 January 1994) art 1131 (NAFTA), the Central America Free Trade Agreement (adopted 5 August 2004) art 10.23 (CAFTA) and the Energy Charter Treaty (adopted December 2014, entered into force 1998) art 34.

[80] Established under art 26.1, the Committee adopts binding interpretations upon a recommendation by the Committee on Services and Investment, in accordance with art 8.44.3(a). Similar provisions are included in the agreement with Vietnam, see, in particular Section 3 (Resolution of Investment Disputes), art 16(4).

[81] CETA (n 77) s 6 (e).

[82] See Lars Markert, 'International Investment Law and Treaty Interpretation - Problems, Particularities and Possible Trends' in Rainer Hofmann and Christian J. Tams (eds), *International Investment Law and General International Law* (Nomos 2011) 53, 63.

[83] Christoph Schreuer, 'International Investment Law and General International Law – From Clinical Isolation to Systemic Integration?' in Hofmann and Tams, ibid., 71, 74.

affected and thus to protect the equality of the parties and legal predictability, especially from the standpoint of the investor.[84]

Imposing upon a tribunal a binding interpretation may be particularly problematic when the interpretation amounts or is perceived as amounting in fact to an amendment of the treaty. This is of particular concern in treaties containing investment protection, as demonstrated by the interpretative note on Article 1105 NAFTA.[85] Only authoritative interpretations that interpret existing treaty rights or obligations without modifying them or creating new ones, and that therefore, do not amount to treaty amendments, can have retroactive effect. As the distinction is at times very difficult to establish, arbitral tribunals have been generally rather prudent in the past in granting retroactive effect to subsequent interpretations.[86] Additionally, if investors are found to hold third-party beneficiary rights, the principles of legitimate expectations and good faith come into play.[87]

VI. NON-DISPUTING PARTY SUBMISSIONS

Several investment treaties give the State(s) not appearing before the arbitral tribunal in investor-State disputes the possibility of submitting formal written submissions on the interpretation of the relevant treaty provisions with a view to assisting the tribunal in its search for the common intention of the parties as recorded in the treaty. [88] Non-disputing party clauses belong to the North

[84] 'EU-Singapore FTA' art 22.22.3 directed the Committee on Trade in Services, Investment and Government Procurement to exercise 'due restraint in recommending interpretations of any provision already submitted to a tribunal in a dispute between a Party and a claimant of the other Party where a final award has yet to be made'. The provision does not appear in the latest version of the agreement (2018). See Free Trade Agreement between the European Union and the Republic of Singapore [2019] OJ L294/3.

[85] Free Trade Commission, 'Notes of Interpretation of Certain Chapter XI Provisions' (31 July 2001) www.sice.oas.org/tpd/nafta/Commission/CH11understanding_e.asp accessed 10 January 2020. For a sharp critique, see *Methanex Corp v United States*, UNCITRAL (NAFTA), Second Opinion of Professor Robert Jennings (6 September 2001).

[86] Cf. *Sempra Energy International v Argentine Republic*, ICSID Case No ARB/02/16, Award (28 September 2007) paras 385-6; *Enron Corporation and Ponderosa Assets, LP v Argentine Republic*, ICSID Case No ARB/01/3, Award (22 May 2007) para 337.

[87] Wälde (n 14) 742, 766–7. In *Enron v Argentina*, ibid., para 337, the Tribunal held that 'States are of course free to amend the Treaty by consenting to another text, but this would not affect rights acquired under the Treaty by investors or other beneficiaries.'

[88] In 2015, the estimation was that well under 1 per cent of investment treaties provide explicitly for submissions by non-disputing parties, see Kathryn Gordon and Joachim Pohl, 'Investment Treaties over Time – Treaty Practice and Interpretation in a Changing World' (2015) *OECD Working Papers on International Investment*

American tradition, although they can also be found elsewhere.[89] Article 1128 NAFTA (Participation by a Party), in particular, reads: 'On written notice to the disputing party, a Party may make submissions to a Tribunal on a question of interpretation of this Agreement.' Article 8.38(2) CETA provides for a similar possibility of intervention.[90]

The idea behind the mechanism is to protect the 'legitimate' [91] or 'systemic'[92] interest of the parties in the correct interpretation of the treaty. States are not restricted to passively monitor the interpretation of treaties they are party to in investment disputes to which they are not party. By applying for a leave to file and eventually filing a non-disputing party submission, they can actively contribute to establish (what they believe is) the meaning of the treaty.

This mechanism is not to be confused with submissions made by *amicus curiae*. These submissions, although technically also filed by 'a non-disputing party' do not stem from other parties to the treaty, but from NGO's, academics etc. In the past, it was notably possible to witness an increased recourse to this instrument by the European Commission, especially in the context of intra-EU disputes.[93] The *raison d'être* of these submissions is completely different from the one of the mechanism discussed here, as their purpose is not to protect any kind of intrinsic interest of the *amici*, but rather to make external expertise available to the arbitral tribunal. Concordantly, these submissions are not limited to interpretative issues, but often concern factual question, for example, in the environmental and technical realm.

Closely linked to the mechanism of non-disputing party submissions are transparency rules. For only when the non-disputing parties are sufficiently informed about the arbitration, can they exercise their right to make submissions on questions regarding the interpretation of the treaty in question. Furthermore, the number of submissions made in a case is not limited. In the

---

2015/02 26 www.oecd.org/investment/investment-policy/WP-2015-02.pdf accessed 10 January 2021.

[89] See, for instance, Peru-Japan BIT (adopted 21 November 2008, entered into force 10 December 2009) art 18(17).

[90] See also CAFTA-DR (n 79) art 10.20.2.

[91] Meg Kinnear, 'Article 1128 – Participation by a Party' in Andrea Bjorklund et al (eds), *Investment Disputes under NAFTA: An Annotated Guide to NAFTA Chapter 11* (Kluwer 2006) Supplement No. 1, 1128-1.

[92] Martins Paparinskis and Jessica Howley, 'Submission by Non-Disputing Party to the Treaty' in Dimitrij Euler et al (eds), *Transparency in International Investment Arbitration* (CUP 2015) 196.

[93] See, however, the rejection of the European Commission's request for permission to intervene in *UP and CD Holding Internationale v Hungary*, ICSID Case No ARB/13/35, Award (9 October 2018) para 98.

past, parties have taken advantage of the mechanism in order to submit several submissions in one dispute.[94]

Tribunals are expected to take into account in good faith the submissions by non-disputing parties and the legal arguments they are based upon. At the same time, they are supposed to consider their relevance as evidence of State practice and, if appropriate, as part of a subsequent agreement, for the purpose of, respectively, Article 31(3)(a) and (b) VCLT. However, as clearly stated in Article 5(4) UNCITRAL Transparency Rules of 2014, arbitral tribunals must ensure that the submission by a non-disputing party to the treaty 'does not disrupt or unduly burden the arbitral proceedings, or unfairly prejudice any disputing party'.

Tribunals must also be cautious about the weight they attach to submissions by non-disputing parties. In *Mesa v Canada*, concerns have been expressed by a member of the tribunal with regard to the material influence these submissions can have on treaty interpretation as the Respondent State and the non-disputing State(s) inevitably 'club together' to share the same interpretation.[95] In the award, a NAFTA tribunal thoroughly went through the different elements of the interpretative process in accordance with Article 31 VCLT. While dealing with the ordinary meaning of 'procurement', it limited itself to note that '[a]ll three NAFTA Parties appear to support the broad notion of procurement as advanced by the tribunals in *ADF* and *UPS*'.[96] It is argued that in this case non-party submissions did not unduly influence the tribunal's interpretation. Since interpreting '[i]nvolves understanding the intention' of the parties,[97] the tribunal could not ignore the agreement of the parties to the treaty on the interpretation of the relevant provision.

The fact that States 'club together' is not necessarily negative. Quite the contrary, it means that the parties to the treaty share the same interpretation. The real risk, as in the case of authentic interpretations, is that the parties to the treaty may be tempted to amend the treaty while pretending that their submissions merely confirm the meaning they have always attached to the treaty. It is the task of the tribunals to carefully draw a clear line between interpretation

---

94 See, for instance, the respective eight submissions by Mexico and the United States in *Pope & Talbot Inc v Canada*, UNCITRAL (NAFTA).

95 *Mesa Power Group LLC v Government of Canada*, UNCITRAL, PCA Case No 2012-17, Concurring and Dissenting Opinion of Judge Charles N Brower (24 March 2016) para 30.

96 Ibid., para 199.

97 Ibid., para 405, quoting with approval *Mobil Investments Inc & Murphy Oil Corporation v Canada*, ICSID Case No ARB(AF)/07/4, Decision on Liability and on Principles of Quantum (22 May 2012) para 254.

and amendment. In this regard, the reply by the applicant to the submissions of non-disputing parties may be of great assistance to the interpreter.

The tribunals' task of delimitation between interpretation and amendment is of particular importance in the field of international investment arbitration, given the special role of the investor, who is a party to the dispute but not to the investment treaty. Until now, there is, however, no indication that its handling in investment cases radiated into other fields of international law.

VII. CONCLUSION

Investment arbitration tribunals, like other international tribunals, are bound by the rules on treaty interpretation codified in the VCLT. The flexibility of these rules, the large amount of decisions rendered by arbitral tribunals, and the hybrid nature of investment arbitration provide a fertile ground for the development of new interpretative approaches and techniques that could in due time have radiating effects across general international law.

Yet, interpretation of investment treaties has often been difficult. On the one hand, several tribunals have struggled to establish the meaning of poorly drafted treaties presenting grammatical and lexical problems. In these cases, interpretation becomes an arduous exercise, regardless of the adequacy of the rules on treaty interpretation and the skills of the interpreter.

On the other hand, in a significant number of cases tribunals have failed to carefully go through the interpretative process set out by Articles 31–33 VCLT and delivered unconvincing interpretations, most prominently regarding the interpretative value of preambles, subsequent practice and other decisions. These cases remain unconvincing departures from the rules contained in the VCLT. Far from influencing other international courts and tribunals, these decisions should serve as a warning for the meticulous application of the VCLT rules on interpretation.

While so far, the approaches adopted by investment tribunals to questions of treaty interpretation have not produced any radiating effects, this might very well happen in the future.

In this respect, three developments need to be mentioned. The first relates to how investment arbitration tribunals have put flesh on the otherwise laconic FET standard. Over the years, they have adopted a case-by-case approach and broken down the standard into a series of concrete principles, mostly borrowed from the experience of domestic courts. By coherently and consistently relying on these principles and ordering them in non-comprehensive lists, they have managed to progressively build up the meaning of the standard. This approach has the potential to radiate into the practice of international tribunals outside the sphere of international investment law. At least in the field of investment law itself, arbitral decisions have already had an important impact on treaty practice. Some States have redesigned the standards in their treaties by incorporating selections of these principles in accordance with their needs. Thus, the interpretative efforts of investment tribunals – which are often qualified – have led to the evolution of more precise and sophisticated standards. This active contribution to the evolution of treaty practice can be considered a distinguishing feature of investment arbitration tribunals. In this regard, they can serve as a role model for other international courts.

The second development concerns submissions by non-disputing States on the interpretation of treaty provisions. Especially with regard to NAFTA, these submissions have proved to be an important tool through which States can ensure that the meaning attached to a treaty by a tribunal corresponds to that agreed upon by the parties at the conclusion of the treaty.

The third development regards the adoption by State parties of authentic interpretations, either at the time of the conclusion of the treaty or any time afterwards. These interpretations certify the meaning the parties intended to record in the treaty and as such are binding for investment tribunals. Several investment treaties expressly provide for the adoption of such interpretations, sometimes through a committee established under the treaty.

The last two developments reveal the attempt of States to assert an effective control over the interpretation of investment treaties. This is important due to the sovereign character of each arbitral tribunal as well as the non-correspondence in investor-State disputes of the parties to the treaty and those to the disputes. Both developments, however, might be a source of inspiration for treaty interpretation in other areas.

5. The temporal scope of application of investment treaties and the effects on general international law

Christina Binder and Jane A. Hofbauer

I. INTRODUCTION

Stephen Hawking begins his exploration of the universe by observing that the quest for answers is ultimately dependent on the physical aspect of time: 'Only time (whatever that may be) will tell'.[1] Time is not only relative in the physical sense, though; also the social construction of time varies greatly. This also extends to the realm of law,[2] with legal periods, crucial dates and – last but not least – the scope of application of legal rules being dependent on a number of circumstances. Thus, the temporal scope of application constitutes one of the most crucial elements of treaty law. While the stages of the life of a treaty – from the moment of its adoption until the end of its legal consequences – depend on the will of the parties, the exercise of such will is embedded in an objective regime governing the legal effects and consequences of each stage.[3]

The interplay between treaty-specific provisions determining the scope of application of a specific agreement and the general law of treaties has particular relevance in the field of investment law, since tribunals are faced with several crucial moments in time which determine the rights and obligations arising under the specific international investment agreements (IIAs). Such moments in time arise both in relation to substantive questions, as well as in

[1] Stephen Hawking, *A Brief History in Time – From the Big Bang to Black Holes* (Bantam Books 1988) 1.

[2] See Christian Djeffal, 'International Law and Time: A Reflection of the Temporal Attitudes of International Lawyers Through Three Paradigms' (2014) 45 *NYIL* 93, 95, who on a more general level provides an excellent discussion of this.

[3] This objective regime is enshrined in numerous provisions of the Vienna Convention on the Law of Treaties (VCLT) (adopted 23 May 1969, entered into force 27 January 1980) 1155 UNTS 331. Of particular relevance in the context of this chapter are arts 25, 28, 37, 54, and 70 VCLT.

direct consequence to the stages of a treaty's life (entry into force, provisional application, scope of dispute settlement clause).[4] Hence, a number of questions of general international law, particularly treaty law, arise in this context. Their investigation is also of special interest given the specific characteristics of investment treaties as treaties for the benefit of investors (third-party beneficiaries). There is thus a triangular relationship which transcends the typically horizontal nature of treaties.

Even though owed to these specific characteristics questions of the general law of treaties may need specific answers in the context of investment law,[5] such answers may nonetheless again feed back into the law of treaties. The symbiotic relationship between general international law and investment law has been observed on several occasions, e.g., in the context of substantive standards,[6] or state responsibility.[7] In light thereof, this contribution continues this investigation and focuses particularly on whether investment law (jurisprudence) provides answers to open questions of the general law of treaties relating to the temporal scope of application. The structure follows the relevant moments in time for a treaty, i.e., its entry into force, its life prior to entry into force by virtue of a treaty's provisional application, and its 'end of life', particularly following mutual termination. Given the wide scope of the topic, not all issues arising in this context are addressed to the same extent. Focus is, however, placed on those cases which have the most to offer with regard to the general law of treaties, i.e., the question of the reach of an openly formulated dispute settlement clause, both with regard to preexisting disputes as well as

---

4 Crucial moments in time, e.g., relate to the question at which time a nationality was acquired or investment made (Does the investor/investment fall within the treaty's scope of application?), as well as to the inquiry into from which moment in time and for how long the afforded protection lasts (When did the treaty enter into force and when was it terminated? Does protection extend beyond the treaty's termination?). Moreover, crucial moments in time relate to the determination when the alleged breach occurred and/or when the dispute 'crystallized', and when the claim was registered (Were relevant cooling off periods respected? Was the claim brought within the foreseen time limitation period?).

5 Cf. *MOX Plant Case (Ireland v United Kingdom)* (Provisional Measures, Order of 3 December 2001) ITLOS Reports 2001, 95, para 51:

> *Considering* also that the application of international law rules on interpretation of treaties to identical or similar provisions of different treaties may not yield the same results, having regard to, *inter alia*, differences in the respective contexts, objects and purposes, subsequent practice of parties and *travaux préparatoires* … .

6 Campbell McLachlan, 'Investment Treaties and General International Law' (2008) 57 *ICLQ* 361.

7 Martins Paparinskis, 'Investment Treaty Arbitration and the (New) Law of State Responsibility' (2013) 24 *EJIL* 617.

continuing or composite acts, and the legal effects of provisional application. Moreover, as a special feature of investment law related to the 'end of life of a treaty', the cancellation of so-called 'sunset clauses'[8] is explored from the perspective of the general law of treaties. Owed to the fact that treaty terminations and withdrawals have become more frequent in the field of investment law,[9] the doctrinal discussion underlying many features of investment law – e.g., the nature of investor rights – but also the general law of treaties, i.e., the question of termination of treaties affording 'third-party rights' may soon be enriched by a significant amount of case law. In a final part, the effects of these developments on general international law are discussed.

II. THE GENERAL SCOPE OF APPLICATION OF IIAS

There is no doubt that IIAs are treaties and as such are governed by general international law, in particular the VCLT.[10] However, given that the law of treaties as encapsulated in the VCLT in many aspects merely constitutes the minimum frame on which the law of treaties rests, answers to open issues in the law of treaties are often found elsewhere. Investment tribunals – through their application and interpretation of treaty law – therefore have a special role to play in the clarification of such open issues as well as in the further development of the field.[11] Such general assessment also proves valid on the specific issue of the 'scope of application' of IIAs; hence, even though the scope of application of IIAs is naturally treaty-specific and therefore often prevails as *lex specialis*, it also is subject to – and thereby informs – the law of treaties as *lex generalis*.

All four facets to a treaty's scope of application (the personal scope of application (*ratione personae*), material scope (*ratione materiae*), territorial scope

---

[8] Sunset clauses are provisions which provide for parts of or the entire treaty content to outlive the date of denunciation. See below in more detail at Section III.C.

[9] See text at n 135.

[10] José E. Alvarez, *The Public International Law Regime Governing International Investment* (Hague Academy of International Law 2011); see also the ICSID Review's special volume dedicated to the intersection between investment arbitration and public international law (2016) 31 *ICSID Review* 255–503.

[11] A similar point has been made also with regard to substantive protection standards and general international law, see McLachlan (n 6), as well as in the context of treaty interpretation (see recently, e.g., Tarcisio Gazzini, *Interpretation of International Investment Treaties* (Hart 2016)). It has also been discussed at length regarding the validity and termination of treaties. See, e.g., Tania Voon and Andrew D. Mitchell, 'Denunciation, Termination and Survival: The Interplay of Treaty Law and International Investment Law' (2016) 31 *ICSID Review* 413.

(*ratione loci*) and temporal scope (*ratione temporis*)) are of key importance when it comes to the application of a relevant IIA – i.e., who is entitled to the privileges and protection of the treaty – and, as a consequence, the jurisdiction of international courts or tribunals. It should come as no surprise that fields guided heavily by practice such as investment law are particularly prone to jurisdictional objections arguing that the specific facts are beyond the scope of the treaty.[12] Terms laying out the scope of application of investments treaties are thus central elements of the investment framework, and feature among the most carefully drafted provisions of bilateral and multilateral investment agreements since they reflect important policy choices of the negotiating partners.[13]

Although partly varying significantly on the precise terms used, the structure of investment treaties is generally very similar.[14] Specific sections at the beginning of the treaty are dedicated to establishing the scope and defining the relevant terms in this regard, i.e., which individuals and legal entities qualify as an 'investor' (*ratione personae*),[15] what qualifies as an 'investment' (*ratione materiae*).[16] While the latter at times also includes definitions on where the investment must be located ('area', 'territory') or whether investments are covered which were made prior to the entry into force of the respective agreement,[17] the territorial and temporal coverage of investment protection

---

[12] Jeswald W Salacuse, *The Law of Investment Treaties* (2nd edn, OUP 2015) 174.

[13] W. Michael Reisman and Mahnoush H. Arsanjani, 'Reflections on the Cogency of Fragmentation: Statutes of Limitation and "Continuing Violations" in Investment and Human Rights Law' in Holger P. Hestermeyer et al (eds), *Coexistence, Cooperation and Solidarity: Liber Amicorum Rüdiger Wolfrum* (Martinus Nijhoff 2011) 265, 266–277; UNCTAD, 'Series on Issues in International Investment Agreements II: Scope and Definition' (1 March 2011) 7 https://investmentpolicy.unctad.org/publications/series/2/international-investment-agreements accessed 10 January 2021.

[14] See in this regard, e.g., Andrew Newcombe and Lluis Paradell, *Law and Practice of Investment Treaties – Standards of Treatment* (Kluwer 2009) 65; Salacuse (n 12) 141.

[15] This typically includes natural persons and entities incorporated or constituted under the laws for the respective contracting parties. Salacuse (n 12) 206–212.

[16] Investment agreements typically include a broad notion of investment (Salacuse (n 12) 176). For example, 'any kind of asset' (Canada-Costa Rica BIT (adopted 18 March 1998, entered into force 29 September 1999)), 'every kind of asset' (Energy Charter Treaty (ECT) (adopted 17 December 1994, entered into force 16 April 1998)) 2080 UNTS 95, art 1(6); or 'every kind of investment in the territory' (Argentina-United States BIT (adopted 14 November 1991, entered into force 20 October 1994)).

[17] UNCTAD Series on Issues in International Investment Agreements II (n 13) 6; See, e.g., Canada-Peru BIT (adopted 14 November 2006, entered into force 20 April 2007) art 1; Ghana-Guinea BIT (adopted 18 May 2001, not yet in force) art 1.

are typically addressed in the final clauses or in specific provisions.[18] Whereas the number and identity of states who are party to the agreement *inter alia* naturally determine the territorial scope, the territorial reach is also dependent on the specific territorial delimitations of the respective parties, and at times defined in specific territorial clauses.[19] As regards the temporal scope, the date of entry into force for each party, the duration of the treaty and potential sunset clauses are relevant, alongside the abovementioned issue whether protection is extended to investments which were made prior to the treaty's entry into force.[20] Additionally, the provisional application of specific treaty provisions may be foreseen prior to treaty's entry into force.[21]

The following will focus on the temporal scope of application since it addresses some of the most crucial and also ambiguous aspects of the law of treaties.[22] The case analysis thereupon demonstrates whether and how investment tribunals deal with the general law of treaties when examining questions arising in this regard.

---

18 For an overview, see also UNCTAD Series on Issues in International Investment Agreements II (n 13) 5–6.

19 See, e.g., United Republic of Tanzania-United Kingdom BIT (adopted 7 January 1994, entered into force 2 August 1996) arts 1 and 12.

20 See, e.g., Philippines-Switzerland BIT (adopted 31 March 1997, entered into force 23 April 1999): art II (Scope of Application):

> The present Agreement shall apply to investments in the territory of one Contracting Party made in accordance with its laws and regulations by investors of the other Contracting Party, whether prior to or after the entry into force of the Agreement.

21 VCLT (n 3) art 25.

22 A large portion of case law dealing with the scope of application of IIAs focuses on the material ('investment') and personal ('investor') scope of application of an IIA. Though naturally treaty-specific, the interpretation of these provisions potentially raises interesting points from the perspective of international law as well, particularly given their relevance with regard to jurisdictional questions. Filippo Fontanelli, *Jurisdiction and Admissibility in Investment Arbitration: The Practice and the Theory* (Brill 2018) lists several examples in this regard, e.g., the repeated use and concretisation of the *Oil Platforms prima facie* test by investment tribunals in determining whether a claim falls within their jurisdictional scope *ratione materiae* (16ff), or questions related to the applicable test on the determination of nationality of corporations (81ff). Also the territorial scope of application of IIAs has been subject of extensive analysis in recent years, in particular in connection with situations involving some element of state succession. For more details see particularly Christian J. Tams, 'State Succession to Investment Treaties: Mapping the Issues' (2016) 31 *ICSID Review* 314; Patrick Dumberry, *A Guide to State Succession in International Investment Law* (Edward Elgar 2018).

III. THE TEMPORAL SCOPE OF APPLICATION OF IIAS

While the VCLT's framework contains default rules for treaties which do not specify their temporal scope of application,[23] bilateral and multilateral investment treaties almost universally resort to treaty-specific rules on their entry into force, validity and termination. In fact, in a comprehensive study conducted in 2013 which analysed more than 2000 IIAs, only two treaties were identified which did not contain such specific clauses.[24] Nevertheless, owing to unclear or ambiguous provisions, a number of tribunals have made statements on the general law of treaties. The following focuses on these cases, in an attempt to identify general patterns and provide answers to open aspects of treaty law.

A. Article 28 VCLT and the Presumption of Non-Retroactivity

The default rule of Article 28 VCLT prescribes the non-retroactivity of treaties unless a different intention of the parties is revealed.[25] Such different intentions

---

[23] The temporal scope of application of treaties is determined by a mix of VCLT provisions. The basis is enshrined in VCLT (n 3) art 28 ('Non-retroactivity of treaties'), however arts 24 (entry into force), 25 (provisional application), and the section on termination and suspension of treaties (arts 54–64) are also of relevance in this regard, as is Section 5, on the consequences of the invalidity, termination or suspension (arts 69–72). See Heike Krieger, 'Article 25 – Provisional Application' in Oliver Dörr and Kirsten Schmalenbach (eds), *Vienna Convention on the Law of Treaties – A Commentary* (Springer 2018) 441, 442.

[24] Joachim Pohl, 'Temporal Validity of International Investment Agreements – A Large Sample Survey of Treaty Provisions' (2013/2014) *OECD Working Papers on International Investment* 7 www.oecd.org/investment/investment-policy/WP-2013_4.pdf accessed 10 January 2021.

[25] VCLT (n 3) art 28 reads:

> Unless a different intention appears from the treaty or is otherwise established, its provisions do not bind a party in relation to any act or fact which took place or any situation which ceased to exist before the date of the entry into force of the treaty with respect to that party.

Article 28 VCLT has been recognised to constitute customary international law in *Questions Relating to the Oligation to Prosecute or Extradite (Belgium v Senegal)* [2012] *ICJ Reports* 422, 457, para 100. VCLT (n 3) art 28 foresees exceptions to the default rule of non-retroactivity, namely in three different cases: First, 'unless a different intention appears from the treaty' covers situations in which the treaty itself explicitly foresees a retroactive application. Second, it also extends to cases where such retroactivity is the result of treaty interpretation, though examples in this regard are scarce. And third, 'unless a different intention … is otherwise established' encompasses those scenarios where the retroactivity is the result of the nature of the treaty itself. In

can directly derive from the treaty itself, as is often argued in the case of IIAs. The specific feature of some IIAs to extend protection to both investments which already exist at the time the IIA entered into force as well as to investments made thereafter[26] therefore generally seems to stand for a wide (temporal) scope of application, and claimants have argued that such provisions constitute an exception from Article 28 VCLT's residual rule. At the same time, however, the temporal provisions of IIAs often limit the IIA's application to disputes ('single exclusion clause'),[27] or even acts or facts ('double exclusion clause'),[28] which have arisen or occurred after the IIA's entry into the force. Claims originating in disputes which have arisen prior to the entry into force are therefore often explicitly excluded from the protection of IIAs. While this provides for more legal certainty,[29] from the viewpoint of general international law, the explicit exclusion might also have appeared necessary,

---

principle, this entails a combination between looking at the object and purpose of the treaty as well as resorting to the supplementary means of treaty interpretation if not in contradiction to the clearly expressed intentions of the parties as discernible through art 31 VCLT's means of treaty interpretation. As Haak argues, there is thus no significant difference stemming from art 28's escape clause than when applying VCLT arts 31, 32 to determine the parties' intentions. Volker Haak, '"Unless the Treaty Otherwise Provides" and Similar Clauses in the International Law Commission's 1966 Draft Articles on the Law of Treaties' (1967) 27 *ZaöRV* 540, 542–545; cf. Frederic Dopagne, 'Article 28 VCLT' in Olivier Corten and Pierre Klein (eds), *The Vienna Conventions on the Law of Treaties: A Commentary* (OUP 2011) 718, 726.

[26] See, e.g., Ecuador-United States BIT (adopted 27 August 1993, entered into force 11 May 1997) art XII(1); Canada-Peru BIT (n 17) art 1; Ghana-Guinea BIT (n 17) art 1; Argentina-Spain BIT (adopted 3 October 1991, entered into force 28 September 1992) art II(2); See generally also Salacuse (n 12) 192–193.

[27] For example, Croatia-United Kingdom BIT (adopted 11 March 1997, entered into force 16 April 1998) art 1: 'the term investment includes all investments whether made before or after the date of entry into force of this Agreement, but the provisions of this Agreement shall not apply to a dispute concerning an investment which arose before its entry into force'; see also Argentina-Spain BIT (n 26); Chile-Peru BIT (adopted 2 February 2000, entered into force 11 August 2001) art 2.

[28] For an example of a double exclusion clause (the broadest possible restriction), see CAFTA, art 10.1(3): 'For greater certainty, this Chapter does not bind any Party in relation to any act or fact that took place or any situation that ceased to exist before the date of entry into force of this Agreement.' (Central America-Dominican Republic Free Trade Agreement (adopted 5 August 2004)). Such clauses resemble the 'Belgian clause' enshrined in many Optional Clause declarations to the PCIJ/ICJ.

[29] On the connection between the rule of law and the principle of non-retroactivity see also Markus Kotzur, 'The Temporal Dimension: Non-Retroactivity and Its Discontents' in Christian J. Tams et al (eds), *Research Handbook on the Law of Treaties* (Edward Elgar 2014) 153, 157f.

as for a long time[30] the general rule on openly formulated dispute settlement clauses – going back to *Mavrommatis Palestine Concessions* – seemed to imply the opposite.[31]

Where such specific clauses are not included in an IIA, this raises interesting points particularly with regard to two aspects related to Article 28 VCLT.[32] These are dealt with in turn: (1) How have investment tribunals treated preexisting disputes, i.e., disputes existing prior to the entry into force of the specific IIA? (2) Which approach can be discerned with regard to continuing or composite acts which have begun before the relevant IIA entered into force and were completed after? As a preliminary point, one should point out that clarity on the temporal scope suffers from the ambiguity attached to the fixing of critical dates as regards preexisting disputes, continuous acts and composite acts. For one, the point in time a 'dispute' crystallises is often difficult to determine and subject to a certain flexibility.[33] Additionally, in certain circumstances,

---

[30] Still in support thereof, e.g., *Anglo-Iranian Oil Co Case (United Kingdom v Iran)* (Preliminary Objections) [1952] *ICJ Reports* 93, 103–106, finding that the jurisdictional clause adopted by Iran had explicitly limited it to the application of treaties accepted after the ratification of the declaration; Rosalyn Higgins, 'Time and the Law: International Perspectives on an Old Problem' (1997) 46 *ICLQ* 501, 502; see also *Case Concerning Application of the Convention on the Prevention and Punishment of the Crime of Genocide* (*Bosnia and Herzegovina v Yugoslavia*) (Preliminary Objections) [1996] *ICJ Reports* 595, 617, para 34.

[31] As was noted by the PCIJ in *Mavrommatis Palestine Concessions*:

> [t]he Court is of opinion that, in cases of doubt, jurisdiction based on an international agreement embraces all disputes referred to it after its establishment. In the present case, this interpretation appears to be indicated by the terms of Article 26 itself where it is laid down that 'any dispute whatsoever … which may arise' shall be submitted to the Court. The reservation made in many arbitration treaties regarding disputes arising out of events previous to the conclusion of the treaty seems to prove the necessity for an explicit limitation of jurisdiction and, consequently, the correctness of the rule of interpretation enunciated above.

Mavrommatis Palestine Concessions (Greece v United Kingdom) (Judgment) (1924) PCIJ Series A No 2, 35.

[32] Another issue which arises is, e.g., how tribunals deal with facts or situations which occur prior to the entry into force of the treaty. As noted by the Tribunal in *Mondev v United States* with regard to facts stemming from prior to the entry into force of NAFTA, 'events or conduct prior to the entry into force of an obligation of the respondent State may be relevant in determining whether the State has subsequently committed a breach of obligation', noting that the earlier approach in *Feldman* (para 62) was too categorical in finding that previous acts and omissions could play no role in the determination of a breach. *Mondev International Ltd v United States of America*, ICSID Case No ARB(AF)/99/2, Award (11 October 2002) paras 69–70.

[33] On the flexibility of the notion of dispute, see also Andrea Gattini, 'Jurisdiction *ratione temporis* in International Investment Arbitration' (2017) 16 *LPICT* 139, noting that this question is particularly complicated by the vagueness pertaining to the

the classification of an act as completed (and thus already the subject of a 'dispute') or continuous is also challenging.[34] As the ILC notes in this regard, this is in part dependent on the primary obligation in question, and in part on the circumstances of the specific case.[35] As will be seen, the flexibility of these aspects result in a wide range of decisions on the matter, sometimes resulting in conflicting outcomes.

1. Prior disputes

Even though the tribunals always possess a certain margin of discretion in determining what they consider the '"real source" of the disputes before them'[36] and there are thus also a number of cases on this matter related to 'single' or 'double exclusion clauses',[37] the following specifically focuses on

---

assessment of when a 'dispute' exists (at 143–144). See also the discussion on this in *Emilio Agustín Maffezini v Kingdom of Spain*, ICSID Case No ARB/97/7, Decision on Objections to Jurisdiction (25 January 2000) paras 90–98. More recently, the ICJ dismissed the *Marshall Islands* cases for the lack of a 'dispute' between the parties. Based on previous case law, it summed up the requirement of 'dispute' to mean: 'disagreement on a point of law or fact, a conflict of legal views or of interests' between parties. In order for a dispute to exist, '[i]t must be shown that the claim of one party is positively opposed by the other' … As reflected in previous decisions of the Court in which the existence of a dispute was under consideration, a dispute exists when it is demonstrated, … that the respondent was aware, or could not have been unaware, that its views were 'positively opposed' by the applicant … In principle, the date for determining the existence of a dispute is the date on which the application is submitted to the Court. See *Obligations concerning Negotiations relating to Cessation of the Nuclear Arms Race and to Nuclear Disarmament (Marshall Islands v United Kingdom)* [2016] *ICJ Reports* 833, paras 37–42 [references omitted]. Note, however, that particularly the element of previous awareness has been criticised.

34 As an example, see also the diverging approaches on how tribunals dealt with earlier domestic decisions in *Empresas Lucchetti SA and Lucchetti Preu SA v Republic of Peru*, ICSID Case No ARB/03/4, Award (7 February 2005) paras 48–59, finding a 'prexisting dispute' and therefore rejecting jurisdiction, and *Jan de Nul NV and Dredging International NV v Arab Republic of Egypt*, ICSID Case No ARB/04/13, Decision on Jurisdiction (16 June 2006) paras 117–131, finding that a new dispute had crystallised, and distinguishing the *Lucchetti* award at length. See also *MCI Power Group LC and the New Turbine, Inc v Republic of Ecuador*, ICSID Case No ARB/03/6, Decision on Annulment (19 October 2009) as discussed below fn 57.

35 ILC, 'Draft Articles on Responsibility of States for International Wrongful Acts, with commentaries' (2001) II(2) *ILC Yearbook* 60, para 4. See also *Impreglio SpA v Islamic Republic of Pakistan*, ICSID Case No ARB/03/3, Decision on Jurisdiction (22 April 2005) paras 312–313, concluding that the act complained of was not of a 'continuing character' but merely possessed 'continuing consequences/effects'.

36 Gattini (n 33) 141.

37 As Jorun Baumgartner, *Treaty Shopping in International Investment Law* (OUP 2016) points out, the matter is also complicated by the fact that some investment tri-

case law related to treaties with broadly formulated dispute settlement clauses or without any specific exclusion clause, both forcing tribunals to directly assess the principle of non-retroactivity as it is enshrined in general international law. That is, absent any specific provision on the issue of preexisting disputes, it remains a source of contention under general international law whether international courts and tribunals enjoy jurisdiction *ratione temporis* over preexisting disputes.[38] The issue arises in circumstances where tribunals are granted jurisdiction to hear a claim on 'existing obligations', without any further specification, but the consent to arbitration has not entered into force yet at the time of the act.[39] The procedural and substantive provisions of an IIA may thus relate to different time periods.[40] While the substantive provisions of IIAs most often are not applicable retroactively – with Article 28 VCLT's presumption applying straightforward in this context[41] – 'existing obligations' covered by the dispute settlement clause could still be found, e.g., under general international law,[42] domestic law[43] or in an earlier treaty.[44, 45]

---

bunals do not clearly distinguish between 'the actors or facts giving rise to the dispute, the dispute itself and the breach of the investment obligation and ensuing injury' (ibid., 176) and some base their reasoning on the principle of non-retroactivity even though dealing with a single exclusion clause (ibid., 177) (as e.g., *Lao Holdings NV v Lao People's Democratic Republic*, ICSID Case No ARB(AF)/12/6, Decision on Jurisdiction (21 February 2014) paras 76, 144).

[38] Gattini (n 33) 142.

[39] Nick Gallus, 'Article 28 of the Vienna Convention on the Law of Treaties and Investment Treaty Decisions' (2016) 31 *ICSID Review* 290, 298–299.

[40] See also Ursula Kriebaum, 'The PCIJ and the Protection of Foreign Investments' in Christian J. Tams and Malgosia Fitzmaurice (eds), *Legacies of the Permanent Court of International Justice* (Martinus Nijhoff 2013) 145, 149.

[41] Sadie Blanchard, 'State Consent, Temporal Jurisdiction, and the Importance of Continuing Circumstances Analysis in International Investment Arbitration' (2011) 10 *Washington Univ Glob Stud LR* 419, 429.

[42] *Paushok v Government of Mongolia*, UNCITRAL, Award on Jursdiction and Liability (28 April 2011) para 468.

[43] *Tradex Hellas v Albania*, ICSID Case No ARB/94/2, Award (29 April 1999) para 194.

[44] *Nordzucker AG v Republic of Poland*, UNCITRAL, Partial Award (10 December 2008) paras 107–109; *Jan de Nul NV and Dredging International NV v Arab Republic of Egypt*, ICSID Case No ARB/04/13, Award (6 November 2008) paras 128–130.

[45] NAFTA serves as an example where jurisdiction was limited to specific violations of the treaty provisions once they entered into force (North American Free Trade Agreement (United States–Canada–Mexico) (adopted 17 December 1992, entered into force 1 January 1994)).

As noted in the ILC's commentary to Article 28 VCLT, jurisdictional clauses providing for the submission to an international tribunal of 'disputes' may also encompass preexisting disputes as:

> by using the word 'disputes' without any qualification, the parties are to be understood as accepting jurisdiction with respect to all disputes *existing* after the entry into force of the agreement. On the other hand, when a jurisdictional clause is attached to the substantive clauses of a treaty as a means of securing their due application, the non-retroactivity principle may operate to limit *ratione temporis* the application of the jurisdictional clause.[46]

The precise formulation of a treaty's jurisdictional or dispute settlement clause is thus essential in determining whether preexisting disputes fall within an international tribunal's jurisdiction or not. In the context of investment law, the relevant instrument in this regard is the respective BIT or multilateral investment agreement,[47] particularly since Schreuer et al.[48] and Waibel[49] both arrive at the conclusion that Article 25 of the ICSID Convention ('any legal dispute') falls in line with the assumption that ICSID tribunals in principle enjoy jurisdiction also over preexisting disputes.

As a consequence, awards dealing with this issue therefore focus on the formulation of the jurisdictional clause in the respective IIA, generally demonstrating a quite restrictive approach to the temporal reach of such clauses. For example, in *Société Générale v The Dominican Republic*, the tribunal held with regard to a clause granting jurisdiction over 'any dispute relating to investment' that 'if the intention had been to allow for retroactivity one would expect that it would require a clear and unequivocal expression of intention to that effect, which is not found in the Treaty or elsewhere.'[50]

---

[46] ILC Articles on State Responsibility (n 35) 212 (Article 24).

[47] Gattini (n 33) 142.

[48] Christoph Schreuer et al, *The ICSID Convention – A Commentary* (2nd edn, CUP 2009) 95.

[49] Michael Waibel, 'Investment Arbitration: Jurisdiction and Admissibility' in Marc Bungenberg et al (eds), *International Investment Law – A Handbook* (Hart 2015) 1212, 1258.

[50] *Société Générale In Respect of DR Energy Holdings Limited and Empresa Distribuidora de Electricidad del Este, SA v Dominican Republic*, UNCITRAL, LCIA Case No UN 7927, Award on Preliminary Objections to Jurisdiction (19 September 2008) para 81. For further cases along this line see, *inter alia*, *Salini Costruttori SpA and Italstrade SpA v Hashemite Kingdom of Jordan*, ICSID Case No ARB/02/13, Decision on Jurisdiction (9 November 2004) para 170, concluding negatively on the retroactive application as regards the phrase 'any dispute which may arise'; *Impreglio v Pakistan* (n 35) para 300, concluding negatively on the retroactive application as regards the phrase 'disputes arising between the Parties': 'Such language – and the absence of specific provision for retroactivity – infers that disputes that may have arisen

Tribunals have been similarly cautious in determining the parties' intent in cases where no specific clause specified the scope in relation to dispute settlement ('unrestrictive clause'). Given the absence of any such clause, tribunals had to further investigate into the intention of the parties in application of the general law of treaties. Particularly noteworthy for its detailed analysis in this regard is *Ping An v Belgium*, discussing the different approaches followed by previous investment tribunals (partly applying the presumption of non-retroactivity, partly rejecting it).[51] In the course of its analysis, the tribunal also expressed doubt as to whether the *Mavrommatis* assumption of covering preexisting disputes still stood as the general principle in this regard, and if it did, that it found 'almost no support in investor-State arbitration'.[52] In the end, the tribunal which was also assessing the relationship between successive BITs explicitly did not 'employ any presumption against retroactivity' to the interpretation of the jurisdictional clause, reasoning that 'in its view the application of a new dispute settlement mechanism to acts which may have been unlawful when they were committed is not in itself the retroactive application of law'.[53] Rather it conducted a detailed exercise of treaty interpretation regarding the specific (later) BIT in question (Belgium-Luxemburg Economic Union-China BIT (2009)), and, based thereupon, concluded that it could not have been the intention of the parties in the specific circumstances at hand to extend protection to preexisting disputes.[54] It is notable in this regard that the tribunal – in line with Article 28 VCLT's formulation – placed significant emphasis on

before the entry into force of the BIT are not covered'; *ABCI Investments NV v Republic of Tunisia*, ICSID Case No ARB/04/12, Decision on Jurisdiction (18 February 2011) paras 169–171, concluding negatively on the retroactive application as regards the phrase 'any legal dispute arising' in reliance on art 28 VCLT. Cf. Gattini (n 33) 143.

[51] *Ping An Life Insurance Company of China Limited, Ping An Insurance (Group) Company of China Limited v Government of Belgium*, ICSID Case No ARB/12/29, Award (30 April 2015) paras 189–191, referencing *Impreglio v Pakistan*, *ATA Construction v Jordan*, *MCI Power v Ecuador*, and *Paushok v Mongolia* applying the presumption; and *Tradex v Albania* rejecting such presumption.

[52] *Ping An Insurance v Belgium* (n 51) para 184. The approach by the PCIJ in *Mavrommatis Palestine Concessions* (n 31) is sometimes also distinguished as being based on the nature and purpose of the specific treaty applicable in that case which by its very nature was meant to be retroactive. Gallus, 'Article 28 of the Vienna Convention' (n 39) 294. See also *Chevron Corporation and Texaco Pretroleum Company v Republic of Ecuador*, UNCITRAL, PCA Case No 34877, Interim Award (1 December 2008) para 246 (Respondent's argument).

[53] *Ping An Insurance v Belgium* (n 51) para 218.

[54] Ibid., paras 192, 218–231.

the *intention* of the parties by also taking the background of the earlier BIT in question rather than simply conducting a textual reading of the relevant BIT.[55]

Along these lines, also the Tribunal in *Lao Holdings NV v Lao People's Democratic Republic* emphasised that the silence does not:

> 'clearly' [manifest] a 'different intention' apparent on the fact of the Treaty. The general presumption favours non-retroactivity and in this Treaty the presumption is not displaced by any different intention 'apparent' on its face. The Tribunal does not view the Treaty as intending to provide legal weapons to investors for the purpose of re-engaging in a pre-existing legal dispute with the Lao Government.[56]

And the Tribunal in *MCI Power Group v Ecuador* noted that:

> The non-retroactivity of the BIT excludes its application to disputes arising prior to its entry into force. Any dispute arising prior to that date will not be capable of being submitted to the dispute resolution system established by the BIT. The silence of the text of the BIT with respect to its scope in relation to disputes prior to its entry into force does not alter the effects of the principle of the non-retroactivity of treaties.[57]

---

[55] Similarly also *Hrvatska Elektroprivreda dd v Republic of Slovenia*, ICSID Case No ARB/05/24, Decision on the Treaty Interpretation Issue (12 June 2009): 'Finally as regards Article 28, it should be underscored that it, unlike Article 31, directs one not just to the text of the 2001 Agreement itself, but also permits the parties' intent of retroactivity to be "otherwise established."' See, however, Jan Paulsson's extensive dissenting opinion to this case, criticising the outcome as too far-reaching, and noting that '[r]etroactivity is not necessary to the object and purpose of the Treaty' (ibid., para 72) and:

> 74. At their para. 201 the majority reason that the expression 'otherwise established' in Article 28 VCLT allow them to look at the 'intention' that flows from 'the very nature' of the Treaty. This seems to be an almost mystical suggestion that any tribunal may do what it pleases by referring to 'the very nature' of a Treaty instead of to its terms. It does not strike me as acceptable legal scholarship.

[56] *Lao Holdings v Lao People's Democratic Republic* (n 37) paras 115–117.

[57] *MCI Power Group LC and the New Turbine, Inc v Republic of Ecuador*, ICSID Case No ARB/03/6, Award (31 July 2007) para 61. Note, however, that the *MCI Power Group* Annulment Committee criticised this interpretation of art 28 VCLT and pointed out that the 'relevant point in time in Article 28 is not when a dispute arose but the time when an act or fact took place or a situation ceased to exist'. The Committee further noted that since Ecuador's failure to pay its alleged debt continued after the entry into force of the BIT, the situation 'could be considered not to have ceased to exist'. *MCI Power Group v Ecuador*, Decision on Annulment (n 34) paras 45–46 (no annulment since arguments on both side were seen to be possible. Despite this criticism, other tribunals have arrived at a similar conclusion, see *ATA Construction Industrial and Trading Company v Hashemite Kingdom of Jordan*, ICSID Case No ARB/08/2, Award (18 May 2010) para 98; similarly also *Mondev v United States* (n 32) paras 68–70.

In *Tecmed*, the tribunal emphasised that the burden of proof regarding the retroactive application of the treaty extending protection to 'investments existing as of the date of its entry into force' to preexisting disputes was on the party making the claim, despite noting that the logical conclusion would be that the 'situations surrounding investments existing at the time do not escape its provisions'.[58]

The approach is not entirely consistent, though. Thus, in *Chevron v Ecuador*, the tribunal affirmed the assumption laid out by the PCIJ in *Mavrommatis Palestine Concessions*, and held that the absence of the mentioning of 'disputes' in the relevant BIT's temporal restrictions resulted in a wide temporal scope, also encompassing preexisting disputes as long as they were tied to 'investments existing at the time of entry into force'.[59] In *Walter Bau v Thailand*, however, relating to a similarly broadly formulated jurisdictional clause, the opposite conclusion was reached by the tribunal.[60]

There are instances where tribunals have distinguished more explicitly between provisions creating substantive and procedural obligations, with both having separate decisive dates regarding their applicability. With regard to the latter, some tribunals have determined the relevant date for the assessment of the application of the dispute resolution provision as the date of filing of the claim.[61] This separate treatment was, however, not only case-specific,[62] but also criticised by the tribunal in *Chevron v Ecuador*, noting that '[t]he principle of non-retroactivity is not different for provisions in treaties dealing with the resolution of disputes, and in particular jurisdictional clauses contained therein'.[63]

---

[58] *Técnicas Medioambientales TECMED SA v United Mexican States*, ICSID Case No ARB(AF)/00/2, Award (29 May 2003) paras 63–65.

[59] *Chevron Corporation and Texaco v Ecuador* (n 52) paras 265, 267, the Tribunal, however, found that the dispute in any event had only arisen after the entry into force of the BIT (ibid., para 269).

[60] *Walter Bau AG (in Liquidation) v Kingdom of Thailand*, UNCITRAL, Award (1 July 2009) para 9.93.

[61] For example, *Nordzucker v Poland* (n 44) paras 107–109; *Jan de Nul v Egypt*, Award (n 44) paras 128–130.

[62] For example, in *Nordzucker v Poland* (n 44) the provision on FET had already entered into force, whereas the provision on arbitration in regard to a FET claim had not yet done so; in *Jan de Nul v Egypt* (n 44) one reason for accepting jurisdiction over preexisting disputes in this regard might have also been motivated by an issue of superseding BITs where the previous BIT did not include a sunset clause; Gallus (n 39) 307–308.

[63] *Chevron Corporation and Texaco v Ecuador* (n 52) paras 169ff, particularly para 173. The tribunal also noted that there might be a different approach to retroactivity in the human rights context, but that such analogy was not strong enough to depart from

While jurisprudence is thus not entirely consistent, most tribunals dealing with treaties not containing any specific exclusion clause engage with Article 28 VCLT's rule of non-retroactivity in a rather strict manner, i.e., unless the treaty clearly stipulates otherwise, preexisting disputes are generally not covered by an IIA, even if its provisions on covered investments[64] and dispute settlement are vague and open. As one tribunal even noted, the express provision against retroactive operation – as a result of the *Mavrommatis* dictum – should 'be seen as states acting under an abundance of caution'[65] and the previous presumption thus seems to have shifted into a more neutral position in favour of non-retroactivity. At times, the parties' intention is primarily, if not exclusively, sought from the specific formulation of the dispute settlement clause itself. This strictness is interesting, particularly as it relates to a jurisdictional precondition where – according to several tribunals – 'there is no principle of either extensive or restrictive interpretation',[66] and where a 'narrow and purely linguistic exercise'[67] is not called for either. Additionally, given that a number of IIAs explicitly include single or double exclusion clauses, the opposite conclusion might have been reached as well, i.e., that without such clause, a broad interpretation is warranted. Other tribunals have therefore conducted a detailed exercise in treaty interpretation in light of Article 28 VCLT's escape clause ('unless a different intention appears from the treaty or is otherwise established'), careful to remain within the parameters of Article 31 VCLT.

2. Continuing and composite acts

The second aspect relating to the temporal scope of application to be investigated in this context relates to continuing[68] or composite acts[69] which span

---

the 'dominant legal framework for retroactivity' (para 176). The same was also concluded by *Paushok v Mongolia* (n 42) para 468.

64 In this regard, Fontanelli (n 22) 52 rightly notes that the application of a treaty to existing investments rather specifies the application *ratione materiae* of the treaty than constitutes indications regarding the competence *ratione temporis* of tribunals.

65 *Walter Bau v Thailand* (n 60) para 9.70. The counsel for the respondent had argued along similar lines, submitting that *Mavrommatis* had been decided at a time of a 'flowering of international law' (para 9.25).

66 *Mondev v United States* (n 32) para 43; see also Schreuer et al, *ICSID Convention Commentary* (n 48) 252–253 for further cases.

67 *Ping An Insurance v Belgium* (n 51) para 218.

68 See ILC Articles on State Responsibility (n 35): art 14(2) stipulates that the 'breach of an international obligation by an act of a State having continuing character extends over the entire period during which the act continues and remains not in conformity with the international obligation.'

69 Composite acts occur when several acts or omissions take place which, taken together, amount to a breach of an international obligation. See also ILC Articles (ibid.)

between the time before the treaty entered into force and the time after the coming into force. The question arises how to deal with such acts which have begun before the relevant IIA has entered into force. Article 13 ARSIWA – reflecting Judge Huber's famous *dictum* on intertemporal law[70] – states that an act of a state does not constitute a breach of an international obligation unless the state is bound by that obligation at the time the act occurs.[71] It follows that states will only breach an international obligation if the relevant act/omission in breach thereof continues past the date of entry into force of that obligation.[72] The issue becomes particularly relevant in those cases where the temporal provision of the relevant IIA limits the application to disputes or and/or acts or fact arising or occurring after the IIA's entry into force.

---

art 15. While there are different categories of composite acts, the field of investment law is particularly concerned with situations where several acts by the state against the same individual amount to a breach of an international obligation. Nick Gallus, 'Recent BIT Decisions and Composite Acts Straddling the Date a Treaty Comes Into Force' (2007) 56 *ICLQ* 491, 492–494, notes that there primarily three different types: first, where the separate act and composite act breach the same obligation (type 'consistent patterns'); second, where the composite act amounts to a different breach of international law than the separate act (which also breach an international law obligation) (type 'aggravation', e.g., murder/genocide); third, where the state acts against different individuals (separate acts) without breaching a specific obligation, but the sum of acts amount to a breach (e.g., discrimination against a national prohibited by a trade agreement, type 'systemic'). With regard to this third type, Gallus notes that there may be some doubt as to whether it amounts to a composite act for the purpose of international law, but finds that the classification is irrelevant as longs as the effects are the same. The difficulty in this context arises *inter alia* also by the fact that such a type of composite act is not explicitly covered by art 15 ARSIWA and the commentary thereto: see ILC Articles on State Responsibility (n 35) 62, para 2. Tribunals have, however, not had difficulties in affirming that such a scenario indeed constitutes a composite act in the sense of art 15 ARSIWA. See, e.g., *Azurix Corp v Argentine Republic*, ICSID Case No ARB/01/12, Award (14 July 2006) para 377; *PSEG Global Inc, the North American Coal Corporation, and Konya Ilgin Elektrik Üretim ve Ticaret Limited Sirketi v Republic of Turkey*, ICSID Case No ARB/02/5, Award (19 January 2007) para 253; *Waste Management, Inc v United Mexican States*, ICSID Case No ARB(AF)/00/3, Final Award (30 April 2004) para 137 'various Mexican agencies conspired together to frustrate the concession, and that the sum of this conduct was greater than its various component parts in terms of causing a violation of Article 1105', dismissed by the Tribunal since no sufficient evidence was presented, ibid., paras 138–139.

[70] '[A] juridical fact must be appreciated in the light of the law contemporary with it, and not of the law in force at the time when a dispute in regard to it arises or falls to be settled.' *Island of Palmas (Netherlands v USA)*, PCA Case No 1925-01, Award (4 April 1928) II RIAA 829, 845.

[71] ILC Articles on State Responsibility (n 35) art 13.

[72] Gallus (n 69) 499.

This criterion seems relatively straightforward with regard to continuing acts, i.e., if the relevant conduct complained of was not completed or did not cease prior to the entry into force, the breach will fall within the temporal scope of the treaty. As tribunals have emphasised, this is also in line with Article 28 VCLT, as well as Article 14(2) ARSIWA,[73] and technically does not constitute a case of retroactivity. In principle, the conduct taking place prior to the treaty's entry into force can be considered as evidence of the factual background informing on the acts/facts post-dating the entry into force.[74] However, as mentioned above, there is some prevailing uncertainty in connection with the determination whether an act may be considered as completed (and thus already the subject of a 'dispute') or continuous.[75] The most frequently applied test on this issue is taken from the *Phosphates in Morocco* case decided by the PCIJ where the Court distinguished between 'the real causes of the dispute' and the 'subsequent factors which either presume the existence or are merely the confirmation or development of earlier situations of facts'.[76]

With regard to *composite acts*, the difficulty in this context arises by virtue of the fact that the separate elements of a composite act on their own may not amount to a breach of international law, and the situation may therefore arise that the acts/omission following the entry into force of a treaty on their own do not violate international law. The ILC Commentary notes with regard to composite acts that if:

> the relevant obligation did not exist at the beginning of the course of conduct but came into being thereafter, the 'first' of the actions or omissions of the series for the purposes of State responsibility will be the first occurring after the obligation came

---

73 ILC, 'Documents of the second part of the seventeenth session and of the eighteenth session' (1966) II *ILC Yearbook* 212 (draft art 24); *Railroad Development Corporation v Republic of Guatemala*, ICSID Case No ARB/07/23, Second Decision on Objections to Jurisdiction (18 May 2010) paras 123–124; *TECMED v Mexico* (n 58) paras 63; *Marvin Roy Feldman Karpa v United Mexican States*, ICSID Case No ARB(AF)/99/1, Interim Decision on Preliminary Jurisdictional Issues of (6 December 2000) para 62; see, however, *Impreglio v Pakistan* (n 35) paras 312–313, as noted above fn 35, where the tribunal denied the 'continuing character' of an act.

74 *Mondev v United States* (n 32) para 69; *Pac Rim Cayman LLC v Republic of El Salvador*, ICSID Case No ARB/09/12, Decision on the Respondent's Jurisdictional Objections (1 June 2012) para 2.105; *MCI Power Group v Ecuador*, Award (n 57) para 62; *Chevron Corporation and Texaco v Ecuador* (n 52) paras 282–283.

75 See references above n 34.

76 *Phosphates in Morocco (Italy v France)* (1938) PCIJ Series A/B No 74; cf. *Case Concerning Certain Property (Liechtenstein v Germany)* (Preliminary Objections) [2005] *ICJ Reports* 6, 23ff; for its use by investment tribunals see, *inter alia, Eurogas Inc and Belmont Resources Inc v Slovak Republic*, ICSID Case No ARB/14/14, Award (18 August 2017) paras 453ff; *ATA Construction v Jordan* (n 57) paras 94ff.

> into existence. This need not prevent a court taking into account earlier actions or omissions for other purposes (e.g. in order to establish a factual basis for the later breaches or to provide evidence of intent).[77]

However, the last sentence thereof was only added at the later stage of the drafting, with earlier drafts still maintaining that 'the only actions or omissions to be taken into consideration are those which occurred while the obligation was incumbent on the State.'[78] While this has since then reversed, it still seems uncertain under which circumstances investment tribunals should 'take into account' earlier actions or omissions.[79]

There are several examples of investment tribunals dealing with composite acts, and generally finding it sufficient if the point of completion takes place after the entry into force of the treaty.[80]

---

[77] ILC Articles on State Responsibility (n 35) 63, para 11.

[78] ILC, 'Report of the International Law Commission on the work of its twenty-eighth session' (1976) II(2) *ILC Yearbook* 94; see also, e.g., Joost Pauwelyn, 'The Concept of a "Continuing Violation" of an International Obligation: Selected Problems' (1996) 66 *BYIL* 415, 447.

[79] Over the past decades, human rights jurisprudence has shed some light on how to proceed concerning 'duration obligations' such as regarding issues of detention. For example, the European Court of Human Rights (ECtHR) stated in *Kalashnikov v Russia* that even though the applicant had been in detention for the majority of time prior to the entry into force of the obligation for Russia, this period had to be taken into account in the assessment of the violation of the obligation. *Kalashnikov v Russia*, App No 47095/99 (ECtHR, 15 July 2002) para 111. The ECtHR has also emphasised in cases regarding art 2 (right to life) or 3 (prohibition of torture) ECHR that a separate 'detachable obligation' relating to procedural aspects (such as the obligation to carry out an effective investigation) will exist even if the substantive aspect fell outside its temporal competence. Such a continuing obligation was not open-ended, but there would need to be a 'genuine connection' between the act 'and the entry into force of the Convention in respect of the respondent State for the procedural obligations'. *Šilih v Slovenia*, App No 71463/01 (ECtHR, 9 April 2009) para 163:

> Thus a significant proportion of the procedural steps required by this provision – which include not only an effective investigation into the death of the person concerned but also the institution of appropriate proceedings for the purpose of determining the cause of the death and holding those responsible to account – will have been or ought to have been carried out after the critical date.

However, it has been warned that the distinct nature of human rights treaties/obligations warrant separate treatment in this regard and that, thus, human rights jurisprudence should not be applied to investment arbitration without due consideration of its specific nature. See also Blanchard (n 41) 440.

[80] Barton Legum et al, 'Ratione Temporis or Temporal Scope' in Barton Legum (ed), *The Investment Treaty Arbitration Review* (3rd edn, The Law Reviews 2018) 24, 27; Sanja Djajic and Petar Djundic, 'Creeping Expropriation – In Search for a More Comprehensive Approach' (2012) 2 *Yearbook Int'l Arb* 239, 249.

An early case in this regard is *Tecmed*, where the tribunal held that measures taken prior to the entry into force of the relevant provisions constituted a composite act together with conduct taken after the treaty had entered into force. On this basis, the tribunal found that Mexico's conduct failed to fulfil the investor's legitimate expectations and thereby violated the fair and equitable treatment standard.[81] The same result was reached in *Walter Bau v Thailand*, focusing on the 'critical date' for the exercise of its jurisdiction:

> Distinction … has to be drawn between breaches which crystallised before October 2004 … and ongoing conduct before that date which crystallised into a dispute after that date. Put in the words of the *Société Générale* tribunal, the Treaty will apply only to acts that will be 'the final result of converging action towards the same result'.[82]

As in *Tecmed*, it was therefore possible to take earlier conduct into account to establish a factual basis for the later breaches. Both cases concerned the question of a breach of legitimate expectations in the context of the fair and equitable treatment standard, but similar statements have also been made with regard to claims for denial of justice or creeping expropriations.[83] By their very nature, these are not 'instantaneous acts' but generally are based on a series of measures.[84]

The dependence on the primary obligation can also be seen in the analysis conducted by the tribunal in *Berkowitz v Costa Rica*. While generally accepting that in the case of composite acts these would fall into the tribunal's temporal jurisdiction, the tribunal declined jurisdiction over conduct which did not constitute a sufficiently autonomous cause of action (i.e., allegations on the adequacy of compensation regarding an act of expropriation which had taken place prior to the entry into force of CAFTA).[85] At the same time, it however held that there was conduct sufficiently independent from conduct occurring prior to the entry into force to find a violation of fair and equitable treatment on the basis of the domestic court proceedings taking place on the assessment

---

81 *TECMED v Mexico* (n 58) paras 172f.

82 *Walter Bau v Thailand* (n 60) para 9.91.

83 See *Société Générale v Dominican Republic* (n 50) paras 87ff, particularly para 91. See also *Siemens AG v Argentine Republic*, ICSID Case No ARB/02/8, Award (17 January 2007) para 263; *CME Czech Republic BV v Czech Republic*, Partial Award (13 September 2001) para 609; *Chevron Corporation and Texaco v Ecuador* (n 52) paras 300–301.

84 Djajic and Djundic (n 80).

85 *Aaron C Berkowitz, Brett E Berkowitz and Trevor B Berkowitz v Republic of Costa Rica*, ICSID Case No UNCT/13/2, Interim Award (25 October 2016) paras 163, 217–218, 280.

of compensation.[86] The distinction between one-time individual acts with continuing effects and continuous/composite acts, where the existence of the wrongful act continues after the treaty's entry into force was thus the key factor in the tribunal's analysis.

In addition to the dependence on the applicable primary obligation, further specifics on this issue may also arise from additional features of investment law. A particular example in this regard can be found in *Société Générale v The Dominican Republic* where the alleged conduct occurred prior to the acquisition of nationality (French) which enjoyed protection under the BIT. While the claimant had attempted to dismiss the argument based on the fact that the 'acts and omissions [were] continuing and composite in nature and scope',[87] the tribunal emphasised the overall objective of the relevant BIT [i.e., to stimulate the transfers of capital and technology between the two countries in the interest of their economic development] and found that it lacked jurisdiction over all acts and events that took place before the investment was acquired by the claimant who enjoyed French nationality.[88]

Hence, in comparison to preexisting disputes, investment practice is more generous in exercising jurisdiction over continuous and composite acts which commence prior to the entry into force of a treaty, but continue or are aggregated only after the treaty's entry into force.[89] As also noted by the *Lucchetti* Annulment Committee, a specific provision is necessary in order to preclude previous facts and occurrences from the tribunal's jurisdiction,[90] particularly in relation to continuous or composite acts. However, tribunals have also sought to carefully guard the temporal scope of application in such circumstances by diligently observing the distinction between composite acts and merely 're-hashed' disputes which in essence were identical to each other.[91] They have thus consistently affirmed the 'real cause' test as applied by the ICJ on such matters. Such 'strictness' can generally also be observed with regard to

---

86 Ibid., para 286.

87 *Société Générale v Dominican Republic* (n 50) para 99.

88 Ibid., para 107.

89 See also the distinction made in *Lao Holdings v Lao People's Democratic Republic* (n 37) para 113. Cf. Stanimir A Alexandrov, 'The Baby Boom of Treaty-Based Arbitrations and the Jurisdiction of ICSID Tribunals: Shareholders as Investors and Jurisdiction *Ratione Temporis*' (2005) 4 *LPICT* 19, 53.

90 *Empresas Lucchetti SA and Lucchetti Preu SA v Republic of Peru*, ICSID Case No ARB/03/4, Decision on Annulment (5 September 2007) paras 94–95.

91 See, e.g., 'the Treaty should not be interpreted as granting it jurisdiction concerning disputes which arose after the entry into force but which are based on actions that have occurred before such entry into force, except for the particular situation of continuing or composite acts'. *Paushok v Mongolia* (n 42) paras 467–468; *Lucchetti v Peru*, Award (n 34) paras 48–59; Fontanelli (n 22) 57ff.

attempts to circumvent the laps of limitation periods which commence from the time of the investor's first knowledge of breach or loss.[92]

As a preliminary conclusion one can make the following observations: First, as some authors have rightly indicated,[93] the use of specific formulations in provisions determining the temporal validity of treaties serves to implement many policy choices of treaty parties. In such circumstances, the clearly expressed intent of the parties, and the particularities of the investment law regime, play a decisive role in any ensuing dispute (see, e.g., *Société Générale v The Dominican Republic*). However, a number of investment tribunals are confronted with dispute settlement provisions without any specific guidance on their temporal reach. As a result, investment tribunals must therefore turn to intertemporal rules as enshrined in the law of treaties (and state responsibility). The frequent reference to Article 28 VCLT's underlying principle by investment tribunals is thus not surprising. While some of the references may initially have been motivated by the fact that the 'arbitrators themselves [appeared] anxious for guidance',[94] the vagueness of Article 28 VCLT's residual rule has forced tribunals to take a further step to determine whether the respective IIA reveals a different intent of the parties than the presumption of non-retroactivity. In doing so they are necessarily confronted with the task of treaty interpretation based on Articles 31f VCLT. It is within this exercise that the approach of tribunals necessarily diverges furthest. While some apply a strictly textual interpretation on the temporal reach of particular provisions or formulations used, other tribunals place more emphasis on finding the intent of the parties. As, however, conceptualised by the drafters of the Vienna Convention, tribunals are keen to remain within the framework of interpretation provided by the VCLT. It follows that while the general approach to Article 28 VCLT seems to depart from a high threshold to overcome the presumption of non-retroactivity, particularly when it comes to establishing jurisdiction for preexisting disputes, inconsistent outcomes are not out of the ordinary[95] and have no bearing on the general validity of Article 28 VCLT. Quite the opposite, the reasoning of

---

[92] *Berkowitz v Costa Rica* (n 85) para 208; Legum (n 80) 27 with further references. For the opposite see *United Parcel Service of America Inc v Government of Canada*, UNCITRAL, Award on the Merits (24 May 2007) para 28.

[93] Reisman and Arsanjani (n 13) 266.

[94] Cf. James Crawford, 'Similarity of Issues in Disputes Arising under the Same or Similarly Drafted Investment Treaties' in Emmanuel Gaillard and Yas Banifatemi (eds), *Precedent in International Arbitration* (Juris 2007) 97, 99.

[95] As noted by Christoph Schreuer on a more general level relating to treaty interpretation, 'different tribunals, even if they faithfully apply Articles 31-33 of the VCLT, are likely to reach different results.' See Christoph Schreuer, 'International Investment Law and General International Law – From Clinical Isolation to Systemic Integration?' in Rainer Hofmann and Christian J. Tams (eds), *International Investment Law and*

certain tribunals has provided important content analysis of the functioning and scope of the underlying maxim (e.g., in cases of continuous or composite acts it seems generally accepted that these fall within the temporal scope of a treaty if they continue or are aggregated after the treaty's entry into force), with the aim of achieving more legal security. Particularly invaluable in this regard are tribunals who put effort on the systematisation of available case law, with focus on the identification of distinguishing elements when departing from other tribunals' approaches (see, e.g., *Ping An v Belgium*, *Berkowitz v Costa Rica*), and those who scrutinise the parties' arguments against their own reading and understanding of general international law. Overall, reliance on the principle of non-retroactivity as enshrined in Article 28 VCLT directly ties the approach to the general law of treaties, thereby providing important judicial authority on the functioning of this rule.

B. Obligations Arising Prior to a Treaty's Entry Into Force, with a Particular Focus on Provisional Application (Art 25 VCLT)

As noted in several of the abovementioned awards, a treaty in general is only relevant once it has entered into force[96] and only in exceptional circumstances extends the application of its provisions retroactively. There are two notable deviations from this default rule, i.e., Articles 18 and 25 VCLT. Given that Article 18 VCLT has not been the key focus in many awards,[97] the following

General International Law – From Clinical Isolation to Systemic Integration (Nomos 2011) 71.

[96] VCLT (n 3) art 24.

[97] Ibid., art 18 contains the obligation not to defeat a treaty's object and purpose prior to its entry into force. Despite the little practice available on this provision, two noteworthy decisions can be mentioned here. In *Tecmed*, the tribunal noted by direct reference to art 18 VCLT that the provision:

> does not only refer to the intentional acts of States but also to conduct which falls within its provision, which need not be intentional or manifestly damaging or fraudulent to go against the principle of good faith, but merely negligent or in disregard of the provision of a treaty or its underlying principles, or contradictory or unreasonable in light of such provisions or principles.

TECMED v Mexico (n 58) para 71 [references omitted]. However, given that in the end the tribunal decided that the investigated conduct constituted a composite act (see also above, text at fn 81), it did not decide on whether these measures amounted to a breach of the Spain-Mexico BIT in question. In contrast, the tribunal in *MCI Power Group v Ecuador* applied a more correct understanding of art 18 VCLT, noting that the:

> wording of Article 18 is not aimed at triggering the early application of the clauses of a treaty, that is, it does warrant retroactive application of the treaty. ... [T]he distinction between the extent of the obligation not to defeat the object and purpose of a treaty and the retrospective application of clauses of that treaty to

places special emphasis on Article 25 VCLT. Said provision[98] relates to the provisional application of a treaty prior to its entry into force in certain circumstances.[99] As Article 25 VCLT stipulates, it is up to the specific treaty and/or the parties to regulate when and how such provisional application may occur. This can be stated either directly in the treaty itself (art 25(1)(a) VCLT), or in any other manner (art 25(1)(b) VCLT), such as in a protocol or annex, or even in an entirely separate agreement.[100]

While Article 25 VCLT thus provides the basis for the provisional application of treaties, it remains unspecific as regards a number of crucial issues arising in this context. For example, Article 25 VCLT remains silent on the forms of expression of intention through which the provisional application is effected,[101] and it also does not address the forms of termination of provi-

---

> situations prior to the date of entry into force of the treaty should not be confused. It has not been proven in the present case that the actions and omissions prior to the entry into force of the BIT and attributable to the Respondent had defeated the object and purpose of the Treaty.

MCI Power Group v Ecuador, Award (n 57) paras 98ff, particularly 108, 116.

[98] Treaty provisions:

1. A treaty or a part of a treaty is applied provisionally pending its entry into force if:
   (a) the treaty itself so provides; or
   (b) the negotiating States have in some other manner so agreed.
2. Unless the treaty otherwise provides or the negotiating States have otherwise agreed, the provisional application of a treaty or a part of a treaty with respect to a State shall be terminated if that State notifies the other States between which the treaty is being applied provisionally of its intention not to become a party to the treaty.

[99] The provisional application of treaties at times is resorted to in order to overcome major treaty crises owed to a prolonged ratification process, e.g., in the case of the Law of the Sea Convention, and is often incorporated into international security arrangements or environmental agreements, where there is a pressing issue at stake (UN Convention on the Law of the Sea (adopted 10 December 1982, entered into force 16 November 1994) 1833 UNTS 3). See also Krieger (n 23) 442.

[100] For example, the Agreement relating to the Implementation of Part XI of the United Nations Convention on the Law of the Sea of 10 December 1982 (adopted 28 July 1994, entered into force 16 November 1994) 1836 UNTS 3. See also Krieger, ibid., 449.

[101] For recent practice on this, see especially *Bernhard von Pezold and others v Republic of Zimbabwe*, ICSID Case No ARB710/15, Award (28 July 2015) paras 338–340, confirming the provisional application on the basis of an exchange of notes; see also William Joseph Simonsick, 'Is Provisional Application on the Rise in International Investment Agreements? The European Union's Recent Treaty Practice and the Curious Case of *Von Pezold*' (2019) 88 *Nordic JIL* 180, 182.

sional application and what the consequences thereof are.[102] Other ambiguous aspects relate to the legal effects of the provisional application of treaties (e.g., whether there is a difference between the provisional application from the date of signature in comparison to such application from the date of ratification), the particular relationship between the provisional application of treaties and relevant provisions of domestic law, and the question whether the provisional application of a treaty has any effect on the scope of the treaty.[103] Hafner has commented in this regard that Article 25 VCLT 'clearly expresses that no reduced application can follow from the provisional application'[104] where no different agreement can be discerned from the parties of the agreement.

This latter point has also been of particular relevance in the context of the Energy Charter Treaty (ECT).[105] Article 45 of the ECT lays down the treaty's provisional application, stipulating that:

> [e]ach signatory which applies the Energy Charter Treaty provisionally in accordance with Article 45(1) and each Contracting Party agrees to apply this Amendment provisionally pending its entry into force for such signatory or Contracting Party to the extent that such provisional application is not inconsistent with its constitution, laws or regulations.[106]

---

[102] Given the numerous unsettled issues arising with regard to the provisional application of treaties, the topic is currently being studied by the ILC with the hope to bring some clarity on many aspects. The current draft guidelines, however, do not shed much light on the disputed aspects.

[103] See also ILC, Second report on the provisional application of treaties, by J M Gómez-Robledo (6 June 2014) UN Doc A/CN.4/675.

[104] Gerhard Hafner, 'The "Provisional Application" of the Energy Charter Treaty' in Christina Binder et al (eds), *International Investment Law for the 21st Century – Essays in Honour of Christoph Schreuer* (OUP 2009) 593, 594–596.

[105] The adoption of the ECT (n 16) in 1994 resulted from the developments in Europe in the late 1980s and early 1990s, and was intended as an instrument to further the integration between East and West following the end of the Cold War, *inter alia* by promoting and protecting investment in the energy sector. It entered into force in 1998, and currently (January 2019) has 54 signatory states, being by far the most widely ratified investment protection agreement. For more details, see also Thomas Roe and Matthew Happold, *Settlement of Investment Disputes under the Energy Charter Treaty* (CUP 2011) 8.

[106] ECT (n 16) art 45; Currently, three states (Australia, Belarus, and Norway) have signed, but not yet ratified the ECT, with Belarus being provisionally bound by virtue of art 45 ECT. Australia and Norway have entered declarations under art 45(2) that they do not accept the ECT's provisional application. Russia signed the ECT and was applying it provisionally until it notified the Secretariat in 2009 that it withdrew from the ECT's provisional application. However, in accordance with art 45(3)(b) ECT, the ECT continues to apply to preexisting investment for a period of 20 years.

The reading and interpretation of this provision – and the question to which extent this provision limited the scope of application of the ECT under certain circumstances – featured prominently in a number of investment cases.[107] This in particular in relation to Article 26 ECT's dispute settlement clause.[108]

As the first case to comprehensively deal with Article 45 ECT, the tribunal in *Kardassopoulos v Georgia* confirmed that the provisional application as encapsulated in Article 25 VCLT should be understood to import 'the application of all its provisions as if they were already in force, even though the treaty's proper or definitive entry into force has not yet occurred'.[109] There has been some debate on the legal effect of provisionally applied treaties, and whether such application produces legally binding rights and obligations.[110] Despite Georgia arguing that the 'provisional application of a treaty does not give rise to legal commitments but [is] only aspirational in nature',[111] the discussion taking place in *Kardassopoulos v Georgia* focused almost exclusively on the procedure for the provisional application of the ECT, as well as its interplay with the domestic law of the involved state parties (Greece and Georgia) in light of Article 45 ECT's limitation clause. Hence, the legal validity of provisional application per se was thereby taken for granted.[112] This is particularly relevant, as it determines to which extent the further VCLT regime is applicable to the treaty in question (in particular arts 18, 24(4) and 46 VCLT, but also, e.g., art 70 VCLT, at a minimum *mutatis mutandis*[113]).

The decade-long *Yukos* proceedings, extending over several judicial instances and *fora*, in principle confirmed a similar conclusion, i.e., the ECT was provisionally applicable by virtue of Article 45 ECT.[114] The essential

---

[107] See, for detailed account, *inter alia*, *Plama Consortium Ltd v Republic of Bulgaria*, ICSID Case No ARB/03/24, Decision on Jurisdiction (8 February 2005) paras 140–142; *Petrobart Ltd v Kyrgyz Republic*, SCC Case No 126/2003, Award (29 March 2005); Tomoko Ishikawa, 'Provisional Application of Treaties at the Crossroads between International and Domestic Law' (2016) 31 *ICSID Review* 270.

[108] ECT (n 16) art 26.

[109] *Ioannis Kardassopoulos v Republic of Georgia*, ICSID Case No ARB/05/18, Decision on Jurisdiction (6 July 2007) para 219.

[110] As demonstrated by Quast Mertsch, the majority seems to regard these treaties as legally binding though. Anneliese Quast Mertsch, *Provisionally Applied Treaties: Their Binding Force and Legal Nature* (Brill 2012) 119–142, 161–173, 198–217; see also René Lefeber, 'The Provisional Application of Treaties' in Jan Klabbers and Rene Lefeber (eds), *Essays on the Law of Treaties* (Martinus Nijhoff 1998) 82, 90.

[111] *Kardassopoulos v Georgia* (n 109) para 84.

[112] Ibid., para 209; cf. ILC, 'Second report on the provisional application of treaties, by Juan Manuel Gómez-Robledo' (9 June 2014) UN Doc A/CN.4/675, para 29.

[113] Ibid., para 83.

[114] It might be added, however, that the tribunals were chaired by the same person in both cases (L. Yves Fortier). This was also made note of in the judgment by District

ground of contention, however, again concerned the interpretation of the limitation clause contained in Article 45 ECT. Two possible interpretations were presented by the parties. First, based on arguments by the Claimant, whether the assessment thereof required to determine if provisional application per se was inconsistent with domestic law or not ('all-or-nothing' approach). Depending on the outcome, either the entire treaty was found provisionally applicable or not at all. Secondly, as advocated for by the Respondent, a 'piecemeal' approach, i.e., an analysis of each provision on its own in light of the limitation clause, thus, also including a separate analysis of the consistency of the dispute settlement provision contained in Article 26 ECT with Russia's constitution, laws or other regulations.

In the Interim Award on Jurisdiction and Admissibility, the tribunal concluded that – based on the general rules of treaty interpretation – 'such provisional application', i.e., 'the provisional application of this Treaty', was to be interpreted as referring to the *entire* treaty rather than *some parts*.[115] It thus agreed with Claimant's 'all-or-nothing' approach and rejected Russia's 'piecemeal' approach. It added in this regard that any other conclusion would run against 'the grain of international law', in shape of the principle *pacta sunt servanda* (as contained in art 26 VCLT) and Article 27 VCLT, prohibiting the invocation of domestic law as a justification for failure to perform a treaty.[116] This 'would undermine the principle that provisional application of a treaty creates binding obligations'.[117]

However, this interpretation and the ensuing result was rejected by the Hague District Court in 2016, setting aside the award. The District Court argued, first, that Article 45's use of the phrase 'to the extent that' indicated that the application was dependent on the compatibility with the respective state's domestic law.[118] Secondly, the District Court emphasised that although Articles 26 and 27 VCLT also applied in the context of a treaty's provisional application, their application in that context was not limitless:

> Signatories to a treaty can explicitly limit the provisional application of treaty provisions, as becomes apparent from Article 25 VCLT … . In this case, the Signatories to the ECT have explicitly laid down in the Limitation Clause in Article 45 paragraph 1 ECT … that the scope of the provisional application is limited to treaty pro-

---

Court of The Hague, Cases C/09/477160 / HA ZA 15-1, C/09/477162 / HA ZA 15-2 and C/09/481619 / HA ZA 15-112, para 5.20.

[115] *Yukos Universal Ltd v Russian Federation*, UNCITRAL, PCA Case No 205-04/ AA227, Interim Award on Jurisdiction and Admissibility (30 November 2009) para 308.

[116] Ibid., paras 312–313.

[117] Ibid., para 314.

[118] Judgment of Hague District Court (n 114) paras 5.7ff.

> visions that are not contrary to national law. Even while it is possible that provisions of national law can stand in the way of the performance of one or more provisions of the ECT, the basis for doing so is encased in the ECT itself – i.e., at treaty level. In other words: a state that relies on a conflict between a treaty provision and national law, on sound grounds and referencing the Limitation Clause, does not act contrary to the *pacta sunt servanda* principle, nor to the principle of Article 27 VCLT.[119]

Based on an analysis of Russian law, the District Court finally concluded that indeed Article 26 ECT would not be covered by the ECT's provisional application given its conflict with the applicable domestic law.[120] Even though the outcome has been criticised, primarily for the effect the judgment may have on the effectiveness of the ECT as a multilateral treaty regime,[121] the piecemeal approach advocated for by Russia – and finding support in the domestic case – has been found to be the more correct by a number of scholars.[122]

The scope and consequences of provisional application as enshrined in Article 25 VCLT may become far more prominent in the near future given the EU's recent trend to include provision application clauses into its newly negotiated trade and investment agreements.[123] The outcome of the *Yukos*

---

[119] Ibid., para 5.19.

[120] Ibid., para 5.48.

[121] See, e.g., Lena U. Serhan, 'Arbitration Unbound: How the Yukos Oil Decision Yields Uncertainty for International-Investment Arbitration' (2016) 95 *Texas LR* 101.

[122] Hafner (n 104) 601; Quast Mertsch (n 110) 100–102, with further references; Alex M. Niebruegge, 'Provisional Application of the Energy Charter Treaty: The Yukos Arbitration and the Future Place of Provisional Application in International Law' (2007) 8 *Chicago JIL* 355. Similarly, Gattini (n 33) 149; against: Simonsick (n 101) 189.

[123] Of the 20 agreements signed by the EU between 2009 and 2022, 18 foresee the possibility of provisional application: '2020 EU-UK' art 12 (Council Decision (EU) 2020/2252 of 29 December 2020 on the signing, on behalf of the Union, and on provisional application of the Trade and Cooperation Agreement between the European Union and the European Atomic Energy Community, of the one part, and the United Kingdom of Great Britain and Northern Ireland, of the other part, and of the Agreement between the European Union and the United Kingdom of Great Britain and Northern Ireland concerning security procedures for exchanging and protecting classified information); '2019 EU-Viet Nam', art 4.13 (Council Decision (EU) 2019/1121 of 25 June 2019 on the signing, on behalf of the European Union, of the Free Trade Agreement between the European Union and the Socialist Republic of Viet Nam [2019] OJ L177/1); 'EU-Singapore', art 4.15 (Free trade Agreement between the European Union and the Republic of Singapore [2019] OJ L294/3); 'EU-Armenia', art 385 (Comprehensive and enhanced Partnership Agreement between the European Union and the European Atomic Energy Community and their Member States, of the one part, and the Republic of Armenia, of the other part [2018] OJ L23/4); 'CETA', art 30.7 (Comprehensive Trade and Economic Agreement between Canada and the European Union [2017] OJ L11/23); '2016 EU-SADC EPA' (Economic Partnership

arbitration was therefore highly anticipated as guidance on 'the status, charac-

Agreement between the European Union and its Member States, of the one part, and the SADC EPA States, of the other part [2016] OJ L250/3); '2015 EU-Kazakhstan', art 281 (Council Decision (EU) 2016/123 of 26 October 2015 on the signing, on behalf of the European Union, and provisional application of the Enhanced Partnership and Cooperation Agreement between the European Union and its Member States, of the one part, and the Republic of Kazakhstan, of the other part [2016] OJ L29/1); '2014 EU-Georgia', art 431 (Association Agreement between the European Union and the European Atomic Energy Community and their Member States, of the one part, and Georgia, of the other part [2014] OJ L/261/4); '2014 EU-Moldova', art 464 (Association Agreement between the European Union and the European Atomic Energy Community and their Member States, of the one part, and the Republic of Moldova, of the other part [2014] OJ L260/4); '2014 EU-Ukraine', art 486 (Association Agreement between the European Union and its Member States, of the one part, and Ukraine, of the other part [2014] OJ L161/3); '2012 EU-CACM', art 353 (although not explicitly termed as such) (Agreement establishing an Association between the European Union and its Member States, on the one hand, and Central America on the other [2012] OJ L346/3); '2012 EU-Colombia, Peru, Ecuador', art 330 (Trade Agreement between the European Union and its Member States, of the one part, and Colombia and Peru, of the other part [2012] OJ L354/3 and Protocol of Accession to the Trade Agreement between the European Union and its Member States, of the one part, and Colombia and Peru, of the other part, to take account of the accession of Ecuador [2016] OJ L356/3); '2012 EU-Iraq', art 117 (limited to certain sections) (Partnership And Cooperation Agreement between the European Union and its Member States, of the one part, and the Republic of Iraq, of the other part [2012] OJ L204/20); '2010 EU-Korea FTA', art 15.10 (Council Decision of 16 September 2010 on the signing, on behalf of the European Union, and provisional application of the Free Trade Agreement between the European Union and its Member States, of the one part, and the Republic of Korea, of the other part [2011] OJ L127/1); '2010 EU-Korea Framework Agreement', art 49 (Council Decision of 10 May 2010 on the signing, on behalf of the European Union, and provisional application of the Framework Agreement between the European Union and its Member States, on the one part, and the Republic of Korea, on the other part [2013] OJ L20/1); '2009 EU-Eastern and Southern Africa States', art 62 (Council Decision of 13 July 2009 on the signing and provisional application of the Interim Agreement establishing a framework for an Economic Partnership Agreement between the Eastern and Southern Africa States, on the one part, and the European Community and its Member States, on the other part [2012] OJ L111/1); '2009 EU-SADC Interim Agreement', art 105 (EC-SADC EPA States Interim Economic Partnership Agreement European Parliament resolution of 25 March 2009 on an Interim Economic Partnership Agreement between the European Community and its Member States, on the one part, and the SADC EPA States, on the other part [2010] OJ C117E/124); '2009 EU-Cameroon', art 98 (Council Decision of 20 November 2008 on the signature and provisional application of the interim agreement with a view to an Economic Partnership Agreement between the European Community and its Member States, of the one part, and the Central Africa Party, of the other part [2009] OJ L57/1). Two of the 19 do not: '2018 EU-Japan' (Agreement between the European Union and Japan for an Economic Partnership [2018] OJ L330/3); '2012 EU-Viet Nam Framework PCA' (Framework Agreement on Comprehensive Partnership and Cooperation between the European Union and its

terization, and obligations imposed by provisional application in international law'.[124] Moreover, the ECT's multilateral nature provides sufficient ground to explore the meaning of one specific framework from the angle of several different arbitral tribunals. However, given the conflicting outcome on some of the most crucial aspects arising in this regard, i.e., the relationship between Article 25 VCLT and Articles 26 and 27 VCLT in connection with the domestic law limitation clause, it is doubtful whether one can already (or even ever given the specific formulation of art 45 ECT) make an assessment on the effect of the discussed awards on general international law relating to the provisional application of treaties. After all, for such an effect, a certain level of consistency in case law is required,[125] and inconsistencies[126] become even more problematic where they, for one, concern the interpretation and application of the same treaty text, and for another, relate to issues resulting in legal uncertainty for the parties as to whether the specific treaty regime even applies (and to which extent).[127]

Member States, of the one part, and the Socialist Republic of Viet Nam, of the other part [2016] OJ L329/8).

[124] Niebruegge (n 122) 368–369.

[125] Even though some investment tribunals have emphasised their case-specific mandate, similar to international commercial arbitration cases, and have warned against exceeding the tasks put before them by placing too much emphasis on wider systemic implications (see, e.g., *Glamis Gold v United States of America*, UNCITRAL, Award (8 June 2009) paras 3–9), an increasing number have also reaffirmed their role as systemic agents of the international legal community (see for many *Churchill Mining PLC and Planet Mining Pty Ltd v Republic of Indonesia*, ICSID Case No ARB/12/14 and 12/40, Decision on Jurisdiction (24 February 2014) where the tribunal noted (at para 85) that:

> it is of the opinion that it must pay due consideration to earlier decisions of international tribunals. Specifically, it deems that, subject to compelling contrary grounds, it has a duty to adopt solutions established in a series of consistent cases. It further deems that, subject to the specific provisions of a given treaty and of the circumstances of the actual case, it has a duty to contribute to the harmonious development of investment law, with a view to meeting the legitimate expectations of the community of States and investors towards certainty of the rule of law.

[126] James Crawford has metaphorically likened the disagreement among investment tribunals to a 'carpet [which] looks very much as if different people have started from different ends without many common threads – a crazy quilt rather than a Persian rug' (James Crawford, 'Treaty and Contract in Investment Arbitration' (22nd Freshfields Lecture on International Arbitration, London, 29 November 2007) https://is.muni.cz/el/law/podzim2010/MVV61K/um/20201574/Crawford-Treaty_and_Contract-2.pdf accessed 10 January 2021).

[127] Inconsistencies relating not to the interpretation of a specific standard or clause but to a question of the 'rules of the game' have been classified as 'unjustifiable inconsistent interpretations', potentially resulting in unfair and unjustifiable surprises *ex post* by Chester Brown et al, 'Lack of Consistency and Coherence in the Interpretation of

In the cases mentioned above, the tribunals and domestic court failed to reach a consistent outcome, owed not only to opposite conclusions on the interpretation of Article 45(1) ECT, but also based on the fact that the issues arising with regard to provisional application are still in development, particularly when it comes to the question how to deal with the reference to domestic law in a limitation clause.

Despite the so far limited case law, however, clarity at minimum seems to have been reached on one issue, i.e., that provisionally applied treaties have legal effect, an issue which the ILC still noted as ambiguous or unsettled until a few years ago.[128] In comparison, it is too soon to reach a valid understanding of domestic limitation clauses and the relationship of Article 25 VCLT with other VCLT provisions. As also noted by the ILC Special Rapporteur Juan Manual Gómez-Robledo in direct reliance on the *Yukos* proceedings, it would therefore be 'premature to advance any conclusions'[129] derived from this ongoing debate. Thus, the final outcome of the Yukos proceedings[130]and other pending proceedings on the matter are indispensable.

C. Treaty Termination by Mutual Consent and Its Legal Consequences for Sunset Clauses (Arts 54, 70 VCLT)

Despite treaties serving the objective of stability and legal security, they may be terminated either as a result of the application of specific treaty provisions or of unforeseen circumstances.[131] In any event, the end of a treaty's life is often marked by turmoil and uncertainty as to the consequences arising for the contracting parties as well as other entities exercising rights under such framework.

Legal Issues' (*EJIL:Talk!*, 5 April 2019). The UNCITRAL Working Group III (UN Doc A/CN.9/935, 14 May 2018) has also noted this as one of the main points of concern related to arbitral outcomes (paras 20ff).

[128] Gómez-Robledo (n 112).

[129] ILC, 'Fourth report on the provisional application of treaties, by Juan Manuel Gómez-Robledo' (23 June 2016) UN Doc A/CN.4/699, para 65.

[130] Enforcement proceedings are underway in a number of other states, *inter alia*, France, Belgium, and the US, see also *Yukos v Russia* (n 115). Most recently, in April 2022, a US court ruled that the stay on enforcement should be lifted (https://globalarbitrationreview.com/us-stay-yukos-awards-lifted-after-six-years accessed 27 August 2022).

[131] See also VCLT (n 3) art 56, containing a rebuttable presumption that aside from treaty specific termination provisions, termination is only possible with the consent of all other parties. Arts 60 (material breach) and 62 (fundamental change of circumstances) serve as notable exceptions thereto.

While there has so far been hardly any case law in the field of investment law on this issue, from the viewpoint of practice, issues arising in connection with treaty termination and the legal consequences thereof have become specifically relevant, and will continue to do so. For example, in a striking move, the representatives of the governments of the member states of the EU issued a Declaration on 15 January 2019 'On the Legal Consequences of the Judgment of the Court of Justice in *Achmea* and on Investment Protection in the European Union' wherein they stated that:

> Union law takes precedence over bilateral investment treaties concluded between Member States. As a consequence, all investor-State arbitration clauses contained in bilateral investment treaties concluded between Member States are contrary to Union law and thus inapplicable. They do not produce effects including as regards provisions that provide for extended protection of investments made prior to termination for a further period of time (so-called sunset or grandfathering clauses). An arbitral tribunal established on the basis of investor-State arbitration clauses lacks jurisdiction, due to a lack of a valid offer to arbitrate by the Member State party to the underlying bilateral investment Treaty.[132]

As a consequence to this political declaration, which is admittedly formulated in a broad and vague manner, member states are to *inter alia* terminate all BITs concluded between them,[133] and discuss any additional steps which might be necessary with regard to the ECT.[134]

Moreover, even though until recently IIA termination has been an infrequent event,[135] recent years have shown growing numbers, particularly in

---

[132] EU Commission, 'Declaration of the Representatives of the Governments of the Member States, of 15 January 2019, on the Legal Consequences of the Judgment of the Court of Justice in *Achmea* and on Investment Protection in the European Union' (15 January 2019). This statement applies to both intra-EU BITs and the ECT to the extent that it provides for intra-EU investor-state arbitration.

[133] For an overview of the consequences of the declaration, see Johannes Tropper, '*Alea iacta est?* Post-*Achmea* Investment Arbitration in Light of Recent Declarations by EU-Member States' (*Völkerrechtsblog*, 24 January 2019). The majority of member states (23 of 27) in fact in 2020 signed an Agreement for the Termination of Intra-EU Bilateral Investment Treaties (OJ L 169).

[134] On the ECT modernization process, see Johannes Tropper, 'Opinion 1/20 and the Conclusion of the Modernisation Negotiations of the Energy Charter Treaty – Hitting the Home Stretch?' (*Kluwer Arbitration Blog*, 25 June 2022).

[135] By September 2014, only 19 investment treaties (of a treaty sample of 1,896 IIAs) had been denounced unilaterally, and two by mutual consent. See Kathryn Gordon and Joachim Pohl, 'Investment Treaties over Time – Treaty Practice and Interpretation in a Changing World' (2015) *OECD Working Papers on International Investment* 18 www.oecd.org/investment/investment-policy/WP-2015-02.pdf accessed 15 January 2021.

relation to many IIAs nearing the expiry of their initial term after which termination becomes possible, and a change in policy by some states.[136] There have also been a growing number of withdrawals from the ICSID Convention.[137] Hence, these developments promise a number of cases in the near future which will have to deal with the end of the temporal scope of protection of investment treaties, and with specific questions arising in the context of Articles 54 and 70 VCLT.

Given the still prevailing absence of investment case law on the matter, the following addresses which aspects of the general law of treaties are particularly relevant for the field of investment law, and whether investment law might – through its practice – shape these rules. The potential of this is given, especially in light of specific questions of treaty law relating to termination and the legal consequences thereof remaining in dire need of practice and clarification. The promising aspect to be clarified relates to the question of third-party rights/acquired rights. However, as will be seen, the field of investment law is also characterised by specific features which might not lend themselves to contributing to the further development of general treaty law on this issue. Article 54 VCLT provides that the 'termination of a treaty or the withdrawal of a party may take place (a) in conformity with the provisions of the treaty; or (b) at any time by consent of all the parties after consultation with the other contracting States'.[138] The VCLT's provisions on the termination or suspension of treaties are largely residual,[139] i.e., in accordance with Article 54(a) VCLT any specific treaty provisions will take precedence. Article 70 VCLT governs the legal consequences arising from the termination of a treaty.[140] The default application of Article 70 VCLT is guided by considerations of 'acquired rights, legal cer-

---

[136] See Tania Voon et al, 'Parting Ways: The Impact of Mutual Termination of Investment Treaties on Investor Rights' (2014) 29 *ICSID Review* 451; August Reinisch and Sara Mansour Fallah, 'Post-Termination Responsibility of States? – The Impact of Amendment/Modification, Suspension and Termination of Investment Treaties on (Vested) Rights of Investor' (2022) 37 *ICSID Review* 101.

[137] ICSID's relevant provisions on withdrawal can be found in arts 71–72 of the Convention (Convention on the Settlement of Investment Disputes between States and Nationals of Other States (adopted 18 March 1965, entered into force 14 October 1966) 575 UNTS 159). See also Reinisch and Mansour Fallah (n 136) 110ff on the relevance of perfected consent.

[138] VCLT (n 3) art 54.

[139] This is explicitly mentioned in VCLT (n 3) art 54 lit. a, art 55, art 56 para 1, art 57 lit. a, art 58 para 1 lit. a para 2, art 60 para 4.

[140] See VCLT (n 3) art 70. Consequences of the Termination of a Treaty:

1. Unless the treaty otherwise provides or the parties otherwise agree, the termination of a treaty under its provisions or in accordance with the present Convention:
   (a) Releases the parties from any obligation further to perform the treaty;

tainty, non-retroactivity of the law, and the doctrine of inter-temporal law',[141] with these aspects however again being subject to party autonomy.[142] In light of this largely residual framework, specific clauses contained in IIAs are of particular relevance. Most often (in more than 90 per cent of the cases) the denunciation of IIAs only is possible after a certain minimum period of application.[143] After this initial period has lapsed, the treaty generally is extended either for another fixed period or for an unlimited time period. In any case, a unilateral denunciation will generally only take effect if given with a certain advance notice.[144] However, even following such denunciation, protection for investments which have already been made[145] most often continues beyond such time period for a certain period of time – especially in the cases of BITs[146] but also in the ECT[147] – by virtue of so-called 'continuing effects', 'survival' or 'sunset' clauses. Owed to the specific nature of investment law,[148] such clauses generally either provide for the entire treaty content to outlive the date

---

(b) Does not affect any right, obligation or legal situation of the parties created through the execution of the treaty prior to its termination.

2. If a State denounces or withdraws from a multilateral treaty, paragraph 1 applies in the relations between that State and each of the other parties to the treaty from the date when such denunciation or withdrawal takes effect.

[141] André Nollkaemper, 'Some Observations on the Consequences of the Termination of Treaties and the Reach of Article 70 of the Vienna Convention on the Law of Treaties' in Ige F. Dekker and Harry H. G. Post (eds), *On the Foundations and Sources of International Law* (Springer 2003) 187.

[142] Stephan Wittich, 'Article 70 – Consequences of the Termination of a Treaty' in Dörr and Schmalenbach (n 23) 1283, 1284.

[143] See, e.g., UK-Albania BIT (adopted 30 March 1994, entered into force 30 August 1995): 'This Agreement shall remain in force for a period of ten years. Thereafter, it shall continue in force until the expiration of twelve months from the date on which either Contracting Party shall have given written notice of termination to the other.' Note that FTAs and EPAs usually do not have an initial period. Pohl (n 24).

[144] Pohl (n 24).

[145] There are few examples which also extend such protection to investments which have not yet been made but have been approved or where commitments have been made, see, e.g., South Africa-Mozambique BIT (adopted 6 May 1997, not yet in force), Canada-Tanzania BIT (adopted 17 May 2013, entered into force 9 December 2013).

[146] Based on Pohl's study, only 1 per cent of the more than 2,000 BITs analysed did not contain such prolonged protection. In contrast, however, almost 90 per cent of FTAs, EPAs and CEPAs failed to include such protection. Pohl (n 24) 15.

[147] ECT (n 16) art 47(3) and art 45(3)(b), applying a sunset clause in relation to the termination of provisional application.

[148] Dolzer and Schreuer describe this well-known fact succinctly:

> [T]he decision to invest in a foreign country initiates a long-term relationship between the investor and the host country. Often, the business plan of the investor is to sink substantial resources into the project at the outset of the investment, with the expectation of recouping this amount plus an acceptable rate of return

of denunciation – i.e., the substantive protection standards as well as access to international dispute settlement – for a certain range of articles, or for a subset of treaty content.[149] In themselves, 'sunset clauses' have no effect on the validity of a denunciation, but they provide for the legal consequences pertaining to such.[150]

Article 54(b) VCLT refers to situations of termination effected by mutual agreement of the parties.[151] It is undisputed that such termination can be effected even if the relevant IIA contains specific termination clauses.[152] Thus, given that the remaining provisions of the IIA are respected (e.g., certain minimum periods of application or sunset clauses),[153] the fact that investors presumably enjoy direct legal entitlements does not constitute a barrier to the subsequent revocation of treaty-based rights.[154] There are numerous examples stemming from practice, with some even extending termination specifically also to sunset clauses. This has often occurred in the context of the conclusion of a new IIA,[155] with recent practice also particularly stemming from the termination of intra-EU BITs.[156] Whether or not it is possible to terminate

---

during the subsequent period of investment, sometimes running up to 30 years or more.

Rudolf Dolzer and Christoph Schreuer, *Principles of International Investment Law* (2nd edn., OUP 2012) 21.

149 Pohl (n 24) 16–17.

150 Karsten Nowrot, 'Termination and Renegotiation of International Investment Agreements' in Steffen Hindelang and Markus Krajewski (eds), *Shifting Paradigms in International Investment Law* (OUP 2016) 227, 242–243.

151 Thomas Giegerich, 'Article 54 – Termination of or Withdrawal From a Treaty Under Its Provisions or by Consent of the Parties' in Dörr and Schmalenbach (n 23) 1015, 1027f.

152 Ibid.; cf. Anthony Aust, *Modern Treaty Law and Practice* (CUP 2007) 288; Moreover, also other VCLT termination provisions, in particular VCLT (n 3) art 62, could be relevant in practice (despite specific termination clauses), as neither art 42(2) nor any other part of the VCLT seem to exclude their application. Cf. Nowrot (n 150) 227, 240ff.

153 See, e.g., the *obiter dictum* in *Eastern Sugar BV (Netherlands) v Czech Republic*, SCC No 088/2004, Partial Award (27 March 2007) paras 174–175; *Marco Gavazzi and Stefano Gavazzi v Romania*, ICSID Case No ARB/12/25, Decision on Jurisdiction, Admissibility and Liability (21 April 2015).

154 Nowrot (n 150) 227, 246. This is also in line with general international law jurisprudence. For an extensive analysis in the field of human rights see Yogesh Tyagi, 'The Denunciation of Human Rights Treaties' (2008) 79 *BYIL* 86.

155 For example, Australia and Chile after terminating their 1996 BIT and concluding a FTA; Peru and South Korea and Singapore, respectively, when consensually terminating their FTAs; Korea and Chile after concluding a new preferential trade agreement. See in detail Voon et al (n 136) 468.

156 For example, the Czech Republic explicitly revoked the sunset clauses when consensually terminating its BITs with Denmark, Estonia, Slovenia, Ireland, and Italy.

sunset clauses by mutual consent is primarily dependent on the formulation of the relevant clause.[157] If the sunset clause is formulated in such a broad manner to also extend the protection afforded by a treaty in cases of mutual termination, and no specific provision allows for its termination, the situation remains uncertain in comparison to cases where this is explicitly foreseen.

To date no case seems to have emerged assessing the legal consequences pertaining thereto.[158] Still, the matter has been discussed extensively in scholarship, thus warranting a brief portrayal of the general issues of treaty law arising on this issue. Given the overall objective of investment law to promote stability and legal security for investors,[159] the core issue arising in this context is whether rights granted under an IIA – and protected beyond the treaty's end of life by virtue of a sunset clause – can in any way be curtailed by one or more state parties terminating the relevant IIA, either by reference to the general law of treaties (e.g., art 62 VCLT)[160] or by mutual consent (art 54 VCLT).

An indispensable preliminary point for the answer to this question is the determination of the nature of investors' rights in IIAs, and whether the specific IIA directly confers rights on the investor, or whether these are 'derivative rights flowing from the host State's duties and the home State's rights under the treaty'.[161] While the majority of scholarship seems to argue in favour of the 'direct rights theory',[162] the 'derivative rights theory'

Christina Binder, 'A Treaty Law Perspective on Intra-EU BITs' (2016) 17 *JWIT* 964, 976.

[157] In fact, some sunset clauses only protect investors in case of unilateral termination to begin with, and consequently do not apply in the case of mutual termination. Binder, ibid., 977.

[158] Tropper (n 133).

[159] For a detailed discussion see also James Harrison, 'The Life and Death of BITs: Legal Issues Concerning Survival Clauses and the Termination of Investment Treaties' (2012) 13 *JWIT* 928, 932–935.

[160] For example, Egypt-United Kingdom BIT (adopted 11 June 1975, entered into force 24 February 1976) art 13:

> in respect of investments made whilst the Agreement is in force, its provisions shall continue in effect with respect to such investments for a period of ten years after the date of termination and without prejudice to the application thereafter of the rules of general international law.

Cf. Harrison (n 159) 939–940.

[161] Voon et al (n 136) 454. The first to comprehensively address this question was Zachary Douglas, 'The Hybrid Foundations of Investment Treaty Arbitration' (2003) 74 *BYIL* 151 and Zachary Douglas, *The International Law of Investment Claims* (CUP 2009); see also Eric De Brabandere, *Investment Treaty Arbitration as Public International Law* (CUP 2014) 55ff.

[162] See, *inter alia*, Campbell McLachlan et al, *International Investment Arbitration: Substantive Principles* (2nd edn, OUP 2017) 75–79; Douglas, 'The Hybrid Foundations

finds support particularly in an often-cited passage from *Loewen v USA* distinguishing between rights of action under private law and investment law.[163] However, even if the majority opinion is followed on this matter, the question arises at which point in time the 'offer to arbitrate' becomes legally binding for the state, i.e., at the moment when it is accepted by an investor[164] or upon the treaty's conclusion/the moment when the offer is expressed.[165] Depending on which theory is followed, it is only at that specific point in time that the offer to arbitration creates legal effects. The ultimate finding on the nature of investor rights and at which moment in time the offer to arbitrate becomes legally binding, however, will depend on the text of the relevant IIA.[166]

Both aspects underlie any further analysis on whether 'acquired rights' of third parties arising from the consent to jurisdiction as potentially protected by Articles 34ff VCLT, particularly Article 37[167] VCLT, and Article 70[168] VCLT on legal consequences of termination, have been affected by denunciation or termination (art 54 VCLT). Hence, the application of Article 54

---

of Investment Treaty Arbitration' (n 161) 182; Andrea K. Bjorklund, 'Private Rights and Public International Law: Why Competition Among International Economic Law Tribunals Is Not Working' (2007) 59 *Hastings LJ* 126; Frederic G. Sourgens, 'Keep the Faith: Investment Protection Following the Denunciation of International Investment Agreements' (2013) 11 *Santa Clara JIL* 335, 379; there are also a number of cases in support of the argument that the relevant IIA conferred a direct legal entitlement for a foreign investor, see *inter alia, BG Group PLC v Argentina*, UNCITRAL, Award (24 December 2007) para 145; *Corn Products International Inc v United Mexican States*, ICISD Case No ARB(AF)/04/01, Decision on Responsibility (15 January 2008) paras 167ff.

[163] *Loewen Group Inc and Raymond L Loewen v United States of America*, ICSID Case No ARB(AF)/98/3, Award (26 June 2003) para 488.

[164] Christoph Schreuer, 'Consent to Arbitration' (2005) 2(5) *TDM* 7.

[165] Michael Nolan and Frederic Caivano, 'Limits of Consent—Arbitration without Privity and Beyond' in Miguel Angel Fernandez-Ballesteros and David Arias (eds), *Liber Amicorum Bernardo Cremades* (La Ley 2010) 873, 877ff.

[166] Voon et al (n 136) 455, 459–460.

[167] Art 37. Revocation or Modification of Obligations or Rights of Third States:

1. When an obligation has arisen for a third State in conformity with article 35, the obligation may be revoked or modified only with the consent of the parties to the treaty and of the third State, unless it is established that they had otherwise agreed.
2. When a right has arisen for a third State in conformity with article 36, the right may not be revoked or modified by the parties if it is established that the right was intended not to be revocable or subject to modification without the consent of the third State.

[168] See above n 140.

VCLT in relation to sunset clauses must be read in light of the concept of the rights of third parties.

There are different opinions on whether investors can be considered as third parties protected by the VCLT's regime on the effects of treaties on third states. On the one hand, it has been argued that even though the VCLT in this regard refers to the right of *third states*, it has since then become recognised to also extend to other non-state entities such as International Organisations or any other third-party right holders.[169] On the other hand, scholars have pointed out the lack of a normative basis to extend the scope of application of Articles 34ff VCLT to non-states actors such as individuals and investors.[170] It has also been warned that such an analogy would stretch too far given the differences between the investment law regime and treaty regime.[171] In particular, the absence of consent by investors to the rights provided to them in an IIA constitutes a notable difference to the requirements established by Article 36 VCLT in relation to consent of third states to treaties providing for rights. It is only once the investor has accepted the offer to arbitrate that such a right could be considered an 'acquired right' and not be revoked without the investor's consent.[172] At latest, this is when the investor has exercised their right, and perfected consent (e.g., by initiating proceedings).[173]

Of potential relevance in this regard is also Article 70(1)(b) VCLT which protects acquired rights in cases where treaties have been terminated.[174] However, Article 70(1)'s introductory part makes explicit reference to the qualification '[u]nless … the parties otherwise agree', clearly emphasising once again the position of states as the 'master of the treaty'.[175] Moreover, as noted by the ILC, the rights and obligations referred to in Article 70 were only intended to encompass those of the contracting parties.[176] The rights of private entities therefore do not seem to fall within the ambit of Article 70 VCLT.[177] Still, it has been maintained that certain rights of private individuals could in

---

[169] Harrison (n 159) 944; Pierre d'Argent, 'Article 37 of the 1969 Vienna Convention' in Corten and Klein (n 25) 944.

[170] Nowrot (n 150) 227, 250.

[171] Binder (n 156) 979; see also Zachary Douglas et al (eds), *The Foundations of International Investment Law* (OUP 2014) 81–82.

[172] Binder (n 156) 979–980.

[173] Ibid., 981–982. The contrary would amount to an extinguishment of exercised rights, see also the findings of the ICJ in *Nottebohm (Liechtenstein v Guatemala)* (Preliminary Objections) [1953] *ICJ Reports* 111, 123.

[174] Wittich (n 142) 1283.

[175] Nowrot (n 150) 251; Binder (n 155) 977; Voon et al (n 136) 467.

[176] *ILC* (n 73) 265, para 3.

[177] Wittich (n 142) 1294.

fact continue to exist by virtue of the general principle of acquired rights, with the caveat that there is however high uncertainty pertaining to the validity and conditions for application of this doctrine.[178]

Finally, whether or not the investor is found to constitute such a third party which has acquired rights under a respective treaty, a further issue which arises is whether the drafters of the relevant provision intended the rights to be irrevocable without the consent of the third party concerned.[179] Harrison, e.g., argues that there are sufficient grounds to assume that the drafters of IIAs – absent any indications of the opposite – might well have intended such rights of third parties to be irrevocable given the nature and terms of IIAs. In particular, he argues that the language used as well as the stability of the investment law framework for investors are decisive elements in this regard.[180] Thus, by virtue thereof, one might argue that the states may have 'implicitly … agreed to an exclusion of the applicability of article 54(b) VCLT *inter se*, at least as far as the observance of minimum periods of applications and survival clauses are concerned'.[181] In any event, however, such an intention should not be assumed lightly,[182] particularly since it relates to the core sovereign power of states to enter into or exit treaty obligations in light of their policy interests.[183]

Despite (still) lacking arbitral practice on these questions arising in connection with the denunciation and termination of IIAs, the above shows that from the perspective of the general law of treaties states enjoy a quite wide discretion to modify or terminate their obligations entered into by mutual consent. While theoretical ambiguities continue to persist on the nature of investor rights, even their status as third-party right-holders would not necessarily provide protection from their rights being rescinded by the state parties, as long as they have not been exercised. From the viewpoint of public international law, states therefore remain the 'masters of the treaty', something that does not seem to change even when applicable in the specific field of investment law.

If investment cases emerge on these issues, would they be capable of developing general international law? Could analogies be drawn between investors as beneficiaries of IIAs and third party rights/acquired rights as mentioned in

---

178 Ibid., 1295, with further references; on the doctrine see also particularly Lord Arnold McNair, 'The General Principles of Law Recognized by Civilized Nations' (1957) 33 *BYIL* 1, 16; for a very critical assessment of the applicability and validity of the doctrine see Voon et al (n 136) 470.

179 Harrison (n 159) 944.

180 Ibid., 946–947.

181 Nowrot (n 150) 252.

182 Giegerich (n 151) 1031–1032.

183 Martins Paparinskis, 'Investment Arbitration and the Law of Countermeasures' (2008) 79 *BYIL* 334, 342.

the VCLT? The majority opinion seems to imply that this is not the case and that the omission in the VCLT was deliberate, thus not serving as an ideal basis for subsuming investor rights thereunder. It seems unlikely that investment tribunals will depart from this interpretation in their assessment of general international law. However, tribunals could be more inclined to place emphasis on the specifics of the field of investment law when assessing the nature of investor rights, particularly when it comes to IIAs which do not contain any specific limitations on sunset clauses.[184]

In contrast to the question when the temporal scope of application of a treaty begins, the end of the temporal reach may therefore develop more independently from the standard assumptions applicable in the general law of treaties.

IV. CONCLUSIONS – THE EFFECTS OF JURISPRUDENCE ON THE TEMPORAL SCOPE OF APPLICATION OF IIAS ON GENERAL INTERNATIONAL LAW

What effect can be hoped for by the analysis of investment jurisprudence with regard to the temporal scope of application of treaties? Despite being a field known for its inconsistency, the application and interpretation of IIAs derives from the law of treaties and, in theory, the sheer number of cases bears the potential to clarify a number of open questions of treaty law.

The interaction between investment law and general international law has been subject to extensive analysis in the past years,[185] yet without significant results as to the effects of investment jurisprudence on general international law. For example, it has been pointed out that more than half of the cases making reference to the ILC Articles on State Responsibility stem from the

---

[184] On a theoretical level, it has been argued, e.g., by Anthea Roberts that the future drafting of IIAs should place more focus on the need to recalibrate the balance of IIAs, and thereby shift from bilateral to triangular treaty relationship. Anthea Roberts, 'Triangular Treaties: The Nature and Limits of Investment Treaty Rights' (2015) 56 *Harvard ILJ* 353.

[185] McLachlan (n 6) 364, noting that the main route through which investment practice contributes to general international law is through the elucidation of general principles of law; Freya Baetens (ed), *Investment Law Within International Law – Integrationist Perspectives* (CUP 2013); De Brabandere (n 161); Stephan W. Schill and Katrine R. Tvede, 'Mainstreaming Investment Treaty Jurisprudence – The Contribution of Investment Treaty Tribunals to the Consolidation and Development of General International Law' (2015) 14 *LPICT* 94.

field of investment law.[186] However, the manner in which tribunals have done so has also been likened to 'a drowning man [who] might grab a stick at sea in the hope of having certainty'.[187] In particular, it has been begrudged that investment tribunals have failed to deal with the substance and methodology of the ILC Articles in a meaningful manner. Others have engaged in a detailed analysis of how investment law has applied rules of general international law, e.g., Articles 31 and 32 VCLT, but have denoted their approach 'a cavalier attitude to treaty interpretation'[188] and avoided making any reference to the reverse impact thereof on general international law. Moreover, it has been remarked by several scholars that the reason why the field of investment arbitration does not always follow public international law in an exact manner or engage in any meaningful analysis might be owed to the often-times prevailing influence of international commercial practice among the selected arbitrators.[189]

Thus, the question may be asked whether the field of investment law has matured enough to clarify open issues of the temporal scope of application of treaties, aside from simply adding to the body of practice. The relevant VCLT provisions – unlike the ILC Articles on State Responsibility – suffer less from the question of validity of norms since the majority of its provisions has long been recognised as customary international law. Investment practice, in this regard, therefore first and foremost consolidates the specific rules stemming from the general law of treaties, e.g., the presumption of the non-retroactivity of treaties unless otherwise intended by the parties (art 28 VCLT). It does so by reference both to general international law cases (particularly *Mavrommatis*) as well as to other investment law cases.[190] However, in contrast to the long-standing *Mavrommatis* presumption in favour of the exercise of jurisdiction *ratione temporis* in cases of openly formulated jurisdictional clauses, the majority of investment tribunals seems to apply a stricter standard on this issue, meaning that where the treaty text does not clearly stipulate otherwise, preexisting disputes are generally not considered as encompassed by the respective IIA's scope of application, even if the provisions on covered investments and dispute settlement are formulated in a vague and open manner. Whether this

---

[186] James Crawford, 'Investment Arbitration and the ILC Articles on State Responsibility' (2010) 25 *ICSID Review* 127, 128.

[187] Ibid.

[188] Michael Waibel, 'International Investment Law and Treaty Interpretation' in Hofmann and Tams (n 95) 29.

[189] James Crawford, 'International Protection of Foreign Direct Investments: Between Clinical Isolation and Systematic Integration' in Hofmann and Tams, ibid., 17, 22; Voon et al (n 136) 473.

[190] On the relevance of considering both with regard to questions of general international law, see also Schill and Tvede (n 185) 103.

reversal will be carried back into general international law is not certain yet. Still, it is noteworthy that the ICJ in the recent *Application of the Convention on the Prevention and Punishment of the Crime of Genocide* (*Croatia v Serbia*) case refrained from affirming the earlier *Mavrommatis* findings despite Croatia arguing in favour of the presumption of the retroactive effect of compromissory clauses.[191] On the other hand, the stricter approach could also be owed to the specific feature of investment law to create an avenue for investors to initiate proceedings at the international level which would otherwise not exist. Offering such to a sometimes unpredictable number of foreign investors is often the result of a detailed cost-benefit analysis conducted by the state.[192] In contrast, under general international law, there are multiple possibilities available for states to settle their disputes peacefully. One could therefore argue that once a state has selected one of these, a broader interpretation of the consent thereto is warranted.

The spillover from investment law to general international law is clearer yet on the matter of the provisional application of treaties. With gaps in theory still persisting until recently on the question of the legal effect of the provisional application of treaties (art 25 VCLT), the consistent affirmation thereof by investment tribunals has clarified this open point in the affirmative. However, at the same time, the inconsistencies remaining with regard to the interpretation of the ECT's domestic limitation clause has been a ground of caution to reach any meaningful conclusions on the further impact thereof.

---

[191] *Application of the Convention on the Prevention and Punishment of the Crime of Genocide* (*Croatia v Serbia*) [2015] *ICJ Reports* 3, 48, para 92:

> [T]he absence of a temporal limitation in Article IX is not without significance but it is not, in itself, sufficient to establish jurisdiction over that part of Croatia's claim which relates to events said to have occurred before 27 April 1992. Article IX is not a general provision for the settlement of disputes. The jurisdiction for which it provides is limited to disputes between the Contracting Parties regarding the interpretation, application or fulfilment of the substantive provisions of the Genocide Convention, including those relating to the responsibility of a State for genocide or for any of the acts enumerated in Article III of the Convention. Accordingly, the temporal scope of Article IX is necessarily linked to the temporal scope of the other provisions of the Genocide Convention.

Note, however, that as remarked above, in *Case Concerning Application of the Convention on the Prevention and Punishment of the Crime of Genocide* (*Bosnia and Herzegovina v Yugoslavia*) (n 30) 617, para 34, the Court still held that art IX of the Genocide Convention did 'not contain any clause the object or effect of which is limit in such manner the scope of its jurisdiction *ratione temporis*'.

[192] Cf. Andrea J. Menaker, 'What the Explosion of Investor-State Arbitrations May Portend for the Future of BITs' in Catherine A Rogers and Roger P Alford (eds), *The Future of Investment Arbitration* (OUP 2009) 157, 160.

The third temporal dimension – the end of a treaty's lifetime and the legal consequences pertaining thereto – so far does not seem to have been subject to (public) investment proceedings. From the perspective of general international law, the field of investment law could particularly shed light on the topic of third-party rights and whether non-state entities could be considered as such for the purpose of the law of treaties. However, the value for the development of general international law will depend on whether investment arbitrators attempt to follow a more traditional public international law approach or whether they afford special attention to the specific features of investment law. At present it seems that this dimension is least likely to contribute to the development of general international law in the near future.

Overall, it is noteworthy that so far only scarce reference can be found to existing investment case law on the question of the temporal scope of application of treaties. For example, among the three most prominent VCLT commentaries, only two reference investment jurisprudence. Villiger (2009) contains no references to investment jurisprudence with regard to the relevant provisions (arts 25, 28, 37, 54, 70).[193] Corten/Klein (2011) merely makes reference to three cases when discussing the specific features of Article 72 ICSID in an excursive point related to Article 70 VCLT.[194] However, the most recent of the three, Dörr/Schmalenbach's second edition (2018), might demonstrate a trend of growing importance. References to investment case law in order to provide a clearer understanding of certain elements can be found regarding the legal effects of provisional application,[195] the question of conduct taking place prior to the entry into force of a treaty,[196] and the question of the validity of the doctrine of acquired rights.[197]

It therefore seems that with investment practice on the temporal scope of application having significantly grown over the past years, and holding the promise to continue to do so, also as regards so far unanswered questions such as the legal consequences of the mutual termination of sunset clauses, future

---

[193] Mark E. Villiger, *Commentary on the 1969 Vienna Convention on the Law of Treaties* (Brill 2009).

[194] Hervé Ascensio, 'Article 70' in Corten and Klein (n 23) 1585, 1606.

[195] Krieger (n 23) 453–454, referencing *Kardassopoulos v Georgia* (n 109) and *Yukos v Russia* (n 115). It also references the debate on the relationship between ECT (n 16) art 45 and domestic law, however without coming to a final conclusion on the issue.

[196] Kerstin von der Decken, 'Article 28 – Non-Retroactivity of Treaties' in Dörr and Schmalenbach (n 23) 507, 515, notes in reference to case law arising under BITs that a lot of ambiguity and legal uncertainty remains with regard to facts occurring before the entry into force of a treaty. Additionally, case law is resorted to for affirming the principle of non-retroactivity (ibid., 516).

[197] Wittich (n 142) 1294–1296.

arbitral practice will undoubtedly become more relevant, also on general questions of treaty law.

6. Ways out of the marshland: International investment law and the law of state succession

Christian J. Tams[1]

I. INTRODUCTION

Three statements, all taken from the Investment Arbitration Reporter website, provide windows into the issues to be addressed in the following contribution:

> In a dramatic holding, UNCITRAL Tribunal finds that Kazakhstan is bound by terms of former USSR BIT with Canada … as a legal successor.[2]
>
> Kazakhstan fends off claims by Canadian gold miner, as tribunal finds it is not a successor to USSR BIT.[3]
>
> Singapore appeals court restores arbitral finding that [1993] Chinese investment treaty extends to Macau [under] the 'moving treaty frontiers' rule.[4]

These statements offer first glimpses of the object of inquiry, viz. the rules of state succession: an area of law that many (incl. public international lawyers of generalist persuasion) find technical and dry. These first glimpses in turn yield three insights into the debate about the allegedly dry and technical rules of state succession, which are marked by controversy, and have real significance and topicality.

---

[1] The author is grateful to Eleni Methymaki (Oxford) for comments and research assistance.

[2] Luke Eric Peterson, 'In a Dramatic Holding, UNCITRAL Tribunal Finds That Kazakhstan Is Bound by Terms of Former USSR BIT with Canada' (*Investment Arbitration Reporter*, 28 January 2016).

[3] Vladislav Djanic, 'Kazakhstan Fends Off Claims by Canadian Gold Miner, as Tribunal Finds It Is Not a Successor to USSR BIT' (*Investment Arbitration Reporter*, 4 August 2020).

[4] Jarrod Hepburn, 'Singapore Appeals Court Restores Arbitral Finding That Chinese Investment Treaty Extends to Macau' (*Investment Arbitration Reporter*, 2 October 2016).

Controversy: The statements suggest that things are anything but straightforward. As per statements #1 and #2, tribunals seem to disagree on whether Kazakhstan is a successor to a BIT concluded with Canada. By the same token, the reference, in statement #3, to the 'restoration' of an award implies that the award needed restoring, because it had previously been quashed.

Significance: The statements hint at the real significance of findings on succession, which can indeed be 'dramatic'. According to statement #1, as a 'legal successor', Kazakhstan was held to the terms of a treaty agreed between Canada and the Soviet Union, at a time when Kazakhstan was but one of 15 republics making up the Union of Socialist Soviet Republics (USSR). If it binds Kazakhstan, would it also bind the USSR's other successor States? And might the same be true for other BITs that the USSR concluded in its dying days? And if, as statement #3 clarifies, a Chinese BIT entered into in 1993, when Macao was administered by Portugal (and would be for another six years), can be invoked by Macao-based investors — does this open up opportunities for litigation under many of China's other early BITs?

Topicality: And finally, the three statements, released in 2016 and 2020, suggest that succession is a live issue in investment arbitration. Tribunals have engaged with it quite frequently over the course of the past decade. In retrospect, one can say that the intriguing *Sanum* litigation (which prompted statement #3) has started a trend: a trend that has seen investment tribunals not only disagree on the fate of the Canada-Kazakhstan BIT (in the *World Wide Minerals* and *Gold Pool* awards, to which statements #1 and #2 refer), but in a number of other disputes. After decades of neglect, investment tribunals have begun to engage with the law of State succession, and their engagement (selective so far, but significant) has prompted renewed academic discussion.[5]

So what has been the impact of this engagement; how have investment lawyers approached the law of State succession? And what, if anything, can general international lawyers learn from their engagement — can the investment practice on State succession radiate into other areas of international law? These questions are at the heart of the present chapter, which proceeds in two main steps: (i) sections II and III continue the stage-setting just begun. They survey the terrain of State succession, by clarifying what it is that investment tribunals engage with when addressing issues of State succession. (As will be shown, they have entered treacherous terrain, perhaps even a marshland.) (ii) sections IV–VI make up the main part of the chapter. Proceeding from the brief

---

[5] Literature has begun to catch up with this trend and offered commentary. The following discussion notably draws on Patrick Dumberry's detailed study, *A Guide to State Succession in International Investment* Law (Edward Elgar 2018); and the author's earlier article, Christian J. Tams, 'State Succession to Investment Treaties: Mapping the Issues' (2016) 31(2) *ICSID Review* 314.

glimpses offered so far, they provide an analysis of investment law practice on state succession, and indicate how this practice has been (or indeed should be) received. That analysis distinguishes between three distinct questions of state succession, and identifies a number of contributions that investment law has made, or could make, to the general discourse of state succession. Section VII offers concluding thoughts and an outlook on 'radiating effects' past and present.

II. THE SETTING: A MARSHLAND

In assessing potential radiating effects of investment law practice, it is useful to start by surveying the field that is meant to be affected. Is it open to be shaped by contributions from special branches of international law (such as investment law)? Is it in need of clarification? In this respect, the field at stake in the present chapter — the general regime of State succession — is particular. State succession is widely considered a treacherous field, a 'marshland', in the words of Tiyanjana Maluwa, which leaves many an innocent traveller trapped: 'an international lawyer seeking a way out of this marshland is as likely as ever to be led into the centre of the miry bog itself'.[6]

This depiction is perhaps exaggerated. It ignores many rather well-defined paths that run through the marshland. To take but one example, international lawyers are on relatively firm ground when discussing the treatment of territorially grounded and boundary treaties, which are deemed to survive instances of State succession.[7] However, the image of a marshland provides a useful starting-point because (notwithstanding decades of debate and many instances of international practice) significant parts of the State succession terrain are treacherous.[8] The centre in particular has remained boggy: the international community's efforts to reach agreement on a default rule, clarifying whether new States are bound by treaties entered into by their predecessors, have

[6] Tiyanjana Maluwa, 'Succession to Treaties in Post-Independence Africa' (1992) 4 *AJIL* 791, 810. See also Matthew Craven, 'The Problem of State Succession and the Identity of States under International Law' (1998) 9 *EJIL* 142, 143.

[7] In the *Gabčíkovo Nagymaros* case, the International Court of Justice noted (citing the work of the International Law Commission) that '"treaties of a territorial character" [had] been regarded both in traditional doctrine and in modern opinion as unaffected by a succession of States', and held that this approach 'reflects a rule of customary international law': see *Case Concerning the Gabčíkovo-Nagymaros Project (Hungary/Slovakia)* [1997] *ICJ Reports* 7, para 123.

[8] Andreas Zimmermann and James G. Devaney, 'Succession to Treaties and the Inherent Limits of International Law' in Christian J. Tams et al (eds), *Research Handbook on the Law of Treaties* (Edward Elgar 2014) 505–506.

proven protracted and only partially successful.[9] Perhaps unsurprisingly, the law is applied cautiously and tentatively, in a process aptly described as 'diplomatic *bricolage*'[10] which, reflecting the absence of clear normative guidance, tends to be dominated by inter-State negotiations, sometimes with depositary input.

These features of the general regime of State succession affect the interaction between international investment practice and general international law. On the one hand, they complicate the task of investment lawyers. Unlike in other fields — among them aspects of the law of treaties codified in the 1969 Vienna Convention,[11] or the law of international responsibility[12] — investment lawyers cannot simply proceed from a generally accepted legal document, which, while perhaps needing to be adapted, provides an accepted point of

---

[9] There are many reasons for this. In addition to the grounds addressed in the text, there is a widespread feeling that, instances of succession — regularly involving major upheaval and rupture — are simply not suitable for codification. Commentators have notably underlined the exceptional nature of succession, which does not happen every day, but rather in waves, each of which takes place in a different political context, frequently in conflict-ridden environments, and presents distinctive characteristics: see, e.g., Rein Mullerson, 'New Developments in the Former USSR and Yugoslavia' (1992–1993) 33 *Va JIL* 299; Rosalyn Higgins et al, *Oppenheim's International Law: United Nations* (OUP 2017) 294–295; Andreas Zimmermann and James Devaney, 'State Succession in Treaties' (2019) *MPEPIL* para 4 https://opil.ouplaw.com/view/10.1093/law:epil/9780199231690/law-9780199231690-e1109 accessed 9 December 2020.

D.P. O'Connell's influential account reflects this understanding: as he noted in the Preface to *State Succession in Municipal Law and International Law*, international law's:

> content necessarily varies according to diplomatic exigencies, so that while its systematic elaboration is a matter of juristic reasoning its practical content must correspond with the realities of international life and intercourse ... The topic of State succession illustrates this interaction perhaps more clearly than any other in the corpus of international law.

Daniel P. O'Connell, *State Succession in Municipal Law and International Law*, vol 1 (CUP 1967) v. 12 years later, having followed long-standing attempts at treaty-making, O'Connell's views had hardened considerably; in his final publication, he considered State succession to be 'a subject altogether unsuited to the processes of codification, let alone of progressive development': see Daniel P. O'Connell, 'Reflections on the State Succession Convention' (1979) 39 *ZaöRV* 725, 739.

[10] Martti Koskenniemi, 'State Succession: Codification Tested Against the Facts' in Pierre-Michel Eisemann and Martti Koskenniemi (eds), *La succession d'Etats: la codification à l' épreuve des faits* (Martinus Nijhoff 1997) 89, 167–168.

[11] Vienna Convention on the Law of Treaties (VCLT) (adopted 23 May 1969, entered into force 27 January 1980) 1155 UNTS 331.

[12] See ILC, Draft Articles on Responsibility of States for Internationally Wrongful Acts, with commentaries (2001) II(2) *ILC Yearbook* 31.

reference. (As will be shown, there is a major document — the 1978 Vienna Convention on Succession of States in respect of Treaties,[13] but it is not generally accepted, at least not in its entirety.) When engaging with State succession, investment lawyers may sometime be on firm ground — but quite often, they need to navigate 'miry bogs'.[14] At the same time, the absence of an agreed framework of reference could very well increase the impact of investment law practice. Precisely because important aspects of the general regime of State succession are uncertain, solutions found within a special field of international law, such as investment law, might very well 'radiate'. To put things bluntly, many general international lawyers, frustrated by long-standing disagreements, would presumably be rather happy for investment lawyers to lead them out of the boggy areas of State succession.

All this presumes too much, though. Before assessing potential impacts of investment practices, it is necessary to survey the general regime in more detail, beyond the first glimpses offered so far. This is done in the subsequent section, which highlights key choices shaping the law of State succession and identifies the most pressing issues arising within it.

III. THE CONTEXT: STATE SUCCESSION TO TREATIES — KEY NOTIONS AND CHOICES

A. Succession

State succession is a curious field that combines fundamental premises of international law with a high degree of technicality. There is agreement on a rather abstract definition of the term 'succession'. The 1978 Vienna Convention on Succession of States in respect of Treaties (VCSST) defines it as 'the replacement of one State by another in the responsibility for the international relations of territory'.[15] (In slightly less convoluted terms, this has been

---

13 Vienna Convention on Succession of States in respect of Treaties (VCSST) (adopted 23 August 1978, entered into force 6 November 1996) 1946 UNTS 3. The most detailed guide to the Convention is Giovanni Distefano et al, *La convention de Vienne de 1978 sur la succession d'États en matière de traités: Commentaire article par article et études thématique* (Bruylant 2016).

14 Maluwa (n 6) 810.

15 VCSST (n 13) art 2. The same approach was followed in the subsequent Vienna Convention on Succession of States in Respect of State Property, Archives and Debts (adopted 8 April 1983, not yet entered into force) (1983) 22 *ILM* 306. The use of terminology can be confusing: 'succession' is used to describe the process of such replacement, but also the legal consequences occurring therefrom. It is important to note that even if a State 'replaces another in the responsibility for the international relations of territory', this does not prejudge the question whether it actually succeeded to rights

put as 'the definitive replacement of one State by another in respect of sovereignty over a given territory'.)[16]Such replacements — involving a predecessor State and a successor State — raise a number of questions: for example, there is a need to address the post-succession rules that apply to predecessor State's property and debts, to responsibility it may have occurred previously, or to the nationality of citizens.[17] However, the field has been shaped by discussion about succession to treaties.

The definition of succession is not only technical, but also quite broad, for there are a number of scenarios that involve one State's replacement by another in respect of sovereignty.[18] New States can gain independence (as happened during decolonisation), existing States can dissolve or separate (as happened with the former Soviet Union or Czechoslovakia), States can merge (Yemen) or one can be incorporated into another (Germany), and territory can change hands between existing States (under peace treaties, or more recently in relation to Hong Kong, Macao or Walvis bay). However, the definition is strict in two other respects, namely by requiring that the predecessor State has to be definitely replaced by the successor State, and that this replacement has to occur in conformity with international law. Both aspects help delineate the scope of the inquiry (section III.B), and have informed attempts at codification (section III.C).

B. Delineations

Many instances of State succession involve ruptures in the organisation of the State concerned. The two cases involving Kazakhstan mentioned in the introductory section illustrate this: the rupture of 1991 — the break-up of the Soviet Union and the emergence of the Republic of Kazakhstan — clearly implicated

---

and obligations of that other State's treaties. In this sense, James Crawford rightly notes that the term is used 'to describe an area … it does not connote any overriding principle, or even a presumption, that a transmission or succession of legal rights and duties occurs in a given case': James Crawford, *Brownlie's Principles of Public International Law* (9th edn, OUP 2019) 409.

[16] Ibid.

[17] These have been the subject of various attempts at codification and clarification: see notably the Vienna Convention on Succession of States in respect of State Property, Archives and Debts (n 15); and the ILC, 'Draft Articles on Nationality of Natural Persons in Relation to the Succession of States' (2000) UN Doc A/Res/55/153, Annex.

[18] For a succinct survey, see Zimmermann and Devaney (n 9) paras 8–14; Gerhard Hafner and Gregor Novak, 'State Succession in Respect of Treaty Relationships' in Duncan Hollis (ed), *The Oxford Guide to Treaties* (2nd edn, OUP 2020) 390–393; Detlev Vagts, 'State Succession: The Codifier's View' (1992–1993) 33 *Va JIL* 275, 285–289.

the rules of State succession. Similar points could be made with respect to the examples of Germany, Yemen, Czechoslovakia and the many instances of decolonisation that reshaped the international system from the 1950s onwards. However, importantly, not all ruptures qualify as State succession, even where they shake the foundations of States. The key concern of the law of State succession is with the legal personality of the State; and with changes to it that occur in accordance with international law. In three respects, this helps keep succession apart from other ruptures.

The first point is straightforward. Changes to a State's internal governance, such as revolutions or momentous changes of government, are not a case of succession, even though they might have dramatic effects on a State's approach to international treaty relations.[19] In this respect, the international community, mindful of preserving the stability of international treaties, has insisted on the principle of continuity: regime changes and revolutions are considered not to affect the legal personality of a State.[20]

The second point is not as straightforward. Not all changes to the territorial reach of a State qualify as succession; even if territorially diminished or extended, a State can continue as the same subject of international law.[21] The key task is to distinguish instances of State identity from State succession. Did Germany post-1945 continue the identity to the defeated Reich — and if so, which Germany? Could Serbia and Montenegro, following the independence of Croatia, Slovenia et al. and the ensuing war of separation, claim to be the same legal subject, as the former Yugoslavia? Did the Russian Federation replace the former Soviet Union in relation to the bulk of former Soviet territory, or did it continue the Soviet Union's personality, territorial reduced? These questions eschew a simple answer; and the international community's preferred approach (often reached after protracted discussion) has been case-by-case, reflecting the views of the potential successor/continuator State, as well as objective factors such as the significance of lost territory or popula-

---

19 O'Connell, 'State Succession' (n 9) 5; Vagts (n 18) 281–282; Andreas Zimmermann, 'Continuity of States' (2006) *MPEPIL* para 9 https://opil.ouplaw.com/view/10.1093/law:epil/9780199231690/law-9780199231690-e1389 accessed 10 December 2020; Crawford (n 15) 413.

20 See Tams (n 5) 320. To illustrate, for the purposes of treaty relations, Cuba remained Cuba notwithstanding the revolution of 1958; and treaties entered into by pre-revolutionary Cuban governments continued to apply to post-revolutionary Cuba. Adjustments to treaty relations were to be pursued through a process of renegotiation rather than the operation of the laws of State succession.

21 For commment on the instances mentioned in the text see Brigitte Stern, 'La succession d'Etats' (1996) 262 *Recueil des cours* 9, 68–82; Mullerson (n 9) 303–305; Higgins et al (n 9) 298–299; Zimmermann and Devaney (n 8) 513–515.

tion.[22] In practice, the line between continuity/identity and succession/replacement has often been fine, perhaps it is indeed 'precarious'.[23] The starting-point is agreed, though: no succession without change of personality.[24]

Finally, there is the question of illegal transfers of territory, or rather, adapting the words of Article 6 of the 1978 Convention: the replacement of States that does not occur 'in conformity with international law'. On this, the law was long held to be settled. If responsibility over territory changed unlawfully, this was to be addressed through a separate set of rules, not the law of State succession.[25] In fact, rules prohibiting the forcible annexation of territory (and the recognition of its effects) are meant to preclude a transfer of sovereignty (which the law of succession recognises).[26] The regime of belligerent occupation seeks to strike a balance between pragmatism (recognising some power of the occupant) and principle (precluding incorporation and steps towards it) — but this balancing assumes the continued sovereignty of the occupied State, not a replacement.[27] All this is worth reiterating firmly as scholars recently have begun to explore the potential application of the law of State succession to a particular controversial instance of annexation, viz.

---

[22] The conventional wisdom suggests the following responses to the questions raised in the text: Russia continues the USSR's legal personality (incl. its permanent Security Council membership); united Germany is the same subject of international law as the Federal Republic of Germany; Serbia and Montenegro succeeded to the former Yugoslavia. See Hafner and Novak (n 18) 397–398, 401 403; Crawford (n 15) 413–414, noting, in relation to the twists and turns of Yugoslavia's case, that '[i]t is difficult to give legal articulation to these episodes'.

[23] Crawford (n 15) 413.

[24] Ibid., 'fundamental distinction'; Zimmermann and Devaney (n 9) para 1; Zimmermann, 'Continuity' (n 19) paras 13–14.

[25] According to its Art 6, the VCSST (n 13); applies only to the effects of a succession of States occurring in conformity with international law and, in particular, the principles of international law embodied in the Charter of the United Nations'. The Convention's Preamble emphasises that 'respect for the territorial integrity and political independence of any State is required by the Charter of the United Nations'.

[26] This is the essence of the Stimson doctrine (LNOJ, Special Supplement 101 (1932) 87–88), as reflected in ILC's Articles on State Responsibility (n 12) Art 41(2) and the ICJ's opinion on *Legal Consequences of the Construction of a Wall in the Occupied Palestinian Territory* (Advisory Opinion) [2004] *ICJ Reports* 136, para 159. See further Rainer Hofmann, 'Annexation' (2020) *MPEPIL* https://opil.ouplaw.com/view/10.1093/law:epil/9780199231690/law-9780199231690-e1376?print=pdf accessed 10 December 2020; Hafner and Novak (n 18) 387.

[27] See Zimmermann (n 19) para 10; Crawford (n 15) 409. See also VCSST (n 13) Art 40, according to which '[t]he provisions of the ... Convention shall not prejudge any question that may arise in regard to a treaty from the military occupation of a territory'.

Crimea.[28] Judging from the publicly available information, these attempts have not so far succeeded; instead tribunals seem to have preferred to argue on the basis of the terms of the applicable treaties, and more specifically the clauses addressing their territorial scope.[29] For investment disputes, this may require some creative argument,[30] but it seems preferable to an approach that discards the firm (and hitherto settled) 'essential distinction'[31] between succession and unlawful territorial changes.

C. The Regime Governing State Succession: A Codification Attempt and Its Fate

The preceding sections map out the contours of State succession as a concept; it remains to outline key feature of the applicable legal rules. This is best done by juxtaposing two competing approaches, and then trace their fate in the most prominent codification attempt, viz. the decade-long negotiations within

---

[28] See, e.g., Daniel Costelloe, 'Treaty Succession in Annexed Territory' (2016) 65 *ICLQ* 343; Odysseas G. Repousis and James Fry, 'Armed Conflict and State Succession in Investor State Arbitration' (2016) 22 *Colum J Eur L* 421; Oddysseas G. Repousis, 'Why Russian Investment Treaties Could Apply to Crimea and What Would this Mean for the Ongoing Russo-Ukrainian Territorial Conflict' (32) 2016 *Arb Int'l* 459. To date, there are at least eight known cases filed by Crimean-based investors against Russia under the Ukraine-Russia BIT and the UNCITRAL Arbitration Rules of 1976. See Advandazy, 'Arbitration Claims by Ukrainian Investors under the Russia-Ukraine BIT: between Crimea and a Hard Place?' (*CIS Arbitration Forum*, 17 February 2016) www.cisarbitration.com/2016/02/17/arbitration-claims-by-ukrainian-investors-under-the-russia-ukraine-bit-between-crimea-and-a-hard-place/ accessed 10 December 2020; Alison Ross, 'Crimea Cases against Russia to Proceed' (*Global Arbitration Review*, 9 March 2017).

[29] Although the decisions on jurisdiction and admissibility are not to date available, parts of the reasoning of the tribunal in the *Everest Estate LLC* has been made public: see Jarrod Hepburn, 'Investigation: Full Jurisdictional Reasoning Comes to Light in Crimea-Related BIT Arbitrations vs Russia' (*Investment Arbitration Reporter*, 9 November 2017).

[30] In *Everest Estate LLC,* the tribunal, e.g., seemed to be persuaded by the argument that — whether Russian or Ukrainian, Crimea was covered by the Russia-Ukraine BIT 'one way or another'. On that basis, it looked primarily at the timing of the investment and found that the BIT indeed applied to investments made in Crimea before the Russian annexation. In *Russian Federation v Ukrnafta,* the Swiss Federal Tribunal, upheld one of the arbitral awards sought by Ukrainian investors by applying the 'moving treaty frontiers rule' to the Russia-Ukraine BIT: see First Civil Law Court, Russian Federation v PJSC Ukrnafta (16 October 2018) 4A_396/2017, 8. Dumberry is rightly cautious: Patrick Dumberry, 'Requiem for Crimea: Why Tribunals Should Have Declined Jurisdiction over the Claims of Ukrainian Investors against Russia under the Ukraine-Russia BIT' (2018) 9 *JIDS* 506.

[31] Gloria Gaggioli, 'Article 6' in Distefano et al (n 13) 206, '*distinction essentielle*'.

the UN International Law Commission, resulting in the adoption of the 1978 Vienna Convention.

These two competing approaches, often portrayed as binaries,[32] are referred to as 'universal succession' and 'clean slate'.[33] Proponents of the former proceed from the need for stability in international treaty relations, and the interest of treaty partners in it: stability in turn requires treaties, as a default rule, to continue throughout the ruptures of succession. The clean slate principle, by contrast, emphasises sovereignty and State consent; put simplistically, it suggests that a new legal subject cannot be born 'with shackles'. This position has found firm support where the emergence of a new State could with some plausibility be described as a freeing from shackles, with decolonisation a case in point.[34] Both approaches — universal succession versus clean slate — mark absolute positions that describe starting-points for a more nuanced discourse. Unsurprisingly, international practice regarding succession has often been equivocal; and has sought to strike a balance between the competing approaches.[35]

This is true for the most important attempt at codification, the 1978 Vienna Convention — even though in retrospect, it is difficult to dispute that the drafters of this Convention got the balance wrong. Drafted at a time when the events of decolonisation were still fresh, the Convention emphasised the importance for newly-independent States to start life with a clean slate. It did however define 'newly independent State' in a particular manner, viz. as a State that, prior to independence, had been 'a dependent territory for the international relations of which the predecessor State was responsible'.[36] By contrast, for States that were not 'newly-independent', the 1978 Convention emphasised treaty stability: hence Article 34 enshrined the principle of universal succession as a default rule, and it did so for a instances of separation/secession as well as the dissolution of States, and for bilateral as well as multilateral treaties.[37] Where territory changes hands between existing States, Article 15

[32] See also Craven (n 6) 143, 'almost total doctrinal schism'.

[33] Zimmermann and Devaney (n 9) para 5; Hafner and Novak (n 18) 388–389.

[34] Zimmermann and Devaney (n 9) para 5; Zimmermann and Devaney (n 8) 516–8.

[35] Hafner and Novak (n 18) 389 ('more sophisticated and more complex rules'); Zimmermann and Devaney (n 8) 518.

[36] VCSST (n 13) Art 16. For a detailed assessment, see Etienne Henry, 'Article 16' in Distefano et al (n 13) 561; for criticism of the distinction between "newly-independent" and other new States, Crawford (n 15) 411, 423–424. For context, see Arman Sarvarian, 'Codifying the Law of State Succession: A Futile Endeavour?' (2016) 27 *EJIL* 789.

[37] VCSST (n 13), Art 34(1) states the 'default rule' of automatic succession, whereas according to Art 34(2) automatic succession does not apply in case that 'the States concerned agree otherwise' (a) or 'it appears from the treaty or is otherwise established that the application of the treaty in respect of the successor State would be

stipulated that the treaty geographical scope would adjust to fit with the States' new territorial scope under the so-called 'moving frontiers' principle.

Cutting across this crucial distinction, the Convention put forward a number of special rules for special treaties. These included provisions providing for the continued application, for all States including for newly-independent States, of territorial and boundary treaties;[38] and a 'without prejudice' clause according to which succession to membership rights within international organisations would primarily be a matter for the institutional regime of that organisation.[39] Lastly, the 1978 Convention offered guidance on the value of certain types of evidence that could reflect the views of States involved in succession. In this respect, it adopted a cautious approach, emphasising that neither statements in a declaration of independence, or in devolution agreements, could be taken to reflect an agreement about how to handle succession issues.[40]

All this made for an ambitious attempt at codification, but not necessarily a successful one. Adopted in 1978, the Convention was slow to attract ratifications, and did not yet apply as treaty law during the wave of successions of the early 1990s. Having finally entered into force in 1996, it is binding today on no more than 23 parties.[41] What is more, unlike with other codification attempts, this low figure cannot simply be taken to reflect inertia — a significant number of States have made clear that they disagreed with aspects of the Convention's regime and preferred to seek pragmatic solutions.[42] This should not be portrayed as a wholesale rejection, as many provisions of the 1978 Convention are broadly accepted and reflect customary international law. However, unlike with respect to other regulatory framework setting out basic rules of general international law, it means that their customary status cannot simply be taken for granted, but needs to be evaluated on an issue-by-issue (or provision-by-provision) basis.

---

incompatible with the object and purpose of the treaty or would radically change the conditions for its operation' (b).

38 VCSST, ibid., Arts 11 and 12. See also Zimmermann and Devaney (n 8) 532–533; Hafner and Novak (n 18) 405–406; *Gabčíkovo-Nagymaros Project* (n 7) para 123.

39 VCSST (n 13), Art 4; and see Section V below.

40 See VCSST, ibid., Arts 8, 9.

41 For details see the information provided in 'Vienna Convention on Succession of States in Respect of Treaties' (*United Nations Treaty Collection*) https://treaties.un.org/Pages/ViewDetails.aspx?src=IND&mtdsg_no=XXIII-2&chapter=23&lang=en accessed 10 December 2021.

42 Matthew Craven, The *Decolonization of International Law. State Succession and the Law of Treaties* (OUP 2007) 15–16 and 29ff; Zimmermann and Devaney (n 8) 508–509; Vagts (n 18) 295.

The subsequent discussion will not assess each and every such provision nor issue. It does not need to, because important aspects of the general regime have not really become relevant in investment practice. To illustrate, the fundamental distinction between newly-independent States and other new States has not become a major issue, for the simple reason that investment agreements of the contemporary era postdate decolonisation;[43] similarly, the particular rules governing territorial treaties have limited relevance for agreement that define investments comprehensively.[44]

In essence, investment practice has engaged with three aspects of the general regime of State succession, which can be put in the form of three straightforward questions:

The first of these is by far the most important: Are new States bound by BITs (or other IIAs) concluded by their predecessors? The two other questions are not of the same practical significance, but offer useful insights as well: Do new States succeed to ICSID membership if their predecessors were members? And what is the impact of cessions on the territorial scope of IIAs?

The subsequent sections address these issues in turn, assessing how investment practice engaged with the general regime, and commenting on the potential impact of their engagement.

IV. NEW STATES AND OLD BITS

Whether old BITs continue to bind new States emerging from processes of State succession is the most relevant question in practice. It has regularly arisen since the 1990s, i.e., in successions that affected predecessor States with BIT policies, and has become more acute as more and more States joined the rapidly expanding BIT network during the 1990s and 2000s. The potential for disagreement on this point is considerable, as every recent instance of State succession implicates a host of prior BITs, and as the number of prior BITs has grown considerably. To illustrate, the fate of seven BITs was at stake when the USSR broke up in 1991: these continued to apply to Russia as a continuator, but perhaps also to the USSR's successor States.[45] When the former Czechoslovakia was replaced by the Czech and Slovak Republics in 1993 16

---

[43] The same cannot be said of all investment contracts: for a helpful analysis see Dumberry (n 4) Chapters 10-14.

[44] Treaties regulating particular types of investment projects could certainly have a territorial component - one need only think of infrastructure projects or geographically defined regimes. However, to the author's knowledge, such treaties have not so far become the subject of succession disputes.

[45] While the number of seven BITs may seem small, in light of the jurisdictional award in the *WWM v Kazakhstan* case (referred to in n 1 above), the seven BITs might

BITs were implicated.[46] At the time South Sudan emerged as an independent State in 2011, its predecessor State, the Republic of Sudan in 2011, was bound by 21 BITs.[47] Finally, Yugoslavia's serial permutations provides a vivid illustration of the increasing relevance of State succession to BITs: The dissolution of SFRY in 1992–1993 cast doubt on the fate of seven BITs then in force for the Socialist Federal Republic of Yugoslavia; by the time Montenegro became independent in 2006, the (then) Republic of Serbia and Montenegro as the predecessor was bound by 33 BITs; by the time Kosovo unilaterally declared its independence in 2008, the number had grown to 40.[48]

So how are such issues to be addressed under the general regime of State succession? And how have investment lawyers approached them? To these questions I now turn.

A. The General Regime

The general regime is, to say the least, uncertain: this indeed is the 'centre of the miry bog'.[49] It is miry because the relatively straightforward approach in favour of universal, automatic succession adopted in Article 34 of the 1978 Vienna Convention (briefly referred to in section III.3 above) has met with scepticism. This scepticism has led States to adopt a 'hands-on' approach to succession, and it has moved debates away from one overarching rule putatively applicable to all treaties, which is said to have been one factor explaining the Convention's poor ratification record.

As regards the former aspect, rather than relying on the operation of one overarching rule, States have sought actively to determine the fate of 'their' treaty rights and obligations post-independence. Inter-State agreements between successor States and the predecessor's treaty partners have been the preferred method of bringing about clarity. Interestingly, the 'hands on' approach adopted by many States has typically led to the outcome that Article 34 envisaged, viz. the continued application of treaties to successor States.

conceivably apply to Russia, the USSR's eleven successor States, and perhaps even the 3 Baltic republics.

[46] See the information available at UNCTAD, Investment Policy Hub, 'Czechia' (*UNCTAD)*) https://investmentpolicy.unctad.org/international-investment-agreements/countries/55/czechia accessed 10 December 2020.

[47] See the information available at UNCTAD, Investment Policy Hub, 'Serbia' (*UNCTAD)* https://investmentpolicy.unctad.org/international-investment-agreements/countries/187/serbia accessed 10 December 2020.

[48] See the information available at UNCTAD, Investment Policy Hub, 'Sudan' (*UNCTAD)* https://investmentpolicy.unctad.org/international-investment-agreements/countries/199/sudan accessed 10 December 2020.

[49] Maluwa (n 6) 810.

In its Report on Aspects of the Law of State Succession, a Committee of the International Law Association captured both trends when noting, in 2002, that 'la pratique de la négociation prévaut concernant la succession en matière de traités', while 'la présomption de la continuité est la prémisse fondamentale en matière de succession d'Etats—afin de sauvegarder la stabilité des relations internationals'.[50] Somewhat mysteriously, the Report concluded by describing that as a general rule, States facing questions of succession sought to solve them through negotiation, on the basis of the principle of continuity, modulated by its exceptions.[51]

Given the dominance of inter-State negotiations, it may indeed be said that the law of State succession in practice has moved from 'substance to procedure' (or 'process').[52] The trend towards process, while understandable, further complicates the search for general principles. Inter-State agreements no doubt clarify the status of particular treaties, but they have left the general regime in a state of flux: outside party agreement on the continuity (or dis- continuity) of a given treaty, there is a rather large grey zone of uncertainty.[53]

Practice and debates over the past two decades can perhaps be read as an attempt to come to terms with this uncertainty. They reflect a move towards nuance and flexibility. The straightforward approach of Article 34 — envisaging automatic succession as a general default rule — seems to have been abandoned: few today would argue that international practice reflected such a rule for all treaties.[54] However, there is significant support for a more nuanced view pursuant to which new States automatically succeed to particular important treaties, notably where these enshrine rights of individuals. From the mid-1990s onwards there has been a recurrent argument that new States, at the very least, are automatically bound by universal human rights and humani-

---

[50] Committee on Aspects of the Law State Succession, 'Rapport final sur la succession en matière de traités' in International Law Association Report of the Seventieth Conference (New Delhi 2002) 22 www.ila-hq.org/index.php/committees accessed 12 December 2021.

[51] Ibid. (authors' translation); see also Committee on Aspects of the Law of State Succession, 'Conclusions on Aspects of the Law on State Succession' (73rd Conference of the International Law Association, Rio de Janeiro 17–21 August 2008) Res 3/2008, Annex, Conclusion 8.

[52] Martti Koskenniemi, 'Report of the Director of Studies of the English-Speaking Section of the Centre' in Eisemann and Koskenniemi (n 10) 65, 132.

[53] Cf. Pierre M. Eisemann, 'Rapport du Directeur de la section de langue française du Centre' in Eisemann and Koskenniemi (n 10) 50–52, arguing that 'confirmatory gestures would inevitably be required in order to determine the status of bilateral treaties' (translation by the author).

[54] For a comprehensive analysis, which offers nuance rather than dismissing the Vienna Convention's preference for succession, see Václav Mikulka, 'Article 34' in Distefano et al (n 13) 1153.

tarian treaties entered into by their predecessors, as rights vested in individuals could not be taken away by a change in the State's personality.[55] The practice of both successor States human rights treaty bodies indicate at least a trend towards continuity in what has been referred to as 'world order' treaties.[56] Whether this trend has hardened into a binding rule remains doubtful though;[57] and cautious voices inevitably note that, in 1996, the ICJ did not endorse the principle of automatic succession in a case turning on the most fundamental of treaties, the Genocide Convention.[58]

In all this, it is important to note that the debate has centred on multilateral treaties. Bilateral treaties, by contrast, have received less attention, and to the extent that they have been addressed, many commentators presented them as reflecting an individual bargain, in which the views of parties are crucial; this in turn has weakened arguments for automatic succession. According to Brigitte Stern, for example, '[l]es traités bilatéraux semblent ne jamais avoir été considérés comme continuant automatiquement à s'appliquer'.[59]

---

[55] *Pars pro toto*, see Human Rights Committee, CCPR, 'General Comment No 26: Continuity of Obligations' (8 December 1997) UN Doc CCPR /C/21/Rev.1/Add.8/Rev.1, para 4, stating that protection under human rights treaties 'devolves with territory and continues to belong to [the beneficiaries], notwithstanding change in government of the State party, including dismemberment in more than one State or State succession'; similarly *Bijelic v Montenegro and Serbia*, App no 19890/05 (ECHR, 11 June 2009) para 69. For much more on this, see Menno T. Kamminga, 'State Succession in Respect of Human Rights Treaties' (1996) 7 *EJIL* 469; Matthew Craven, 'The *Genocide* Case, the Law of Treaties and State Succession' (1997) 68 *BYIL* 127; Oscar Schachter, 'State Succession: The One and Future Law' (1992–1993) 33 *Va JIL* 253, 259. Much earlier Jenks had argued that the clean slate theory cannot be applied in respect of treaties of a law-making character and those that have a particular impact on the rights of individuals, such as the International Labour Conventions, see Wilfred Jenks, 'State Succession in Respect of Law-Making Treaties' (1952) 29 *BYIL* 105.

[56] See Craven, ibid., 158–159 and references in the last footnote.

[57] For a more 'sober' analysis, see Akbar Rasulov, 'Revisiting State Succession to Humanitarian Treaties: Is There a Case for Automaticity?' (2003) 14 *EJIL* 141; also Hafner and Novak (n 18) 407–409.

[58] *Case Concerning Application of the Convention on the Prevention and Punishment of the Crime of Genocide* [1996] *ICJ Reports* 595, para 23. Judges Weeramantry and Shahabuddeen disagreed: see ibid., 634 and 640ff.

[59] Stern (n 21) 315; and see further Patrick Dumberry, 'State Succession to Bilateral Treaties: A Few Observations on the Incoherent and Unjustifiable Solution Adopted for Secession and Dissolution of States under the 1978 Vienna Convention' (2015) 28 *LJIL* 13; Alexandre Genest, 'Sudan Bilateral Investment Treaties and South Sudan: Musings on State Succession to Bilateral Treaties in the Wake of Yugoslavia's Breakup' (2014) *TDM* 3. Under the VCSST (n 13), bilateral treaties would typically be covered by the general rules, e.g., Art 34 or Art 12. For newly independent States, the Convention does envisage a relatively flexible regime, under which the parties can expressly or by impli-

B. The Impact of Investment Practice

Investment lawyers have had to deal with questions of succession to BITs since the early 1990s, but only in the recent past has the issue become more acute. Two forms of engagement with the regime of State succession can be distinguished:

The first is a confirmation of the general approach to state succession. In line with the ambivalent trends captured in the ILA Committee Report,[60] investment treaty practice reflects a move towards 'process' and negotiation, and at the same time underlines the importance of treaty stability. Successor States and their treaty partners have regularly clarified the fate of BITs by entering into explicit agreements listing treaties that continue to apply, and those that do not. In the clear majority of instances, such lists envisage the continued application of prior BITs in relation to the successor State. To illustrate, the Czech Republic, over time, agreed on the continued application of 14 of the CSSR's 16 BITs; with the remaining two treaty partners, it entered into new agreements.[61] In a considerable number of proceedings, arbitral tribunals have given effect to the treaty parties' intentions, typically in no more than a few lines, and at times without even noting that succession had been agreed.[62]

As is clear from the examples mentioned in the Introduction, not all investment disputes could be resolved so easily. Not all States have been as diligent as the Czech Republic in clarifying the fate of 'their' BITs — and not all treaty partners have been as willing to go along with such clarification. In a relevant number of arbitral proceedings, investors have begun to 'test' the regime. They have done so by initiating proceedings against successor State on the basis of BITs concluded by their predecessors (and not yet addressed in negotiations). Should these BITs continue to apply even in the absence of an explicit inter-party agreement? Responses given by investment tribunals mark the second, more recent, phase of engaging the general regime. This engagement is on-going[63] and, as highlighted by the short references to the

---

cation decide to keep the treaty in force: see VCSST (n 13) Art 24 and further VCSST, ibid., Art 28 for the case of provisional application.

60 ILA (n 50) 50.

61 Tams (n 5) 330–331; Dumberry (n 5) paras 3.10–3.13.

62 See, e.g., *Ronald S Lauder v Czech Republic*, UNCITRAL, Final Award (3 September 2001) paras 2 and 10; and for much more, Dumberry, *A Guide to State Succession* (n 5) paras 6.08–6.15.

63 As if to prove the point, the High Court of Justice of England and Wales, following the completion of this chapter, rendered judgment in the case of *Gold Pool JV Ltd v Republic of Kazakhstan, PCA Case No. 2016-23* [2021] EWHC 3422. In the judgment of 15 December 2021, Baker J decided to set aside the earlier *Gold Pool* arbitral award dated 30 July 2020 pursuant to s. 67 Arbitration Act 1996. Contrary to the arbitral tri-

Gold Pool and *World Wide Minerals* cases offered at the start of this chapter, seems to produce results that are difficult to reconcile. However, this is not the only problem affecting the analysis. More immediately, such analysis is complicated by the fact that the three most relevant awards (the two ones just mentioned, plus *Deripaska v Montenegro*) have not been published in full. Drawing on publicly available summaries of the case-law, the subsequent discussion has to remain tentative.[64] But three points can be made:

First, based on the available information, tribunals seem to have shown relatively little appetite to get drawn into abstract discussions about the nature of bilateral investment treaties, and how this would affect succession. Their reasoning avoids conceptual arguments at times advanced by commentators, who have asked questions such as: Should BITs be viewed as bilateral 'inter-party bargains' that because of their bilateral nature simply cannot continue in force for new States?[65] Or should the focus, by contrast, be on the quasi-multilateral nature of the web of investment treaties which, akin to human rights treaties, benefits third parties (which might support, as it seems to have for human rights treaties, an argument for continuity)?[66] Tribunals so far seem to have preferred to argue on narrower, factual grounds, avoiding the grand schisms. However, the *Deripaska* award offers one important clarification. Based on its analysis of succession practice, the tribunal saw no support for a theory of automatic succession to BITs: according to a passage of the award quoted in the Investment Arbitration Reporter summary, States do not seem to 'proceed from a generally shared expectation of automaticity'.[67] In the absence of such practice, automaticity could not simply be deduced from the perceived nature of BITs.

Second, tribunals have been serious in exploring contextual factors which could help identify the intention of parties. Judging from the available sum-

---

bunal, Baker J held that the arbitrators did have jurisdiction *ratione voluntatis* to hear the claims; as a result, the case was remitted to the arbitrators to deal with the substantive claims on the merits.

[64] There is a further reason for the present author to put matters tentatively: following a completion of a first draft of this chapter, he became involved, as an expert, in the proceedings in *Oleg Deripaska v Republic of Montenegro* (PCA Case No 2017-07).

[65] See, e.g., Patrick Dumberry, 'An Uncharted Question of State Succession: Are New States Automatically Bound by the BITs Concluded by Predecessor States before Independence?' (2015) 6 *JIDS* 74; Dumberry (n 59) 13; Genest (n 59) 9–12.

[66] For hints in this direction, see Zimmermann and Devaney (n 9) paras 19–20; Tams (n 5) 334–336; Vagts (n 18) 281.

[67] See Vladislav Djanic, 'Revealed: Reasons Surface for Tribunal's Decision That Montenegro Was Not Bound by the Russia-Yugoslavia BIT' (*Investment Arbitration Reporter*, 3 July 2020).

maries, they have looked at a broad range of materials and drawn from them support for or against succession, including the following:

- treaty databases of an official or private nature, in which a controversial BIT may or may not have been listed;[68]
- references to the controversial BIT in subsequent treaties;[69]
- statements by State parties to the controversial BIT;[70]
- the practice of the successor State (and its partner) in addressing the fate of other treaties;[71]
- statements made in the context of the successor State's move to independence, e.g., pledges to respect international obligations,[72] which indeed can provide a 'rich source of data on the law on succession'.[73]

While this list is not exhaustive, it indicates the level of detail and granularity of investment awards seeking to make address the question of succession to BITs.

Third, implicit in all this is a focus on succession by conduct, or by tacit agreement, which at least marks a shift of emphasis. Whereas the general debate about succession had emphasised formal processes of addressing succession (notably through inter-State negotiations and treaty inventories), recent investment awards explore a much wider range of evidentiary materials. This is not to say that tribunals have lightly accepted succession by conduct: the parties' tacit agreement needs to be established carefully, and is certainly

---

68 Djanic (n 67).

69 For example, in the context of the *World Wide Minerals* and *Gold Pool cases,* commentators have referred to the Preamble to the 1997 Trade Agreement between the Government of Canada and the Government of the Republic of Kazakhstan, which mentioned the Canada-USSR BIT: see Baro Huelmo, 'Is Kazakhstan a State Successor to the USSR? A Perspective from Investment Treaty Arbitration' (2018) 36(2) *ASA Bulletin* 295, 309; Luke Eric Peterson, 'After Failure of Claim Under Kazakh Statute, Canadian Miner Hopes That USSR-Canada Investment Treaty Permits Arbitration with Kazakhstan' (*Investment Arbitration Reporter*, 18 December 2013) 1.

70 Peterson (n 2); Djanic (n 67) 7–8; Djanic (n 3) 1.

71 Djanic (n 67) 7–8; Peterson (n 68) 1; as well as Ministry of Justice (Kazakhstan), 'The Republic of Kazakhstan won a multimillion arbitration brought by Canadian company "Gold Pool"' (Press Release, 3 August 2020) https://www.gov.kz/memleket/entities/adilet/press/news/details/respublika-kazahstan-vyigrala-mnogomilionnyy-arbitrazhnyy-process-protiv-kanadskoy-kompanii-gold-pool-arbitrazhnyy-tribunal-podtverzhdaet-chto-kazahstan-ne-svyazan-sovetskim-soglasheniem?lang=en accessed 3 December 2021.

72 Djanic (n 66) 3.

73 Cf. Tai-Heng Cheng, *State Succession and Commercial Obligations* (Transnational Publishers 2006) 262, referring to devolution agreements and statements made in the run-up to independence.

not the rule. However, tribunals have clearly considered succession by conduct to be an option. And perhaps one could say that in their willingness to engage with a wide range of materials, the recent investment practice marks a return to the non-formalist practice of the decolonisation era in which succession was often considered to have been effected by conduct — and when a leading commentator would observe that '[s]o far as the case of bilateral treaties is concerned, ... States can agree, even in the most informal fashion, to keep treaties in force'.[74]

The three awards just mentioned are recent, and it would be premature to expect them to have shaped the general regime. In fact, given their confidential nature, one wonders how they could: summaries of awards are a weak basis for radiation; things that remain in the dark cannot radiate. However, the tentative summaries offered in the preceding section suggest that, if they were (to become) public, the awards could have a very beneficial effect on the general debate. They could notably shine a spotlight on bilateral treaties, which the debate of 1990s and 2000s, focused as they were on world order treaties, often treated in passing. What is more, careful analysis of investment awards such as *World Wide Minerals*, *Deripaska* and *Gold Pool* could advance debates about the requirements for succession based on conduct and tacit agreement: this would be an extremely useful contribution which could point a way out of the sometimes stale debates between 'clean slate' and 'strict continuity' approaches.

At present, investment practice remains in the early stages: in order to shape the general regime, awards will need to be made public, and the approaches will need to mature, and be tested further. However, the potential for beneficial radiating effects is clearly there — precisely because in the 'centre of the miry bog',[75] the general regime fails to deliver certainty. A handful of properly reasoned arbitral awards would likely be warmly welcomed by the State succession community. Even the three awards just summarised might, should they become publicly available, would likely be seen as a significant first steps towards clarification.

---

[74] O'Connell, 'Reflections' (n 9) 733. This informality is reflected in VCSST (n 13) Arts 24 and 29 which envisage the continued application of bilateral treaties if the parties 'by reason of their conduct they are to be considered as having so agreed'. As noted above n 59, in the framework of the VCSST, ibid., Arts 24 and 28 only apply to treaties agreed by newly independent States in the sense of Art 16; for other States, the general rules (Art 34) would typically result in automatic succession.

[75] Maluwa (n 6) 810.

V. NEW STATES AND ICSID MEMBERSHIP

Whilst succession to BITs is the most relevant problem in practice, investment lawyers have had to deal with two other 'succession scenarios'. Treaties establishing international organisations provide the first case in point.

A. The General Regime

Treaties establishing international organisations are curious creatures. They are contractual agreements, typically between States, but they establish a normative framework within which that arrangement can evolve, centred on the bond of membership. The general regime of succession — similar to the general regime of treaty law[76] — reflects as much. Article 4 of the 1978 Vienna Convention confirms the application of the general regime to 'any treaty which is the constituent instrument of an international organization'; but it states that this is 'without prejudice to the rules concerning acquisition of membership and without prejudice to any other relevant rules of the organization'.[77] This latter proviso recognises the primary relevance of rules of international institutional law. And while most constituent documents are silent on the question of succession, international institutional law traditionally did offer clear guidance: it viewed membership in an international organisation as a personal status that, unless the organisational statute envisaged it, could not be succeeded to.[78] In his detailed study, Konrad Bühler in this respect spoke of the 'traditional axiom of non- succession'.[79]

During the 1990s, it looked as if this axiom might come under pressure. Economic and financial institutions such as the International Monetary Fund, the World Bank, or the European Bank for Reconstruction and Development

---

[76] See VCLT (n 11) art 5.

[77] VCSST (n 13) Art 4(a). In practice, the 'without prejudice' part of the provision has been treated as determinative: 'membership of an organisation is a question for the constitution of the organisation and not one for a general rule of international law, as the State Succession Convention makes clear', noted O'Connell 'Reflections' (n 9) 732. See further O'Connell, *State Succession* (n 9) vol II, 183; Mullerson (n 9) 304–305; cf. Hafner and Novak (n 18) 410; Sarvarian (n 36) 803.

[78] Hafner and Novak (n 18) 410; Karl Zemanek, 'State Succession After Decolonisation' (1965) 161 *Recueil des cours* 182, 253; Paul R. Williams, 'State Succession and the International Financial Institutions: Political Criteria v. Protection of Outstanding Financial Obligations' (1994) 43 *ICLQ* 776, 784; Zimmermann and Devaney (n 9) para 21.

[79] Konrad G. Bühler, *State Succession and Membership in International Organizations: Legal Theories Versus Political Pragmatism* (Martinus Nijhoff 2001) 30.

were keen to preserve the financial assets of States like Yugoslavia and Czechoslovakia, and perhaps more so, to avoid default on outstanding loans and financial obligations.[80] After the break-up of Yugoslavia and Czechoslovakia, successor States (the Czech and Slovak Republics, Croatia, Slovenia, etc.) were admitted to continue their predecessors‘ former membership status rather than seek admission as new members. In the view of some commentators writing at the time, this suggested that traditional axioms were giving way to a pragmatic approach. Bühler notably advanced an influential distinction based on the character of the organisation concerned, excluding succession to membership within political organisations emphasising close integration, while admitting it in principle for 'universal-technical organisations' aimed at wide participation.[81]

B. The Impact of Investment Practice

International organisations generally play a rather limited role in investment law. The field lacks overarching multilateral organisations of the WTO- or IMF-type; horizontal treaty-making remains the norm. The International Centre for Settlement of Investment Disputes (ICSID) is the main exception to this general rule: while not heavily integrated, it possesses autonomous legal personality,[82] enjoys privileges and immunities[83] and grants contracting parties rights to participate in the organisation's decision-making process.[84] Since the 1990s, new States such as Czech or Slovak Republics, the member States of the former Yugoslavia, and more recently Montenegro or South Sudan, could have sought to succeed to the ICSID membership of their predecessors. Given the Centre's close institutional links with the World Bank (which, as noted above, approached succession to membership quite pragmatically during the 1990s), such an approach might have been at least plausible: in Bühler's dis-

---

80 For many details, see Williams (n 78); for a short summary, Zimmermann and Devaney (n 9) paras 21–22.

81 Konrad Bühler, 'State Succession, Identity/Continuity and Membership in The United Nations' in Eisemann and Koskenniemi (n 10) 227–233. As Williams notes (n 78) 794–808, the pragmatic approach reflected 'the desire to preserve the assets of successor States … the political desire to exclude the participation of Serbia/ Montenegro, and the financial desire to provide for complete assumption of the debt obligations of the predecessor States'.

82 Convention on the Settlement of Investment Disputes between States and Nationals of Other States (ICSID Convention) (adopted 18 March 1965, entered into force 14 October 1966) 575 UNTS 159, Art 18.

83 Ibid., Arts 19–24.

84 See, e.g., ibid., Arts 4(1) and 6 (composition and powers of the Administrative Council).

tinction, ICSID certainly qualifies as a 'universal-technical organisation' that should permit succession to membership.

However, ICSID institutional practice points in a different direction. No new State so far has sought to succeed to the membership of a predecessor State. Quite the opposite, all new States that have wanted to join the Centre have joined as new members pursuant to Article 67 of the Convention.[85] The ICSID website provides all the required details, and unlike the website of other treaties (e.g., multilateral human rights treaties, the UN Charter, or disarmament treaties), the information is quite straightforward. No complex distinctions between forms of acquiring or continuing membership are drawn, no explanatory footnotes required to set out the views of depositaries: without exceptions, all successor States that emerged during the ruptures of the 1990s are listed as new members.[86]

Why this straightforward approach was preferred, is a matter for speculation. The most obvious explanation may be that not that much hinges on ICSID membership. Unlike in international financial institutions, ICSID has no major institutional interest in preserving existing membership ties (with a view to determining the fate of assets of the predecessor State). What is more, Article 67 makes it easy to join as a new member. Unlike more integrated organisations, ICSID is a very 'open shop'; in essence, all World Bank members can join if they so wish, without any need to be admitted by a vote. So complex arguments about succession might not be worth making.

Given the relatively low stakes, it is not surprising that succession to membership has raised few real issues. In the one case that did arise — *MNSS B.V. and others v Montenegro* brought in 2011 — the problem was resolved quickly. When the claimants realised that at the time of the arbitration request Montenegro had not yet joined ICSID,[87] and could thus not be a contracting

---

[85] Ibid., Art 67 states:

> This Convention shall be open for signature on behalf of States members of the Bank. It shall also be open for signature on behalf of any other State which is a party to the Statute of the International Court of Justice and which the Administrative Council, by a vote of two-thirds of its members, shall have invited to sign the Convention.

See the 'List of Contracting States and Other Signatories of the Convention' (*ICSID*) https://icsid.worldbank.org/resources/lists/icsid-3 accessed 3 December 2020.

[86] See 'Joining ICSID' https://icsid.worldbank.org/en/Pages/about/Joining-ICSID.aspx accessed 3 December 2020; and further Tams (n 5) 320–324; Zimmermann and Devaney (n 9) para 21.

[87] Montenegro signed the ICSID Convention (n 82) on 19 July 2012 and ratified it on 10 April 2013, becoming thus a contracting party on 10 May 2013 as provided under Art 68(2) of the ICSID Convention.

party for the purposes of Article 25 of the ICSID Convention,[88] they requested their claims to be registered under the ICSID Additional Facility Rules. The request was granted by the Secretariat and a formal notice of Arbitration was eventually filed on 6 December 2012.[89]

All this suggests that, in the main, investment practice is fully in line with the 'traditional axiom of non-succession'.[90] It reflects the continuing appeal of the traditional approach that views membership as something each State must acquire in its own right and name. To the extent that this traditional approach had come under pressure during the 1990s, investment practice would seem to confirm it.

VI. INVESTMENT TREATIES AND CESSIONS OF TERRITORY

As noted above, not all instances of State succession involve new States and new legal persons. The notion of 'succession', as understood in international legal discourse, also covers ruptures of a different type: one State can 'definitive[ly] replac[e] ... another in respect of sovereignty over a given territory'[91] without changes to its legal personality.[92] Sometimes, this does involve major upheavals, as in Germany's recent history: the country's (re-)unification was dramatic and complex by any standard, but was rationalised as an incorporation of the GDR into the FRG, which left the latter's legal personality unaffected. Yet the typical scenario of this type of succession is not incorporation, but the cession of territory.[93] Traditionally a standard mode of allocating territorial sovereignty — whether as part of purchases (e.g., Alaska, Louisiana), land

---

[88] Pursuant to the ICSID Convention (n 82) Art 25(1):

> [t]he jurisdiction of the Centre shall extend to any legal dispute arising directly out of an investment, between a Contracting State (or any constituent subdivision or agency of a Contracting State designated to the Centre by that State) and a national of another Contracting State, which the parties to the dispute consent in writing to submit to the Centre.

[89] See Jarrod Hepburn, 'Montenegro to Face Second Known Investment Treaty Claim, This Time over Bankrupt Steelworks' (*International Arbitration Reporter*, 10 December 2012). For the final award in which no mention is made of this preliminary 'conundrum', see *MNSS BV and Recupero Credito Acciaio NV v Montenegro*, ICSID Case No ARB(AF)/12/8, Award (4 May 2016).

[90] Bühler (n 79) 30.

[91] Crawford (n 15) 409.

[92] For comment on the scope of the definition, see the ILC, 'Draft Articles on Succession of States in Respect of Treaties with commentaries' (1974) II(1) *ILC Yearbook* 208.

[93] For a succinct account, see Oliver Dörr, 'Cession' (2019) *MPEPIL*, especially paras 20–22 https://opil.ouplaw.com/view/10.1093/law:epil/9780199231690/

swaps (of the '*Heligoland v Sansibar*' type) or most commonly, imposed in peace treaties — such cessions have become less common today, and the rules against annexation of territory limit their validity.[94] However, territory continues to change hands between States — as has happened, in recent times, with respect to Walvis Bay, the Red Sea islands of Tiran and Yotvat and Macao and Hongkong/Kowloon. At least one of these recent examples has focused the attention of investment lawyers, as the subsequent discussion illustrates.

A. The General Regime

From the perspective of State succession, cessions of territory are viewed as a straightforward matter. There is little need to engage with arguments about clean slates or the conditions under which new States emerge. As long as the cession is a complete one, resulting in the integration of the transferred territory into the cessionary's legal order, the general regime of succession offers a refreshingly simply solution, which is neither very complex nor much disputed. The basic principle is that for each State — cedent and cessionary — prior treaties remain in force on their respective territories. The transferred piece of territory simply moves from one State's treaty regime into the other's.[95] This is referred to as the 'moving treaty-frontiers' principle (or rule) and codified in Article 15 VCSST, which is considered to reflect customary international law.[96] The default rule is viewed as an extension in time of the general principle of treaty law set out in Article 29 of the 1969 Vienna Convention on the Law of Treaties,[97] namely the 'presumption [that] ... when a State concludes a treaty, the latter applies to the entire territory of the State',[98] and perhaps because of this pedigree has prompted little debate. Like other

---

law-9780199231690-e1377 accessed 11 December 2021; for further details A. Tanzi and L. Iapichino, 'Article 15' in Distefano et al (n 13) 543.

94 See *supra* Section III.B. for comment on lawful versus unlawful instances of succession.

95 See the ILC's commentary to draft Art 14 (n 92) 208 (eventually becoming VCSST (n 13) Art 15), stating that 'on a territory's undergoing a change of sovereignty, it passes automatically out of the treaty régime of the predecessor sovereign into the treaty régime of the successor sovereign'.

96 See Zimmermann and Devaney (n 8) 520; Andreas Zimmermann, *Staatennachfolge in völkerrechtliche Verträge* (Springer 2000) 449, 823; Hafner and Novak (n 18) 397.

97 VCLT (n 11) Art 29 states: 'Unless a different intention appears from the treaty or is otherwise established, a treaty is binding upon each party in respect of its entire territory.' The commentary to VCSST draft Art 14 (eventually Art 15) specifically refers to Art 29 VCLT: (n 91) 208.

98 See Mark Villiger, *Commentary on the 1969 Vienna Convention on the Law of Treaties* (Brill 2009) 392.

default rules, it comes with exceptions: as Article 15 clarifies, treaty frontiers do not move if it 'appears from the treaty or is otherwise established that the application of the treaty to that territory would be incompatible with the object and purpose of the treaty or would radically change the conditions for its operation'. But these have so far prompted relatively little debate.[99]

B. The Impact of Investment Practice

A side aspect of the general regime of successions, cessions of territory have been the site of much recent debate among investment lawyers. The reason for this is simple: prominent recent decisions have highlighted controversial aspects of the general regime as just outlined. In the course of proceedings in the *Sanum* cases, an UNCITRAL tribunal,[100] the Singapore High Court,[101] and the Singapore Court of Appeal[102] have disagreed on whether the China-Laos BIT concluded in 1993 applied to Macao, a territory formerly administered by Portugal and reverting to China in 1999, and could be invoked by Macao-based investors.[103] While concerning the same dispute, the three decisions, read together, offer a fairly clear (and recent) exposition of the moving treaty frontiers principle and its limits.

The limits mattered in particular, as Macao's reversion was an unusual case of cession: rather than fully integrating with China, under the joint Chinese-Portuguese Protocol of 1999 it would retain a particular status, often captured in the formula of 'one country, two systems'.[104] In light of this, the arbitral tribunal and the two Singapore courts wondered whether (adapting the words of Article 15 (b) VCSST), 'it appear[ed] from [the China-Laos BIT] or [was] otherwise established that the application of the treaty to [Macao] would

[99] To illustrate, see the instructive analysis by Tanzi and Iapichino (n 93) 553–554, which accords no more than a handful of paragraphs to exceptions.

[100] *Sanum Investments Ltd v Lao People's Democratic Republic*, PCA Case No 2013-13, Award on Jurisdiction (13 December 2013).

[101] *Government of the Law People's Democratic Republic v Sanum Investment Ltd* [2015] SGHC 15.

[102] *Sanum Investment Ltd v Government of the Law People's Democratic Republic* [2016] SGCA 57.

[103] See the Joint Declaration on the Question of Macao (with annexes) (China-Portugal) (13 April 1987) 1498 UNTS 228. For comment on the *Sanum cases*, see notably Dumberry (n 5) paras 6.48–6.98; John Shijian Mo, 'The Dilemma of Applying Bilateral Investment Treaties of China to Hongkong and Macao' (2018) 33 *ICSID Review* 125; Christina Binder, 'Sanum Investments Limited v The Government of the Lao People's Democratic Republic' (2016) 17 *JWIT* 280.

[104] For much more, see Odysseas G. Repousis, 'On Territoriality and International Investment Law: Applying China's Investment Treaties to Hong Kong and Macao' (2015) 37 *Michigan JIL* 113.

be incompatible with [its] object and purpose ... or would radically change the conditions for its operation'. The treaty itself was silent on this; and the three decisions were split in what can indeed be described as 'a textbook example of the difficulties arising from the application of the general international law of state succession to a particular situation'.[105] The arbitral tribunal applied the moving treaty frontier principle; the Singapore High Court considered the parties to have agreed otherwise (and quashed the award);[106] the Singapore Court of Appeal overruled the High Court decision and held that the BIT did apply to Macao.[107]

Much of this back and forth reflected differing assessments of the evidence (and its admissibility). When considering that the parties had agreed not to follow the moving treaty frontier rule, the Singapore High Court placed emphasis on *Notes Verbales* exchanged by the Laotian Ministry of Foreign Affairs and the Chinese Embassy in Vientiane.[108] These indeed reflected the parties' views that the BIT did not apply to Macao — but these views were expressed in 2014, i.e., after the arbitral award had been rendered, and for that reason could not have been taken into account by the arbitral tribunal. The Singapore Court of Appeal, for its part, considered the *Notes Verbales*, submitted after the critical date, could not change the result reached through the regular means of treaty interpretation.[109]

Beyond these evidentiary matters, three aspects of the *Sanum* trias of decisions deserve to be noted. The first concerns the starting-point of the analysis. All three decisions considered the moving treaty frontier principle to apply presumptively;[110] none of them felt that investment treaties (which do display

---

[105] Binder (n 13) 290.

[106] *Sanum*, High Court Decision (n 101) paras 70ff and 110–111. For a critical appraisal on whether the court really established the intention of the parties, see Naomi Hart and Sriram Srikumar, 'Investor-State Arbitration before the High Court of Singapore: Territoriality, Nationality and Arbitrability' (2014) 4 *CJICL* 191, 197–198.

[107] China subsequently refuted the Singapore Appeals Court judgment supporting the view that the 'geographical scope of application' of an investment agreement is a 'question of fact' for the contracting parties to decide themselves, and that in principle Chinese investment agreements do not apply to Macao: see Foreign Ministry Spokesperson, 'Regular Press Conference' (21 October 2016) www.italaw.com/sites/default/files/case-documents/italaw7687.pdf accessed 3 December 2020.

[108] *Sanum*, High Court Decision (n 101) paras 39–40 (where the *Notes Verbales* were viewed as a subsequent agreement pursuant to VCLT (n 11) Art 31(3)).

[109] *Sanum*, Court of Appeal Decision (n 102) paras 101–121. The same applied to two further *Notes Verbales* issued in 2015: see ibid., paras 27–35.

[110] See, for example, *Sanum*, Arbitral Award (n 100) paras 278–295; *Sanum* High Court Decision (n 101) paras 61–62; *Sanum*, Court of Appeal Decision (n 102) paras 47–50.

particular characteristics) should be governed by a special set of rules.[111] In this first respect, investment practice is fully in line with the general approach, and could be said to consolidate it further. Second, the analysis also points to considerations that could help rebut the presumption. As with respect to new States and old BITs (discussed above[112]), the listing practice of international institutions matters, as does the wider treaty practice of the cessionary. In this sense, the decisions e.g., noted that a WTO Report of 2001 had not listed the China-Laos BIT among the treaties that would henceforth apply to Macao; and all distinguished the China-Laos BIT from other Chinese BITs that regulated their territorial scope explicitly.[113] Third, beyond these particular considerations, the trias of *Sanum* decisions reflects the strength of the presumption in favour of moving treaty frontiers. All three decisions considered the presumption to apply notwithstanding Macao's continued autonomy, post reversion. In line with this, solutions were sought on the basis of the China-Laos BIT. The fact that under the terms of the China-Portuguese Joint Declaration of 1987, this cession, unusually, followed the logic of 'one country, two systems' was in itself not enough to justify an exception from the moving treaty frontiers principle.[114] The Singapore Court of Appeal notably did not accept that the China-Portugal Joint Declaration could operate as a 'contract-out' from the customary moving treaty frontiers rule since it constituted an agreement *inter partes* which did not create rights and obligations for third parties.[115]

So what remains of the three decisions' detailed engagement with the moving treaty frontier? The more recent literature correctly considers *Sanum* to support the moving treaty frontier principle;[116] but given the strong support it enjoys already, this is unlikely to make much of a difference. Beyond that, international lawyers will find in the three decisions significant guidance on how exceptions to the principle should be construed. In this respect, investment practice offers valuable detail on an oft-neglected issues, notably on the

---

[111] A point noted by Binder (n 103) 293.

[112] See *supra* Section IV.B.

[113] See, e.g., *Sanum*, Arbitral Award (n 100) paras 243–251; *Sanum*, High Court Decision (n 101) paras 83–86 and 107–109; *Sanum*, Court of Appeal Decision (n 102) paras 88–89 and 95–99. By way of illustration, see the Protocol to the China-Russia 2006 BIT (adopted 9 November 2006, entered into force 1 May 2009) which excludes Hong Kong and Macao from the treaty's territorial scope.

[114] See, e.g., *Sanum*, Arbitral Award (n 100) paras 243–251; *Sanum*, High Court Decision (n 1001) para 74, drawing on the parties' agreement reflected in the *Notes Verbales*, in which 'one country, two systems' was one of a number of considerations; *Sanum*, Court of Appeal Decision (n 102) paras 72–82.

[115] See *Sanum*, Court of Appeal Decision (n 102) paras 75–78. This position could draw on VCSST (n 13) Art 8, which limits the influence of devolution agreements.

[116] See, e.g., Hafner and Novak (n 18) 397; Crawford (n 15) 411.

limited impact of the Joint Declaration.[117] At the same time, given the unusual nature of the cession arrangements reached for Macao, international lawyers may not have much opportunity (nor need) to draw on this valuable detail — and the fact that Macao's unusual position within China did not as such justify an exception to the moving treaty frontier principle means that even for these, there is no bright-line rule. The case of Hong Kong, which equally was to follow the rationale of 'one country, two systems', is the most obvious analogue;[118] yet Hong Kong's status is explicitly addressed in many treaties, which limits the scope for investment-related practice to radiate. All things considered, the trias of *Sanum* decisions is perhaps best seen as a curious foray into the 'outer rim' of the realm of succession.[119]

VII. CONCLUDING THOUGHTS

The preceding considerations highlight rather different ways in which investment practice has engaged with rules of State succession. Overall, it seems investment lawyers have moved cautiously: they have not rushed 'into the centre of the miry bog itself',[120] but tread softly and, where possible, kept to the well-defined paths, or stuck to the margins. This cautious attitude is understandable, and perhaps it is wise. However, it has affected the impact of investment practice on the general regime of State succession: despite the number of decisions addressing succession, none of the succession awards breaks dramatic new ground; one looks in vain, so far, for a decision of the *Tadic*, *Kadi* or *Nicaragua* type. And in fact, the most likely contender, *World Wide Minerals v Kazakhstan* (which has been called 'dramatic')[121] cannot really break new ground because the parties have so far preferred to keep it confidential.

If the preceding, diverse, reflections leave an overall impression, they suggest that investment lawyers work from within the general regime, fully aware—and availing themselves — of its flexibility. As Zimmermann and Devaney have argued, despite the fact that the law of State succession faces novel challenges with the rise in the international scene of actors other than States, 'it is unlikely that this area of international law will fundamentally

---

[117] Dumberry (n 5) para 6.96; Binder (n 103) 294, investment practice 'keeps general international law "alive", it details and further specifies it'.

[118] But cf. *Sanum*, Court of Appeal Decision (n 102) para 90, criticising simple analogies between Hong Kong and Macao.

[119] See further Dumberry (n 5) para 6.96–6.98.

[120] Maluwa (n 6) 810.

[121] Peterson (n 2).

change. Rather it is more likely that … current principles and doctrine will be adapted to accommodate … new influences instead of succumbing to them.'[122]

This is not to say that investment lawyers merely give effect to a pre-defined general regime. Working from within it, they mould it, at times confirming trends, adding texture, specificity and nuance. In four respects, investment practice, as assessed in the preceding sections, does seem relevant for the general discourse on State succession:

(1) Diplomatic practice regarding BITs confirms the two general features of the law of State succession to bilateral treaties. Successor States and treaty partners frequently enter into negotiations about the fate of old treaties — BIT practice affirms the move towards 'process', reflected in frequent inter-party agreements on questions of succession. And in a clear majority of cases, these negotiations result in the continued application of the treaty: succession is the preferred option, stability the premise: even if not required by law, it marks the default starting-point.

(2) Arbitral practice is gradually beginning to clarify the position in the absence of explicit inter-party agreement. Academics will surely hope for bold arbitral guidance on whether new States automatically succeed to BITs. However, investment tribunals should not be expected to solve this complex puzzle — they cannot 'drain the marshland' alone, and they certainly cannot do so if parties prefer their awards to remain confidential. However, the emerging jurisprudence indicates a willingness to engage with arguments about succession by conduct; and even the informal summaries of awards point towards factors that determine arguments about implied consent. This is a welcome 'new influence' that the general regime of succession can and should 'accommodate', and which will result in a more down-to-earth, grounded, discourse on succession: perhaps future generations of treaty succession specialists will credit investment tribunals with having added to the hitherto lofty discourse, based on sweeping conceptual claims, an earthly layer of down-to-earth arguments in which listing practices feature prominently and diplomatic interactions are scrutinised in detail. While not ground-breaking, this would be an eminently useful contribution.

(3) ICSID's institutional practice reflects the special nature of succession to membership in international organisations. It underlines that, as a default position, membership status cannot be succeeded to, but it is rather something a State acquires in its own name. In this respect, investment practice confirms the traditional approach.

[122] Zimmermann and Devaney (n 8) 512.

(4) Arbitral awards have shed light on peculiar instances of cessions of territory, such as that of Macao. They proceed from the moving treaty frontiers rule, a rule whose customary status has not been questioned. They have shone a spotlight on the hitherto neglected limits of the rule, but so far read these limits very narrowly, thus affirming the dominance of the default rule.

PART III

Investment law and the law of international responsibility

7. Investment arbitration as an engine of development of the rules of attribution – with particular focus on *lex specialis* and *de facto* state organs

Stephan Wittich[1]

I. THE RELEVANCE OF THE RULES OF ATTRIBUTION

If state responsibility is at the heart of international law inasmuch as it is the ultimate test of the effectiveness of any legal order, then attribution is in the thick of responsibility, if only because attribution as a *fait générateur* is one of the two essential 'conditions' for – or, in the words of the ILC Articles on Responsibility of States for Internationally Wrongful Acts (ARSIWA) – 'elements' for the origin of responsibility.[2] In other words, there is no responsibility without attribution. And, as relevant as State responsibility is to international investment law as a special 'branch' of international law, it may safely be assumed that, vice versa, investment law, particularly through the practice of investment arbitration, has become enormously relevant to the general law of State responsibility. With particular focus on the application of the rules of attribution in investment arbitration, it was rightly stated by one commentator that arbitral awards in investment disputes have become a 'testing ground' for the ARSIWA.[3] This is no surprise, given the fact that

---

[1] The author wishes to thank Haris Huremagic and Koloman Roiger-Simek for their valuable research assistance.

[2] ILC, 'Draft Articles on Responsibility of States for International Wrongful Acts, with commentaries'(2001) II(2) *ILC Yearbook*, Article 2 (ARSIWA):

> Elements of an internationally wrongful act of a State. There is an internationally wrongful act of a State when conduct consisting of an action or omission:
> (a) is attributable to the State under international law; and
> (b) constitutes a breach of an international obligation of the State.

[3] Kaj Hobér, 'State Responsibility and Attribution' in Peter Muchlinski et al (eds), *The Oxford Handbook of International Investment Law* (OUP 2008) 550, 582.

most investment tribunals invariably have to deal with questions of breaches of international obligations potentially entailing the responsibility of the host State. It is this potential repercussion of the practice of investment law on the law of international responsibility with a focus on selected aspects of attribution that is the topic of this chapter.

As a general concept, attribution describes the process by which a specific conduct, fact, or result is ascribed to a particular person and thus usually implies a measure of accountability. This is particularly important for States which, as social constructs in the form of legal entities, cannot but act through organs, ultimately human beings, representing them in their international (as well as domestic) transactions. The nature or character of rules of attribution may be either normative/prescriptive or factual/descriptive. On the one hand, the normative approach would consider attribution as being based on criteria determined by law and require a legal assessment according to prescriptive legal norms and not on the mere recognition of a link of factual connection of causation. The descriptive or factual approach, on the other hand, would tie attribution to the factual perception of the person applying the law; in other words, the descriptive approach does not view attribution as a technical legal operation, but as a simple empirical statement by the interpreter of a specific factual situation.[4]

There is general agreement in the doctrine that rules of attribution in international law are normative or prescriptive rather than factual or descriptive.[5] The decisive criteria for attribution are assigned by international law in the first place, and do not follow from an empirical interpretation of facts that would establish a causal link between the act at issue and the State 'behind' it.[6] This, of course, does not mean that attribution is detached from the factual circumstances or details of the particular case. Not only would this be in outright

---

[4] Luigi Condorelli and Clauss Kress, 'The Rules of Attribution: General Considerations' in James Crawford, Alain Pellet and Simon Olleson (eds), *The Law of International Responsibility* (OUP 2010) 221, 226.

[5] See particularly James Crawford, *State Responsibility. The General Part* (CUP 2013) 114. For more recent statements to this effect see Georgios Petrochilos, 'Attribution. State Organs and Entities Exercising Elements of Governmental Authority' in Katia Yannaca-Small (ed), *Arbitration under International Investment Agreements. A Guide to the Key Issues* (2nd edn, OUP 2018) 332; Csaba Kovács, *Attribution in International Investment Law* (Kluwer 2018) 27.

[6] The ILC commentaries to the ARSIWA make this clear by stating that '[t]he attribution of conduct to the State as a subject of international law is based on criteria determined by international law and not on the mere recognition of a link of factual causality', see ILC Articles on State Responsibility (n 2) 38–39 (Part I, Chapter II, para 4); See also Chia Lehnardt, *Private Militärfirmen und völkerrechtliche Verantwortlichkeit* (Mohr Siebeck 2011) 124.

tension with the essential purpose of law to regulate factual conduct; it would also ignore the fundamental idea that 'normative processes must demonstrate sensitivity to the facts of each case',[7] if only in order to be effective. Therefore, any operation of attribution, and the rules governing that process, will necessarily be guided by the perception of factual reality, but that applies of course to the application of law at large. On that very general basis, international law is full of rules of attribution, those in the law of State responsibility probably being the most prominent, but certainly not the only ones.[8]

Furthermore, issues of attribution of conduct may also arise in the context of investment disputes involving international organisations although this is still an underdeveloped field and occurs only in exceptional or unusual situations. But as cases such as *Electrabel v Hungary*[9] and the transfer of competences for foreign direct investment within the European Union demonstrate, investment cases involving an international organisation may arise more frequently in the future. Such cases may and probably will raise delicate questions of allocation of competences, of attribution of conduct and ultimately of responsibility.[10]

---

[7] Crawford (n 5) 114.

[8] Understood in a broad sense, attribution is also relevant for questions of causation and evidence, as well as in sources doctrine. For instance, the Vienna Convention on the Law of Treaties (adopted 23 May 1969, entered into force 37 January 1980) 1155 UNTS 331, Article 7 tells us who is considered as representing a State for the purpose of performing certain acts relating to a treaty. That presumption is applied in practice, and by analogy, also to ascertain who may enter into legally binding unilateral acts on behalf of a State, see *Nuclear Tests (Australia v France)* [1974] *ICJ Reports* 253, 269 para 49; *Armed Activities on the Territory of the Congo (New Application: 2002) (Democratic Republic of the Congo v Rwanda)* [2006] *ICJ Reports* 6, 28 paras 46–47. Similarly, in the context of customary to 'qualify as State practice, the conduct in question must be "of the State"', meaning the conduct 'of any State organ', ILC, 'Draft Conclusions on Identification of Customary International Law' (2018) UN Doc A/73/10, 132. The law of State immunity equally contains a number of rules that perform an attributive function in that they ascribe a specific result or effect to the conduct of a person or entity in relation to the State. For an overview, see Christina Binder and Stephan Wittich, 'A Comparison of the Rules of Attribution in the Law of State Responsibility, State Immunity and Custom' in Gabor Kajtár (ed), *Secondary Rules of Primary Importance in International Law: Attribution, Causality, Evidence, and Standards of Review in the Practice of International Courts and Tribunals* (OUP 2022) 242.

[9] *Electrabel SA v Hungary,* ICSID Case 3 No ARB/07/19, Decision on Jurisdiction, Applicable Law and Liability, Award (30 November 2012); see also *AES Summit Generation Ltd and AES-Tisza Erömü Kft v Hungary,* ICSID Case No ARB/07/22, Award (23 October 2010); *Ioan Micula et al v Romania,* ICSID Case No ARB/05/20, Award (11 December 2013).

[10] Stephan Wittich, 'International Investment Law' in André Nollkaemper and Ilias Plakokefalos (eds), *The Practice of Shared Responsibility in International Law* (CUP 2017) 822, 835–848.

It will be interesting to see what influence these developments may have on both the ARSIWA and the ILC Articles on the Responsibility of International Organizations and on how the complex relationship between the two will play out in practice.

Given the enormous 'popularity' the ARSIWA have enjoyed in investment arbitration – a popularity that is continuing to increase both in quantity and density – the practice of investment tribunals on questions of attribution has attracted a considerable body of literature which has dealt with these questions already in great detail.[11] Therefore, the following contribution will be confined to look at two aspects which have been the subject of more recent case law, that is, the question of special rules of attribution under investment agreements (*lex specialis*) and the concept of *de facto* State organs under Article 4(2) ARSIWA. Both have a certain potential to contribute to the further development of the general rules enshrined in the ARSIWA.

II. THE RULES OF ATTRIBUTION AND THEIR APPLICATION IN INVESTMENT ARBITRATION

Investment tribunals have recognised the customary nature of the ARSIWA, usually without any discussion, either in their entirety, or in relation to particular rules of attribution.[12] In general, it is safe to say that '[i]nvestment treaty tribunals have had no difficulty in relying on State responsibility principles to decide issues of attribution'.[13] Through their case law, they have endorsed, applied and confirmed the rules of attribution as codified in the ARSIWA.[14] An extensive study on the rules of attribution concerning State entities or enterprises[15] has shown that after the adoption of the ARSIWA by the ILC in

---

[11] Most importantly, see Luca Schicho, *State Entities in International Investment Law* (Nomos 2012); Jonas Dereje, *Staatsnahe Unternehmen. Die Zurechnungsproblematik im Internationalen Investitionsrecht und weiteren Bereichen des Völkerrechts* (Nomos 2016); Simon Olleson, 'Attribution in Investment Treaty Arbitration' (2016) 31 *ICSID Review* 457; Kovács (n 5); Petrochilos (n 5) 332; Carlo de Stefano, *Attribution in International Law and Arbitration* (OUP 2020).

[12] See the extensive list of investment cases concerning the customary nature of the ARSIWA in Dereje (n 11) 254–256.

[13] *Flemingo DutyFree Shop Private Ltd v Republic of Poland,* UNCITRAL, Award (12 August 2016) para 420.

[14] See Simon Olleson, 'The Impact of the ILC's Articles on Responsibility of States for Internationally Wrongful Acts – Preliminary Draft' (*British Institute of International and Comparative Law*, 2007) www.biicl.org/files/3107_impactoftheartic lesonstate_responsibilitypreliminarydraftfinal.pdf accessed 15 April 2002; James Crawford, 'Investment Arbitration and the ILC Articles on State Responsibility' (2010) 25 *ICSID Review* 127.

[15] Dereje (n 11) 258–365.

2001, investment tribunals have tended to stick to both the structure and the substance of the ARSIWA rules of attribution.

On their face, the rules of attribution are straightforward. The ILC Articles draw a distinction between attribution of conduct 'directly' through State organs (Articles 4–6) and 'indirect' attribution where the conduct is initially performed by private persons or entities (Articles 8–11). In the practice of investment tribunals, the most relevant provisions are Articles 4, 5, and 8. Article 4 deals with State organs in a twofold sense. On the one hand, it establishes attribution to the State of conduct by organs that hold this formal status according to internal law (so-called *de jure organs*). As a matter of course, this rule attributes any conduct of any organ, whether it 'exercises legislative, executive, judicial or any other functions, whatever position it holds in the organization of the State, and whatever its character as an organ of the central government or of a territorial unit of the State' (Article 4 para 1). While this rule of attribution proceeds from the formal characterisation of an organ under domestic law, this is, for purposes of attribution under the law of State responsibility, not the end of the matter. For Article 4 para 2 makes clear that, in order to assess organ status, this reference to domestic law is not exhaustive. Rather, organ status may also derive from the domestic practice of a State. In such a case, 'reference exclusively to internal law would be misleading' because 'the term "organ" used in internal law may have a special meaning, and not the very broad meaning it has under article 4'.[16] The commentary concludes that, '[a]ccordingly, a State cannot avoid responsibility for the conduct of a body which does in truth act as one of its organs merely by denying it that status under its own law'.[17] This 'special' status has become known as '*de facto* organ', particularly in the case law of the International Court of Justice (ICJ).[18]

Furthermore, under Article 5, the conduct of persons, groups or entities not constituting an organ of the State under Article 4 may nevertheless be attributable to the State if and to the extent they exercise elements of governmental authority. The rationale of this rule is clear: where certain governmental, regulatory, or other public functions have been delegated to parastatal entities or private corporations, any conduct by such entities or corporations in the exercise of these functions is attributable to the State.[19] Again, if such conduct were not attributable, a State could easily escape international responsibility through various means of 'outsourcing'. Articles 8 and 11, respectively, attribute conduct by private individuals if it is directed or controlled by the State

16 ILC Articles on State Responsibility (n 2), Commentary to Article 4, para 11.
17 Ibid.
18 See below Section IV.A.
19 ILC Articles on State Responsibility (n 2), Commentary to Article 5, para 1.

(Article 8), or if the State subsequently acknowledges and adopts such conduct (Article 11).

As stated above, the general picture of investment arbitration is that tribunals have largely followed the structure and substance of the rules of attribution in the ARSIWA. Furthermore, they have also been more inclined to incorporate into their reasoning the case law of the ICJ which, again, will have the effect of reinforcing the rules of attribution under public international law. With an increasing density of arbitral practice, the approach of tribunals to questions of attribution under the ARSIWA has become not only better structured but also sufficiently argued and reasoned.[20] However, there are also less fortunate tendencies to be found in the treatment of the ARSIWA rules of attribution by investment tribunals, some of which are unique to investment arbitration, while others may be found in other courts and tribunals as well.

As to systemic flaws, it certainly goes too far to apply the rules of attribution to breaches of contract unless these simultaneously constitute breaches of international law.[21] In such circumstances, the rules of attribution are prayed in aid in relation to issues which in reality have nothing to do with questions of State responsibility. Such an extension of the scope of the rules on attribution is conceptually misleading, even though probably warranted by pragmatic considerations in that it would be unreasonable to invent applicable rules that would be different from those in the law of State responsibility, the more so as these are based on well-founded considerations of reason and logic. However, for a number of conceptual reasons, the question whether a State is a party to a contract and thus might incur responsibility pursuant to an umbrella clause following a breach of that contract is not to be answered on the basis of attribution rules under international law.[22] Rather, this is a question that falls to be decided pursuant to the proper law governing the contract.[23]

---

[20] See the exemplary list in de Stefano (n 11) 119, note 87. See also *LESI SpA et ASTALDI SpA v Democratic Peoples' Republic of Algeria,* ICSD Case No ARB/05/3, Award (12 November 2008) paras 102–118.

[21] See, e.g., *Bayindir Insaat Turizm Ticaret VE Sanayi A.Ş v Pakistan,* ICSID Case No ARB/03/29, Award (27 August 2009) paras 111–139; *SwemBalt AB, Sweden v Republic of Latvia*, UNCITRAL, Award (23 October 2003) para 37; *Nykomb Synergetics Technology Holding AB v Republic of Latvia,* SCC, Award (16 December 2003) para 4.2. See also Hobér (n 3) 582; Michael Feit, 'Responsibility of the State under International Law for the Breach of Contract Committed by a State-Owned Entity' (2010) 28 *Berkeley JIL* 142, 153–156.

[22] See, e.g., James Crawford, 'Treaty and Contract in Investment Arbitration' (2008) 24 *Arb Int'l* 351, 363, 369; Crawford (n 14) 134.

[23] James Crawford and Paul Mertensкötter, 'The Use of the ILC's Attribution Rules in Investment Arbitration' in Meg Kinnear et al (eds), *Building International*

A repeated problem encountered in analysing investment awards is that tribunals at times proceed in an unstructured way when engaging in determining attribution. To some extent, this is owed to poor party submissions that fail to provide any information as to the particular rule(s) of attribution invoked[24] and hence offer only little guidance to tribunals. In other cases, however, this is a genuine problem of the tribunal itself. A perusal or arbitral practice yields cases where the tribunal does not state the rule of attribution, if any, it applies,[25] where it presents several rules of attribution in some kind of product list to

---

Investment Law. The First 50 Years of ICSID (Kluwer 2016) 27, 34–35; Olleson (n 11) 465–466; de Stefano (n 11) 123–129.

[24] Sometimes tribunals do not shy away from criticising such obscure submissions. A good example in this respect is *F-W Oil Interests, Inc v Republic of Trinidad and Tobago*, ICSID Case No ARB/01/14, Award (3 March 2006) para 187, desperately complaining that:

> it derived no assistance whatever from the undifferentiated way in which the claimant continued, throughout both the written phases of the case and the oral argument, to plead its case in terms of 'T&T', the expression apparently being intended to be understood to cover indiscriminately any or all of the entities and agencies involved.

Similarly, the Tribunal in *Gustav F W Hamester GmbH & Co KG v Republic of Ghana,* ICSID Case No ARB/07/24, Award (18 June 2010) complained of the poor submissions of claimant (footnotes omitted from original; emphasis in the original):

> 148. To summarise the Claimant's position is simple: it considers that Cocobod must be completely assimilated to the Government of Ghana. The analysis leading to this conclusion has, however, been somewhat imprecise and has evolved in the course of the case …
>
> 150. … It therefore seems that the Claimant considers that the acts of Cocobod, a State entity, are attributable to the Government as sovereign acts. Furthermore, it considers that, as contractual acts, they are capable of violating the obligation in Article 9(2) of the BIT to respect contractual obligations undertaken by the Government. A few paragraphs later, without any legal analysis, the Claimant also states that Cocobod 'at all times acted as an organ of the Respondent'.
>
> 151. In its Reply, the Claimant's analysis is expanded, but the main contention seems to be that Cocobod is a State *organ*, either *de jure* or *de facto*. …
>
> 159. The Claimant argues that 'the fact of State instruction and direction or "effective control" ... is objectively established,' without elaborating on the basis for this conclusion.
>
> 160. As noted by the Respondent in its Rejoinder, the Claimant's analysis, overall, is somewhat unclear, as 'Hamester appears to be confusing ILC Article 5 with Articles 4 and 8'.

[25] *Waste Management, Inc v United Mexican States (II)*, ICSID Case No ARB(AF)/00/3, Award (30 April 2004) para 75: 'For the purposes of the present Award, however, it will be assumed that one way or another the conduct of Banobras was attributable to Mexico for NAFTA purposes.'; *EnCana Corporation v Republic of Ecuador,* UNCITRAL, LCIA Case No UN3481, Award (3 February 2006) para 154; *Ioannis Kardassopoulos v Georgia,* ICSID Case No ARB/05/18, Award (3 March

choose from,[26] alternates between different rules of attribution,[27] and, very frequently, combines individual criteria of different rules without properly distinguishing between these.[28] The latter is particularly flawed in that it ignores the distinct consequences that may follow depending on the particular attribution rule applied. For instance, both Article 4(2) and Article 8 allow for attribution of the acts of private entities or individuals to the State on condition that the latter has control over the former. However, the difference in the degree of control required (full control versus effective control) leads to different results pursuant to the different rules. As will be seen, this is particularly important for the concept of *de facto* organ which, if applicable, leads to attribution of all and any conduct whereas mere effective control under Article 8 results in attribution of the conduct over which the State had (if only effective) control in the particular case.[29] Therefore, it is always important to clearly identify the applicable rule of attribution invoked or applied, difficult as it may be in individual cases.

III. *LEX SPECIALIS* AS A DRIVING FORCE FOR DEVELOPMENT?

As is well-known, the ARSIWA are residual and only apply in the absence of an agreement in which the parties may establish their own rules of attribution and thus displace (partly or entirely) those of the ARSIWA. Accordingly, Article 55 expressly allows for special rules on the 'conditions for the existence of an internationally wrongful act', this being a clear reference i.e., to the

2010) para 280, holding that the relationship between the relevant entities and the State 'bears all of the hallmarks of attribution under international law'.

[26] *Chevron Bangladesh Block Twelve, Ltd et al v People's Republic of Bangladesh,* ICSID Case No ARB/06/10, Award (17 May 2010) para 171: 'In all the circumstances, and having regard to the provisions of Articles 4, 5 and 8 of the ILC Articles, and Article 8 in particular, the Tribunal has no hesitation in concluding that Petrobangla's actions are attributable to Bangladesh.'

[27] *United Parcel Service of America Inc (UPS) v Government of Canada,* ICSID Case No UNCT/02/1, Award on the Merits (24 May 2007) para 76. See also *Toto Costruzioni Generali SpA v Republic of Lebanon,* ICSID Case No ARB/07/12, Decision on Jurisdiction (11 September 2009) para 44.

[28] de Stefano (n 11) 121–123.

[29] See below nn 72–76 and accompanying text.

rules of attribution,[30] which is put beyond doubt by the commentary to Article 55.[31]

Yet, despite this generous possibility allowing for theoretically far-reaching deviations by agreement in the exercise of party autonomy, international investment law hardly knows of special rules of attribution barring perhaps some specific definitions of State entities in Model BITs.[32] While, admittedly, some tribunals apparently have detected *leges speciales* in certain investment treaties, or treaties including provisions on investment protection, a closer analysis shows that the approach taken and the reasons given by these tribunals are, as will be shown below, ultimately unconvincing.

Several reasons might explain the scarcity of express references to the *lex specialis* principle as a tool for determining the relationship between 'general' international law and 'special' regimes. First, and on a very general note, 'specialized' areas of international law, which are primarily concerned with the content of 'their' own distinct rules, may foster a lack of perspective of general international law.[33] In that sense, ignorance of a broader perception is probably owed to organisational or institutional blindness. Furthermore, and with particular focus on the rules of attribution, there will usually not be a need for *leges speciales*, as the relevant provisions in the ARSIWA are couched in sufficiently broad terms so as to allow investment tribunals to subsume the vast majority of attribution questions under the general rules. In the course of this operation, tribunals will necessarily adapt the abstract general rules to the particulars of the individual case, a process that renders special rules in most instances somewhat redundant.

However, institutional blindness, coupled with 'the parsimonious behavior of certain arbitrators … as to the application of general international law',[34]

---

30 The issue of *lex specialis* may also arise unrelatedly to attribution, see, e.g., *Archer Daniels Midland Company v Mexico,* ICSID Case No ARB (AF)/04/5, Award (21 November 2007) (finding that the NAFTA lays down its own rules on countermeasures). Similarly, *Corn Products v Mexico,* ICSID Case No ARB(AF)/04/1, Decision on Responsibility (15 January 2008).

31 See ILC Articles on State Responsibility (n 2), Commentary to Art 55, para 3: 'A particular treaty might impose obligations on a State but define the "State" for that purpose in a way which produces different consequences than would otherwise flow from the rules of attribution in Chapter II.'

32 See the US Model BIT of 2012, reprinted in Rudolf Dolzer and Christoph Schreuer, *Principles of International Investment Law* 2nd edn, (OUP 2012) 376;

33 Bruno Simma and Dirk Pulkowski, 'Of Planets and the Universe: Self-Contained Regimes in International Law' (2006) 17 *EJIL* 483, 488; Bruno Simma, 'Two Worlds, But Not Apart: International Investment Law and General International Law' in Marc Bungenberg et al (eds), *International Investment Law* (CH Beck 2015) 361, 364 MN 7.

34 de Stefano (n 11) 109.

may also lead to the opposite result and encourage tribunals to liberally assume the existence of special rules of attribution where there are simply none. One problem encountered in the analysis of alleged special rules by tribunals is the confusion between, on the one hand, primary norms establishing specific obligations of the State and its various organs, and, on the other hand, secondary rules of attribution that merely ascribe a specific conduct that may, or may not, be compatible with the obligation under the primary norm.

Thus, some tribunals have interpreted Articles 1502(3)(a) and 1503(2) of the former NAFTA, dealing with monopolies and State enterprises,[35] as constituting a combined *lex specialis* to the general rules of attribution under the ARSIWA. Most notably, the tribunal in *United Parcel Service v Canada* considered these provisions as constituting special rules of attribution to the effect of entirely derogating Articles 4 and 5 of the ARSIWA.[36] This view was advanced also in other cases, for instance in *Mesa v Canada* where the tribunal asserted that NAFTA established in fact 'a special regime',[37] as well as shared in the literature.[38] Similarly, the tribunal in *Tamimi v Oman* stated that even if the facts of the case allowed for an attribution because of effective control (implicitly referring to Article 8 ARSIWA), 'this [was] not relevant to the test for attribution under Article 10.1.2 of the US-Oman FTA',[39] thus obviously assuming that the purported special rule had exclusive effect.

---

[35] According to these provisions, each party:

> shall ensure, through regulatory control, administrative supervision or the application of other measures, that any … monopoly [or] state enterprise … acts in a manner that is not inconsistent with the Party's obligations under this Agreement [or] with the Party's obligations under Chapters Eleven (Investment) and Fourteen (Financial Services) … wherever such a monopoly exercises any regulatory, administrative or other governmental authority that the Party has delegated to it.

[36] *UPS v Canada* (n 27) para 33.

[37] *Mesa Power Group, LLC v Canada*, UNCITRAL, PCA Case No 2012-17, Award (24 March 2016) paras 362–364. Note that the tribunal misunderstood the relation between general rule and *lex specialis* when it stated that the NAFTA 'regime' could not 'be displaced by the ILC Articles' (para 362). For a similar approach, see *Adel A Hamadi Al Tamimi v Sultanate of Oman*, ICSID Case No ARB/11/33, Award (3 November 2015) paras 321–324, concerning a similar provision in the US-Oman Free Trade Agreement. See also *Genin v Estonia*, ICSID Case No ARB/99/2, Award (25 June 2001) para 327.

[38] Crawford (n 14) 132–133; Monique Sasson, *Substantive Law in Investment Treaty Arbitration* (Kluwer 2010) 4–5; Kovács (n 5) 52–53. See also Dolzer and Schreuer (n 32) 220; Petrochilos (n 5) 332, 348, expressing a balanced view but leaving the question open.

[39] *Adel A Hamadi Al Tamimi v Sultanate of Oman*, ICSID Case No ARB/11/33, Award (3 November 2015) para 322. Oddly, while the Tribunal held that Article 5 ARSIWA was not applicable to the case, it still regarded Article 5 as providing 'a useful

However, it is highly doubtful whether the relevant rules in plurilateral or bilateral investment treaties really provide for special rules of attribution that would derogate, or even exclude, the existing general rules of attribution of the ARSIWA. Given the different sources for such alleged special rules (e.g., NAFTA, ECT, BITs), it would be unsound to treat the different provisions alike, and a thorough analysis and interpretation in each case is called for. Yet, a careful reading of the relevant provisions, particularly Articles 1502 and 1503 of the former NAFTA or Article 22 ECT,[40] suggests that these establish specific or additional primary norms containing substantive obligations of result.[41] On that basis, the cases referred to above would seem to mistake attribution for breach (or vice versa), and thus to confound the two elements of responsibility. In international investment law, like in many other 'branches' of public international law, States may be obliged to perform positive acts, particularly to protect the foreign investment against physical violence or harassment under the standard of full protection and security,[42] and it is up to that primary norm itself to determine the scope *ratione materiae* and *ratione personae* of the obligation.[43]

---

guide as to the dividing line between sovereign and commercial acts' (ibid., para 324). In a similarly enigmatic manner, the tribunal stated that while ARSIWA Article 5 was not applicable, and '[a]lthough State responsibility for the conduct of State organs is not directly expressed in the text of the US-Oman FTA, the attribution of such conduct to the State is broadly supported in international law' (ibid., para 344, referring in note 706 to ARSIWA Article 4).

[40] Article 22. State and Privileged Enterprises

1. Each Contracting Party shall ensure that any state enterprise which it maintains or establishes shall conduct its activities in relation to the sale or provision of goods and services in its Area in a manner consistent with the Contracting Party's obligations under Part III of this Treaty.
2. No Contracting Party shall encourage or require such a state enterprise to conduct its activities in its Area in a manner inconsistent with the Contracting Party's obligations under other provisions of this Treaty.
3. Each Contracting Party shall ensure that if it establishes or maintains an entity and entrusts the entity with regulatory, administrative or other governmental authority, such entity shall exercise that authority in a manner consistent with the Contracting Party's obligations under this Treaty.
4. No Contracting Party shall encourage or require any entity to which it grants exclusive or special privileges to conduct its activities in its Area in a manner inconsistent with the Contracting Party's obligations under this Treaty.
5. For the purposes of this Article, 'entity' includes any enterprise, agency or other organization or individual.

[41] Dereje (n 11) 365–396; de Stefano (n 11) 109–110. See also Kovács (n 5) 176.

[42] Schicho (n 11) 18–21; Dolzer and Schreuer (n 32) 162–163.

[43] For instance, whether the standard to be applied is that of due diligence and what that means in detail See, e.g., *Wena Hotels Ltd v Egypt,* ICSID Case No ARB/98/4,

Furthermore, it has to be borne in mind that the exclusive purpose of the international law of attribution, be it under the general rules of the ARSIWA or alleged special treaty-based rules, is to attribute a certain conduct to the State in order to determine the existence of that State's international responsibility. It is not their task to establish, identify, interpret, or delineate the content and extent of substantive State obligations.[44]

It is therefore more convincing to view such treaty provisions not as establishing specific rules of attribution but as imposing particular positive obligations on the treatment and protection of foreign investments.[45] The tribunal in *F-W Oil Interests v Trinidad & Tobago* took a very balanced approach when, after analysing the relevant provision in the BIT, it concluded that it 'is to all intents and purposes indistinguishable from the position under general international law', in the case at hand 'as exemplified by Article 5' ARSIWA.[46] Thus, while the tribunal may have assumed the formal existence of a *lex specialis* on attribution, it considered it devoid of any practical effect as it was identical to the parallel customary rule. It then continued to state in a dictum that despite the generally available possibility to include in the BIT special rules, under the specific treaty such a possibility would more accurately operate 'at the level of primary obligation'.[47] Similarly, the tribunal in *Windstream v Canada* stated that Article 1503(2) of the former NAFTA only clarified, by examples, the scope and extent of Article 5 ARSIWA.[48] With regard to Article 22 ECT,

---

Award (8 December 2000) para 84. See generally Giuditta Cordero Moss, 'Full Protection and Security' in August Reinisch (ed), *Standards of Investment Protection* (OUP 2008) 131; August Reinisch and Christoph Schreuer, *International Protection of Investments. The Substantive Standards* (CUP 2020) 558–586.

[44] See ILC Articles on State Responsibility (n 2) Introductory Commentary, paras 5–7. See also Crawford and Mertenskötter (n 23) 42, as to the question on the applicability of the ARSIWA to umbrella clause determinations. To the same effect Olleson (n 11) 463.

[45] As stated in *Bosh International, Inc v Ukraine,* ICSID Case No ARB/08/11, Award (25 October 2012) para 183:

> The Tribunal does not agree with the Claimants that the effect of Article II(2)(b) is to render the conduct of the University attributable to Ukraine. Rather, it imposes a positive obligation on Ukraine to ensure that any 'State enterprise' that exercises governmental authority acts in a manner that is consistent with Ukraine's obligations under the BIT.

[46] *F-W Oil Interests v Trinidad and Tobago* (n 24) para 203. See also Carlo de Stefano, 'Case Comment: Adel Hamadi Al Tamimi v Sultanate of Oman' (2017) 32 *ICSID Review* 267, 273.

[47] Ibid., para 206. See also *Ulysseas, Inc v Ecuador,* UNCITRAL, Final Award (12 June 2012) para 135, where the tribunal seems to have equated the relevant provision in the BIT as to its content to Article 5.

[48] *Windstream Energy LLC v Canada,* PCA Case No 2013-22, Award (27 September 2016) para 233, stating that Article 1503(2) NAFTA was 'consistent with

the (albeit scarce) arbitral practice equally favours this approach. Thus, in *Nykomb v Latvia*, the tribunal assumed attribution under general international law without addressing the ECT.[49] Obviously, therefore, the tribunal did not view Article 22 as establishing a rule of attribution, at least not one deviating from the ARSIWA. In *AMTO v Ukraine*, the tribunal considered Article 22 ECT merely from the viewpoint of substantive obligations without addressing issues of attribution.[50]

On a side note, it is of course true that in many cases the result of either approach will be virtually identical[51] because every act by a State enterprise inconsistent with the obligations of a party to an investment agreement amounts to a breach by that party of the agreement, and that breach invariably or *ipso facto* establishes attribution. However, there may be cases where a State entity, while neither being a *de jure* organ under Article 4(1), nor coming within the scope of Article 5 (because it does not exercise governmental authority), may still be considered a *de facto* State organ under Article 4(2). If the application of the *lex specialis* rule(s) on attribution does not establish attribution and if further, the *lex specialis* derogates the general rules entirely, the result will be a significant and unwarranted restriction of State responsibility. This is precisely what happened in *UPS v Canada* and in *Tamimi v Oman*,[52] and it is highly doubtful whether this really was the effect intended by the parties to the treaty.[53]

It is therefore argued in the doctrine that a purported policy of States to have recourse to party autonomy and:

> stipulate *inter partes* rules of attribution that are narrower than the prongs provided by the ARSIWA ... should not be supported, in that it entails in fact a circumvention of the primary rules embodied in the applicable treaty and, consequently, a diminished international protection of covered investors.[54]

Article 5 of the ILC Articles'. See also *Noble Ventures, Inc v Romania,* ICSID Case ARB/01/11, Award (12 October 2005) para 69: 'The rules of attribution can only be found in general international law which supplements the BIT in this respect.'

[49] *Nykomb v Latvia* (n 21) 31 para 4.2.

[50] *Limited Liability Company AMTO v Ukraine,* SCC Arbitration No 080/2005, Award (26 March 2008) para 112.

[51] Kovács (n 5) 176.

[52] In the latter case, this was expressly stated by the tribunal when it found that the relevant Article of the BIT was 'significantly narrower than the several grounds of attribution provided under the ILC Draft Articles on State Responsibility', *Al Tamimi v Oman* (n 39) para 322 in note 675.

[53] Jürgen Kurtz, 'The Paradoxical Treatment of the ILC Articles on State Responsibility in Investor-State Arbitration' (2010) 25 *ICSID Review* 200, 208–210.

[54] de Stefano (n 46) 273.

Based on considerations of legal policy, this argument may or may not have its merits, but it can certainly not do away with the basic freedom of States to establish their 'own' rules of attribution with effect *inter partes*. As long as the underlying general rules are *jus dispositivum* – and neither the ARSIWA (as made abundantly clear in Article 55)[55] nor investment law would indicate otherwise – there is nothing in the law to prevent the parties from finding a solution agreed upon as they please.

As a matter of principle, it is an open question whether the protective ambit of the rules of attribution is preferably to be extended or may equally be restricted. By generally allowing for party autonomy in Article 55, the ARSIWA take a neutral position, and if parties to an investment treaty choose to deviate from these (i.e., Articles 4–11), it is up to them, and them alone, whether they want to expand or restrict their scope of application. The *a priori* denial of 'negative derogation' from the general rules of attribution on account of a purported erosion of primary rules or inconsistency 'with the basic structure of the customary international law on State responsibility' is neither dogmatically nor empirically justified.[56] However, what the limited practice in investment law indeed shows is that it is unwarranted to liberally assume the existence of special rules in investment treaties in general, and special rules that would completely derogate the general ones in particular. A *lex specialis* cannot be presumed but must be clearly established,[57] particularly if it is supposed to be a 'hard' *lex specialis*, that is, one aimed at excluding the operation of the general rules of attribution altogether. Given that none of the tribunals merely assuming a special rule of attribution did substantiate their reasoning,[58] their handling of the issue of *lex specialis* is a missed opportunity to clarify this question.

In conclusion, it may be said that investment treaties are silent on questions of attribution. Special rules on attribution are hard to discern, practice to that effect is either insignificant or unconvincing, or leads to an overall inconclu-

---

55 Confirmed by the ICJ in *Application of the Convention on the Prevention and Punishment of the Crime of Genocide (Bosnia and Herzegovina v Serbia and Montenegro)* [2007] *ICJ Reports* 43, 201 para 408.

56 As argued by de Stefano (n 20) 115–116:

> Derogation *ad minus* of rules of attribution of internationally wrongful acts would entail an indirect erosion or eventual circumvention of the relevant international primary rules. This is not desirable, since such agreements *inter se* would be inconsistent with the basic structure of the customary international law on State responsibility.

57 *Elettronica Sicula SpA (ELSI) (USA v Italy)* [1989] *ICJ Reports* 15, 42, para 50.

58 See Kurtz (n 53) 209, speaking of 'a troubling thinness to the reasoning of the *UPS* tribunal' which only 'offered a generalized laundry list of reasons to support [its] conclusion'.

sive result at best. And even those treaty provisions that may charitably be considered as establishing a *lex specialis* on attribution do not produce an outcome different from that achieved through the application of the general rules. In sum, therefore, investment law offers little to nothing concerning special rules of attribution. As a rule, investment tribunals apply the existing framework and, through that, confirm the customary nature of the general rules of attribution as laid down in the ARSIWA.

IV. THE DEVELOPMENT OF THE CONCEPT OF *DE FACTO* ORGANS IN INVESTMENT ARBITRATION

A. General International Law

While investment tribunals have not established new rules of attribution by resorting to *leges speciales*, they have had an influence on the development of existing rules within the framework of the ARSIWA. One particular aspect of the status as an organ that has been taken up by investment tribunals more recently is the distinction between *de jure* and *de facto* organs. That distinction has gradually developed in general international law and, while it is implicitly contained in Article 4 ARSIWA, it was only in the *Bosnian Genocide* case in the ICJ that the concept assumed a clearer shape.

As to terminology, *de jure* organs are those holding the formal status as organs under the domestic law, whereas *de facto* organs, though not classified as organs under internal law, are factually integrated into the State to such a degree that they, as much as *de jure* organs, 'make up the organization of the State and act on its behalf'.[59] In other words, a *de facto* organ acts in essentially the same way as a *de jure* State organ.[60] It is nowadays generally recognised that the term *de facto* organ should be confined to the rule in Article 4,[61] even though

[59] ILC Articles on State Responsibility (n 2), Commentary to Article 4, para 11. The source for this category may not only be the domestic law, but also internal practice (ibid).

[60] Marko Milanović, 'State Responsibility for Genocide' (2006) 17 *EJIL* 553, 582, referring to the statement of the Chairman of the ILC Drafting Committee in 1998.

[61] See, e.g., Crawford (n 5) 124–126; James Crawford, *Brownlie's Principles of Public International Law* (8th edn, OUP 2012) 545; James Crawford and Simon Olleson, 'The Character and Forms of International Responsibility' in Malcom D Evans (ed), *International Law* (4th edn, OUP 2014) 454; Djamchid Momtaz, 'Attribution of Conduct to the State: State Organs and Entities Empowered to Exercise Elements of Governmental Authority' in Crawford et al (n 4) 237, 243.

the term is sometimes also used in the context of Article 5[62] or of Articles 8,[63] 10 and 11.[64] A main source of that confusion no doubt is the fact that the concept as it stands now in Article 4 was previously part of current Article 8.[65] Furthermore, a clear distinction between the attribution rules in Articles 4 and 5 is not always easy to make, as there may be cases where *de facto* organs also exercise elements of governmental authority.[66]

As is well known, the distinction between *de jure* and *de facto* organs was developed by the ICJ initially in *Nicaragua* where the Court, in a somewhat ambiguous manner, raised the question whether conduct by private individuals could be attributed to a State if the relationship between the two is 'one of dependence on the one side and control on the other'.[67] It implicitly stated that the required threshold to equate that conduct was that of 'complete dependence'.[68] In the *Genocide* case, the Court clarified that concept in three major respects. First, it clearly distinguished the test of complete dependence of *de facto* organs under Article 4 from that of effective control under Article 8. The Court thus established two separate tests, already in fact in *Nicaragua*,[69] but ultimately put that beyond doubt in *Genocide*.[70] Second, it justified the attri-

---

[62] *Jan de Nul NV and Dredging International NV v Arab Republic of Egypt,* ICSID Case No ARB/04/13, Award (6 November 2008) para 144, argument by claimants. Particularly in the German-speaking doctrine, the term *de facto* organ is used in the context of Article 5, see among others Andreas von Arnaud, *Völkerrecht* (4th edn, CF Müller 2019) 173; Markus Beham et al, *Völkerrecht verstehen* (2nd edn, Facultas 2019) 413, referring to the term *de facto* organ in the context of Article 5 as misleading though.

[63] Jörn Griebel and Milan Plücken, 'New Developments Regarding the Rules of Attribution? The International Court of Justice's Decision in *Bosnia* v. *Serbia*' (2008) 21 *LJIL* 601; Yoram Dinstein, *War Aggression and Self-Defence* (5th edn, CUP 2011) 224.

[64] See, e.g., Condorelli and Kress (n 4) 221, 230–231. See also Paolo Palchetti, 'De Facto Organs of a State' in Rüdiger Wolfrum (ed), *The Max Planck Encyclopedia of Public International Law*, vol II (OUP 2012) 1048.

[65] Crawford (n 5) 126.

[66] de Stefano (n 11) 53.

[67] *Military and Paramilitary Activities in and against Nicaragua (Nicaragua v United States of America)* Merits [1896] *ICJ Reports* 14, 62 para 109.

[68] Ibid., 62–63 para 110.

[69] Ibid., 139 para 277. See also Dereje (n 11) 131–132; Milanović (n 60) 577; Crawford (n 5) 125 in note 7.

[70] *Bosnian Genocide* case (n 55) 297 para 397. The Court implicitly confirmed that in *Armed Activities on the Territory of the Congo (Democratic Republic of the Congo v Uganda)* [2005] *ICJ Reports* 168, 226 para 160 where the Court refers to 'the requisite *tests* … for sufficiency of control'. de Stefano (note 11) 52 fittingly – and wittily – states that the Court in the *Genocide* case 'cons[e]crated the category of *de facto* organs to be intended in its normative autonomy'.

bution of the conduct of *de facto* organs by the fact that otherwise, States were allowed 'to escape their international responsibility by choosing to act through persons or entities whose supposed independence would be purely fictitious' because in reality, these were ultimately only agents of the State.[71] And third, by requiring the high threshold of complete dependence, the Court considered that condition to be met only in very exceptional circumstances.[72]

In the doctrine, the complete dependence test has been criticised for lack of need of such a rule of attribution as conduct under the effective control of the State is at any rate covered by Article 8.[73] However, this view ignores the essential difference in threshold between the two tests, complete dependence being obviously much stricter than mere effective control. On the other hand, and that follows directly from the distinction between Articles 4 and 8, if it is established that the person or entity acts under complete dependence from the State, all the actions performed in such capacity as a *de facto* organ would be attributable to the State for purposes of international responsibility.[74] In contrast, under Article 8 'conduct will be attributable to the State only if it directed or controlled the specific operation and the conduct complained of was an integral part of that operation'. Article 8 'does not extend to conduct which was only incidentally or peripherally associated with an operation and which escaped from the State's direction or control'.[75] Furthermore, under Article 8 the control relates to the specific conduct, whereas under Article 4 the control is that over the person or entity acting.[76] In the latter case, it is not decisive whether the State has control over the particular conduct to be attributed (or not). Finally, while conduct of a *de facto* organ is also attributable even if the organ exceeds its authority or contravenes instructions (Article 7), such *ultra vires* acts are beyond the reach of Article 8.[77] Thus, the rule of attribution concerning *de facto* organs strikes a reasonable balance in that it is narrower and broader than that under Article 8 at the same time.

As mentioned, the ICJ has approved the concept of *de facto* State organ and provided some clarifications of its main aspects, yet it has never 'positively' applied it but has regularly denied that the high bar of complete dependence and strict control was met in the given case. In a well-known award rendered just one year after the *Nicaragua* judgment, the Iran-US Claims Tribunal seems to have actually applied the concept of *de facto* organ and, as a result,

---

71 *Bosnian Genocide* case (n 55) 205 para 392.
72 Ibid., 205 para 393.
73 Schicho (n 11) 93–94.
74 *Bosnian Genocide* case (n 55) 207 para 397.
75 ILC Articles on State Responsibility (n 2), Commentary to Article 8, para 3.
76 Dereje (note 11) 174.
77 ILC Articles on State Responsibility (n 2), Commentary to Article 7, para 9.

established attribution of the acts of the Iranian Revolutionary Guards at a time where they were not (yet) part of the formal institutional structure of the State.[78] However, the fact that in support of its decision, the Tribunal cited Article 8 of the first reading draft, which was split into current Articles 8 and 9 in the process of second reading, and in fact applied essentially Article 9 ('conduct carried out in the absence or default of the official authorities'), renders the authority of this case as an example for the current understanding of *de facto* organ status rather doubtful.[79]

The issue now to be addressed is the approach taken by investment tribunals towards the concept of *de facto* organs, and whether arbitral practice in the field of investment law has developed it further.

B. *De Facto* Organs in Investment Arbitration

1. General

Investment arbitration has generally been very compliant in adopting the concept of *de facto* organs in Article 4.[80] A main reason for this is that in investment law, many cases of attribution concern State entities that are in some way or the other controlled by the State, but do not assume 'official'

---

[78] *Kenneth P Yeager v Islamic Republic of Iran,* Case No 10199, Partial Award (2 November 1987) 103 para 42:

> The question … arises whether the acts at issue are attributable to Iran under international law. While there is some doubt as to whether revolutionary 'Komitehs' or 'Guards' can be considered 'organs' of the Government of Iran, since they were not formally recognized during the period relevant to this Case, attributability of acts to the State is not limited to acts of organs formally recognized under internal law. It is generally accepted in international law that a State is also responsible for acts of persons, if it is established that those persons were in fact acting on behalf of the State. See ILC-Draft Article 8 (a). An act is attributable even if a person or group of persons was in fact merely exercising elements of governmental authority in the absence of the official authorities and in circumstances which justified the exercise of those elements of authority. See ILC-Draft Article 8 (b).

[79] See ibid., para 43:

> The Tribunal finds sufficient evidence in the record to establish a presumption that revolutionary 'Komitehs' or 'Guards' after 11 February 1979 were acting in fact on behalf of the new government, or at least exercised elements of governmental authority in the absence of official authorities.

But see de Stefano (n 11) 51. In that respect, it is telling the ILC cites this case not in support of Article 4 but of both Articles 8 and 9; see ILC Articles on State Responsibility (n 2), Commentary to Article 8, para 7 in note 169, and Commentary to Article 9, para 2. See also André de Hoogh, 'Articles 4 and 8 of the 2001 ILC Articles on State Responsibility' (2001) 72 *BYIL* 255, 271.

[80] See the extensive references in Dereje (n 11) 400–401.

or 'formal' organ status under domestic law as required by the concept of *de jure* organs. There have been an increasing number of cases in which claimants have invoked *de facto* organ status, which has prompted some tribunals to address the status of *de facto* organs *eo nomine*.[81] These are essentially cases decided after the delivery of the judgment in *Bosnian Genocide* where the International Court used the term *de facto* organ in the 'proper' context. However, in a number of other cases, it is apparent that tribunals have applied the concept implicitly, that is, without expressly invoking it under the name *de facto* organ status. Admittedly, there have also been cases in which the tribunal has rejected the concept as a matter of principle. As Dereje convincingly argues, the tribunals in these cases were guided merely by the ILC commentary to Article 4, which is not very informative in this respect,[82] and did not consult the case law of the International Court, partly because the Court's judgment in *Genocide* was rendered after the decision in the respective investment case. Finally, up until today, there has apparently been just a single case, in which the tribunal has 'positively' applied the concept in that it considered the high threshold of complete dependence being met.[83] This seems to testify to the exceptional character of that particular rule of attribution.

Despite that development, however, the picture remains quite mixed, especially because the approaches taken and the reasons provided by the tribunals are far from uniform. The most difficult task in properly assessing the approach of investment tribunals to the concept of *de facto* organs is to identify the threshold of complete dependence established or applied. As a deliberately vague term, its concrete application to a given case requires a more detailed specification of its substance on the basis of the broader context which may vary from case to case. Obviously, this holds true for any indeterminate legal term, but it is particularly obvious in the present instance since the concept of *de facto* organs under general international law has developed in the setting of paramilitary or other armed groups, whereas in investment law, the potential *de facto* organs are usually enterprises, instrumentalities or other entities either owned or controlled by the State. Usually, the conduct of the former will be based on completely different premises, guided by totally different purposes, pursuing very different policies, and performed with entirely different means than that of the latter.[84] As a consequence, the nature of the relationship between a State and a paramilitary group under its control will vary significantly from the relationship between a State and a dependent commercial

---

[81] Most notably see *Deutsche Bank AG v Democratic Socialist Republic of Sri Lanka,* ICSID Case No. ARB/09/02, Award (31 October 2012).

[82] Dereje (n 11) 401, with further references.

[83] *Flemingo v Poland* (n 13) para 435.

[84] Dereje (n 11) 141, 402–404; de Stefano (n 11) 141.

enterprise, and this in turn may have repercussions on the legal rules governing that relationship. In addition to the issue of *lex specialis* addressed above, this raises the question as to the 'adaptability' of the concept. This point was for instance made by the tribunal in *Bayandir v Pakistan*, when it said that it was:

> aware that the levels of control required for a finding of attribution under Article 8 in other factual contexts, such as foreign armed intervention or international criminal responsibility, may be different. It believes, however, that the approach developed in such areas of international law is not always adapted to the realities of international economic law and that they should not prevent a finding of attribution if the specific facts of an investment dispute so warrant.[85]

While this statement was made against the backdrop of Article 8, it holds true *a fortiori* for attribution under Article 4. Given the many options available to States to organise their activities through persons, agencies, instrumentalities, bodies, companies or other entities not formally integrated into the structure of the State, in addition to the 'extraordinary expansion of public authority activity',[86] a myriad of potential elements characterising that relationship may have to be taken into account and will be relevant in assessing the existence (or not) of complete dependence and strict control.[87] Much will depend on the particulars of the individual case, not the least on the many ways in which the State can exert actual or material influence on the conduct of the (separate) entity.

---

85 *Bayindir Insaat Turizm Ticaret VE Sanayi AŞ v Pakistan,* ICSID Case No ARB/03/29, Award (27 August 2009) para 1.

86 *Salini Costruttori SpA and Italstrade SpA v Kingdom of Morocco*, ICSID Case No ARB/00/4, Decision on Jurisdiction (23 July 2001) para 35.

87 This was e.g., made clear by the tribunal in *F-W Oil v Trinidad and Tobago* (n 24) para 203, when it stated in relation to Article 5:

> Indeed the ILC consciously refrained from including in the draft even elements towards defining its application in particular cases. Rather, the Commission took the view, as expressed in paragraph (6) of the Commentary to draft Article 5, that the notion had to be judged in the round, in the light of the area of activity in question, and in the light of the history and traditions of the country in question. In short, the notion is intended to be a flexible one, not amenable to general definition in advance; and the elements that would go in its definition in particular cases would be a mixture of fact, law and practice. Moreover – and the point is of some importance – it is not the case that the same answer would necessarily emerge on every occasion; in some of its activities a State enterprise might fall on one side of the line, in others on the other. Considerations of a very similar kind would apply to the case lying on the outer edge of the spectrum of possibilities described above, that in which the State enterprise was not exercising "governmental authority" as such, but has to be regarded as acting in fact on State instructions, or under State direction, or under State control.

The basic guidance for refining that test provided by the International Court is its two-pronged nature.[88] Accordingly, the entity must be completely dependent on the State in that the latter potentially controls each and every activity of the latter which therefore lacks any real independence and becomes merely the instrument or agent of the State.[89] Secondly, it is moreover necessary that the State in fact make use of this potential dependency by exercising strict control over the actions of the entity, for instance by devising the strategy and directing the tactics of the latter.[90]

2. Elements of 'complete dependence' in investment arbitration

In an attempt to categorise the various elements that have been taken into consideration by investment tribunals in assessing *de facto* organ status, several general propositions follow from an analysis of the case law. First, as is dictated by the flexibility of the complete dependence test as well as the great diversity of aspects that may describe the structural or functional relationship between the State and the entity,[91] tribunals look at all available circumstances that might provide an indication as to the organ status, and while they may focus on a particular aspect of special importance to the case, that will usually not be dispositive of the matter. This holds particularly true for the status of the entity under domestic law, which is only one source of information of that entity's 'real' status.[92] For example, with regard to separate legal personality, the tribunal in *Almås v Poland* stated that:

> internal status does not necessarily imply that an entity is not a State organ if other factors, such as the performance of core governmental functions, direct day-to-day subordination to central government, or lack of all operational autonomy, point the other way.[93]

In *Deutsche Bank v Sri Lanka*, the tribunal stated that 'the fact that [a state enterprise] takes the form of a separate legal entity is not decisive' for *de facto* organ status.[94] This is in line with numerous other investment awards holding that the mere existence of separate legal personality by the entity in question does not of itself rule out the possibility of that entity still being a *de facto*

---

[88] Dereje (n 11) 133–134.

[89] *Bosnian Genocide* case (n 55) 205–206, paras 392, 394.

[90] *Nicaragua* case (n 67) 62 para 110.

[91] Dereje (n 11) 402.

[92] Petrochilos (n 5) 337–340.

[93] *Mr Kristian Almås and Mr Geir Almås v Republic of Poland,* UNCITRAL, PCA Case No 2015-13, Award (27 June 2016) para 207.

[94] *Deutsche Bank v Sri Lanka* (n 81) para 405(b).

organ.[95] The tribunal in *InterTrade v Czech Republic* resorted to mere logic in justifying this approach:

> If the Claimant's analysis were to be accepted, i.e. that a State is automatically responsible for all the acts of its separate public entities, this would completely blur the distinction between Article 4 and 5, and the provision of two distinct bases of responsibility.[96]

If anything, the separate legal personality of an entity under domestic law may establish a presumption of institutional separateness against characterisation as a *de jure* State organ.[97] However, and quite obviously, where an overall assessment of the structural and functional relationship between the entity and the State reveals that the entity 'is distinguishable from the State solely on account of its legal personality'[98] or that the 'juristic personality' of the entity merely serves the purpose of giving it 'an aura of independence' with 'deep and pervasive State control',[99] the presumption will be to the contrary.

The same considerations apply to formal control through mere economic ownership of a company by a State which does not convert that entity into an organ[100] but is, at best, only indicative of organ status, an indication, however,

---

[95] *Salini v Morocco* (n 86) para 35; *Nykomb v Latvia* (n 21) para 4.2; *Eureko BV v Republic of Poland,* UNCITRAL, Partial Award (19 August 2005) paras 127–134; *LESI v Algeria* (n 20) para 108, note, however, that the tribunal ultimately considered attribution established under Article 5, ibid., para 118). See further Petrochilos (n 5) 340ff, speaking of the legal cloth as a 'mere form'. Admittedly, there are cases in which the tribunal seemingly held the opposite, see, e.g., *Noble Ventures v Romania* (n 48) para 69. However, upon analysis the tribunal, like others to the same effect, confined itself to addressing the *de jure* organ status of the entity involved but did not consider the possible *de facto* organ status and continued to focus on Article 5. See also *Saipem SpA v People's Republic of Bangladesh*, ICSID Case No ARB/05/07, Decision on Jurisdiction (21 March 2007) para 146.

[96] *InterTrade Holding GmbH v Czech Republic,* UNCITRAL, Final Award (20 May 2012) para 177.

[97] *Almås v Poland* (n 93) para 209; Petrochilos (n 5) 342.

[98] *Salini v Morocco* (n 86) para 35. See also *Consortium RFCC v Kingdom of Morocco*, ICSID Case No ARB/00/6, Decision on Jurisdiction (16 July 2001) para 40: '*une entité que seul son statut juridique distingue de l'Etat*'.

[99] *Deutsche Bank v Sri Lanka* (n 81) para 405(a).

[100] *Waste Management v Mexico (II)* (n 25) para 75: 'The mere fact that a separate entity is majority-owned or substantially controlled by the state does not make it *ipso facto* an organ of the state.' Similarly *Emilio Agustín Maffezini v Kingdom of Spain,* ICSID Case No ARB/97/7, Decision on Jurisdiction (25 January 2000) para 84; *EDF (Services) Ltd v Romania,* ICSID Case No ARB/05/13, Award (8 October 2009) para 190; *Electrabel SA v Republic of Hungary,* ICSID Case No ARB/07/19, Award (30 November 2012) para 7.96. *Tulip Real Estate Investment and Development Netherlands BV v Republic of Turkey,* ICSID Case No ARB/11/28, Award (10 March

that must be supplemented by additional factors indicating complete dependence.[101] Also, the fact that a State entity or enterprise was established by the State or whether it was established by statutory law, decree or private law act, is of little importance in establishing *de facto* organ status.[102] Thus, investment tribunals, in line with both Article 4 and the case law of the International Court, have approached the matter of *de facto* organs from a substantive perspective and have discarded purely formal criteria as largely insignificant.

As to substantive criteria, the influence of the State on the composition of the Board of Directors managing the activity of the entity is crucial. Again, however, the question who is entitled to appoint and dismiss the members of the Board, or the question whether only public officials in office are eligible to serve on the Board will depend on the particular circumstances, especially the institutional or corporate structure of the entity. If, for instance, the Board is composed of State officials on account only of their status as officials, this will provide a strong presumption in favour of *de facto* organ status.[103] Similarly, the fact that the government has a direct right to appoint and/or remove the Board will be important to determine *de facto* organ status.[104] In such a case of 'dual capacity' of public officials, the strategic interests and the policies of the

2014) para 289: 'The position of the Tribunal is that, whilst state ownership may, in certain circumstances, be a factor relevant to the question of attribution, it does not convert a separate corporate entity into an 'organ' of the State.' According to the ILC Commentary to Article 8, para 6, mere ownership does not even suffice to establish the much lower threshold of effective control.

[101] Minority ownership by the State will generally evidence a lack of any significant control by, even less so dependence on, the State, see, e.g., *Lao Holdings NV v Lao People's Democratic Republic,* ICSID Case No ARB(AF)/12/6, Award (6 August 2019) para 81: 'It is clear that a minority shareholding in a corporation is not sufficient in international law ... of itself, to attribute the acts of a corporation to its shareholders.'

[102] Dereje (n 11) 139–140, 405.

[103] See, e.g., *Salini v Morocco* (n 86) para 32; *Consortium RFCC v Maroc* (n 98) para 36; *Chevron Bangladesh v Bangladesh* (n 26) para 164(iii); note, however, that the tribunal already found the relevant entity to be a *de jure* organ (ibid., paras 146–148). See also *Ampal-American Israel Corp et al v Arab Republic of Egypt,* ICSID Case No ARB/12/11, Decision on Liability and Heads of Loss (21 February 2017) paras 137–147, although the tribunal in the end applied Articles 8 and 11; *MCI Power Group LC and New Turbine, Inc v Republic of Ecuador,* ICSID Case No ARB/03/6, Award (31 July 2007) paras 224–225, note that the tribunal only invoked 'the customary rules codified by the ILC', without applying a particular provision.

[104] *Flemingo v Poland* (n 13) para 430; *Deutsche Bank v Sri Lanka* (n 81) para 405.b); *LESI v Algeria* (n 20) para 107(iii) and (iv). But see *Ortiz Construcciones y Proyectos SA v People's Democratic Republic of Algeria,* ICSID Case No ARB/17/1, Award (29 April 2020) para 176, where the tribunal found that even though the members of both the Board and the Assembly were nominated by a government agency, the entity still maintained a sufficient degree of operational autonomy.

relevant governmental body will almost invariably control the entity's actions which, therefore, will lack substantive independence. Where, however, the State enjoys limited control over the composition of the Board, for instance the right to appoint and remove only the director or president, or the respective deputy, tribunals have not considered the entity a *de facto* organ.[105]

The same applies to cases where the members of the Board are appointed by the government in exceptional circumstances, for instance because the Supervisory Council, who would normally be entrusted with appointment, is temporarily eliminated.[106] Here again, much will depend on the circumstances, and a perfunctory application of a single criterion will not be enough. For example, the fact that the Board members are designated by government officials and that the Board members appointed include government officials may be indicative for dependence but not suffice in itself. As the tribunal in *Unión Fenosa Gas v Egypt* stated, as much as an ordinary private company, a State-owned company is commercially controlled by its owner, and '[p]rivate parent corporations routinely appoint their officers as members of the boards of directors of their wholly-owned subsidiaries without thereby losing shareholder immunity from liability'.[107]

A further criterion taken into consideration by investment tribunals is that of the entity being under binding orders or directions by the government[108] or subject to instructions.[109] However, that criterion too requires some clarification. First, it is necessary to assess the 'true' nature of the instruction or direction. Thus, in *Hamester v Ghana*, the tribunal did not consider the right to give 'directions of a general character', rather than specific instructions, as decisive. Furthermore, it emphasised that these 'general policy directions' could only be made after consultation with the Board of Directors.[110] Secondly, it is important to determine whether the entity is generally under instructions, or whether this occurs only in specific situations. In the latter case, that fact might rather come within the scope of Article 8. Finally, the relevance of instructions for purposes of controlling the entity may vary in two ways. On the one hand, it will make a difference whether the instructions are binding on the entity under

---

[105] *Almås v Poland* (n 93) para 213.

[106] *Staur Eiendom AS, EBO Invest AS and Rox Holding AS v Republic of Latvia*, ICSID Case No ARB/16/38, Award (28 February 2020) paras 332, 336.

[107] *Unión Fenosa Gas, SA v Arab Republic of Egypt,* ICSID Case No ARB/14/4, Award (31 August 2018) para 9.106.

[108] *Deutsche Bank v Sri Lanka* (n 81) para 405(b), where the tribunal added that it would not matter whether those directions are in the best interests of the entity.

[109] *Chevron Bangladesh v Bangladesh* (n 26) para 162.

[110] *Hamester v Ghana* (n 24) para 187.

the given circumstances,[111] or whether they only have 'recommendatory' character. On the other hand, one will also have to distinguish a formal or 'official' power to give instructions from the right to give mere factual ones. There may well be cases where the Board, while not formally under instructions, acts in a way that pursues the interests of the State rather than that of the entity. Such a possibility may exist in situations where members of the Board 'obey' such informal instructions out of fear not to be re-appointed or to be removed or to suffer similar disadvantages.[112]

Some tribunals have also taken into account the financial relationship between the State and the relevant entity, in particular the extent to which the latter depended financially on the former. Relevant factors will for instance include whether the entity has an autonomous budget,[113] its own bank account or holds property in its own name,[114] or funds owned by the State private ownership,[115] in which cases tribunals have denied *de facto* organ status. Conversely, if the entity is funded exclusively by the State, for instance by funds originating 'from the amounts allocated in the State budget',[116] this will militate in favour of such status.

Tribunals have additionally considered whether the entity was created with a view to carrying out (exclusively) governmental functions.[117] By contrast, 'where an entity engages on its own account in commercial transactions, even if these are important to the national economy',[118] or where an entity, while carrying out public activities, is required to be managed in accordance with business practice without any commitment by the governmental systems and conditions,[119] the fact that the activities are performed in the general interest of the State does not render that entity a *de facto* organ. However, this criterion must certainly put into perspective, as the organ status under Article 4 exists on account of the close structural or insti-

---

[111] See, e.g., *EDF v Romania* (n 100) para 205. Note, however, that the tribunal's findings were made under Article 5.

[112] See, in detail, Schicho (n 11) 197–198.

[113] *Jan de Nul v Egypt* (n 62) para 161.

[114] *Almås v Poland* (n 93) para 213.

[115] *Unión Fenosa v Egypt* (n 107) para 9.101.

[116] *Toto Costruzioni Generali SpA v Republic of Lebanon,* ICSID Case No ARB/07/12, Decision on Jurisdiction (11 September 2009) para 52, note, however, that the tribunal ultimately attributed the conduct under Article 5. See also *LESI v Algeria* (n 20) para 107.v; *Deutsche Bank v Sri Lanka* (n 81) para 405(b). See also Petrochilos (n 5) 342.

[117] *Flemingo v Poland* (n 13) para 428, confirming *de facto* organ status (para 435). See also *Salini v Morocco* (n 86) para 33; *Emilio Agustín Maffezini v Kingdom of Spain,* ICSID Case No ARB/97/7, Award (22 October 2015) para 53. Note, however, that the tribunal applied the 'functional' test under Article 5.

[118] *Almås v Poland* (n 93) para 210. See also *Ortiz v Algeria* (n 104) paras 183, 188; *Tulip v Turkey* (n 100) para 287.

[119] *Jan de Nul v Egypt* (n 62) para 161.

tutional relationship between the State and the entity, and not because an entity is authorised to exercise governmental authority. For the conduct of an organ under Article 4 (*de jure* and *de facto*) is attributable to the State irrespective of whether the specific act or omission was carried out in the exercise of public authority, provided of course that the organ acts in its capacity as an organ.[120] As a distinct criterion, the exercise of governmental authority is relevant only under Article 5.

The clearest example of complete dependence is the fact that the entity lacks (any) operational[121] or real autonomy.[122] In such circumstances, the overall picture of the relationship between the State and the entity reveals in and of itself a complete dependence of the latter on the former. If a total lack of operational or real autonomy results from an aggregate assessment of the context, a further investigation into the existence and actual exercise of strict control may be dispensed with.[123]

3. Requirement of strict control

Where the overall assessment of the circumstances reveals a complete dependence of the entity, the State will potentially have full control over it. Given the exceptional character of *de facto* organ status, the International Court requires furthermore that the State actually exercise that strict control. This requirement will however be difficult to prove in practice. Therefore, it is important to determine whether the State has 'used' the entity for pursuing its own interests rather than those of the entity itself. In *Deutsche Bank v Sri Lanka*, for instance, the tribunal considered it significant that the entity was required to follow any written directions of the Minister, 'regardless of whether those directions are in the best interests of [the entity]'.[124] Thus, if the entity has no choice in its commercial activities, but is merely the principal vehicle by which the State implements its own policy or other decisions,[125] and the entity does not perform any meaningful activities of its own, the requirement of strict control may readily be presumed to be met.

V. CONCLUDING REMARKS

This brief review of the practice of investment tribunals regarding selected issues of attribution shows an overall remarkable 'embeddedness' of invest-

---

[120] ILC Articles on State Responsibility (n 2), Commentary to Article 4, paras 3 and 6.

[121] *Almås v Poland* (n 93) para 209; *Ortiz v Algeria* (n 104) para 177.

[122] *Unión Fenosa v Egypt* (n 107) para 9.106.

[123] Dereje (n 11) 412, with further references.

[124] *Deutsche Bank v Sri Lanka* (n 81) para 405b.

[125] *Chevron v Bangladesh* (n 26) para 163(ii); *Nykomb v Latvia* (n 21) 31.

ment law in general international law. As to possible *leges speciales* on attribution, tribunals have overwhelmingly discarded such an option and considered the relevant provision(s) in the applicable treaties as either containing attribution rules that are substantially identical to those under the ARSIWA, or as establishing distinct primary norms containing substantive obligations rather than rules of attribution. The few decisions in which tribunals have affirmed the existence of a *lex specialis* remain isolated which comes as no surprise given their disturbingly scant and flawed reasoning. This obvious lack of need for *leges speciales* on attribution in the field of investment law clearly confirms and reinforces the general rules of attribution.

As to the concept of *de facto* organ, the practice of investment arbitration has somehow revived a specific rule of attribution under the general system of State responsibility, a rule that, while already expounded by the ICJ in the *Nicaragua* case, somehow lay dormant in practice. Until the Court's more detailed treatment of the concept in the *Bosnian Genocide* case, the case law of investment tribunals has developed in an organic, yet unorganised way. In many earlier cases, most tribunals addressing *de facto* organ status have done so implicitly – or perhaps intuitively – rather than dogmatically or in a well-structured manner. However, after the adoption of the ARSIWA and, particularly, the Court's *Bosnian Genocide* judgment, *de facto* organ status was increasingly argued by claimants in investment arbitration, and tribunals addressed and, as a matter of principle, expressly approved the concept.

As to the application of the concept, the practice of investment arbitration shows a clear 'policy' of tribunals not to pick out individual aspects and treat them in isolation from each other. There is no single decisive criterion that would establish *de facto* organ status. Rather, tribunals look at the legal and factual ties of the (separate) entity and the whole set of elements existing between the State and the entity; they engage in an overall assessment of the circumstances in order to determine the existence of the criteria of *de facto* organs.[126] In doing so, they have remained within the structure and framework of the ARSIWA and the ILC's master plan, but added flesh to the bone of a concept rarely used in general international law. In line with the view of the ICJ that *de facto* organ status is of an exceptional character, investment tribunals have applied the concept very restrictively. While there are numerous cases where tribunals have reviewed the facts through the lens of Article 4(2)

---

[126] Such an overall assessment was conducted in a very detailed manner by the tribunal in *LESI v Algeria* (n 20) which concluded (at para 108): '*Il ressort de l'ensemble de ces éléments que l'ANB est certes une entité dotée d'une personnalité juridique distincte, mais qu'elle dépend étroitement de l'Etat algérien*'. And further: '*Pour le Tribunal arbitral, il ressort de cette analyse que l'ANB peut être assimilée à cet égard à l'Etat algérien.*'

and ultimately found the conditions not to be met, there is apparently only one case to date in which the tribunal has explicitly established attribution under the concept of *de facto* organ.[127] To be sure, the case law is still in development and on occasion inconsistent, as tribunals have assessed the same or similar facts and criteria differently. However, this appears to be a well-known, probably unavoidable systemic problem of investment arbitration that is not specific to the issues studied in this chapter.

In conclusion, the contribution of investment arbitration to the general rules of attribution in the law of State responsibility is modest, but it is perceptible, and it is continuing. Using the concept of *de facto* organ under Article 4(2) as an example, it was shown that the general rule is reasoned, well-founded and flexible enough to be transposed to the investor-State context. Investment arbitration has adapted it to the special needs of investment law, particularly as regards the different criteria to be applied. It may reasonably be assumed that this overall conclusion can also be transferred to other rules of attribution. Thus, by applying, interpreting and adapting the ILC Articles on attribution, international investment law has clarified and consolidated the general rules and continues to shape a solid fundament on which future tribunals may build their cases.

---

127 *Flemingo v Poland* (n 13) para 435.

8. The impact of investment arbitration in the development of state responsibility defences

Federica I. Paddeu

I. INTRODUCTION

International law recognises six general defences to State responsibility: consent, self-defence, countermeasures, *force majeure*, distress and state of necessity. These are included in Chapter V of Part One of the Articles on the Responsibility of States for Internationally Wrongful Acts (ARS), adopted by the International Law Commission and noted by the UN General Assembly in 2001.[1] To a great extent, Chapter V constitutes a codification of the customary

[1] ILC, Articles on Responsibility of States for Internationally Wrongful Acts, with commentaries (2001) II(2) *ILC Yearbook* 31, arts 20–25 (ARS). On this category in general see: Federica Paddeu, 'Circumstances Precluding Wrongfulness' (2015) *MPEPIL* https://opil.ouplaw.com/view/10.1093/law:epil/9780199231690/law-9780199231690-e215 accessed 6 January 2021, and references cited therein. The term 'defence' is used here to refer to the circumstances in Chapter V of Part One of the ARS. The term seems better suited for the task, as it is agnostic in respect of the classification of any given circumstance as a circumstance precluding wrongfulness (justification) or a circumstance precluding responsibility (excuse), both of which will be defined in Section V.A below. Note, however, that the term 'defence' is also used in a much wider sense, to refer to what Crawford has called the 'armoury of defensive arguments' at the disposal of a State, and which range from objections to jurisdiction and admissibility to waivers of the claim, see James Crawford, *State Responsibility: The General Part* (CUP 2013) 275. When used in this chapter, 'defence' will refer to *substantive* defensive arguments, namely defensive arguments which aim to defeat a claim on the merits. This usage is not unknown in international law. By way of example, Greece referred to its arguments relating to the exception of non-performance (at one point proposed in the ILC as a candidate for inclusion in Chapter V of Part One) and countermeasures as 'Defences' in *Application of the Interim Accord of 13 September 1995 (FYR of Macedonia v Greece)* [2011] *ICJ Reports* 644. See *Interim Accord*, Counter-Memorial of Greece (19 January 2010) 178 ('Other Possible Defences'); Rejoinder of Greece, (27 October 2010) 185 ('Chapter 8: Defences to the FYROM's claim of breach of

international law on defences. Nevertheless, some doubts remain as to the customary recognition of certain conditions and requirements of the various provisions, as well as in respect of the characterisation of the defences as circumstances precluding wrongfulness or circumstances precluding responsibility. Like the ARS themselves, the defences are of general application, insofar as they are available in respect of all international obligations without any distinctions as to the source, origin or content of those obligations.[2] The defences are, therefore, applicable across the whole range of international law including specialised fields of international law,[3] such as investment law.[4]

The defences are regularly invoked in disputes involving investment law (broadly understood, as will be explained later): *force majeure* played a significant role in the Iranian defence against US nationals' claims before the Iran-US Claims Tribunals,[5] countermeasures were relied upon by Mexico in response to claims by US investors in the high-fructose corn syrup disputes,[6] and state of necessity was a central piece of Argentina's defence strategy in the claims brought against it by foreign investors in the wake of the financial crisis of the early 2000s.[7] More recently, *force majeure* and state of necessity have been, and are likely to be, invoked by respondent States in claims arising in connection with the events of the Arab Spring[8] and the emergency measures taken by States in response to the SARS-Cov-2 pandemic.[9] A bird's eye view of the decisions of international courts and tribunals shows that, at least since the adoption of the ARS in 2001, the majority of the practice in respect of the

the Interim Accord'). This term is to be preferred as it is agnostic as to the character of any one of the provisions in ARS (n 1) arts 20–26 as justifications (namely, circumstances precluding wrongfulness) or excuses (namely, circumstances precluding responsibility).

[2] ILC, Articles on State Responsibility (n 1) art 12.

[3] Subject, of course, to any relevant *lex specialis*, as per ARS (n 1) art 55.

[4] For an analysis of the defences in the context of investment law, see: Martins Paparinskis, 'Circumstances Precluding Wrongfulness in International Investment Law' (2016) 31 *ICSID Review* 484.

[5] On which see, David Caron, 'The Basis of Responsibility: Attribution and Other Trans-Substantive Rules' in Richard Lillich et al (eds), *The Iran-US Claims Tribunal: Its Contribution to the Law of State Responsibility* (Transnational Publishers 1998) 173–177.

[6] This case law will be considered below in Section IV.

[7] This case law will be considered below in Section V.

[8] See, e.g., *Unión Fenosa Gas SA v Arab Republic of Egypt*, ICSID Case No ARB/14/4, Award (31 August 2018) para 8.20 (Respondent) and para 8.36 (Claimant). See further: Cherine Foty, 'The Impact of the Arab Spring on the International Arbitration Landscape' (*Kluwer Arbitration Blog*, 26 July 2019).

[9] See Federica Paddeu and Kate Parlett, 'COVID-19 and Investment Treaty Claims' (*Kluwer Arbitratoin Blog,* 30 March 2020).

defences in the law of responsibility has come from investor-State dispute settlement.[10]

This chapter will consider the contribution of investment arbitration towards the development of the defences in the law of State responsibility. It will focus on the three defences mentioned in the previous paragraph, as these are the most commonly invoked in investment disputes. It will show that the precursors of the current investment treaty regime, namely disputes in relation to damage caused to the property of foreigners decided by the Permanent Court of International Justice (PCIJ) and other mixed claims commissions and arbitral tribunals, had a significant impact on the development of the plea of *force majeure*. It will then review the current engagement of investment treaty tribunals with the pleas of countermeasures and state of necessity. In both of these cases, the tribunals took as a starting point the codification of these defences in the ARS. Crucially, none of the States parties to the disputes contested the customary status of these defences – despite the fact that they had been far from uncontroversial during the drafting of the ARS.[11] These decisions have

---

[10] To exemplify this contrast, the International Court of Justice (ICJ) has considered defences in the law of responsibility only a handful of times since 2001: *Case Concerning Oil Platforms (Islamic Republic of Iran v United States of America)* [2003] *ICJ Reports* 161, the parties argued ARS art 21, though the Court did not expressly address this provision in its judgment; *Legal Consequences of the Construction of a Wall in the Occupied Palestinian Territory* [2004] *ICJ Reports* 136, the Court briefly rejected a potential plea of necessity by Israel; *Armed Activities on the Territory of the Congo (DRC v Uganda)* [2005] *ICJ Reports* 168, Uganda invoked consent and self-defence, and referred to the relevant provisions in ARS in its pleadings, but the Court did not refer to the ARS provisions in its decision; *Application of the Interim Accord of 13 September 1995* (n 1), Greece invoked countermeasures in response to FYR Macedonia's claim. Countermeasures have also been invoked in the disputes relating to the jurisdiction of the ICAO Council, between Bahrain, Egypt, Saudi Arabia and UAE, on the one hand, and Qatar, on the other, which are currently pending before the Court, and were briefly addressed in the parties' arguments, though not by the Court in its judgment, in *Jurisdictional Immunities of the State (Germany v Italy: Greece intervening)* [2012] *ICJ Reports* 99. Beyond the ICJ, the UNGA, 'Report of the UN Secretary-General: Responsibility of States for internationally wrongful acts - Compilation of decisions of international courts, tribunals and other bodies' (20 June 2017) UN Doc A/71/80/Add.1, 8, shows that art 23 (*force majeure*) was referenced in only one decision of the European Court of Human Rights, and art 20 (consent) was referenced in only one decision in the WTO.

[11] For a brief overview of the controversies regarding countermeasures during the drafting of the ARS, see Federica Paddeu, *Justification and Excuse in International Law: Concept and Theory of General Defences* (CUP 2018) 259–261. Interestingly, Mexico, which invoked countermeasures before investment tribunals as will be seen later, was critical of the inclusion of countermeasures in the ARS. For example, in 1993, Mexico commented in the Sixth Committee that: 'legitimizing the imposition of unilateral sanctions by one or more States in response to the wrongful conduct of

contributed to the consolidation of the defences in customary law. What is more, in grappling with the application of these general and abstract rules to the particular circumstances of each dispute, tribunals have had to specify the situations that meet the requirements and conditions of each: thus adding meat to the (bare) bones of these rules. Perhaps more relevantly for our purposes, these tribunals have had to engage with situations not addressed by the ARS (or in their drafting history) and even with fundamental aspects of these rules. To illustrate, this chapter will consider the question of the permissibility of countermeasures affecting the rights of investors, as an example of the former type of engagement, and the classification of state of necessity as an excuse rather than a justification, as an example of the latter.

In addition to this introduction, this chapter is divided into five sections. Section II provides some preliminary remarks on judicial legal development in international law in general and, in particular, the role that investment tribunals play in development of the law of State responsibility. Sections III, IV, and V, then move on to consider each of the examples mentioned: *force majeure*, countermeasures and state of necessity, respectively. Section VI concludes with an assessment of the impact (or potential impact) of investment arbitration on the development of these defences.

The analysis in this study will take the adoption of the ARS in 2001 as the critical date by reference to which the development of the defences will be assessed. The ARS, and the formulation of the defences contained therein, will therefore be taken as a snapshot of where the customary law on the defences stands, and any changes and modifications will be assessed by reference to the provisions in this document. This point of reference is necessary, since customary law is not static but is (or can be, at any rate) in constant evolution.

---

another State was contrary to norms of international law and might exacerbate international conflicts. All provisions on countermeasures should be deleted': UNGA, 'Summary Record of the 27th Meeting' (4 November 1993) UN Doc A/C.6/48/SR.27, 13, para 60. In 2001, it 'regretted' their inclusion in the ARS ('Comments and observations received from Governments' (2001) II(1) *ILC Yearbook* 83, para 1.) but was ultimately satisfied with the balance struck in their regulation (UNGA, 'Summary Record of the 14th Meeting' (13 November 2001) UN Doc A/C.6/56/SR.14, 3–4, para 16. For the controversies surrounding the adoption of the plea of necessity, see Paddeu, *Justification and Excuse*, ibid., 398–401. Only in one case, under the Argentina–UK BIT, claimants contested the customary status of the defence, relying on the United Kingdom's objection. In their view, the defence was either not part of customary law or, at any rate, not applicable under the BIT since the UK had been a 'persistent objector': *BG Group Plc v Republic of Argentina,* UNCITRAL, Award (24 December 2007) para 400. The Tribunal did not address this issue for, 'whether the Tribunal rejects or accepts' its application, the defence would fail: ibid., para 407.

Any potential change must therefore be assessed by reference to a static point in time, by reference to what the customary law was 'on a given day'.[12]

II. INVESTMENT ARBITRATION AS A MOTOR FOR THE DEVELOPMENT OF THE LAW OF DEFENCES?

Whether international tribunals can make or develop international law, in addition to just applying the law to specific facts, is a persistent and thorny question in international law.[13] Many eminent scholars have turned their attention to the issue,[14] and their works show that this is a question which eschews simple answers. It is not possible to do justice to the richness of this literature in the context of this chapter, but it is nevertheless important, to frame the discussion to follow, to consider two preliminary questions, one general and one specific. First, do international courts and tribunals contribute to the development of international law?[15] Second, can (and do) international investment tribunals contribute to the development of the law of State responsibility?

A. International Courts and the Development of International Law

As to the first question, the starting point is the perhaps obvious observation that international courts and tribunals are not law-makers: they have no express legislative mandate.[16] As a general rule, decisions of international tribunals are binding only on the parties to them,[17] and are not a formal source of the law. Indeed, Article 38(1)(d) of the Statute of the International Court of Justice

---

[12] James Crawford and Thomas Viles, 'International Law on a Given Day' in James Crawford (ed), *International Law as an Open System: Selected Essays* (Cameron May 2002) 69.

[13] Christian J. Tams and Antonios Tzanakopoulos, 'Barcelona Traction at 40: The ICJ as an Agent of Legal Development' (2010) 23 *LJIL* 781, 782, 784.

[14] One of the most important texts on this question is Hersch Lauterpacht, *The Development of International Law by the International Court* (Stevens & Sons 1958). For more recent works considering this question, see the collection of essays edited by Christian J. Tams and James Sloan (eds), *The Development of International Law by the International Court of Justice* (OUP 2013), and the 2015 Gaetano Morelli Lectures, published in Enzo Cannizzaro et al (eds), *Decisions of the ICJ as Sources of International Law?* (International and European Papers Publishing 2018). Other reference works will be referred to throughout this chapter, as they become relevant.

[15] The question whether they should is a separate one, which will not be considered in this chapter.

[16] Tams and Tzanakopoulos (n 13) 782.

[17] See, e.g., Statute of the International Court of Justice (adopted 24 October 1945, published 18 April 1946) 33 UNTS 993, art 59.

(ICJ) mentions them as 'subsidiary means for the determination of rules of law'.[18] Decisions of international courts and tribunals are, in the words of Shabtai Rosenne, 'the store-house from which the rules of heads (a), (b) and (c) [of Article 38(1) of the ICJ Statute] can be extracted'.[19] For this reason, international decisions have also been described as 'documentary sources' that indicate where we can find evidence of the existence of the rules of international law.[20] Nevertheless, it is undeniable that the decisions of international courts and tribunals can have an impact on the development of international law.[21] As noted by Rosalyn Higgins, former President of the ICJ, 'the very determination of specific disputes, and the provision of specific advice, does develop international law'.[22] This is certainly true of the ICJ.[23] It is also true of other international tribunals within their own substantive fields of law. Thus, specifically in the context of investment arbitration, Stephan Schill has remarked that to understand international investment law 'means knowing the practice of investment treaty tribunals'.[24] But the contribution of these tribunals can go beyond their own specialised fields.[25]

More specifically, tribunals can have an impact in the development of customary international law – the source of (much of) the law of State responsi-

---

[18] Ibid., art 38(1)(d).

[19] Malcom Shaw, *Rosenne's Law and Practice of the International Court: 1920-2015*, vol 3 (5th edn, Brill/Nijhoff 2016) 1607.

[20] Alain Pellet and Daniel Müller, 'Article 38' in Andreas Zimmerman and Christian J. Tams (eds), *The Statute of the International Court of Justice: A Commentary* (3rd edn, OUP 2019) 945.

[21] See, e.g., Robert Y Jennings, 'The Judiciary, International and National, and the Development of International Law' (1996) 45 *ICLQ* 1, 3; Alain Pellet, 'Article 38' in Andreas Zimmerman et al (eds), *The Statute of the International Court of Justice: A Commentary* (OUP 2006) 789; James Crawford, *Brownlie's Principles of Public International Law* (8th edn, OUP 2012) 39-40.

[22] Rosalyn Higgins, *Problems and Process: International Law and How We Use it* (Clarendon 1994) 302.

[23] See, generally, Lauterpacht (n 14). See further: Christine Chinkin and Alan Boyle, *The Making of International Law* (OUP 2007) 268; Alain Pellet, 'Shaping the Future of International Law: The Role of the World Court in Law-Making' in Mahnoush H Arsanjani et al (eds), *Looking to the Future: Essays on International Law in Honor of W Michael Reisman* (Brill 2010) 1065; Pellet and Müller, 'Article 38' (n 20) 954ff and Chester Brown, 'Article 59' in Zimmerman and Tams (n 20) 1587ff.

[24] Stephan W. Schill, 'Sources of International Investment Law: Multilateralization, Arbitral Precedent, Comparativism, Soft Law' in Samantha Besson and Jean d'Aspremont (eds), *The Oxford Handbook of the Sources of International Law* (OUP 2017) 1104.

[25] See, e.g., Chinkin and Boyle (n 23) 300.

bility.[26] Christine Chinkin and Alan Boyle have identified three ways in which this contribution can materialise.[27] First, international courts and tribunals can declare existing law. Second, during the phase of formation of a customary rule, tribunals can crystallise the rule by revealing its existence on the basis of assessments of the practice and *opinio juris* of States.[28] Third, they can 'generate or constitute a rule where the decision becomes a focal point for the subsequent practice and *opinio juris* of States'. These three processes may appear distinct at least at an analytical level, but the distinctions between them are blurred in practice. More particularly, assessments as to whether courts and tribunals have generated customary law, or merely revealed or crystallised it, cannot escape some degree of subjectivity. Superimposed on these three mechanisms, courts and tribunals can also contribute to legal development in the application of the (existing) law to specific facts. It is usual to distinguish between, on the one hand, application/clarification of the rules,[29] and, on the other hand, the development of the rules. [30] But, once again, these two processes are not clearly distinct be it conceptually or practically, and the boundaries between them are fuzzy and relatively subjective.[31]

---

[26] It is broadly accepted that many of the provisions in the ARS (n 1) are part of customary international law.

[27] Chinkin and Boyle (n 23) 283.

[28] For an example, see the ICJ's decision in *Jurisdictional Immunities of the State* (n 10).

[29] For example, by assisting in the clarification of uncertain aspects of rules that are already established as part of customary international law. See, e.g., Tarcisio Gazzini, 'The Role of Customary International Law in the Field of Foreign Investment' (2007) 8 *JWIT* 691, 692–693. See also Tams and Tzanakopoulos (n 13) 784.

[30] For example, by expanding (or restricting) their scope of application. See: Patrick Dumberry, 'The Role and Relevance of Awards in the Formation, Identification and Evolution of Customary Rules in International Investment Law' (2016) 33 *J Int'l Arb* 269, 278. An example, in this regard, is the expansion of the category of high-ranking officers entitled to absolute immunity by the ICJ in *Case Concerning the Arrest Warrant of 11 April 2000 (DRC v Belgium)* [2002] *ICJ Reports* 3. The Court reasoned teleologically in that case, rather than on the basis of State practice and *opinio juris*. Nevertheless, in their practice subsequent to this judgment, States have for the most part endorsed the scope of absolute immunities for the 'troika' of high-ranking officers: Head of State, Head of Government and Foreign Affairs Ministers. On this development, see Roger O'Keefe, 'Jurisdictional Immunities' in Tams and Sloan (n 14) 118–120.

[31] Karol Wolfke, *Custom in Present International Law* (2nd edn, Nijhoff 1993) 72–73:

> A decision of the court on what is the law is always based, to a greater of lesser degree, on free evaluation. Hence it is a truism to say that a judicial organ ascertaining customs to some extent creates them … A statement by the court that a certain rule applies in settling a dispute involves a law-creating factor.

Not all decisions of international tribunals, however, contribute to the development of international law. There are, as Jan Paulsson wrote, 'awards and awards, some destined to become ever brighter beacons, others to flicker and die near-instant deaths'.[32] Judicial legal development is limited and contingent. To begin with, international courts and tribunals, while they may participate in the development of the law, are but one such participant. So the impact of their decisions on legal development will be dependent on interactions with other actors in this process including, most importantly, States.[33] Formally, of course, it is the wear of the decisions in the practice of States which will be determinative of their contribution to legal development: whether States are willing to follow the particular decision and to do so out of a sense of legal obligation.[34] In practice however, other international bodies may play a role. Thus, other international tribunals may follow the decision in question, the ILC could include the finding in one of its projects,[35] or the UN General Assembly may adopt a declaration on the basis of an advisory opinion of the Court.[36] But this is not all. In order to enter these interactive processes of legal development, the relevant decisions must persuade other actors. In this connection, the literature has identified a series of external and internal factors that may be relevant in the assessment of a decision's potential impact on legal development. Externally, the impact of courts as agents for legal development

---

See further Anthea Roberts, 'Power and Persuasion in Investment Treaty Interpretation: The Dual Role of States' (2010) 104 *AJIL* 180, 188.

[32] Jan Paulsson, 'International Arbitration and the Generation of Legal Norms: Treaty Arbitration and International Law' (2006) 5 *TDM*.

[33] Chinkin and Boyle (n 23) 301; Christian J. Tams, 'The Development of International Law by the International Court of Justice' in Cannizzaro et al (n 14) 97–98.

[34] For indeed, other actors can choose to overrule or ignore the decisions in question: Tams and Tzanakopoulos (n 13) 785.

[35] An example is the attribution rule on acknowledgement and adoption in ARS (n 1) art 11. This basis of attribution was not included in the first draft of the ARS, which had completed consideration of the provisions on attribution in 1973. Attribution on the basis of subsequent endorsement of private conduct was relied upon in 1980 by the ICJ in *Case Concerning United States Diplomatic and Consular Staff in Tehran* [1980] *ICJ Reports* 3. This basis of attribution was subsequently included in the ARS by Special Rapporteur Crawford in 1998: James Crawford, 'First Report on State Responsibility' (1998) II(1) *ILC Yearbook* 54–55. For a brief overview of the ILC's work on this article, see Olivier de Frouville et al, 'Attribution of Conduct to the State: Private Individuals' in James Crawford et al (eds), *The Law of International Responsibility* (OUP 2010) 273–275.

[36] While these are not binding, according to Jennings, States may find it imprudent not to follow them: Robert Jennings, 'What Is International Law and How Do We Tell It When We See It?' in Robert Jennings, *Collected Writings of Sir Robert Jennings*, vol 2 (Kluwer 1983) 741.

is dependent on opportunity (namely, the cases and legal issues brought before them) and what Christian J. Tams has referred to as the 'receptiveness' of the particular field to judicial development.[37] Internally, the impact of decisions towards legal development relates to certain attributes of the decision including the authority of the tribunal, the composition of the tribunal, the context of the decisions, the size of the majority, and the quality of the reasoning.[38] Not all decisions will have the same weight and value by reference to these attributes, and therefore not all will successfully exert influence on the development of the law. To be sure, this is not a check-list and, as demonstrated by the influence of the ICJ's *obiter dicta* on *erga omnes* obligations in *Barcelona Traction*,[39] the contribution of judicial or arbitral decisions to legal development is to some extent unpredictable. Few generalisations seem possible in this area,[40] and a case-by-case approach is to be preferred.

B. International Courts and Tribunals and the Development of the Law of State Responsibility

As to the second point, case law has played an important role – but certainly not an exclusive one[41] – in the development of the customary law of State responsibility.[42] Questions of responsibility frequently come before courts and tribunals, so there is plenty of opportunity for such development. Indeed, questions

---

37 Tams (n 33) 95.

38 Commentary to Conclusion 13: ILC, 'Report of the ILC on the work of its Sixty-eight session: Draft Conclusions on the Identification of Customary International Law' (Advance version, 18 August 2016) UN Doc A/71/10, GAOR, Supp No 10, para 3. See also Christoph Schreuer, 'The Development of International Law by ICSID Tribunals' (2016) 31 *ICSID Review* 728, 738–739; Chinkin and Boyle (n 23) 300–310.

39 *Barcelona Traction, Light and Power Company, Ltd (Belgium v Spain)* Judgment [1970] *ICJ Reports* 3. On the impact of this judgment, see Tams and Tzanakopoulos (n 13); Niels Petersen, 'Lawmaking by the International Court of Justice — Factors of Success' (2011) 12 *German LJ* 1296, 1304–1311.

40 Gilbert Guillaume, 'The Use of Precedent by International Judges and Arbitrators' (2011) 2 *JIDS* 5, 10.

41 See Patrick Daillier, 'The Development of the Law of Responsibility through the Case Law' in Crawford et al (n 35) 38; Christian J. Tams, 'Law-Making in Complex Processes: The World Court and the Modern Law of State Responsibility' in Christine Chinkin and Freya Baetens (eds), *Sovereignty, Statehood and State Responsibility: Essays in Honour of James Crawford* (CUP 2015) 288.

42 Thomas Buergenthal, 'Lawmaking by the ICJ and Other International Courts' (2009) 103 *ASIL Proceedings* 403, 404; Pellet (n 23) 1078; Alain Pellet, 'Remarques sur la jurisprudence récente de la Cour International de Justice dans le domaine de la responsabilité internationale' in Marcelo Kohen et al (eds), *Perspectives of International Law in the 21st century: Liber Amicorum Professor Christian Dominicé in Honour of his 80th Birthday* (Martinus Nijhoff 2012) 321; James Crawford, 'The

of State responsibility had arisen in over two-thirds of the ICJ's cases,[43] and a significant proportion of the cases coming before specialised tribunals, like human rights courts or investment tribunals, involve question of State responsibility for the violation of the particular treaty regime. Furthermore, the law of responsibility is particularly receptive to judicial development.[44] The rules of State responsibility are formulated in general and abstract terms, since they must cater to the 'infinite variety', to borrow Richard Baxter's expression,[45] of obligations that States undertake in their international relations. Likewise, they are general because tribunals require flexibility to address the equally infinite variety of ways in which States may (or may not) comply with these obligations. Case law is therefore crucial for the specification and clarification of these rules. But the 'receptiveness' of this field to judicial development is now relatively constrained: tribunals are, after all, operating within the legal framework set in the ARS.[46]

The ARS and its Commentary bear out the role of case law in the development of the law of responsibility. As remarked by Patrick Daillier, the ARS 'are based principally on case law precedents, to a far greater extent than on State practice and doctrine, references to which are far less systematic'.[47] International decisions were indeed frequently referred to in the work of the ILC on State responsibility, and many of these decisions feature in the Commentary to (almost all of) the provisions in the ARS.[48] The Commentary includes references to the case law of the ICJ (and its predecessor, the PCIJ), but also to decisions of tribunals of limited or specific jurisdiction. This should not be surprising: if the law of State responsibility is applicable generally, across all fields of international law, then the practice upon which its rules are

International Court of Justice and the Law of State Responsibility' in Tams and Sloan (n 14) 74; Tams (n 33) 76.

43 At least, as at 2021. See Federica Paddeu, 'The ICJ and the Law of State Responsibility' in Kate Parlett and Carlos Esposito (eds), *Cambridge Companion to the International Court of Justice* (CUP 2022) (forthcoming).

44 Tams (n 41) 304.

45 R. Baxter, 'International Law in "Her Infinite Variety"' (1980) 29 *ICLQ* 549.

46 On which see Tams (n 41) 297. This observation appears to be valid more generally as well, see Vaughan Lowe and Antonios Tzanakopoulos, 'The Development of the Law of the Sea by the International Court of Justice' in Tams and Sloan (n 14) 193, on the impact of codification and multilateral treaty-making on the scope for judicial development.

47 Daillier (n 41) 41.

48 Daillier notes that the references to international decisions are absent from the commentaries of the following Articles only: art 18 (coercion); arts 19, 28 and 46, on plurality of injured States; arts 53 (termination of countermeasures) and 54 (measures taken by States other than the injured State); and art 56 (questions not regulated by the Articles): ibid.

founded must also be found across all of international law. It is insufficient, that is, for the practice relating to a rule of the law of State responsibility to exist solely within one field of international law (whatever this may be) – if that were the case, then it would likely be a special rule of responsibility within that field, rather than a rule of the general law of State responsibility. By implication, the case law of all international courts and tribunals, whether they are courts of general jurisdiction or operating within certain fields of international law, like investment tribunals, in respect of any given rule of State responsibility, such as the defences in the ARS, can potentially contribute to their development, to the extent at least that they are engaged in interpreting and applying that rule as a rule of customary international law.

For present purposes, it is noteworthy that the ILC's Commentary to the ARS frequently refers to decisions of investment tribunals. 'Investment tribunal' is here understood broadly to encompass arbitral tribunals established under bilateral investment treaties, as well as other tribunals concerned with the application of the law for the protection of the property of foreigners. These latter tribunals include the Iran-US Claims Tribunal,[49] which has dealt with claims involving harm to the property of US nationals, and what may be considered the 'predecessors' of investment tribunals, namely the early 20th century mixed-commissions and *ad hoc* tribunals dealing with claims involving injury to the property of aliens.[50] References to this case law are most evident in the provisions of Part One of the ARS, since these are applicable in respect of all obligations of the State – regardless of the character of the beneficiary of the obligation.[51] A clear example are the rules on attribution, as many of these rules were developed in the case law of the mixed commissions of the

---

[49] On the value of Iran-US Claims Tribunal decisions in the development of the law of State responsibility, see Lillich et al (n 5). Further, on the relevance of the Tribunal's decisions in investment arbitration, see Christopher Gibson and Christopher Drahozal, 'Iran-US Claims Tribunal Precedent in Ivestor-State Arbitration' in Christopher Gibson and Christopher Drahozal (eds), *The Iran-US Claims Tribunal at 25: The Cases Everyone Needs to Know for Investor-State & International Arbitration* (OUP 2007) ch 1.

[50] See, broadly, Rudolf Dolzer and Christoph Schreuer, *Principles of International Investment Law* (2nd edn, OUP 2012) 1–7.

[51] ILC Articles on State Responsibility (n 1), Commentary to art 12, para 6:

> the regime of State responsibility for breach of an international obligation under Part One is comprehensive in scope, general in character and flexible in its application: Part One is thus able to cover the spectrum of possible situations without any need for further distinctions between categories of obligation concerned or the category of the breach.

This is in contrast to the provisions of Parts Two and Three which are applicable in inter-State relations only. See ARS (n 1) art 33.

early 20th century.[52] Investment decisions also featured in the Commission's work on the defences to State responsibility, especially in relation to Articles 23 (*force majeure*) and 25 (state of necessity). For its work on these defences, the Commission benefitted from an extensive survey of practice prepared by the UN Secretariat in 1979, which contained a lengthy section on 'arbitral decisions' including decisions of mixed-commissions on claims involving damages to the property of foreigners.[53] The Survey is referred to generally in the first footnote of the Commentary to Article 23,[54] as are a number of other decisions of the mixed-claims commissions and the Iran-US Claims Tribunal.[55] The Commentary to Article 25, on state of necessity, also refers to *French Company of Venezuelan Railroads*,[56] a claim against Venezuela involving damage to the property of a foreign investor, and the *LAFICO v Burundi* case.[57] It is noteworthy that these decisions are included in the Commentary, given Daillier's observation that, despite the importance of case law to the development of the law of responsibility, references to decisions of international tribunals in the ARS Commentary 'are relatively few in number and not particularly diverse, given the existing body of case law'.[58]

The decisions of investment tribunals have historically contributed to the development of the law of State responsibility, as Section III below will show. There is nothing in contemporary international law to prevent the continued role of these tribunals in the development of the general law of State responsibility, insofar as they engage with the 'secondary' rules codified in the ARS.

---

52 See, e.g., the analysis of the development the rules on attribution of private acts to the State in Tal Becker, *Terrorism and the State. Rethinking the Rules of State Responsibility* (Hart 2006) ch 2.

53 UN Secretariat, '"Force majeure" and "Fortuitous event" as Circumstances Precluding Wrongfulness: Survey of State Practice, International Judicial Decisions and Doctrine' (1978) II(1) *ILC Yearbook* 148–187. While the survey focused on *force majeure* and fortuitous event, the practice included in it is cited in the Commentary to both arts 23 and 25 (n 51).

54 ILC Articles on State Responsibility (n 1), Commentary to art 23, note 366.

55 Ibid.: references to the practice of mixed-claims commissions in ibid., note 376; and the case-law of the Iran-US Claims Tribunal in ibid., note 381.

56 *French Company of Venezuelan Railroads* (1904) 10 RIAA 285, referred to in ARS Commentary (n 51) art 23, note 410.

57 *Libyan Arab Foreign Investment Company (LAFICO) v Burundi* (1991) 96 ILR 279, referred to in ARS Commentary (n 51) art 23, note 413.

58 Daillier (n 41) 42.

III. FOREIGN PROPERTY IN INTERNAL CONFLICTS: DEVELOPMENT OF THE PLEA OF *FORCE MAJEURE*

The plea of *force majeure* is a good example of a rule whose development was influenced by the decisions of tribunals. This example predates the contemporary field of investment law and investment arbitration, but it is nevertheless relevant to the present analysis as it concerns the precursor to this field: the law on the treatment of aliens and their property and the case law concerning responsibility for injuries to the property of foreigners. This example, indeed, shows that the contribution of investment tribunals, broadly understood to include the mixed claims commissions and arbitral tribunals of the early 20th century, as well as tribunals addressing aspects of the law on the protection of foreign property, such as the PCIJ, to the development of the law of State responsibility is not a recent phenomenon.

Force majeure is an old concept, but its acceptance as a defence in international law was contested for much of the 19th century.[59] Throughout this century, the plea was frequently invoked by States to deny claims for damage to foreign property which had occurred during internal strife, including revolutions, insurrections and other low-level revolts within their territories. But the invocation of the plea was controversial, due to the broad understanding espoused by the invoking States, which denied any responsibility for any damage caused to foreign property in the context of such internal troubles. For example, Belgium rejected claims for compensation presented by the UK and the US, among others, on behalf of their subjects for damage to their property during the Belgian Insurrection of 1830. For Belgium, the damage, which had occurred during the bombardment of Antwerp, was the '[consequence] of open war [which] are events of chance or of superior force, for which no one is responsible'.[60] Similar denials of responsibility were common throughout the period, and many foreigners whose property had suffered damage during the fighting remained without compensation – even when the damage had been caused by the State's own forces. It is not difficult to see why the notion of *force majeure* as employed in this context was harshly criticised by many scholars and was objected to by several States.[61] For example, in response to

---

[59] These developments are traced in Federica Paddeu, 'A Genealogy of Force Majeure in International Law' (2011) 82 *BYIL* 381, 398-436.

[60] (1841–1842) 30 BFSP 224, cited in UN Secretariat (n 53) 106.

[61] See, e.g., E. Brusa, 'Responsabilité des Etats à raison des dommages soufferts par des étrangers en cas d'émeute ou de guerre civile' (1898) 17 *Annuaire IDI* 96; Carlos Wiesse, *Reglas de derecho internacional aplicables a las guerras civiles* (2nd edn, Torres-Aguirre 1905) 78–79; Julius Goebel, 'The International Responsibility of

Belgium's position just quoted, the UK contested the attribution of the damage to the 'event of chance or of superior force' and maintained that Belgium was nevertheless responsible since the damage had been caused by Belgian volunteers, whose injurious acts 'were not unavoidable'.[62]

Broad invocations of *force majeure*, like the Belgian one, may have resulted from a number of features of the 19th century international system.[63] One of these features was the denial by home States of any obligation to protect foreigners and their property in these circumstances. As such, many States considered that there was no legal basis for the claims. When an event of *force majeure* occurred, such as an internal conflict, there was a fortiori no question of the home State's responsibility. A second feature was the understanding of conflict as an event the occurrence of which was outside the bounds of the law, akin to a natural event, which States could not only not foresee, but that they could not control.[64] In the face of these events, the State's will was nullified and everything the State did in addressing the event was, in a sense, compelled by the superior force. Hence, the State could not be held responsible for any of the ensuing damage. Last, was the manner of the presentation of claims prevalent at the time: these were presented collectively, by the home State, for a total sum of compensation through diplomatic means. The broad formulation of the claims was met with a broad disclaimer of responsibility – and thus, a broad understanding of *force majeure*. These features began to change towards the late 19th century. States began accepting obligations involving the treatment of foreigners and their property within their territory in circumstances of conflict (internal and international as it was); it was slowly recognised that wars and other internal conflicts did not obliterate the State's will and that so long as the State remained in control of the behaviour of its armed forces, it could be responsible; and, finally, increasing resort to third-party dispute settlement (through mixed commissions or *ad hoc* tribunals) resulted in a more detailed and individualised presentation of claims: claims were now submitted individually, or in groups of related claims arising from the same set of events, which required the parties to elaborate on the legal bases of their respective positions in respect of each – be it to ground the claim or to ground the defence. These changes paved the way for the recognition of the plea of *force majeure*, as we now understand it, in the first half of the 20th century.

States for Injuries sustained by Aliens on account of Mob Violence, Insurrections and Civil Wars' (1914) 8 *AJIL* 802, 813.

62 (1841–1842) 30 BFSP 232, in UN Secretariat (n 53) 106.

63 This is a brief summary of developments reviewed in Paddeu (n 59).

64 For an overview of this position, see Quincy Wright, 'Changes in the Conception of War' (1924) 18 *AJIL* 755, 763–767 (and sources cited therein).

During the first half of the 20th century, tribunals considered pleas of *force majeure* in, among others, *French Company of Venezuelan Railroads*,[65] *Russian Indemnity*,[66] *Serbian Loans*[67] and *Brazilian Loans*.[68] In all these cases, the claims involved injury suffered by foreigners in their property against the background of armed conflict – internal and international. The first thing to note about these decisions is that none of the issuing tribunals provided any evidence for the recognition of *force majeure* in international law at the time. They did not 'reveal' its existence by assessing the practice and the assent of States, for example, or by confirming its recognition in the domestic legal systems, in line with Article 38(1)(c) of the ICJ Statute. They rather asserted that the defence was recognised in international law. Only the *Russian Indemnity* tribunal provided some justification for its consideration of *force majeure* as a matter of international law: this defence 'may be pleaded in opposition in public as well as in private international law' because 'international law must adapt itself to political necessities.'[69] And yet, the recognition of the plea at the time was far from certain: *force majeure* was only briefly and obliquely mentioned during the preparatory work of the Hague Codification Conference in 1930, and it was not included as one of the situations in which States could disclaim responsibility in the report prepared by José Gustavo Guerrero for the Conference's Preparatory Committee or in the Bases of Discussion for the Conference produced by the Preparatory Committee itself.[70]

These decisions were also instrumental in settling the content and scope of the defence. Indeed, we can begin to discern in the decisions of this period the contours of our current defence of *force majeure*, as codified in ARS Article 23. Thus, the case law was crucial for the consolidation of *force majeure* as

---

65 *French Company of Venezuelan Railroads* (1904) 10 RIAA 285.

66 *Russian Indemnity Case (Russia/Turkey)* (1912) Scott Hague Court Rep 297.

67 *Case Concerning the Payment of Various Serbian Loans Issued in France (France v Kingdom of the Serbs, Croats and Slovenes)* (1929) PCIJ Series A No 20, 5.

68 *Case Concerning the Payment of Various Brazilian Loans Issued in France (France v Brazil)* (1929) PCIJ Series A No 21, 93.

69 *Russian Indemnity* (n 66) 317.

70 See Paddeu (n 59) 433–436. It is possible that no mention of *force majeure* was included in the report as the report focused on obligations owed to foreigners and, as such, obligations requiring the attainment of a standard of diligence. Insofar as diligence cannot require a State to do what is impossible, *force majeure* is irrelevant as a defence: where compliance with the obligation is rendered impossible, the State has not fallen foul of compliance with its obligation. This said, not all obligations owed to foreigners are due diligence obligations: States have obligations not to directly injure foreigners or their property, which are different from their obligations to prevent damage occurring to foreigners and their property. In relation to the former (obligations not to injure foreigners and their property), *force majeure* could still potentially be available as a defence.

a defence arising from an impossibility to perform an obligation resulting from the occurrence of an unforeseen and irresistible event; as a defence, that is, that involved an involuntary non-performance of an obligation. During the 19th century the conception of *force majeure* prevalent in the literature and practice was descriptive and aprioristic: the expression was used to refer, literally, to 'superior forces'. Once the superior force materialised, this was understood to nullify the will of the State such that no damage occurring in connection with the superior force could be attributed to the State in question. Broad disclaimers of responsibility for damage caused during internal struggles followed from this conception: if these were a superior force, then no damage caused in connection with them entailed the State's responsibility. In the first part of the 20th century this conception was left behind in favour of what may be termed a 'global'[71] or 'situation-based'[72] conception of *force majeure*, focused on impossibility of performance. The difference is important. Unlike under the descriptive conception, under the global conception of *force majeure*, the State would be exonerated only if the internal conflict had made it impossible for it to comply with the specific obligation at issue and not merely as a result of its occurrence.

This shift in the understanding of *force majeure* can be seen in the decisions in *French Company of Venezuelan Railroads*[73] and *Russian Indemnity*.[74] In the latter case, for example, the Ottoman Empire argued that a series of unforeseen events, including several insurrections and its participation in international wars,[75] had caused for it an 'impossibility to service' its debt to the Russian government as an indemnity for losses suffered by Russian subjects during the 1877/1878 war;[76]

---

[71] The term is Paul-Henri Antonmattei's: *Contribution à l'étude de la force majeure* (LGDJ 1992) 9–10.

[72] Sandra Szurek spoke of 'events' of *force majeure* and 'situation' of *force majeure* to distinguish the two conceptions mentioned here: Sandra Szurek, *La force majeure en droit international*, vol 2 (doctoral thesis - Université Paris II Panthéon-Assas, 1996) 409–16. This distinction has been drawn by domestic law scholars as well. For example, Antonmattei refers to two techniques in the determination of the notion of *force majeure*: an *a priori* one, pursuant to which certain categories of events are themselves 'constitutive of *force majeure ipso facto*', and a 'global approach', requiring the circumscription of abstract 'elements' of *force majeure*, see Antonmattei (n 71) 9–10.

[73] *French Company of Venezuelan Railroads* (n 65) esp 327.

[74] *Russian Indemnity* (n 66) 317–318. The Ottoman Empire invoked *force majeure* since a series of unforeseen events had caused for it an 'impossibility to service' its debts to the Russian Empire, see: *Contre-Mémoire présenté au nom du Gouvernement de l'Empire Ottoman* (1911) 44, para 123.

[75] On which see Michael Waibel, *Sovereign Defaults before International Courts and Tribunals* (CUP 2011) 89.

[76] *Contre-Mémoire présenté au nom du Gouvernement de l'Empire Ottoman* (1911) 44, para 123.

for Turkey this was, as Russia too had recognised in diplomatic correspondence, an 'absolute impossibility'.[77] The tribunal unfortunately conflated the Ottoman Empire's arguments about self-preservation and *force majeure*. Despite the respondent's warnings to the tribunal that the two were not 'la même chose',[78] the tribunal held that the plea was not met because it was an 'exaggeration' to admit that the payment of the debt 'would imperil the existence of [Turkey] or seriously compromise its internal or external situation'.[79] Be that as it may, the tribunal's consideration of the plea is compatible with the situation-based approach to *force majeure*: the tribunal queried whether the series of unforeseen events referred to by Turkey had produced an impossibility of performance, rather than hold that because of the occurrence of these unforeseen events Turkey could not perform its obligations. It required, in short, that the events cause an impossibility to perform – quite aside from the question of the degree of such impossibility.[80]

The same approach was then followed by the PCIJ in Serbian and Brazilian Loans,[81] and by States in their arguments in Société Commerciale de Belgique (Socobelge).[82] In Serbian Loans, the PCIJ had to consider a claim against Serbia for its failure to service debts to French bond-holders in gold-francs, against the background of World War I and the ensuing economic crisis. Serbia invoked *force majeure* as a defence to this claim. Serbia's defence did not involve an assertion that the war was an event of *force majeure* and that it was, consequently, exonerated for its failure to pay. Rather, Serbia focused on its own (in)ability to continue to comply with the obligation in the circumstances. In particular, it argued that a French Law of 1914 imposing a forced-currency

[77] Ibid., 64, para 183.

[78] *Contre-Réplique présentée au nom du Gouvernement de l'Empire Ottoman* (1912) 28, para 280. For an analysis of the parties' arguments on self-preservation and *force majeure*, see Paddeu (n 11) 295–297.

[79] *Russian Indemnity* (n 66) 317.

[80] Namely, whether the impossibility required was absolute, in the sense that the Ottoman Empire would have had no choice not to comply (e.g., it had run out of money), or relative, in the sense that it would have had the option to comply with it but only at the cost of self-destruction of the Ottoman Empire.

[81] *Brazilian Loans* (n 68) 120. For Brazil's invocation of *force majeure* which, it said, rendered the payment of its debt impossible, see *Brazilian Loans* (Memorial) PCIJ Rep Series C No 16, 153; *Brazilian Loans* (Counter-Memorial) PCIJ Rep Series C No 16, 235, 241, 243.

[82] *Société Commerciale de Belgique (Belgium v Greece)* (1939) PCIJ Series A/B No 78, 160. The Court did not have to decide the dispute, since Belgium dropped its claim once Greece acknowledged on record that it did not intend to repudiate its obligation towards *Socobelge*: ibid., 174–175. The parties' pleadings on *force majeure* were extensive, for a summary, see Paddeu (n 59) 430–433.

regime had made it 'materially impossible'[83] to obtain gold-francs to pay the debt. The Court rejected the plea on the facts since the gold-franc was a standard of value, but upheld the formulation of the defence as pleaded by Serbia. As the Court explained, the plea was concerned with 'impossibility of performance' and it seemed indeed that obtaining gold-francs had become impossible. However, the gold-franc was a standard of value and, for this reason, payment remained possible *in specie*.[84]

By the time the ILC began its work on the plea of *force majeure* in 1979,[85] there were no doubts within the Commission or in the Sixth Committee of the UN General Assembly, that *force majeure* was a defence which was recognised as part of (customary) international law.[86] To be sure, there were disagreements within the Commission and the Sixth Committee of the UNGA about the formulation of the defence, or certain of its specific requirements (such as the kind and degree of impossibility required).[87] But there were no doubts that this defence was recognised in international law in roughly the same terms set out in the case law just considered, which features prominently in the Commentary to Article 23: as a defence which concerns the impossibility to perform an obligation caused by an external and irresistible force. After the many disagreements over the concept of *force majeure* in the 19th century, it was the investment case law (broadly understood) that settled the defence into international law. Claims involving damage to the property of foreigners had provided the opportunity for development, in an area that was receptive to such development.

IV. COUNTERMEASURES, INVESTORS AND THE RIGHTS OF THIRD PARTIES

The articles on defences in the ARS, like the law of State responsibility in general, are stated in general and abstract terms. This ensures that tribunals have the flexibility required in assessing difficult cases: these cannot be

---

83 As Serbia explained the situation in its Memorial, *Case Concerning the Payment of Various Serbian Loans Issued in France (France v Kingdom of the Serbs, Croats and Slovenes)* (1929) PCIJ Series C, No 16-III(3), 459.

84 *Serbian Loans* (n 67) 34–35.

85 Special Rapporteur Roberto Ago's report on *force majeure* was submitted this year: Roberto Ago, 'Eighth Report on State Responsibility' (1979) II(1) *ILC Yearbook* 66ff.

86 For a review of the relevant statements in the Sixth Committee, see Paddeu (n 59) 487–490.

87 For an overview, see Paddeu (n 11) 308–320. Specifically on the standard of impossibility, which is often misunderstood in the literature, see the explanation as to the kind and degree of impossibility required by ARS (n 1) art 23: ibid., 320–323.

decided by reference to formulas, but need to respond to the circumstances of each case.[88] Thus, whenever tribunals apply rules of the law of responsibility, including the defences, they need to engage in some measure of clarification: to bring the general down to the particular. In this connection, tribunals contribute towards the determination of the scope of the relevant rules by deciding, on a case-by-case basis, which factual patterns fall within that rule. This involves, to some extent, the development of that rule as it may require the application of the rule to situations not previously considered. Some might see these as instances of clarification of the rules involved. But on occasion, as will be seen, this 'clarification' can be quite innovative.

An example of this is the question of the permissibility of countermeasures affecting the rights of investors. The issue came up in three investment disputes brought by US investors against Mexico under NAFTA. All disputes arose from the same set of facts: the imposition by Mexico of, among others, a 20 per cent tax on any drink containing sweetener other than cane sugar, a measure which affected US importers of high-fructose corn syrup (HFCS). In all three cases, Mexico argued that the tax was a countermeasure against the imposition of market restrictions on Mexican sugar by the US, a measure which it considered to be in breach of NAFTA. A central issue in all three cases was whether countermeasures taken by Mexico against the USA (the two treaty-parties) could involve measures affecting the rights of US investors.[89]

This question was not directly answered by the ARS. The Articles and their Commentary do not mention the rights of investors in the provisions on countermeasures. ARS Article 50(1), which enumerates the obligations which cannot be affected (let alone directly targeted) by countermeasures, does not include obligations towards foreign investors in this list. Indeed, the drafting history of this article shows that there was considerable uncertainty as to the permissibility of this type of countermeasures. Special Rapporteur Gaetano Arangio-Ruiz raised the issue during his consideration of potential restrictions on the right to take countermeasures, in particular those restrictions based on human rights law and 'other humanitarian values'. At the time, there were scholars who argued that the right to property should be protected from the right to take countermeasures.[90] But as Arangio-Ruiz's overview of practice and scholarly opinion showed, these views were not at all unanimous. While

---

[88] The observation was made by Crawford in relation to the ICJ and inter-State disputes, but the observation seems relevant more broadly. See Crawford (n 42) 74.

[89] For a detailed analysis of the three decisions, see Kate Parlett, 'The Application of the Rules on Countermeasures in Investment Claims' in Chinkin and Baetens (n 41) 389.

[90] See, e.g., Ignaz Seidl-Hohenveldern, 'Reprisals and the Taking of Private Property' (1962) 9 *Neth ILR* 470, 475.

there was broad agreement that takings could not be justified as countermeasures, opinions differed in respect of asset-freezing.[91] Such divergence of views was echoed in the ILC itself, as evidenced by the discussions on this point.[92] In a cautious assessment, Omer Elagab noted that, at least with respect to asset-freezing, 'the majority of instances of State practice … would suggest that alien property may be frozen as a counter-measure', but, he continued, States had not 'expressed clearly defined views on this point'. The available evidence related to 'mere episodes' and thus there remained some doubt as to 'whether the freezing of alien property can be justified as a counter-measure'.[93]

Notwithstanding the absence of a specific restriction in this regard in the ARS, potential limitations to countermeasures affecting foreign property may be inferred from other aspects of the regime of countermeasures.[94] One such potential limitation may be inferred from Article 49, according to which countermeasures can only be 'directed against' the offending party. The implication, as drawn in the Commentary, is that countermeasures cannot be directed against a third party.[95] Or, to put it another way, the rights of third parties may not be the object of countermeasures. The Commentary refines this implication further, by adding that third-party rights may not be 'affected', even incidentally, by a countermeasure adopted against the offending State. In practice, it is not uncommon for countermeasures taken against the offending party to have incidental effects on 'the position of third States or indeed other third parties.[96] For example, 'if the injured State suspends transit rights with the responsible State … other parties, including third States, may be affected thereby'.[97] These incidental effects may indeed be inevitable in an interconnected world. However, the Commentary draws a distinction between countermeasures which incidentally affect the rights owed by the invoking State to a third State from countermeasures which incidentally affect the interests of

[91] See, e.g., Linos-Alexandre Sicilianos, *Les réactions décentralisées à l'illicite* (LGDJ 1990) 360; Carlo Focarelli, *Le contromisure nel diritto internazionale* (Giuffrè 1994) 13–36, 510. For further references, see Gaetano Arangio-Ruiz, 'Third Report on State Responsibility' (1991) II(1) *ILC Yearbook* 33–34; Arangio-Ruiz, 'Fourth Report on State Responsibility' (1992) II(1) *ILC Yearbook* 30–32.

[92] ILC, 'Report of the Commission on the work of its forty-fourth session' (1992) II(2) *ILC Yearbook* 33, para 233.

[93] Omer Yousif Elagab, *The Legality of Non-Forcible Counter-Measures in International Law* (OUP 1988) 108–109.

[94] As noted by Arangio-Ruiz, 'Fourth Report' (n 91) 32 para 83.

[95] ARS Commentary (n 51) art 49, para 4. Note, in this regard, that the position of third parties is not equally protected in the case of self-defence: ARS Commentary (n 51) art 21, para 5.

[96] Ibid., art 49, para 5.

[97] Ibid.

third States.[98] Only in the former case will countermeasures be impermissible, and then only vis-à-vis that third State.[99] So, while the rights of foreign investors are not included in the list of impermissible countermeasures in Article 50, the Article 49 limitation in respect of third parties could potentially render them impermissible.

All three tribunals decided that Mexico's countermeasures were unlawful, but they did so for different reasons. Two tribunals held that the countermeasures were impermissible because they affected the rights of investors. In *CPI* the Tribunal held that Mexico owed substantive obligations under NAFTA directly to investors, which were autonomous and distinct from those of their home State.[100] Therefore, their rights could not be affected by a countermeasure directed against the home State.[101] Likewise, the Tribunal in *Cargill* asserted that countermeasures could not justify the infringement of obligations owed to third parties, including 'specific obligations owed to nationals of the offending State'.[102] In contrast to the tribunal in *CPI*, however, the *Cargill* tribunal maintained that the substantive or procedural character of investor rights was irrelevant in this regard. So long as investors possessed direct rights as against the invoking State and these were affected by the countermeasures, then the latter would be impermissible.[103] The third tribunal, in the *ADM* case, reached the opposite conclusion: countermeasures affecting investors were permissible, insofar as the rights of investors under NAFTA were procedural in character.[104] The inconsistencies between the tribunals on the (im)permissibility of countermeasures affecting investors hinged on the character of investor rights as substantive or procedural – thus, on a matter of investment law.[105] But from the standpoint of the law of countermeasures, there is a common thread underlying these three decisions: the tribunals all approached the question from the Article 49/third party rights angle.

---

[98] Ibid., paras 4–5. See also *Cysne (Responsibility of Germany for Acts committed subsequent to 31 July 1914 and before Portugal entered the war) (Portugal/Germany)* (1930) 2 RIAA 1035, 1056–1057.

[99] The measures could nevertheless remain lawful vis-à-vis the responsible State.

[100] *Corn Products International, Inc v Mexico*, ICSID Case No ARB/(AF)/04/1, Decision on Responsibility (15 January 2008) paras 168–169.

[101] Ibid., para 176.

[102] *Cargill, Inc v Mexico*, ICSID Case No ARB/(AF)/05/2, Award (18 September 2009) para 422.

[103] Ibid., para 426.

[104] The plea was dismissed because the Mexican measure did not meet the requirements of countermeasures, see *Archer Daniels Midland Company v Mexico*, ICSID Case No ARB/(AF)/04/5, Award (21 November 2007) para 180.

[105] Moreover, one that is likely to be dependent on the specific treaty in question.

The approach taken by the tribunals may have seemed like the simple application of a limitation of the right of countermeasures already present in international law, just a question of clarifying who 'third parties' are in the sense of ARS Article 49. But in reality, it involved some element of innovation and, therefore, of development. Scholars have offered conflicting assessments of these three awards, in particular in respect of the question whether investors can be considered as 'third parties' in the relevant sense at all. Some, like Martins Paparinskis have agreed with the tribunals on this point arguing that investors are third parties in a 'State responsibility' sense. Paparinskis argues that third parties in the law of responsibility are in a qualitatively different position to third parties within the law of treaties. In the context of responsibility, a third party is any subject which is not involved in the relation between the wrongdoing State and the injured State. This is, in his view, the rationale of the human rights exclusion in ARS Article 50(1)(b) and this same rationale should be extended to other private parties who derive rights from treaty-regimes – such as investors.[106] But others, like Junianto James Losari and Michael Ewing-Chow have criticised the tribunal's characterisation of investors as 'third parties'. In their view, investors are in a rather different position than that of a third State which is not a party to the relevant investment agreement and whose rights may be affected by a countermeasure between the investment-treaty parties. Indeed, even if investors possess substantive rights under investment treaties, these rights are to some extent dependent on the rights of their home States, and they are subject to modification, suspension or termination by their home State, as well as subject to the interpretations agreed upon by the States parties.[107] It might be added, as recognised by the tribunal in *Cargill*, that should the investors' claim be espoused by their home State in exercise of diplomatic protection, the countermeasure would be valid for, in accordance with the fiction of diplomatic protection, '[i]n the case of diplomatic espousal … the claim is owned by the espousing State and the espousing State is the named party'.[108] This would render the permissibility of countermeasures in these circumstances somewhat arbitrary, dependent not on legal principle but on the contingent question of the formulation of claims. Avoiding this arbitrariness, Eran Sthoeger and Christian J. Tams have argued in favour of a 'third-party beneficiary' approach to this question: in their view, as beneficiaries of rights granted by States, investors cannot posses more rights

[106] Martins Paparinskis, 'Investment Arbitration and the Law of Countermeasures' (2008) 79 *BYIL* 264, 334–345.

[107] Junianto J. Losari and Michael Ewing-Chow, 'A Clash of Treaties: The Lawfulness of Countermeasures in International Trade Law and International Investment Law' (2015) 16 *JWIT* 274, 299–300.

[108] *Cargill v Mexico* (n 102) para 424.

than thoser enjoyed by their home States. By implication, investor rights would be subject to the same limitations as those of their home States – including their being liable to breach by way of countermeasures.[109]

Taking a broader systemic view, Kate Parlett has noted that the tribunals' approach may lead to a situation where 'States may be compelled to compensate nationals of the wrongdoing State for the impact of the countermeasure', thus rendering the taking of countermeasures futile in practice.[110] Since the majority of foreign investment is located in developing States, such a development may significantly hamper the ability of these States to take countermeasures against developed States. Indeed, while countermeasures may be formally available to all States, the material inequalities among States result in countermeasures being taken by those who can, not by those who may wish to take them,[111] and those who can are usually more powerful States. The ability to take countermeasures affecting foreign investors has been seen as a way of rebalancing these material inequalities.[112]

No further cases involving countermeasures have been decided by investment tribunals since these decisions were issued. Likewise, States have not offered their views on this matter: a review of States' comments in the context of the Sixth Committee's consideration of the future status of the ARS – while sometimes touching on the institution of countermeasures[113] – does not show any direct engagement by States with this issue. It may be too soon to tell what the 'wear' of these decisions will be in the practice of States and other international courts and tribunals. However, given the defensible criticism of the tribunals' decisions and their reasoning, and the systemic implications of this approach for the ability of developing States to take countermeasures, it is likely that these decisions may not wear well in the subsequent practice of States. Be that as it may, the decisions may stimulate the further development of the law by raising important, and unresolved, issues about the institution of countermeasures ranging from which rights of which third parties are safe-

---

[109] Eran Sthoeger and Christian J. Tams, 'Swords, Shields and Other Beasts: The Role of Countermeasures in Investment Arbitration' (2022) 37 *ICSID Review* 121, 134–136.

[110] Parlett (n 89) 404.

[111] Julio Barboza, 'Contramedidas en la reciente codificación de la responsabilidad de los Estados: fronteras con la legítima defensa y el estado de necesidad' (2003) 12 *Anuario Argentino DI* 15, 19.

[112] Christian Tomuschat, 'Are Counter-Measures Subject to Prior Recourse to Dispute Settlement Procedures?' (1994) 5 *EJIL* 77, 78–79.

[113] For an overview of States' concerns in respect of countermeasures, as expressed in their comments to the UNGA Sixth Committee, see Federica I. Paddeu, 'To Convene or Not to Convene? The Future Status of the Articles on State Responsibility: Recent Developments' (2017) 21 *Max Planck Yearbook UN Law* 83, 106.

guarded from being affected by countermeasures (an issue which goes beyond investment law and which will be increasingly relevant as the participation of individuals and other non-State actors in the legal order increases), to their effectiveness as the only mechanism equally available to all States (at least formally) to enforce their rights in the international legal order. In this sense, at least, these decisions may still be seen as a 'motor' of legal development.

V. STATE OF NECESSITY: JUSTIFICATION OR EXCUSE?

Investment tribunals have also shown themselves willing to go beyond consolidating the rules and clarifying the detail and engaging with the fundamentals of the defences in the law of responsibility. This is most evident in their handling of the plea of necessity, and the tribunals' consideration of whether this defence provides a justification or an excuse to the invoking States. The most notable of the decisions on this issue is that of the Annulment Committee in *CMS v Argentina*.[114] The decision of the Committee stated that the defence of necessity 'is an excuse which is only relevant once it has been decided that there has otherwise been a breach of [the] substantive obligations'.[115] The Committee came to this conclusion after a careful comparison between the plea of necessity and the essential security interests exception in the BIT, taking into account the language, effect and relationship between the two. According to the Committee, a tribunal must first determine whether there had been a breach of the treaty (an analysis which required consideration of the essential security interests exception), and only after it had found that a breach existed could the analysis move on to consider 'whether Argentina's responsibility could be precluded in whole or in part' by the plea of necessity.[116] The Committee presented its decision as simply stating the position of the ILC on the matter: 'if state of necessity in customary international law goes to the issue of responsibility', said the Committee, 'it would be a secondary rule of international law – and this was the position taken by the ILC'.[117]

This decision has been endorsed by subsequent investment tribunals, as will be seen later. But the decision may be more innovative than it presents itself to be: it is, indeed, a fundamental reassessment of the character of the defence of necessity in international law. Given the equivocation and confusion which exists in relation to the notions of justification and excuse, the position of the

---

[114] *CMS Gas Transmission Company v Argentine Republic*, ICSID Case No ARB/01/8, Annulment (25 September 2007) para 134.

[115] Ibid., para 129.

[116] Ibid., para 134.

[117] Ibid.

ARS in this regard, and the (current) characterisation of the plea of necessity, it is necessary to take a pause and clarify these issues, so as better to appreciate the *CMS* Committee's decision.

A. A Preliminary Clarification: Justification and Excuse in International Law

Not all defences, as it is known, exonerate in the same way. The two main ways in which defences get defendants 'off the hook', to put it colloquially, is by either justifying their conduct, or excusing the actors from the consequences of their wrongful conduct. These two kinds of defences can be defined as follows: Justifications are defences that arise from properties or characteristics of acts, which render conduct lawful; excuses arise from properties or characteristics of actors and, while not affecting the illegality of conduct, they relieve the actor of the consequences of his wrongful conduct.[118] These definitions represent the common core of agreement between legal scholars and theorists on the meaning of these two terms.[119] To be sure, there are disagreements at the margins of the distinction.[120] Likewise, there remain debates as to whether the distinction is or should be recognised in any given legal order. But the core meaning of these concepts, as just defined, is no longer disputed. At its core, the distinction is both clear and resolved.[121]

Whether the distinction is recognised in international law is unclear. But a good argument can be made that the distinction should be recognised since it can give rise to important practical consequences.[122] Among others, the distinction can have an impact on the responsibility of accessories to the internationally wrongful act. For example, a State will be responsible for aiding and assisting another State only insofar as the action of the assisted State is itself wrongful.[123] If the act of the assisted State is lawful, then no responsibil-

---

[118] Douglas Husak, 'Justifications and the Criminal Liability of Accessories' (1989–1990) 80 *J Crim L & Criminology* 491, 496.

[119] These definitions largely track the meaning of these notions in ordinary language. See, in this respect, the *Oxford English Dictionary* definitions of both words: justification is '[t]he action of justifying or showing something to be just, right, or proper; vindication of oneself or another' (3), and excuse is the 'attempt to clear (a person) wholly or partially from blame, without denying or justifying his imputed action' (I.1.a).

[120] For an overview, see Kimberly Kessler Ferzan, 'Justification and Excuse' in John Deigh and David Dolinko (eds), *The Oxford Handbook of Philosophy of Criminal Law* (OUP 2011) 239.

[121] The question whether the distinction is useful, or has any practical implications, is a separate and distinct one.

[122] See generally Paddeu (n 11) ch 2.

[123] On which see ARS (n 1) art 16.

ity can arise for the assisting State. Thus, whether the assisted State benefits from a justification (such that its conduct is lawful) or an excuse (such that its conduct remains unlawful) can affect the responsibility of the assisting State. Likewise, the distinction between the two types of defences can have normative implications. Justifications, after all, single out conduct which is permissible in accordance with the legal order. Thus a finding of justification in any given case can have an impact beyond that particular case: other actors finding themselves in the same circumstances ought to be able to successfully plead the justification in question. Excuses, instead, do not have this effect insofar as they reinforce that certain conduct – even when adopted in exceptional circumstances – is wrongful. The distinction reinforces the conduct guiding function of law, by clarifying which conduct is permissible and which conduct the law prohibits.[124] Vaughan Lowe thus argued, before the ILC completed its work on the ARS, that all defences in the ARS should be classified as excuses since this might in practice strengthen the normative pull of rules.[125] This latter concern is one which has been raised by investment tribunals when addressing the plea of necessity, as will be seen later.

The ILC did not classify the defences included in the ARS as justifications or excuses. During the first reading, Special Rapporteur Ago strongly defended the view that all the circumstances acted as justifications, and his view ultimately determined the terminology used in the text of the ARS themselves (i.e., the language of 'preclusion of wrongfulness'). The use of this language notwithstanding, the Commission was not as assertive in its position that all the circumstances operated as justifications.[126] The debates in the Commission during the first reading of the Articles show that the question was left unresolved and that it would be the subject of subsequent discussion.[127] But

---

[124] George Mousourakis, 'Justification and Excuse' (1998-1999) 7 *Tilburg Foreign LR* 35, 44.

[125] Vaughan Lowe, 'Precluding Wrongfulness or Responsibility: A Plea for Excuses?' (1999) 10 *EJIL* 405.

[126] It is significant in this regard that the commentary to the draft ARS adopted on first reading stated that the circumstances excluded wrongfulness 'in the normal case', thus leaving open the possibility that they may operate to exclude responsibility. See, on this point, Paddeu (n 11) 45.

[127] The ILC Report of 1973 records that 'only some members' of the Commission agreed with Ago's view 'for the time being': ILC, 'Report of the Commission on the work of its twenty-fifth session' (1973) II *ILC Yearbook* 176, commentary to draft art 1, para 12. Ago's Eighth Report to the ILC in 1979, which tackled the question of the character of the defences, selectively quoted from the 1973 report, and asserted that the Commission 'had already had occasion to state its view' on the matter and that it had done so in agreement with Ago's view. He omitted from his reference the fact that only 'some members' had agreed and that, moreover, they had done so 'for the time being': Ago, 'Eighth Report' (n 85) para 44. The passage from Ago's report was subsequently

that subsequent discussion did not take place (or, at least, there is no public record of it having taken place in the ILC's yearbooks). On second reading, Special Rapporteur Crawford raised the issue once again but decided that, on balance, the ARS should not strictly classify the various circumstances as justifications or excuses.[128] The Commission endorsed this suggestion and, as a result, no discussion on these two concepts or on the classification of each defence took place.

In light of the above, it can be concluded that the ARS do not determine, definitely or definitively, the character of the individual circumstances therein recognised. It is against this background that the use of the expression 'circumstances precluding wrongfulness' in the title of Chapter V of Part One, and the use of the terms 'justification' and 'excuse' throughout the Commentary must be viewed: the use of these terms is not an indication of the Commission's definitive views, nor of its confusion as to the meaning of these terms. Rather, the wording employed in the ARS and their Commentary should be seen as evidencing that the question of the classification of the circumstances into justifications or excuses remains to be settled.

B. State of Necessity as a Justification

Individual defences are not inherently justifications or excuses. The same defence can be formulated as one or the other, and this is usually the case with the plea of necessity.[129] The choice as to the classification of any given defence

---

copied verbatim in the 1979 Report: ILC, 'Report of the Commission on the work of its thirty-first session' (1979) II(2) *ILC Yearbook* 106, para 2.

[128] Special Rapporteur Crawford stated that:

> On balance the Special Rapporteur is not persuaded that a categorical distinction needs to be made as between the circumstances to be covered by chapter V. There is in truth a range of cases, and a clear example of distress or even necessity may be more convincing as a circumstance precluding wrongfulness than a marginal case of self-defence. It seems sufficient to deal with all the circumstances under the existing general rubric of chapter V, making the specific distinctions and qualifications between them that have been proposed.

James Crawford, 'Second Report on State Responsibility' (1999) II(1) *ILC Yearbook*, para 355.

[129] State of necessity is classified as a justification in some legal systems (see, e.g., the US Model Penal Code, section 3.02), as an excuse in others (see, e.g., the decision of the Supreme Court of Canada, *Perka v The Queen* (1984) 2 SCR 232), and as both a justification and an excuse in others still (Germany, e.g., recognises a justification and an excuse of necessity in its Criminal Code, at secs 34 and 35 respectively. For the text of these provisions, see Klaus Bernsmann, 'Private Self-Defence and Necessity in German Penal Law and in the Penal Law Proposal - Some Remarks' (1996) 30 *Israel LR* 171, at 180 and 184, respectively. Bohlander refers to excusing necessity in sec 35

as a justification or an excuse depends on a range of factors including the premises and assumptions underlying the legal order, normative or other policy considerations and, sometimes, the institutional structure of the legal system, which may or may not be able to accommodate (or give practical meaning to) one or other typology of defence.[130] Once the choice is made on any of these bases or a combination thereof, the defence can be formulated following the patterns of justification or excuse or, since often the defences will be codified before classifications are made and, besides, classifications may change over time, the defence can be re-interpreted or re-formulated to follow those patterns.[131] Theories of justification and excuse provide the patterns to be followed in either case.

The plea of necessity can be formulated as a choice of evils (or lesser evils) defence. Formulated in this way, the plea concerns the situation of an agent who must choose whether to comply with her obligations at the cost of harm to one of her essential interests, or to protect her essential interest at the cost of breaching one of her obligations and, thereby, harming an innocent party. This formulation calls for a consequentialist calculus: which of the two courses of conduct (is predicted to) consist in the lesser evil, or to prevent a greater evil? The classic example is that of the hiker who breaks into a cabin to protect herself from a storm.[132] The hiker infringes the right of a third innocent party (the owner of the cabin), but her actions save her life. In these circumstances, her actions are justified (and therefore lawful) because they exclude a greater evil (the loss of life). Lesser-evils is indeed a (consequentialist) theory of justification pursuant to which conduct that achieves a greater good is deemed lawful by the legal order.[133]

State of necessity can also be formulated as an excuse. When cast in this way, the defence focuses on the circumstances of the agent and, in particular, on the degree of coercion or compulsion caused by external circumstances on

---

as 'duress' in his English translation of the German Criminal Code: Michael Bohlander, *The German Criminal Code: A Modern English Translation* (Hart 2008) 44–45.)

[130] For an excellent example of a tribunal deciding on the character of a defence, see the Canadian Supreme Court's consideration of the plea of necessity in *Perka v The Queen* (n 129).

[131] This is a streamlined and unrefined explanation of a much more complex analysis, on which see Ferzan (n 120) 239.

[132] This thought experiment was developed by Joel Feinberg, and has subsequently been used to explore different aspects of the necessity defence. For Feinberg's original formulation, see: Joel Feinberg, 'Voluntary Euthanasia and the Inalienable Right to Life (Tanner Lecture)' (1978) 7 *Philosophy and Public Affairs* 93.

[133] See Joshua Dressler, 'Justifications and Excuses: A Brief Review of the Concepts and the Literature' (1986–1987) 33 *Wayne LR* 1155, 1163.

the agent's free will. The conduct of the agent is still physically voluntary,[134] but it is said to be morally or normatively involuntary:[135] as a result of the circumstances, the agent's 'choice to break the law is no true choice at all, as it is remorselessly compelled by normal human instincts'.[136] Such involuntariness is measured 'on the basis of society's expectation of appropriate and normal resistance to pressure'.[137] This is why some scholars refer to this type of necessity as 'compulsion of circumstance'[138] and why certain legal systems, like the English one, refer to it as 'duress of circumstances'.[139]

The plea of necessity in Article 25 of the ARS is formulated as a lesser-evils defence. Thus, the plea is only available where the invoking State acts to protect one of its 'essential interests' against a 'grave and imminent peril', and its actions do not impair an 'essential interest' of the affected party. State of necessity is therefore formulated as a justification. Some States endorsed the classification of state of necessity as an excuse during the drafting of the ARS,[140] but by and large States invoking the plea of necessity have tended to do so by way of justification; namely to argue that their behaviour is lawful (and not that they are excused for their unlawful behaviour).[141] In investment arbitration,

---

[134] It is not involuntary in the same sense as, e.g., the conduct of a sleepwalking person.

[135] On the concept of normative involuntariness, see George Fletcher, *Rethinking Criminal Law* (OUP 2000) 802–807. Note, however, that there are disagreements in the literature as to the rationale of this excuse and, in particular, on whether necessity excuses because the conduct is involuntary (in the moral/normative sense described) or on the basis of a moral evaluation of the defendant's conduct and its compatibility with what would be required from a person of reasonable firmness. On these debates, see Fletcher, ibid., 798–810; A. P. Simester et al, *Criminal Law: Theory and Doctrine* (7th edn, Hart 2019) 813–814. The text above refers to the involuntariness rationale as this seems more easily applicable to States (in the sense that it is possible to assess, and indeed some rules of international law relate to, the degree of coercion on a State's free will) than the rationale based on the 'person of reasonable firmness'.

[136] *Perka v The Queen* (n 129) 249 (per Dickson J).

[137] Ibid., 259 (per Dickson J).

[138] Fletcher (n 135).

[139] See, e.g., David Ormerod and Karl Laird, *Smith, Hogan, and Ormerod's Criminal Law* (15th edn, OUP 2018) 344–345; Simester et al (n 135) 808–811.

[140] France, India, Japan, Russia and the UK considered that state of necessity was an excuse. For references to the relevant sources, see Paddeu (n 11) 400–401.

[141] For further references, see ibid., 401–413.

Argentina,[142] Egypt,[143] and Zimbabwe[144] have all invoked the plea as a justification.

C. State of Necessity in Investment Arbitration: Towards an Excuse?

The *CMS* Committee provided two sources to back up its finding that state of necessity provides an excuse but neither actually supports this proposition. The award first refers to Special Rapporteur Crawford's report on state of necessity to the ILC.[145] However, at no point in the pages mentioned does Crawford support, explicitly, the characterisation of state of necessity as an excuse. On the contrary, at one point, he states that: 'It should also be stressed that (unlike *rebus sic stantibus*) the plea of necessity only operates by way of a temporary preclusion of wrongfulness' – so, as a justification.[146] Second, it refers to the Commentary to Chapter V of Part One of the ARS, in particular paragraphs

---

[142] *Sempra Energy International v Argentine Republic,* ICSID Case No ARB/02/16, Award (29 September 2007) para 333, a 'concept precluding wrongfulness'; *Enron Corporation and Ponderosa Assets LP v Argentine Republic,* ICSID Case No ARB/01/3, Award (22 May 2007) para 294, a 'concept precluding wrongfulness'; *Continental Casualty Company v Argentine Republic,* ICSID Case No ARB/03/9, Award (5 September 2008) para 160, actions 'entirely lawful'; *Metalpar SA and Buen Aire SA v Argentine Republic* ICSID Case No ARB/03/5, Award (6 June 2008) para 137, 'justification … under international law'; *National Grid plc v Argentine Republic,* UNCITRAL, Award (3 November 2008) para 205, conduct is 'licit'; *EDF International SA, SAUR International SA and Leon Participaciones Argentinas SA v Argentine Republic,* ICSID Case No ARB/03/23, Award (11 June 2012) para 1163, conduct is 'justified'; *EDF (Annulment)* para 317, plea invoked in case of finding of a 'prima facie breach of the BIT'; *Total SA v Argentine Republic,* ICSID Case No ARB/04/1, Annulment (1 February 2016) para 229, plea invoked as a 'circumstance that precludes the wrongfulness of an act contrary to the obligation allegedly violated'. The pleadings of Argentina are not public, so the following list of examples relies on the tribunal's own summary of the Argentine argument. It would seem reasonable to assume that Argentina's position on the plea of necessity under customary law was consistent throughout the various disputes brought against it. Nevertheless, tribunals have used inconsistent and equivocal language in their description of Argentina's argument, sometimes using the language of justification and other times the language of excuse. Troublingly, they have often done so within the same award.

[143] *Unión Fenosa v Egypt* (n 8) para 8.21: '[T]he state of necessity caused by the revolution that erupted in Egypt and whose after-effects persist to this day precludes any wrongfulness of the conduct alleged to constitute a violation of the Spain-Egypt BIT …'.

[144] *Bernard von Pezold and Others v Republic of Zimbabwe*, ICSID Case No ARB/10/15, Award (28 July 2015) para 616.

[145] The Committee refers to Crawford, 'Second Report' (n 128) 73–74, 85.

[146] Ibid., para 293.

2–4 and 7 of the Commentary. Paragraphs 2–4 are concerned with the character of defences as 'shields' and not 'swords', and clarifies that, unlike analogous provisions in the law of treaties, the defences have no effect on the continued validity of the underlying obligation(s). In explaining the character of defences as 'shields', the Commentary states that they 'provide a justification or excuse' for non-performance. Paragraph 7, in turn, addresses the distinction between what one may term 'affirmative' or 'substantive' defences, on the one hand, and other types of defensive arguments that States may raise, such as objections to jurisdiction and admissibility, on the other. Again, the Commentary states that the defences in Chapter V 'operate like defences or excuses in internal legal systems'. None of these paragraphs lend support to the proposition that state of necessity is an excuse or that this is the ILC's understanding of Article 25. Rather than simply re-stating the views of the ILC which, as noted, did not express any views on the matter, the *CMS* Committee was re-evaluating the basis upon which the plea of necessity operates in international law: after all, the formulation of the plea as a lesser-evils, and the practice of States invoking the plea before international courts and tribunals, had moved in the direction of recognising state of necessity as a justification.

The *CMS Annulment* decision scores relatively highly in the internal factors mentioned in Section II as affecting the potential impact of a decision on the development of the law. Thus, the Committee was composed of very experienced and reputable arbitrators: two of the arbitrators were ICJ judges during, at least, a part of the proceedings (Gilbert Guillaume and Nabil Elaraby),[147] and the other arbitrator was the final Special Rapporteur to the ILC on State Responsibility (James Crawford, now himself a Judge in the ICJ). It is also a well-reasoned and argued decision, if not supported adequately by the materials it relied upon. And yet, the 'wear' of the decision in the subsequent practice of States and other international bodies is somewhat inconsistent.

Some tribunals have explicitly endorsed the Annulment Committee's finding as to the characterisation of the plea of necessity as an excuse,[148] at least unambiguously so.[149] But many others have done so only implicitly:

---

[147] Judge Guillaume served on the ICJ until 2005, and Judge Elaraby until 2006. See 'All Members' (*International Court of Justice*) www.icj-cij.org/en/all-members accessed 6 January 2021.

[148] For example *Continental Casualty v Argentina* (n 142) fn 236.

[149] It is unclear whether the Annulment Committee in *Sempra v Argentina* (n 142) also intended to follow the *CMS (Annulment)* (n 114) approach. The *Sempra* committee explained (at para 200) that:

> … Article 25 is concerned with the invocation by a State Party of necessity 'as a ground for precluding the wrongfulness of an act not in conformity with an international obligation of that State'. Article 25 presupposes that an act has been

essentially, by reaching a similar or consistent result, but following a different reasoning path. Indeed, such choice may also be implicitly buttressed by those investment tribunals which have criticised the plea of necessity as a justification on the basis of the normative implications of this classification. These tribunals expressed concern that to accept the legality of Argentina's measures would have an impact on the fabric of investment treaties worldwide. In short, to accept that Argentina had acted lawfully would be tantamount to signalling to other host States that, in similar conditions, they too could lawfully impair the rights of investors – that their obligations under investment treaties, in other words, were only applicable insofar as circumstances were unexceptional. In the words of the *Suez-InterAguas* tribunal:

> The severity of a crisis, no matter the degree, is not sufficient to allow a plea of necessity to relieve a state of its treaty obligations ... The reason of course is that given the frequency of crises and emergencies that nations, large and small, face from time to time, to allow them to escape their treaty obligations would threaten the very fabric of international law and indeed the stability of the system of international relations.[150]

These tribunals were not ready to accept that the government had acted lawfully when, in adopting measures to face the crisis, it had acted incompatibly with its obligations under the relevant investment treaties.

> committed that is incompatible with the State's international obligations and is therefore 'wrongful'...

and that 'Article 25 deals with a situation where a State Party is in breach of a Treaty obligation and seeks to justify its breach by a plea of necessity' (para 203). The substance of the Committee's description (art 25 applies when there is a breach/wrongful act) would seem to suggest so as it reflects the role of excuses, though its use of language (art 25 is a 'circumstance for precluding wrongfulness' which 'justifies') suggests the opposite. The same can be queried of the *El Paso* award. There, the tribunal expressly quotes, and endorses, the *CMS (Annulment)* approach (of the plea as an excuse), and yet it refers to state of necessity as a 'circumstance precluding wrongfulness' and describes its operation as the 'setting aside' of the illegality of the conduct, see *El Paso Energy International Company v Argentine Republic,* ICSID Case No ARB/03/15, Award (31 October 2011) paras 553–554.

[150] *Suez Sociedad General de Aguas de Barcelona SA and InterAguas Servicios Integrales del Agua SA v Argentine Republic,* ICSID Case No ARB/03/17, Liability (30 July 2010) para 236. See also *Suez Sociedad General de Aguas de Barcelona SA and Vivendi Universal SA v Argentine Republic,* ICSID Case No ARB/03/19, Liability (30 July 2010) para 258.

Nevertheless, these tribunals also acknowledged the difficult situation that Argentina had faced at the time. The tribunal in *Suez-InterAguas*, for example, noted that:

> The crisis into which Argentina fell in 2001–2003 was undoubtedly one of the most severe in its history. It was characterized by extreme social disturbance, riots, violence, and almost total breakdown of the political system. Evidence in the record in the present case clearly shows its severity.[151]

In an attempt to mediate between the government's predicament and the concern over the impact of the necessity justification, tribunals opted for what Charles Leben has referred to as a 'Solomonic solution':[152] they disallowed the defence but nonetheless took the economic crisis into account in assessing the quantum of compensation.[153] In a sense, these tribunals had it both ways: they maintained the illegality of the conduct of Argentina, while nevertheless making some concessions for the extraordinary situation that the country was facing. The *Sempra* tribunal was quite explicit in this regard. The issue was not, it said, 'one of lowering the standards of protection set under the Treaty or the law'.[154] It remained the case, however, that 'the manner in which the law has to be applied cannot ignore the realities resulting from a crisis situation, including how a crisis affects the normal functioning of any given society. This is the measure of justice that the Tribunal is bound to respect'.[155]

Other tribunals have, nevertheless, continued to apply state of necessity as a justification. For example, the tribunals in *von Pezold v Zimbabwe* and *Unión Fenosa v Egypt* treated the defence as raised by the respective respondents, namely as a justification. Perhaps more relevantly, those States, Zimbabwe and Egypt, eschewed the *CMS* Committee's characterisation and pled state of necessity as a justification – suggesting that, despite the stature of the members of the Annulment Committee, the quality of the reasoning, the defensibility of the rationale (especially in respect of the normative implications of the classification), States have been unwilling to reconsider the status of the plea.

While there has been opportunity and receptiveness to this legal development in respect of the classification of the plea of necessity as an excuse, and

---

[151] *Suez-InterAguas v Argentina* (n 150) para 235. See also *Suez-Vivendi v Argentina* (n 150) para 257; *CMS Gas Transmission Company v Argentine Republic*, ICSID Case No ARB/01/8, Award (12 May 2005) para 322.

[152] Charles Leben, 'L'état de nécessité dans le droit international de l'investissement' (2005) 349 *Gazzette du Palais* 19, 20.

[153] See, e.g., *CMS v Argentina* (n 151) paras 356, 406; *Sempra v Argentina* (n 142) paras 396–397; *National Grid v Argentina* (n 142) para 274.

[154] *Sempra v Argentina* (n 142) para 397.

[155] Ibid.

the *CMS* Annulment Committee's finding meets many of the relevant factors mentioned earlier, this decision has not worn well in the subsequent practice of States and other international actors – at least as at this point in time.

VI. AN ASSESSMENT

The 'secondary rules' of responsibility are a set of general principles. Indeed, if there is a basic feature that sets them apart from so-called 'primary rules' is precisely their generality. In Crook and Bodansky's words:

> [w]hat defines the scope of the [ARS] is not their 'secondary' status but their generality: the [ARS] represent those areas where the ILC could identify and reach consensus on general propositions that can be applied more or less comprehensively across the entire range of international law.[156]

This is not just in the spatial sense, so to speak, of applying across all areas of international law. But also in the broader sense of being abstract: after all, if they are to apply across all areas of international law, the rules cannot be too specific for otherwise they could not cater to the 'infinite variety' of obligations that States undertake in their international relations. The 'secondary rules' are therefore general and abstract – the bare bones – so as to ensure flexibility to the tribunals and other international decision-makers that must apply them to the array of situations that come before them.

Their generality and abstract character make them particularly receptive to development by case law. As demonstrated by the example of *force majeure*, this was true historically, and continues to be true today. Furthermore, it was true of decisions of the PCIJ and, currently, the ICJ, and also of decisions of investment tribunals, broadly understood. Of course, the latitude allowed to international courts and tribunals for the development of the law of responsibility has fluctuated considerably: where the PCIJ was able to lay down the foundational principles of this area of international law, tribunals today, including the ICJ, operate within a much more constrained field where the basic decisions as to the structure of the law of responsibility and its parameters are set by the ARS. But they continue to contribute to the development of this area of international law. Indeed, as noted by Jennings: 'The great value of decided cases for the development and clarification of the law is largely because truth is stranger than fiction, and real life throws up circumstances which the most imaginative writers never thought of.'[157]

---

156 Daniel Bodansky and John Crook, 'Symposium: The ILC's State Responsibility Articles: Introduction and Overview' (2002) 96 *AJIL* 773, 780–781.

157 Jennings (n 36) 744.

The decisions of investment tribunals, by far the largest number of decisions involving defences since the adoption of the ARS, have contributed to the consolidation of these rules. Modest as it might seem, this is nevertheless an important contribution. The articles on defences in the ARS are often taken for granted, forgetting that many of these rules were far from uncontroversial among States at the time the ARS were adopted in 2001. For example, States expressed opposing views about the status of the necessity plea as a rule of customary law and many vehemently objected to the inclusion of a regime of countermeasures in the ARS at all. Mexico and the US were at opposite ends of the spectrum on the topic of countermeasures during the drafting of the ARS: where Mexico objected to their inclusion in the ARS and wanted them tightly limited if they were to be included,[158] the US objected to the tight regulation imposed on this institution by the ILC.[159] Less than a decade later, Mexico would rely on countermeasures in the high-fructose corn syrup disputes: a 180-degree shift. The decisions of investment tribunals since 2001 do not, at all, betray any of these disagreements: the parties, and the tribunals along with them, have taken these rules as settled.

Furthermore, the investment case law has also had the important effect of fleshing out the various aspects of the defences – of putting the meat on the bones, as it were. For example, we may now have a better sense of what interests of the State are 'essential': not just the survival of the State, but also the wellbeing of a States' population through access to public services, the maintenance of public order, and the functioning of public institutions.[160] It has also highlighted areas of uncertainty, which will require further attention from States.[161] These include, for instance, the requirement of non-contribution in the plea of necessity: Is this a purely causal or a fault-based element? In the absence of any prior practice on this requirement (which was introduced by the

[158] See sources above in n 10.

[159] See, e.g., 'Comments and observations received from Governments' (n 11) 84: the US 'continues to believe that the restrictions in articles 50–55 that have been placed on the use of countermeasures do not reflect customary international law or State practice, and could undermine efforts by States to settle disputes peacefully. The United States therefore strongly believes that these articles should be deleted'.

[160] See *Sempra v Argentina* (n 142) para 326; *BG Group v Argentina* (n 11) para 393; *National Grid v Argentina* (n 142) para 245.

[161] For an overview and assessment of the investment case law on the defence of necessity, see Federica Paddeu and Michael Waibel, 'Necessity 20 Years On: The Limits of Article 25 ARSIWA' (2022) 37 *ICSID Review* 160–191.

ILC),[162] tribunals have struggled to interpret this standard and have therefore taken opposing views on the point.[163]

Investment tribunals have also dealt with meatier questions, such as the ones addressed in this contribution. Are investors third parties in the Article 49 sense? Is state of necessity a justification or an excuse? It is difficult to say whether tribunals' decisions on these issues have had an impact on the development of the law of responsibility. In a narrow sense, it is tempting to conclude that they have not had any effect. No further cases involving countermeasures affecting investors have been decided (publicly at least), and States have not commented on the issue. Further, States invoking state of necessity have continued to plead it as a justification – even years after the Committee's decision in *CMS*. But it may be too soon to tell. A relatively short period of time has elapsed since these decisions were issued. To be sure, time is not an independent consideration for the development of customary rules, it is rather instrumental to the generality and uniformity of the relevant practice. This practice may accumulate over a short period of time, as the ICJ acknowledged in *North Sea Continental Shelf*,[164] or it may require a considerably longer period. In respect of the defences, it seems reasonable that more time will be necessary for the accumulation of practice since the defences concern exceptional circumstances or situations which occur only rarely.

The contribution of tribunals need not necessarily be judged by whether the specific dictum was adopted by States and other international actors. Insofar as their findings propel or catalyse legal development, whether this is in accordance with their views or in a different direction, they may be seen as 'motors' of legal development. Thus, it may be that States' assertion that the

---

[162] On which see Gebhard Bücheler, *Proportionality in Investor-State Arbitration* (OUP 2015) 280, referring to cases or State practice involving economic emergencies; Ryan Manton, *Necessity in International Law* (unpublished PhD thesis, University of Oxford, 2016) 190.

[163] Contrast the approaches in *Impregilo SpA v Argentine Republic,* ICSID Case No ARB/07/17, Award (21 June 2011) para 356, in which the Tribunal held that 'contribution' did not require conduct that was 'deliberate … reckless or negligent, or even caused by a lesser degree of fault'; and in *LG&E Energy Corp, LG&E Capital Corp, LG&E International Inc v Argentine Republic,* ICSID Case No ARB/02/1, Liability (3 October 2006) para 256; *Enron Corporation and Ponderosa Assets LP v Argentine Republic,* ICSID Case No ARB/01/3, Award (22 May 2007) para 311; *Sempra Energy International v Argentine Republic,* ICSID Case No ARB/02/16, Award (29 September 2007) para 353, all of which required at least negligence, and *Urbaser SA and Consorcio de Aguas Bilbao Bizkaia, Bilbao Biskaia Ur Partzuergoa v Argentina* ICSID Case No ARB/07/26, Award (8 December 2016) para 711, which required intent or recklessness.

[164] *North Sea Continental Shelf Cases (FR Germany/Denmark; FR Germany/Netherlands)* [1969] *ICJ Reports* 3, 43, para 74.

plea of necessity operates as a justification, following the decisions of the *CMS* Committee and other investment tribunals, may consolidate the status of this defence as a justification. Or it may be that, after the high-fructose corn syrup disputes States may be prudent and not resort to countermeasures affecting foreign investors. These will in themselves be important developments given the existing ambiguities on these points. It is unlikely that States will ignore the investment case law on the defences (or on the law of responsibility more generally) in the negotiations of a treaty on State responsibility – should the UNGA convene a conference for the adoption of a treaty on State responsibility, an option which continues to gain support in the UNGA's Sixth Committee.[165] For indeed, in considering facts which are often 'stranger than fiction' and which even the 'most imaginative writers never thought of', investment arbitral tribunals have had the important role of fleshing out these skeletal rules.

[165] As at 2016, at least 100 States had supported the adoption of a treaty on State responsibility, and about 22 had opposed this course of action. For an overview of the data, see Paddeu (n 113) 87–92.

9. Remedies for wrongful conduct: Lessons from investment arbitration

Dirk Pulkowski[1]

I. INTRODUCTION

As the Roman law adage goes, *ubi jus ibi remedium*—where there is a right, there is a remedy. Given the significance of remedies in legal practice, the number of international law cases between States in which a court or tribunal has ordered 'restitution' or awarded 'compensation' is surprisingly small. Leaving aside the Iran-United States Claims Tribunal, compensation, in particular, appears to have been awarded in only four recent inter-State proceedings – two damages awards of the Eritrea-Ethiopia Claims Commission at the Permanent Court of Arbitration (PCA), the judgment of the International Court of Justice (ICJ) in the *Diallo* case, the judgment of the International Tribunal for the Law of the Sea (ITLOS) in the *Saiga* case, and the arbitral award in the *Arctic Sunrise* case at the PCA. The most common remedy in inter-State cases remains 'satisfaction' – the third remedy under the general international law on State responsibility, available 'insofar as [the injury] cannot be made good by restitution or compensation'.[2]

In investor-State dispute settlement (ISDS), on the other hand, compensation is the primary remedy.[3] Satisfaction has some significance as an additional

[1] All views expressed are personal. I am grateful to Nismah Adamjee and Iuliia Samsonova, formerly Assistant Legal Counsel at the Permanent Court of Arbitration, for their inspired research assistance. The bulk of this chapter was finalised in October 2017. Subsequent developments, until May 2021, are reflected to a more limited extent.

[2] As one commentator has noted, at the ICJ 'satisfaction has become the most frequently awarded remedy', Helmut Philipp Aust, 'Investment Protection and Sustainable Development' in Steffen Hindelang and Markus Krajewski (eds), *Shifting Paradigms in International Investment Law* (OUP 2016) 209.

[3] In the present chapter, the term 'compensation' is used in the same manner as by the International Law Commission in Articles on Responsibility of States for Internationally Wrongful Acts, reproduced with commentaries in (2001) II(2) *ILC Yearbook* 31. For a different usage, distinguishing between compensation and damages,

remedy: besides damages, claimants frequently request a declaration that the host State has breached the investment treaty in question. A finding of breach by an international tribunal is recognised as a form of satisfaction.[4] Restitution, however, is rarely sought, and even less frequently ordered.

The present chapter explores the reasons for the apparent discrepancy between the practices of inter-State courts and tribunals established under general international law, on the one hand, and investment tribunals, on the other hand. What remedies are available in the event of a breach of a primary rule contained in an investment treaty? Do the available remedies differ from those under general international law? Are there lessons to be learnt by inter-State courts and tribunals from the practice of investment tribunals? And if, so, have general international courts and tribunals been willing to take the experience of investor-State arbitration into account?

II. APPLICABLE LAW

Turning to the practice of investment tribunals, a first question is what law such tribunals should apply when ordering remedies. As will be shown, given that the treaty parties have tended to provide limited or no direction in investment treaties themselves, tribunals have by necessity sought guidance in the customary international law of State responsibility.

A. *Lex Specialis*: Remedies Specified in the Investment Agreement

Investment treaties set out the applicable standards of investment protection (primary rules, in the terminology of the International Law Commission (ILC)) and provide for the jurisdiction of arbitral tribunals. However, they rarely address the consequences of a breach of such standards (secondary rules).

Few investment agreements expressly contemplate restitution as a remedy. Notable exceptions include Article 1135 of the North American Free Trade Agreement (NAFTA), which vests arbitral tribunals with the power to award 'restitution of property' while providing the State party to the dispute with the option to 'pay monetary damages and any applicable interest in lieu of

---

see Stephan Wittich, 'Investment Arbitration: Remedies' in Marc Bungenberg et al (eds), *International Investment Law: A Handbook* (Nomos 2015) MN 5ff and 27ff.

4 Christoph Schreuer, 'Alternative Remedies in Investment Arbitration' (2015) 3 *J Damages IL* 1. But see Wittich (n 3) MN 70, who argues that, in the investment context, 'a declaration of wrongfulness would not assume the form of a distinct remedy as it would only be the precondition for the damages award and thus be absorbed by the latter'.

restitution'[5] and some bilateral investment treaties (BITs) containing similar or identical language.[6]

More commonly, investment agreements contain provisions defining the standard of compensation. Notwithstanding some variation in terminology, the majority of these follow the Hull formula and require compensation to be 'prompt, adequate and effective'.[7] Other investment agreements provide for 'fair and equitable' compensation[8] or 'just' compensation.[9] Again other BITs, such as the United States-Rwanda BIT, go one step further and clarify the meaning of the phrase 'prompt, adequate and effective',[10] while others clarify the standard of compensation by referring to the 'genuine value' or 'market value' of the investment. For example, the Energy Charter Treaty (ECT) provides that expropriation should be 'accompanied by the payment of prompt, adequate and effective compensation', which 'shall amount to the fair market value of the Investment expropriated'.[11]

---

[5] North-American Free Trade Agreement (adopted 17 December 1992, entered into force 1 January 1994) art 1135(1)(b).

[6] Central America-Dominican Republic-United States Free Trade Agreement (adopted 5 August 2004, entered into force 1 January 2009) art 10.26; United States-Chile Free Trade Agreement (adopted 6 June 2003, entered into force 1 January 2004) art 10.25; United States-Peru Trade Promotion Agreement (adopted 12 April 2006) art 10.26; Canada-South Africa BIT (adopted 27 November 1995, not yet entered into force) art XIII; Italy-Mexico BIT (adopted 24 November 1999, entered into force 5 December 2002) Annex on the Settlement of Disputes Mechanisms [sic] art 9(1)(b); United States Model Bilateral Investment Treaty (2004) art 34(1)(b).

[7] For example, Canada-Egypt BIT (adopted 13 November 1996, entered into force 3 November 1997) art 8(1) provides:

> Investments or returns of investors of either Contracting Party shall not be nationalized, expropriated or subjected to measures having an effect equivalent to nationalization or expropriation … except for a public purpose, under due process of law, in a non-discriminatory manner and against prompt, adequate and effective compensation.

[8] Morocco-United Kingdom BIT (adopted 30 October 1990, entered into force 14 February 2002); India-China BIT (adopted 21 November 2006, entered into force 1 August 2007).

[9] See Ecuador-Italy BIT (adopted 25 October 2001, entered into force 1 February 2005) art 5(3); Ecuador-Netherlands (adopted 27 June 1999, entered into force 1 July 2001) art 6(c).

[10] Rwanda-United States of America BIT (adopted 19 February 2008, entered into force 1 January 2012) art 6(2) of the stipulates:

> [t]he compensation … shall (a) be paid without delay; (b) be equivalent to the fair market value of the expropriated investment immediately before the expropriation took place ('the date of expropriation'); (c) not reflect any change in value occurring because the intended expropriation had become known earlier; and (d) be fully realizable and freely transferable.

[11] Energy Charter Treaty (adopted 17 December 2014, entered into force 16 April 1998) art 13(1)(d).

However, such provisions are generally limited to compensation for lawful expropriation. While States occasionally argue in dispute settlement proceedings that the same standard should also govern compensation for unlawful conduct, tribunals have tended to reject such an approach. If a treaty spells out the standard for compensation only in the context of lawful expropriation, it follows, *e contrario*, that it may not be presumed that the drafters of the treaty necessarily intended the same standard to apply across the board, including in respect of unlawful conduct.

For example, the tribunal in *ADC v Hungary* noted that the Hungary-Cyprus BIT stipulated the standard of compensation for lawful expropriation but did not address the standard for unlawful expropriation and held that the default standard of customary international law applied to the assessment of damages for unlawful expropriation.[12] The tribunal in *Siemens v Argentina* distinguished compensation under the treaty standard for lawful expropriation, which was limited to the value of the expropriated investment, from compensation under customary international law, which was intended to wipe out all the consequences of the illegal act by additionally providing consequential damages.[13] Similarly, the tribunal in *Vestey Group Ltd v Venezuela* endorsed the customary international law standard of full reparation and held that 'an unlawful expropriation must be remedied by an award covering the full value of the property taken'.[14]

B. An Interpretive Presumption Specific to Investment Law?

In the absence of specific provisions in investment treaties, investment tribunals will typically need to look elsewhere for guidance as to which remedies they should order. It has been argued that the 1965 ICSID Convention[15] may embody a default position for international investment law generally, which could inform the interpretation of all investment agreements.[16] In its enforcement chapter, the Convention states that every contracting State must 'enforce the pecuniary obligations imposed by that award within its territories as if it were a final judgment of a court of that State' (art 54(1)). Commentators have thus argued that the Convention implies the existence of forms of

[12] *ADC Affiliate Ltd and ADC & ADMC Management v Republic of Hungary*, ICSID Case No ARB/03/16, Award (2 October 2006) paras 479–494.

[13] *Siemens AG v Argentine Republic*, ICSID Case No ARB/02/8, Award (17 January 2007) paras 349–353.

[14] *Vestey Group Ltd v Bolivarian Republic of Venezuela*, ICSID Case No ARB 06/4, Award (15 April 2016) paras 330–334.

[15] Convention on the Settlement of Investment Disputes Between States and Nationals of Other States (adopted 18 March 1965, entered into force 14 October 1966) 575 UNTS 159.

[16] Michelle Bradfield and John Christopher Thomas, 'Non-Pecuniary Remedies: A Missed Opportunity?' (2015) 30 *ICSID Review* 635, 639.

non-pecuniary relief. The drafting history of the Convention, which the same commentators have consulted, provides ample confirmation of that point.[17]

It is far from obvious, however, on what basis the ICSID Convention should be considered as interpretive authority for individual investment treaties, to the point that it could establish a default interpretive presumption for the meaning of such treaties. The Convention is not an 'instrument which was made by one or more parties in connection with the conclusion of the [investment treaty] and accepted by the other parties as an instrument related to the treaty' (art 31(2) of the Vienna Convention).

It remains conceivable to have regard to the Convention as an instrument setting out 'relevant rules of international law applicable in the relations between the parties' (art 31(3)(c) of the Vienna Convention). However, it would go too far to draw any general conclusions in respect of the interpretation of investment treaties from the mere fact that the negotiators of the ICSID Convention ostensibly assumed the existence of remedies other than compensation. A significant argument is that the drafters, in the early 1960s, did not necessarily envisage the Convention as a complement to bilateral investment treaties – only few such treaties had been concluded at that time,[18] and not all of them would provide for compulsory dispute settlement. Rather, they devised an instrument for investment disputes more generally, including – at that time predominantly – contractual disputes.

At best, the position under the ICSID Convention would seem to lend additional support to conclusions that remain to be drawn on the basis of other, stronger authority.

C. Customary International Law

In the absence of a treaty-based *lex specialis*, it seems natural to turn to international custom. Since the adoption of the ILC of the Draft Articles on State Responsibility in 2001,[19] practitioners of investment law tend to refer to the Articles and the accompanying commentary as an authoritative expression of the customary international law in the area.

---

[17] Ibid., 637.

[18] According to the database of the United Nations Conference on Trade and Development (UNCTAD), 48 investment agreements had been concluded by 1965 (see 'International Investment Agreements Navigator' (UNCTAD) http://investmentpolicyhub.unctad.org/IIA accessed 25 September 2021).

[19] See ILC Articles on State Responsibility (n 3) chap. IV. E.1.

1. Possible objections to the application of the ILC Articles

Such a 'shortcut', avoiding the need to establish *consuetudo* and *opinio iuris* more specifically, disregards the fact that the ILC Articles are intended to combine elements of both 'codification' and 'progressive development'.[20]

There is another, more formal objection to the applicability of the ILC Articles – that the Articles were not drafted with investor-State arbitration, but rather with a paradigm of inter-State disputes, in mind.[21] Some commentators have argued, in response, that the Articles cover all international obligations of a State, including not only those owed to States but also those owed to an individual or group, or to the international community as a whole, regardless of whether they are based on treaties or customary international law or derive from a general principle applicable within the international legal order.[22] Others have suggested that the Articles should at least apply in relations between States and foreign investors insofar as these are subject to international law such as in the ECT.[23]

In any event, the objection cannot apply in the same manner across all sections of the Articles. As James Crawford has pointed out, Part I of the Articles spells out the conditions under which international responsibility of a State can be engaged;[24] this Part focuses only on the infringing State, and is not concerned with the nature of the other party to which a primary obligation may be owed and which may invoke responsibility. Part I can thus apply to ISDS without systemic difficulty. The key question is that of the scope of the applicable *lex specialis* – the investment treaty – as is illustrated in the contributions of Federica Paddeu and Stephan Wittich in this volume.

---

[20] The ILC was tasked by the General Assembly with the mandate under art 13 of the Charter of the United Nations to 'initiate studies and make recommendations for the purpose of ... encouraging the progressive development of international law and its codification'.

[21] James Crawford, 'Investment Arbitration and the ILC Articles on State Responsibility' (2010) 25 *ICSID Review* 127, 130.

[22] Kaj Hobér, 'State Responsibility and Investment Arbitration' (2008) 25 *J Int'l Arb* 545, 547.

[23] Karl-Heinz Böckstiegel, 'Applicable Law to State Responsibility under the Energy Charter Treaty and other Investment Protection Treaties' in Clarisse Ribeiro (ed), *Investment Arbitration and the Energy Charter Treaty* (JurisNet 2006) 257, 259. See also *Noble Ventures, Inc v Romania*, ICSID Case No ARB/01/11, Award (12 October 2005); *Bernhard von Pezold and Others v Republic of Zimbabwe*, ICSID Case No ARB/10/15, Award (28 July 2015) para 691: 'Although this dispute arises between an investor and a State, it is apparent that the ILC Articles will be of considerable guidance to this Tribunal.'

[24] James Crawford, 'Investment Arbitration and the ILC Articles on State Responsibility' (2010) 25 *ICSID Review* 127, 129.

Part III concerns the invocation of responsibility in the relations between States. It represents a digest, as it were, of the international legal history of claims brought by one State against another State. It is evident that the provisions of that Part cannot automatically apply to ISDS proceedings. This was recognised by the tribunal in *Archer Daniels Midland v Mexico*, which explained:

> it is a matter of the particular provisions of [NAFTA] Chapter Eleven to determine whether and to what extent persons or entities other than States are entitled to invoke responsibility on their own account. ... Customary international law – pursuant to which only sovereign States may invoke the responsibility of another State – does not therefore affect the rights of non-State actors under particular treaties to invoke state responsibility. This rule is not only true in the context of investment protection, but also in the human rights and environmental protection arena.[25]

However, it is not excluded that ISDS tribunals would find that certain characteristic elements of the invocation of international responsibility in inter-State proceedings might also apply to ISDS proceedings.

Part II, finally, contains the provisions of interest here – regarding the 'content of the international responsibility of a State'; this part also addresses the remedies available under customary international law in the case of a breach of a primary rule. As Article 33, entitled 'Scope of international obligations set out in this part', demonstrates, the provisions regarding remedies for breaches of international law were drafted with an inter-State paradigm in mind:

> 1. The obligations of the responsible State set out in this part may be owed to another State, to several States, or to the international community as a whole, depending in particular on the character and content of the international obligation and on the circumstances of the breach.
> 2. This part is without prejudice to any right, arising from the international responsibility of a State, which may accrue directly to any person or entity other than a State.

Technically, the ILC Articles describing the obligation to make reparation for injury would thus apply only in inter-State relations. ISDS would seem to fall under the 'without prejudice clause' of paragraph 2.

A different conclusion could be warranted if it were the case that investors, in ISDS proceedings, invoke delegated (or derivative) rights that are vested with their home State. On this construction, one might say that Part II of the ILC Articles can apply literally in ISDS proceedings, as the Investor enforces

[25] *Archer Daniels Midland Company v United Mexican States*, ICSID Case No ARB (AF)/04/5, Award (21 November 2007) para 118.

'obligations of the responsible State … owed to another State'.[26] On the other hand, if investment treaties are understood to endow investors with their own individual rights, reference to Part II would be more questionable.

2. Relevance of the case law underlying the ILC's codification

It would however seem that the formal status of the investor, pursuant to legal doctrine, should not be determinative for the purpose of determining the applicability of the ILC Articles. It bears recalling what the ILC Articles represent, and how they were made: the Articles are an extraction by leading jurists of key holdings from a reservoir of court and tribunal decisions. Such decisions by courts and tribunals underlying the ILC's codification work would seem highly relevant for ISDS proceedings. Many cases referred to in the commentary to the Articles regarding forms of reparation concerned diplomatic protection claims – claims brought by home States in respect of injury to their nationals. The fact patterns and legal problems are often astonishingly close to what we nowadays see in ISDS proceedings, as is demonstrated by the following examples.

(a) Norwegian Claims Case (USA v Norway) (1922)

The case was mentioned in the commentary to Article 36 (Compensation) at paragraphs 28 and 30 to illustrate different claims for loss of profit. The case concerned a dispute regarding the amount of compensation for requisitioned ships that at the time of requisition were in the process of being built for 15 Norwegian owners. The tribunal fixed the amount of compensation on the basis of the fair market value, representing the total value of the shipping contracts, and awarded interest for a period of five years.

(b) Delagoa Bay Railway Arbitration (USA, UK v Portugal) (1900)

The case was mentioned in the commentary to Article 36 (Compensation) at paragraphs 27 and 36 (n 561, 575) to illustrate the availability of compensation for lost profits in the context of concessions and other contractually protected interest. The case concerned a dispute between a concessionnaire and Portugal regarding the construction of a railway in Mozambique. The tribunal found that Portugal acted unlawfully when it unilaterally decreed that a final part of the railway, not included into the original concession, had to be built in eight

---

[26] Martins Paparinskis, 'Investment Treaty Arbitration and the (New) Law of State Responsibility' (2013) 24 *EJIL* 636. See also Robert Volterra, 'ILC Articles on State Responsibility and Investor-State Arbitration: Do Investors Have Rights?' (2010) 25 *ICSID Review* 218, 222.

months and obliged Portugal to pay a total of 15,314,000 French francs in compensation, plus 5 per cent interest, to the claimants.

(c) *Spanish Zone of Morocco Claims (Great Britain v Spain) (1924)*

The case was mentioned in the commentary to Article 35 (Restitution) at paragraph 3 (n 493) to illustrate the award of compensation once restitution has become impossible. The case concerned a dispute between British subjects and protégés and Spain for damage caused between 1913 and 1921 in the Spanish Zone of Morocco during riots and civil unrest – a fact pattern that bears resemblance to situations implicating the guarantee of 'full protection and security' in modern investment treaties.

(d) *Oscar Chinn Case (UK v Belgium) (1934)*

The case was mentioned in the commentary to Article 36 (Compensation) at paragraph 32 (n 577) as an example of a situation where 'lost profits have been excluded on the basis that they were not sufficiently established as a legally protected interest'. The case concerned a dispute between a British national, Oscar Chinn, and Belgium regarding the loss of Chinn's shipping business in Belgian Congo due to the reduction of carriage charges. In its judgment of 12 December 1934, the Permanent Court of International Justice (PCIJ) denied the British claims on the basis that there was no nationality-based discrimination.

While all four cases just mentioned were inter-State cases, it would not seem unreasonable for arbitral tribunals in ISDS proceedings to take guidance from these awards and judgments in respect of the content of responsibility under an investment treaty. The fact patterns resemble those at issue in modern investment disputes, as do many of the legal questions. In view of the continuing relevance of the case law underlying the ILC Draft Articles, ISDS tribunals are justified in making careful reference to Part II of the Articles, as a shortcut to an authoritative body of decisions by courts and tribunals that reflect the customary international law on the treatment of aliens.[27]

Indeed, investor-State tribunals have referred to Part II of the Articles in a large number of cases since the finalisation of the ILC Draft Articles in 2001. Given the relatively small number of compensation claims at the ICJ and ITLOS, and the more self-contained approach of the human rights courts (see below), investor-State tribunals have even been the primary judicial appliers of Part II of the Articles. Despite conceptual doubts as to the direct applicability

---

[27] Helmut Aust has in this context referred to the ILC Articles as 'the most important source of inspiration with respect to remedies', see Helmut Philipp Aust, 'Investment Protection and Sustainable Development' in Hindelang and Krajewski (n 2) 219.

of the Articles, investor-State tribunals have thus arguably contributed more than other courts or tribunals to the confirmation and consolidation of the rules of reparation under general international law as codified by the ILC.

A number of fundamental assumptions endorsed by the ILC in 2001 were not as settled at the time as one might think from today's vantage point. For example, Martins Paparinskis has pointed out that several States and influential members of the ILC had in fact opposed the unqualified principle of full reparation as enunciated in *Chorzów Factory* and ultimately reflected in the Draft Articles; they urged the ILC instead to limit the scope of recoverable compensation by excluding (at least) damages that could deprive a State's population 'of its own means of subsistence'.[28] In the meantime, the repeated affirmation in investor-State arbitration of the unqualified principle of full reparation without regard for political or economic considerations, coupled with the virtual absence of contradiction by States, 'provides a strong, if implied endorsement of the 2001 ILC Articles' on that point.[29]

III. FORMS OF REPARATION

Having thus established the relevance of the customary international law regarding remedies for investor-State arbitration, I will explore how such tribunals have approached questions of reparation more specifically. The focus in this regard will be on awards of restitution and reparation. As will become apparent, investor-State tribunals have in some ways confirmed the pre-2001 practice that formed the basis of the ILC Draft Articles and commentary, and in other ways charted a different course. The latter notably applies in respect of the relationship between the remedies of restitution and compensation.

A. Restitution

Whether investment tribunals are empowered to order restitution of the *status quo ante* remains controversial. Some have argued that, in the absence of specific provisions empowering them to do so, investment tribunals are not competent to award restitution.[30] The proponents of this point of view tend to emphasise practical difficulties associated with the enforcement of such

---

28 Martins Paparinskis, 'A Case Against Crippling Compensation in International Law of State Responsibility' (2020) 83 *MLR* 1246, 1256ff.

29 Ibid., 1266.

30 Zachary Douglas, 'Other Specific Regimes of Responsibility: Investment Treaty Arbitration and ICSID' in James Crawford et al (eds), *The Law of International Responsibility* (OUP 2010) 815, 829; Andreas Kulick, *Global Public Interest in International Investment Law* (CUP 2012) 209.

remedy, in particular in ICSID arbitrations,[31] and contend that the availability of restitution could be seen as an infringement on the power of the State to expropriate.[32] Others counter that view by pointing out that there are no restrictions as to the available remedies to be found in the great majority of investment treaties, the ICSID Convention or the New York Convention.[33] Even those who believe that restitution is in principle available, however, note that there are reasons why an arbitral tribunal may not wish to exercise such a power, such as the rarity of claims for non-pecuniary relief, the difficulty of performing an order for restitution in cases of unlawful expropriation, and the difficulty of obtaining the cooperation of the respondent State in enforcing an order for restitution in its territory.[34]

Similarly, there is no consistent line of jurisprudence regarding the availability of the restitution in investor-State arbitration proceedings. To the extent that tribunals have expressly considered questions of restitution they mostly appear to have arrived at the conclusion that restitution should not be categorically excluded.

1. What ISDS awards say about the availability of restitution

(a) Restitution available

In *LG&E v Argentina*, one of the cases brought against Argentina in the aftermath of the Argentine financial crisis in 2001 and 2002, the tribunal initially referred to the ILC Articles on State Responsibility. Acknowledging that '[r]eparation can thus take the form of restitution or compensation',[35] the tribunal did not regard restitution as appropriate in that case:

> The judicial restitution required in this case would imply modification of the current legal situation by annulling or enacting legislative and administrative measures that make over the effect of the legislation in breach. The Tribunal cannot compel Argentina to do so without a sentiment of undue interference with its sovereignty.

---

[31] Douglas (n 30) 829. As noted above, art 54(1) of the ICSID Convention reserves the Convention's special enforcement regime to 'pecuniary obligations imposed by [the] award'.

[32] Kulick (n 30) 209. But see the convincing critique of this view in Aust (n 27) 218.

[33] Borzu Sabahi, *Compensation and Restitution in Investor-State Arbitration: Principles and Practice* (OUP 2011) 63–65.

[34] Carole Malinvaud, 'Non-Pecuniary Remedies in Investment Treaty and Commercial Arbitration' in Albert van den Berg (ed), *50 Years of the New York Convention* (Wolters Kluwer 2009) 209, 230; see also Christoph Schreuer, 'Non-Pecuniary Remedies in ICSID Arbitration' (2004) 20 *Arb Int'l* 325; Bradfield and Thomas (n 16) 655–661.

[35] *LG&E Energy Corp, LG&E Capital Corp and LG&E International Inc v Argentine Republic,* ICSID Case No ARB/02/1, Award (25 July 2007) para 32.

> Consequently, the Tribunal arrives at the same conclusion: the need to order and quantify compensation.[36]

Similarly, in *Petrobart v Kyrgyz Republic*, the tribunal made reference to the ILC Articles but held that in the particular case compensation was to be preferred:

> The Arbitral Tribunal notes Petrobart's explanation that the company no longer has any activity in the Kyrgyz Republic and that its supply contract with Uzneftegazdobicha is no longer in operation. In such circumstances, the Arbitral Tribunal considers that specific performance is no longer a practical option and finds that also in regard to lost profits monetary compensation would be the only appropriate remedy in this case.[37]

In *Occidental v Ecuador*, the tribunal recognised that restitution is generally available as a remedy, but could only be awarded where that was possible in the circumstances of a particular case:

> Restitution in kind is never guaranteed to an injured claimant. Whether restitution in kind is possible or impossible must necessarily and logically be ascertained when a tribunal is seized of the matter. At that point, it is not disputed that for purposes of making an injured claimant whole, specific performance should be granted to it, unless impossible or disproportionate when compared to compensation. In other words, in the event of injury suffered as a result of an illegal act, the injured claimant has a right to specific performance unless specific performance is impossible.[38]

In *Burlington Resources v Ecuador*, the tribunal noted in a procedural order:

> With respect to international law, Article 35 of the ILC Articles on State responsibility provide for restitution which includes specific performance unless it is materially impossible or wholly disproportionate. Whether specific performance is impossible or disproportionate is a question to be dealt with at the merits stage. It is true that the view has been expressed that the right to specific performance is not available under international law where a concession agreement for natural resources has been terminated or cancelled by a sovereign State. In the instant case, the PSCs are in force which makes it unnecessary to consider that view. As far as Ecuadorian law is concerned, it appears to provide for the remedy of specific performance pursuant to Article 1505 of the Civil Code.[39]

---

[36] Ibid., para 87.

[37] *Petrobart Ltd v Kyrgyz Republic,* SCC Case No 126/2003, Award (29 March 2005) 78.

[38] *Occidental Petroleum Corp and Occidental Exploration and Production Co v Republic of Ecuador (II)*, ICSID Case No ARB/06/11, Decision on Provisional Measures (17 August 2007) para 75, see also paras 76–85.

[39] *Burlington Resources, Inc v Republic of Ecuador*, ICSID Case No ARB/08/5, Procedural Order No 1 (29 June 2009) para 70.

(b) Primacy of restitution or compensation

Assuming that restitution is in principle available, the question arises whether restitution or compensation should be the primary remedy (assuming that both remedies are possible in a particular case). In *Nykomb Synergetics Technology Holding v Latvia*, the tribunal emphasised the primacy of restitution overcompensation:

> it seems to be agreed between the parties, that the question of remedies to compensate for losses or damages caused by the Respondent's violation of Article 10 of the Treaty must primarily find its solution in accordance with established principles of customary international law. Such principles have authoritatively been restated in the International Law Commission's Draft Articles on State Responsibility adopted in November 2001 … According to Articles 34 and 35 ILC restitution is considered to be the primary remedy for reparation.[40]

The tribunal further emphasised that restitution was conceivable 'either through a juridical restitution of provisions of Latvian law … or through a monetary restitution to Nykomb's subsidiary of the missing payments [under the relevant contract]'.[41] With respect to the missing payments up to the time of the award, the tribunal decided that compensation would be more appropriate, because 'restitution must primarily be seen as an appropriate remedy in a situation where the Contracting State has instituted actions directly against the investor [not against its subsidiary]'.[42]

In *ADC v Hungary*, the tribunal confirmed the primacy of restitution, although the tribunal found that in the particular case only compensation was possible:

> The remaining issue is what consequence does application of this customary international law standard have for the present case. It is clear that actual restitution cannot take place and so it is, in the words of the Chorzów Factory decision, 'payment of a sum corresponding to the value which a restitution in kind would bear', which is the matter to be decided.[43]

The tribunal in *CMS Gas Transmission Company v Argentina* recognised the primacy in principle of restitution but applied a somewhat different test than that under the ILC Articles to determine whether such restitution was owed. According to the tribunal, where restitution—involving in case the reinstate-

---

[40] *Nykomb Synergetics Technology Holding AB v Republic of Latvia*, SCC, Award (16 December 2003) para 5.1.

[41] Ibid., para 154.

[42] Ibid.

[43] *ADC v Hungary* (n 12) para 495.

ment of the gas regulatory framework – was 'utterly unrealistic', compensation should be awarded:

> Restitution is by far the most reliable choice to make the injured party whole as it aims at the reestablishment of the situation existing prior to the wrongful act. In a situation such as that characterizing this dispute and the complex issues associated with the crisis in Argentina, it would be utterly unrealistic for the Tribunal to order the Respondent to turn back to the regulatory framework existing before the emergency measures were adopted, nor has this been requested.[44]

In *Mr Franck Charles Arif v Moldova*, the tribunal, while qualifying restitution as the preferred remedy, considered that the respondent State should have a (free) choice between restitution and compensation. In that case, the tribunal did not feel that it should order restitution as the sole remedy because the respondent had not positively confirmed the possibility of restitution. Instead, a combination of restitution and conditional compensation was ordered:

> The Tribunal notes that the general position in international law is that the injured State may elect between the available forms of reparation and may prefer compensation to restitution. On the other hand, restitution is more consistent with the objectives of bilateral investment treaties, as it preserves both the investment and the relationship between the investor and the Host State.
>
> The Tribunal considers restitution to be the preferable remedy, but as in the present case Respondent has not been able to confirm that restitution is possible, and the Tribunal cannot supervise any restitutionary remedy, the best course is to order restitution and compensation as alternatives, with the remedy of compensation suspended for a period of ninety days.[45]

In contrast to the case just mentioned, the tribunal in *ATA Construction v Jordan* was faced with a situation where compensation was, in the tribunal's view, incapable of repairing the harm caused to the investor, notably because the material damage caused by the extinction of the investor's right to arbitrate was uncertain. Instead:

> The situation to be re-established was the *status quo ante*, specifically, the arbitral clause. The only way effecting that was by negating, as a matter of international law, the mandatory extinguishment of the arbitration agreement … This necessarily resulted in the restoration of the arbitration agreement *in toto*.[46]

---

44 *CMS Gas Transmission Co v Argentine Republic,* ICSID Case No ARB/01/8, Award (12 May 2005) para 407.

45 *Mr Franck Charles Arif v Republic of Moldova,* ICSID Case No ARB/11/23, Award (8 April 2013) paras 700–701.

46 *ATA Construction, Industrial and Trading Company v Hashemite Kingdom of Jordan,* ICSID Case No ARB/08/2, Decision on Interpretation (7 March 2011) para 40.

In *Goetz v Burundi*, the tribunal found that the withdrawal of the free zone certificate conferring tax and customs exemptions to the investors constituted a measure tantamount to expropriation. The investors had requested that the tribunal order the respondent State, Burundi, to cancel the withdrawal of the certificate and pay compensation. The tribunal decided:

> it falls to the Republic of Burundi, in order to establish the conformity with international law of the disputed decision to withdraw the certificate, to give an adequate and effective indemnity to the claimants as envisaged in Article 4 of the Belgium-Burundi investment treaty, unless it prefers to return the benefit of the free zone regime to them. The choice lies within the sovereign discretion of the Burundian government. If one of these two measures is not taken within a reasonable period, the Republic of Burundi will have committed an act contrary to international law the consequences of which would be left to the Tribunal to ascertain.[47]

Technically, the decision in *Goetz* does not fall under the law of State responsibility – a regime dealing with the legal consequences of internationally wrongful acts. Rather, the tribunal appears to have provided Burundi with the choice to pay the required compensation or to provide restitution of the free zone certificate to prevent the expropriation from becoming unlawful. The parties in that case reached a settlement.

(c) Restitution unavailable

In *Enron Corporation and Ponderosa Assets v Argentina*, on the other hand, the tribunal observed that '[t]he Treaty does not specify the damages to which the investor is entitled in case of breach of the standards of treatment different from expropriation, i.e., fair and equitable treatment or the breach of the umbrella clause'. The silence in the treaty did not however cause the tribunal to apply the customary international law on State responsibility. Rather, the tribunal suggested that '[a]bsent an agreed form of restitution by means of renegotiation of contracts or otherwise, the appropriate standard of reparation under international law is compensation for the losses suffered by the affected party'.[48] Similarly, the tribunal in *CME v Czech Republic* appears to have regarded compensation as the self-evident and only remedy when it noted that 'international law requires that compensation eliminates the consequences of the wrongful act'.[49] In *LIAMCO v Libya*, the arbitrator opined that an order of

---

[47] *Antoine Goetz et consorts v République du Burundi*, ICSID Case No ARB/95/3, Award (10 February 1999) para 133.

[48] *Enron Corporation and Ponderosa Assets, LP v Argentine Republic,* ICSID Case No ARB/01/3, Award (22 May 2007) para 359.

[49] *CME Czech Republic BV v Czech Republic,* UNCITRAL, Final Award (14 March 2003) para 501.

restitution 'would constitute in fact an intolerable interference in the internal sovereignty of States'.[50]

While this position appears to be a minority view in the case law (despite the widespread practice in ISDS proceedings of awarding solely compensation), it has gained significant traction at the policy level. Doubts have been expressed as to whether an order of restitution is appropriate in investment proceedings. The Investment Policy Framework for Sustainable Development (IPFSD), elaborated by the United Nations Conference on Trade and Development in 2012 and updated in 2015, while ostensibly limited to highlighting policy options for States, presumes that restitution is necessarily more onerous and less desirable than compensation. The IPFSD suggests that States may consider 'limit[ing] available remedies to monetary compensation and restitution of property (or to compensation only)'.[51] This option is reflected in the treaty practice, although it is not the predominant approach.[52]

UNCTAD's objective may have been to exclude from the scope of available remedies any order of restitution that would negate (what we might today call) a State's 'right to regulate'. While such intention is understandable, there remain many scenarios in which restitution makes economic sense for the investor and policy sense for the host State. One may recall that, in *Franck Charles Arif v Moldova*, it was the host State that argued quite forcefully that it should be permitted 'to determine if it can provide some form of restitution … in lieu of whatever damages the Tribunal might determine'.[53] The claimant in that case had speculated that 'the reality is that Respondent is unwilling or unable to extend a firm offer for restitution, backed by adequate guarantees' and accordingly requested damages. The tribunal, however, considered that 'restitution is more consistent with the objectives of bilateral investment treaties, as it preserves both the investment and the relationship between the investor and the Host State'.[54] An advantage of restitution was to 'restore Claimant to the position he would have been in without any violation of the BIT' while avoiding 'the uncertainties of the calculation of damages, including the possibility of risk free windfall profits'.[55] The case shows that it may be inappropriate to exclude the remedy of restitution altogether.

---

[50] *Libyan American Oil Company (LIAMCO) v Libya*, Award (12 April 1977) 62 ILR 140, 196.

[51] UNCTAD, 'Investment Policy Framework for Sustainable Development' (2015) UNCTAD/DIAE/PCB/2015/5, 109.

[52] See the treaties enumerated in note 6.

[53] *Arif v Moldova* (n 45) para 568.

[54] Ibid., para 570.

[55] Ibid., para 569.

2. Why not restitution? A procedural problem

While there seems to be little conceptual resistance on the part of ISDS tribunals to restitution, the reality remains that restitution is rarely contemplated, and even more rarely ordered, in investor-State proceedings. One reason for such hesitation on the part of tribunals may be the perception, which was articulated in some of the awards just cited, that an order of restitution could be seen by the respondent State as an encroachment upon its sovereignty, and may potentially cause the State to refuse compliance with the tribunal's award. Another reason, however, may be procedural. The fact that compensation is often the only remedy considered by tribunals may be a result of neither party specifically requesting restitution.

In many cases, claimants express a preference for compensation. In situations where the claimant is not interested in restitution and requests compensation, however, it falls to the respondent to object to the claimant's choice of remedy, and insist that restitution be awarded if liability is found. If no such objection is raised, the tribunal must assume that the respondent State does not contest the claimant's preference for compensation.[56]

Insisting on restitution, however, may put the respondent in an awkward position if its primary interest is to deny liability. It would have to argue, for instance, that a particular decree constitutes a legitimate exercise of government authority, which was adopted in a democratic process and pursues legitimate policy objectives. It would have to argue concurrently that, should the tribunal disagree, it would prefer to revoke that decree rather than pay any compensation. The State may feel that such argumentation could be seen as weakening its position on liability, as it might indicate either a lack of confidence in the strength of its case or, worse, a disguised hint to the tribunal that the arbitrators should resolve the case by ordering restitution and 'sparing the treasurer's purse'.

As a result, the most likely scenario for an award of restitution is one in which the investor insists on restitution as its preferred remedy. This was the case in the recent arbitrations of *Philip Morris Asia v Australia*[57]

---

56 See Wittich (n 3) MN 59.

57 In *Philip Morris*, the claimant requested that the tribunal:

(1) order Respondent to withdraw the Plain Packaging Measures or refrain from applying them against Claimant's investments; or in the alternative,
(2) award damages of at least USD 4,160 million, plus compound interest at the Australian bank cash management account rate running from the date of breach to the date of Respondent's payment of the Award; and
(3) award Claimant all of its fees and expenses, including attorney's fees, incurred in connection with this arbitration; and (4) award such other relief as the Tribunal deems just and appropriate.

Philip Morris Asia Ltd v Commonwealth of Australia, PCA Case No 2012-12, Award on

and *Von Pezold v Zimbabwe*).[58]

It is fair to conclude that the relative paucity of investor-State precedent ordering restitution is not due to any unique applicable law (different from the general rules of State responsibility), nor does there appear to be a failure on the part of tribunals to appreciate the possibility of restitution. Rather, the procedural circumstances in which tribunals are called upon to select an appropriate remedy are often unconducive to an order of restitution.

B. Compensation

Turning to the second remedy, compensation (the most frequent remedy in investor-State arbitration), it is worth exploring whether there are any relevant differences in the stance of investor-State tribunals as compared to courts and tribunals established under general international law.

1. Legal standard and practice in ISDS proceedings

The starting point of virtually every investor-State award of compensation is the pronouncement of the PCIJ in the *Chorzów Factory* case, namely that, under international law, 'reparation must, as far as possible, wipe out all the consequences of the illegal act and re-establish the situation which would, in all probability, have existed if that act had not been committed'. The amount of compensation, according to the PCIJ, should 'correspond ... to the value which a restitution in kind would bear'.[59]

In investment disputes, the value of restitution in kind is generally established by reference to the 'fair market value' – the amount that a willing buyer would have paid on the valuation date to a willing seller in the market.[60] The value of the investment may reflect profits that the investor reasonably expected to incur, and which the wrongful conduct by the State has prevented it from realising.[61]

There are three main approaches to determine an investment's 'fair market value':

Jurisdiction and Admissibility (17 December 2015) para 89.

[58] In *von Pezold v Zimbabwe* (n 23) para 670: '[t]he Claimants [sought] declaratory relief, restitution in kind (i.e., the reinstatement of title to the Zimbabwean Properties) and compensation for losses not covered by restitution in kind. In the alternative, they [sought] declaratory relief and compensation'.

[59] *Chorzów Factory (Germany v Poland)*, Award on the Merits, Judgment No. 13, PCIJ Series A (1928) 47.

[60] Sabahi (n 33) 102.

[61] Sergey Ripinsky and Kevin Williams, *Damages in International Investment* Law (BIICL 2015) 279.

(1) the income-based approach, often assessed by reference to a discounted cash flow method, which is used to calculate the present value of a business's expected cash flows;
(2) the market-based approach, which estimates the business' value by making a comparison to other similar businesses;
(3) the asset-based approach, which determines the value of a business by calculating the value of its tangible and intangible assets.[62]

Among these three methods, the first two appear to be most commonly used in practice. The last method is used sparingly but may be useful where the value of a business is significantly determined by its assets and no competitors in a comparable market situation exist, or where reliable financial data is not available. Besides these three principal methods, tribunals may choose to estimate the market value of an investment by calculating the total amount which the investors have spent on the investment[63] or adopt a hybrid approach, which combines backward-looking elements (the amount invested by the claimant or the value of tangible assets) and forward-looking elements (the loss of future benefits).[64]

All of the valuation methods just described involve the submission of detailed evidence by the claimant, typically followed by similarly detailed rebuttal evidence by the respondent. Such evidence extends to the economic circumstances of the industry in question, the financial situation of the claimant (or claimant's company) and its prospects of earning future profits. In some cases, financial statements have been considered sufficient evidence for a damages claim.[65] Such statements demonstrating 'the nature, date and amount of the expenditure' and proving that this invested amounts were 'directly connected with the investment project'[66] were accepted by the tribunals in *PSEG v Turkey*,[67] *Autopista v Venezuela*,[68] and *Tecmed v Mexico*.[69] More commonly, however, investment tribunals will determine damages based on a combination of financial documents,

---

62 Ibid., 193.

63 See *Vivendi v Argentina*, ICSID Case No ARB/97/3, Award (20 August 2007); *Metaclad v Mexico*, ICSID Case No ARB(AF)/97/1, Award (30 August 2000); *Tecmed v Mexico*, ICSID Case No ARB (AF)/00/2, Award (29 May 2003).

64 Ripinsky and Williams (n 61) 231.

65 Ibid., 272.

66 These are the requirements set out in *SPP v Egypt*, ICSID Case No ARB/84/3, Award (20 May 1992) para 200.

67 *PSEG v Turkey*, ICSID Case No ARB/02/5, Award (19 January 2007) paras 320–321.

68 *Autopista v Venezuela*, ICSID Case No ARB/00/5, Final Award (23 September 2003) paras 247–248.

69 *Tecmed v Mexico* (n 63) para 195.

written expert reports submitted by the parties, cross-examination of the parties' experts at a hearing[70] and, increasingly, the concurrent discussion in front of the tribunal of salient points by the experts of both sides (so-called expert conferencing or 'hot-tubbing').[71] Less common in investment proceedings is the appointment by the tribunal of its own expert, but reliance on a tribunal-appointed expert may be particularly appropriate where the respondent State has chosen not to participate in the arbitration.[72]

A difficult question concerns the permissibility of having regard to equitable considerations in awarding damages for material loss. Technically, the applicable standard of full reparation would seem to allow little room for equity: the State is under an obligation to make the injured party whole, and it is the tribunal's task to assess as precisely as possible what it takes to achieve that objective. Accordingly, the discussion within the investment law community has gone in the direction of limiting the discretion of tribunals and increasing the 'scientific' predictability of arbitral awards.[73]

A recent counterpoint to that trend is offered by the award in *Perenco v Ecuador*. The tribunal, chaired by a former president of the ICJ, emphasised that 'the assessment of damages whether in contract, tort or under a treaty, is "not an exact science" nor an exercise in economic theory'; rather a tribunal is tasked with 'estimating a reasonable figure to compensate [the claimant] for the damage which it has suffered as a result of [the respondent State's]

[70] Nigel Blackaby and Alex Wilbraham, 'Practical Issues Relating to the Use of Expert Evidence in Investment Treaty Arbitration' (2016) 31 *ICSID Review* 655, 656–658; see also Dana H. Freyer, 'Assessing Expert Evidence' in Lawrence W. Newman and Richard D. Hull (eds), *The Leading Arbitrators' Guide to International Arbitration* (2nd edn, Juris Publishing 2008) 429, 430–432; Brooks W. Daly et al, *A Guide to the PCA Arbitration Rules* (OUP 2014) para 5.142.

[71] Jonathan Lee, 'Controlling Expert Evidence in International Commercial Arbitration' (2017) 19 *Asian Disp Rev* 4, 8–9; Frances P. Kao et al, 'Into the Hot Tub – A Practical Guide to Alternative Expert Witness Procedures in International Arbitration' (2010) 44 *Int'l Lawyer* 1035, 1040–1041; Kabir Singh et al, 'The 'Additional Weapon': Practical Tips for Effective Expert Conferencing in Arbitration' (*Kluwer Arbitration Blog*, 28 March 2016).

[72] See, e.g., PCA Press Release (15 August 2016) in *Airport Belbek LLC and Mr Igor Valerievich Kolomoisky v Russian Federation,* PCA Case No 2015-07. See also Blackaby and Wilbraham (n 70) 664.

[73] Joshua B. Simmons, 'Valuation In Investor-State Arbitration: Toward A More Exact Science' (2012) 30 *Berkeley JIL* 196. See also John A. Trenor (ed), *The Guide to Damages in International Arbitration* (Global Arbitration Review 2016) Part III: Approaches and Methods for the Assessment and Quantification of Damages, with multiple references.

breaches'.[74] Similarly, some commentators have welcomed an element of equitable discretion in the quantification of damages an opportunity for balancing 'between host state and investor interests', to 'recognise the "shades of grey" which may exist in the relationship between the investor and host state as opposed to requiring an "all or nothing" approach'.[75]

While the concerns expressed about the 'all or nothing' nature of the international law on reparation is understandable, it would seem that tribunals should exercise caution in introducing equitable elements in the absence of a specific mandate to that effect in the investment agreement at hand. The IPFSD published by UNCTAD, for example, contemplates that States wishing to grant tribunals such a mandate may include in their treaties language limiting compensation to an amount that is 'equitable in light of the circumstances of the case' or 'commensurate with the country's level of development'.[76]

Claims for moral damages are relatively rare in investment arbitration. A notable recent example is the cases of *Pezold v Zimbabwe*, where an amount of US$ 1 million in moral damages was awarded to a member of the Pezold family on account of the failure of the Zimbabwean police to protect him from death threats and physical violence by 'settlers' on his farm.[77]

While the amount of US$ 1 million may have appeared comparatively small to the arbitrators, faced with a large claim for pecuniary damages, it is dramatically higher than what Mr Pezold could have expected to receive from a human rights court. Awards of 'just satisfaction' by the European Court of Human rights (ECtHR), for example, have been shown to remain below EUR 25,000 (with a median of only EUR 3,000 and a mean of EUR 4,053).[78] The examples surveyed by Judge Greenwood in his separate opinion in the *Diallo* case (discussed in more detail below) are equally instructive:

---

[74] *Perenco Ecuador Ltd v Republic of Ecuador*, ICSID Case No ARB/08/6, Award (27 September 2019) para 69.

[75] Margaret B. Devaney, 'Remedies in Investor-State Arbitration: A Public Interest Perspective' (*Investment Treaty News*, 22 March 2013).

[76] UNCTAD, *Investment Policy Framework for Sustainable Development* (UNCTAD 2015) UNCTAD/DIAE/PCB/2015/5, 109.

[77] *von Pezold v Zimbabwe* (n 23). See also Mark W. Friedman and Floriane Lavaud, 'Damages Principles in Investment Arbitration' in John A. Trenor (ed), *The Guide to Damages in International Arbitration* (Global Arbitration Review 2016) 93 (with a further example).

[78] Anne Peters et al, 'Measuring Violations of Human Rights: An Empirical Analysis of Awards in Respect of Non-Pecuniary Damage under the European Convention on Human Rights' (2016) 76 *ZaöRV* 1.

> So far as detention is concerned, the European Court of Human Rights in *Al-Jedda v. United Kingdom* (Grand Chamber, application No. 27021/08, judgment No. 27021/08) considered a figure of €25,000 (equivalent to approximately US$36,000 at the rate of exchange on the date of that judgment) sufficient for a detention which lasted more than three years (judgment of 7 July 2011, 147 *International Law Reports* 107). In *Lupsa v. Romania* (application No. 10337/04, judgment of 8 June 2006), the same Court considered that a sum of €15,000 (approximately US$19,000 at the rate of exchange on the date of that judgment) was equitable in respect of both moral and material damage in the case of a man who was unlawfully expelled from the respondent State after residing there for fourteen years, during which he had founded a family and established a business in the country. The Inter-American Court of Human Rights in *Gutiérrez-Soler v. Colombia* (judgment of 12 September 2005) awarded US$100,000 to a man who had been tortured into signing a false confession, persecuted for an offence he had not committed and separated from his family for so long that he lost all contact with his child for several years.[79]

Such discrepancies in the amounts awarded in different areas of international adjudication are undesirable. There is no reason why an individual should be awarded more generous moral damages than other persons subject to a comparable wrong – in *von Pezold*, by a factor of 30 – only because his or her claim can be presented as an add-on to a pecuniary damages claim in an investment dispute rather than a human rights claim.[80]

2. Legal standard and practice of international courts and tribunals

How does the case law of ISDS tribunals compare with the practice of courts and tribunals under general international law, notably the ICJ, ITLOS, and inter-State arbitration? How do human rights courts, such as the ECtHR, assess compensation?

(a) Inter-State proceedings

The practice of the ICJ in respect of compensation is sparse, to say the least. Until recently, the only case in which the Court was asked to determine the amount of compensation was its very first contentious case – the 1949 *Corfu*

---

[79] *Gutiérrez-Soler v Colombia*, Judgment, Inter-American Court of Human Rights Series C No 132 (12 September 2005).

[80] For a similar view, see Luke Eric Peterson, 'Moral Damages in Investment Arbitration' (*Kluwer Arbitration Blog*, 15 May 2011).

Channel case – in which it awarded the UK total sum of GBP 843,947, taking account of a report prepared by Court-appointed experts.[81]

In the recent *Diallo* judgment – an example of injury to an individual with elements of a human rights case and an investment dispute – the ICJ considered, as a first head of damages, Guinea's claim for moral damages. According to the Court, such 'non-material injury can be established even without specific evidence'.[82] The Court awarded Mr Diallo an amount of US$ 85,000. The Court explained that the quantification of moral damages necessarily rested on equitable considerations.

As Judge Greenwood rightly observed, however, the Court made little effort to indicate which principles or factors it applied in reaching the particular figure.[83] The lack of principled justification is particularly concerning as the Court's figure departs significantly from the practice of human rights courts (see above), so that it cannot be argued that the Court's decision was self-evident in light of generally applied principles.

In the *Arctic Sunrise* arbitration, the arbitral tribunal distinguished the situation of the crew members from those of Mr Diallo, noting that the Netherlands had based its claim on the amount awarded by the ICJ in respect of Mr Diallo. It concluded that 'the circumstances of the *Diallo* case are more extreme' and that the 30 crew members of the Arctic Sunrise 'can be said to have been held in conditions that were, to use the words of one of their Russian lawyers who observed the situation first-hand, "not optimal"'.[84] The tribunal then went on to discuss the case law of the ECtHR, concluding however that significant inconsistencies remained. The tribunal, using its discretion, awarded a lump sum amount of EUR 600,000 in respect of all 30 crew members, an amount that would appear to be roughly consistent with the 'scales' used by human rights courts.

In *Diallo*, in addition to moral damages, Guinea asserted 'three heads of material damage: alleged loss of personal property; alleged loss of professional remuneration (referred to by Guinea as 'loss of earnings') during Mr Diallo's detentions and after his expulsion; and alleged deprivation of 'potential earnings'.'[85]

---

[81] *Corfu Channel, Assessment of the amount of compensation due from the People's Republic of Albania to the United Kingdom of Great Britain and Northern Ireland* [1959] *ICJ Reports* 244, 250.

[82] *Ahmadou Sadio Diallo* (*Republic of Guinea v Democratic Republic of the Congo*) (Compensation) [2012] *ICJ Reports* 324, para 21.

[83] Ibid., Declaration of Judge Greenwood.

[84] *The Arctic Sunrise Arbitration (Netherlands v Russian Federation)*, PCA Case No 2014-02, Award on Compensation (10 July 2017) para 76.

[85] Ibid., para 14.

Interestingly, equity played an important role under these heads of damage, too. The Court shied away from an all-or-nothing approach based on evidentiary considerations – the Court could have refrained from awarding any compensation, based on the argument that Guinea had not proven that the property was actually lost and that it had failed to specify the value of Mr Diallo's possessions on an itemised basis. Instead, the Court awarded the amount of US$ 10,000, 'based on equitable considerations' noting that it was convinced that some 'material injury to Mr. Diallo with respect to personal property' must have occurred.[86]

As regards Mr Diallo's lost profit claims, the Court found that Guinea had presented no evidence for any 'lost earnings'. As Judge Greenwood explains in further detail,

> The second reason for the comparatively small sum recovered by Guinea lies in the lack of evidence presented in support of the claim for material damage allegedly sustained by Mr. Diallo. Guinea claimed in excess of US$7 million for loss of earnings and loss of Mr. Diallo's personal property. For Guinea to succeed in that claim, it had to produce evidence which demonstrated that Mr. Diallo had sustained the loss claimed and that that loss had been caused by the unlawful acts of the DRC. Guinea has not, however, produced any evidence to that effect. If one takes the claim for loss of earnings, there is no evidence whatsoever of what Mr. Diallo was earning prior to, or following, his detention and expulsion from the DRC.[87]

The Court therefore declined to award any compensation in respect of past or future lost income. For the (rather commonplace) proposition that the Court cannot award damages that are purely 'speculative', the Court referred to human rights cases but refrained from citing the case law of ISDS tribunals[88] even though dozens of investor-State awards would have supported the same proposition. This hesitation of the Court to derive direct conclusions from investor-State case law is in line with the position the Court had taken in the merits phase of the case. In its 2007 judgment, the Court had acknowledged that 'various international agreements, such as agreements for the promotion and protection of foreign investments and the Washington Convention, have established special legal regimes governing investment protection'. However, the Court had declined to deduce any 'change in the customary rules of diplomatic protection'[89] from

---

[86] Ibid., paras 33 and 36.

[87] *Ahmadou Sadio Diallo* (n 82) Declaration of Judge Greenwood.

[88] Ibid., paras 49 and 53.

[89] *Ahmadou Sadio Diallo* (*Republic of Guinea v Democratic Republic of the Congo*) Preliminary Objections [2007] *ICJ Reports* 582, para 90.

that practice and adopted a restrictive stance in relation to the protection of shareholders.[90]

A result of the Court's approach may have been some uncertainty on Guinea's part as to how the Court wished to approach questions of compensation, including in respect of evidence. It is difficult to imagine that a professionally represented claimant in an investor-State arbitration would have submitted a damages memorial without documenting earnings through specific evidence. A more satisfactory outcome might have resulted had the Court put the parties on notice, either at the beginning of the damages phase or after the receipt of the Congo's counter-memorial on damages, that it expected to receive specific proof of any material losses that were alleged. It is understandable that a court would be hesitant to request further submissions in a case involving an individual, who, as Mr Diallo, had already waited 11 years for the proceedings to conclude. Nonetheless, an opportunity for the submission of further evidence on Guinea's part and counter-evidence on the Congo's part, while further prolonging the proceedings by a few months, would have allowed the Court either to award compensation on a sound evidentiary basis or to reject the claim confidently, rather than referring to the paucity of the record.

While the Court's approach in *Diallo* has met with considerable scholarly interest, *Diallo* remains, factually and legally, a simple case limited to wrongful conduct to which a single individual was exposed (with consequences for his economic activity). Reparation questions of far greater complexity have been at issue in the reparation phases of Certain Activities Carried Out by Nicaragua in the Border Area (*Costa Rica v Nicaragua*) and Armed Activities on the Territory of the Congo (*Democratic Republic of the Congo v Uganda*). The latter case, in particular, in which Uganda's compensation claims alone amounted to over US$ 11 billion, is one of the most significant inter-State compensation cases in modern history.[91] And

---

[90] The Court's judgment was received critically. One commentator, who however acknowledged that he had acted as counsel for Guinea, argued that 'there is no obstacle in international law to the expression of the will of States through treaties being at the same time an expression of practice and of the *opinio juris* necessary for the birth of a customary rule if the conditions of it are met', Alain Pellet, 'The Case Law of the ICJ in Investment Arbitration' (2013) 28 *ICSID Review* 223, 226, citing *Sempra Energy International v Argentine Republic*, ICSID Case No ARB/02/16, Decision on Jurisdiction (11 May 2005) para 156.

[91] According to Johnny Veeder's calculations, the claimed amounts, as indeed the amounts at stake in any known contemporary dispute settlement proceedings, pale compared to the sums awarded in the *Alabama* arbitration. According to Veeder, 'as compensation, the tribunal ordered Great Britain to pay the sum of US$ 15.5 million in gold to the United States, with simple interest—equivalent, in today's money (taking into

while the factual matrices of environmental damages and armed conflict have little in common with a breach of investment treaty obligations, at a technical level, investor-State case law has clearly informed various concepts deployed in the written and oral pleadings of the applicants and respondents. Counsel notably referred to legal authorities from investor-State arbitrations to elucidate the following concepts:

- the limits of compensation which does not cover 'speculative and uncertain damage';[92]
- the character of satisfaction, which must not be punitive;[93] and
- the time from which interest accrues.[94]

Other important reference points in the counsel pleadings in *Congo v Uganda* were the awards of the Eritrea-Ethiopia Claims Commission.[95] As a result of years of armed hostilities, the Eritrea-Ethiopia Claims Commission faced a challenging evidentiary record. The Commission rationalised and explained its approach in some detail. As far as the standard of proof is concerned, the Commission adopted the high standard of 'clear and convincing evidence' to prove liability of one of the States parties 'because the Parties' claims frequently involved allegations of serious – indeed, sometimes grave – misconduct by a State'.[96] For the quantification of injury, however, such a high standard was inappropriate:

> the Commission recognizes the enormous practical problems faced by both Parties in quantifying the extent of damage following the 1998–2000 war.

---

account relative British GDPs) to about US$225 billion dollars'. See VV Veeder, 'The Historical Keystone to International Arbitration: The Party-Appointed Arbitrator—From Miami to Geneva' (2013) 107 *ASIL Proceedings* 387, 390.

92 See Memorial of Uganda on Reparation (28 September 2016), vol I, para 2.39 (citing *Amco Asia Corporation and Others v Republic of Indonesia*, ICSID Case No. ARB/81/1, Award (20 Nov. 1984), para. 238).

93 See Oral Proceedings (Uganda), Verbatim Record 2021/8 of 22 April 2021, p 62 (Pellet).

94 See Memorial of the Democratic Republic of the Congo (Sept. 2016), vol I, para 7.57.

95 Counsel for both parties, but especially those representing Uganda, referred repeatedly to the Eritrea-Ethiopia Claims Commission. In the written pleadings alone, the Commission was referred to 16 times: see Memorial of Uganda on Reparation (28 September 2016), vol I, paras 2.9, 2.10, 2.11, 2.17, 2.28, 2.45, 2.46, 2.47, 2.52, 2.55, 2.56, 2.58, 2.59, 2.60, 3.13; and Memorial of the Democratic Republic of the Congo (Sept. 2016), vol I, para 1.21.

96 Eritrea-Ethiopia Claims Commission, PCA Case No 2001-02, Final Award – Eritrea's Damages Claims and Final Award - Ethiopia's Damages Claims (17 August 2009) para 35.

> Requiring proof of quantification of damage by clear and convincing evidence would often – perhaps almost always – preclude any recovery. This would frustrate the Commission's agreed mandate to address 'the socio-economic impact of the crisis on the civilian population' under Article 5(1) of the Agreement.[97]

In view of these difficulties, the Commission decided to proceed with 'judgment and approximation', making 'the best estimates possible on the basis of the available evidence'.[98] Even so, the Commission made a notable effort to make the bases of its damages calculation explicit. The Commission sketched the main considerations – including specific figures to the extent they existed – that it took into account, although such considerations remained at a rather high level of abstraction given the large number of incidents to which the proceedings related.

No comparable difficulties in quantifying pecuniary damages arose in the other two recent inter-State proceedings already mentioned, the *Saiga* case and the *Arctic Sunrise* case. In *Saiga*, ITLOS affirmed at the outset the principle that, under international law:

> Saint Vincent and the Grenadines is entitled to reparation for damage suffered directly by it as well as for damage or other loss suffered by the *Saiga*, including all persons involved or interested in its operation. Damage or other loss suffered by the Saiga and all persons involved or interested in its operation comprises injury to persons, unlawful arrest, detention or other forms of ill-treatment, damage to or seizure of property and other economic losses, including loss of profit.[99]

ITLOS went on to note that 'Saint Vincent and the Grenadines has submitted substantial documentation' in support of its claims. While 'Guinea challenges the validity of some claims and the reasonableness of the amounts presented', ITLOS conducted a 'careful scrutiny of invoices and other documents submitted' and thus decided to 'award compensation in the total amount of US$ 2,123,357'.[100] By contrast, the tribunal dismissed the claim for compensation in respect of allegedly lost registration revenue, noting that 'no evidence has been produced by Saint Vincent and the Grenadines that the arrest of the Saiga caused a decrease in registration activity under its flag, with resulting loss of revenue'.[101] The reasoning of

---

97 Ibid., para 36.
98 Ibid., para 37.
99 *The M/V 'SAIGA' (No. 2) Case (Saint Vincent and the Grenadines v Guinea)* (Judgment, 1 July 1999) ITLOS Case No 2, para 172.
100 Ibid., paras 174–175.
101 Ibid., para 177.

the tribunal, however, does not allow any further insights as to why certain alleged losses were regarded as compensable and not others, or indeed which specific positions were included within the compensable amounts.

The *Arctic Sunrise* Tribunal, on its part, provided a more detailed break-down of the specific positions claimed. The tribunal discussed the calculations advanced by the Netherlands in detail, explaining why it considered it appropriate to depart from them in some respects. Finally, the tribunal relied on the opinion of tribunal-appointed experts, namely a maritime surveying expert and an accounting expert. The thoroughness of the *Artic Sunrise* Tribunal's approach is reminiscent of the ICJ's approach in *Corfu Channel*. Such an approach to the analysis of compensation should be regarded as the yardstick for future inter-State proceedings.

(b) European Court of Human Rights

The starting point of the ECtHR, finally, purports to be the same as that of ISDS tribunals or courts and tribunals under general international law – namely that the yardstick that compensation must wipe out all the consequences of the breach.[102] The approach in the relevant Article 41 of the European Convention on Human Rights differs, however, from the language used today in the context of State responsibility, in that it distinguishes situations in which 'reparation' is available and situations in which 'the internal law of the High Contracting Party concerned allows only partial reparation to be made'. In the latter case, the 'Court shall, if necessary, afford just satisfaction to the injured party'.

The Convention's language ('just' in English or '*équitable*' in French) may explain the emphasis by the Court on equity, pervading its practice in respect of both pecuniary and moral damages. Many commentators have criticised the approach of the Court as non-transparent and difficult to reverse-engineer based on the amount of compensation awarded.[103] The Court has also been criticised for its sparse reasoning on compensation, which sometimes does not go beyond the affirmation that a particular amount was arrived at 'on an equitable basis'.[104] As one commentator put

[102] Monica Carss-Frisk, 'A Guide to the Implementation of Article 1 of Protocol No. 1 to the European Convention on Human Rights' (2001) Human Rights Handbooks No 4 www.echr.coe.int/LibraryDocs/DG2/HRHAND/DG2-EN-HRHAND-04(2003).pdf) accessed 5 July 2020.

[103] Ingrid Nifosi-Sutton, 'The Power of the European Court of Human Rights to Order Specific Non-Monetary Relief: A Critical Appraisal from a Right to Health Perspective' (2010) 23 *Harvard HRJ* 51, 56.

[104] See Jacobs et al, *The European Convention on Human Rights* (6th edn, OUP 2014) 44; Jane Wright, *Tort Law and Human Rights* (Hart 2001) 40, analysing damages

it, 'there appears to be little consistency in the Court's approach to the affording of just satisfaction. Many decisions lack convincing reasoning for the awards', and '[the] phrase ["what is equitable"] recurs over and over again in the case-law and frequently covers a complete lack of reasoning in the Court's decision for the award of a particular sum'.[105] Despite such criticism, however, human rights lawyers are aware of the amounts of compensation the Court is typically prepared to award for particular types of injury, notably for forms of moral injury. The range of moral damages is thus not unpredictable.

What the Court seems to have refrained from doing is to refer to the practice of investor-State tribunals in its case law. In its landmark judgment in *Cyprus v Turkey*, for instance, the Court had no difficulty in referring to the *Diallo* case of the ICJ in considering whether international law recognises certain forms of damages in inter-State proceedings.[106] The separate opinions suggest that the Court may have also considered historic arbitral awards rendered in the 1920s to 1950s.[107] However, no comparable reference to investor-State cases appears to have been made when the Court was faced with a complaint from an individual against a State party.

IV. ONE LEGAL STANDARD, DIFFERENT PRACTICES?

The practice just discussed demonstrates one notable commonality: all international courts and tribunals, whether established under general international law or international investment treaties, profess to apply a similar legal standard in determining the remedies to which the party injured by unlawful State conduct is entitled. Courts and tribunals have endorsed the principle of full reparation, often by reference to the *PCIJ's Chorzów Factory* case.

The implementation of this legal standard, however, is less consistent. A first dividing line concerns the forms of remedies most commonly ordered. While satisfaction and restitution are the primary remedies in inter-State proceedings, compensation is the norm in mixed proceedings,

under the UK Human Rights Act 1998; Nifosi-Sutton (n 103) 54.

[105] Robin White, 'Remedies in a Multi-Level Legal Order: The Strasbourg Court and the UK' in Claire Kilpatrick et al (eds), *The Future of Remedies in Europe* (OUP 2000) 191, 196–198.

[106] *Cyprus v Turkey*, App No 25781/94 (ECtHR, Grand Chamber, 12 May 2014) (Just satisfaction) para 46.

[107] Ibid., Concurring Opinion of Judge Pinto de Albuquerque, joined by Judge Vučinić, para 15.

involving a private investor (in ISDS) or an individual (in human rights cases). A second dividing line relates to the preferred approach to ascertaining the amount of compensation that is due. While ISDS tribunals have tended towards a scientific, evidence-based methodology for ascertaining pecuniary damages, inter-State courts and human rights courts have tended to emphasise the equitable element in the determination of any damages, including pecuniary ones. The latter tendency appears to be less marked in inter-State arbitration or at ITLOS.

Moreover, when awarding moral damages (an exercise that by necessity implies a degree of discretion), courts and tribunals have had little regard for the practice in other fora. The award by the ICJ and certain investor-State tribunals of equitable compensation for moral damages in amounts markedly higher from those typically awarded by human rights courts is a case in point. While one may criticise the amounts awarded by human rights courts as too low, it is certainly undesirable that investment tribunals – once ironically referred to as 'human rights treat[ies] for a special-interest group',[108] namely foreign investors – value comparable moral injury multiple times higher than human rights courts.

The general picture, however, is that investor-State tribunals readily and routinely refer to decisions by courts and tribunals under general international law or other legal authorities evidencing the position under general international law. Occasionally, that tendency to 'inscribe' the tribunal's decision within a larger international law jurisprudence has even caused tribunals to refer to general international law where technically no such reference was warranted.[109]

In contrast, courts and tribunals under general international law have been noticeably more reserved in their use of investor-State case law. As a recent study shows, while ISDS tribunals are eager to cite external international sources, their awards, in turn, are among the sources least frequently cited by other courts and tribunals. For example, while the ICJ's case law is cited in investor-State decisions on over 600 occasions, there is not a single ICJ judgment that cites an investor-State award.[110] This quantitative evidence lends further support to the impression that the effect of investor-State case law regarding remedies on courts and tribunals under general international law has been rather limited.

---

[108] José Alvarez, 'Critical Theory and the North American Free Trade Agreement's Chapter Eleven' (1997) 28 *U Miami Inter-American LR* 303, 308.

[109] See the discussion above, regarding the extent to which investor-State tribunals should seek guidance in the ILC Articles on State responsibility.

[110] Damien Charlotin, 'The Place of Investment Awards and WTO Decisions in International Law: A Citation Analysis' (2017) 20 *JIEL* 279, 288.

It would be simplistic, however, to equate a lack of formal reference to a lack of impact. As the recent pleadings in *Congo v Uganda* and *Costa Rica v Nicaragua* show, the ICJ is being made aware by parties of the practice of investor-State tribunals in complex compensation cases. While the judgment in *Costa Rica v Nicaragua* makes no express reference to investor-State case law, and one may venture to predict that a similarly economical approach will prevail in *Congo v Uganda*, this does not mean that judges would not take guidance from such case law in their consideration of an inter-State compensation case. Moreover, until the Court recently adopted a limitation on the 'arbitration activities of the Members of the Court',[111] a considerable number of ICJ judges, including several of its presidents, gained first-hand experience with investor-State arbitrations as party-appointed or presiding arbitrators. It can thus not be presumed that the ICJ would be ignorant of the investor-State practice in respect of remedies.

In any case, there is much that investment tribunals, inter-State courts and tribunals, and human rights courts can learn more from one another. Despite imperfections in each process, it is fair to say that inter-State tribunals highlight the significance of remedies other than financial compensation for resolving disputes between States; investment tribunals have sought to establish a more rigorous and evidence-based process for evaluating claims for compensation in respect of material losses and lost profits than is habitual in general international law tribunals; the jurisprudence of human rights courts, finally, provides a yardstick for the quantification of moral damages.

In particular, the substantial body of investor-State decisions addressing questions of remedies as well as the reactions to those decisions by States and other stakeholders warrant closer attention by other international courts and tribunals. While the ILC Draft Articles may identify the critical issues that can arise in international claims for reparation, on a number of points the ILC's 2001 codification is founded on a fairly limited number of decisions. Investment arbitration has proved to be a veritable laboratory for testing the ILC's codification in modern legal practice. The results generated in that laboratory are not always consistent, nor are all decisions convincing; but investment proceedings have highlighted important challenges that may arise in the application of the general international law on

---

[111] Compilation of decisions adopted by the Court concerning the external activities of its Members, adopted on 8 September 2020, incorporating a decision concerning arbitration activities of Members of the Court adopted on 2 October 2018.

State responsibility, many of which are pertinent for international legal practice more generally.

For example, while the principle of the primacy of restitution appears firmly established in the customary international law on State responsibility, investment proceedings have raised doubts whether such primacy necessarily reflects a desirable policy. While in some cases host States have preferred restitution overcompensation, there are other circumstances in which an order of restitution was seen as an unjustified encroachment on a State's sovereign regulatory powers.

The investor-State case law has also highlighted the difficulty of implementing the principle of full reparation in compensation cases. Even though some tribunals have questioned the usefulness of 'scientific' valuation methods for international law proceedings, there has been a strong trend towards a more rigorous use of formal valuation methods and modelling in assessing the value of expropriated investments or compensation in the event of a treaty breach.[112]

Relatedly, the experience in the investor-State field suggests that treaty parties may wish to give express consideration to the remedies that should be available under a treaty, including whether there should be limitations on the availability of restitution, whether a standard of compensation other than the fair market value should apply, or whether compensation should be affected by equitable considerations.

Finally, while the basic international law principles of causation are largely uncontroversial, investment cases have demonstrated that various important concepts – including proximate causation in the event of multiple causes, the reasonable foreseeability of the injury by the investor, or questions of contributory fault – may present considerable difficulty in practice. On some of these points, investor-State cases constitute the only contemporary international authorities available.

Investment tribunals have for some time now sought to grapple with complex questions of remedies. Their decisions have been exposed to critique from States, other stakeholders, and the academia, and subsequent tribunals have sought to learn from decisions that were perceived as defi-

[112] Cf. the recent establishment of a Task Force on Damages in International Arbitration by the International Council for Commercial Arbitration (ICCA) and the American Society of International Law (ASIL). See ICCA, 'ICCA-ASIL Task Forces on Damages' www.arbitration-icca.org/projects/ICCA-ASIL-Task-Force-on-Damages.html accessed 25 September 2021. While the Task Force is not exclusively concerned with investor-State arbitration, it has drawn substantially on investment cases, and its products are intended to apply in investor-State arbitration.

cient. There is no reason why other courts and tribunals should not benefit from that collective learning experience.

PART IV

Investment law and the general regime of dispute resolution

10. Investment arbitration as incubator of evidentiary principles in international and transnational law

Frédéric Gilles Sourgens

I. INTRODUCTION

The relationship between general international law and investment law is rocky. One recent example of this rocky relationship comes in the form of the recent memorandum on general principles of law in international law.[1] That memorandum addresses the use of general principles by inter-State arbitral tribunals.[2] It further addresses the work of international courts.[3] The memorandum does not address investor-state arbitral decisions. That is despite the fact that investor-state jurisprudence has added significantly to the object of the memorandum's study.[4] The omission thus feels like an intentional snub.

Another example is the other UN organ charged with custody of general international law. The International Court of Justice (ICJ) has frequently left opportunities pass it by to include reference to the work of investor-State tribunals in its own decisions.[5] More recently, the ICJ became more direct in its apparent rebuke of efforts by a litigant before it to rely upon the doctrine of legitimate expectations developed in the fair and equitable treatment context by investor-State tribunals in the context of a dispute relating to coastal access.[6] In response, the Court noted 'that references to legitimate expectations

[1] ILC, 'General Principles of Law, Memorandum by the Secretariat' (12 May 2020) UN Doc A/CN.4/742.

[2] Ibid., 24–35.

[3] Ibid., 36–80.

[4] Michael D. Nolan and Frédéric G. Sourgens, 'Issues of Proof of General Principles in International Arbitration' (2009) 3 *WAMR* 505.

[5] See Alain Pellet, 'The Case Law of the ICJ in Investment Jurisprudence' (2013) 28 *ICSID Review* 223.

[6] *Obligation to Negotiate Access to the Pacific Ocean (Bolivia v Chile)* [2018] *ICJ Reports* 507, para 161.

may be found in arbitral awards concerning disputes between a foreign investor and the host State that apply treaty clauses providing for fair and equitable treatment'.[7] But it concluded that '[i]t does not follow from such references that there exists in general international law a principle that would give rise to an obligation on the basis of what could be considered a legitimate expectation'.[8] The point in its own context was reasonably unremarkable (it dealt with the question whether good faith in international law requires actual reliance – a point which vexed the Court for instance in the *Nuclear Tests* cases).[9] Its warning about the demarcation of the *lex specialis* of investment protection from general international law was nevertheless immediately understood.[10]

One might surmise that the Court's caution (and rebuke) is political. It would not have gone unnoticed among the Court's membership that participation in investor-State arbitrations is an argument made against the re-election of judges on the Court. In fact, the Court has since prohibited such engagements.[11] Open reliance upon investment arbitration decisions would strengthen this point. Much of the influence of investment arbitration may therefore operate beyond the surface. (For example, it is entirely possible to conceive of the jurisprudence of investor-State tribunals regarding fair and equitable treatment in terms of reliance.[12] The rebuke by the Court in *Obligation to Negotiate Access to the Pacific Ocean* may thus have been informed by the jurisprudence it rejected – though its reasoning is opaque on this point.)

Evidence may provide a welcome reprieve from such avoidance of investor-State jurisprudence in general international law. Proof of facts, and the law governing this proof of facts is a central piece of investor-State arbitration. Stanimir Alexandrov, himself now a leading arbitrator of investor-State disputes, once challenged a room packed full of investment arbitration practitioners to do the following: read only the fact section of any investor-State decision[13]

---

7 Ibid., para 162.

8 Ibid.

9 Ibid., para 161. For a full discussion of the good faith point in general international law, see Frédéric G. Sourgens, 'Reconstructing International Law as Common Law' (2015) 47 *George Wash ILR* 1.

10 Martins Paparinskis, 'Tweet' (*Twitter*, 1 October 2018).

11 H E Mr Abdulqawi A Yusuf, 'Speech' (Seventy-Third Session of the United Nations General Assembly, New York, 25 October 2018) www.icj-cij.org/public/files/press-releases/0/000-20181025-PRE-02-00-EN.pdf accessed 1 November 2020. For a discussion, see Frédéric G. Sourgens, 'Failing the Hague Stress Test' (*EJIL:Talk!*, 6 November 2018).

12 See Frédéric G. Sourgens, 'Supernational Law' (2017) 50 *Vanderbilt JTL* 155, 181–195.

13 Stanimir Alexandrov, 'Remarks' in Ian Laird and Todd Weiler (eds), *Investment Treaty Arbitration and International Law* (Juris 2009) 205.

– then guess who prevailed. Dr Alexandrov surmised that in almost every case, they would guess correctly.[14]

As this chapter will discuss, the law governing such proof of facts developed from, and further refined, evidentiary rules in public international law. The developments in investor-State arbitration therefore are not alien to a public international law way of thinking about evidence. Rather, they are a direct continuation of general international law.

Further, as Lucinda Low, the former president of the American Society of International Law noted in a keynote address to be published as a part of a volume on international law and investment arbitration, investor-State arbitration provides by far the most primary materials of any international law adjudication mechanism. With more than 1,000 reported disputes, it is the largest pool of primary materials on how a general international law perspective might address evidentiary questions in the context of an ably developed and argued record.[15]

Finally, one can hope that the use of rules of evidence in investor-State arbitration is politically innocuous. Concerns raised with regard to investor-State arbitration ranged the gamut of substantive concerns about the substantive rules applied by investor-State tribunals, the incoherence of arbitral awards, and the alleged pro-investor bias of some arbitrators. It did not make any allegations regarding the core fact finding mission of these tribunals. Incorporating the evidentiary reflections of investor-State tribunals therefore may be less controversial than relying upon investor-State arbitral decisions for substantive rules of international law governing the treatment of aliens.

This hope may soon find a test case. At its 69th session in the summer of 2017, the International Law Commission (ILC), on the recommendation of the Working Group on its Long-term Programme of Work included the topic of 'evidence before international courts and tribunals' as one of two new potential topics to be addressed by the ILC.[16] This development is significant given the selection criteria adopted by the ILC:

> the topic: (a) should reflect the needs of States in respect of the progressive development and codification of international law; (b) should be at a sufficiently advanced stage in terms of State practice to permit progressive development and codification; (c) should be concrete and feasible for progressive development and codification;

---

[14] Ibid.

[15] Lucinda Low, 'Keynote' in Meriam N. Alrashid et al (eds), *Investment Treaty Arbitration and International Law* - Volume 14 (2021) https://arbitrationlaw.com/library/keynote-address-chapter-13-investment-treaty-arbitration-and-international-law-volume-14 accessed 11 January 2021.

[16] ILC, 'Report of the International Law Commission on the Work of its sixty-ninth session' (1 May–2 June and 3 July–4 August 2017) UN Doc A/72/10, Annex B.

> and (d) that the Commission should not restrict itself to traditional topics, but could also consider those that reflect new developments in international law and pressing concerns of the international community as a whole. The Commission would welcome the views of States on those new topics.[17]

Some members of the Commission at least, in other words, believe that there is a sufficient bulk of practice to codify the rules of evidence in international law. As much of this bulk of practice developed in the context of investor-State arbitration one may hope that evidence will provide a welcome means of open engagement by general international legal bodies with the jurisprudence of investor-State tribunals. Such engagement would be particularly welcome as the jurists on the tribunals in question are among the most highly esteemed international judges and practitioners.

This of course leaves the question whether the ILC would wish to receive these materials as authoritative even in this limited context. This concern, however, may turn out to be too narrow. Given the ILC's current composition, it is certainly familiar with investor-State arbitration. Several members of the ILC have significant investor-State experience.[18] The wealth of material in the investor-State context may thus provide the Commission with a means to sharpen its thinking even its reliance upon investor-State arbitration would occur sub rosa. While such a development would be a sad continuation of the connivance by international jurists in the politicisation of international law dispute resolution writ large, it would also suggest that any true engagement of evidentiary rules in international law must contend with the developments in investor-State arbitration. It is only then that one might see where some of the potentially unatrributed refinements of evidentiary rules in international law came to be.

The chapter will analyse four key topics, which are likely to be at the heart of the ILC's work on evidence. It will consider first the question of burdens and standards of proof. It will then proceed to an examination of the law of presumption and inferences. It will continue with an inquiry regarding the availability and scope of exclusionary rules of evidence. A brief conclusion highlights key findings of the inquiry.

Each of the sections below will begin with a brief genealogy. This genealogy will place investor-state arbitration in the context of general international law. Drawing on the work done in *Evidence in International Investment Arbitration*, it will present how the issue in question has evolved in investment

---

[17] Ibid., para 32.

[18] ILC, 'Membership' (*ILC*, 2 May 2018) https://legal.un.org/ilc/ilcmembe.shtml accessed 11 January 2021.

arbitration.[19] It will append a full proposed codification of evidentiary rules in investment arbitration from that book, as well, for reference purposes.[20] Finally, it will outline how this codification might be of help in the general international law context. The chapter will thus hope to outline in concrete ways how the practice of investor-state tribunals might come to impact the progressive development of general international law.

II. BURDENS AND STANDARDS OF PROOF

The law of burdens and standards of proof is the first building block of the law of evidence. Burdens of proof determine who must show that a fact exists. The failure to meet a burden of proof means that a fact has not been shown to exist. It thus means that the party relying upon this fact as part of its case will be deprived of a crucial means to make out its case. The burden of proof – and its allocation to one party or another – can frequently prove dispositive. The standard of proof on the other hand concerns not who must prove but by what kind of measure they must prove. Depending upon context, different allegations must be made out by different measures of proof in order to meet one's burden. It is therefore important to bear both burden and standard in mind when considering the first building block of the law of evidence of who must prove and by how much.

A. Foundations in General International Law

Burdens and standards of proof have deep roots in general international law. This chapter will look to the early crystallisation and application of these general rules in the practice of the ICJ due to the sophisticated statement of reasons, influence and relative volume of ICJ jurisprudence compared to other forms of public international law dispute resolution. Investor-State arbitration expressly adopts and builds upon these foundations. Consequently, the further refinement of burdens and standards of proof in investor-state arbitration are relevant for the further progressive development of general international law: they are part of the same legal discourse. The foundations of burdens and standards of proof in general international law are discussed in turn.

---

[19] Frédéric G. Sourgens et al, *Evidence in International Investment Arbitration* (OUP 2018) *passim*.

[20] See Appendix to this chapter.

1. Burdens of proof

The international law foundation of the rules governing burdens of proof in investor-State foundation are made express in one of the early investor-State arbitral awards, *Asian Agricultural Products Limited (AAPL) v Sri Lanka.*[21] The *AAPL* tribunal stated that 'in order to handle the legal issues related to evidence', it had to 'tak[e] into consideration [certain] established international law rules'.[22] The tribunal began that '[t]here exists a general principle of law placing the burden of proof upon the claimant'.[23] It continued that 'The term actor in the principle *onus probandi actori incumbit* is not to be taken to mean the plaintiff from the procedural standpoint, but the real claimant in view of the issues involved,' i.e., 'the burden of proof rests upon the party alleging the fact'.[24] Finally, '[a] Party having the burden of proof must not only bring evidence in support of his allegations, but must also convince the Tribunal of their truth, lest they be disregarded for want, or insufficiency, of proof'.[25]

AAPL also dealt with questions of reversals of burden of persuasion. It explained that

> In exercising the 'free evaluation of evidence' provided for under the previous Rule, the international tribunals 'decided the case on the strength of the evidence produced by both parties', and in case a party 'adduces some evidence which *prima facie* supports his allegation, the burden of proof shifts to his opponent.[26]

The context for the comment by the *AAPL* decision should highlight that the question is not burden of proof as such. Rather, it concerns the evaluation of evidence. Thus, the question in this case is one of burdens of persuasion. These burdens can switch even though the technical burden of proof remains on the original party.

The *AAPL* tribunal principally relied in its early discussion of the placement of the burden of proof on the moving party on Bin Cheng's work on general principles of international law.[27] Bin Cheng included the adage as one the general principles of law recognised by international courts and tribunals.[28] As Cheng explained, the

---

[21] *Asian Agricultural Products Limited (AAPL) v Republic of Sri Lanka*, ICSID Case No ARB/87/3, Award (27 June 1990).

[22] Ibid., para 56.

[23] Ibid.

[24] Ibid.

[25] Ibid.

[26] Ibid.

[27] Ibid., citing Bin Cheng, *General Principles of Law as Applied by International Courts and Tribunals* (CUP 1987); Durvard V. Sandifer, *Evidence Before International Tribunals* (University Press of Virginia 1975).

[28] Bin Cheng, *General Principles of Law as Applied by International Courts and Tribunals* (Stevens & Sons 1953) 327.

point of a burden of proof is that 'a party having the burden of proof must not only bring evidence in support of his allegations, but must also convince the Tribunal of their truth, lest they be disregarded for want, or insufficiency, of proof'.[29] The burden of proving a fact thus is equivalent to an assignment of default positions – a court or tribunal will assume the absence of a fact until the party moving to prove its existence has persuaded the tribunal otherwise.

As Cheng explains, general international law historically distinguished this burden of proof from a broader burden to produce evidence.[30] Both parties to a judicial or arbitral proceeding shared in the burden to bring forth materials in their possession upon which a court or tribunal might rest its decision.[31] In other words, the assignment of a burden of proof did not give license to the responding party to destroy evidence or fail to bring forward materials relevant to the tribunal's line of inquiry. It did, however, give the respondent party the proverbial benefit of the doubt.

The principle that the burden of proof rests on the moving party has remained a trite truism of international legal jurisprudence since. The ICJ recently took up the classic distinction between burdens of proof and burdens of production in the *Genocide Convention* case between Croatia and Serbia.[32] It explained that '[w]hilst the burden of proof rests in principle on the party which alleges a fact, this does not relieve the other party of its duty to cooperate 'in the provision of such evidence as may be in its possession that could assist the Court in resolving the dispute submitted to it'.[33] As the Court explained in *Diallo*, this burden might be relaxed by reference to context such as when a party sets out to prove a negative fact by reference to a presumption.[34] These statements of the burden of proof in general international law continue to remain generally consistent with the foundations of the law of burden of proof in investor-State arbitration.

2. Standards of proof

Investor-State arbitration is similarly indebted to general international law for its treatment of standards of proof. Investor-State arbitration further have referenced the standard of intimate conviction of the judge followed in general

[29] Ibid., 329.
[30] Ibid., 327–9.
[31] Ibid.
[32] *Application of the Convention on the Prevention and Punishment of the Crime of Genocide (Croatia v Serbia)* [2015] *ICJ Reports* 3, 73.
[33] Ibid., quoting *Case Concerning Pulp Mills on the River Uruguay (Argentina v Urugay)* [2010] *ICJ Reports* 14, 71.
[34] *Case Concerning Ahmadou Sadio Diallo (Republic of Guinea v Democratic Republic of the Congo)* [2010] *ICJ Reports* 639, 661.

international law.[35] Investor-State tribunals note that the standard of proof might be relaxed in some circumstances, referring to general international law for the proposition that difficulty of proof of a particular fact can reduce the applicable standard of proof to the provision of *prima facie* evidence.[36] Investor-State arbitration follows Judge Higgins separate opinion in the *Oil Platforms* case to more persuasive evidence than might otherwise suffice to make out a claim in cases of significantly grave allegations of wrongdoing or submission of improbable facts.[37]

This discussion of the standard of proof arises originally in one of the classic decisions of the ICJ, *Corfu Channel*.[38] In *Corfu Channel*, the UK claimed that Albania had permitted mines to be laid in Albanian waters that in turn damaged His Majesty's navy while passing innocently through Albanian waters.[39] One of the allegations raised by the UK government was that the mines had been laid by the Yugoslav navy and that Albania had permitted the Yugoslav navy to do so. The UK offered testimony from a (former) Lieutenant-Commander Kovacic in the Yugoslav navy that he saw mines being loaded upon two vessels at port in Sibenik and saw them return 'a few days after the occurrence of the explosions'.[40]

In dealing with Lieutenant-Commander Kovacic's testimony, the Court relied entirely upon the applicable standard of proof:

> [w]ithout deciding as to the personal sincerity of the witness Kovacic, or the truth of what he said, the Court finds that the facts stated by the witness from his personalknowledge are not sufficient to prove what the United Kingdom Government considered them to prove.[41]

The Court explained that '[a] charge of such exceptional gravity against a State would require a degree of certainty that has not been reached here'.[42] The narrowest holding that might be inferred from *Corfu Channel* is that the graver the allegation, the more directly the evidence must prove it (i.e., while circumstantial evidence is permissible, the inference to be drawn must be minimal.) One

---

[35] *Churchill Mining Plc v Republic of Indonesia*, ICSID Case No ARB/12/14, Award (6 December 2016) paras 240–244.

[36] *AAPL v Sri Lanka* (n 21) para 56.

[37] *Libananco Holdings Ltd v Republic of Turkey*, ICSID Case No ARB/06/8, Award (31 August 2011) para 125; *Churchill Mining Plc v Indonesia* (n 35) paras 240–244.

[38] *Corfu Channel (United Kingdom v Albania)* [1949] *ICJ Reports* 4.

[39] Ibid., 12–16.

[40] Ibid., 16.

[41] Ibid., 17.

[42] Ibid.

might also infer a broader holding from *Corfu Channel*, namely that the gravity of the allegation changes – that is heightens – the applicable standard of proof.

The procedural posture of *Corfu Channel*, however, would militate in favour of the narrower reading: Yugoslavia was not a party to the *Corfu Channel* proceedings.[43] Yugoslavia consequently did not present evidence.[44] Yugoslavia's evidence would have been directly relevant to the question of whether the Yugoslav navy vessels observed by LCdr Kovacic had laid the mines in question – but the evidence was simply not procedurally available and no inference could be drawn from its absence given Yugoslavia's status in the proceedings. The Court in essence was placed in a position in which an inference against Albania would penalise Albania for the absence of evidence Albania could not control. Thus, it is reasonable to require that the leap from direct evidence to inference be minimal so as to safeguard against this risk. This dilemma – how persuasive is the evidence in supporting an inference as opposed to how high is the standard of proof – is precisely the same as the one encountered in the early investor-State arbitration cases such as *AAPL*.[45]

The concept of standard of proof in contemporary ICJ jurisprudence remains faithful to these shared beginnings in *Corfu Channel* and *AAPL*. Most recently, the issue of standard of proof again resurfaced in the context of genocide-related proceedings before the Court. The Court in 2007 confirmed the continued applicability of the *Corfu Channel* ruling.[46] In a later such proceeding between Croatia and Serbia, the Court in its 2015 judgment again relied upon the *Corfu Channel* case as well as its 2007 judgment.[47] It thus confirmed that the gravity of the charge 'requires that it be fully convinced that allegations made in the proceedings, that the crime of genocide or the other acts enumerated in Article III have been committed, have been clearly established'.[48]

---

[43] Ibid., 17:

> On its side, the Yugoslav Government, although not a party to the proceedings, authorized the Albanian Government to produce certain Yugoslav documents, for the purpose of refuting the United Kingdom contention that the mines had been laid by two ships of the Yugoslav Navy. As the Court was anxious for full light to be thrown on the facts alleged, it did not refuse to receive these documents. But Yugoslavia's absence from the proceedings meant that these documents could only be admitted as evidence subject to reserves, and the Court finds it unnecessary to express an opinion upon their probative value.

[44] Ibid.

[45] *AAPL v Sri Lanka* (n 21) para 56.

[46] *Case Concerning Application of the Convention on the Prevention and Punishment of the Crime of Genocide (Bosnia and Herzegovina v Serbia and Montenegro)* [2007] *ICJ Reports* 43, 129.

[47] *Genocide Case (Croatia v Serbia)* (n 32).

[48] Ibid.

B. Maturity in Investor-State Arbitration

The practice of investor-State tribunals has significantly developed the state of the law on both burdens and standards of proof to a point that it is possible progressively to codify or restate a set of substantive rules followed by investor-State tribunals. As outlined below, this development of the law of burdens and standards of proof remains fully consistent with the early common starting points for analysis between investor-State arbitration and general international law. It is also arguably consistent with the development of general international law of evidence in other dispute resolution mechanisms.

As outlined in *Evidence in International Investment Arbitration*, a progressive codification exercise of the rules of burdens and standards of proof as crystallised from the practice investor-State tribunals is descriptive.[49] It is premised upon a review of all available investor-State arbitration cases. On the basis of this review, it is possible to categorise both the actions of tribunals with regard to the burden and standard of proof in investor-State proceedings and to compare those actions to the State rationale of leading investor-State arbitral awards. To the extent that there is a significant overlap between actions and a plausible means to distill a common rationale for these actions it is then possible to codify the rules of evidence at work in investor-State arbitration. The full extent of that work would be beyond the scope of this chapter. Instead, this section outlines the result of the work in question with a brief explanation of the salient rules on burden and standard of proof.

1. Burden of proof

The practice of investor-State tribunals permits the formulation of three rules applied with broad agreement across different investor-State proceedings with regard to the burden of proof. The first of these rules is the basic shared starting point already mentioned above: *actori incumbit onus probandi* – the moving party bears the burden of proof.[50] The practice of investor-State tribunals, however, also permits a more granular understanding of this burden of proof. In the first place, it allows the conclusion that the burden of proof can be met in four alternative ways: by the submission of direct evidence,[51] circumstantial

49 Sourgens et al (n 19).

50 Ibid., 291 (Evidentiary Principles §1(1)). *AAPL v Sri Lanka* (n 21) para 56; *Tokios Tokelés v Ukraine*, ICSID Case No ARB/02/18, Award (26 July 2007) para 121; *Michael Ballantine and Lisa Ballantine v Dominican Republic*, UNCITRAL, PCA Case No 2016-17, Award (3 September 2019) 506–7.

51 Sourgens et al (n 19) 291 (Evidentiary Principle §1(1)(a)). *Caratube International Oil Co LLC v Republic of Kazakhstan*, ICSID Case No ARB/08/12, Award (5 June

evidence,[52] evidence otherwise supporting an inference in its favour,[53] or proof that a presumption in favour of the moving party renders submission of such direct, or indirect evidence unnecessary.[54] In other words, it might well be true that the preferred way to discharge a burden of proof is by the submission of direct evidence of the fact in question. But it does not defeat a claim that this is not possible. (This conclusion, famously, is consistent with the ICJ's conclusion in *Corfu Channel* – but provides further support and jurisprudence as to each of the different ways in which a case can be proved.)[55]

There are several points of potential distinction to the jurisprudence of other international courts and tribunals. First, the possibility of carrying one's burden of proof by means of an inference is not well-articulated in some other international decisions. One such example is the *Duzgit Integrity PCA* arbitration between Malta and São Tomé and Príncipe under the UN Law of the Sea Convention.[56] One of the issues in that arbitration was whether São Tomé and Príncipe breached Article 225 of the United Nations Law of the Sea Convention by the way that it caused a Maltese flagged vessel to operate a transfer of ship to ship transfer while under the control of the São Tomé and Príncipe coastguard.[57] Particularly, Malta claimed that São Tomé and Príncipe exposed the marine environment to an unreasonable risk.[58]

In dealing with Malta's submission, the award outlines the pieces of proof proffered by Malta.[59] These pieces of evidence included witness statements.[60] They also included indirect pieces of evidence such as lapsed registration certificates, etc.[61]

The tribunal engaged this evidence as follows:

2012) para 436; *Besserglick v Mozambique*, ICSID Case No ARB(AF)/14/2, Award (28 October 2019) para 368.

[52] Sourgens et al (n 19) 291 (Evidentiary Principle §1(1)(b)). *Caratube International Oil v Kazakhstan* (n 51) para 436.

[53] Sourgens et al (n 19) 291 (Evidentiary Principle §1(1)(c)). *Gemplus SA v Mexico*, ICSID Case No ARB(AF)/04/3, Award (16 June 2010) 13–99; *Perenco Ecuador Ltd v Republic of Ecuador*, ICSID Case No ARB/08/6, Award (27 September 2019) para 316; *Besserglick v Mozambique* (n 50) paras 368–370.

[54] Sourgens et al (n 19) 291 (Evidentiary Principle §1(1)(d)).

[55] *Corfu Channel* (n 38) 18.

[56] *In the Matter of the Duzgit Integrity Arbitration (Malta v São Tomé and Príncipe)*, PCA Case No 2014-07, Award (5 September 2016).

[57] Ibid., paras 108–111.

[58] Ibid., para 284.

[59] Ibid., para 292.

[60] Ibid.

[61] Ibid.

> the determination of whether the marine environment was exposed to an unreasonable risk by the STS operation between 19 and 23 October 2013 must be made on the basis of the actual circumstances under which the operation was carried out, irrespective of whether it was carried out in full compliance with any national laws.[62]

It then concluded '[b]ased on the evidence before it, the Tribunal is not persuaded that São Tomé exposed the marine environment to an unreasonable risk in breach of Article 225. Accordingly, the Tribunal determines that Malta has failed to meet its burden of proof under this head of claim'.[63]

From an evidentiary perspective, such a conclusion is very untidy to say the least. What does the tribunal mean when it says a determination 'must be made on the basis of the actual circumstances?'[64] As this is the only statement purporting to analyse the evidence summarised immediately before, one could read into this statement that witness statements and other indirect evidence are not probative of actual circumstances. Such a conclusion is not internally consistent, as the tribunal notes inconsistent (be it self-interested) eye-witness testimony in its summary of Malta's evidence. So what did the tribunal mean?

The point is non-trivial as some of the evidence submitted by Malta appeared to set up an inference. (The knowing operation of a vessel that is out of registration would support an inference of disregard for safety procedures. This could well be the predicate for a conclusion that the respondent exposed the marine environment to undue risk.) So why not draw that inference? The decision reads as if inferences are insufficient as not evidence of 'actual circumstances'.

Confusingly, the same tribunal later on its decision addresses the question of inferences on another head of claim.[65] The tribunal in that setting makes a determination of fact obviating the need for an inference, rejecting that the inference could appropriately be drawn.[66] The tribunal thus appears to suggest that inferences can support a claim, but does not set out why this was not appropriate in in the context of Article 225 of UNCLOS.

The point here is not to castigate a particular tribunal. The point is rather that carrying of burdens of proof by means of inferences is not as fully and consciously developed in other international legal proceedings as it is in investor-State proceedings. Thus, it may not seem odd to the reader of the Malta award that the tribunal would have dispensed with questions of proof in

---

62 Ibid., para 293.
63 Ibid.
64 Ibid.
65 Ibid., para 277.
66 Ibid.

such a conclusory fashion – to the contrary that is presumably why the award was issued the way it was. But this conclusion would strike one as underdeveloped from the perspective of investor-State arbitration.

As the Malta Tribunal appeared to allow that inferences could be used to carry a party's burden of proof this provides a helpful opening for study of the more detailed investor-State decisions. Investor-State decisions can provide more granular guidance how inferences interact with burdens of proof. It thus provides a helpful opening tertium comparationis for other international legal proceedings.

Second, fairly, the fact that a party failed to meet its burden of proof with regard to a fact carries an implication of its own: 'the event or occurrence submitted as a fact did not take place'.[67] Investor-State tribunals are reasonably willing to draw such a factual conclusion from the record. This stands in contrast to some jurisprudence of the ICJ, which applies burdens of proof to avoid making factual findings, at all.[68] Investor-State tribunals in most instances follow the facts to their logical conclusion and make findings.[69] This making of findings is important for potential questions of res judicata or collateral estoppel should need for the doctrines arise in ancillary proceedings and is therefore reasonably prudent to the extent that is premised in careful and prudent analysis by the tribunal.[70]

Investor-State tribunals further have significantly refined the question of the burden of proof in the jurisdictional setting.[71] By way of example, the question of burdens of proof on jurisdiction is facially confusing. Decisions such as *Fisheries Jurisdiction* have announced the rule that there is no jurisdictional burden of proof.[72] This line of decisions, however, concerns questions of jurisdiction ratione voluntatis only – i.e., whether there is consent to jurisdiction.[73] It in principle should not extend further on factual questions whether the Court has jurisdiction ratione personae or ratione materiae. The canonical statement

---

67 Sourgens et al (n 19) 291 (Evidentiary Principles §1(2)).

68 *Pulp Mills Case* (n 33) 75, 77, 93, 95, 97-100.

69 See *Rompetrol Group NV v Romania*, ICSID Case No ARB/06/3, Award (6 May 2013) para 179.

70 See R. Doak Bishop and Silvia Marchili, *Annulment under the ICSID Convention* (OUP 2012) 207–210.

71 Sourgens et al (n 19) 291 (Evidentiary Principles §2).

72 *Fisheries Jurisdiction Case (Spain v Canada)* [1998] *ICJ Reports* 432, 450.

73 See ibid. For a broader discussion, see Michael D. Nolan and Frédéric G. Sourgens, 'Limits of Consent - Arbitration Without Privity and Beyond' in Miguel Ángel Fernández Ballesteros and David Arias Lozano (eds), *Liber Amicorum Bernardo Cremades* (Kluwer 2010) 873.

that there is no burden of proof on jurisdiction, however, does not articulate these distinctions and in fact can fairly be read to contradict them.[74]

Part of the reason for this imprecision is reasonably straightforward. Jurisdictional objections in many non-investor-State proceedings are legal in nature. They concern the meaning and scope of a potential jurisdictional undertaking.[75] The issue therefore is not front of mind in the same way, even if they could arise upon occasion (e.g., whether a dispute is admissible due to the exhaustion of local remedies in the context of a claim of diplomatic protection).[76]

In investor-State arbitration evidentiary issues are frequently dispositive of jurisdictional questions, as issues of fact arise that bear on the tribunal's jurisdiction. Assigning the burden correctly as to who must prove the relevant fact therefore is of the utmost importance. The ground rule reflected in investor-State jurisprudence is that the 'party invoking the jurisdiction of the tribunal must submit evidence that, if unrebutted, would meet the standard of proof to establish jurisdiction'.[77] It thus bears the burden of proof on jurisdictional facts.[78] The party invoking jurisdiction also 'must plead, but not prove, sufficient facts to assert a claim for which relief may be granted'.[79] The starting

---

[74] *Fisheries Jurisdiction* (n 72).

[75] Nolan and Sourgens (n 73).

[76] *Case Concerning Ahmadou Sadio Diallo (Republic of Guinea v Democratic Republic of the Congo)* (Preliminary Objections) [2007] *ICJ Reports* 582, 599; *Interhandel Case (Switzerland v United States of America)* (Preliminary Objections) [1959] *ICJ Reports* 6, 26–27.

[77] Sourgens et al (n 19) (Evidentiary Principle §2(1)).

[78] *Ambiente Ufficio SpA and Others (Case formerly known as Giordano Alpi and Others) v Argentine Republic*, ICSID Case No ARB/08/9, Decision on Jurisdiction and Admissibility (8 February 2013) para 312:

> [T]he burden of proof that the Claimants are Italian nationals falls on the Claimants themselves, while the burden to disprove the negative elements – i.e., of not being Argentine (or, for that matter, dual) nationals and of not have been domiciled in Argentina for more than two years—would fall on the Respondent's side;

Apotex Inc v United States of America, UNCITRAL (NAFTA), Award on Jurisdiction and Admissibility (14 June 2013) para 150. 'Apotex (as Claimant) bears the burden of proof with respect to the factual elements necessary to establish the Tribunal's jurisdiction.'

[79] Sourgens et al (n 19) 291 (Evidentiary Principle §2(2)); *Methanex Corporation v United States of America*, UNCITRAL (NAFTA), Preliminary Award on Jurisdiction and Admissiblity (7 August 2002) para 116; *SGS Société Générale de Surveillance SA v Republic of the Philippines*, ICSID Case No ARB/02/6, Decision on Objections to Jurisdiction (29 January 2004) para 26; *Salini Construttori SpA v Jordan*, ICSID Case No ARB/02/13, Decision on Jurisdiction (9 November 2004) paras 139–151.

position thus is that a party wishing to invoke the jurisdiction of a tribunal must prove that the tribunal is in fact vested with jurisdiction all else being equal.

Problematically, the respondent in investor-State jurisprudence typically does not rest on the insufficiency of evidence submitted by the claimant. Rather, frequently 'introduce[s] evidence to rebut the jurisdictional submission'.[80] When a respondent does so, however, it 'may not introduce evidence at the jurisdictional stage that would rebut only merits submissions advanced by the claimant'.[81] Further, to the extent that a respondent makes a submission of fact that goes beyond testing the sufficiency of the evidence submitted by the claimant, it becomes the moving party as to that fact. When it does so, it 'bears the proof ... with regard to its jurisdictional submissions' alleging new facts not already contained in the record.[82] This assignment of the burden of proof thus sensibly elaborates who has what burden when and why. It thus provides a very robust framework for a tribunal's establishment of its own jurisdiction borne out by the habitual testing of jurisprudence by respondent States.

Finally, investor-State tribunals also have had frequent occasion to address questions of burden of proof when it comes to the remedies stage.[83] This is an area of particular importance in investor-State arbitration – and of relatively different import in traditional State-to-State dispute resolution. Investor-State tribunals generally require that the 'party seeking a remedy must submit evidence that, if unrebutted, would meet the relevant standard of proof that the remedy requested is appropriate'.[84] Particularly, when a party seeks damages

---

[80] Sourgens et al (n 19) 291 (Evidentiary Principle §2(3)); *Inceysa Vallisoletane SL v Republic El Salvador*, ICSID Case No ARB/03/26, Award (2 August 2006) para 48; *World Duty Free Co Ltd v Kenya*, ICSID Case No ARB/0/7, Award (4 October 2006) para 105; *Plama Consortium Ltd v Republic of Bulgaria*, ICSID Case No ARB/03/24, Award (7 August 2008) paras 101–105; *Phoenix Action Ltd v Czech Republic*, ICSID Case No ARB/06/5, Award (15 April 2009) paras 34-43; *Metal-Tech Ltd v Uzbekistan*, ICSID Case No ARB/10/3, Award (4 October 2013) paras 278–280.

[81] Sourgens et al (n 19) 291 (Evidentiary Principle §2(3)) (Evidentiary Principle §2(4)); *Gustav F W Hamester GmbH & Co KG v Republic of Ghana*, ICSID Case No ARB/07/24, Award (18 June 2010) para 143.

[82] Sourgens et al (n 19) 291 (Evidentiary Principle §2(5)); *Bernhard von Pezold v Zimbabwe*, ICSID Case No ARB/10/15, Award (28 July 2015) para 174; *Plama Consortium Ltd v Republic of Bulgaria*, ICSID Case No ARB/03/24, Decision on Jurisdiction (8 February 2005) paras 177–178; *Ioan Micula v Romania*, ICSID Case No ARB/05/20, Decision on Jurisdiction and Admissibility (24 September 2008) para 95.

[83] Sourgens et al (n 19) 291 (Evidentiary Principles §3).

[84] Ibid. (Evidentiary Principle §3(1)); Thomas W. Wälde and Borzu Sabahi, 'Compensation, Damages, and Valuation' in Peter Muchlinski et al (eds), *The Oxford Handbook of International Investment Law* (OUP 2008) 1110.

as its remedy, it 'must submit evidence that, if unrebutted, would meet the relevant standard of proof that the remedy requested is not speculative'.[85]

Obviously, the manner in which remedies are proved and calculated should not differ markedly across different international fora. It should be noted, however, that the calculation of damages, based upon sophisticated records and a subsequent challenge of these records, is something that happens more frequently in investor-State dispute resolution than in other fora. Investor-State proceedings are nearly exclusively about damages. They are not about other potential international remedies. It is for this reason that there is naturally more record engagement with damages cases in investor-State arbitration.[86]

Again, the respondent is not left simply with the option of attacking the sufficiency of the evidence submitted by its claimant. Rather, it 'may submit evidence to rebut submissions made by its opponent'.[87] To the extent that these submissions contain the assertion of a new fact not already in issue, however, 'the respondent bears the burden of proving its submission' on that point.[88]

2. Standard of proof

The practice of investor-State tribunals permits the formulation of approximately half a dozen rules applied with broad agreement across different investor-State proceedings with regard to the standard of proof. In the first place, the general standard of proof applied by investor-State tribunals requires that the party with the burden of proof convince a tribunal that it is more probable than not that a factual contention the party advances is true.[89]

Investor-State arbitration since has further developed the rules governing the standard of proof. Investor-State jurisprudence begins from the premise that the weighing of evidence – and the application of the standard of proof is

---

85 Sourgens et al (n 19) 291 (Evidentiary Principle §3(2)); *Achmea BV (formerly Eureko BV) v Slovak Republic*, UNCITRAL, PCA Case No 2008-13, Award (7 December 2012) para 323; *Al Bahloul v Tajikistan*, SCC Case No V. (064/2008), Award (8 June 2010) para 39; *Impregilo SpA v Argentine Republic*, ICSID Case No ARB/07/17, Award (21 June 2011) para 371.

86 For a discussion on the relationship between general international law and investor-state arbitration on this point, see Borzu Sabahi, *Compensation and Restitution in Investor-State Arbitration Principles and Practice* (OUP 2011).

87 Sourgens et al (n 19) 291 (Evidentiary Principle §3(3)); Irmgard Marboe, *Calculation of Compensation and Damages in Investment Law* (OUP 2009) 125.

88 Sourgens et al (n 19) 291 (Evidentiary Principle §3(4)).

89 Ibid. (Evidentiary Principles §5); *Kardassopoulos v Georgia*, ICSID Case Nos ARB/05/18 and ARB/07/15, Award (3 March 2010) para 229; *von Pezold v Zimbabwe* (n 81) para 177.

a question of tribunal discretion.[90] This discretion, however, is not unbounded. Rather, a tribunal must exercise its discretion in good faith.[91] It is possible to assess whether a tribunal exercises its discretion in good faith by reference to three factors: whether the exercise of discretion is broadly consistent and appropriate to the record; whether the exercise of discretion is consistent with the principle of the equality of the parties; and whether the exercise of discretion is otherwise consistent with natural justice.[92]

As tribunals exercise their discretion in a manner appropriate to their fact-finding task, the jurisprudence of investor-State tribunals again allow for a more granular understanding of standards of proof in operation (as opposed to in principle). Investor-State jurisprudence consistently looks to four factors in exercising tribunal discretion. First, tribunals thus look to the gravity of the allegation made by a party, consistent with *Corfu Channel*.[93] Second, tribunals then assess the quantity of evidence submitted by a party alleging a fact – did a party submit a single piece of evidence to establish a central and unexpected fact or did it submit multiple pieces of evidence to support its contention? – bearing in mind the quantity of rebuttal evidence submitted by the non-moving party.[94] Third, tribunals assess how credible and probative the evidence is of the submission advanced by the moving party and the non-moving party respectively, that is how credible is each piece of evidence and if it is credible how directly does it establish that the fact submitted by a party actually is

---

90 Sourgens et al (n 19) 292 (Evidentiary Principles §4(1)); *Alapli Elektrik BV v Republic of Turkey*, ICSID Case No ARB/08/13, Decision on Annulment (10 July 2014) para 234.

91 Sourgens et al (n 19) 292 (Evidentiary Principle §4(2)).

92 Ibid., *Fraport AG Frankfurt Airport Services Worldwide v Republic of the Philippines*, ICSID Case No ARB/03/25, Decision on the Application for Annulment (23 December 2010) paras 180–217; *Victor Pey Casado and President Allende Foundation v Republic of Chile*, ICSID Case No ARB/98/2, Annulment (Dec. 18, 2012) paras 71–82; *Caratube International Oil Co v Republic of Kazakhstan*, ICSID Case No ARB/08/12, Decision on Annulment Application (21 February 2014) para 97.

93 Sourgens et al (n 19) 292 (Evidentiary Principle §4(3)(a)); *Corfu Channel* (n 38) 17.

94 Sourgens et al (n 19) 292 (Evidentiary Principle §4(3)(b), (d)). See *Fireman's Fund Insurance Co v United Mexican States*, ICSID Case No ARB(AF)/02/01, Award (14 July 2006) para 213; *International Thunderbird Gaming Corp v United Mexican States*, UNCITRAL–NAFTA, Award (26 January 2006) para 136; *Rompetrol Group NV v Romania*, ICSID Case No ARB/06/3, Award (6 May 2013) para 224, noting that testimonial evidence required further external corroboration due to questions of credibility.

true?[95] Fourth, and finally, investor-State tribunals consider the availability of direct evidence to support a contention.[96]

This approach is broadly consistent with other international proceedings but remains helpfully additive to it. One useful example is the arbitration between Guyana and Suriname regarding their maritime boundary delimitation.[97] The key question on point was whether there existed special circumstances 'to justify a departure from the median line approach' to boundary delimitation.[98]

After a legal discussion to establish that navigation rights constituted special circumstances, the tribunal turned to the evidence. The tribunal began with its conclusion: 'the record amply supports the conclusion that the predecessors of the Parties agreed upon a N10°E delimitation line'.[99] The tribunal then looked at how the record so supported the conclusion. It noted first that '[c]ontrary to Guyana's assessment … , Suriname has presented evidence of navigation in the western channel, albeit of small local craft, rather than large ocean-going vessels'.[100] Reading between the lines, there was thus more than one piece of evidence that allowed a specific conclusion as to what type of vessels navigated in the channel. It is also implicit in the statement that Guyana had not submitted probative evidence to rebut this conclusion. This is thus consistent with the approach in investor-State arbitration.

While this reading of the award is plausible, it requires a certain amount of guess work. That is, the tribunal does not come right out and say what the basis of its conclusion is. Rather, it again makes observations in reasonably conclusory terms. Here, the practice of investor-State tribunals while consistent is

---

95 Sourgens et al (n 19) 292 (Evidentiary Principle §4(3)(c), (e)). See *Siag v Arab Republic of Egypt*, ICSID Case No ARB/05/15, Award (1 June 2009) paras 211–215; *Europe Cement Investment & Trade SA v Republic of Turkey*, ICSID Case No ARB(AF)/07/2, Award (11 August 2009) para 158; *Feldman v United Mexican States*, ICSID Case No ARB(AF)/99/1, Award (12 December 2002) para 131, determining how to deal with a he-said-he-said situation of contradictory direct evidence; *Middle East Cement Shipping and Handling Co SA v Arab Republic of Egypt*, ICSID Case No ARB/99/6, Award (12 April 2002) para 94; *Tradex Hellas SA v Republic of Albania*, ICSID Case No ARB/92/2, Award (29 April 1999) para 84; *AAPL v Sri Lanka* (n 21) para 56.

96 Sourgens et al (n 19) 292. See *Alpha Projektholding GmbH v Ukraine*, ICSID Case No ARB/07/16, Award (8 November 2010) para 373; *Tokios Tokelès v Ukraine* (n 50) para 14; *Rumeli Telekom AS v Republic of Kazakhstan*, ICSID Case No ARB/05/16, Award (21 July 2008) paras 444, 709; *Zeevi Holdings v Republic of Bulgaria*, UNCITRAL Case No UNC 39/DK, Award (25 October 2006) paras 944–945.

97 *In the Matter of an Arbitration between Guyana v Suriname*, PCA Case No 2004-04, Award (17 September 2007).

98 Ibid., para 298.

99 Ibid., para 306.

100 Ibid.

simply more precise and thus helpful to establish the reasoning process in the engagement of record evidence.

The Suriname-Guyana decision then comes to its main piece of evidence. It 'must take account of Guyana's own admissions that there was recognition of a N10°E line for 3 nm'.[101] This evidence is particularly probative ('own admission.') The record cite for this admission, however, is briefing rather than pieces of proof. One can therefore understand why the tribunal did not begin its record analysis there but rather first established the record basis for the same conclusion and then gave probative weight to these assertions contained in the record in light of the admission made in pleadings.

Again, the point must be made out between the lines. The tribunal does not say that this is what is going on. It lets the reader infer it. It therefore helps to have a more granular set of decisions in investor-State arbitration that can support the inference as to what international tribunals actually do when they make evidentiary findings in more general, and not always record-cited terms.

Returning to the elements as used in investor-State arbitration, the fourth element is of particular importance. It provides helpful, additional support for principles developed in only a handful of cases that by their nature appear idiosyncratic. Thus, consistent with the narrower reading of *Corfu Channel* above, investor-State jurisprudence tends to prefer direct evidence when it is available.[102] Direct evidence is immediately relevant to, and probative of, the fact to be proved.[103] Eye-witness testimony from Benvolio that Benvolio saw Romeo stab Tybalt is immediately probative of the assertion that Romeo stabbed Tybalt.[104] Of course, this does not end the inquiry into direct evidence.[105] It is still necessary to establish whether we can believe the eye-witness account. The tribunal must ascertain whether the evidence is in fact credible.[106] This credibility question again has two components. First, is the eye-witness sincere?[107] In our context, Benvolio is Romeo's cousin and friend. It would therefore be reasonable to assume his testimony is sincere as he would have little

---

101 Ibid.

102 Sourgens et al (n 19) 292 (Evidentiary Principle §7); *Certain Activities Carried out by Nicaragua in the Border Area (Costa Rica v Nicaragua)* [2015] *ICJ Reports* 665, 733, noting the absence of direct evidence submitted by Nicaragua as a significant factor in its decision; Simone Halink, 'All Things Considered: How the International Court of Justice Delegated its Fact Assessment to the United Nations in the Armed Activities Case' (2008) 40 *NYU JILP* 13, 22.

103 Sourgens et al (n 19) 292 (Evidentiary Principle §7(2)).

104 William Shakespeare, *Romeo and Juliet*, III:1.

105 Kevin Jon Heller, 'The Cognitive Psychology of Circumstantial Evidence' (2006) 105 *Michigan LR* 241, 248.

106 Sourgens et al (n 19) 292 (Evidentiary Principle §8).

107 Heller (n 105) 248–251.

known motive to lie. Assuming that the tribunal determines that the evidence is sincere, it must still establish whether it is competent.[108] Could the witness see? Assume that Benvolio testified that he looked away in fright for the last minute of the altercation between Romeo and Tybalt, did Benvolio really see the alleged blow? The testimony is only direct evidence if Benvolio actually saw what he says he saw (Romeo slew Tybalt) and sincerely reports his observations. That said, if a tribunal does find direct evidence credible in the sense that it is sincere and competent, the fact it supports has been established. To continue to doubt the fact is only as sane as to continue to doubt the credibility of the direct evidence.

Of course, there are many cases in which such direct evidence is not available. *Corfu Channel* highlights such a scenario. In that instance, investor-State jurisprudence also permits proof by circumstantial and hearsay evidence.[109] This circumstantial evidence, however, is subject to additional review by the tribunal beyond an appraisal of its credibility. Investor-State tribunals typically look for corroboration of such circumstantial or hearsay evidence.[110] This additional step makes sense, as a person can be both sincere (i.e., credible) and misinformed if they did not in fact witness the events about which they testify.

This more granular understanding of the operations of standards of proof help to add context to the *Corfu Channel* approach to standards of proof in the context of particularly grave allegations.[111] Investor-State jurisprudence follow in *Corfu Channel*'s footsteps that a tribunal 'may apply a higher standard of proof than balance of the probabilities to make determinations of particular gravity'.[112] At the same time, investor-State annulment jurisprudence is express that investor-State tribunals may not heighten the standard of proof to one that requires proof beyond a reasonable doubt.[113] What then does a tribunal due when it faces a charge of particular gravity?

As outlined above, however, this heightened standard of proof can now be seen in context. Proof of the contention by direct evidence is likely to remain unaffected by a heightened standard of proof. The tribunal has to determine that the evidence is credible no matter the standard of proof it applies. If such

---

[108] Ibid.

[109] Sourgens et al (n 19) 292 (Evidentiary Principle §9).

[110] Ibid. (Evidentiary Principle §9(3)); *Rompetrol v Romania* (n 69) para 215; *Generation Ukraine Inc v Ukraine*, ICSID Case No ARB/00/9, Award (16 September 2003) para 19.4; *Gemplus v Mexico* (n 53) paras 4.172–4.175.

[111] *Corfu Channel* (n 38) 17.

[112] Sourgens et al (n 19) 292 (Evidentiary Principle §6(1)).

[113] *Fraport v Philippines*, Annulment (n 92) paras 180–217. The author participated as counsel for Fraport AG in the proceedings.

direct evidence is credible, it is likely to meet any standard proof given that it is immediately probative of the event to which it testifies.[114]

The heightened standard of proof therefore concerns not proof by direct evidence but proof by indirect evidence. The heightened standard is likely to require a different kind of corroboration of indirect evidence. Most directly, it will look to find additional corroboration. This additional corroboration adds pieces of evidence, i.e., adds weight with regard to the second factor considered by tribunals in weighing evidence outlined above. Different corroboration requires a qualitatively different approach to indirect evidence – the corroboration needs to be more material. It needs to shorten the distance between the pieces of evidence and the conclusion to be drawn from them, i.e., add weight with regard to the third factored considered by tribunals in weighing evidence outlined above. The heightened standard of proof in other words is an organic part of the ordinary fact-finding mission of international tribunals rather than an external imposition upon it. In other words, it is firmly grounded in the tribunal's discretionary powers to establish the facts of the dispute rather than imposing external legal constraints on how such a process is permitted to operate.

C. Informing Perspectives

Investor-State jurisprudence can act as an incubator for the development of evidentiary principles in general international law. The problem faced in the general international law of dispute resolution before bodies such as the ICJ is meaningfully the same as the problem faced by investor-State tribunals.

It might at this point be objected that the investment regime differs from international adjudication before the ICJ in important respects and that these differences limit the relevance of investor-State arbitration. First, it might be submitted that ICJ has significantly fewer powers to call for the production of evidence than an investor-State tribunal. This would mean that ICJ cases and investor-State proceedings are meaningfully different.

Such a distinction would look to Articles 49 and 50 of the ICJ Statute as well as Article 56 of the Rules of Court. In principle, such an argument would submit, the Court has the power to request the production of evidence but has no means to compel it. All Article 49 authorises is that '[f]ormal note shall be taken of any refusal'.[115]

---

[114] *Fraport v Philippines*, ICSID Case No ARB/03/25, Award (16 August 2007) para 399. The author participated for Fraport AG in the proceedings.

[115] Statute of the International Court of Justice (adopted 24 October 1945, published 18 April 1946) 33 UNTS 993, art 49.

This distinction should not, however, be taken too far. Thus, Article 43 of the ICSID Convention reasonably mirrors Article 49 of the ICJ Statute when it provides that 'Except as the the Tribunal may, if it deems it necessary at any stage of the proceedings, (a) call upon the parties to produce documents or other evidence.'[116] An ICSID tribunal has limited to no power actually to compel production. All it can do is ask.

ICJ practice and ICSID practice further both admits to the possibility of the drawing of adverse inferences from non-production of documents. Famously, in *Corfu Channel*, the ICJ asked for a specific document, document XCU, to be produced by the Admiralty and threatened the drawing of an adverse inference in case of non-production.[117] ICSID tribunals have used the same approach. In both instances, the express drawing of adverse inferences in reasonably rare. *Corfu Channel* did not draw an adverse inference that passage was less than innocent despite non-production of the document in question.[118] And in investor-State cases, even the shadow of an adverse inference may well motivate a sometimes successful annulment request.[119]

It might further be objected that ICJ proceedings are not as fact intensive as investor-State proceedings. One might thus disagree that one can read only the findings of fact in an ICJ decision and already know the outcome of the case on the basis of such findings. Three points should be considered in rebuttal of such an argument. First, one should fairly re-examine whether such scepticism is actually warranted. Consider the decision in *Corfu Channel* discussed throughout so far. That decision studiously fashions its factual findings. There is no reason to doubt the good intentions of the UK in passing through the straits (document XCU notwithstanding).[120] There is no reason to believe collusion in the mining of the straits with Yugoslavia. But there is also every reason to believe that Albania knew of the presence of the mines and did not warn the British.[121] Tell these facts to any person with a strong moral compass and ask: what should a court do? The answer is likely to be what the ICJ actually did.

---

[116] Convention on the Settlement of Investment Disputes between States and Nationals of Other States (adopted 18 March 1965, entered into force 14 October 1966) 575 UNTS 159, art 43.

[117] W. Michael Reisman, *The Quest for World Order and Human Dignity in the Twenty-First Century: Constitutive Process and Individual Commitment* (Brill 2012) 455–472.

[118] Ibid.

[119] *Fraport v Philippines*, Annulment (n 92).

[120] Reisman (n 117) 455–472.

[121] *Corfu Channel* (n 38) 9–18.

Second, it might be objected that *Corfu Channel* is an exception that proves the rule due to its obvious geo-political ramifications and in any event is an old case. Here, one might consider the Suriname/Guayana PCA arbitration discussed above.[122] The case is a border delimitation without the geo-political ramifications of *Corfu Channel*. And yet, how should one expect the arbitration to come out after the tribunal has informed us that Guyana has admitted that Suriname's assertion of navigational rights is actually factually correct?[123] This factual conclusion as presented in the award practically invites one to say 'estoppel'. The facts thus do a lot of weight-bearing work even in recent decisions that appear routine to all but the parties involved.

Third, it is on the whole likely that factual questions and fact finding will take on increasing importance in their own right. The ICJ decision in *Pulp Mills* here is instructive.[124] *Pulp Mills* concerns a complicated international environmental law claim about the effects of economic activity on a river. Such a claim lives and dies on its facts.[125] To say that such claims are receding or not of the gravest concern in the current moment seems unrealistic. We thus are likely to see fact finding become increasingly important in many general international adjudications lending credence to the statement that investor-State arbitration encountered meaningfully the same problem to which general international dispute resolution must face up in turn.

The starting point for investor-State jurisprudence is the same as the starting point for general international law. As discussed in the previous section, investor-State jurisprudence begins its engagement with evidence through its reception of ICJ jurisprudence on point. The development in investor-State arbitration therefore can meaningfully assist in the development of general international law standards on standards and burdens of proof for the reasons outlined above – the problems in general international law are meaningfully similar and engagement with these problems is more detailed in investor-State jurisprudence due in part to the far greater number of cases and attempts by counsel to distinguish prior case law.

As the discussion in the preceding sections has attempted to outline, the jurisprudence of investor-State tribunals on burdens and standards of proof is particularly helpful as a source for general international law codification and progressive development efforts. The jurisprudence of investor-State tribunals on burdens and standards of proof can readily be restated into cogent principles

---

[122] *Guyana v Suriname* (n 97).

[123] Ibid., para 306.

[124] *Pulp Mills Case* (n 33).

[125] Ibid.

governing the taking of proof. This means that it can serve as an inspiration for the future codification of evidentiary principles in general international law.

This inspiration can at a minimum serve as a *tertium comparationis* whether the general international jurisprudence follows meaningfully in the same footsteps as investor-State arbitration. In other words, the work in the investor-State arbitration context has provided a rubric for the detailed examination of general international law developments on burdens and standards of proof. At a minimum, this rubric will thus assist in sharpening the understanding of general international law by highlighting differences between its modalities of fact-finding through the prisms of burdens and standards of proof and those at work in general international law. This comparative approach thus will greatly assist in the development of more precise general international law rules on burdens and standards of proof.

Hopefully the work done in the context of investor-State arbitration will prove to be even more helpful. The evidence outlined above suggests that general international law and investor-State arbitration have developed from the same source materials and have taken reasonably similar trajectories. This would suggest that the differences between the doctrinal efforts to restate the rules on burdens and standards of proof in investor-State arbitration should be immediately valuable to the progressive codification of general international law. They can serve as a blueprint that can be applied mutatis mutandis to other specific international law dispute resolution contexts. If this more ambitious conclusion will be borne out by the work of the ILC, investor-State jurisprudence will have served an outsized role in testing and refining the rules of standards and burdens of proof in general international law.

III. INFERENCES AND PRESUMPTIONS

The law of burdens and standards of proof already points to the next building block of the law of evidence: inferences and presumptions. Inferences are a means to prove a case not on the basis of the indirect retelling of direct evidence (hearsay evidence) but rather to proof the existence of Fact A by proving the existence of Fact B, a fact that typically only appears when Fact A is also present. If one finds oneself in a windowless conference room, one cannot observe whether it is raining outside. If however one sees a colleague walking into the conference room in an overcoat and folding up a wet umbrella, one can infer from the overcoat that the person walked in from outside and from the wet umbrella that it must be raining. Presumptions in turn are legally recognised correlations between such Fact A and Fact B that exist either as a matter of substantive law or as a matter of independent proof as to generalizable correlations.

The use of inferences and presumptions is one of the key means in which evidence is taken in international adjudication. Direct evidence, while broadly preferred, is rarely available as to key factual disputes. Further, it is also rare to find second-hand accounts of such direct evidence. Recourse to inferences and presumptions therefore is a necessary fact of international legal life. This second building block is therefore instrumental in understanding how proof in international dispute resolution works.

A. Foundations in General International Law

The use of inferences and presumptions in investor-State arbitrations have deep roots in general international law. This section provides a brief overview with regard to the roots of investor-State arbitration in the general international law of inferences and presumptions in ICJ jurisprudence respectively. The next section will outline their further development as investor-State jurisprudence matured.

1. Inferences

General international law permits courts and tribunals to rely upon inferences. The *Corfu Channel* case, already discussed above, provides an early example of the permissive use of inferences. The *Corfu Channel* court noted that:

> By reason of this exclusive control, the other State, the victim of a breach of international law, is often unable to furnish direct proof of facts giving rise to responsibility. Such a State should be allowed a more liberal recourse to inferences of fact and circumstantial evidence. This indirect evidence is admitted in all systems of law, and its use is recognized by international decisions.[126]

The *Corfu Channel* case readily identifies that inferences are typically a secondary means of fact finding, i.e., a court or tribunal should utilise them only when direct proof of facts is not available.[127] It further confirms that proof by inference is a general principle of law.[128]

The *Corfu Channel* approach remains good law. For instance, the Court more recently applied similar proof by inference in the genocide context. In the *Genocide* case between Croatia and Serbia, Croatia asserted that Serbia

---

[126] *Corfu Channel* (n 38) 18.
[127] Ibid.
[128] Ibid.

had specific genocidal intent by way of inference.[129] It relied upon 17 factors to support such an inference. Specifically:

(1) the political doctrine of Serbian expansionism which created the climate for genocidal policies aimed at destroying the Croat population living in areas earmarked to become part of 'Greater Serbia';
(2) the statements of public officials, including demonization of Croats and propaganda on the part of State-controlled media;
(3) the fact that the pattern of attacks on groups of Croats far exceeded any legitimate military objective necessary to secure control of the regions concerned;
(4) contemporaneous video footage evidencing the genocidal intent of those carrying out the attacks;
(5) the explicit recognition by the JNA that paramilitary groups were engaging in genocidal acts;
(6) the close co-operation between the JNA and the Serb paramilitary groups responsible for some of the worst atrocities, implying close planning and logistical support;
(7) the systematic nature and sheer scale of the attacks on groups of Croats;
(8) the fact that ethnic Croats were constantly singled out for attack while local Serbs were excluded;
(9) the fact that during the occupation, ethnic Croats were required to identify themselves and their property as such by wearing white ribbons tied around their arms and by affixing white cloths to their homes;
(10) the number of Croats killed and missing as a proportion of the local population;
(11) the nature, degree and extent of the injuries inflicted (through physical attacks, acts of torture, inhuman and degrading treatment, rape and sexual violence), 'including injuries with recognizable ethnic characteristics';
(12) the use of ethnically derogatory language in the course of acts of killing, torture and rape;
(13) the forced displacement of Croats and the organized means adopted to this end;
(14) the systematic looting and destruction of Croat cultural and religious monuments;
(15) the suppression of Croat culture and religious practices among the remaining population;
(16) the consequent permanent and evidently intended demographic changes to the regions concerned; and
(17) the failure to punish the crimes which the Applicant alleges to be genocide.[130]

[129] *Genocide Case (Croatia v Serbia)* (n 32) 119.
[130] Ibid., 119–120.

The Court followed Croatia's invitation to assess whether Serbia had such specific intent by way of an inference. The Court in other words did not require direct proof of this intent. The Court found that

> of the 17 factors suggested by Croatia to establish the existence of a pattern of conduct revealing a genocidal intent, the most important are those that concern the scale and allegedly systematic nature of the attacks, the fact that those attacks are said to have caused casualties and damage far in excess of what was justified by military necessity, the specific targeting of Croats and the nature, extent and degree of the injuries caused to the Croat population.[131]

The Court ultimately did not make a finding of fact consistent with Croatia's suggested inference.[132] The Court's rationale for its decision is that Croatia had failed prove that the intent of genocide was the only reasonable inference to be drawn from the evidence.[133] The Court pointed in particular to acts of evacuation by Serbian forces of the Croatian civilian population as fundamentally inconsistent with the inference that Serbian forces intended to commit genocide.[134] It therefore inferred to the contrary that genocidal intent against Croatians was absent.

General international law also recognises the availability of adverse inferences from the conduct of the parties in judicial proceedings. Again, *Corfu Channel* stands out as an early precedent.[135] Albania in *Corfu Channel* contested that British passage through the mined straights was in fact as innocent as the UK had claimed.[136] It requested production of British orders for the passage in question.[137] The Court order that the document be produced.[138] The Court warned that failure to produce the document could lead to the drawing of an adverse inference.[139]

Interestingly, the UK did not in fact produce the document in question.[140] The Court nevertheless stayed its hand and did not in fact draw an adverse inference.[141] Rather, the Court reasoned that the document was unlikely to contain the kind of damning evidence that Albania suggested it did.[142] The

---

131 Ibid., 121
132 Ibid., 128.
133 Ibid.
134 Ibid., 127.
135 *Corfu Channel* (n 38) 17.
136 Ibid., 16–18.
137 Ibid., 32.
138 Ibid.
139 Ibid.
140 Ibid.
141 Ibid.
142 Ibid.

Corfu Channel case therefore stands for the proposition that adverse inferences are permissible as a matter of general international law, but that they are generally disfavoured.

The use of inferences in investor-State arbitration is generally conscious of, and follows the guidance of, general international law. In summarising investor-State arbitral jurisprudence on the use of inferences, the *Rumeli v Kazakhstan* tribunal held that:

> In general, international tribunals have given full weight to circumstantial evidence. Two independent factors are considered by Arbitral Tribunals when assessing the weight that should be given to such evidence:
>
> - the first factor is the party's attitude in the proceedings. If a party, as was the case with Respondent, does not comply with its obligations, for instance by refusing to produce the requested documents and witnesses, the Arbitral Tribunal is authorized to draw adverse conclusions from the party's behavior. The same applies when witnesses manifestly lack independence, as was the case with those produced by Respondent;
> - the second factor is whether direct evidence of fact is unavailable. In this respect, the International Court of Justice decided in the *Corfu Channel* case that '[T]he other State [the claimant], the victim of a breach of international law, is often unable to furnish direct proof of facts giving rise to responsibility. Such a State should be allowed a more liberal recourse to inferences of facts and circumstantial evidence. This indirect evidence is admitted in all systems of law, and its use is recognized by international decisions.' In *AAPL v Sri Lanka*, an ICSID Arbitral Tribunal listed the international rules regarding evidence and concluded: 'Finally, in cases where proof of a fact presents extreme difficulty, a tribunal may thus be satisfied with less conclusive proof, i.e. prima facie evidence.'[143]

More recently, the *Lao Holdings v Laos* merits decision again expressly incorporated the *Corfu Channel* standard on record inferences as informative of its own decisionmaking.[144] The tribunal in *Mesa Power v Canada* in a procedural order outlined an approach that in substance followed the general international law on adverse inferences.[145]

2. Presumptions

General international law permits international courts and tribunals to find facts by reference to presumptions. The use of presumptions is one of the key

---

[143] *Rumeli Telekom AS v Kazakhstan*, ICSID Case No ARB/05/16, Award (29 July 2008) para 444 (footnotes omitted).

[144] *Lao Holdings NV v Lao People's Democratic Republic*, ICSID Case No ARB(AF)/12/6, Decision on Merits (10 June 2015) para 11.

[145] *Mesa Power Group LLC v Government of Canada*, UNCITRAL, PCA Case No 2012-17, Procedural Order (23 August 2013) para 29.

staples identified in Durward Sandifer's reference work on evidence before international courts and tribunals.[146] The ICJ continues to rely in its contemporary jurisprudence upon presumptions as part of its fact-finding process.[147]

The literature on international legal presumptions doctrinally split presumptions into two separate categories. The first category consists of presumptions based in applicable law.[148] One such famous presumption in municipal law is the presumption of innocence in criminal proceedings.[149] Such presumptions must be proved in the same way as any other rule of law before an international court or tribunal.

Second, international law recognises judicial presumptions. Judge Kreća in a separate opinion explained how such judicial presumptions operate as a matter of general international law:

> Judicial presumption, along with legal presumption, is one of the main sorts of presumption in international law. It means that a certain fact or state of affairs, even though it has not been proved, is taken by an international tribunal as truthful. As such it does not necessarily coincide with, or is not equivalent to, the fact or the state of affairs. As far as the reasoning of the existence of judicial presumption is concerned, considerations of a practical nature are prevalent. Judicial presumption is a weapon to avoid waiting to get to know precisely the facts and situation on which is dependent the existence, content or cessation of the right that would have adverse consequences for interested subjects or that would render difficult due course of legal proceedings.[150]

Investor-State arbitration follows general international law. Investor-State arbitration allows proof by presumption. One of these presumptions is the presumption in favour of the validity of domestic legal acts. As the *Paushok v Mongolia* tribunal elaborated:

> Every year, governments around the world propose the adoption of tax measures which constitute either new initiatives or amendments to existing fiscal legislation. There is a presumption of validity in favor of legislative measures adopted by a State

[146] Sandifer (n 27) 107, 142–143.

[147] *Case Concerning Land and Maritime Boundary between Cameroon and Nigeria (Cameroon v Nigeria: Equatorial Guinea intervening)* [2002] *ICJ Reports* 303, 340, presumption that parties determined the border; *Case Concerning the Frontier Dispute (Burkina Faso v Republic of Mali)* [1986] *ICJ Reports* 554, 579.

[148] Robert Kolb, *The Elgar Companion to the International Court of Justice* (Edward Elgar 2014) 241–243.

[149] François Quintard-Morénas, 'The Presumption of Innocence in the French and Anglo-American Legal Traditions' (2010) 58 *AJCL* 107, 140–141.

[150] *Case Concerning Legality of Use of Force (Serbia and Montenegro v United Kingdom)* (Separate Opinion of Judge ad hoc Kreća) [2004] *ICJ Reports* 1307, 1394, 1400–401.

> and the burden of the proof is upon those who challenge such measures to demonstrate their invalidity.[151]

This presumption, like others, is anchored in general international law. As Mojtaba Kazazi explained 'there are many precedents founding rebuttable presumptions on general principles of law such as ... regularity and validity of acts of sovereigns to international law'.[152]

B. Maturity in Investor-State Arbitration

The practice of investor-State tribunals has significantly advanced the state of the law on both inferences and presumptions to a point that it is possible codification and progressive development of a set of substantive rules followed by investor-State tribunals. As outlined below, this advancement of the law of inferences and presumptions remains fully consistent with the early common starting points for analysis between investor-State arbitration and general international law. It is therefore instructive for the codification and progressive development of general international law rules. Again, a full elaboration of the underlying codification effort is beyond the scope of this chapter. Instead, this section outlines the result of the work in question with a brief explanation of the salient rules on burden and standard of proof.

1. Inferences

The current practice of investor-State arbitration permits the formulation of three general rules governing the drawing of inferences in investor-State arbitration. To begin with, the current practice of such tribunals makes it possible to provide a more precise definition of what inferences are and how they are drawn. An inference is a finding of fact. It is premised not upon direct evidence or indirect, hearsay evidence that would establish the fact immediately. Instead, it finds the fact by inductive reasoning from context.[153] This is broadly consistent with the practice of other inter-State proceedings.[154]

---

[151] *Sergei Paushok, CJSC Golden East Company and CJSC Vostokneftegaz Company v Government of Mongolia,* UNCITRAL, Order on Interim Measures (2 September 2008) para 81. The author served as counsel for Mongolia in the proceedings.

[152] Mojtaba Kazazi, *Burden of Proof and Related Issues: A Study on Evidence before International Tribunals* (Brill 1996) 246.

[153] Sourgens et al (n 19) 295 (Evidentiary Principle §26(2)).

[154] See *Railway Land Arbitration (Malaysia v Singapore)*, PCA Case No 2012-1, Award (30 October 2014) para 132; *Frontier Dispute (Burkina Faso v Niger)* [2013] *ICJ Reports* 44, 90; *Case Concerning Sovereignty over Pedra Branca/Pulau Batu Puteh, Middle Rocks and South Ledge (Malaysia v Singapore)* [2008] *ICJ Reports* 12, 35.

Importantly, investor-State arbitrations are alive to the fact that more than one inductive inference can be drawn from context.[155] Each of these inferences can be reasonable on their face.[156] The fact of a person walking in from the outdoors in January in Kansas wearing an overcoat and folding a wet umbrella could support the conclusion that it is raining. It could also support the inference that it is snowing. Unless we were made aware of the alternative, reasonable inference, we would likely accept either explanation for the wet umbrella without great hesitation.

To account for the multiplicity of potential reasonable inferences from any given context, investor-State arbitration does not exclusively rely upon a reasonable inference test. Rather, investor-State tribunals draw inferences if they are plausible as opposed to if they are only reasonable.[157]

---

[155] See, e.g., *Rompetrol v Romania* (n 69) para 232; *Cambodia Power Co v Kingdom of Cambodia*, ICSID Case No ARB/09/18, Decision on Jurisdiction (22 March 2011) paras 82–83, 94–95; *Waguih Elie George Siag and Clorinda Vecchi v Arab Republic of Egypt*, ICSID Case No ARB/05/15, Award (1 June 2009) para 12; *Tokios Tokelès v Ukraine* (n 50) para 3; *Methanex Corporation v United States of America*, UNCITRAL (NAFTA), Final Award on Jurisdiction and Merits (3 August 2005) paras III.52–III.57; *CDC Group Public Ltd Co v Republic of Seychelles*, ICSID Case No ARB/02/14, Award (17 December 2003) paras 45–51; *Marvin Roy Feldman Karpa v United Mexican States*, ICSID Case No ARB(AF)/99/1, Dissenting Opinion of Jorge Covarrubias Bravo (3 December 2002) paras 32–37.

[156] Sourgens et al (n 19) 150–153.

[157] Ibid., 295 (Evidentiary Principle §28). See, e.g., *Rompetrol v Romania* (n 69) para 232:

> As to the coincidence in time, by contrast, the Tribunal would itself have inclined to the view that the thrust of the Talpes report, taken together with the bodies and authorities to whom it was in due course forwarded, made it more probable than not that there was a connection of some kind between the report and the initiation of the original investigation by the PNA into the Petromidia privatization. But even with that connection as the working hypothesis, it carries one nowhere, in the Tribunal's opinion …

Cambodia Power Co v Cambodia (n 155) paras 82–83, 94–95, setting out disputing views whether the inference could be drawn that multiple contracts formed part of a single transaction for purposes of consolidation under one consent to arbitration; *Siag v Egypt* (n 155) para 12, 'There was no real dispute as to the primary facts and the sequence of events relevant to the dispute as opposed to the inferences and legal conclusions to be drawn from those facts'; *Tokios Tokelès v Ukraine* (n 50) para 3, stating that the record was by and large clear but that the parties sought contradictory inferences as to the ultimate facts in dispute; *Methanex Corp v United States*, Final Award (n 154) paras III.52–III.57:

> The Tribunal can understand Methanex's conviction that all of these 'dots', if (i) they were to be taken as the only dots; (ii) they were to be accepted at face value as submitted by Methanex; and, moreover, (iii) they were carefully connected as Methanex proposes, would show that the 'real' reason Governor Davis enacted

As will be discussed in more detail below, this is an important point of distinction with general international law adjudication and arbitrations. It is far more typical that international adjudication simply looks to its preferred inference and defend it as reasonable than that it present multiple different inferences and determine which of these is most plausible. To provide one such example, the ICJ in *Burkina Faso v Mali* rejected an inference requested by Burkina Faso, which had submitted that the wording of a particular document drawn up by a relevant Geographical Service suggested the implication of a 'modification of the boundaries ... as previously fixed'.[158] The Court rejected this inference because it was 'obvious that the Geographical Service would not have been able to ascertain' relevant facts 'on the ground' because it admitted to lacking knowledge that would have been instrumental to forming a view about facts on the ground.[159] It continued to follow its own train of thought that:

> the fact that the Geographical Service found that the draft submitted to it did not correspond, for the points indicated, to the maps it had available, may mean that this draft made changes to the existing officialmaps; it does not warrant a finding that the legally-established boundaries were likewise altered.[160]

The use of 'obvious' by the Court suggests that it does not consider that a contrary view could reasonably be held.[161] This, however, tends to put conclusion before reasoning. There is nothing facially unreasonable about the suggestion that 'changes to existing official maps' intended to make changes to legally-established boundaries even in the face of a lack of knowledge of facts of the ground.

The plausibility of inferences measures which of multiple reasonable inferences is more likely the to be the case in light of the relevant context proved by the parties. In the ordinary course of events, a tribunal will look to five factors to determine which inference is plausible in any given circumstance. First, the tribunal will seek to establish how difficult it would be to prove the fact

---

> Executive Order D-5-99 was to favour ethanol and to harm Methanex and methanol. Methanex's difficulties, however, are manifold ... The Tribunal is not averse to trying to 'connect the dots' as a way of testing Methanex's hypothesis, but the dots Methanex has provided and which it affects to find so vivid, have all but faded into chiaroscuro in the course of this adversarial procedure ...

CDC Group v Seychelles (n 155) paras 45–51, discussing the inferences to be drawn from commercial conduct of the claimant; *Marvin Roy Feldman Karpa v Mexico* (n 155) paras 32–37, setting out both the disagreement within the tribunal and between the parties regarding the relevant inferences to be drawn from record evidence.

[158] *Frontier Dispute (Burkina Faso v Mali)* (n 154) 610

[159] Ibid.

[160] Ibid.

[161] Ibid.

by direct evidence.[162] The easier it is to prove the fact by direct evidence, the less likely a tribunal will be to draw any significant inference in favour of the party with the burden of proof. Second, the tribunal will need to determine how significant the inference is for the case. The more significant the inference, the stronger the inductive link between context and fact to be inferred will have to be.[163]

With these framework points in mind, tribunals then go about their task of establishing plausible inferences in much the same way. Tribunals establish whether the evidence submitted to them supports the finding of context facts.[164] In other words, is the evidence upon which an inference would be based credible in its own right? Importantly, this determination is a finding of fact in its own right, i.e., either a specific context does or does not exist. (The colleague did or did not walk into the room holding an umbrella.) Each of these contextual facts will then become the basis for the tribunal to draw specific inferences.

Once it is established that contextual evidence is credible in its own right, the tribunal tests the relative strength of the connection between the contextual fact and the rival inferences to be drawn.[165] The stronger the correlation between a contextual fact and the inference, the more plausible the inference. The fact that it is January is a contextual factor for the inference that it is snowing. In most places, it would not be a factor with a strong correlation to snow on any given day in January. The fact that a person is wearing sun glasses is a contextual factor for the inference that it is sunny outside. All else being equal, the wearing of sun glasses has a stronger correlation to sunshine than the fact that it is January to it snowing.

Fourth, inferences become more plausible the more different contextual factors independently supporting the same inference have been proved.[166] The fact that it is January does not of itself have a strong correlation with snowfall. The presence of a wet umbrella would itself weakly correlate to snow. But

---

[162] Sourgens et al (n 19) 295 (Evidentiary Principle §28(a)).

[163] Ibid. (Evidentiary Principle §28(e)); *Quasar de Valores SICAV SA et al v Russian Federation*, SCC Case No 24/2007, Award (20 July 2012) para 175; *Fraport v Philippines*, Award (n 114) paras 469–481.

[164] Sourgens et al (n 19) 295 (Evidentiary Principle §28(c)); *Marvin Roy Feldman Karpa v Mexico* (n 95) para 131, determining how to deal with a he-said-he-said situation of contradictory direct evidence; *Middle East Cement v Egypt* (n 95) para 94; *Tradex Hellas v Albania* (n 95) para 84; *AAPL v Sri Lanka* (n 21) para 56.

[165] Sourgens et al (n 19) 295 (Evidentiary Principle §28(b)); *SGS Société Générale de Surveillance SA v Republic of Paraguay*, ICSID Case No ARB/07/29, Decision on Jurisdiction (12 February 2010) para 6.

[166] Sourgens et al (n 19) 295 (Evidentiary Principle §28(d)); *Fireman's Fund v Mexico* (n 95) para 213.

the combination of both factors (wet umbrella in January) would significantly increase the plausibility of snowfall. On its own, it would overcome the evidence of the presence of sunglasses as evidence of sunshine as opposed to snowfall. Add a heavy overcoat, wet winter boots, and gloves and the correlation to snowfall would have been strengthened still further and so on.

The practice of investor-State tribunals also allows the drawing of inferences on the basis of party misconduct in the proceedings. Tribunals in doing so assess the severity of the misconduct, its relationship to the fact to be inferred (i.e., destruction of evidence relating to the wiring of funds to government officials), the procedural good faith of the party seeking the inference, the plausibility of the inference on the record without reference to the misconduct, and the overall significance of the inference.[167] Importantly, these factors already suggest that tribunals will draw record inferences if at all possible to avoid drawing adverse inferences.[168]

The finder of fact is unlikely to draw an adverse inference outright. In comparing the relative plausibility of the respective record inferences requested by the parties, the finder of fact takes into account whether the ultimate fact as to which a party requests an inference could have been easily proved in the ordinary course of events by that same party. If that same party destroyed evidence or otherwise engaged in procedural misconduct with regard to the inference in question, this misconduct will be weighed by the tribunal in the making of record inferences.[169] It thus explains how tribunals are sensitive to the procedural comportment of parties appearing before them without resorting to the admittedly heavy-handed tool of adverse inferences.

2. Presumptions

The current practice of investor-State arbitration permits the formulation of four general rules governing the use of presumptions in investor-State arbitration. Following general international law, investor-State arbitration follows the distinction between legal presumptions and juridical presumptions.[170] Investor-State tribunals have relied upon either type of presumption.[171]

---

[167] Sourgens et al (n 19) 295 (Evidentiary Principle §29).

[168] Ibid. (Evidentiary Principle §29(d)).

[169] See Steven Hammond, 'Spoliation in International Arbitration: Is It Time to Reconsider the 'Dirty Wars' of the International Arbitral Process?' (2009) 3 *Disp Resolution Int'L* 5; Peter Ashford, 'Document Production in International Arbitration' (2012) 10 *Loyola U Chicago ILR* 1, 9; see also *Lao Holdings NV v Lao People's Democratic Republic*, ICSID Case No ARB(AF)/12/6, Ruling on Motion to Amend the Provisional Measures Order (30 May 2014) para 70.

[170] Sourgens et al (n 19) 293 (Evidentiary Principle §13).

[171] Ibid.

Investor-State arbitration further has not established a hierarchy between these presumptions.[172]

Investor-State jurisprudence recognises legal presumptions. These presumptions are rules of the applicable law to be applied by the tribunal.[173] Although the applicable law governs the operation of these presumptions, investor-State tribunals treat legal presumptions as rebuttable as a default rule, meaning that a party would have to convince the tribunal that a presumption cannot be rebutted as a matter of applicable law.[174]

The use of a legal presumption by a tribunal is premised not upon a finding of fact, as such. Rather, the determination that a legal presumption is applicable is a matter of legal reasoning.[175] Its applicability must be proved in the same manner as any other legal rule is proved to the tribunal. Any failure by the tribunal to apply or not to apply a legal presumption thus would be reviewable as an *exces de pouvoir* in the same manner as any other failure in the application of law by the tribunal.[176]

Investor-State jurisprudence also routinely relies upon judicial presumptions. A juridical presumption rests upon a finding of a particular kind of fact: the existence of a habit, routine, or general practice or usage.[177] If the tribunal finds that such a habit, routine or general practice or usage applies, a party can submit that it acted consistently with the habit, routine or general practice or usage in question.[178] This finding by a tribunal is a finding of fact rather than

---

[172] Ibid. (Evidentiary Principle § 14). *Hussein Nuaman Soufraki v United Arab Emirates*, ICSID Case No ARB/02/7, Decision on the Application for Annulment (5 June 2007) paras 60–63; *Franck Charles Arif v Republic of Moldova*, ICSID Case No ARB/11/23, Award (8 April 2013) para 356, n 126; *Ambiente Ufficio SpA v Argentina* (n 77) para 318; *Tza Yap Shum v Republic of Peru*, ICSID Case No ARB/07/6, Decision on Jurisdiction and Competence (19 June 2009) para 63; *Ioan Micula v Romania* (n 82) para 87; *Waguih Elie George Siag and Clorinda Vecchi v Arab Republic of Egypt*, ICSID Case No ARB/05/15, Decision on Jurisdiction (11 April 2007) para 153.

[173] Sourgens et al (n 19) 293 (Evidentiary Principle §15(1)).

[174] Ibid. (Evidentiary Principle §15(2)).

[175] Ibid. (Evidentiary Principle §16(1)); *Soufraki v United Arab Emirates* (n 172) paras 60–63.

[176] Sourgens et al (n 19) 293 (Evidentiary Principle §16(2)).

[177] Ibid., 294 (Evidentiary Principle §20).

[178] Ibid. *Micula v Romania,* ICSID Case No ARB/05/20, Award (11 December 2013) para 673, addressing presumptions of regulatory stability by reference to reasonableness criteria; *Phoenix Action v Czech Republic* (n 80) para 127, looking to the practice of purchasing bankrupt companies to reorganize them for a profit to determine whether an investor had assumed risk; *CDC Group v Seychelles* (n 155) para 47, addressing the 'common practice of lenders in charging for time spent and expenses incurred in connection with the investigation and processing of applications for loans'; *Bridas SAPIC v Government of Turkmenistan*, Partial Award [1999] ICC-9058/FMS/

a matter of legal reasoning.[179] A tribunal therefore can act with the same discretion in making such findings of juridical presumptions as it can with regard to other evidence.[180]

Despite this broad discretion on the part of tribunals, the jurisprudence of investor-State tribunals nevertheless follows certain common factors in the finding of such juridical presumptions. In the first place, proof that a routine practice or habit is followed in the relevant industry will significantly strengthen the case for the application of a juridical presumption.[181] Second, the party relying upon the presumption will have to show that the circumstances at bar in fact fit within the scope of the routine or general practice.[182] Further, the party relying upon the presumption strengthens its case if it can show that it acted consistently with the routine practice openly towards its counterparty either during the making of the investment, in the course of performance of the investment transaction or in other contexts related to the investment.[183] Much like legal presumptions, juridical presumptions are rebuttable.[184]

Investor-State arbitration adds to general international law in important respects. The first such addition comes from the nature of dispute resolution in investor-State arbitration. The main form of investor-State arbitration, ICSID arbitration, makes available annulment proceedings as an option. ICSID annulments have in fact reviewed the use of presumptions as such.[185] It is thus one of the few fora in which such a review is in fact possible – and has in fact occurred.

Second, and as further discussed below, the frequency with which presumptions have entered investor-State dispute resolution is itself important. It provides an important critical mass of decisions on how presumptions can be

---

KGA, para 139, n 13, relying upon usage of trade to explain the good faith nature of a transaction structure.

[179] Sourgens et al (n 19) 294 (Evidentiary Principle §21(1)).

[180] Ibid. (Evidentiary Principle §21(2)).

[181] Ibid. (Evidentiary Principle §22(a)); *Joseph Charles Lemire v Ukraine*, ICSID Case No ARB/06/18, Award (28 March 2011) para 169: 'If it can be proven that in the normal cause of events a certain cause will produce a certain effect, it can be safely assumed that a (rebuttable) presumption of causality between both events exists, and that the first is the proximate cause of the other'. Cf. Klaus Peter Berger, *The Creeping Codification of the New Lex Mercatoria* (2nd edn, Kluwer 2010) 198–199.

[182] Sourgens et al (n 19) 293 (Evidentiary Principle §22(b)); *Burlington Resources Inc v Republic of Ecuador*, ICSID Case No ARB/08/5, Decision on Jurisdiction (2 June 2010) paras 327–329.

[183] Sourgens et al (n 19) 293 (Evidentiary Principle §22(c)–(e)).

[184] Ibid. (Evidentiary Principle §20(2)).

[185] *Soufraki v United Arab Emirates* (n 172) paras 60–63.

used and proved. This critical mass is itself helpful in further assessing how the proof of a presumption can be approached in other contexts.

Investor-State jurisprudence in addition has crystallised a number of legal presumptions of its own as that jurisprudence has matured that arose out of the specific, repeat fact-patterns it has encountered. These legal presumptions cover jurisdictional, merits, and remedies questions.[186] A complete list of these presumptions is beyond the scope of the current chapter. This transformation, however, seems to have combined the use of juridical presumptions in jurisprudence with an interpretive hardening of these juridical presumptions into the applicable legal instruments such as bilateral investment treaties. The willingness of tribunals to rely upon the earlier pronouncements by investor-state tribunals on juridical presumptions further suggests that the line between juridical and legal presumptions is a fluid one.

C. Informing Perspectives

The discussion above should readily showcase the value of investor-State arbitration for the further development or codification of the general international law of evidence. The development in investor-State arbitration permits a more granular understanding how tribunals draw inferences when applying general international law. The development of investor-State arbitration further provides a ready window into how a party can go about proving a presumption – and how new presumptions can arise through judicial or arbitral decisionmaking.

The utility of investor-State arbitration is particularly pronounced in the context of the plausibility rationale supporting the drawing of inferences at play in investor-State arbitration.[187] This rubric is superior to the general international law understanding of inferences as premised in their reasonableness.[188] It is further a superior mode of explaining jurisprudence of the ICJ requiring that an inference be the only reasonable inference from the record.[189] The plausibility analysis outlined above is more attuned to the fact that in most instances multiple inferences can reasonably be drawn from record facts. It thus provides a means to distinguish between the inferences in a more transparent and predictable fashion. And it does so in a manner that is largely consistent with the findings of fact by general international law tribunals.

---

[186] Sourgens et al (n 19) 293–294 (Evidentiary Principle §§ 17–19).
[187] Ibid., 150–153.
[188] Kazazi (n 152) 259; Sandifer (n 27) 154.
[189] *Genocide Case (Croatia v Serbia)* (n 32) 119.

The Croatian *Genocide* case against Serbia discussed above here serves as a good illustration.[190] That case stands for the problem of a reasonableness standard in the drawing of inferences. One should surmise that the standard employed by the Court for the drawing of inferences – that a fact must the only reasonably inference from the record – is a tacit admission.[191] The case concerned the question whether Serbian forces had genocidal intent. The tacit admission by the Court's adoption of its standard is that genocidal intent would be a reasonable inference a person could draw from the record. If such an inference were not possible, a lesser standard would have sufficed to resolve the factual question before the Court. The fact that the Court tacitly admitted to the multiplicity of reasonable inferences created a dilemma of how to choose between the different reasonable candidates. The Court's standard apparently would return us to the burden of proof – i.e., the party that submits a fact must prove that it is the existence of the fact in question is the only reasonable inference from the record. This standard, however, simply creates an absurdity: it would mean that in most any case in which the parties are represented by competent counsel, proof by inference would be unavailable. All a party would have to do to frustrate the drawing of an inference would be that a different inference could also be drawn from the record. As proof would then return to a question of burdens, courts would have to find for the non-moving party in all instances.

The Croatian *Genocide* case highlights that this not how the ICJ approaches the drawing of inferences vel non. Rather, the Court was keenly aware of the relative strengths of the different inferences in light of the overall record evidence.[192] It appears to have made its findings upon this relative appraisal of strength of the different alternatives.[193]

The importance of this difference in approach cannot be overstated. The Court did not find that Serbia may have had genocidal intent but that such an inference was technically improper due to the operation of the international law of evidence.[194] This, however, would have been the logical result of the application of the Court's announced standard. Rather, the Court made the stronger finding that all things considered Serbia lacked the intent in question because it was on the whole more plausible that Serbia acted without such intent than with it.[195] The Court's findings strove to do material justice in the context of a complex record. It did not abdicate its responsibility to do so on

---

190 Ibid.
191 Ibid.
192 Ibid., 119–127.
193 Ibid.
194 Ibid., 119.
195 Ibid., 119–127.

the basis of a technical invocation of the rules governing the law of proof. In other words, the plausibility analysis is both a better explanation of the Court's own analysis and a better result for international justice itself. Rather than being dependent upon unyielding technicality, international justice can adapt to the circumstances and make difficult factual determinations with eyes wide open.

The plausibility analysis further permits finders of fact to bring their procedural concerns to bear when drawing record inferences. This has multiple advantages. To begin with, this approach permits one to explain in doctrinally coherent terms what counsel already suspect: procedural misconduct matters even if it is not the formal basis for decision in an arbitral award. By providing a doctrinally sound explanation how and why finders of fact are permitted to bear procedural comportment in mind, the plausibility analysis gets away from the appearance of tribunal subterfuge or insincerity. More importantly still, it provides a more precise instrument for the consideration of procedural misconduct in the drawing of inferences as it embeds procedural (mis)conduct in a specific context. It can thus better distinguish between important and collateral misconduct in the fact-finding process.

The plausibility analysis is likely to influence how general international law fact finders will go about their missions. As general international law disputes become increasingly complex, the rival requests for inferences before international courts and tribunals is likely to increase. This means that international courts and tribunals will need a more nuanced tool for the drawing of inferences than an analysis of their reasonableness alone. Investor-State arbitration has provided just such a tool by the repeated refinement in investor-State jurisprudence of inferential proof.

In the context of presumptions, the jurisprudence of investor-State tribunals further provides a ready means to identify how such presumptions can be proved. This is particularly helpful in the context of judicial presumptions, which are part of the broader fact-finding mission of the tribunal.[196] The factors identified in the context of investor-State arbitration will necessarily have to be adapted to the general international law context – the factors identified in the context of investor-State disputes are embedded in the investor-State relationship. General international law does not govern an investor-State relationship, but rather a State-to-State relationship.

Despite this difference in context, the factors identified in the context of investor-State disputes should be readily translatable to the State-to-State context. Rather than relying upon a particular custom in an industry, such judicial presumptions would look to usages in State-to-State conduct. These

196 Kolb (n 148) 241–243.

usages are not customary international law – the usages in question do not occur due to a sense of legal compulsion. Rather, they describe the manner in which the relevant State-to-State business is normally conducted as a matter of convenience. Similarly, when such a custom would be the basis for a presumption, it will be important to query whether the exchange at bar would ordinarily have been governed by the usage in question. Finally, past instances of such usage *inter partes* will provide further indicia of reliability for the use of a judicial presumption in the case at bar. In other words, the factors identified in investor-State arbitration are flexible and can be moved from context to context.

As even general international law comes to incorporate an ever-greater scope of relationships, evidence of this flexibility is important. The ICJ is no longer tasked with sitting exclusively over disputes in which the facts of the dispute is confined to diplomatic or military exchanges between sovereigns. Rather, the Court is tasked with resolving factual disputes that involve different relationships between States or quasi-State actors on the one hand and individuals on the other in the context of diplomatic protection claims, human rights claims, and, sadly, claims relating to the prevention of the crime of genocide.[197] In each of these settings, key fact gathering will inevitably have to rely upon judicial presumptions as proof of each element of the underlying dispute by discrete evidence will be close to impossible. The fact that investor-State arbitration has relied upon adaptable features to prove judicial presumptions – adaptable features that are context sensitive – provides a means to divine how judicial presumptions could be proved in these other, non-traditional contexts of the application of general international law.

On a more critical note, however, the development of presumptions – and particularly the hardening of judicial into legal presumptions through jurisprudence – suggests that fact-finding might suffer from a certain degree of fragmentation across different dispute resolution bodies. Nascent legal presumptions in investor-State arbitration may clash with presumptions established in the State-to-State context. It is in this context interesting that the Court has actively sought to avoid such clashes in the context of *Yugoslav* cases in which the ICTY made relevant findings to a dispute at bar before the Court.[198] Such attempts at harmonisation are less likely to succeed when the Court hears a case, in which a presumption is potentially applicable but in which a sister court or tribunal has not ruled on related facts. This difference in context is likely to bring out the different policy prerogatives of the sister courts and tribunals and therefore lead to a potential clash between presumptions.

[197] *Genocide Case (Croatia v Serbia)* (n 32) 121.

[198] Ibid., 126–127.

In the inevitable future instances of a clash, it will be important to return to the underlying functional basis for the use of presumptions in the first place to overcome this spectre of fragmentation – the principle of good faith. This use of the principle of good faith to 'defragment' fact-finding poses its own challenges that are beyond the scope of this chapter. The fact that investor-State arbitration raises this issue, however, again supports the view that investor-State arbitration will be instrumental in the future development of general international law: investor-State arbitration poses a question that general international law will need grapple with and answer.

IV. CONCLUSION

This chapter has outlined the case why general international lawyers interested in the law of evidence should play close attention to investor-State arbitration, which has provided a fertile ground for the codification of rules of evidence from a consistent and steady flow of precedent. This flow of precedent is premised upon a reception and an interpretation of the same general international law starting points that inform decisionmaking before other international courts and tribunals. The solutions that investor-State arbitration has been able to provide further are such as to improve transparency, predictability, and thus the quality of justice available before its bar.

As the ILC continues its work on the law of evidence, it is therefore quite likely that investor-State arbitration will provide a helpful point of comparison and development for general international law. The ILC naturally will have a far greater scope of work than an investor-State scholar or practitioner. But there is reason to believe that this greater scope will only tend to confirm that the solutions generated in investor-State arbitration will prove useful in other settings. The problems of proof encountered in investor-State arbitration are hardly unique to its field. And the abilities of a tribunal to get at the truth in investor-State arbitration are no more capacious or less capacious than they are in other international contexts.

In one thing the ILC can most certainly take heart. The task it has set for itself is indeed achievable. The law of evidence and the process of proof is amenable to codification and progressive development. As the ILC sets about this work, the Commission can further infuse a needed normative vision of what international justice should serve and how processes of proof can support this mission. But this normative vision need not stand in for the wisdom of practice. Practice is indeed abundant. And – though at the edges subject to reform through calm, common-sense reflection – practice is sound.

APPENDIX – EVIDENTIARY PRINCIPLES IN INVESTOR-STATE ARBITRATION[1]

Part I – The Burden of Proof

§1 Actori Inucumbit Onus Probandi

(1) Either party asserting a fact in order to establish an element of a claim, counter-claim, affirmative defence or propriety of a remedy must:

   a. present admissible, relevant and material direct evidence to support such assertion;
   b. present admissible, relevant and material circumstantial evidence sufficient to support such assertion;
   c. sustain that sufficient evidence has been submitted to support an inference of the truth of the assertion, or
   d. sustain that a presumption renders proof of the fact in question by admissible, relevant and material evidence unnecessary.

(2) A finding by the arbitral tribunal that a party failed to present such evidence or sustain the applicability of a presumption entails that the event or occurrence submitted as a fact did not take place.

§2 Burden of Proof and Jurisdiction

(1) The party invoking the jurisdiction of the tribunal must submit evidence that, if unrebutted, would meet the standard of proof to establish jurisdiction.

(2) At the jurisdictional stage, the party invoking the jurisdictional of the tribunal further must plead, but not prove, sufficient facts to assert a claim for which relief may be granted it (the pro tem rule).

(3) The party objecting to jurisdiction may introduce evidence to rebut the jurisdictional submission.

(4) The party objecting to jurisdiction may not introduce evidence at the jurisdictional stage that would rebut only merits submissions advanced by the claimant.

(5) The party objecting to jurisdiction bears the burden of proof as set out in §1 with regard to its jurisdictional submissions made pursuant to point (3) above.

§3 Burden of Proof Merits and Remedies

(1) The party seeking a remedy must submit evidence that, if unrebutted, would meet the relevant standard of proof that the remedy requested is appropriate.

(2) The party seeking damages must submit evidence that, if unrebutted, would meet the relevant standard of proof that the remedy requested is not speculative.

(3) The respondent may submit evidence to rebut submissions made by its opponent pursuant to sub-sections (1) and (2).

(4) The respondent bears the burden of proving its submission pursuant to sub-section (3).

---

[1] First published in Sourgens et al (n 19) 291ff.

Part II – The Standard of Proof

§4 Free Evaluation of Evidence

(1) Subject to this Part, the arbitral tribunal has discretion in determining the standard of proof to be applied to any specific type of allegation.
(2) The arbitral tribunal must exercise its discretion in good faith such that its decisions are
  a. consistent and appropriate;
  b. respect the equality of the parties; and
  c. otherwise conform with natural justice.
(3) The following factors guide the arbitral tribunal in its evaluation of evidence:
  a. the gravity of the charge advanced by the party with the burden of proof;
  b. the quantity of evidence submitted by the party with the burden of proof;
  c. the materiality of evidence submitted by the party with the burden of proof;
  d. the quantity of evidence submitted in rebuttal;
  e. the materiality of evidence submitted in rebuttal;
  f. the availability of direct evidence.

§5 The Balance of Probabilities

The arbitral tribunal must determine in its inner conviction that the party with the burden of proof has submitted evidence sufficient to establish that its contention is more probable than not unless a heightened standard of proof applies.

§6 Heightened Standard of Proof

(1) The arbitral tribunal may apply a higher standard of proof than balance of the probabilities to make determinations of particular gravity.
(2) The arbitral tribunal must not apply a standard of proof that allegations have been proved beyond a reasonable doubt.

Part III – Direct and Circumstantial Evidence

§7 Preference for Direct Evidence

(1) The arbitral tribunal when possible shall make findings of fact by means of direct evidence.
(2) Direct evidence is testimony or documentary proof immediately and directly relevant to the establishment of a fact without aid or any intervening fact or process.

§8 Credibility as Criterion for Direct Evidence

(1) To support the finding of a fact on the basis of direct evidence, the arbitral tribunal must determine the evidence to be credible.
(2) The arbitral tribunal has discretion to make credibility findings.

§9 Circumstantial Evidence (Hearsay)

(1) A tribunal may make findings of fact premised upon hearsay evidence.
(2) In the investor-state arbitration context, hearsay evidence is a statement made by a declarant not subject to cross-examination submitted for the truth of the matter asserted.
(3) To the extent an arbitral tribunal relies upon hearsay evidence, I tmust corroborate the hearsay evidence in question with other direct or indirect evidence or by way of an inference.
(4) To the extent credible direct evidence is available, an arbitral tribunal must not rely upon hearsay evidence to contradict the direct evidence in question.

Part IV – Shifting Burden of Evidence

§10 Shifting the Burden of Evidence

A submission by a party of sufficient evidence to meet its burden and standard of proof with regard to a specific fact, claim, or contention shifts the burden of evidence to its opponent.

§11 Rebuttal of Shifted Burdens of Evidence

In order to contest the point in issue, the party to whom the burden of evidence has been shifted must submit further evidence in rebuttal.

§12 Burden of Evidence and Burden of Proof

Shifting of the burden of evidence does not disturb the burden of proof.

Part V – Presumptions

§13 Presumptions in General

(1) The arbitral tribunal may make findings of fact premised upon presumptions consistent with applicable standards of proof.
(2) Use of a presumption means that a fact is supported by general practices and circumstances beyond the specific project at issue in the dispute due to the applicability of a:

    a. Legal presumption; or
    b. Judicial presumption.

§14 Types and Hierarchy of Presumptions

Presumptions may be either legal presumptions or judicial presumptions.

§15 Legal Presumptions (*Praesumptiones iuris*)

(1) A legal presumption is a norm that assumes that certain facts are established in a given situation as a matter of applicable law.

(2) Unless expressly displaced by a rule of applicable law, a legal presumption is rebuttable.

§16 Proof of Legal Presumptions

(1) An arbitral tribunal's determination of the existence of a legal presumption constitutes a legal ruling that a rule of relevant applicable law exists in contradistinction to a finding of fact.

(2) Proof of a legal presumption is reviewable as a manifestex cess of power in the arbitral tribunal's application of the law.

§17 Rebuttable Legal Presumptions Reflected in Investor-State Jurisprudence on Jurisdiction

Investor-state arbitral tribunals have in the past recognised the following legal presumptions in the jurisdictional context:

a. official home state certification of the nationality of a natural person entails the rebuttable presumption that the natural person has the nationality in question;

b. registration in the shareholder registry of a juridical person entails the rebuttable presumption that the person so registered is the owner of the shares;

c. roof of majority ownership of a juridical person entails the rebuttable presumption of control by the majority owner over the juridical person;

d. proof of effective control over a juridical person at a certain point in time entails the rebuttable presumption that effective control was continuous;

e. proof that an investment was made entails the rebuttable presumption that the investment contrib- uted to the host state's economy; and

f. submission without more of the text of a standard most-favoured-nations clause entails the rebuttable presumption that the clause was not intended to apply to dispute resolution provisions.

§18 Rebuttal Legal Presumptions Reflected in Investor-State Jurisprudence on the Merits

Investor-state arbitral tribunals have in the past recognised the following legal presumptions:

a. proof of an official government act entails the rebuttable presumption that the act was valid as amatter of host state law;
b. proof that the investment was made in a specific regulatory environment without more entails the rebuttable presumption that the regulatory environment was subject to reasonable change;
c. proof that otherwise comparable investors received disparate treatment entails the rebuttable presumption that the host state discriminated between them;
d. proof that a legal instrument was made on a certain date entails the rebuttable presumption that it was not intended to have retroactive effect; and
e. submission without more of the text of an exceptions clause entails the rebuttable presumption that the clause is not self-judging.

§19 Rebuttable Legal Presumptions Reflected in Investor-State Jurisprudence on Remedies

Investor-state arbitral tribunals have in the past recognised in the remedies context that the submission of audited financial statements gives to the rebuttable presumption that the financial information included in the statements is accurate and reliable.

§20 Judicial Presumptions (*Praesumptiones hominis*)

(1) A judicial presumption is an assumption that as a matter of fact, the facts of the given case follow habitual, routine, or general practices applicable to the transactions, circumstances, or relationships in question.
(2) Unless expressly displaced by a rule of applicable law, a judicial presumption is rebuttable.

§21 Proof of Judicial Presumptions

(1) An arbitral tribunal's determination of the existence of a judicial presumption constitutes a finding of fact.
(2) An arbitral tribunal has discretion to make such a finding consistent with the principles of evidence governing proof of facts.

§22 Factors Relevant in Establishing Judicial Presumptions

In determining whether a judicial presumption should be established, the following circumstances are significant:

a. Evidence of a general usage, custom, or practice in the relevant industry;
b. Relationship between the transaction and the general usage,custom or practice;
c. Statements made by the parties during negotiations or prior to the making of the investment;
d. Evidence of past conduct by one or both of the parties consistent with the proposed presumption; and
e. The course of performance between the parties.

Part VI – Judicial Notice and Iura Novit Curia

§23 Judicial Notice as Permissible Means to Supplement the Record

Subject to the rules of natural justice, the arbitral tribunal may on its own motion or upon application of one the parties supplement the record by means of judicial notice.

§24 Instances in Which Judicial Notice May Be Taken

Judicial notice is appropriate when facts are so well known or can be so accurately and easily established by reference to authoritative sources as not to be subject to reasonable doubt.

§25 Iura Novit Curia

Arbitral tribunals know the law without need of additional proof or submission by the parties if:

a. the rule of law in question is a general rule of international law and central to the arbitral tribunal's ability to administer its arbitral function; or
b. the tribunal can take judicial notice of the rule in question.

Part VII – Inferences

§26 Inferences in General

(1) The arbitral tribunal may make findings of fact by means of inferences.
(2) An inference is a conclusion made in the absence of sufficient direct or indirect and probative evidence that as a matter of plausibility, a fact nevertheless must have occurred or circumstance must be the case in light of other relevant record evidence and party conduct in the arbitral proceedings.
(3) The plausibility of an inference is governed by the same standard of proof as the proof of the relevant fact or circumstance by direct or indirect evidence.
(4) An arbitral tribunal must give all parties a reasonable opportunity to comment upon a proposed inference.

§27 Inferences Outside of the Merits Context

Consistent with applicable standards of proof, the arbitral tribunal has the power to draw inferences in every context.

§28 Factors Relevant in Drawing Inferences

In determining whether an inference is made plausible by other record evidence, the following circumstances are significant:

a. the difficulty of proving the fact by direct evidence;
b. the relationship between the inference to be drawn and the fact proved by direct evidence;
c. the strength of direct evidence supporting the inference;
d. the number of different pieces of proof supporting the same inference;
e. the significance of the inference for the satisfaction of the requisite standard of proof.

§29 Inferences Arising from the Misconduct of the Parties in Arbitral Proceedings

(1) The arbitral tribunal is empowered to draw adverse inferences from party misconduct in the arbitration.
(2) In determining whether an inference is made plausible by the conduct of one of the parties to the arbitral proceedings, the following circumstances are significant:
   a. the severity of the party's misconduct in the arbitral proceedings;
   b. the relationship between them is conduct and the fact to be proved by means of an inference;
   c. the procedural good faith of the party seeking the inference;
   d. the plausibility of the same inference from the record absent considerations of party misconduct;
   e. the overall significance of the requested inference.

Part VIII – Exclusionary Rules of Evidence

§30 Exclusionary Rules in General

(1) The arbitral tribunal as master of the taking of evidence in the arbitral proceedings may take guidance in the exclusion of evidence from the IBA Rules on the Taking of Evidence in International Arbitration.
(2) Typically, the exclusion of evidence is warranted in investor-state arbitration in three limited categories of circumstances
   a. when its inclusion would violate another party's right to be heard;
   b. when its inclusion would violate the equality of the parties;or
   c. when its inclusion would violate fundamental principles of international public policy.

§31 Burden of Proof regarding Exclusion of Evidence

The party requesting that evidence be excluded from the record carries the burden of proof to establish a basis for the exclusion of the evidence in question.

§32 Privilege in General

(1) An arbitral tribunal may exclude evidence from the record to the extent the evidence in question is covered by privilege.
(2) An arbitral tribunal in its discretion may take action other than the exclusion of evidence to protect the privilege interests of the parties. Other actions may include:
   a. Redactions;
   b. In camera review;
   c. Review by an independent expert; or
   d. Other similar mechanisms intended to protect the privacy interest of the party invoking the privilege as well as the evidentiary interest of the party seeking disclosure or admission.

§33 Applicable Law and Privilege

To determine whether to exclude evidence on the basis of privilege, the municipal law governing the party, the municipal law governing the asserted privilege, and international law and practice recognising a privilege are relevant.

§34 Types of Privileges

(1) Privileges that have been asserted in investor-state arbitration are:
  a. Attorney-client privilege;
  b. Work product privilege;
  c. Privilege of communications with in house counsel;
  d. Cabinet privilege; and
  e. Secrecy of ongoing investigations.

(2) Tribunals may recognise other privileges consistent with applicable law and investor-state tribunal practice.

§35 Factors Relevant to Privileges in General

Factors relevant in the context of excluding evidence on the ground of privilege are the need of excluding the evidence in question:

a. to permit a party to be meaningfully represented in legal proceedings or instructuring transactions,
b. to permit a party to solicit and receive unbiased advice in internal decisionmaking,
c. legitimate expectations of privacy by the party claiming the privilege recognised by municipal law or international law,
d. prior conduct by a party in consistent with the claim of privilege, and
e. the recognition of a privilege with regard to similar communications of the other party by the tribunal at an earlier stage of the proceedings.

§36 Attorney Client Privilege

(1) The arbitral tribunal may exclude evidence falling under the attorney-client relationship or informa- tion or evidence derived therefrom.

(2) Communications between natural persons or juridical persons and their attorney are privileged under attorney-client privilege when the communications in question arise
  a. to seek legal advice without interference, or
  b. to advance a legal claim without interference.

(3) The privilege extends to communications with third parties acting as agents for attorney if:
  a. the agents act to facilitate the provision of legal advice by the attorney; and
  b. the communications were made pursuant to the broader agency relationship.

§37 Work Product Privilege

(1) The arbitral tribunal may exclude evidence falling under the work product privilege or evidence derived therefrom.

(2) Documents are work product when they are created in anticipation of and for the purpose of preparing for litigation or arbitration.

§38 Privilege of Communications with In House Counsel

A tribunal may exclude evidence generated by in house counsel or other evidence derived therefrom if it determines that the recognition of an in-house privilege is appropriate as a matter of applicable law.

§39 Cabinet Privilege

(1) Documents the release of which would compromise the national security of the host state constitute state secrets and are privileged as such.
(2) Evidence arising from deliberative and policy making processes at high levels of government ar eprivileged to the extent the government's interest in confidentiality outweighs the public interest of disclosure.
(3) Claims for cabinet privilege must be pled with specificity.

§40 Secrecy of Ongoing Investigations

In addition to the privileges in §§41–44, jurisprudence has recognised a privilege of secrecy of ongoing investigations to the extent the government's interest in confidentiality outweighs the materiality of the evidence in light of the claims raised in the arbitration proceedings.

§41 Waiver of Privilege

(1) Privilege is waived by the purposeful disclosure of privileged documents or information.
(2) A party may limit waiver upon showing of good cause that the disclosure was inadvertent.

§42 Confidentiality

(1) A tribunal may choose to exclude evidence from the record even if the evidence in question is not covered by privilege to the extent that the legitimate confidentiality interests of the party opposing the introduction of evidence into the record significantly outweigh the probative value of the evidence.
(2) An arbitral tribunal in its discretion may take action other than the exclusion of evidence to protect the confidentiality interests of the parties. Other actions may include:
    a. Redactions;
    b. In camera review;
    c. Review by an independent expert; or
(3) Other similar mechanisms intended to protect the privacy interest of the party invoking confidentiality as well as the evidentiary interest of the party seeking disclosure or admission.

§43 Factors Relevant to Confidentiality in General

Factors relevant in the context of excluding evidence on the ground of confidentiality are:

a. the potential probative value of the evidence,
b. the materiality of the evidence to core factual issues in dispute between the parties,
c. legitimate expectations of privacy by the party asserting confidentiality,
d. the potential harm suffered by the party opposing introduction of evidence into the record should the evidence be made public, and
e. the efficacy of alternative means to protecting the respective interests of the parties.

§44 Commercial & Technical Confidentiality

(1) A tribunal may exclude documents or passages from documents on the basis of commercial, as well as technical confidentiality.
(2) Commercial and technical confidentiality interests may be established on the basis of:
  a. municipal law; or
  b. industry practice,usage, or custom.

§45 Instances of Commercial Confidentiality Recognised in Jurisprudence

Subject to the factors outlined in §43, investor-state arbitral tribunals have in the past recognised the following types of evidence to give rise to commercial confidentiality interests:

a. Bid documents
b. Pricing and costing information
c. Marketing planning data
d. Strategic planning data
e. Market share data and
f. Internal accounting or financial records.

§46 Instances of Technical Confidentiality Recognized in Jurisprudence

Subject to the factors outlined in §43, investor-state arbitral tribunals have in the past recognised the following types of evidence to give rise to commercial confidentiality interests:

a. Testing data and other information underlying patent applications
b. Location, depths and angles of drillholes
c. Metal assays and other analysis from drill cores
d. Coordinates, elevation, azimuth, inclination and total depth of different samples taken from drillcore
e. Three dimensional modelling in the extractive industries; and
f. Maps generated as a result of explorative activities.

§47 Other Confidentiality Interests

(1) Arbitral tribunals may protect confidentiality interests other than commercial or technical information.
(2) Subject to the factors outlined in §43, jurisprudence has recognized the following instances of additional confidentiality interests:
  a. Confidential governmental communications
  b. Medical records.

§48 Exclusion of Evidence Threatening a Party's Right to Be Heard

Arbitral tribunals may exclude evidence the submission into the record of which would threaten its opponents right to be heard.

§49 Exclusion of Evidence Submitted Outside the Ordinary Course

(1) Arbitral tribunals may exclude evidence if it is proffered outside of the ordinary course of proceedings as set out in the arbitral tribunal's procedural orders.
(2) Factors relevant to the exclusion of evidence as untimely are
 a. Availability of the evidence at an earlier stage;
 b. Materiality of the evidence;
 c. The conduct of the parties in making discovery of the evidence onerous or time consuming;
 d. Ability to cross-examine witnesses relevant to the new evidence;
 e. Ability to comment during the ordinary course of the proceedings; and
 f. Feasibility of permitting comment or cross-examination in an expeditious manner with a few to rendering an award or decision in a reasonable time after the close of the hearing.

§50 Exclusion of Evidence Threatening the Equality of Arms Between the Parties

Arbitral tribunals may exclude evidence the submission into the record of which would threaten the equality of the arms between the parties.

§51 Exclusion of Evidence to Protect Fundamental Principles of International Public Policy

Arbitral tribunals may exclude evidence the submission into the record if the evidence was obtained in a manner that is inconsistent with fundamental principles of international public policy.

Part IX – Documents and Document Production

§52 Taking of Evidence by the Tribunal in General

The arbitral tribunal is the master of the procedural organisation of the taking of written evidence and evidence at the hearing subject to the principles below.

§53 Document Defined

(1) Investor-state tribunals have followed the definition of 'document' as provided by the IBA Rules on the Taking of Evidence (2010).
(2) Consequently, 'document' means 'means a writing, communication, picture, drawing, program or data of any kind, whether recorded or maintained on paper or by electronic, audio, visual or any other means'. (IBA Rules on Evidence, Definition.)

§54 Contemporaneous Documents

(1) Documents generated contemporaneously with the events to which they pertain are prima facie more reliable in their description of those events than statements

generated at a later point in time by persons affiliated with the party benefited by the evidence in the proceedings.

(2) Other evidence, such as non-contemporaneous documents or witness or expert testimony, serves to:
   a. Complete the record for facts as to which no such contemporaneous documents exist;
   b. Provide further context for the contemporaneous documents; or
   c. Contest the probative value of the contemporaneous documents submitted by the opposing party.

§55 Translation of Documents

(1) The arbitral tribunal is tasked to determine the official language of the proceedings at the outset of the arbitration consistent with the consent instrument and applicable arbitral and institutional rules.

(2) Documents in a language other than the official language of the proceedings must be translated, in whole or in part, by the party submitting the document.

(3) In determining whether a document requires translation in full or in part, the arbitral tribunal may take into account:
   a. The length of the document;
   b. The cost of translation;
   c. The relevance of the document as a whole to the portion of the document relied upon by the party submitting it.

§56 Authenticity of Documents

(1) Unless challenged by a party, the authenticity of documents is presumed by the arbitral tribunal.

(2) A party challenging the authenticity of a document may for good cause or against placement of security request inspection of an original of the document in question.

(3) In determining contested authenticity, arbitral tribunals may consider factors including:
   a. Signatures;
   b. Ink and printing processes;
   c. Paper stock;
   d. Seals and stamps.

(4) In non-paper media, other factors relevant to the medium in question apply by analogy.

§57 Requests for Production of Documents in General

(1) Arbitral tribunals limit the production of documents to requests that do not seek evidence in the hope of uncovering material to serve as a foundation for an argument not yet formally advanced in the arbitration.

(2) A party requesting production of documents bears the burden to prove that production of the document(s) requested should be ordered.

§58 Request to Produce

(1) Document production begins with a request to produce documents. The request to produce must state:
   a. The relevance of the document(s) requested to be produced;
   b. The materiality of the document(s) requested to be produced;
   c. Identify relevance of the document(s) requested to be produced narrowly and with specificity;
   d. State why production would not impose an unreasonable burden on the producing party; and
   e. State the basis upon which the requesting party has determined that the document(s) are likely to be in the possession, custody, or control of the party of whom the request is made.

(2) The party of whom production is requested may accede to the request without objection, object to production, or produce responsive documents while lodging an objection. An objection to production may:
   a. Argue that the party requesting production has failed to meet its burden with regard to formulating the reasons set out in (1)(a)–(e); or
   b. Assert that the documents requested fall within one of the exclusionary rules in §§30–51;

(3) The party requesting production may be allowed to respond to objections by reformulating its requests or otherwise address any arguments newly raised under §56(2)(b).

(4) The arbitral tribunal in its discretion will resolve any remaining disputes between the parties by ordering production of documents as requested, denying the request, or ordering production of a narrower set of documents than requested.

(5) An order to produce documents by the arbitral tribunal imposes a duty upon the party so ordered diligently to search for the document(s) at issue in the order, produce the documents within the time limit set by the tribunal, or report that the documents requested do not exist or could not be located following a diligent search.

(6) Parties remain under continuing obligation to supplement their production of documents if they become aware of documents responsive to requests as to which they have been ordered to make production or as to which they have not raised an objection following their original production of documents consistent with the arbitral tribunal's procedural orders.

§59 The Request must be Relevant to the Case

(1) A document is relevant if a reasonable arbitrator could conclude that the document renders a fact contested between the parties more or less probable to have occurred.

(2) An arbitral tribunal's assessment of relevance during the document production phase is without prejudice to its ultimate conclusion on the relevance of evidence to its ultimate decision on disputed facts in the arbitral proceedings.

§60 The Request must be Material to the Outcome

(1) A document is material to the outcome of the dispute if it is particularly probative of a disputed issue of fact.

(2) In determining materiality, an arbitral tribunal may consider:

a. The quantity of other available evidence to support or weaken the factual assertion to which the document is relevant;

b. The prima facie quality of the evidence in supporting or weakening the factual assertion to which the document is relevant; and

c. The importance of the factual assertion, if proved or disproved, to the dispute as a whole.

(3) An arbitral tribunal's assessment of materiality during the document production phase is without prejudice to its ultimate conclusion on the relevance of evidence to its ultimate decision on disputed facts in the arbitral proceedings

§61 The Request must be Narrow and Specific

(1) The request of a single document stating a date, author, and subject matter is narrow and specific.

(2) Arbitral tribunals assess the narrowness and specificity of requests for the production of classes of document by reference:

a. to the detail with which the subject-matter is identified;

b. the date range with regard to which the request would require a diligent search of responsive documents;

c. the identification of authors and recipients of the documents; and

d. the custodians of the documents believed currently to havepossession, custody, or control of the documents.

§62 The Request Must Not Impose an Unreasonable Burden on the Producing Party

In determining the reasonable burden, a party may be asked to bear in responding to requests for document production, the following factors may be relevant

a. the general availability of the class of documents requested to the party making the request;

b. the expense of conducting a diligent search for responsive documents;

c. the materiality of responsive documents;

d. the placement in issue of a fact to which responsive documents would be material by the party of which production is requested; and

e. a comparison of the respective burdens of production of the parties to the arbitration.

§63 Belief that the Documents are in Possession, Custody, or Control of Documents Requested

(1) A requesting party must assert a basis for its reasonable belief that the documents requested are in the possession, custody, or control of the party of which it requests production.
(2) A party may discharge its burden to state such a reasonable belief by reference to other record evidence permitting the inference that the documents requested existed and were under the power of the party of which production is requested.
(3) A party may further discharge its burden by reference to judicial presumptions with regard to classes of documents kept in the ordinary course by entities like the one of which production is requested.

§64 Privilege Logs and Appointment of Experts

(1) A party withholding otherwise responsive documents from its production may, at the tribunal's discretion, identify the documents so withheld and the basis in law for its exclusion from production in a log.
(2) The log must be transmitted consistent with the arbitral tribunal's procedural orders to the party requesting production of documents.
(3) The requesting party may object to the exclusion of documents from production by challenging the legal basis stated in the log.
(4) The arbitral tribunal may resolve the dispute by:
    a. Reviewing the log and the objection to the log by the requesting party;
    b. Reviewing the log, the objection to the log, as well as the document at issue in camera;
    c. Delegating its authority to resolve the party's dispute regarding the exclusion of certain documents from production to a tribunal-appointed expert.

§65 Failure to Comply with Document Production Obligations

The arbitral tribunal may take the failure of a party to comply with its document production obligations into account when drawing adverse inferences pursuant to §29.

Part X - Witnesses

§66 Purpose of Witness Testimony

Parties may rely upon witnesses in order to:
a. testify to facts that cannot be established upon the basis of documentary evidence;
b. impeach the authenticity, credibility, or significance of record evidence proffered by the other side; and
c. provide further context for record.

§67 Evidence-in-Chief, Defined

The direct testimony of a witness constitutes that witness' evidence in chief upon which the arbitral tribunal and the parties may rely in advancing and resolving factual submissions.

§68 Written Testimony as Evidence-in-Chief

(1) Party witnesses give their evidence-in-chief in written witness statements.
(2) Counsel may assist the witness in memorialising the witness' testimony in writing for submission in the proceedings.

§69 Timing of Evidence-in-Chief

(1) Written witness statements must be submitted with the earliest pleading to which they pertain or at the earliest time at which their introduction was reasonably feasible.
(2) Witnesses may amend their witness statements in writing with successive pleadings to report on new events or circumstances, which occurred after submission of the respective earlier witness statement or to respond to new allegations raised in later pleadings by the party opponent, an amicus curiae, or a tribunal witness.

§70 Substance of Evidence-in-Chief

(1) Written witness statements must be sufficient detailed to permit an understanding, on the face of the document, of the facts to which the witness testifies.
(2) A witness should, when possible, refer to contemporaneous documents of which the witness had personal knowledge at the time the events to which the witness is testifying took place.
(3) Witnesses must in any event identify the source from which they draw their testimony, including:
    a. Personal action or observation;
    b Conversations with third persons;or
    c. Review of the relevant documentation.

§71 Additional Formal Requirements for Evidence-in-Chief

(1) Written witness statements must provide:
    a. The name and address of the witness;
    b. A description of the relationship of the witness to the parties; and
    c. Personal background information.
(2) The witness must affirm the truth of the witness statement.
(3) The witnesss statement must be signed, dated, and state its place of execution.

§72 Language of the Testimony

(1) A witness may choose to provide evidence-in-chief in the language of the proceedings or in another language.
(2) If a witness provides his or her evidence-in-chief in a language other than the original language of the proceedings,
    a. the witness statement must identify the original language of the statement;
    b. the witness must identify the language in which he or she would testify if called for cross-examination; and
    c. the party proffering the witness must submit a translation of the statement together with the original.
(3) The parties must make reasonable efforts to agree with the arbitral tribunal upon a manner of interpretation and transcription of witness testimony given at the hearing

in a language other than an official language of the proceedings. Absent a ruling by the arbitral tribunal to the contrary,
  a. Interpretation should, if reasonably feasible, proceed simultaneously;
  b. Unless provided by the arbitral institution, the party proffering the witness must make efforts to obtain an interpreter satisfactory to the tribunal; and
  c. Transcription of testimony will occur in an official language of the proceedings but the tribunal may also permit transcription in the language of the testimony.

(4) A party wishing to object to the translation of testimony must do so at the earliest possible time or in accordance with a procedure set forth by a tribunal.

§73 Calling Witnesses for Cross-Examination

(1) A party wishing to call a witness for cross-examination must provide reasonable notice to the party proffering the witness to be cross-examined.
(2) Absent extraordinary circumstances, parties can only call witnesses for cross-examination who have already submitted their evidence-in-chief.
(3) The arbitral tribunal is tasked with setting the date at which and the manner in which the parties must notify each other of the witnesses they seek to examine.
(4) The arbitral tribunal may within a reasonable time after the exchange by the parties of lists of witnesses whom they wish to cross-examine call additional witnesses for cross-examination.

§74 Objection to Call of a Witness for Cross-Examination

(1) Parties may object in exceptional circumstances to the request for cross-examination of a witness within a reasonable time of the notice calling the witness.
(2) The arbitral tribunal will determine in its discretion whether the party objecting to the cross- examination of a witness has provided a good cause why the witness should be excused.

§75 In-Person and Remote Cross-Examination

(1) Absent an order of the arbitral tribunal to the contrary, witnesses as a default rule will be cross-examined in person before the arbitral tribunal.
(2) Arbitral tribunals may order the party wishing to proffer a witness remotely via audio or video-link to pay for reasonable fees incurred by the examining party to be represented in the room in which the witness will provide testimony.
(3) Arbitral tribunals have accepted as good cause for the remote cross-examination of witnesses:
  a. The arrest or detention of the witness;
  b. The existence of an Interpol Red Notice for the witness;
  c. Natural disasters;
  d. Threat to the personal safety of the witness;
  e. Unreasonable costs of bringing the witness to the place of the hearing;
  f. Technical facilities to permit reliable remote examination; and
  g. The consent of the parties.

§76 Order of Cross-Examination

Absent good cause shown, arbitral tribunals ordinarily proceeds with the examination of the fact witnesses proffered by the moving party, followed by the fact witnesses proffered by the responding party, followed by an examination of the experts.

§77 Time Allocation for Cross-Examination

(1) The arbitral tribunal may allocate time for cross-examination to the parties in its discretion subject to securing the equality of the parties and each party's right to be heard.
(2) Absent good cause shown, arbitral tribunals proceed on the basis of an equal allocation of time to both parties.

§78 Exclusion of Witnesses from Cross-Examination of Other Witnesses (Sequestration of witnesses)

On its own motion or upon request by a party, the arbitral tribunal may exclude witnesses from the hearing room during the cross-examination of other witness to avoid the contamination of later cross- examination testimony.

§79 Direct Examination of Witnesses at the Hearing

(1) Absent extraordinary circumstances, the direct examination of witnesses at the hearing is limited.
(2) Subject to the supervision by thearbitral tribunal, the direct hearing examination may:
    a. Introduce the witness to the tribunal;
    b. Affirm the correctness of the evidence in chief;
    c. Make necessary corrections to the evidence-in-chief to address statements the witness considers to be false or misleading at the time of his or her live testimony;
    d. Update the arbitral tribunal with regard to relevant and material developments regarding the subject matter of the witness' testimony occurring since the last written statement submitted by the witness.

§80 Scope of Cross-Examination

(1) Counsel may always cross-examine a witness with regard to facts, events, or circumstances within the scope of the witness' evidence-in-chief.
(2) With the express leave of the arbitral tribunal, counsel may cross-examine a witness with regard to facts, events, or circumstances as to which the witness has personal knowledge.
(3) Counsel may establish personal knowledge on the basis of:
    a. Record documentary evidence;
    b. General responsibilities; and
    c. Other witness testimony.

§81 Permissible Types of Cross-Examination

(1) Cross-examination serves to elicit testimony regarding relevant and material facts not already submitted in the witness' evidence-in-chief or to impeach the witness' testimony or character of the witness for truthfulness.

(2) To impeach a witness, counsel may:
   a. Elicit a statement from the witness inconsistent with other record documentary or witness evidence;
   b. Confront the witness with prior inconsistent statements made by the witness;
   c. Test the basis for statements made by the witness;
   d. Test the memory of the witness; and
   e. Establish bias.

(3) Impeachment by prior inconsistent statement requires that the witness be given an opportunity to address the asserted inconsistency upon review of the allegedly inconsistent statement.

§82 Permissibility of Leading Questions

(1) To the extent reasonable, Counsel may ask witnesses questions that the witness can answer only by affirming or denying a fact.

(2) After answering the question, the witness may provide further testimony explaining his or her statement.

§83 Conduct of Hearing Examination

(1) The arbitral tribunal may ask the witness questions at any time.

(2) Parties may object to the arbitral tribunal with regard to a line of questioning by opposing counsellor as needed including on the basis that:
   a. The witness is providing untimely evidence-in-chief as part of hearing direct testimony;
   b. Counsel's questions are unduly leading and do not permit the witness to testify in their own voice to relevant and materials facts;
   c. Questions are beyond the scope of the written testimony;
   d. The witness lacks personal knowledge to answer the question;
   e. A question of statement mischaracterises the testimony of the witness;
   f. A question is hypothetical calling for irrelevant speculation;
   g. A question calls for uncorroborated hearsay testimony;
   h. A question or line of questioning is confusing or badgering the witness;
   i. Counsel is testifying;
   j. A question is calling for evidence subject to exclusion on grounds set out in §§§30–51; or
   k. A question is calling for testimony, which is potentially prejudicial to the witness in pending criminal proceedings.

(3) Parties may further request the arbitral tribunal instruct an unresponsive or evasive witness to answer the question posed during cross-examination.

(4) A party will be given an opportunity to re-direct examine a witness with regard to questions posed during the witness' hearing examination within the scope of the hearing examination.

§84 Consequence of Non-Appearance of a Party Witness

(1) The arbitral tribunal will disregard the evidence-in-chief of a witness who failed to appear for cross- examination as ordered by the tribunal.
(2) In exceptional circumstances, the arbitral tribunal may excuse the non-appearance of a witness.
(3) Arbitral tribunals have excused the non-appearance of a witness when the witness expressed a reasonable fear of criminal prosecution, civil contempt, loss of employment or unreasonable deterioration of his or her health should the witness testify as ordered.

§85 Tribunal Fact Witnesses

Arbitral tribunals may on their own motion or upon the application of a party call a witness who has not given evidence-in-chief as part of the arbitral proceedings.

§86 Party Application to Call a Tribunal Fact Witnesses

(1) A party applying to call a tribunal witness will need to satisfy the arbitral tribunal of the need to call the witness in question.
(2) Arbitral tribunals take the following factors into consideration when making such a determination:
    a. Timeliness of the application;
    b. Relevance and materiality of the potential testimony; and
    c. Unavailability of alternative evidence.

§87 Scope of Testimony of a Tribunal Fact Witness

The arbitral tribunal in consultation with the parties will set the scope of testimony for a tribunal witness prior to calling the witness to testify.

§88 Evidence-in-Chief of a Tribunal Fact Witness

(1) At the witness' election, the witness may provide his or her evidence-in-chief by means of live hearing testimony.
(2) The arbitral tribunal gives due regard to requests by the witness to testify remotely.
(3) The parties in collaboration with the arbitral tribunal are tasked to determine the most appropriate manner to conduct a direct examination.
(4) All parties have a right to examine the tribunal witnesses either by means of direct or cross-examination.

§89 Consequence of Non-Appearance of a Tribunal Witness

(1) The arbitral tribunal may disregard record documentary evidence authored by the tribunal witness who failed to appear for live examination or any other hearsay statements attributed to him by other witness or documentary evidence.
(2) The arbitral tribunal may further make such inferences as are appropriate on the basis of the witness' absence from the proceedings.

§90 Expert Opinion, Defined

The direct testimony of an expert constitutes that expert's opinion upon which the arbitral tribunal and the parties may rely in advancing and resolving factual and technical submissions.

§91 Purpose of Expert Testimony

Parties may rely upon experts in order to:

a. testify to facts that cannot easily be established upon the basis of documentary evidence including technical standards and commercial practices;
b. testify to legal issues relevant and material to the resolution of the dispute; and
c. provide an opinion regarding the consequence of the dispute for a party including the valuation of its losses.

§92 Written Report as Opinion Testimony

(1) Party experts give their evidence-in-chief in written expert reports.
(2) Counsel may assist the expert in memorialising the witness' testimony in writing for submission in the proceedings.

§93 Timing of Expert Opinions

(1) Written expert reports must be submitted with the earliest pleading to which they pertain or at the earliest time at which their introduction was reasonably feasible.
(2) Experts may amend their witness statements in writing with successive pleadings to opine on new events or circumstances, which occurred after submission of the respective earlier expert report or to respond to new allegations raised in later pleadings by the party opponent, an amicus curiae, or a tribunal witness or expert.

§94 Substance of Expert Opinions

(1) Written expert reports must be sufficient detailed to permit an understanding, on the face of the document, of the expert's conclusions and reasons for those conclusions.
(2) Experts must in any event identify the source from which they draw their testimony, including:
    a. Assumptions and instructions provided by counsel
    b. Personal action or observation;
    c. Conversations with third persons; or
    d. Review of documentation.
(4) Absent extraordinary circumstances, experts must submit the documents upon which they rely to form their expert opinion.

§95 Additional Formal Requirements for Expert Opinions

(1) Written witness statements must provide:
    a. The name and address of the experts involved in submitting the report;
    b. The qualifications of the expert(s);and
    c. A description of the relationship of the expert to the arbitral tribunal, the parties, as well as their counsel.
    d. A statement of independence and imparitiality.
(2) The expert(s) must affirm their independence and affirmation that the conclusions in the reporter are the genuine belief of the expert(s).
(3) The expert report must be signed, dated, state its place of execution, and identify the portions for which each expert is responsible as appropriate.

§96 Tribunal Expert

(1) The arbitral tribunal may on its own motion or upon the application of a party appoint a tribunal expert.
(2) The arbitral tribunal must consult the parties prior to the appointment of an expert to receive comments as to the need, appropriate scope, and identity of a tribunal expert.
(3) The arbitral tribunal upon consideration of party comment may take such action it deems appropriate.
(4) Tribunal experts must make available their expert opinion in the same manner as a party-appointed expert.

§97 Calling an Expert for Cross-Examination

(1) A party wishing to call an expert for cross-examination must provide reasonable notice to the party proffering the witness to be cross-examined.
(2) The arbitral tribunal is tasked with setting the date at which and the manner in which the parties must notify each other of the experts they seek to examine.
(3) The arbitral tribunal may within a reasonable time after the exchange by the parties of lists of wit- nesses whom they wish to cross-examine call additional witnesses for cross-examination.

§98 Method of Live Examination

(1) The arbitral tribunal may call an expert for cross-examination similar to the examination of fact witnesses.
(2) Cross-examination serves to elicit relevant and material opinion evidence not already submitted in the expert report or to impeach the expert's opinion.
(3) To impeach a witness, counsel may:
    a. Probe the qualifications of the expert;
    b. Confront the assumptions made by the expert;
    c. Confront the expert with prior inconsistent statements made by the expert in other settings;
    d. Test the evidentiary basis for expert's opinion;
    e. Test the method employed by the witness, including the scope of its adoption in the relevant field; and
    f. Establish bias or lack of independence of the expert.
(4) Impeachment by prior inconsistent statement requires that the witness be given an opportunity to address the asserted inconsistency upon review of the allegedly inconsistent statement.
(5) Alternatively, the arbitral tribunal may examine the experts jointly, including by permitting the experts to exchange with each other on the witness stand.

§99 Consequence of Non-Appearance of an Expert

(1) The arbitral tribunal will disregard the opinion of an expert who failed to appear for cross-examination as ordered by the tribunal.
(2) In exceptional circumstances, the arbitral tribunal may excuse the non-appearance of an expert.
(3) When reports are authored by a team of experts, only the team member relevant to the proposed cross-examination need appear.
(4) Arbitral tribunals otherwise have excused the non-appearance of an expert in a manner analogous to §81.

11. On the contribution of investment arbitration to issues of evidence and procedure before other international courts and tribunals

James G. Devaney

I. INTRODUCTION

This chapter examines the contribution of investment arbitration to international dispute settlement more generally in relation to matters of evidence and procedure. Part II examines the practice of a number of inter-State dispute settlement fora in an attempt to gauge the contribution of the considerable body of practice of investment arbitration which has been built up over the course of the last few decades. It is shown that, at least at this point in time, this contribution is difficult to discern and appears to vary from one context to another.

Part III argues that investment arbitration is in practice an important point of reference for the resolution of 'cross-cutting' issues of evidence and procedure, with significant potential to influence the handling of similar issues before other courts and tribunals. For instance, certain issues such as the challenge and disqualification of decision-makers, abuse of process, or admissibility of illegally-obtained evidence have received extensive consideration in investment arbitration. The manner in which such issues have been dealt with by investment arbitrators, it is argued, forms part of an increasingly rich corpus of practice from which other courts and tribunals can potentially draw inspiration.

Accordingly, the strict position taken by some inter-State tribunals to date, which circumscribes reference to investment arbitration practice on account of it not being a relevant source of law, is undesirable. For international courts and tribunals to willfully deprive themselves of this potentially fruitful source of inspiration and guidance on issues of evidence and procedure is unnecessarily isolationist and potentially harmful to international law as a discipline more generally.

II. THE VARIABLE AND UNEVEN INFLUENCE OF INVESTMENT ARBITRATION ON INTER-STATE DISPUTE SETTLEMENT FORA

This chapter argues that the corpus of investment arbitration practice regarding the handling of 'cross-cutting' issues of procedure and evidence is a potentially valuable source of inspiration for other international courts and tribunals. As such, as a preliminary issue, it is necessary to clarify what exactly is meant by cross-cutting issues of procedure and evidence, which are distinguished from substantive primary or secondary international legal rules or principles.[1] A broad definition of procedure is adopted, encompassing 'all rules and principles regulating the manner in which the proceedings (*le procès*) are conducted … [and] the way in which the parties' requests are dealt with … from the institution of proceedings until the moment of the final decision'.[2] Any attempt to assess such procedural issues, which are both varied and various across the different contexts within which the courts and tribunals mentioned operate, is necessarily selective. Nevertheless, an attempt is made to draw upon practice which can be said to be representative or significant for the stated purpose of attempting to understand the contribution that investment arbitration can make to the development of international law more generally.

Furthermore, the primary metric through which influence is measured throughout is citations. Of course, this is an imperfect metric, open to the criticism that some citations may be merely symbolic or ornamental, as well as criticism that citations alone cannot capture the full extent of the influence of investment arbitration practice. While the limitations of the methodological approach adopted in this chapter are clear, a broader conception of influence would entail alternative methods of inquiry, such as sociolegal methods which fall outside the scope of this chapter. As such, the conclusions drawn from the current approach which focuses primarily on citations in the following pages should be understood with this in mind.

With regard to the 'cross-cutting' nature of such issues of evidence and procedure, practice demonstrates that, despite different constitutive instruments,

---

1 Hélène Ruiz Fabri and Joshua Paine, 'The Procedural Cross-Fertilization Pull' (2019) *MPIL Lux Research Paper Series* No 2019(6) 5 https://papers.ssrn.com/sol3/papers.cfm?abstract_id=3441701 accessed 6 January 2022; Chester Brown, *A Common Law of International Adjudication* (OUP 2007) 8; Sergey Punzhin, 'Procedural Normative System of the International Court of Justice' (2017) 30 *LJIL* 662.

2 Robert Kolb, 'General Principles of Procedural Law' in Andreas Zimmermann and Christian J. Tams (eds), *The Statute of the International Court of Justice: A Commentary* (3rd edn, OUP 2019) 965; Malcolm Shaw, *Rosenne's Law and Practice of the International Court 1920–2015* (5th edn, Brill Nijhoff 2016) 1049ff.

parties and legal contexts, when it comes to procedure and evidence 'certain common problems' arise in the process of adjudication or arbitration.[3] For instance, the admissibility of evidence or abuse of process are common challenges for international courts and tribunals. That courts and tribunals look to each other to find common solutions to these common problems is a result of the simple fact that in reality 'there are a finite number of ways to resolve such problems in a manner that is both efficient and just'.[4] Looking to other fora in this manner has most often been termed in the literature 'cross-fertilization'.[5] Such cross-fertilisation is only able to occur due to the fact different international courts and tribunals perform the same broad dispute settlement and judicial or arbitral function.[6]

Reference to the existing practice of other international courts and tribunals is appealing to decision-makers for a number of reasons, ranging from demonstrating that their preferred solution to a procedural issue under consideration is not arbitrary,[7] and increasing the acceptability of their approach by referring to other (perhaps more authoritative) tribunals who have done likewise.[8]Cross-fertilisation has been described as a complex phenomenon due to the fact that it is rather indeterminate in nature, implying communication

---

[3] John Crook, 'Procedural Convergence in International Courts and Tribunals' in Chiara Giorgetti and Mark Pollack (eds), *Beyond Fragmentation: Competition and Collaboration Among International Courts and Tribunals* (CUP 2022) 87, quoted in Ruiz Fabri and Paine (n 1).

[4] Ibid.

[5] Ulf Linderfalk, 'Cross-Fertilization in International Law' (2015) 84 *Nordic JIL* 428, 431; Chester Brown, 'The Cross-Fertilization of Principles Relating to Procedure and Remedies in the Jurisprudence of International Courts and Tribunals' (2008) 30 *Loy LA Int'l & Comp LR* 219; Anne-Marie Slaughter, 'Judicial Globalization' (1999–2000) 40 *Va JIL* 1103; Tulio Treves, 'Cross-Fertilization Between Different International Courts and Tribunals: The Mangouras Case' in Holger Hestermeyer et al (eds), *Coexistence, Cooperation and Solidarity: Liber Amicorum Rudiger Wolfrum* (Martinus Nijhoff 2001) 1798ff; Chiara Giorgetti, 'Cross-Fertilization of Procedural Law among International Courts and Tribunals: Methods and Meanings' in Arman Sarvarian et al (eds), *Procedural Fairness in International Courts and Tribunals* (British Institute of International and Comparative Law 2015); Ruth Teitel and Robert Howse, 'Cross-Judging: Tribunalization in a Fragmented But Interconnected Global Order' (2009) 41 *NYU JILP* 959.

[6] Brown (n 5) 230.

[7] Ruiz Fabri and Paine (n 1) 5; Erik Voeten, 'Borrowing and Non-Borrowing among International Courts' (2010) 39 *J Leg Stud* 547, 553.

[8] On the particular issue of precedent, see Niccolo Ridi, '"Mirages of an Intellectual Dreamland"? *Ratio, Obiter* and the Textualization of International Precedent' (2019) 10 *JIDS* 361; Nathan Miller, 'An International Jurisprudence? The Operation of "Precedent" across International Tribunals' (2002) 15 *LJIL* 483; Gilbert Guillaume, 'The Use of Precedent by International Judges and Arbitrators' (2011) 2 *JIDS* 5, 6.

between courts and tribunals, but not saying anything as to 'the directions of this communication or whether there is some hierarchy or reciprocity in the processes, or established patterns'.[9] Furthermore:

> cross-fertilization is used to cover a plurality of methods or techniques (e.g., citation to the decisions or practices of other tribunals (whether in a specific or general way), drawing analogies or distinctions with the decisions or practices of other tribunals, or considering how other tribunals have resolved an issue for the purposes of learning or adaptation).[10]

Interestingly, however, aside from Chester Brown's influential *A Common Law of International Adjudication*,[11] and a small number of other pieces of scholarship,[12] significantly less attention has been paid to the procedural aspects of cross-fertilisation compared to cross-fertilisation of substantive international law.[13] It is in this context that the present contribution seeks to examine cross-fertilisation in relation to the topic of the present volume, namely the contribution of investment arbitration to international law more generally.

Evidentiary issues are given a particularly prominent place in the following analysis owing to the considerable attention that has been paid to these particular procedural issues in recent times. Such attention is evident not only in the submissions to, and decisions of, international courts and tribunals in the last decade or so,[14] but also in the ink spilled on such issues in international legal scholarship.[15] In addition, the issue of evidence before international

---

9 Ruiz Fabri and Paine (n 1) 4.

10 Ibid; see also Giorgetti (n 5) 225.

11 Brown (n 1).

12 See (n 5).

13 Ruiz Fabri and Paine (n 1) 4.

14 See, e.g., *Case Concerning Pulp Mills on the River Uruguay (Argentina v Uruguay)* [2010] *ICJ Reports* 14, and in particular the Dissenting Opinion of Judges Al-Khasawneh and Simma; *Armed Activities on the Territory of the Congo (Democratic Republic of the Congo v Uganda)* [2005] *ICJ Reports* 168; *Whaling in the Antarctic (Australia v Japan: New Zealand intervening)* [2014] *ICJ Reports* 226 to mention but a few.

15 Anna Riddell and Brendan Plant, *Evidence Before the International Court of Justice* (British Institute of International and Comparative Law 2009); Loretta Malintoppi, 'Fact Finding and Evidence Before the International Court of Justice (Notably in Scientific-Related Disputes)' (2016) 7 *JIDS* 421; James G. Devaney, *Fact-Finding Before the International Court of Justice* (CUP 2016); Kenneth J Keith, 'The Development of Rules of Procedure by the World Court Through Its Rule Making, Practice and Decisions' (2018) 49 *Vict Univ Well LR* 511; Mohammed Bennouna, 'Experts before the International Court of Justice: What For?' (2018) 9 *JIDS* 345; James Flett, 'When Is an Expert Not an Expert?' (2018) 9 *JIDS* 352;

courts and tribunals has been, *inter alia*, a topic of study for a Committee of the International Law Association (ILA)[16] and proposed as such for the International Law Commission (ILC).[17] That evidence is such a prominent issue in a range of contexts provides an additional justification for the analysis which follows. This increased attention to issues of evidence and procedure has already seen some courts and tribunals including the ICJ implement procedural responses, such as the ICJ's newly-introduced policy prohibiting 'moonlighting'.[18] Most interestingly for our purposes, this also provides an indirect link between the practice of the ICJ and ISDS, to which we will return below. Taken together, such factors strongly suggest that the time is right to assess whether international investment arbitration is having any influence on this process.

A. Inter-State Arbitration – Uneven Receptiveness to Investment Arbitration

Due to the fact that inter-State arbitration appears to be the preferred legal dispute settlement method for States today,[19] consideration of this method of

---

Geoffrey Senogles, 'Some Views from the Crucible: The Perspective of an Expert Witness on the Adversarial Principle' (2018) 9 *JIDS* 361; Joan E. Donoghue, 'Expert Scientific Evidence in a Broader Context' (2018) 9 *JIDS* 379; Isabelle Van Damme, 'The Assessment of Expert Evidence in International Adjudication' (2018) 9 *JIDS* 406; Kate Parlett, 'Parties' Engagement with Experts in International Litigation' (2018) 9 *JIDS* 440; Brendan Plant, 'Expert Evidence and the Challenge of Procedural Reform in International Dispute Settlement' (2018) 9 *JIDS* 464, Laurence Boisson de Chazournes et al, 'One Size Does Not Fit All – Uses of Experts before International Courts and Tribunals: An Insight Into Practice' (2018) 9 *JIDS* 477.

[16] See Committee on the Procedure of International Courts and Tribunals, 'Interim Report' in International Law Association Report of the Seventy-Eight Conference (Sydney 2018).

[17] ILC, 'Report of the International Law Commission on the Work of its Sixty-ninth Session' (1 May – 2 June and 3 July – 4 August 2017) UN Doc A/72/10, Annex B. Further emblematic of the importance of such issues, a recent project to commemorate 70 years of the International Court of Justice surveyed 71 top international legal practitioners about their views regarding dispute settlement before the Court. The issue raised most often was that of evidence and fact-finding; Amelia Keene, 'Outcome Paper for the Seminar on the International Court of Justice at 70: In Retrospect and in Prospect' 7 *JIDS* 238.

[18] H E Mr. Abdulqawi A Yusuf, 'Speech' (Seventy-Third Session of the United Nations General Assembly, New York, 25 October 2018) www.icj-cij.org/public/files/press-releases/0/000-20181025-PRE-02-00-EN.pdf accessed 1 November 2020.

[19] A. Alexander Marie Stuyt, *Survey of International Arbitrations: 1794-1989* (Martinus Nijhoff 1990); see also Christine Gray and Benedict Kingsbury, 'Developments in Dispute Settlement: Inter-State Arbitration Since 1945' (1992) 63

dispute settlement is an obvious place to start. The arbitral practice explored below addresses a diverse range of evidentiary and procedural issues, ranging from challenge and disqualification of arbitrators to the hearing of testimony via a video-conference. Through consideration of these issues of evidence and procedure, we can discern a number of different approaches to investment arbitration, each of which are set out more fully in the following sections. Perhaps most remarkable are the strict approaches adopted by the *Chagos Marine Protected Area* (*Chagos MPA*) and *Abyei* arbitrations, particularly in the case of the former, in which the tribunal flatly refused to consider any mixed arbitral practice. This explicit refusal allows us to talk of a specific, strict approach in accordance with which the decision only to consider inter-State practice is not only acknowledged but also justified.

The *ad hoc* nature of these inter-State arbitrations may raise doubts as to the viability of saying anything generally about issues of procedure and evidence due to their potentially diverging applicable procedural rules. Nevertheless, while it is true that arbitral tribunals most commonly have the discretion to adopt their own rules of procedure (through consultation with the parties),[20] practice shows that rules relating to procedure and evidence tend to be similar. For instance, arbitrations under Annex VII of UNCLOS, such as in the *Guyana/Suriname* case, most often adopt Rules of Procedure based on the PCA Optional Rules.[21] This results in a high degree of commonality between

---

BYIL 97, 100; Jacomijn J. van Haersolte-van Hof, 'The Revitalization of the Permanent Court of Arbitration' (2007) 54 *Neth ILR* 395; The recent revitalisation of inter-State arbitration is often attributed to two main factors. The first is the dispute settlement procedure set out in Annex VII of the United Nations Convention on the Law of the Sea (UNCLOS) which makes inter-State arbitration the fall-back option when no other agreement can be reached between the parties; The second is the adoption of the series of Optional Procedural Rules as part of the New Directions Initiative of the PCA. These procedural rules sought to address the underuse of the PCA through diversification and making arbitration under the auspices of the PCA more flexible and appealing to disputing parties (following on from the success of the UNCITRAL Rules used in the Iran-US Claims Tribunal); Tjaco T. Van den Hout, 'Resolution of International Disputes: The Role of the Permanent Court of Arbitration – Reflections on the Centenary of the 1907 Convention for the Pacific Settlement of International Disputes' (2008) 21 *LJIL* 643.

[20] See United Nations Convention on the Law of the Sea (UNCLOS) (adopted 10 December 1982, entered into force 16 November 1994) 1833 UNTS 3, Annex VII, art 5.

[21] Compare *Guyana v Suriname,* PCA Case No 2004-04, Rules of Procedure for the Arbitral Tribunal Constituted under Annex VII to the United Nations Convention on the Law of the Sea (24 February 2004) and PCA, 'Optional Rules for Arbitrating Disputes Between Two States' (1992) https://pca-cpa.org/wp-content/uploads/sites/6/2016/01/Optional-Rules-for-Arbitrating-Disputes-between-Two-States_1992.pdf accessed 6 January 2022.

such arbitrations and those brought on an *ad hoc* basis, such as the *Abyei* arbitration, which also use the PCA Optional Rules as a basis for their Rules of Procedure. In reality, the various sets of rules of procedure, such as the 2012 PCA Rules of Procedure, Optional Rules for Arbitrating Disputes Between Two States and Optional Rules for Arbitrating disputes between Two Parties of which Only One Is a State, all contain broadly similar provisions.[22]

Arbitral practice is rather uneven in terms of receptiveness to investment arbitration practice on procedure and evidence. In fact, in certain cases we can discern a stricter approach of close adherence to the constitutive instruments of various dispute settlement bodies, and a related unwillingness to consider outside influences, while in others we see greater openness and readiness to look to investment arbitration and to take its practice into account. In the case of the former approach, it is impossible to say whether investment arbitration is a motor for the development of rules of procedure and evidence due to the fact that such tribunals see it as inappropriate to take investment arbitration into account. The latter case, however, is different and allows us to say something on the present and potential role for investment arbitration as a motor for the development of international law more generally.

1. Refusal to consider investment arbitration: The strict approach of the Chagos MPA arbitration

An example of the first of these approaches is the *Chagos MPA* arbitration between the United Kingdom and Mauritius. In this case Mauritius challenged Judge Greenwood's selection as arbitrator by the UK on account of his previous dealings with the British Government which, they alleged, compromised his impartiality.[23] In considering this challenge, the arbitral panel necessarily had to first of all establish which standard it ought to apply when considering the allegations. Mauritius had sought to have the 'appearance of bias' standard applied in order to assess Judge Greenwood's impartiality. Challenge

---

[22] See Article PCA, 'Arbitration Rules 2012' (2012) art 27(3) https://docs.pca-cpa.org/2015/11/PCA-Arbitration-Rules-2012.pdf; PCA Optional Rules for Arbitrating a Dispute Between Two States, ibid art 24(3); PCA, 'Optional Rules for Arbitrating a Dispute between Two Parties of Which Only One is a State' (1993) art 24(3) https://docs.pca-cpa.org/2016/01/Optional-Rules-for-Arbitrating-Disputes-between-Two-Parties-of-Which-Only-One-is-a-State-1993.pdf both accessed 4 November 2020; Rules of Procedure in *Guyana v Suriname*, ibid art 11(2); *MOX Plant Arbitration (Ireland v United Kingdom),* PCA Case No 2002-01, Rules of Procedure (25 October 2001) art 12(2); UNCITRAL, 'Arbitration Rules' (15 December 1976) A/RES/31/98, art 24(3) or UNCITRAL, 'Arbitration Rules as revised in 2010' (2010) UNGA Res 65/22, art 27(3).

[23] See *Chagos Marine Protected Area Arbitration (Mauritius v United Kingdom),* PCA Case No 2011-03, Reasoned Decision on Challenge (1 December 2011).

of arbitrators in international investment proceedings, whether conducted in accordance with ICSID[24] or UNCITRAL[25] rules, is relatively commonplace. While earlier case law had required 'not a possible lack of the quality, but a quasi-certain, or to go as far as possible, a highly probable' lack of independence or impartiality, the standard adopted by tribunals in the course of the last few years appears to show a move towards the lower 'appearance of bias' standard.[26] This has been generally welcomed by commentators for bringing clarity to an issue that had been unsettled in ICSID jurisprudence for some

---

24 Convention on the Settlement of Investment Disputes between States and Nationals of Other States (adopted 18 March 1965, entered into force 14 October 1966) 575 UNTS 159, art 57 states that a party can seek disqualification of an arbitrator 'on account of any fact indicating a manifest lack of the qualities required by paragraph (1) of Article 14' – art 14 requiring that arbitrators be of 'high moral character' and a person 'who may be relied upon to exercise independent judgement'; art 57 has been described as imposing 'a heavy burden on the party making the proposal [to disqualify]'; Christoph Schreuer et al, *The ICSID Convention: A Commentary* (2nd edn, CUP 2009) 1202. Under art 58 of the Convention an arbitrator can be replaced if such claims made under art 14 are proven to show a 'manifest lack' of impartiality or independence.

25 In contrast, under the relevant instruments which govern United Nations Commission on International Trade Law (UNCITRAL), London Court of International Arbitration (LCIA) and Stockholm Chamber of Commerce (SCC) proceedings, a manifest lack need not be shown but rather mere circumstances that 'give rise to justifiable doubts' about independence or impartiality, UNCITRAL Arbitration Rules 2010 (n 22) art 12(1); UNCITRAL, 'Model Law on International Commercial Arbitration' (21 June 1985) UN Doc A/40/17, Annex 1, art 12(2); LCIA, 'Arbitration Rules' (1 October 2014) art 10.1 www.lcia.org/Dispute_Resolution_Services/lcia-arbitration-rules-2014.aspx; Arbitration Institute of the SCC, 'Arbitration Rules' (1 January 2010) art 15(1) https://sccinstitute.com/media/29361 8/skiljedomsregler-eng-arb-2010.pdf. Furthermore, art 11 of the EU Commission's recent Transatlantic Trade and Investment Partnership (TTIP) Proposal on ethics contains a mechanism for challenging the independence of arbitrators in accordance with a similar standard, see European Union Commission, 'Proposal on Transatlantic Trade and Investment Partnership' (16 September 2015) art 11 referring to Annex II: Code of Conduct for Members of the Tribunal, the Appeal Tribunal and Mediators, art 2 http://trade.ec.europa.eu/doclib/docs/2015/september/tradoc_153807.pdf all accessed 5 November 2021.

26 *Blue Bank International & Trust (Barbados) Ltd v Bolivarian Republic of Venezuela*, ICSID Case No ARB/12/20, Award (26 April 2017); see Baiju Vasani and Shaun Palmer, 'Challenge and Disqualification of Arbitrators at ICSID: A New Dawn?' (2015) 30 *ICSID Review* 194; Karel Daele, '*Saint Gobain v Venezuela* and *Blue Bank v Venezuela*: The Standard for Disqualifying Arbitrators Finally Settled and Lowered' (2014) 29 *ICSID Review* 296; *Burlington Resources Inc v Republic of Ecuador*, ICSID Case No ARB/08/5, Decision on the Proposal for Disqualification of Professor Francisco Orrega Vicuña (13 December 2013); *Raiffeisen Bank International AG and Raiffeisenbank Austria dd v Republic of Croatia*, ICSID Case No ARB/17/34, Decision on the Proposal to Disqualify Stanimir Alexandrov (17 May 2018).

years, with some arguing that it will increase the predictability and consistency of the ICSID system as a whole.[27]

However, the tribunal in the *Chagos MPA* arbitration was not receptive to the argument made by Mauritius. Instead of considering the claim that the not inconsiderable body of practice in international investment law ought to be taken into account for the purposes of the present case, it rather insisted that this practice was of little relevance. The tribunal took this position on the back of its rather formalistic appraisal of the situation that, owing to the fact the tribunal was dealing with an inter-State dispute, only other inter-State practice and rules of procedure were relevant.

In the tribunal's own words, it decided that the law applicable to this Annex XII dispute was that of UNCLOS 'supplemented by the law and practice of international courts and tribunals in inter-State cases'.[28] Similarly, it saw no reason to consider the challenge 'on grounds other than those contained in the law and practice of international courts and tribunals concerned only with inter-State cases'.[29] In taking this position the tribunal explicitly rendered the practice of investment tribunals and other relevant standards such as the International Bar Association Guidelines on Conflicts of Interest in International Arbitration irrelevant for the purposes of that particular arbitration.

In doing so, the tribunal deprived itself of recourse to guidelines which, despite being 'soft law', have had significant influence in investment arbitration practice.[30] The Chairman of ICSID's Administrative Council has described the IBA's Guidelines as 'widely recognized in international arbitration as the pre-eminent set of guidelines for assessing arbitrator conflicts' and its standards are widely followed particularly in relation to applications made for disqualification during the course of the arbitration.[31] In particular it has

---

27 Daele (n 26) 305.

28 *Chagos MPA Arbitration* (n 23) para 165.

29 Ibid. (emphasis added).

30 See International Bar Association, 'Guidelines on Conflicts of Interest in International Arbitration' (23 October 2014) www.ibanet.org/Publications/publications_IBA_guides_and_free_materials.aspx accessed 1 November 2020. In fact, in international investment law these rules have become so influential that the recently announced investment tribunal in the Canada-EU Free Trade Agreement specifically compels arbitrations to comply with the IBA standards in art 8.30(1). Interestingly, under art 8.30(2) any challenge to the impartiality of an arbitrator is to be sent to the President of the International Court of Justice for determination – perhaps this will lead to the influence of investment arbitration into inter-State practice, since judges will be used to using these standards? The IBA Rules have been particularly influential in recent times in the context of investment arbitration.

31 Ibid.

been suggested that these Guidelines were an important influencing factor in the approach of ICSID tribunals in applying a less stringent test to the issue of disqualification of arbitrators.[32]

The tribunal justified its position in the orthodox manner, citing the fact that inter-State dispute settlement is based on the consent of parties and 'more specifically upon the rules of public international law, the sources of which are set out in Article 38(1) of the Statute of the ICJ'.[33] Under this strict interpretation of what the tribunal could and could not consider, it is clear why the tribunal felt it could not take into account rules adopted by non-governmental institutions such as the IBA. The tribunal found that Mauritius had failed to demonstrate that such rules had been expressly adopted by States, nor indeed that they in fact formed part of a general practice accepted as law. Finally, the tribunal found that such rules, most often employed in investment arbitration, did not fall within any other of the sources of international law enumerated in Article 38(1) of the Statute of the ICJ (without considering whether the IBA standards could be said to be capable of being or becoming general principles of law in the sense of Article 38(1)(c) of the Court's Statute).

In taking such a strict position on the relevance of, *inter alia*, investment arbitration practice, the tribunal aligned itself with the traditional approach of older, inter-State tribunals such as the ICJ.[34] In referring to UNCLOS's dispute settlement apparatus, specifically to Article 287 UNCLOS, the tribunal made the connection that 'it cannot have been the intention behind that framework that different conditions would apply to the independence and impartiality of adjudicators in the third forum (arbitration under Annex VII) in comparison with the ICJ or ITLOS'. Accordingly, the tribunal concluded that:

> In this context, where an Annex VII tribunal is an alternative forum to ITLOS or the ICJ, the Tribunal takes the view that only the rules applying to, and practice of, inter-State tribunals are of relevance to the qualification and challenge of arbitrators in proceedings under Annex VII.[35]

As a result, the tribunal rejected the appearance of bias standard prominent in international investment law on the basis that, absent a foundation in the appli-

---

32 Luke Sobota, 'Repeat Arbitrator Appointments in International Investment Disputes' in Chiara Giorgetti (ed), *Challenges and Recusals of Judges and Arbitrators in International Courts and Tribunals* (Martinus Nijhoff 2015) 297.

33 *Chagos MPA Arbitration* (n 23) para 167.

34 Ibid., para 168: 'It follows that the Tribunal is not persuaded that such additional rules, which cannot be considered as a source of law as regards judges of ITLOS or the ICJ, are any more relevant to arbitral tribunals established under Annex VII of the Convention than they are to judges of ITLOS or the ICJ.'

35 Ibid.

cation, 'such an approach risks supporting a wholly subjective standard'.[36] The tribunal's position in this regard raises a number of questions which are considered further in section III, but for the moment it suffices to note the attitude of the tribunal to the potential contribution of international investment law.

2. Strict but inconsistent: The approach of the *Abyei* and *Indus Waters Kishenganga* arbitrations

A similarly strict approach to the potential contribution of investment law can be discerned, at least in relation to certain issues, in the *Abyei* arbitration. This particular arbitration arose out of an agreement signed between the State of Sudan and the Sudan People's Liberation Movement (SPLM/A, which would later become the governing party of South Sudan) at a time before South Sudan had become a sovereign State. Although not strictly an inter-State arbitration, the tribunal in *Abyei* took a similar approach in relation to the potential contribution of international investment law.

The Government of Sudan had sought to rely on Article 2(a) of the Arbitration Agreement it had signed with the SPLM/A to establish that there had been serious procedural irregularities rendering a previous commission's findings on the fixing of a boundary void due to an excess of mandate. However, the arbitral tribunal found that it could only consider those narrow grounds for excess of mandate under Article 2(a) of the Arbitration Agreement and could not consider 'concepts of nullity or invalidity of arbitral awards, or incorporate the well-known grounds for invalidity or nullity based on procedural or due process violations included in instruments such as the 1958 New York Convention [or] the ICSID Convention …'. Ultimately, the arbitral tribunal concluded that there was '… no basis for expanding this single ground for invalidity to include other grounds that were not specified'.[37]

Crucially, however, the tribunal was not completely consistent in its approach. For instance, in relation to certain other issues, the tribunal did in fact draw upon arbitral practice in relation to a different procedural issue. In considering the appropriate standard for the setting aside of arbitral awards on the grounds of failure to state reasons, the tribunal examined a broad number of investment cases (noting the '*jurisprudence constante*'[38]) including annulment committees in *Klöckner*,[39]

---

[36] Ibid., para 169.

[37] *The Government of Sudan/The Sudan People's Liberation Movement/Army (Abyei Arbitration)* PCA Case No 2008-07, Award (22 July 2009) para 441.

[38] Ibid., para 528.

[39] *Klöckner Industrie-Anlagen GmbH and Others v United Republic of Cameroon and Société Camerounaise des Engrais*, ICSID Case No ARB/81/2, Decision of the Ad Hoc Committee (3 May 1985) para 151.

MINE,[40] *Amco*[41] and *Vivendi*.[42] The Tribunal in Abyei made reference to this investment law jurisprudence, along with that of the ICJ, as evidence of '"general principles of law and practices" applicable to the setting aside of arbitral awards on the ground of failure to state reasons'.[43] This is significant and stands in stark contrast to the more formalistic position taken in the *Chagos MPA* arbitration.

Other examples can also be found in which the inter-State arbitral tribunals appear to be more open to considering investment arbitration practice. For instance, in the *Indus Water Kishenganga* arbitration between India and Pakistan, conducted under the auspices of the PCA, the tribunal went so far as making a procedural order which specifically referred to investment arbitral practice. In its Procedural Order No. 10, the tribunal informed the parties that video-conferencing was an acceptable substitute for in-person cross-examination in certain circumstances, explicitly citing practice in investment arbitration to this effect.[44] The tribunal included mixed investment arbitration among other examples of 'international arbitral hearings' in citing practice in support of its position.[45]

---

[40] *Martime International Nominees Establishment v Republic of Guinea,* ICSID Case No ARB 84/4, Decision of the Ad Hoc Annulment Committee (22 December 1989) para 5.09.

[41] *Amco Asia Corporation and others v Republic of Indonesia,* ICSID Case No ARB/81/1, Ad Hoc Committee Decision on the Application for Annulment (16 May 1986) paras 41–44.

[42] *Compania de Aguas del Aconquija SA and Vivendi Universal SA v Argentine Republic*, ICSID Case No ARB/97/3, Decision on Annulment (3 July 2002) paras 61–65.

[43] *Abyei Arbitration* (n 37) para 531.

[44] See Procedural Order No 10, *Concerning Pakistan's Request for Permission to Present Dr Acreman for Cross-Examination by Telephone Link* (15 August 2012) para 6 quoted in *Indus Water Kishenganga Arbritration (Parkistan v India)* PCA Case No 2011-01, Partial Award (18 February 2013) para 111.

[45] Procedural Order No. 10, ibid: Hearing Tr., (21 August 2012) 1:3-7 and in footnote 1 the tribunal referred to investment law practice including: *Murphy Exploration and Production Company International v Republic of Ecuador*, ICSID Case No ARB/08/4, Award on Jurisdiction (15 December 2010) para 16; *SD Myers, Inc v Government of Canada*, UNCITRAL, Second Partial Award (21 October 2002) para 76; *Sergei Paushok, CJSC Golden East Company and CJSC Vostokneftegaz Company v Government of Mongolia*, UNCITRAL, Award on Jurisdiction and Liability (28 April 2011) para 61; *Fraport AG Frankfurt Airport Services Worldwide v Republic of the Philippines*, ICSID Case No ARB/03/25, Award (16 August 2007) para 43; *EDF (Services) Ltd v Romania*, ICSID Case No ARB/05/13, Award (8 October 2009) para 38; *SGS Société Générale de Surveillance SA v Republic of Paraguay*, ICSID Case No ARB/07/29, Award (10 February 2012) para 23.

Taken together, this selection of recent inter-State arbitration practice reveals a somewhat unclear picture. There is some evidence of a strict approach to the potential influence of international investment arbitration, adhering to the traditional State-centric conception of dispute settlement. There are also examples, as we have seen, of strict adherence to the constitutive instruments of various dispute settlement bodies, and a related unwillingness to consider outside influences. In contrast, there are also signs of greater openness and readiness to look to investment arbitration and to take its practice into account, as was the case to some extent in *Abyei* and *Kishenganga*. But how do things stand in relation to the strictly State-centric bodies such as the World Trade Organization and the International Court of Justice?

B. The World Trade Organization: Clinical Isolation After All?

Despite some authors urging otherwise,[46] with regard to issues of evidence and procedure, the adjudicatory bodies of the WTO have been reluctant to make reference to investment arbitration to date. In fact, both WTO panels and the Appellate Body (AB) in general stand out as being among the least willing to take into account the practice of other international courts and tribunals.[47] Despite the early insistence that the WTO adjudicatory bodies did not operate in 'clinical isolation' from the rest of international law,[48] in practice there are few references in panel or AB reports to the practice of other tribunals, aside from the ICJ and its predecessor the PCIJ.[49]

The practice of the adjudicatory bodies of the WTO in relation to referencing external jurisprudence in general stands in stark contrast to that of investment arbitration. For instance, a recent empirical study has shown that, while one in five citations in investment arbitration are to external sources, the figure in

---

[46] Mary Footer, 'On the Laws of Attraction: Examining the Relationship Between Foreign Investment and International Trade' in Roberto Echandi and Pierre Sauvé (eds), *Prospects in International Investment Law and Policy* (CUP 2013) 137; Adrian Johnston and Michael Trebilcock 'Fragmentation in International Trade Law: Insights from the Global Investment Regime' (2013) 12 *World Trade Rev* 621.

[47] Damien Charlotin, 'The Place of Investment Awards and WTO Decisions in International Law: A Citation Analysis' (2017) 20 *JIEL* 279.

[48] James Bacchus, 'Not in Clinical Isolation' in Gabrielle Marceau (ed), *A History of Law and Lawyers in the GATT/WTO* (CUP 2015) 507.

[49] Charlotin (n 47) 290. For a rare example see the Panel citing the ICJ and investment practice in relation to the concepts of equity and even-handedness in WTO, *China - Measures Related to the Exportation of Rare Earths, Tungsten and Molybdenum – Panel Report* (26 March 2014) WT/DS431/R, 7.32ff; but cf. the claim in Michelle Zang, 'Shall We Talk? Judicial Communication between the CJEU and WTO Dispute Settlement' (2017) 28 *EJIL* 273.

the WTO context is a mere one in 100.[50] Similarly, while investment tribunals make reference to external authority on a wide range of substantive issues, the practice of the WTO adjudicative bodies is markedly different, only doing so in relation to a narrow range of issues, most usually treaty interpretation.[51] This, it has been suggested, represents 'a relative severance from other international law fora' on the part of the adjudicative bodies of the WTO.[52] This is true both in relation to external jurisprudence in general and specifically in relation to investment arbitral practice more specifically, with WTO decision makers usually 'chos[ing] to steer (rather) a solitary course'.[53]

There are rare examples of engagement with investment arbitral practice, such as US-Stainless Steel in which the AB addressed the issue of the role of precedent in WTO jurisprudence. In seeking to justify the informal or de facto system of precedent in WTO dispute settlement the AB relied on Article 3.2. DSU and the reference contained therein to 'security and predictability'. More interestingly for our purposes, however, it also included a footnote to a passage in the ICSID case of *Saipem S.p.A. v People's Republic of Bangladesh* in which the tribunal had used similar reasoning in stating that it was under 'a duty to adopt solutions established in a series of consistent cases' in order to meet the 'legitimate expectations of the community of States and investors towards certainty of the rule of law'.[54]

Nevertheless, such references remain the exception rather than the rule, in that it has not been commonplace in WTO jurisprudence to rely on investment awards in order to substantiate a position taken by the adjudicatory bodies.[55] Of course, there may be a number of sound reasons as to why the WTO operates in this way in practice and these will be considered below,[56] but for the moment is suffices to note the position taken thus far, before turning our attention to the ICJ.

---

50 Charlotin (n 47) 287; Joost Pauwelyn, 'The Role of Public International Law in the WTO: How Far Can We Go?' (2001) 95 *AJIL* 535, 577.

51 Charlotin (n 47) 290–291.

52 Ibid.

53 Ibid., 296, aside from *China – Rare Earths (Panel)* (n 49) and WTO, *United States – Final Anti-Dumping Measures on Stainless Steel from Mexico - Report of the Appellate Body* (30 April 2008) WT/DS34/AB/R.

54 *US – Stainless Steel* (n 53) para 160, quoting *Saipem SpA v People's Republic of Bangladesh*, ICSID Case No ARB/05/07, Decision on Jurisdiction and Recommendation on Provisional Measures (21 March 2007) para 67.

55 Petros Mavroidis, 'No Outsourcing of Law? WTO Law as Practiced by WTO Courts' (2008) 102 *AJIL* 421, 467; Robert Howse, 'The World Trade Organization 20 Years On: Global Governance by Judiciary' (2016) 27 *EJIL* 9, 72.

56 See, e.g., Lorand Bartels, 'Applicable Law in WTO Dispute Settlement Proceedings' (2001) 35 *JWT* 499.

C. International Court of Justice and Investment Arbitration: A Bridge too Far?

It is not difficult to find examples of how the jurisprudence of the World Court has made a contribution to international investment law in relation to issues of procedure.[57] That having been said, it is significantly more difficult to find any evidence vice versa. The following section shows that it is difficult to discern whether investment arbitration has had any influence on its practice. Historically, the Court's approach to making reference to external sources in its majority opinions was clear. In the first decades of the Court's operation, it exclusively cited its own jurisprudence, adhering to an 'unwritten rule'[58] that excluded even inter-State arbitral awards on the grounds that they could not 'give rise to generalization going beyond the special circumstances of each case'.[59] However, in the mid-1980s this began to change and today the situation is markedly different.[60] Since then, and in light of the proliferation of international courts and tribunals since the 1990s,[61] the Court has made reference in its majority opinions to the jurisprudence of various other fora such as ITLOS,[62]

---

[57] For instance, ICSID arbitrations have relied heavily on ICJ jurisprudence when making provisional measures under the openly-worded ICSID Convention (n 24) art 47, perhaps unsurprisingly given that this provision was modelled on the Statute of the International Court of Justice (adopted 26 June 1945, published 8 April 1946) 33 UNTS 993, art 41; Christoph Schreuer, *The ICSID Convention: A Commentary* (CUP 2001) 766–7, para 53.

[58] Hugh Thirlway, *The Law and Procedure of the International Court of Justice*, vol 1 (OUP 2013) 248: 'the existence, at the time the writer entered the service of the Court [1968], of an unwritten rule of drafting that the Court only referred specifically to its own jurisprudence, never to arbitral awards. This rule now appears to have been abandoned'.

[59] *Case Concerning the Barcelona Traction, Light and Power Company, Limited (Belgium v Spain)* (Judgment) [1970] *ICJ Reports* 3, para 63, cf. *Nottebohm Case (Liechtenstein v Guatemala)* (Judgment) [1953] *ICJ Report* 111, 119, making reference to *Alabama claims of the United States of America against Great Britain*, Award (14 September 1872) (1871) 29 RIAA 125.

[60] Vladyslav Lanovoy, 'The Authority of Inter-State Arbitral Awards in the Case Law of the International Court of Justice' (2019) 32 *LJIL* 561, 579.

[61] See generally Philippe Sands, 'Reflections on International Judicialization' (2017) 27 *EJIL* 885.

[62] *Territorial and Maritime Dispute (Nicaragua v Colombia)* (Judgment) [2012] *ICJ Reports* 624, paras 125, 178, 241, referring to *Delimitation of the Maritime Boundary in the Bay of Bengal (Bangladesh/Myanmar)* (Judgment) ITLOS Reports 2012, 86; *Maritime Delimitation in the Caribbean Sea and the Pacific Ocean (Costa Rica v Nicaragua) and Land Boundary in the Northern Part of Isla Portillos (Costa Rica v Nicaragua)* (Judgment) [2018] *ICJ Reports* 139, paras 135, 153, referring to *Bangladesh/Myanmar*, ibid.

human rights treaty bodies,[63] regional courts[64] and perhaps most notably international criminal tribunals.[65] In particular, the ICJ has made use of international criminal law jurisprudence in relation to issues of evidence; a practice for which it has been criticised by some commentators who have argued that the Court has effectively outsourced its fact-finding role.[66] While such accusations may be overstated, there is no doubt that in certain cases the ICJ and international criminal tribunals have engaged in significant judicial dialogue.[67]

In this sense reference to such external influences is by no means taboo.[68] In fact, particularly more recently it has been said that the ICJ has 'moved well beyond being its own echo chamber to participating in a much more open

---

[63] See, e.g., *Questions relating to the Obligation to Prosecute or Extradite (Belgium v Senegal)* (Judgment) [2012] *ICJ Reports* 422, para 101 which makes reference to a number of decisions of the Committee against Torture including Committee Against Torture, 'O.R.M.M. and M.S. v Argentina' (23 November 1989) UN Doc CAT/C/WG/3/DR/1, 2 and 3/1988; see also *Legal Consequences of the Construction of a Wall in the Occupied Palestinian Territory* (Advisory Opinion) [2004] *ICJ Reports* 136, paras 109–113 and 136 which makes reference to decisions of the Human Rights Committee, and CCPR, 'General Comment No 27: Article 12 (Freedom of Movement)' (2 November 1999) UN Doc CPPR/C/21/Rev.1/Add.9 in considering the 'constant practice of the Human Rights Committee'.

[64] See, e.g., *Case Concerning Ahmadou Sadio Diallo (Republic of Guinea v Democratic Republic of the Congo)* (Judgment) [2012] *ICJ Reports* 324, paras 18, 24, 33, 40, 49, making reference to, *inter alia*, IACtHR and ECtHR judgments.

[65] See, e.g., *Application of the Convention on the Prevention and Punishment of the Crime of Genocide (Croatia v. Serbia)* (Judgment) [2015] *ICJ Reports* 3 and *Case Concerning Application of the Convention on the Prevention and Punishment of the Crime of Genocide (Bosnia and Herzegovina v Serbia and Montenegro),* (Judgment) [2007] *ICJ Reports* 43, making reference to a number of ICTY judgments; see Devaney (n 15) 88.

[66] Richard Goldstone and Rebecca Hamilton, 'Bosnia v. Serbia: Lessons from the Encounter of the International Court of Justice with the International Criminal Tribunal for the Former Yugoslavia' (2008) 21 *LJIL* 95, 104.

[67] See, e.g., *Application of the Convention on the Prevention and Punishment of the Crime of Genocide (Bosnia and Herzegovina v. Serbia and Montenegro)*, (Judgment) *ICJ Reports* 43, paras 402–403.

[68] *Nottebohm Case* (n 59) 119; *Arbitral Award of 31 July 1989 (Guinea-Bissau v Senegal)* (Judgment) [1991] *ICJ Reports* 53, para 46; see also *Case Concerning the Continental Shelf (Tunisia/Libyan Arab Jamahiriya)* (Judgment) [1982] *ICJ Reports* 18, paras 66 and 111; *Land, Island and Maritime Frontier Dispute (El Salvador/ Honduras: Nicaragua intervening)* (Judgment) [1992] *ICJ Reports* 351, 591–92, para 391; *Case Concerning Maritime Delimitation and Territorial Questions between Qatar and Bahrain (Qatar v Bahrain)* (Judgment) [2001] *ICJ Reports* 40, 70–71, paras 100, 117; *Case Concerning Sovereignty over Pulau Ligitan and Pulau Sipadan (Indonesia/ Malaysia)* (Judgment) [2002] *ICJ Reports* 625, 682, para 135; *Case Concerning the Land and Maritime Boundary between Cameroon and Nigeria (Cameroon v Nigeria: Equatorial Guinea intervening)* (Judgment) [2002] *ICJ Reports* 303, 414–15, para 222.

discourse, fostering the cross-fertilization of legal authorities'.[69] However, the Court has to date only ever made one reference to investment arbitral practice, namely *Biloune v Ghana Investments Centre*, in the Preliminary Objections phase of the *Diallo* case in 2007, in dismissing Guinea's claims that there had been any change in the customary rules of diplomatic protection.[70] Furthermore, most recently, in the *Bolivia v Chile* case the Court rather summarily rejected the relevance for arbitral awards in determining whether the doctrine of legitimate expectations exists in international law more generally, stating that '[i]t does not follow from such references [to investment arbitration practice] that there exists in general international law a principle that would give rise to an obligation on the basis of what could be considered a legitimate expectation'.[71]

This is the case even where the Court or its judges could have usefully done so. For instance, in relation to the use of experts, a common practice in investment arbitration, no explicit reference was made to this practice. To give but one example, in the *Pulp Mills* case the Court's approach to evaluating the complex and scientific evidence put before it by the parties was heavily criticised both by commentators and from within the Court itself.[72] However, investment law practice was not been cited as a potential source of inspiration for reform. Rather, in the case of Judge Simma and Al-Khasawneh's Separate Opinion in the *Pulp Mills* case it was in fact the practice of the World Trade Organization that the judges chose to highlight. In relation to the appointment of experts to assist tribunals in dealing with particularly complex or scientific issues the judges stated that:

> [i]t is perhaps the World Trade Organization ... which has most contributed to the development of a best practice of readily consulting outside sources in order better to evaluate the evidence submitted to it; in fact, it was devised as a response to the needs of the dispute resolution process in cases involving complex scientific questions.[73]

---

[69] Lanovoy (n 60) 579.

[70] For a rare reference to an investment treaty award in the Court's jurisprudence, see *Ahmadou Sadio Diallo (Republic of Guinea v Democratic Republic of the Congo)* (Judgment) [2007] *ICJ Reports* 582, 615, para 90.

[71] For example, *Obligation to Negotiate Access to the Pacific Ocean (Bolivia v Chile)* (Judgment) [2018] *ICJ Reports* 507, para 162.

[72] See, e.g., *Pulp Mills* (n 14) Dissenting Opinion of Judges Al-Khasawneh and Simma, para 2; Devaney (n 15); Goldstone and Hamilton (n 66); Katherine Del Mar, 'Weight of Evidence Generated Through Intra-Institutional Fact-Finding Before the International Court of Justice' (2011) 2 *JIDS* 393.

[73] *Pulp Mills* (n 14), Dissenting Opinion of Judges Al-Khasawneh and Simma, para 2.

This is of course just one example plucked from a dissenting opinion in one case, but the fact that in this case it is the WTO adjudicative bodies and not international investment arbitration that is cited as best practice is nonetheless significant in itself. [74] One commentator has remarked on the Court's seemingly increasing comfort in making reference to inter-State arbitral awards which 'may be contrasted with the absence of similar reliance on investor-state arbitral awards, notwithstanding their volume, the level of interest in them, and the areas of substantive overlap'.[75] The traditional bias towards inter-State dispute settlement fora is certainly one possible explanation, and commentators will inevitably argue that the sovereign nature of the parties before the ICJ justifies its more insular approach, but the Court's apparent view of citing investment arbitration as being a bridge too far, at least for the moment, remains remarkable.

Accordingly, using the metric of citations alone, it is not possible to speak of any influence of investment arbitration on the ICJ. That is not to say, however, that the ICJ is blind to developments in investment arbitration which potentially have an impact on its functioning.[76] A clear example of this is the President of the ICJ's announcement to the United Nations General Assembly in 2018 that the Court's judges would no longer engage in so-called 'moonlighting', i.e., the practice of acting as legal decision-makers in other fora.[77] The President's announcement came on the back of the publication of an influential report which highlighted that ICJ judges had been involved in around 10 per cent of all known investment arbitrations,[78] and at a time when a debate on the problematic issue of 'double-hatting' is being played out in international legal scholarship.[79] Accordingly, in order to 'place beyond reproach

---

[74] See Devaney (n 15) 36. See, e.g., WTO, *United States — Import Prohibition of Certain Shrimp and Shrimp Products – Report of the Panel* (15 May 1998) WT/DS58/R and WTO, *United States — Import Prohibition of Certain Shrimp and Shrimp Products – Report of the Appellate Body* (12 October 1998) WT/DS58/AB/R. See WTO, *European Communities – Measures Affecting the Approval and Marketing of Biotech Products – Panel Reports* (29 September 2006) WT/DS291/R, WT/DS292/R, WT/DS293/R, 7.16.

[75] Lanovoy (n 60) 570.

[76] Nathalie Bernasconi-Osterwalder and Martin Dietrich Brauch, 'Is "Moonlighting" a Problem? The Role of ICJ Judges in ISDS' (2017) International Institute for Sustainable Development www.iisd.org/sites/default/files/publications/icj-judges-isds-commentary.pdf accessed 6 January 2020.

[77] Yusuf (n 18).

[78] Bernasconi-Osterwalder and Brauch (n 76) 1; Marie Davoise, 'Can't Fight the Moonlight? Actually, You Can: ICJ Judges to Stop Acting as Arbitrators in Investor-State Disputes' (*EJIL:Talk!*, 5 November 2018).

[79] See further Malcolm Langford et al, 'The Revolving Door in International Investment Arbitration' (2017) 20 *JIEL* 301.

the impartiality and independence of Judges in the exercise of their judicial functions', the ICJ's judges decided that the that 'they will not normally accept to participate in international arbitration. In particular, they will not participate in investor-State arbitration or in commercial arbitration'.[80] It is interesting to note that, while participation in commercial or investment arbitration is specifically prohibited by the Court's new policy, participation in inter-State arbitration in certain limited circumstances is not, harking back to the Court's traditionally favourable opinion of inter-State arbitration.

Overall, one may wonder why, if the problematic actions of the Court's judges before other dispute settlement fora can bring about a particular procedural reform from the ICJ, why can other, more positive actions (such as the considered development of a standard for the admissibility of illegally-obtained information) not also do so. This, as well as a number of more general ruminations on the potential influence of international investment arbitration in future cases, are considered in the following section.

III. THE UNTAPPED POTENTIAL OF INVESTMENT ARBITRATION PRACTICE

With regard to the implications of the current state of the art, it is argued any strict approach that consists of refusing to rely on investment arbitral practice in relation to procedure and evidence is, all things considered, undesirable. Each of the courts and tribunals examined above are tasked with performing the same general function, are faced with the same 'cross-cutting' issues of procedure and evidence, and, crucially, as Judge Greenwood has stated:

> International law is not a series of fragmented specialist and self-contained bodies of law, each of which functions in isolation from the others; it is a single, unified system of law and each international court can, and should, draw on the jurisprudence of other international courts and tribunals, even though it is not bound necessarily to come to the same conclusions.[81]

There is much to be gained from international courts and tribunals at least (and perhaps at most) taking into account investment arbitration practice, as Greenwood advocates. To give one example in this respect, the issue of admissibility of illegally-obtained evidence is a cross-cutting issue of procedure and evidence which has arisen repeatedly in investment arbitral practice of late.[82]

---

80 Yusuf (n 18).

81 *Ahmadou Sadio Diallo* (n 64) Declaration of Judge Greenwood, 394, para 8.

82 See Cherie Blair and Ema Vidak Gojković, 'Wikileaks and Beyond: Discerning an International Standard for the Admissibility of Illegal Obtained Evidence' (2018) 33

Traditionally, international courts and tribunals (save for international criminal tribunals[83]) have operated in accordance with the general rule of *liberté de la preuve* or 'the free admissibility of evidence' (with only a small number of exceptions).[84] In contrast to domestic evidentiary regimes which most often have sophisticated rules of admissibility, such rules 'have no place in international adjudication, where the relevance of facts and the value of evidence tending to establish facts are left to the appreciation of the court'.[85] One of the limited exceptions has been said to be that of illegally-obtained evidence. Nevertheless, even this limited circumstance has been closely circumscribed in practice, with, for example, the ICJ never having excluded evidence on this ground,[86] despite it being an issue in a number of cases.[87]

Recent investment arbitration practice, however, is illuminating for other courts and tribunals who may be faced with this cross-cutting issue again before long. For example, in one of the *Yukos* awards, *Hulley Enterprises*, the tribunal made extensive use of leaked cables between the US State Department and Yukos's auditor PricewaterhouseCoopers, released by Wikileaks.[88] In this particular dispute the tribunal seemed content to rely on evidence which had

---

ICSID Review 235.

83 See, e.g., ICTY, 'Rules of Procedure and Evidence' (24 July 2009) IT/Rev.43, Rule 89(C), which states that '[a] Chamber may admit any relevant evidence which it deems to have probative value', which has in fact been described as 'arguably the most frequently used provision in the Rules'; see Patricia Viseur Sellers, 'Rule 89 (C) and (D): At Odds or Overlapping with Rule 96 and Rule 95?' in Richard May et al (eds), *Essays on ICTY Procedure and Evidence in Honour of Gabrielle Kirk McDonald* (Martinus Nijhoff 2001). Rule 89(D) even permits the exclusion of evidence on the grounds that it lacks probative value, although this provision has not been the subject of extensive jurisprudence. See also Gideon Boas, 'Admissibility of Evidence under the Rules of Procedure and Evidence of the ICTY: Development of the "Flexibility Principle"' in May et al, ibid., 265.

84 See *Mavrommatis Palestine Concessions (Greece v Britain)* (Judgment) PCIJ Rep Series A No 2; Brown (n 1) Chapter 3.

85 Shabtai Rosenne and Yael Ronen, *The Law and Practice of the International Court, 1920–2005* (4th edn, Martinus Nijhoff 2006) 557; see also Charles N. Brower, 'The Anatomy of Fact-Finding Before International Tribunals: An Analysis and a Proposal Concerning the Evaluation of Evidence' in Richard B Lillich (ed), *Fact-Finding Before International Tribunals* (Transnational 1992) 147.

86 Keith Highet, 'Evidence, the Court, and the Nicaragua Case' (1987) 81 *AJIL* 1, 46.

87 See W. Michael Reisman and Eric E. Freedman, 'The Plaintiff's Dilemma: Illegally Obtained Evidence and Admissibility in International Adjudication' (1982) 76 *AJIL* 737, 739; Hugh Thirlway, 'Dilemma or Chimera – Admissibility of Illegally Obtained Evidence in International Adjudication' (1984) 78 *AJIL* 622, 633.

88 *Hulley Enterprises Limited (Cyprus) v Russian Federation*, UNCITRAL, PCA Case No 2005-03/AA226, Final Award (18 July 2014) paras 1218, 1223.

been obtained illegally, at least under the law of the US, without offering any opinion as to the issue of the admissibility of illegally-obtained evidence more generally.[89] This position is in line with the traditional approach taken by other courts and tribunals, mentioned above.

In *Methanex v United States*, the issue of illegally-obtained information arose once again, this time not as a result of Wikileaks but rather a more traditional (unlawful) method of 'dumpster diving'. In this particular case, the NAFTA tribunal found that the illegally-obtained documents were in fact inadmissible, going against the traditional position on the admissibility of illegally-obtained evidence before international courts and tribunals, highlighting the duty of good faith and the principles of justice and fairness.[90] While it is notable that an international tribunal would consider such evidence inadmissible, it should be taken into account that in this particular case it was the party seeking to rely on the evidence that had committed the unlawful act in order to obtain it, that the tribunal considered the documents to be of marginal materiality, and as such that excluding these documents from proceedings would not have any significant impact.[91]

In contrast, in *EDF v Romania*, EDF sought to rely upon a recording between one of its employees and the President of Romania regarding the payment of a bribe required to continue its business in Romania.[92] While the tribunal found that the tape recording had been obtained by EDF illegally, it showed its willingness to look to the practice of other courts and tribunals and found that:

> Generally, international tribunals take a liberal approach to the admissibility of evidence. The Tribunal is of the view, however, that such discretion is not absolute. In the Tribunal's judgment, there are limits to its discretion derived from principles of general application in international arbitration, whether pursuant to the Washington Convention or under other forms of international arbitration. Good faith and procedural fairness being among such principles, the Tribunal should refuse to admit evidence into the proceedings if, depending on the circumstances under which it was obtained and tendered to the other Party and the Tribunal, there are good reasons to believe that those principles of good faith and procedural fairness have not been respected.[93]

---

[89] Blair and Vidak Gojković (n 82) 248; See further James Boykin and Malik Havalic, 'Fruits of the Poisonous Tree: The Admissibility of Unlawfully Obtained Evidence in International Arbitration' (2015) *TDM* 5.

[90] *Methanex Corporation v United States of America,* UNCITRAL/NAFTA, Final Award of the Tribunal on Jurisdiction and Merits (3 August 2005) para 55.

[91] Ibid., para 56.

[92] *EDF (Services) Ltd v Romania,* ICSID Case No ARB/05/13, Procedural Order No 3 (29 August 2008) para 15.

[93] Ibid., para 47.

As such, in this particular case, the tribunal took into account that a number of factors in determining the admissibility of the evidence, including, *inter alia*, the actions of the party seeking to rely on the evidence, and its reliability.[94] Tribunals also considered the admissibility of illegally-obtained evidence in other cases, excluding such evidence in cases such as *Libanano v Turkey*.[95] Other tribunals have landed somewhere in the middle, such as *Caratube v Kazakhstan*, in which Caratube sought to rely on certain documents that had been leaked as part of the so-called 'KazakhLeaks' incident in 2016.[96] In this case, the tribunal allowed the admission of certain non-privileged documents which had been illegally-obtained but excluded other, privileged documents.[97]

This rich investment arbitral practice on this cross-cutting issue of evidence and procedure has allowed commentators to draw larger conclusions from this practice in an attempt to develop the doctrine. For instance, Blair and Vidak Gojković have argued that this recent practice shows that when faced with such questions tribunals have tended to ask a number of additional questions, including: (i) has the evidence been obtained unlawfully by a party who seeks to benefit from it? (ii) does public interest favour rejecting the evidence as inadmissible? And (iii) do the interests of justice favour the admission of evidence?[98] Taken together, this represents a clear example of the potential added value of taking investment arbitral practice into account.

The issue of illegally-obtained evidence is just one example chosen to illustrate the rich corpus of investment law practice which could act as a driver of the development of international law more generally.[99] For this potential to be realised, however, other courts and tribunals would have to embrace Judge Greenwood's advice that international courts can, and should, draw on the jurisprudence of other international courts and tribunals – even if they are not bound necessarily to come to the same conclusions.[100] The question then becomes whether courts and tribunals are likely to do so. The final section offers some hope in this regard, speculating that courts and tribunals will find

---

94 Blair and Vidak Gojković (n 82) 254.

95 *Libananco Holdings Co Ltd v Republic of Turkey*, ICSID Case No ARB/06/8, Decision on Preliminary Issues (23 June 2008) para 82.

96 *Caratube International Oil Company LLP and Devincci Salah Hourani v Republic of Kazakhstan*, ICSID Case No ARB/13/13, Award (27 September 2017) para 150.

97 Ibid., paras 669, 1259.

98 Blair and Vidak Gojković (n 82) 259.

99 Other cross-cutting examples such as abuse of process could have been selected, see, e.g., Yuka Fukunaga, 'Abuse of Process under International Law and Investment Arbitration' (2018) 33 *ICSID Review* 181.

100 Greenwood (n 81).

it increasingly difficult to avoid such engagement as long as parties continue to rely on investment arbitration practice in their submissions.

IV. CONCLUDING THOUGHTS: INTERNATIONAL COURTS AND THE UNSUSTAINABILITY OF ISOLATIONISM

Chester Brown's influential work on the development of a so-called common law of international adjudication, mentioned above, identifies a range of factors which he argues facilitate procedural cross-fertilisation between courts and tribunals.[101] More than a decade on, it is instructive to take Brown's work as a reference point and reflect on the extent to which these facilitating factors have been borne out in practice. Overall, the courts and tribunals considered here have not been particularly forthcoming in their dicta on any potential development of a common law of international adjudication or procedural cross-fertilisation. Brown cites the relatively small size of the 'international bar', and 'international judiciary' as a factor capable of contributing to converging approaches to procedural issues.[102] However, while empirical research carried out in the intervening years has confirmed that a relatively small group of individuals appear in the majority of investment arbitration cases. [103] This does not seem to have been mirrored by any increase in citations of investment arbitral practice.

Similarly, although Brown suggests that international courts and tribunals may utilise 'customary rules developed in international judicial practice, and general principles of law, both of which are well established as sources of judicial procedure' to justify cross-fertilisation, tribunals have not yet explicitly relied on such argumentation.[104] In fact, even when presented with the

---

[101] Brown (n 1) 230; These factors included (i) similar constitutive instruments or procedural rules, (ii) that courts look to each other's existing practice when an issue arises in proceedings before them, (iii) certain approaches to treaty interpretation which allow different provisions to be interpreted in a similar manner, (iv) resort to customary international law and general principles of law which are common to courts and tribunals, (v) the ability to make reference to inherent powers, (vi) the similar function performed by courts and tribunals, (vii) the existence of an 'international bar', (viii) competition among international courts, (ix) a perception of commonality between courts as being a generally positive development, (x) the similar relationship between parties and the tribunal, (xi) parties themselves pleading the relevance of the practice of other courts, and finally (xii) norm-intrinsic reasons such as fairness.

[102] Ibid.

[103] Sergio Puig, 'Social Capital in the Arbitration Market' (2014) 25 *EJIL* 387.

[104] Brown (n 1) 229.

opportunity of doing so, as in the case of the *Chagos MPA* arbiration above,[105] regarding whether the widely-accepted IBA Guidelines represented general principles of law, the tribunal demurred.

More generally, it is difficult to discern whether courts and tribunals consider such cross-fertilisation to be a positive practice, as Brown suggested they may. This is perhaps to be expected, given the principle of judicial economy[106] but it nevertheless leaves us attempting to look for any such developments 'between the lines' of judgments and awards. As such, the rather mixed picture presented in Part 1 above suggests that the limiting factors which may hamper procedural cross-fertilisation also mentioned by Brown may still be an impediment. These limiting factors include the fact that, while some constitutive instruments and rules of procedure may be similar,[107] other regimes are significantly different on certain issues, and that interpretation can only bridge some of this gap.[108] Other limiting factors are the particular function assigned to each tribunal and the nature of the parties which appear before it.[109] For instance, the apparent reluctance of the ICJ to rely on investment arbitration practice (compared at least to inter-State arbitration) examined above,[110] may be to some extent rooted in, in my opinion misplaced, misgivings regarding the mixed nature of investment arbitration.

Ultimately, another factor identified by Brown is most likely to determine the long-term influence of investment arbitration: the extent to which parties themselves rely on arbitral practice in their submissions. It was through such submissions that the ICJ made its first and second mentions of investment law practice in recent times, even if it did not ultimately rely on such practice.[111] In this vein, the more that parties cite investment practice with regard to evidence and procedure, it seems likely the courts and tribunals will find it difficult to resist some form of engagement with it. Of course, some courts and tribunals may continue to attempt to hold back the tide and refuse to consider investment arbitration practice for formalistic (as in the case of *Chagos MPA*) or other reasons. However, doing so would be a mistake, and it is much more fruitful to 'take into account' the practice of investment arbitration, particu-

---

[105] See above Section II.A.

[106] Ridi (n 8).

[107] Brown (n 1) 226; This may be because a number of different sets have rules have a common ancestor, such as those of the International Court of Justice, the International Tribunal for the Law of the Sea, and the European Court of Human Rights, which were all modelled to a greater or lesser extent on the Statute of the Permanent Court of International Justice.

[108] Ibid., 234.

[109] Ibid., 234ff.

[110] See above Section II.C.

[111] Ibid.

larly that which is relied upon by parties in their own submissions. And, as we have seen, as long as cross-cutting issues of evidence and procedure such as the admissibility of illegally-obtained evidence continue to be thoughtfully handled (and the law developed accordingly), it is highly likely that parties and their counsel will continue to turn to investment arbitration practice in the hope of bolstering their legal arguments.

All this comes at a time when some scholars are writing of procedural cross-fertilisation fostering an 'emerging model of due process' which itself produces 'certain common expectations and apparent deviations from the model must be explained'.[112] Others talk of a 'brave new world' of authority sharing, in which it is necessary to 'pay greater attention than ever before to authorities originating from other dispute settlement peers that are dealing with similar questions.[113] Whether or not one agrees that we are indeed living in a brave new world, today it is at the very least difficult to maintain that international law is 'a series of fragmented specialist and self-contained bodies of law, each of which functions in isolation from the others'.[114] Rather, as Part 2 argued, international courts can, and should, draw on the jurisprudence of other international courts, and the rich corpus of investment arbitration practice should be paid just as much attention as any inter-State court or tribunal.

---

[112] Ruiz Fabri (n 1) 24.

[113] James Crawford, 'Continuity and Discontinuity in International Dispute Settlement' (2010) 1 *JIDS* 3, 22.

[114] Greenwood (n 81).

12. Review and enforcement of arbitral awards in international investment law and general public international law

Michail Risvas[1]

I. INTRODUCTION

In the last three decades international investment arbitration cases grew exponentially.[2] While arbitral proceedings before investment tribunals are expensive and relatively long, a final award is not always the end of the dispute between the parties. In arbitrations conducted under the auspices of the International Centre for Settlement of Investment Disputes (ICSID) of the World Bank, the parties may only apply to annul the award before a three-member ad hoc committee – and not before any domestic court.[3] The members of the committee are selected by ICSID from the 'Panel of Arbitrators'.[4] This self-contained regime for review

---

[1] The author is grateful to the editors of the present book, Professors Stephan Schill, Rainer Hofmann, and Christian J. Tams, as well as Dr Odysseus Repousis and Dr Michail Dekastros for their comments. The author is also grateful to Mr Maximilian Schalkowski for his research assistance. The views presented, and any errors or omissions, are those of the author's alone.

[2] According to UNCTAD, '[a]s of 1 January 2018, the total number of publicly known ISDS claims had reached 855': UNCTAD, 'Investor-State Dispute Settlement: Review of Developments in 2017' (June 2018) IIA Issues Notes 2, 2 https://unctad.org/system/files/official-document/diaepcbinf2018d2_en.pdf accessed 20 November 2020. By contrast, until 2000, the total number of investment treaty arbitrations was less than 35, see UNCTAD, Investment Policy Hub, 'Case name and number' (*UNCTAD*) http://investmentpolicyhub.unctad.org/ISDS/FilterByYear accessed 20 November 2020.

[3] The Convention on the Settlement of Investment Disputes between States and Nationals of Other States (ICSID Convention) (adopted 18 March 1965, entered into force 14 October 1966) 575 UNTS 159, art 53(1) stipulates that '[t]he award shall be binding on the parties and shall not be subject to any appeal or to any other remedy except those provided for in this Convention'.

[4] See ICSID Convention, ibid., art 52(3). See further Christoph Schreuer, 'From ICSID Annulment to Appeal Half Way Down the Slippery Slope' (2011) 10 *LPICT*

and annulment of awards has created considerable case law (consisting of approximately 100 decisions). In non-ICSID arbitrations, which include arbitrations conducted under the auspices of the ICSID Additional Facility, the unsuccessful party can (and sometimes does) challenge the arbitral award before the courts of the jurisdiction in which the arbitral tribunal was seated.[5] Thus, a number of cases of pivotal legal and political importance regarding the review of arbitral awards have been brought before domestic courts in the United States,[6] Canada,[7] United Kingdom,[8] France,[9]

211; Carolyn B. Lamm, 'Internationalization of the Practice of Law and Important Emerging Issues for Investor-State Arbitration' (2011) 354 *Recueil des cours* 35; *ICSID*, 'Background Paper on Annulment For the Administrative Council of ICSID' (2012) 27 *ICSID Review* 443.

[5] On the interaction between domestic courts and international investment tribunals, see generally Gabrielle Kaufmann-Kohler and Michele Potestà, 'Investor-State Dispute Settlement and National Courts: Current Framework and Reform Options' (2020) *EYIEL*, in particular Chapter 3 ('The Interplay Between Investor-State Arbitration and Domestic Courts in the Existing IIA Framework'). On whether the parties can waive their right to apply to set aside the award in advance, see Maxi Scherer, 'The Fate of Parties' Agreements on Judicial Review of Awards: A Comparative and Normative Analysis of Party-Autonomy at the Post-Award Stage' (2016) 32 *Arb Int'l* 437. At the same time, the parties' agreement to *expand* the scope of review of the arbitral award by the domestic court would be usually unenforceable, see, ibid., 445; *Hall Street Associates, LLC v Mattel, Inc*, 552 US 576 (2008); France, Court of Cassation, *Société Buzzichelli Holding v Hennion* (6 April 1994) in (1995) *Revue de l'arbitrage* 263; *Guangzhou Dockyards Co v ENE Aegiali I* [2010] EWHC 2826 (Comm) para 30. Contra, German Supreme Court (1 March 2007) *ASA Bulletin* 810.

[6] See, e.g., *BG Group PLC v Republic of Argentina*, 572 US 25 (2014); see also Andrea K. Bjorklund, 'Case Comment: Republic of Argentina v BG Group PLC' (2012) 27 *ICSID Review* 4.

[7] See, e.g., *United Mexican States v Metalclad Corporation* (2001) BCSC 664; *United Mexican States v Marvin Roy Feldman* (2003) No 03-CV-23500 (Ont SC) and (2005) 193 OAC 213, 248 DLR (4e) 443 (Ont CA); *The Attorney General of Canada v SD Myers, Inc* (2004) FC 38; *Bayview Irrigation District #11 v United Mexican States* [2008] OJ No 1858, 2008 CanLII 22120 (Ont SC); *United Mexican States v Cargill Incorporated* (2010) ONSC 4656 (Ont SC) and *United Mexican States v Cargill Incorporated* (2011) ONCA622 (Ont CA).

[8] See, e.g., *The Republic of Ecuador v Occidental Exploration & Production Co* [2006] EWHC 345 (Comm); *GPF GP Sàrl v The Republic of Poland* [2018] EWHC 409 (Comm).

[9] See, e.g., CA Paris, *République Tchèque c Monsieur Pren Nreka* (25 September 2008) No 07/04675; CA Paris, *République du Kirghizistan c Monsieur Valeriy Belokon* (21 February 2017) No 15/01650.

the Netherlands,[10] Singapore,[11] and other jurisdictions. While until 2015 only one investment treaty arbitral award has been set aside by a domestic court (*Metaclad v Mexico*),[12] since then the picture changed rapidly: investment treaty awards have been set aside in different jurisdictions, including the Netherlands,[13] Singapore,[14] France,[15] and the UK.[16] At the same time, courts in other jurisdictions resist such trend. In Switzerland courts have 'never upheld an application to annul an investment award' to date, despite 15 known attempts to do so.[17]

Arbitral tribunals do not interpret investment treaties in clinical isolation from international law but frequently refer to the jurisprudence of the International Court of Justice (ICJ),[18] and other international courts and tribu-

---

[10] District Court of The Hague, Consolidated Court Cases no 386934 / HA ZA 11-402 and 408948 / HA ZA 11-2813 (*The Republic of Ecuador v Chevron Corporation (USA) and Texaco Petroleum Company*); District Court of The Hague, Cases C/09/477160 / HA ZA 15-1, C/09/477162 / HA ZA 15-2 and C/09/481619 / HA ZA 15-112 (*The Russian Federation v Veteran Petroleum Limited, The Russian Federation v Yukos Universal Limited, The Russian Federation v Hulley Enterprises Limited*); Court of Appeal of The Hague, Cases no C/09/477160 / HA ZA 15-1, C/09/477162 / HA ZA 15-2 and C/09/481619 / HA ZA 15-112 (*Veteran Petroleum Limited, The Russian Federation v Yukos Universal Limited, The Russian Federation v Hulley Enterprises Limited v The Russian Federation*). The Dutch Supreme Court upheld Russia's appeal on 5 November 2021.

[11] *Swissbourgh Diamond Mines (Pty) Ltd and others v Kingdom of Lesotho* [2018] SGCA 81; *Kingdom of Lesotho v Swissbourgh Diamond Mines (Pty) Ltd and others* [2017] SGHC 195.

[12] *Metalclad Corporation v United Mexican States*, ICSID Case No ARB(AF)/97/1, Award (30 August 2000); *United Mexican States v Metalclad Corporation* (n 7); Shotaro Hamamoto, 'Domestic Review of Treaty-Based International Investment Awards: Effects of the Metalclad Judgment of the British Columbia Supreme Court' in Machiko Kanetake and André Nollkaemper (eds), *The Rule of Law at the National and International Levels: Contestations and Deference* (Hart Publishing 2016) 100; see also Section III below.

[13] *The Russian Federation v Veteran Petroleum Limited, The Russian Federation v Yukos Universal Limited, The Russian Federation v Hulley Enterprises Limited* (n 10); reinstated by the Court of Appeal. The Court of Appeal's decision was set aside by the Supreme Court and the case was remanded to the Amsterdam Court of Appeal.

[14] *Swissbourgh Diamond Mines v Kingdom of Lesotho* (n 11); *Kingdom of Lesotho v Swissbourgh Diamond Mines (Pty)* (n 11).

[15] CA Paris, *République du Kirghizistan c Monsieur Valeriy Belokon* (21 February 2017) No 15/01650.

[16] *GPF GP Sàrl v The Republic of Poland* [2018] EWHC 409 (Comm) (overturning parts of the tribunal's award on jurisdiction).

[17] Kaufmann-Kohler and Potestà (n 5) 66–72.

[18] See, e.g., Alain Pellet, 'The Case Law of the ICJ in Investment Arbitration' (2013) 28 *ICSID Review* 223.

nals, such as the European Court of Human Rights (ECtHR),[19] and, to a lesser extent, the WTO Panels and the Appellate Body.[20] Nonetheless, little attention has been paid to the influence that investment tribunals had or could have on the decisions rendered by other international courts and tribunals either generally or regarding the issue of review of arbitral awards in particular.[21] This is perhaps not surprising given the stance of the ICJ towards investment treaty arbitration, ranging from skepticism to covert hostility. In *Diallo* the ICJ refused to take into consideration the practice under investment treaties regarding the protection of shareholders when interpreting the customary international law on this issue:

> [t]he fact invoked by Guinea that various international agreements, such as agreements for the promotion and protection of foreign investments and the Washington Convention, have established special legal régimes governing investment protection, or that provisions in this regard are commonly included in contracts entered into directly between States and foreign investors, is not sufficient to show that there has been a change in the customary rules of diplomatic protection; it could equally show the contrary.[22]

More recently, in *Bolivia v Chile* the ICJ also refused to consider that the (rich) investment arbitration jurisprudence on legitimate expectations had any relevance for general public international law:

> The Court notes that references to legitimate expectations may be found in arbitral awards concerning disputes between a foreign investor and the host State that apply treaty clauses providing for fair and equitable treatment. It does not follow from such references that there exists in general international law a principle that would give rise to an obligation on the basis of what could be considered a legitimate

---

[19] See, e.g., *Philip Morris Brands Sàrl, Philip Morris Products SA and Abal Hermanos SA v Oriental Republic of Uruguay*, ICSID Case No ARB/10/7, Award (8 July 2016) paras 398–399; see also Pierre-Marie Dupuy et al (eds), *Human Rights in International Investment Law and Arbitration* (OUP 2009).

[20] See, e.g., *Continental Casualty Company v Argentine Republic*, ICSID Case No ARB/03/9, Award (5 September 2008); see also Jürgen Kurtz, 'The Use and Abuse of WTO Law in Investor-State Arbitration: Competition and Its Discontents' (2009) 20 *EJIL* 749; Robert L. Howse and Efraim Chalamish, 'The Use and Abuse of WTO Law in Investor-State Arbitration: A Reply to Jürgen Kurtz' (2010) 20 *EJIL* 1087.

[21] For an exception, see Stephan W. Schill and Katrine Tvede, 'Mainstreaming Investment Treaty Jurisprudence: The Contribution of Investment Treaty Tribunals to the Consolidation and Development of General International Law' (2014) 14 *LPICT* 94, and the chapters in this volume.

[22] *Case Concerning Ahmadou Sadio Diallo (Republic of Guinea v Democratic Republic of the Congo* (Judgment) [2007] *ICJ Reports* 582, 615, para 90.

> expectation. Bolivia's argument based on legitimate expectations thus cannot be sustained.[23]

In 2018, the ICJ changed its policy of allowing the ICJ judges to participate as arbitrators in international arbitration under investment treaties or contracts, with a limited exception of inter-State arbitrations.[24] Even within the realm of investment treaty arbitration, it appears that domestic judgments concerning the review of arbitral awards have no or little influence on arbitral tribunals.[25]

To the best of the author's knowledge, the only exception of an international court or tribunal referring to, and drawing inspiration from, the review of arbitral awards in the realm of investment arbitration is the Government of *Sudan v Sudan People's Liberation Movement/Army* (the *Abye* arbitration).[26]

---

[23] *Obligation to Negotiate Access to the Pacific Ocean (Bolivia v Chile)* (Judgment) [2018] *ICJ Reports* 507, para 162.

[24] H E Mr Abdulqawi A. Yusuf, President of the International Court of Justice, 'Speech' (Seventy-Third Session of the United Nations General Assembly, New York, 25 October 2018) 11–12:

> Over the years, the Court has taken the view that, in certain circumstances, its Members may participate in arbitration proceedings. However, in light of its ever-increasing workload, the Court decided a few months ago to review this practice and to set out clearly defined rules regulating such activities. As a result, Members of the Court have come to the decision, last month, that they will not normally accept to participate in international arbitration. In particular, they will not participate in investor-State arbitration or in commercial arbitration. However, in the event that they are called upon, exceptionally, by one or more States that would prefer to resort to arbitration, instead of judicial settlement, the Court has decided that, in order to render service to those States, it will, if the circumstances so warrant, authorize its Members to participate in inter-State arbitration cases. Even in such exceptional cases, a Member of the Court will only participate, if authorized, in one arbitration procedure at a time. Prior authorization must have been granted, for that purpose, in accordance with the mechanism put in place by the Court. Members of the Court, will, however, decline to be appointed as arbitrators by a State that is a party in a case pending before the Court, even if there is no substantial interference between that case and the case submitted to arbitration. This is essential to place beyond reproach the impartiality and independence of Judges in the exercise of their judicial functions. Finally, I cannot stress enough that any participation of Members of the Court in such inter-State arbitrations is subject to the strict condition that their judicial activities take absolute precedence.

www.icj-cij.org/public/files/press-releases/0/000-20181025-PRE-02-00-EN.pdf accessed 10 November 2020.

[25] For example, 'the Metalclad judgment exert[s] little influence over the subsequent tribunals, while the vacated part of the *Metalclad* award continues to be quoted and relied on', Hamamoto (n 12) 112.

[26] *The Government of Sudan / The Sudan People's Liberation Movement / Army (Abyei Arbitration)*, PCA Case No 2008-07, Award (22 July 2009); see also Schill and

In that case the tribunal was called to review not an arbitral award but the decision of committee of technical experts (the 'Abyei Boundaries Commission' or 'ABC') regarding the delimitation of Abyei area in Sudan. In examining whether the ABC exceeded its mandate (agreed by the Government of Sudan and the Sudan People's Liberation Movement), the tribunal held that:

> [i]n public international law, it is an established principle of arbitral and, more generally, institutional review that the original decision-maker's findings will be subject to limited review only. The relevant case law draws a clear distinction between an appeal on the merits – to determine whether the original decision was legally and factually 'right or wrong' – and a review of whether the decision-maker that rendered a decision exceeded its powers. A reviewing body that is seized of the issue of putative excess of powers will not 'pronounce on whether the [original] decision was right or wrong,' as this question is legally irrelevant within an excess of powers inquiry.[27]

Citing the annulment decisions of ICSID ad hoc committees in *Vivendi v Argentina* and *CDC Group v Seychelles*, the tribunal further clarified that:

> [t]here is no dearth of international case law confirming that the remedy of annulment of arbitral awards is granted only under exceptional circumstances. Reviewing bodies have noted that only 'weighty' or'"exceptional circumstances' will justify a finding of invalidity and that the party seeking to impugn an arbitral award bears a 'very great' burden of proof. In addition, reviewing bodies have limited their review to'"clear' cases and have noted that the reviewing body must 'not intrude into the legal and factual decisionmaking of the [original decision-making body].' This body of case law suggests that the scope of review in international proceedings leading to the annulment of a prior decision is generally very limited.[28]

Thus, the tribunal concluded that '[t]he practice of courts and tribunals in public international law is broadly supportive of the proposition that an instance of review must defer, and give special weight, to the interpretation of a jurisdictional instrument by the decision-making body designated under that instrument'.[29] For reaching that conclusion the Tribunal did not only rely on the relevant jurisprudence of the ICJ,[30] but also on the case law of ICSID ad hoc committees.[31]

Leaving the notable exception of the *Abyei* arbitration aside, the jurisprudence of ICSID ad hoc Committees and domestic courts in relation to

---

Tvede (n 21).

27 *Abyei Arbitration*, ibid., para 403.

28 Ibid., para 405.

29 Ibid., para 505.

30 Ibid., paras 505–510.

31 Ibid., paras 507 and 512.

the review of arbitral awards, despite consisting of dozens of cases, has had little influence on international courts and tribunals and did not influence the development of international law. However, an important methodological caveat must be made. 'Influence' is usually equated with explicit citations or refences. Nonetheless, one can certainly make the argument that international investment law (and, in fact, any specialised branch of public international law) could influence other regimes of international law indirectly. In other words, the lack of explicit references to international investment law does not necessarily mean that the practice of ICSID ad hoc Committees or domestic courts in relation to the review of arbitral awards does not influence international law more generally; it speaks more to the international law scholars' limitations to discern more indirect influences. Naturally, this opens up an area of further, methodologically difficult research which cannot be explored in the confines of this chapter.

This chapter examines the law regulating the review of arbitral awards by the ICJ (section II), domestic courts (section III) and ICSID ad hoc committees (section IV) and makes the case for greater cross-fertilisation between (i) the case law regarding review of arbitral awards and (ii) other regimes of international law (section V).

II. REVIEW OF ARBITRAL AWARDS IN THE JURISPRUDENCE OF THE INTERNATIONAL COURT OF JUSTICE

Even before the international arbitration 'revolution' which occurred in the late 20th century and the beginning of the 21st century, public international law was not agnostic to legal questions arising out in the context of the review of arbitral awards. The ICJ had (some rare) opportunities to review (inter-State) arbitral awards and pronounce on the appropriate standard of such review in two case: the Arbitral Award of 31 July 1989 case between Guinea-Bissau and Senegal[32] and Arbitral Award made by the King of Spain on 23 December 1906.[33]

[32] *Case Concerning the Arbitral Award of 31 July 1989 (Guinea-Bissau v Senegal)* (Judgment) [1991] *ICJ Reports* 53.

[33] *Case concerning the Arbitral Award made by the King of Spain on 23 December 1906 (Honduras v Nicaragua)* [1960] *ICJ Reports* 192. In the *Monetary Gold* case, the ICJ would have been called to review the award rendered by the arbitrator, had it not been for the application of the eponymous principle that precluded the examination of the merits of the case, *Case of the Monetary Gold Removed from Rome in 1943* (Preliminary Question) [1954] *ICJ Reports* 19.

In Arbitral Award made by the King of Spain on 23 December 1906 Honduras initiated proceedings before the ICJ complaining that Nicaragua's failure 'to give effect to the arbitral award made on 23 December 1906 by His Majesty the King of Spain constitutes a breach of an international obligation' and called the ICJ to rule that Nicaragua 'is under an obligation to give effect to the award'.[34] On its part Nicaragua argued (*inter alia*) that the arbitral award contained 'obscurities and contradictions which made this execution impossible', 'is vitiated by essential errors', 'is not supported by an adequate statement of reasons', and 'the King exceeded his jurisdiction'.[35] Nicaragua also 'expressed readiness to submit to arbitration or mediation the disagreement between itself and the Government of Honduras concerning the validity of the said so-called arbitral decision'.[36] In the light of the fact that '[n]o question was at any time raised in the arbitral proceedings before the King with regard either to the validity of his designation as arbitrator or his jurisdiction as such',[37] the ICJ summarily dismissed Nicaragua's allegation that 'the designation of the King of Spain as arbitrator to decide the boundary dispute between the two Parties was invalid'.[38] The ICJ had no difficulty rejecting Nicaragua's argument on the alleged expiration of the Treaty providing for arbitration also on the basis that 'no objection was taken before the King of Spain to his proceeding with the arbitration on the ground that the Gamez-Bonilla Treaty had already expired'.[39] The Court then examined Nicaragua's submission that the award was invalid due to 'excess of jurisdiction', 'essential error', 'lack or inadequacy of reasons in support of the conclusions arrived at by the Arbitrator' and the award 'is in any case incapable of execution by reason of its omissions, contradictions and obscurities'.[40]

---

34 *Arbitral Award by the King of Spain* (n 33) 195. The award fixed 'the dividing line between the Republics of Honduras and Nicaragua from the Atlantic to the Portillo de Teotecacinte', ibid., 202.

35 Ibid., 197.

36 Ibid.

37 Ibid., 207.

38 Ibid.

39 Ibid., 209. See also, ibid.:

> the Court considers that, having regard to the fact that the designation of the King of Spain as arbitrator was freely agreed to by Nicaragua, that no objection was taken by Nicaragua to the jurisdiction of the King of Spain as arbitrator either on the ground of irregularity in his designation as arbitrator or on the ground that the Gamez-Bonilla Treaty had lapsed even before the King of Spain had signified his acceptance of the office of arbitrator. and that Nicaragua fully participated in the arbitral proceedings before the King, it is no longer open to Nicaragua to rely on either of these contentions as furnishing a ground for the nullity of the Award.

40 Ibid., 210.

First, the ICJ briefly articulated the applicable standard of review:

> even if there had not been repeated acts of recognition by Nicaragua which, as the Court has found, debars it from relying subsequently on complaints of nullity and even if such complaints had been put forward in proper time, the Award would, in the judgment of the Court, still have to be recognized as valid. The Court will proceed to indicate very briefly the reasons for arriving at this conclusion. Before doing so, the Court will observe that the Award is not subject to appeal and that the Court cannot approach the consideration of the objections raised by Nicaragua to the validity of the Award as a Court of Appeal. The Court is not called upon to pronounce on whether the arbitrator's decision was right or wrong. These and cognate considerations have no relevance to the function that the Court is called upon to discharge in these proceedings, which is to decide whether the Award is proved to be a nullity having no effect.[41]

Subsequently, the ICJ applied that standard and rejected Nicaragua's arguments without offering an extensive analysis.[42]

The second case in which the ICJ reviewed an international arbitral award concerned an award rendered by a three-member tribunal constituted pursuant to an 1985 arbitration agreement between Guinea-Bissau and Senegal. The tribunal's mandate was (1) to decide on whether the 1960 agreement delimiting the maritime boundary between the two countries concluded by Portugal and France (the former colonial powers of the two countries respectively) was binding and (2) in case of a negative answer to that question, to delimit that boundary.[43] In 1989 the arbitral tribunal (composed by Mohammed Bedjaoui and André Gros as co-arbitrators, and Julio Barberis as presiding arbitrator)

---

41 Ibid., 214.

42 Ibid., 216:

> The last ground of nullity raised by Nicaragua is the alleged lack or inadequacy of reasons in support of the conclusions arrived at by the arbitrator. However, an examination of the Award shows that it deals in logical order and in some detail with all relevant considerations and that it contains ample reasoning and explanations in support of the conclusions arrived at by the arbitrator. In the opinion of the Court, this ground is without foundation.

Ibid., 217:

> In view of the clear directive in the operative clause and the explanations in support of it in the Award, the Court does not consider that the Award is incapable of execution by reason of any omissions, contradictions or obscurities.'

43 See *Arbitral Award of 31 July 1989* (n 32) 58:

1. Does the Agreement concluded by an exchange of letters on 26 April 1960, and which relates to the maritime boundary, have the force of law in the relations between the Republic of Guinea-Bissau and the Republic of Senegal?
2. In the event of a negative answer to the first question, what is the course of the line delimiting the maritime territories appertaining to the Republic of Guinea-Bissau and the Republic of Senegal respectively?

rendered its award. The arbitral tribunal ruled that the 1960 agreement delimit the boundary of the maritime zones that existed in 1960 (territorial sea, the contiguous zone and the continental shelf) but not those which did not exist at the time (exclusive economic zone[44] and fishery zone). However, the tribunal invoked the 'evolutionary interpretation' of the concept of the continental shelf. The presiding arbitration issued a declaration clarifying that the 1960 agreement 'does not have the force of law with respect to the waters of the exclusive economic zone or the fishery zone'.[45] Guinea-Bissau argued that 'the so-called "award" of 31 July 1989 is inexistent in view of the fact that one of the two arbitrators making up the appearance of a majority in favour of the text of the "award", has, by a declaration appended to it, expressed a view in contradiction with the one apparently adopted by the vote'.[46] '[S]ubsidiarily', Guinea-Bissau argued that the arbitral tribunal did not comply with the arbitration agreement by failing to proceed to decide on the disputed maritime areas between the two countries.[47] The ICJ ruled that:

> [t]he Tribunal found, in reply to the first question, that the 1960 Agreement had the force of law in the relations between the Parties, and at the same time it defined the substantive scope of that Agreement. Such an answer did not permit of a delimitation of the whole of the maritime areas of the two States, and a complete settlement of the dispute between them. It achieved a partial delimitation. But that answer was nonetheless both a complete and an affirmative answer to the first question; it recognized that the Agreement of 1960 had the force of law in the relations between Senegal and Guinea-Bissau. The Tribunal could thus find, without manifest breach of its competence, that its answer to the first question was not a negative one, and that it was therefore not competent to answer the second question. In this respect

---

[44] The Exclusive Economic Zone (EEZ) was one of the main legal innovations of the United Nations Convention on the Law of the Sea (UNCLOS) (adopted 10 December 1982, entered into force 16 November 1994) 1833 UNTS 3. Already in 1982 (12 years before the UNCLOS entered into force) the ICJ held that the EEZ 'may be regarded as part of modem international law', *Continental Shelf (Tunisia / Libyan Arab Jamahiriya)* (Judgment) [1982] *ICJ Reports* 18, 74, para 100. However, it is rather uncontroversial that this concept was unknown in international law in 1960. See also Maria Gavouneli, *Functional Jurisdiction in the Law of the Sea* (Brill 2007) 61–62.

[45] *Arbitral Award of 31 July 1989* (n 32) 60.

[46] Ibid., 56.

[47] See ibid.:

> [the] so-called decision is absolutely null and void, as the Tribunal failed to reply to the second question raised by the Arbitration Agreement, whereas its reply to the first question implied a need for a reply to be given to the second, as it did not comply with the provisions of the Arbitration Agreement by which the Tribunal was asked to decide on the delimitation of the maritime areas as a whole, to do so by a single line and to record that line on a map, and as it has not given the reasons for the restrictions thus improperly placed upon its jurisdiction.

> also, the contention of Guinea-Bissau that the entire Award is a nullity must be rejected.[48]

As a result, the ICJ summarily rejected Guinea-Bissau's arguments:

> [t]he Court is unable to uphold the contention that the reasoning of the Tribunal was insufficient on this point. The reasoning mentioned above is, once again, brief but sufficient to enlighten the Parties and the Court as to the reasons that guided the Tribunal. It found that the boundary line fixed by the 1960 Agreement was a loxodromic line drawn at 240º from the point of intersection of the prolongation of the land frontier and the low-water line of the two countries, represented for that purpose by the Cape Roxo lighthouse. Since it did not reply to the second question, it did not have to define any other line. It thus considered that there was no need to draw on a map a line which was common knowledge, and the definitive characteristics of which it had specified.[49]

What the analysis of these two ICJ cases shows is that the Court focused on specific aspects of the disputes before it, rather than making more general pronouncements on the subject of review. This, coupled with the absence of more cases of similar nature, explains why the ICJ jurisprudence on the review of arbitral awards is only part of the relevant international practice; ICSID ad hoc Committees and domestic courts have generated a much richer jurisprudence on the review of awards rendered by investment treaty tribunals, which will be considered in the next two sections.

III. THE REVIEW OF INVESTMENT TREATY ARBITRAL AWARD BY DOMESTIC COURTS

Domestic courts regularly review the validity of international arbitral awards either in the course of set-aside proceedings (before the courts of the jurisdiction in which the arbitral tribunal was seated)[50] or in the course of enforcement proceedings (usually on the basis of Convention on the Recognition and

---

[48] Ibid., 73, para 60.

[49] Ibid., 74, para 63.

[50] See UNCITRAL, 'Model Law on International Commercial Arbitration' (21 June 1985) UN Doc A/40/17, as amended in 2006, art 1(2). On the controversial question whether an arbitral award, which has been set aside by the courts of the jurisdiction of the seat of the arbitral tribunal, could be enforced in another jurisdiction see Rashda Rana; 'The Enforceability of Awards Set Aside at the Seat: an Asian and European Perspective' (2017) 40 *Fordham ILJ* 813; Albert Jan van den Berg, 'Should the Setting Aside of the Arbitral Award Be Abolished?' (2014) 29 *ICSID Review* 263; Emmanuel Gaillard, 'The Enforcement of Awards Set Aside in the Country of Origin' (1999) 14 *ICSID Review* 16; Georgios Petrochilos, 'Enforcing Awards Annulled in Their State of Origin Under the New York Convention' (1999) 48 *ICLQ* 856.

Enforcement of Foreign Arbitral Awards (the 'New York Convention')).[51] Such review of arbitral awards is limited. If the arbitral award is being enforced in a State party to the New York Convention, the domestic courts of that jurisdiction can refuse the enforcement of that award only for very specific reasons, pertaining to the composition or the (lack of) jurisdiction of the arbitral tribunal, as well as procedural propriety and public policy.[52] Article V of the New York Convention circumscribes that limited review:

> (1) Recognition and enforcement of the award may be refused, at the request of the party against whom it is invoked, only if that party furnishes to the competent authority where the recognition and enforcement is sought, proof that:
>
> (a) the parties to the agreement referred to in article II were, under the law applicable to them, under some incapacity, or the said agreement is not valid under the law to which the parties have subjected it or, failing any indication thereon, under the law of the country where the award was made; or
>
> (b) the party against whom the award is invoked was not given proper notice of the appointment of the arbitrator or of the arbitration proceedings or was otherwise unable to present his case; or
>
> (c) the award deals with a difference not contemplated by or not falling within the terms of the submission to arbitration, or it contains decisions on matters beyond the scope of the submission to arbitration, provided that, if the decisions on matters submitted to arbitration can be separated from those not so submitted, that part of the award which contains decisions on matters submitted to arbitration may be recognized and enforced; or
>
> (d) the composition of the arbitral authority or the arbitral procedure was not in accordance with the agreement of the parties, or, failing such

---

[51] Convention on the Recognition and Enforcement of Foreign Arbitral Awards (adopted 10 June 1958, entered into force 7 June 1959) 330 UNTS 3. As of October 2018, 159 States have ratified the New York Convention. On the New York Convention see Marike Paulsson, *The 1958 New York Convention in Action* (Wolters Kluwer 2016). ICSID, 'Additional Facility Rules' (April 2006) ICSID/11, Schedule C: Arbitration (Additional Facility) Rules, art 19 provides that 'Arbitration proceedings shall be held only in States that are parties to the 1958 UN Convention on the Recognition and Enforcement of Foreign Arbitral Awards'.

[52] See Hossein Abedian, 'Judicial Review of Arbitral Awards in International Arbitration: A Case for an Efficient System of Judicial Review' (2011) 28 *J Int'l Arb* 553, 554; see generally Farshad Ghodoosi, *International Dispute Resolution and the Public Policy Exception* (Routledge 2017); Leon Trakman, 'Domestic Courts Declining to Recognize and Enforce Foreign Arbitral Awards: A Comparative Reflection' (2018) 6 *Chinese J Comp L* 174.

agreement, was not in accordance with the law of the country where the arbitration took place; or

(e) the award has not yet become binding on the parties, or has been set aside or suspended by a competent authority of the country in which, or under the law of which, that award was made.

(2) Recognition and enforcement of an arbitral award may also be refused if the competent authority in the country where recognition and enforcement is sought finds that:

(a) the subject matter of the difference is not capable of settlement by arbitration under the law of that country; or

(b) the recognition or enforcement of the award would be contrary to the public policy of that country.[53]

Article 34(2) of the UNCITRAL Model Law (which has influenced a plethora of domestic arbitration laws) is very similar and provides:

An arbitral award may be set aside by the court specified in article 6 only if:

(a) the party making the application furnishes proof that:

(i) a party to the arbitration agreement referred to in article 7 was under some incapacity; or the said agreement is not valid under the law to which the parties have subjected it or, failing any indication thereon, under the law of this State; or

(ii) the party making the application was not given proper notice of the appointment of an arbitrator or of the arbitral proceedings or was otherwise unable to present his case; or

(iii) the award deals with a dispute not contemplated by or not falling within the terms of the submission to arbitration, or contains decisions on matters beyond the scope of the submission to arbitration, provided that, if the decisions on matters submitted to arbitration can be separated from those not so submitted, only that part of the award which contains decisions on matters not submitted may be set aside; or

(iv) the composition of the arbitral tribunal or the arbitral procedure was not in accordance with the agreement of the parties, unless such agreement was in conflict with a provision of this Law from which the parties cannot derogate, or, failing such agreement, was not in accordance with this Law; or

(b) the court finds that:

(i) the subject matter of the dispute is not capable of settlement by arbitration under the law of this State; or

(ii) the award is in conflict with the public policy of this State.[54]

---

[53] New York Convention (n 51) art V.

[54] UNCITRAL Model Law (n 50) art 34(2).

Thus, both national legislation and international legal instruments establish a (rebuttable) presumption in favour of the validity of arbitral awards.[55] As the Court of Justice of the European Union (CJEU) has emphasised:

> it is in the interest of efficient arbitration proceedings that review of arbitration awards should be limited in scope and that annulment of or refusal to recognize an award should be possible only in exceptional circumstances.[56]

The absence of, or the difficulty in reaching, a common approach regarding the standard of review of arbitral awards in international commercial arbitration is highlighted by the *Dallah Real Estate & Tourism Holding Co v Ministry of Religious Affairs, Government of Pakistan*, where Lord Collins observed that:

> in most national systems, arbitral tribunals are entitled to consider their own jurisdiction, and to do so in the form of an award. But the last word as to whether or not an alleged arbitral tribunal actually has jurisdiction will lie with a court, either in a challenge brought before the courts of the arbitral seat, where the determination may be set aside or annulled, or in a challenge to recognition or enforcement.[57]

---

[55] Committee on International Commercial Arbitration, 'Final Report on Public Policy as a bar to enforcement of international arbitral awards' in Interational Law Assocation Report of the Seventhieth Conference (New Delhi 2002) para 6, 'Many courts have expressed a policy favouring enforcement'; Gary B Born, *International Commercial Arbitration* (2nd edn, Kluwer Law International 2014) 3413.

[56] CJEU, C-126/97 *Eco Swiss China Time Ltd v Benetton International NV* [1999] ECR. I-3055, para 35. The CJEU abandoned its pro-arbitration stance recently in Case C-284/16 *Slowakische Republik v Achmea BV* [2018] ECLI:EU:C:2018:158, paras 52–59. See also the judgment of the US Supreme Court in *Mitsubishi Motors Corp v Soler Chrysler-Plymouth, Inc*, 473 US 614, 631 (1985):

> *The Bremen* and *Scherk* establish a strong presumption in favor of enforcement of freely negotiated contractual choice-of-forum provisions. Here, as in Scherk, that presumption is reinforced by the emphatic federal policy in favor of arbitral dispute resolution. And at least since this Nation's accession in 1970 to the Convention, see [1970] 21 U.S.T. 2517, T.I.A.S. 6997, and the implementation of the Convention in the same year by amendment of the Federal Arbitration Act, that federal policy applies with special force in the field of international commerce.

[57] *Dallah Real Estate & Tourism Holding Co v Ministry of Religious Affairs, Government of Pakistan* [2010] UKSC 46, para 86, per Lord Collins. See also ibid., para 25, per Lord Mance and *China Minmetals Materials Import & Export Co, Ltd v Chi Mei Corp*, 334 F.3d 274, 288 (3d Cir. 2003), 'it appears that every country adhering to the competence-competence principle allows some form of judicial review of the arbitrator's jurisdictional decision'. See also CA Paris, *Gouvernement du Pakistan v Societe Dallah Real Estate & Tourism Holding Co* (17 February 2011) No 09/28533; see also Carolyn B. Lamm and Eckhard R. Hellbeck, 'The Enforcement of Awards' in Chiara Giorgetti (ed), *Litigating International Investment Disputes: A Practictioner's Guide* (Brill 2014) 496, 479. Cf. *Kabab-Ji SAL (Lebanon) v Kout Food Group (Kuwait)*

Matters are even more complicated in investment treaty arbitration.[58] In particular, as explained above,[59] domestic courts have yet to create a *jurisprudence constante* in relation to the appropriate standard of review,[60] which will be the focus of this section.

The first question in relation to the appropriate standard of review of arbitral awards rendered pursuant to an investment treaty is whether that standard is (or should be) different from the one applied to the review of arbitral awards rendered pursuant to contracts governed by domestic law. One view is that the review of commercial arbitral awards by domestic courts is qualitatively different from the review of investment treaty awards.[61] This is due to the different manner by which consent to arbitrate is given,[62] or the public nature of

---

[2020] EWCA Civ 6 and CA Paris *Kabab-Ji (Lebanon) v Kout Food Group (Kuwait)*, (23 June 2020) No 17/22943.

[58] See Stephan W. Schill, *The Multilateralization of International Investment Law* (CUP 2009) 253–256.

[59] See above Section I.

[60] Céline Lévesque, '"Correctness" as the Proper Standard of Review Applicable to 'True' Questions of Jurisdiction in the Set-Aside of Treaty-Based Investor-State Awards' (2014) 5 *JIDS* 69, 70.

[61] See also W. Michael Reisman, 'Reflections on the Control Mechanism of the ICSID System' in Emmanuel Gaillard (ed), *The Review of International Arbitral Awards* (JurisNet 2008) 218–219:

> International commercial arbitration has intentionally designed a control mechanism that does not include appeal because of the conviction that 'such a mechanism, with an inherently far-reaching scope' would have reduced the attractiveness of international commercial arbitration and its utility to the world economy. International investment arbitration, by contrast, has elements of both inter-State or public international arbitration and international commercial arbitration. This is reflected in the control mechanism which the Washington Convention designed. Its Article 52 bears some resemblance to Article V of the New York Convention. But it and, indeed, its context, are actually very different.

[62] See Lévesque (n 60) 71:

> One aspect that differentiates the set-aside of commercial awards based on contracts from treaty-based investor-State awards is the nature of consent. Indeed, for awards rendered under IIAs the source of consent is multilayered. In most investor-State arbitrations, consent is provided on the basis of an IIA that commits State Parties to submitting to arbitration when an investor (of another Party) makes a claim of breach of the treaty against one of them. Consent is perfected when the investor accepts the 'offer' of arbitration in the treaty by serving a notice of arbitration upon a State Party. As such, when evaluating the 'intention of the parties' as regards to who should have the last word on questions of jurisdiction, a court cannot only consider the specific consent of the investor and the State to arbitrate the current dispute (as would happen in international commercial arbitration) but it must also consider the general consent offered by the States in the treaty.

investment treaty arbitration.[63] Another view is that the fact that in investment treaty arbitration consent to arbitrate is not given in a contract between two parties, but in an international treaty concluded between two States, does not justify a different approach. This is the view adopted by the *US Supreme Court in BG v Argentina*:

> the question before us is who—court or arbitrator—bears primary responsibility for interpreting and applying Article 8's local court litigation provision ... In answering the question, we shall initially treat the document before us as if it were an ordinary contract between private parties. Were that so, we conclude, the matter would be for the arbitrators. We then ask whether the fact that the document in question is a treaty makes a critical difference. We conclude that it does not.[64]

In *Achmea*, the CJEU held that the judicial review of arbitral awards by domestic courts is inadequate for safeguarding the application of EU law by arbitral tribunals, due to the limited character of that review.[65] For reaching that conclusion, the CJEU distinguished commercial arbitration from investment arbitration: for the former, the limited review of arbitral awards by domestic courts was unproblematic, but this was not the case for investment treaty awards:

> [i]t is true that, in relation to commercial arbitration, the Court has held that the requirements of efficient arbitration proceedings justify the review of arbitral

---

[63] Gabriel Bottini, 'Present and Future of ICSID Annulment: The Path to an Appellate Body?' (2016) 31 *ICSID Review* 712, 713. However, while generally true, this argument does not necessarily apply to commercial arbitrations involving a State or a state entity.

[64] *BG Group v Argentina* (n 6) 26. For a criticism of the majority's approach, see Jarrod Wong, 'BG Group v. Republic of Argentina: A Supreme Misunderstanding of Investment Treaty Arbitration' (2016) 43 *Pepperdine LR* 541 and Anthea Roberts and Christina Trahanas, 'Judicial Review of Investment Treaty Awards: BG Group v. Argentina' (2014) 108 *AJIL* 750, 750: 'The dissent's approach is preferable because it appreciates the public international law basis and public law nature of investment treaty arbitration, which differs in important ways from contractual arbitration between private parties.'

[65] *Achmea* (n 56) paras 52–59. Cf. CJEU, Case C-284/16 *Slowakische Republik v Achmea BV*, Opinion of Advocate General Wathelet [2017] ECLI:EU:C:2017:699, para 239:

> In the case of Article 8 of the BIT, the awards made by the arbitral tribunals cannot avoid review by the national courts. That review may be carried out in the context of an action to set aside the arbitral award before the courts of the seat of the arbitration or in the context of an objection to a request for recognition and enforcement of the award before the courts of the country in which recognition and enforcement of the award are sought in accordance with the Convention for the Recognition and Enforcement of Foreign Arbitral Awards, signed at New York on 10 June 1958.

> awards by the courts of the Member States being limited in scope, provided that the fundamental provisions of EU law can be examined in the course of that review and, if necessary, be the subject of a reference to the Court for a preliminary ruling (see, to that effect, judgments of 1 June 1999, *Eco Swiss*, C-126/97, EU:C:1999:269, paragraphs 35, 36 and 40, and of 26 October 2006, *Mostaza Claro*, C-168/05, EU:C:2006:675, paragraphs 34 to 39).
>
> However, arbitration proceedings such as those referred to in Article 8 of the BIT are different from commercial arbitration proceedings. While the latter originate in the freely expressed wishes of the parties, the former derive from a treaty by which Member States agree to remove from the jurisdiction of their own courts, and hence from the system of judicial remedies which the second subparagraph of Article 19(1) TEU requires them to establish in the fields covered by EU law (see, to that effect, judgment of 27 February 2018, *Associação Sindical dos Juízes Portugueses*, C-64/16, EU:C:2018:117, paragraph 34), disputes which may concern the application or interpretation of EU law. In those circumstances, the considerations set out in the preceding paragraph relating to commercial arbitration cannot be applied to arbitration proceedings such as those referred to in Article 8 of the BIT.[66]

The second question which divided domestic courts regarding the appropriate standard of review is how much deference they should accord to the arbitral tribunal which rendered the award. The judgments in *United Mexican States v Metalclad Corp* in Canada,[67] *SwemBalt v Latvia* in Denmark,[68] and *Sanum v Laos* in Singapore,[69] lie at the one end of the spectrum, showing little deference to the findings of the arbitral tribunal. At the other end of the spectrum, domestic courts (as in e.g., *BG v Argentina*[70] and *Occidental v Ecuador*[71]) decided to accord considerable deference to the arbitral tribunal. It is worth highlighting that even within a single jurisdiction courts have failed to adopt a uniform standard of review of investment treaty awards.[72]

---

66 *Achmea* (n 56) paras 54 and 55.

67 *United Mexican States v Metalclad Corporation* (n 7).

68 Maritime and Commerical Court of Copenhagen, *Republic of Latvia v SwemBalt Ltd,* Case S-22-01 (7 January 2003); see also Walid Ben Hamida, 'Two Nebulous ICSID Features: The Notion of Investment and the Scope of Annulment Control' (2007) 24 *J Int'l Arb* 287, 303–304.

69 *Government of the Lao People's Democratic Republic v Sanum Investments Ltd* [2015] SGHC 15, Reversed in the Court of Appeals, *Sanum Investments Ltd v The Government of the Lao People's Democratic Republic* [2016] SGCA 57; see also Odysseas G. Repousis, 'On Territoriality and International Investment Law: Applying China's Investment Treaties to Hong Kong and Macao' (2015) 37 *Michigan JIL* 113.

70 *BG Group v Argentina* (n 6).

71 'The test for the Court is this: was the Tribunal correct in its decision on jurisdiction? The test is not: was the Tribunal entitled to reach the decision that it did': *Ecuador v Occidental Exploration* (n 8) para 7.

72 Regarding Canada and Sweden, see Lévesque (n 60) and Kateryna Bondar, 'Annulment of ICSID and Non-ICSID Investment Awards: Differences in the Extent of

IV. REVIEW OF ARBITRAL AWARDS BY ICSID AD HOC COMMITTEES

The ICSID Convention provides for an autonomous, self-contained mechanism for the review and annulment of awards rendered by arbitral tribunals under the auspices of ICSID.[73] The annulment mechanism is available for both ICSID treaty and contract arbitrations.[74] Article 53(1) of the ICSID Convention makes clear that '[t]he award shall be binding on the parties and shall not be subject to any appeal or to any other remedy except those provided for in this Convention'.[75] Up to date, more than 90 annulment proceedings have been commenced at ICSID by both investors and States, and the rate of annulment (partial or full) is rather low (approximately 3 per cent of the registered cases and 6.6 per cent of all awards).[76] Article 52 of the ICSID Convention provides a closed, exhaustive list[77] containing the very exceptional grounds for which annulment of an ICSID arbitral award could be sought:

> Either party may request annulment of the award by an application in writing addressed to the Secretary-General on one or more of the following grounds:
> (a) that the Tribunal was not properly constituted;
> (b) that the Tribunal has manifestly exceeded its powers;
> (c) that there was corruption on the part of a member of the Tribunal;
> (d) that there has been a serious departure from a fundamental rule of a procedure; or
> (e) that the award has failed to state the reasons on which it is based.[78]

Review' (2015) 32 *J Int'l Arb* 621, 648–649 respectively.

[73] On the history of the ICSID annulment mechanism, see ICSID, 'Updated Background Paper on Annulment for the Administrative Council of ICSID' (5 May 2016) 2-9 https://icsid.worldbank.org/sites/default/files/Background%20Paper%20on%20Annulment%20April%202016%20ENG.pdf accessed 22 November 2020 and J. Christopher Thomas and Harpreet Kaur Dhillon, 'The Foundations of Investment Treaty Arbitration: The ICSID Convention, Investment Treaties and the Review of Arbitration Awards' (2017) 32 *ICSID Review* 459, 475–479.

[74] On annulment in the context of ICSID contract arbitrations, see Gabrielle Kaufmann-Kohler, 'Annulment of ICSID Awards in contract and Treaty Arbitrations: Are There Differences?' in Emmanuel Gaillard and Yas Banifatemi (eds), *Annulment of ICSID Awards* (Jurisnet 2004).

[75] ICSID Convention (n 3) art 53(1); see also Lisa M. Bohmer, 'Finality in ICSID Arbitration Revisited' (2016) 31 *ICSID Review* 236.

[76] ICSID Background Paper on Annulment (n 73) 10 and 30.

[77] See *RSM Production Corporation v Grenada (I)*, ICSID Case No ARB/05/14, Decision on the Application of RSM Production Corporation for a Preliminary Ruling (7 December 2009) para 21.

[78] ICSID Convention (n 3) art 52(1); see also Christoph Schreuer, 'ICSID Annulment Revisited' (2003) 30 *LIEI* 103; Bottini (n 63); Philippe Pinsolle, 'Jurisdictional Review

As David Caron aptly put it, these grounds relate to the '"legitimacy" of the process of decision', rather than the 'substantive correctness of decision'.[79] The factual determinations of ICSID tribunals are not reviewable by the annulment committees,[80] and tribunals have also discretion in adopting the most appropriate valuation method with their choice being not reviewable by the annulment committee.[81]

The interpretation and application of Article 52(1) of the ICSID Convention by ad hoc Committees has not led to consistent results. Importantly, while *ad hoc* committees agree that their review should not be confused with, and is more limited than, appeal review,[82] there have been fundamentally different

---

of ICSID Awards' (2004) 5 *JWIT* 619; R. Doak Bishop and Silvia M. Marchili, *Annulment Under the ICSID Convention* (OUP 2012).

[79] David D. Caron, 'Reputation and Reality in the ICSID Annulment Process: Understanding the Distinction between Annulment and Appeal' (1992) 7 *ICSID Review* 21, 24.

[80] *Quiborax SA, Non Metallic Minerals SA and Allan Fosk Kaplún v Plurinational State of Bolivia*, ICSID Case No ARB/06/2, Decision on Annulment (18 May 2018) para 112, departing from the annulment decision in *Caratube International Oil Company LLP v Republic of Kazakhstan*, ICSID Case No ARB/08/12, Decision on the Annulment Application of Caratube International Oil Company LLP (21 February 2014) para 158:

> [f]actual findings and weighing of evidence made by a tribunal are outside the powers of review of an annulment committee, except if the applicant can prove that the errors of fact are so egregious, or the weighing of evidence so irrational, as to constitute an independent cause for annulment …

See also *Occidental Petroleum Corporation and Occidental Exploration and Production Company v Republic of Ecuador*, ICSID Case No ARB/06/11, Decision on Annulment of the Award (2 November 2015) para 373:

> These are all factual findings, which the Tribunal adopted after having reviewed the extensive evidentiary record, heard the witnesses and weighed the available evidence. The Tribunal is best placed to perform this task, and its conclusions should not be second-guessed by an ad hoc committee – save in exceptional circumstances, when the errors of fact committed by the tribunal are so egregious as to give rise to one of the grounds for annulment established in Article 52(1) of the Convention.

See also Pierre Mayer, 'To What Extent Can an *Ad Hoc* Committee Review the Factual Findings of an Arbitral Tribunal' in Gaillard and Banifatemi (n 74) 243.

[81] See *Quiborax* (n 80) paras 154–193. On the calculation of damages in investment treaty arbitration, see Christina L. Beharry (ed), *Contemporary and Emerging Issues on the Law of Damages and Valuation in International Investment Arbitration* (Brill Nijhoff 2018); Irmgard Marboe, *Damages in Investor-State Arbitration: Current Issues and Challenges* (Brill 2018); Borzu Sabahi, *Compensation and Restitution in Investor-State Arbitration: Principles and Practice* (OUP 2011).

[82] *Venoklim Holding BV v Bolivarian Republic of Venezuela*, ICSID Case No ARB/12/22, Decision on Annulment (2 February 2018) para 189.

approaches in relation to the correct standard of review.[83] In the words of the annulment decision in *CDC v Seychelles*, '[t]hat annulment is not the same thing as appeal is a principle acknowledged although applied unevenly in the various decisions of ad hoc Committees'.[84] At least four (or even five) generations of ICSID annulment decisions have been identified depending on how intensely the *ad hoc* Committees scrutinise the ICSID awards.[85] These inconsistent results have led some scholars to criticise the current system[86] and to propose to replace it with an appellate mechanism modelled after, or, at least, inspired by, the WTO Appellate Body.[87] Others argue that on balance

---

83 On the standard of review, see Gabrielle Kaufmann-Kohler and Michele Potestà, 'Can the Mauritius Convention Serve as a Model for the Reform of Investor-State Arbitration in Connection with the Introduction of a Permanent Investment Tribunal or an Appeal Mechanism? Analysis and Roadmap' (3 June 2016) para 118 www.uncitral.org/pdf/english/CIDS_Research_Paper_Mauritius.pdf accessed 20 November 2020, 'Assuming the appellate tribunal's area of review extends to both issues of law and fact, the question arises whether the appellate tribunal should review these issues de novo or whether it should accord some degree of deference to the findings of the first adjudicator'.

84 *CDC Group plc v Republic of Seychelles*, ICSID Case No ARB/02/14, Decision on Annulment (29 June 2005) para 34, citing Christoph Schreuer, 'Three Generations of ICSID Annulment Proceedings' in Gaillard and Banifatemi (n 74) 42. See also Pierre Lalive, 'On the Reasoning of International Arbitral Awards' (2010) 1 *JIDS* 55, 59: ICSID ad hoc committees 'do not as yet compose a clear general picture or provide one authoritative interpretation of Article 52(1) (lit. e)'.

85 Schreuer, ibid.; Bondar (n 72) 636–637.

86 See, e.g., Andreas R. Ziegler, 'Is It Necessary to Avoid Substantive and Procedural Overlaps with Other Agreements in IIAs?' in Armand De Mestral and Céline Lévesque (eds), *Improving International Investment Agreements* (Routledge 2013) 174; David Collins, 'ICSID Annulment Committee Appointments: Too Much Discretion to the Chairman?' (2013) 30 *J Int'l Arb* 333; Dohyn Kim, 'The Annulment Committee's Role in Multiplying Inconsistency in ICSID Arbitration: The Need To Move Away From An Annulment based System' (2011) 86 *NYU LR* 242, 270; William Burke-White and Andreas von Staden, 'Private Litigation in the Public Law Sphere: The Standard of Review in Investor-State Arbitrations' (2010) 35 *Yale JIL* 283, 300; David A. Gantz, 'An Appellate Mechanism for Review of Arbitral Decisions in Investor–State Disputes: Prospects and Challenges' (2006) 39 *Vanderbilt JTL* 39; Bottini (n 63) 725.

87 Yenkong Ngangjoh-Hodu and Chikodili Ajibo, 'ICSID Annulment Procedure and the WTO Appellate System: The Case for an Appellate System for Investment Arbitration' (2015) 6 *JIDS* 308; see also Don McRae, 'The WTO Appellate Body: A Model for an ICSID Appeals Facility?' (2010) 1 *JIDS* 371. On a comparison between the investment treaty arbitration and the WTO regimes, see Dan Sarooshi, 'Investment Treaty Arbitration and the World Trade Organization: What Role for Systemic Values in the Resolution of International Economic Disputes?' (2014) 49 *Texas ILJ* 445.

the current ICSID system of annulment committees should be preserved.[88] Essentially, the dividing line of these antithetical approaches revolves around the 'the right balance between the award's finality and the legitimacy of both the arbitral process and the award'.[89] This is inevitably 'a subjective exercise': '[s]ome will emphasize the need for efficient settlement of disputes and of legal security; others will advance the importance not only of correctness but also of fairness in dispute resolution, among other societal values'.[90]

Finally, the recent practice of the EU has not only moved away from investment treaty arbitration and towards a permanent 'Investment Court System', but also abandoned the decentralised annulment system of limited review. The Investment Protection Agreement (EU-Singapore), the Comprehensive Economic and Trade Agreement (CETA), and the Investment Protection Agreement (EU-Vietnam), all establish 'Appeal' or 'Appellate' Tribunals. The scope of review of these 'Appeal' or 'Appellate' Tribunals includes, but is not limited to, the grounds contained in Article 52(1) of the ICSID Convention; it also involves an assessment of any errors in the interpretation or application of the applicable law, and any manifest errors in the appreciation of the salient facts (including domestic law).[91]

---

[88] See, e.g., Christian J. Tams, 'Is There a Need for an ICSID Appellate Structure?' in Rainer Hoffman and Christian J. Tams (eds), *The International Convention for the Settlement of Investment Disputes: Taking Stock After 40 Years* (Nomos 2007) 250; Jan Paulsson, 'Is an Investment Dispute Appellate Mechanism Desirable?' in Karl P. Sauvant and Michael Chiswick-Patterson (eds), *Appeals Mechanism in International Investment Disputes* (OUP 2008); Barton Legum, 'Options to Establish an Appellate Mechanism for Investment Disputes' in Sauvant and Chiswick-Patterson, ibid., 238. However, the latter recalibrated his position in light of the recent wave of mega-regional trade and investment agreements, see Barton Legum, 'Appellate Mechanisms for Investment Arbitration: Worth a Second Look for the Trans-Pacific Partnership and the Proposed EU-U.S. FTA?' in Jean E. Kalicki and Anna Joubin-Bret (eds), *Reshaping the Investor-State Dispute Settlement System Journeys for the 21st Century* (Brill Nijhoff 2015) 438.

[89] Bottini (n 63) 713.

[90] Ibid.

[91] Investment Protection Agreement (EU-Singapore) (adopted 19 October 2018, entered into force 21 November 2019) art 3.19 provides:

> The grounds for appeal are: (a) that the Tribunal has erred in the interpretation or application of the applicable law; (b) that the Tribunal has manifestly erred in the appreciation of the facts, including the appreciation of relevant domestic law; or, (c) those provided for in Article 52 of the ICSID Convention, in so far as they are not covered by (a) and (b).

Investment Protection Agreement (EU-Vietnam) (adopted 30 June 2019) art 3.54 provides:

> The grounds for appeal are: (a) that the Tribunal has erred in the interpretation or application of the applicable law; (b) that the Tribunal has manifestly erred in the

V. TOWARDS MORE CROSS-FERTILISATION?

To date there is limited influence of international investment law (as far as review of arbitral awards either by ICSID Committees or domestic courts is concerned) on the practice of other international courts and tribunals.[92] It is not possible to comprehensively examine the relationship between the ICJ (and other international courts) on the one hand, and the international investment treaty regime (including the role of domestic courts in it) on the other in this chapter. Such examination presupposes, *inter alia*, a detailed consideration of the different criticisms which have been levelled against the Investor-State Dispute Settlement System. The argument put forward in this chapter is more circumspect. It argues that international courts and tribunals should engage with the jurisprudence of *ad hoc* ICSID Committees or domestic courts in relation to the review of investment treaty awards because such jurisprudence constitutes an invaluable corpus of national and international decisions grappling with difficult but common issues of review. As similar questions have arisen, and will arise in the future, in international adjudication, it would be immensely helpful to examine the approach taken by domestic courts or ICSID *ad hoc* Committees. This is irrespective of whether the ICJ will rely on, or disagree with, that approach. Moreover, a closer engagement by the ICJ or other international courts with the case law of ICSID *ad hoc* Committees or national courts in relation to questions of review of arbitral awards will also create the opportunity of a virtuous cycle of judicial dialogue, as ICSID ad hoc Committees or national courts will in turn consider how the ICJ treated their jurisprudence. As Vadi observed:

> [i]nternational judicial borrowing, that is, borrowing decisions from other international fora in the interpretation of international law, would be compatible with the unity of public international law and would promote its coherence. Judicial dialogue

---

> appreciation of the facts, including the appreciation of relevant domestic law; or (c) those provided for in Article 52 of the ICSID Convention, in so far as they are not covered by subparagraphs (a) and (b).

The Comprehensive Economic and Trade Agreement (EU-Canada) (adopted 30 October 2016, not provisionally entered into force 21 September 2017) Investment Chapter, art 8.28(2):

> The Appellate Tribunal may uphold, modify or reverse the Tribunal's award based on: (a) errors in the application or interpretation of applicable law; (b) manifest errors in the appreciation of the facts, including the appreciation of relevant domestic law; (c) the grounds set out in Article 52(1) (a) through (e) of the ICSID Convention, in so far as they are not covered by paragraphs (a) and (b).

[92] See above Section I.

> is feasible and possible: informal linkages already exist. Some arbitrators have been professors of public international law or judges in other international fora.[93]

Three areas can be indicatively identified in which the case law of ICSID *ad hoc* Committees or national courts could be helpful to other international courts or tribunals. Naturally, these areas do not exhaust the universe of potential international law questions which international courts and tribunals deal with and to which the case law regarding the review of investment treaty arbitral awards could be particularly useful. Nor, the short analysis below does justice to the importance or complexity of the relevant issues, which can and should be explored further in the future.

The first and obvious area is precisely the review of arbitral awards. The ICJ was called to review arbitral awards in two occasions in 1991 and 1960, before the emergence of international investment law.[94] Had the ICJ (or another international court or tribunal) be called to review an arbitral award today, it would have at its disposal a rich jurisprudence generated by different domestic courts and ICSID ad hoc Committees. Whether in the light of its stance towards investment treaty arbitration described above,[95] the ICJ would have actually chosen to engage with, rather than ignore, the relevant case law is difficult to tell. However, as this chapter made clear it should.

The second area of potential cross-fertilisation relates more broadly to the concept of the 'standard of review'. International courts and tribunals are often called to review decisions of other bodies (adjudicative, administrative or other),[96] and, in that context, examine complex questions regarding proce-

---

93 Valentina Vadi, 'Critical Comparisons: The Role of Comparative Law in Investment Treaty Arbitration' (2010–2011) 39 *Denver JILP* 67, 95. See also the excellent analysis between investment treaty jurisprudence and the law on State responsibility in Martins Paparinskis, 'Investment Treaty Arbitration and the (New) Law of State Responsibility' (2013) 24 *EJIL* 617.

94 See above Section II.

95 See above Section I.

96 See generally Lukasz Gruszczynski and Wouter Werner, *Deference in International Courts and Tribunals - Standard of Review and Margin of Appreciation* (OUP 2014); Yuka Fukunaga, 'Margin of Appreciation as an Indicator of Judicial Deference: Is It Applicable to Investment Arbitration?' (2019) 10 *JIDS* 69; Johannes H. Fahner, 'From Dispute Settlement to Judicial Review? The Deference Debate in International Investment Law' in Michiel Duchateau et al (eds), *Evolution in Dispute Resolution. From Adjudication to ADR?* (Eleven International Publishing 2016) 61; Caroline Henckels, 'Balancing Investment Protection and the Public Interest: The Role of the Standard of Review and the Importance of Deference in Investor–State Arbitration' (2013) 4 *JIDS* 197; Stephan W. Schill, 'Deference in Investment Treaty Arbitration: Re-conceptualizing the Standard of Review' (2012) 3 *JIDS* 577.

dural guarantees[97] and the appropriate deference to be accorded to the original decision-maker. The *Abyei* arbitration is one example,[98] but it should not remain the only one. The *Whaling in Antarctica* case could have been another example. In that case, the ICJ analysed the appropriate standard of review to determine whether the special permits for killing and hunting whales allegedly for scientific purposes granted by Japan were consistent with the International Convention for the Regulation of Whaling.[99]

Finally, the third area in which the case law of national courts on the review of investment treaty awards could be particularly interesting relates more broadly to the role of domestic courts in the application, interpretation and development of international law.[100] This is because the review of arbitral awards by domestic courts, and in particular those awards rendered pursuant to investment treaties, constitutes one of the most important areas of legal interaction between domestic courts and international law instruments (treaties) and practice (international adjudication). In that context, the relevant body of jurisprudence sheds light on the relationship between international and domestic courts and tribunals and offers invaluable insights to the interpretation and application of international law by domestic courts. Such questions cannot be explored in this chapter further, but they should be the object of research by international law scholars and careful consideration by all international law adjudicators.

VI. CONCLUSIONS

Although the practice of domestic courts and ICSID annulment committees in relation to the review of investment treaty awards is vast it has yet failed to constitute a 'motor' for the development of international law. Nonetheless,

---

[97] This is particularly relevant for example in the context of cases regarding the Convention for the Protection of Human Rights and Fundamental Freedoms (adopted 4 November 1950, entered into force 3 September 1953) 213 UNTS 221, art 6 guaranteeing fair trial.

[98] See above Section I.

[99] *Whaling in the Antarctic (Australia v Japan: New Zealand intervening)* (Judgment) [2004] *ICJ Reports* 226, paras 62–69.

[100] See Antonios Tzanakopoulos and Christian J. Tams, 'Domestic Courts as Agents of Development of International Law' (2013) 26 *LJIL* 531; Roger O'Keefe, 'Domestic Courts as Agents of Development of the International Law of Jurisdiction' (2013) 26 *LJIL* 541; Rosanne van Alebeek, 'Domestic Courts as Agents of Development of International Immunity Rules' (2013) 26 *LJIL* 559; Devika Hovell, 'A Dialogue Model: The Role of the Domestic Judge in Security Council Decision-Making' (2013) 26 *LJIL* 579; Anthea Roberts, 'Comparative International Law? The Role of National Courts in Creating and Enforcing International Law' (2011) 60 *ICLQ* 57.

this chapter made the case for greater cross-fertilisation and offered suggestions as to which areas the practice of ICSID Committees or domestic courts reviewing arbitral awards could be particularly illuminating. The creation of the 'Investment Court System', promoted by the EU, with its expanded 'appellate' review, as well as enhanced judicial dialogue between different domestic courts, could – and should – lead towards greater harmonisation, or, even, towards a formation of a 'common law' of review of arbitral awards in international law.[101]

[101] The concept of a 'common law' of review of arbitral awards is inspired by the influential monograph, Chester Brown, *A Common Law of International Adjudication* (OUP 2007).

Index